Routing *the* Golf Course

The art & science that forms the golf journey

Routing *the* Golf Course

The art & science that forms the golf journey

Forrest L. Richardson, ASGCA

Foreword by
Peter Oosterhuis

John Wiley & Sons, Inc.

The routing of golf holes and the design of golf courses must be approached with the hands-on participation of a professional golf course architect. No book can possibly provide a complete how-to manual for such a complex undertaking. Each individual project comes with its own set of circumstances, and these must be researched and evaluated by a professional engaged specifically for that project. This book is intended to serve only as a guide for those involved or interested in the subject of routing golf courses.

The author and contributors express general opinions and offer typical guidelines, customary practices, and examples. The publisher, author, or contributors will not be held liable for any representation made, regardless of its form, accuracy, or intent.

Included within this edition are designs, architectural plans, photo representations, and names of golf holes, features, and courses. They are reproduced to support the educational nature of this subject matter. Regardless of their format, such representations may have associated copyright, trademark, patent, design patent, and trade dress protection. All designs, architectural plans, photo representations, and names of golf holes, features, and courses included should be presumed the intellectual property of the golf course architects, planners, architects, engineers, owners, developers, agencies, or organizations responsible for their creation. Accordingly, they may not be copied, implemented, or integrated with other plans without express consent. The presence, or lack thereof, of copyright, trademark, patent, or design patent information associated with photos, drawings, diagrams, or descriptions does not necessarily constitute the full extent of ownership or rights that may exist.

This book is printed on acid-free paper. ♾

Published by John Wiley & Sons, Inc., Hoboken, New Jersey.
Published simultaneously in Canada.

For general information on our other products and services or for technical support, please contact our Customer Care Department within the United States at (800) 762-2974, outside the United States at (317) 572-3993 or fax (317) 572-4002.

Wiley also publishes its books in avariety of electronic formats. Some content that appears in print may not be available in electronic books.

Library of Congress Cataloging-in-Publication Data:

ISBN 0471-43480-9

Printed in the United States of America.

10 9 8 7 6 5 4 3 2 1

To my father,

who taught me to persevere,

and who watched the Golf Channel

in his final days,

reporting all he could to a son

who was busy writing.

Contents

Foreword

It is certainly a privilege to be able to write the foreword to Forrest Richardson's grand work, *Routing the Golf Course.* Forrest's decision to take on this most demanding project goes to show his tremendous commitment to his craft. This work will surely become recognized as the most complete study of an oft overlooked attribute of a golf course. Forrest carefully blends core information, historical references, personal experiences, enlightening interviews, and much of the wisdom of Jack Snyder, his mentor and inspiration.

In my conversation with Forrest in Hole 12, I admit that my appreciation of golf course design blossomed only after I had given up full-time tournament play on the the PGA Tour. After time spent as a director of golf at a challenging Charles Banks course (Forsgate in New Jersey) and at a George Thomas masterpiece (Riviera), I had a much greater admiration for those ladies and gentlemen who strive to create challenging but enjoyable golf courses. I do regret not keeping a detailed record of all the courses I played around the world; I suppose I was too busy trying to finish at the top of the leaderboard!

Few golf course designers become household names, but that doesn't stop many talented and focused individuals from pursuing their dreams of designing and building wonderful golf courses that can be enjoyed by golfers of all abilities.

I can imagine Forrest's book not only inspiring and informing a potential golf course architect, planner, or developer, but also helping all golfers better understand and appreciate the layout of any course they might play — perhaps to the benefit of their score!

I'm sure you will relish the opportunity to add to your knowledge of golf course architecture. Enjoy the book, and good golfing!

— Peter Oosterhuis

Acknowledgments

In formally thanking people for helping to pull a project together, you try not to miss anyone, yet you must move swiftly. You can almost hear the theme music of the Academy Awards beginning to drown you out before you finish. My apologies if this drags on, but I cannot type any faster.

I am indebted to each of the golf course architects who trusted me with this work and encouraged me along the way. This applies not only to this book, but also to my career, which was shaped by many. To Geoffrey Cornish, Robert Muir Graves, and Bill Amick: Thank you for your faith in this project and my earlier writings. To the late Desmond Muirhead who passed away not long after the last word had been written: Your insights about routing could fill many books. Thank you for sharing them and giving me such good advice. I wish you had been able to hold the finished book. And to Jack Snyder, known elsewhere in this book as Arthur Jack Snyder: I cannot thank you enough for mentoring me. Without your experience and the gift for being able to pass some of it my way, I would be no further than Hole 2 or 3 by now.

Guest writers include the renowned Gil Martinez in Hole 6, "Real Estate, the Almighty Influence," and the esteemed Dr. Ed Sadalla in Hole 10, "The Psychology of the Golf Journey." They are joined by my interview with Peter Oosterhuis in Hole 12, "What Makes a Great Golf Course." And, as if he has not already done enough to help me, Jack Snyder keeps on giving by offering a few insights in the aptly titled Hole 17, "Never Assume Anything!" The thoughts of these professionals could be packaged into a conference of its own, but here you get them without the bad coffee and the uncomfortable chairs.

The organizations that came to the rescue are many. Special thanks are due to the American Society of Golf Course Architects (ASGCA); to Rand Jerris and Maxine Vigliotta at the United States Golf Association (USGA); to Peter Lewis and Fiona McDougall at the British Golf Museum; and to Alan McGregor, Peter Mason, and Liz Taylor at the St. Andrews Links Trust. For their help during my trips to unearth the history of routing and to visit even more golf courses, I must thank my good friends George Farrow, Wyn Thompson, and all of the Gransburys up in the North of England, and, down south, John Mercer and Mo Webster. Your hospitality, transport service, and cooking were above and beyond. Why is it that you put up with this foreigner?

A picture is worth 10,000 words, as the saying is supposed to go. Great thanks to each of the golf course architects who spent time sorting through their files for old routing plans, photos, and information for use throughout the book. The clubs, archives, and photographers who provided images are all heroes in their own right.

My editors, Margaret Cummins and Elizabeth Roles at John Wiley & Sons, were terrific and enthusiastic guides who brought everything together. Their counterpart in my office was my capable assistant, Mike Hopkins. Although I know he would rather have been doing real routing plans instead of fiddling with all of the examples, diagrams, illustrations, and charts, he poured himself into this project from beginning to end, many times working until the daylight came around a second time. Mike wears many hats in this small office, as I do. We wore even more during this effort, and it cannot be adequately expressed how well the work all seemed to go.

Last, but not least, appreciation goes to my family for long ago seeing to it that I had a junior set of golf clubs and transportation to the local courses. If not for my parents, my Uncle Maurice, and my brother Bill, golf might have escaped my radar. And more recently to everyone for their support during writing, traveling, editing, and more writing. Not everyone is lucky enough to work alongside their spouse—I am. My wife, Valerie, an accomplished graphic designer, took on the tedious job of accounting for all the images in these pages and remained mostly patient. She managed to keep everything in order, including our personal life. My daughter, Haley, could not have been better to me. I regret the late nights when she was already asleep before I could say good night. Thank you for chipping with me in the backyard.

— FORREST RICHARDSON

Introduction

There are 35,000 golf courses across the world, and it's my guess that among the 50 million golfers who occupy their fairways, it is a rare instance to hear one say something along the lines of "Gee, the routing of this course is very interesting." Quite simply, the routing of golf courses is taken mostly for granted. The process of getting from point A to point B in a round, one of the unique aspects of this beloved game, is overshadowed by the happenings of each individual hole, that breathtaking view at the par-3, or all of the individual and minute events that are piled together to make up a complete round of golf. Routing is something that golfers are subconsciously aware of, but never to the point that it can be appreciated on its own merit. A golf course might feel right—but why?

Routing is the anatomy of a golf course, and a golf course is the framework for the entire game on a given day in the life of a golfer. Of all the millions of individual components that go into golf, the routing is the glue that holds them in place. It is a common thread that ties the beginning with the end, attaches each hole to the next, and supports the golfer to make a mark, be it good or not-so-good. Even though years of opinion may finally spell the end of a disliked bunker on a course, or some grand old tree dies, or a new lake is added, the routing will almost always endure. When neighborhoods once full of children are redeveloped into neighborhoods full of the children of the children who grew up there, the golf course that winds its way beside these homes will, very likely, begin at the same point and go in the identical direction it did on the day it first opened for play. It is rare to see a golf course significantly rerouted, and there is a good explanation for this: It is costly. Just as you cannot easily change the anatomy of a living person, you cannot easily change the anatomy of a living golf course. Yes, of course you can alter its appearance and shift a few things around. But generally, you have only so much space to work with, and where the holes go is where they will continue to go.

The effect of routing is powerful. It is a rather permanent condition. As such, it occupies an important part of the design of golf courses—far more important than typically regarded. In my work as a golf course architect, I have seen routing plans that were expertly created and also plenty that look as if they had been thrown together at the last minute. What a shame. To take such a precious part of the game—the treasure map we provide the golfer—and assume that things will work themselves out once the magic of the bulldozers is performed and the bare ground disappears to unveil shades of green turf.

I think of golf courses as snowflakes—no two exactly alike. And why? The answer has considerably more to do with routing than any other variable. In the mathematical realm, two golf holes on earth *do* have a sporting chance of being *nearly* identical. As evidence, take a look at the extreme efforts to construct replica holes in the past few years. Some developers have gone to tremendous lengths to have a famous golf hole sophisticatedly mapped and, once it is recreated in another place, to then detail the entire setting right down to the identical species of vegetation and the exact type of sand used in the bunkers. But how many entire golf courses do you suppose will ever be successfully cloned?

The ingredients that make routings so crucial and influential are the setting of a golf course together with its climate and the hundreds of other details of a particular locale. Multiply those specifics by the multitude of options in the sequence and the unfolding of golf holes as they link together on a particular day, and you will begin to appreciate the command of a routing plan. No matter how you dissect it, when we speak of *routing,* we are speaking of a *journey.* And no two journeys can ever be the same.

Although this book has a narrow focus—*golf course routing*—it remained my goal throughout the writing to apply the information to a wide range of readers. The content is not solely directed to the golf course architects, land planners, and landscape architects who are often first on the scene when it comes to looking at land for a golf course, although I admit this was tempting. Nor was the makeup aimed only toward land developers, home builders, resort operators, golf management companies, and politicians, even though it is their great influence that more often than not defines a completed golf course. The writing is geared to the golf enthusiast. Every so often, you will find the text interrupted to examine the game itself. This is by design. Most of the people I meet who are connected with golf share a fascination with the overall experience of the game. To present thoughts about golf course routing and to not send a periscope up to look around at the many facets of the game would be a disservice.

Much has been written about golf course routing, although most of it falls within isolated chapters in books of broader topic or, occasionally, in articles and opinions from early golf architects. I am indebted to the writers before me and have expounded on their thinking and wisdom with the greatest possible care and regard.

I hope that once you have "played through" this book, it comes more naturally for you to distinguish good routings from bad, and great from not bad. But this objective in understanding routing remains only part of the plan. That there will be a greater push for excellence when it comes to golf course routing is the ultimate goal.

In a game where the participants move from one short act to another, it's essential to have an infinite understanding of what goes into making this progression work. Among my favorite adjectives, a golf course routing can be "intriguing," "exciting," "mysterious," "beautiful," "efficient," "safe," "challenging," and "dramatic." The list continues...and keep in mind there is an opposite for each and every word you can possibly think of!

To *route* means to *direct.* An expanded definition will very often go a step further: "to divert in a specified direction along an intended path."

How lucky we are to be a part of a game in which the limits of play are defined not only by a very specialized form of architecture but also by the customized story that gets written each and every time a player makes his or her way from beginning to end. What a bore it would be if we did not have this topic to consider.

Using This Book

If the truth be known, I planned only 14 chapters when this book was in process, but by classifying the guest writings solicited to complete the topic as full-fledged chapters, it became possible to reinforce a theme with 18 tidy chapters—referred to as *holes*—and a most essential "19th Hole." Beyond this bit of trivia, there are really only seven things that will be helpful for the reader to know:

1. The book is divided into four sections, each consisting of groupings of "holes" that may be thought of as chapters. The book is arranged this way by design. It helps to recall topics in groups, just as golf holes can often be recalled better by this method.
2. "The Opening," which consists of Holes 1 through 6, is a background and sets the stage. Some readers may have a good handle on this, but I encourage reading it anyway.
3. "Making the Turn," which consists of Holes 7 through 9, comprises information essential to any good understanding of routing.
4. "The Heart," which consists of Holes 10 through 15, is really the how-to portion (but I would not suggest skipping right to it.)
5. "The Finish," which consists of Holes 16 through 18 plus the "19th Hole," is a collection of advice on presenting, wisdom on a variety of routing topics, and final thoughts on the future of golf courses and routing. Like all real-world 19th Holes, this area is a place to ponder and reflect.
6. Intermingled within this "round" is a collection of short stories based on real-life personal experiences. I hope the stories break up the material in a positive way. If any of these seem uninteresting to you, by all means feel free to skip ahead.
7. This book's outer margins have been put to use. Here you will find interesting quotes, facts, and trivia.

PART ONE

The Opening

The Evolution of Golf Course Routing

HOLE NO. 1

When a fellow passenger on a flight back home from one of my trips asked what I was writing so feverishly, I thought and responded with a clarity that had, until then, not been so evident. "I'm writing about getting from point A to point B," I said. And with that began a conversation about golf, like so many before and on so many flights.

"Getting from point A to point B" does not sound nearly as impressive as "Routing the Golf Course," but it is honestly simple. When you boil it all down, a golf course is just a series of paths, some physical and some mental. How they are traveled is up to the golfer. The golf course has significant influence in this matter; it is an expanse of living, breathing nature that dares and beckons while at the same time lying motionless and remaining speechless

In our modern times, however, golf courses are anything but speechless. They have been given voice through the cleverness of the golf course designer, a relatively new breed of professional that was, until the great growth of golf in the early 1900s, as unnecessary as the lob wedge. Where golf layouts were originally set by nature, they began to be defined by the human hand. This transformation—from all natural to mimicking natural—has significantly changed the art of golf course routing.

> *Numberless games with club and ball have been played for the past two thousand years, and doubtless for millenniums before; but no game with more than one club and with a separate ball for each player, and no game having as its goal adesignated hole in the ground.*
> —*Charles Blair Macdonald,* Scotland's Gift—Golf

This book is about the why and where—and how—of routing golf courses. The topic at first may seem straightforward, like A to B, but then it opens many doors that lead to many more. The why, for example, is quite difficult to pin down. In order to appreciate the routing of golf courses, it seems only appropriate to have an idea of why indeed they came to be routed in the first place. And to resolve this, a discussion of the origins of the game of golf is warranted. This chapter begins at that discussion. It opens the first door.

ANCIENT TIMES

No one knows for sure exactly when golf began, but this has not in the least deterred people from asking. Peter Lewis, director of the British Golf Museum in St. Andrews, Scotland, and historian to the Royal and Ancient Golf Club, relates that it is among the most pressing of questions asked by visitors to the museum. "When exactly was the first game of golf played?" is the "simple" question. To which Mr. Lewis begins a very long and wide answer that has an equally long and wide margin of error. The fact is that we do not know when the first game of golf was played. We can only theorize.

Long before The Old Course at St. Andrews, which has become known as The Home of Golf, there were rumblings of golf. Just how golf-like these rumblings were is a matter of debate, to which there can be no sure conclusion. They are worthy of thought, though, especially in the context of how golf courses finally came to be routed.

Sticks & Balls

It would be presumptuous to consider that the earliest people did not occasionally amuse themselves by whacking a round stone or fruit with a stick. Imagine the bored kid on his way back to the cave, a stick with a slight curve at the end, and a nearly spherical projectile. Whack! One bounce, and down a rabbit hole. You may well have just visualized the first ever hole-in-one.

More formal studies suggest games involving sticks and balls were played by the ancient Egyptians, Greek, Romans, Chinese, and Japanese, among others. But none of these games had much in common with golf; researchers depict them as mostly hockey-like and played on formal courts. The same holds true for games played by the ancient Indian civilizations of North America. The format of these games was generally one team against another. That lone kid returning to the cave was certainly doing something more golf-like than were a bunch of Egyptian linemen screaming for their teammates to pass the ball within rectangular arenas framed with sandstone blocks. Ancient stick-and-ball games took the form of arena sports. Their relationship to golf lies only in the use of a club and the hitting of a ball.

A. V. Velde pinx.
J. Aliamet Sculp.
LES AMUSEMENS DE L'HIVER
Dédié a Messire Louis - Antoine de la Roche, Marquis de Rambures,
Maréchal de Camp des Armées du Roy. Par son très-humble et très-obeissant serviteur Aliamet.
Gravé d'après le Tableau Original du Cabinet de Mr. Mariette.

Old European Games

A more appropriate header might be "Defunct European Games," as each of the games discussed here are gone from the scope. However, many scholars have spent many hours promoting the connection to modern golf of certain stick-and-ball games in the cultures of emerging Europe.

Take, for example, the Dutch game *kolven* (also *kolf* or *colf*). This game, mostly played between two opposing groups, has origins dating to the year 1297. There was also *choule* (or *chole*), a game popular in France and the Netherlands during the Middle Ages. This game originally involved play by two teams attempting to hit into a guarded goal. And then there was *pall-mall,* a game of French or Italian origin (there is uncertainty as to which), usually played in rectangular fenced enclosures with posts at each end. Pall-mall spread throughout Europe and was played widely in England. Suddenly, however, it seemed to drop off the face of the earth at the beginning of the eighteenth century. A derivative game, *mail à chicane* (or *jer du mail*) endured in the south of France and a few other places.

FIGURE 1-1
A classic engraving showing the Dutch game *kolf* being played across open expanses of ice around the middle of the thirteenth century. The game of golf, whether or not it was influenced by *kolf,* established itself on the linksland of Scotland well before 1457 when the game was banned.

SOURCE: *GOLF ILLUSTRATED,* JANUARY 1916

THE APPLE TREE GANG
Often thought of as America's first golf club, the St. Andrews Golf Club of Yonkers, New York, was founded in 1888 by six men who had been introduced to the game by Robert Lockhart, an immigrant Scottish linen merchant. Lockhart and his followers had laid out a three-hole course the year before but arrived at the conclusion that the club needed more holes to accommodate the increasing popularity of this "new" game. John Reid was elected the club's first president. The apple tree reference was to the many apple trees that defined the eventual six-hole layout and accounted for the course's primary obstacles.

So what about these games? Just how golf-like were they? In contrast to pall-mall or *choule,* which were court games, in *het kolven,* players were occasionally known to have the object of playing toward a distant target, although this target took on a variety of forms. There are also suggestions that although a kolven match was usually played in an enclosed area, it was sometimes played across more open country, through villages and down roads. But history is very loose on the matter of actual holes in *kolven*—and, for that matter, what the playing ground was referred to for each individual target. It must be told that *kolven* was often played on ice, and the most common illustrations of it show a target as a stake or post—not a hole at all. The nineteenth-century writer Andrew Lang, in *The Badminton Library* (1890), summed up *kolven (kolf)* in this way: "[G]olf is no more kolf than cricket is poker."

In one similarity to golf, pall-mall has been linked to play with multiple clubs, usually no more than two. But even this is a sketchy fact. It is thought that when two clubs were used, one was for long shots and one for difficult lies. The object was to reach the post at the opposite end of the enclosure, a flat courtyard.

Each of these games, including *choule* and *mail à chicane,* had its own quirks. Clearly, though, none were golf. In not one of these archaic games was there more than a single isolated element of the four ingredients of golf: (1) a range of clubs, (2) the player's own ball, (3) a simple hole dug into the ground—not ice, and (4) the infinite variety of play achieved by playing across natural land set up purposefully with hazards en route. Indeed, we should take note that this last quality is the essence of *routing.*

The Cross-Country Element

As this look into games played with sticks and balls has demonstrated, golf is as much about *golf courses* as it is anything else. For it is the distinction of the limitless and ever-changing playing ground that unmistakably sets golf apart from other games and pastimes. This distinction holds true regardless of whether the discussion is about the ancient games involving sticks and balls or any modern game that attempts a comparison. The nature of traversing the land is among golf's greatest legacies.

Although there are references to cross-country stick-and-ball activity, such as in the translation of *Roman de Brut* (1155–1200), from which the passage "driving balls wide over the fields" comes, this was probably not golf. As has been established, in none of the old games typically mentioned as predecessors to golf are there reliable accounts of formats played cross-country where a ball assigned to a particular individual was hit until it rolled into a hole. Certainly there are none where the process is repeated all over again to another hole located a varied distance away. This is the great distinction in golf. Golf involves much more than a stick and ball and well more than hitting the two together to propel the ball past an opponent or to outmaneuver another team. Without the element of playing across the land—on golf courses—golf may appear almost

Golfers of the Scottish Renaissance. St. Andrews 1543 A.D.

FIGURE 1-2
The Trio of St. Andrews Golfers, a project of historical illustrator Jurek Alexander Putter, who works from his studio in St. Andrews, Scotland, captures the Scottish Renaissance of 1543. The subjects of Putter's work, like the detail of the town's buildings, were painstakingly researched and are shown in the likely regalia of such golfers of their time. Little did the practitioners of the game in 1543 know that their provincial pastime would survive in Scotland and eventually emerge, in literal terms, to çonquer the world.
COURTESY OF JUREK ALEXANDER PUTTER: www.jurekputter.freeserve.co.uk

similar to some of the games mentioned. That modern-day practice range located alongside the highway, if transported back in time to the year 1200, may well look like ancient *het kolven* players mingling on the village square, or perhaps pall-mall teams practicing for the afternoon match. Without the invention of the golf course, we really have no golf.

It would be neglect to discuss the influences of cross-country and sticks and balls without mentioning the element of golf related to the hunt. My collaborator, Dr. Ed Sadalla, whose insightful comments about human psychology as it relates to golf course routing appear in Hole 10, "The Psychology of Journey," covers this topic. Let me just say that there is a direct relationship between hunting and marching out over the moors in pursuit of a projectile just struck, bringing it to a dead state in the fewest of shots, and then starting the whole procedure over again. When we play golf, we are after something—*we are hunting.*

Let us but ask ourselves why golf originated on links-land and immediately it becomes clear that without hazards there would have been no golf.
—*Robert Hunter,* The Links

So Who Invented Golf?

Despite the many books written on the subject—which, by the way, reach numerous and varied conclusions—there is really a simple answer. It is offered here for anyone who may ever ask: *Golf was invented by whomever invented the golf course.* For without golf courses, as it has already been established, there are only sticks and balls. Sticks and balls and the process of hitting them together are only a fraction of golf. Golf is more.

The above conclusion conveniently bypasses the longstanding jockeying for position by the Scottish and the Dutch. Which of them was responsible for golf is rather a contested question. The Dutch scholars point to their ancestors' game *het kolven* and a number of similarities to golf, but they are unable to point to *golf courses* dotting the Dutch landscape. The Scots, in an effort to thwart the Dutch claims to golf-like clubs, balls, targets, and the sketchy history of cross-country *kolven* play, try like the devil to push their origins of golf as early as possible. Nothing would be more welcomed by the Scots than the unearthing of a long-lost diary of a golf course operator writing about the troubles of damage from knights in heavy armor trampling across their "course." What matters in finding the origin of golf is finding the origin of the golf course. In this area, the Scots are well in command.

FIGURE 1-3
The infamous Act of Parliament from 6 March 1457 is the first mention of golf ever discovered. The Act itself, by King James II, banned golf and other pastimes because they interfered with archery practice.
SOURCE: THE SCOTTISH PARLIAMENT PROJECT, UNIVERSITY OF ST. ANDREWS, SCOTLAND

ITEM it is decretyt and ordanyt that wapinschawingis be haldin be the lordis ande baronys spirituale and temperale four tymis in the zere And at the fut ball ande the golf be vtterly cryt doune and not vsyt Ande at the bowe merkis be maide at ilk paroch kirk a paire of buttis and schuting be vsyt ilk sunday And that ilk man schut sex schottis at the lest vnder the payne to be raisit apone thame that cumis not at the lest ij d to be giffin to thame that cumis to the bowe merkis to drink And this to be vsyt fra pasche till alhallomess efter And be the nixt mydsomer to be reddy with all ther graith without failze And that ther be a bowar and a fleger in ilk hede towne of the schyre And at the towne furnys him of stuf and graithe efter as nedis him therto that he may serve the cuntre with And as tuichande the futball and the golf we ordane it to be punyst be the baronys vnlawe And gif he takis not the vnlaw that it be takin be the kingis officiaris Ande gif fie parrochin be mekill that ther be iij or iiij or fyue bow merkis in sik placis as ganys ther for And that ilk man within that parrochin that is within fyfte and passit xij zere sall vse schuting and that men that is outwith and past thre scoir zeiris sal vse vther honest gammys as efferis

Item, it is decreed and ordained that weaponshowings be held by the lords and barons, spiritual and temporal, four times yearly, that football and golf be utterly cried down and not used, that the bow marks be made at every parish church, a pair of targets, and shooting to be practiced every Sunday, and that each man shoot at least six shots under the pain to be raised upon those that do not attend at least 2 pence, to be given to those that come to the bow marks for drink. This is to be done from Easter until All Hallows, and by the next midsummer [men are] to be ready with all their equipment without fail. And that there be a bower and a fletcher in each head town of the shire, and that the town furnish him with goods after his needs in order that he may serve the country. And, touching the football and golf, we ordain it to be punished by the baron's unlaw. And if he [the baron] does not take the unlaw, that it be taken by the king's officers. And if the parish is large, that there be 3, 4 or 5 bow marks in such places as gain thereby. And that each man within the parish who is younger than fifty and past twelve years shall use shooting, and that men who are outwith and passed sixty shall use other honest games as are appropriate.

The most famous written account in support of the Scottish origin of golf is the 6 March 1457 Act of Parliament in which golf was banned because it was interfering with the archery practice of its citizens. Logically, to be banned in the first place, golf must have been popular well before this time. Keep well in mind that this 1457 written account is the first mention of *golf* ever found. All of the previous historical references were to other games or were merely generic accounts concerning clubs and balls.

In support of the Dutch argument is the *Book of Hours* of 1530, which shows paintings of people playing *kolven* with clubs that resemble what we have come to know as golf clubs. These players are striving to knock balls into an actual hole in the ground. *Kolven* has been traced to the year 1297, and this is not widely disputed. The distinction between the two accounts is that the 1457 Scottish act was unmistakably about a cross-country game called *golf* in which players controlled their own ball and played with it until holing out to a distant target that changed each time the players repeated their pursuit. The name *golf* has stuck ever since. There is no reason to believe golf has ever been anything but a game played across a rambling landscape on what has come to be known as a *course.* On the other hand, there is every reason to believe that Dutch *het kolven,* at least what we know about its play up to the written mention of golf by the Scots, was about play in courtyards, through villages, and, very often, on ice.

Although it will continue to be debated, the Scots were the first to define golf, and there can really be no dispute when the word *define* is used. Ancient Scotland is where golf came into being. Although it is very likely that influences such as *kolven* and other games may have helped parts of it to develop, golf, with its distinct ingredients, is a product of Scotland.

THE TERMS *BUNKER & TRAP*

The word *bunker,* meaning "a chest or box, often one also used as a seat" and, also, "an earthen seat or bank located in a field," is recorded in Scots from the 1500s. The golf meaning emerged in the 1800s and reflected the "deep, chest-like" qualities of the original (*Source: Scottish National Dictionary Association*). One wonders what pits of sand were called before. Likely not *traps,* as this term came into popular use in America after the late Harry Vardon's caddie exclaimed, "Mr. Vardon, you're *trapped.*" during the 1913 U.S. Open at The Country Club. Both *bunker* and *trap* are acceptable terms. It is surmised that *bunker* is more used in the British Isles due to its origin there and that *sand trap,* when used, is more common in the United States for the same reason.

LINKSLAND, SCOTLAND & GOLF

The game of golf—the game played across open fields with holes—came into being in Scotland sometime before the 1457 Act of Parliament by King James II banning "golfe" for interfering with archery practice. Two reigns later in 1502, King James IV became an avid golfer himself, and the development of the royal nature of the game was underway. As we have explored, exactly how long golf was being played before the 1457 ban is uncertain. Its origins can only be conjectured in light of the obvious claim that if it was prevalent enough to be banned, it had surely been around for quite some time. Keep in mind that in this period there were no mass media and the nearest thing to a high-speed connection was a laborious cart ride across dangerous battlefields. Time moved slowly. Unlike today, fads took decades to spread.

KOLF VERSUS GOLF

When the seventeenth-century Dutch ship *Lastrager* sank off Scotland's coastline, it carried five brass objects among its treasures. In the 1970s, these were recovered along with other cargo, but researchers wracked their brains for 16 years trying to figure out what the odd brass objects could have been used for. Finally, in 1992, Robert Sténuit identified them as *kolfsloffen*—literally, in Dutch, "kolf slippers." They were the clubheads used in the popular Dutch game kolf. Sténuit's find strengthened two theories: (1) that Dutch traders were sure to have brought their game to Scotland's shores during their visits, and (2) that the Dutch game in this era was significantly different from golf, as evidenced by the design of the clubheads, which were sized for hitting much larger balls than the golf clubheads of the same period.

The Word *Golf*

Because this book is about golf course routing, it will prove useful to cover a small bit about the word *golf.* The words *course* and *routing* probably need no explanation, athough it might be pointed out that *course* first indicated that portion of the links (the whole of the links often referred to as the *green*) between hazards and along the line to the hole. In essence, course first meant "fairway," although that term was not yet in use. *Course* quickly moved up the ranks and soon, as if to think positively, golfers began describing the entirety of the links as "a course," where just years before the term meant only the smooth bits.

Now to *golf.* While many believe the connection between the words *golf* and *kolf* to be compelling, the spellings of *golf* through medieval times varied widely. It was not uncommon for words to have significant spelling differences, even within the same document. *Gowffe, gouffe,* and *golfe* are but a few of the many examples.

In *The Story of Golf, From Its Origins to the Present Day* (1972), author Tom Scott offers some interesting thoughts on where the Scots may have come up with *gouffe.* Besides discussing its possible roots in *kolf,* Scott points out an old Scottish word, *howffe,* which meant "meeting place." He makes an excellent case that in a country of varied dialects, such as Scotland, such a progression involving the sounds of "*h*" and "*g,*" would not be too unordinary. Golfers, after all, had to have places to meet, and golf links could very well have been named for this big-picture need. Interestingly, Scott does not connect *howffe* to the Dutch word *hof,* a word for "courtyard." Perhaps this would only add fuel to the Dutch argument that golf might have come from their game *kolven.* It is also quite thought-provoking of Scott to call attention to the Scottish word *gulfe,* which means "bay." Could there be a connection between these words? It would have been quite logical for the word *golf* to have roots in a word that describes land along the coast where golf had become popular.

Golf has so much to do with the physical ground—the land, the course, and the meeting place—that it would make great sense if its name somehow stems from these elements. Ah, but until someone uncorks that cellar door behind which are writings about golf that have not seen the light of day for some seven or eight-hundred years, we will never know for sure exactly where the word *golf* comes from. We can only speculate. Or argue.

Linksland

The British Isles are synonymous with *linksland.* The word *links* comes from the Old English *hlincas,* meaning "ridges." The Scottish term *links* came to mean the undulating sandy ground near a shore, which was full

One of the best, if not *the* best, descriptions of how linksland evolved was penned by Sir Guy Campbell in *A History of Golf in Britain.* I believe anyone who might attempt a better explanation of how the land on which the first natural golf courses were discovered would be foolish. For this reason, six paragraphs of this eloquent writing are included:

> *In the formation and over-all stabilization of our island coastlines, the sea at intervals of time and distance gradually receded from the higher ground of cliff, bluff and escarpment to and from which the tides once flowed and ebbed. And as during the ages, by stages, the sea withdrew, it left a series of sandy wastes in bold ridge and significant furrow, broken and divided by numerous channels up and down which the tides advanced and retired, and down certain of which the burns, streams and rivers found their way to the sea.*
>
> *As time went on, these channels, other than those down which the burns, streams and rivers ran, dried out and by the action of the winds were formed into dunes, ridges and knolls, and denes, gullies and hollows, of varying height, width and depth.*
>
> *In the course of nature these channel-threaded wastes became the resting, nesting and breeding places for birds. This meant bird droppings and so guano or manure, which, with the silt brought down by the burns, streams and rivers, formed tilth in which the seeds blown from inland and regurgitated from the crops of the birds germinated and established vegetation. Thus eventually the whole of these areas became grass-covered, from the coarse marram on the exposed dunes, ridges and hillocks, and the finer bents and fescues in the sheltered dunes, gullies and hollows, to the meadow grasses round and about the river estuaries and the mouths of the streams and burns. Out of the spreading and intermingling of all these grasses which followed, was established the thick, close-growing, hard-wearing sward that is such a feature of true links turf wherever it is found.*
>
> *On these areas in due course and where the soil was suitable, heather, whins, broom and trees took root and flourished in drifts, clumps, and covets; terrain essentially adapted to attract and sustain animal life.*
>
> *Nature saw to this. First came the rabbits or "cunnings" as an ancient St. Andrews charter describes them; and after the "cunnings" as naturally came the beasts of prey, followed inevitably by man.*
>
> *This sequence had a definite effect on these wastes or warrens. In them the rabbits bred and multiplied. They linked up by runs their borrows in the dunes and ridges with their feeding and frolicking grounds in the straths and sheltered oases flanked and backed by whins and broom. The runs were then gradually worn into tracks by foxes, and man the hunter in his turn widened the tracks into paths and rides. Generations later when man the sportsman, having adopted golf as a pastime, went in search of ground suitable for its pursuit, he found it waiting for him, in these warrens, almost ready to hand. In form it was certainly primitive, but it supplied lavishly what today are regarded as the fundamental and traditional characteristics of golfing terrain.*
>
> —*Sir Guy Campbell,* A History of Golf in Britain

Sir Campbell's writing describes perfectly the east coast of Scotland, and it is here that golf is thought to have developed. The conditions were right. This terrain that seemed useless for any other purpose contributed to the spread of golf in Scotland. Whether at the coast or just slightly inland, golf and linksland seemed inseparable, and would remain so for many years.

of ridges of windswept sand and hills formed by the forces of the weather and sea. In no other language is there a word to define, with such precision, this distinctive form of land.

Although it would be charming if a linksland were the site of the first golf course, nothing in history necessarily confirms this. Golf could very well have begun in the hinterlands. But if it did, the game then moved to the coasts, where it eventually flourished. It could be that golf rooted in linksland because (1) the land was easier to come by, or (2) its followers might simply have enjoyed the game on this terrain. Or perhaps a little of both was at play.

A practical reason linksland would have been chosen lies in its unsuitability for farming and building. It was naturally open and available for roaming by the population. Games could be played there without conflicting with the order of the day. What is more, the seaside population was significant, so there was a supply of golfers.

The more romantic rationale for linksland being chosen for golf is that it was infinitely more *interesting*. That golf is played over an obstacle course cannot have been an accident, for much simpler games could—and would—be played on more much more refined terrain. Linksland, a topsy-turvy land that seems at first to go against ease and gravity, provides a contradiction that is not seen in most sports. Imagine soccer played on rough hillocks with the occasional sand pit. (Say, perhaps there is a concept there.) In golf, the objective of choosing from an array of routes that single path to the hole that will produce the best possible result has been forever shaped by the influences of the links. Golfers recognized an aspect of fun in this land that would forever make golf unique among all sports and games. In a way, these pioneers of golf purposefully antagonized themselves by playing their game over land that was neither flat nor confined. In fact, the land chosen for the first golf course was so ill suited to the purpose of easily advancing a small ball that this quality in itself has become golf's greatest hallmark.

But, despite its apparent ruggedness, hidden amongst linksland is a field-like quality. Although the land is rough in appearance, there are everywhere natural reprieves winding their way in and among the dunes and tall grasses. These reprieves constituted the first golf courses, although in the early stages of golf there were only paths on which play was carried out from one place to the next. Crude by today's standards, these paths would one day become holes.

ANCIENT DISTANCES

A good drive for a golfer in 1813 was about 165 yards with the old feather ball (the *feathery*). In 1848, the gutta-percha ball was introduced; its distance was about 25 yards farther than the feathery, or around 190 yards. In 1898, Coburn Haskell of Cleveland got the idea to manufacturer a golf ball in a fashion similar to rubber-cored baseballs. His invention, the Haskell Ball, introduced a few years later, added another 25 yards, or just over 200 yards for decent drives.

EARLY HOLES & COURSES

It was not until the early 1800s that golf courses—that is, series of holes that formally constituted a course—were recorded in reliable map form or described well enough for this distinction. Until this time, holes and their combinations with one another were largely whatever golfers defined them to be. Golf was anything but standardized. Play was over naturally occurring land with few or no improvements. The hole in the ground was about all that was formal.

GOLF COURSE ROUTING HISTORIC TIMELINE

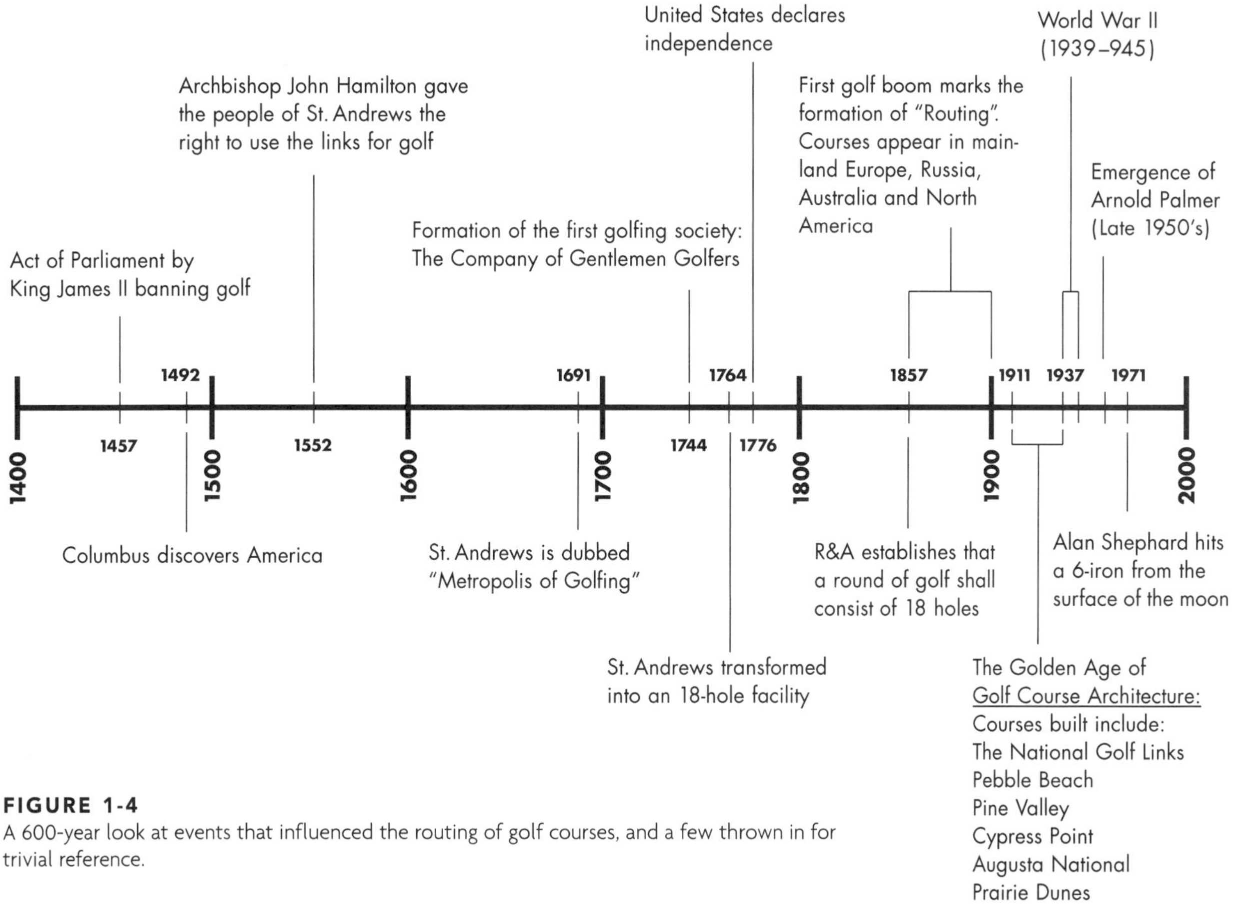

FIGURE 1-4
A 600-year look at events that influenced the routing of golf courses, and a few thrown in for trivial reference.

The Beginning of Golf Holes

Literally, a "hole" in golf's early development meant only the hole dug into the ground, not what we typically think of today—the assemblage of tees, fairway, hazards, and green that make up a "golf hole." As can be seen from the earliest maps of Scotland's oldest golf courses, the dug holes in the terrain were given names, and play was from just adjacent to the one previously holed out to the next one in line.

The earliest golf holes were most likely laid out as a matter of convenience. Beginning near a town or gathering place where the finishing hole was established, the line of play for the first hole was toward another hole dug in the ground, and so on. Citizens roaming over the land trampled the grass and kept it low. Rabbits nibbled at the grass, and larger animals, such as the sheep who grazed there, took cover at the low points and hunkered in to get away from the strong winds.

The "greens," which did not include defined places to putt as we have today, nor nomenclature to define them, were simply the areas most calm in terms of terrain and were usually matted down nicely by

THE STYMIE

The stymie was a situation created when a player's ball came to rest between the cup and an opponent's ball. Under old golf rules, the obstructing ball could not be moved, and the player farther away could indirectly strike the offending ball in the process of playing his own ball. Rescinded from the Rules of Golf (for obvious reasons!) in 1951, the stymie is just one example of how the play of golf has changed dramatically through the years. Like the movement to stroke play from traditional match play, such changes significantly altered the way golf was played and, ultimately, the way courses were routed, designed, and constructed.

golfers and others. The tees were one and the same with these "greens." There were no separately built platforms as we have today. Play was from a few steps to the right or left of where you had just holed out. The hazards were the hollows created by animals combined with the naturally occurring hills of sand held together with tufts of grass at the top and sides. Presumably, the first bunkers were created by animals, who knew that, as the modern-day adage says, a bunker is a relatively good place to be should lightning catch you by surprise. *Bunker,* by the way, is Scottish for "wooden storage chest" and appropriate to describe the natural pits of despair that very likely interrupted the landscape of early golf links.

As golfers went from target to target, the areas between the obstacles became worn smooth. This is where the grass would be kept low. Today we call these areas *fairways,* but there was no such distinction back then. Where it was not desirable to walk—or hit a ball—the land remained rugged and evil. These were the *roughs.* And they were.

The object of early holes was quite simply to commit the fewest number of strokes en route, typically against an opponent of one or more. It is well confirmed that early golfers often played in large groups. There is cause to believe that a match might have been against several other players, at times a small army of golfers trekking across the links.

What the early golf holes lacked was any relation to a par or standard. There were no par 3s, 4s, or 5s. Indeed, there was no concept of par until the 1890s, when it was first formulated as an "ideal fixed score." The object before this concept emerged was a simple matter of counting up the hole-by-hole winners. The winner was whoever won the greatest number of holes among the quantity that all the contestants agreed to play.

Also, because there was little constraint to the width and seldom any traffic on individual golf holes, there were abundant opportunities and considerable choice in how to get from point A to point B. Sadly, this quality that so influenced the development of golf is being quietly snuffed out by the influences that tend to pinch the width of golf holes. Golf holes with wide-open choices, even intruding onto adjacent fairways, are now replaced by defined corridors that guide golfers along a single path from one hole to the next. Development on neighboring lands, the desire to use minimal acreage, and heightened litigation have all contributed to this condition.

The Formation of Courses

The task of chaining golf holes together was all about play from one hole dug in the ground to another. Eventually you would need to return (hey, you might as well be golfing on the way back!), and this whole process of chaining and returning was what formed golf courses. The act of returning is the most significant landmark in the formation of golf courses, or *links,* as they were referred to in the beginning.

Returning to the point at which you began golfing is at the core of golf course routing. This is precisely how golf courses were formed, and it gave them their original out-and-back quality. Golfers played so many

FIGURE 1-5
Pacific Dunes, the second course at the Bandon Dunes Golf resort in Oregon, is a classic links layout created in the twenty-first century. Designed by golf architect Tom Doak, the par-71 layout follows the land—and not the rules. The par sequence of the back nine (par 37) is worth mentioning, as it features four par 3s, three par 5s, and only two par 4s.
MIKE HOUSKA, PHOTOGRAPHER; COURTESY OF DOGLEG STUDIOS

holes on their way *out* and, generally, the same holes on their way back in. Because play began near a hole dug in the ground that would generally be the last played during a match, the first dug hole in the ground that a golfer reached was often the next to the last that he encountered on the way back. That is, if the golfer were to come all the way back. As noted, golf in this time was whatever it needed to be. Holes were not always numbered. Play could change form from day to day and round to round. It is very likely that play could have begun on some links midway on the routing; players simply began and ended where they preferred, or where convenient.

The method whereby early courses were laid out can only be surmised. This was undoubtedly an outgrowth both of the natural hazards coming into play and choosing the path of least resistance among them. It would be sad to think, however, that there was not also an element of being clever and cunning in the process of determining where these holes would be set. Even though there was no such profession as golf course architect, most certainly decisions were made that were identical to those being carried out today. Routing was taking place, albeit as a more casual undertaking.

The Element of Sequence

In early golf, the occasional excitement of playing from the end of one hole to another hole very likely took the form of determining the target without regard to sequence. For example, the play decided upon might have been two or more holes away from the starting point. Effectively, this amounted to turning 200-yard holes into 600-yard holes, or whatever may have seemed right at the moment.

This peculiarity led to an absence of a set number of holes for golfing grounds. A links (the term most used to describe a series of holes as golf developed) consisted of any number of golf holes. Perhaps only one, or maybe as many as 50. Without the standard of par, a round was whatever

[T]o learn golf architecture one must know golf itself, its companionships, its joys, its sorrows, its battles — one must play golf and love it.
— George C. Thomas Jr., Golf Architecture in America

golfers deemed it to be. You could play a few holes, go out and back once, or, as they ultimately decided at the famous Leith Links, a round would require playing Leith's five-hole layout three times in succession. Leith, by the way, is considered among the oldest formal golf clubs ever established. Certainly, Leith was among the very first formal courses, and it is quite significant to this idea of randomness that it consisted of just five holes, and no one seemed bothered that St. Andrews, not too far away, had 22. The concept of a golf course being defined by the golfers who played it was an important concept of early golf. Certainly it sets apart the layouts of long ago from anything in the last few hundred years. Golf, at its formation, was about making up the game to be played. Courses were literally whatever the golfers of a group deemed them to be. "Let's play six out and six back today, Malcolm." "No, ol' chap, I prefer to round all 12."

THE ERA OF STANDARDIZATION

Standardization began at what we now affectionately refer to as The Old Course at St. Andrews. Only two chapters of this book are devoted exclusively to specific courses; the selection of St. Andrews as one was easy to justify. In this upcoming chapter, the many influences of St. Andrews are explored and considered. Unquestionably, no place is more dedicated to golf, and none has sparked such rich traditions. The effects of St. Andrews on the golfing world are second to none.

As a preface to Hole 2, "The Influence of St. Andrews," it is important to pass on that it was at The Old Course at St. Andrews where golf received its most recognizable standard: 18 holes. Since 1764, when this monumental decision to have 18 holes was made, standardization has come a long way beyond the 18-hole tradition. Long after the move to 18 holes was adopted, we still find golf being standardized. A continual tug-of-war seems to pit naturalness and randomness against standards of all types.

Changes by Early Societies & Greenkeepers

However they may have come into being, the early routings of links were not 100 percent sacred. The decisions of early golfing societies, which were influential in creating new rules and bylaws, eventually changed the way golf was played, and this led to changes in the way golf courses were configured. Private golf societies, whose members played on the public links, were made up of the aristocrats and influencers of the time. Their members got their way, even if it meant making modifications to the natural links that were spread over public lands. The Company of Gentlemen Golfers, established in 1744, is regarded as the first such golfing society. (At least it is the first we know about.) These few enthusiastic golfers played over just five holes at Leith Links, but they did so for nearly half a century before moving to Edinburgh and changing their charter to The Honourable Company of Edinburgh Golfers, now settled at Royal Muirfield.

Changes made to links by the order of golfing societies were generally related to new policies or rules. Therefore, equally influential as the members themselves were those who cared for golfing grounds. It would have been futile for societies to vote to change policy without having someone capable of actually making the changes to the physical ground.

The role of early greenkeepers in routing, up to and including the legacy of Old Tom Morris at St. Andrews, was one of convenience. Who better to help determine whether a change or improvement would work than the guy responsible for making sure the holes were dug crisply, the flags in place, and damage repaired whenever necessary? Although greenkeeping was a rather casual process at early courses, there is evidence of designated managers who cared for the links and were ultimately responsible for readying them for competition and doing all of the jobs we now associate with the "keeping of the green."

In their landmark book *The Architects of Golf,* authors Geoffrey Cornish and Ron Whitten go so far as to proclaim Allan Robertson (1815–1859) the first-ever golf course architect. Robertson, a ball-maker and supervisor of the links at St. Andrews, was given the job of improving the links under the umbrella direction of the Society of St. Andrews Golfers. Robertson is credited with implementing many changes at St. Andrews and went on to consult on the layout of courses nearby. One in particular, a ten-hole layout, eventually became what is now Royal Carnoustie.

Links and golf, it may be said, go hand in hand; where there is no links there can be no golf.

—From a pamphlet entitled Historical Gossip About Golf and Golfers, *1863, author unknown*

FIGURE 1-6
Portrait of Allan Robertson, considered the first golf architect for his 1848 modifications to The Old Course at St. Andrews. Among his vocations, Robertson was a ball-maker at St. Andrews, and he was the first golfer to break 80 there.

COURTESY OF THE USGA ARCHIVE

Clearly, golf is no more kolf than cricket is poker."
—Andrew Lang, The Badminton Library, *1890*

Early Golf Routings

Early golf architecture has been referred to often, but never has it been well pinpointed in terms of years. In this book, and by authority of those who contributed to and reviewed its content, it is defined as the period in which courses began to be laid out instead of found, up to the great proliferation of golf in the United States, where the game finally took hold on the single country that would change its course for the next several generations.

The *beginning* of this period, let's say, would be at the last part of the nineteenth century, roughly the 1870s. This is when we began to see golf professionals assume the responsibility of golf course routing for newly founded courses. They were also active in bringing golf to parts of the world where no golf had gone before. Mostly Scottish emigrants, these evangelists began introducing golf to Europe and the British Empire as well as to America. Clubs were established in New Zealand (1871), Canada (1873), Australia (1882), Belgium (1888), Spain (1891), Switzerland (1892), Holland (1893), Germany (1895), Russia (1895), Italy (1898), and the United States, in New York (1888).

The last decade of the nineteenth century saw the formation of routing. It was a time when a consciousness about the layout of courses began to be documented. For example, at Portmarnock in Ireland, W. C. Pickeman and George Ross went against the grain of going out and coming in, instead routing ingenious side-by-side and returning nines that offered a variety of directions. Their pre-1900 work was among the first purposeful routings of an 18-hole course that did not follow the out-and-back principle. Muirfield was another. Here, Old Tom Morris is credited with establishing a course with a configuration different from other links. All of the holes are within a short walk of the clubhouse, and only three holes—the third, fourth, and fifth, play along the same direction in succession. The two loops of nine holes begin with the "front" nine, a clockwise-oriented outer loop, and end with the "back" nine, a mostly counterclockwise inner loop.

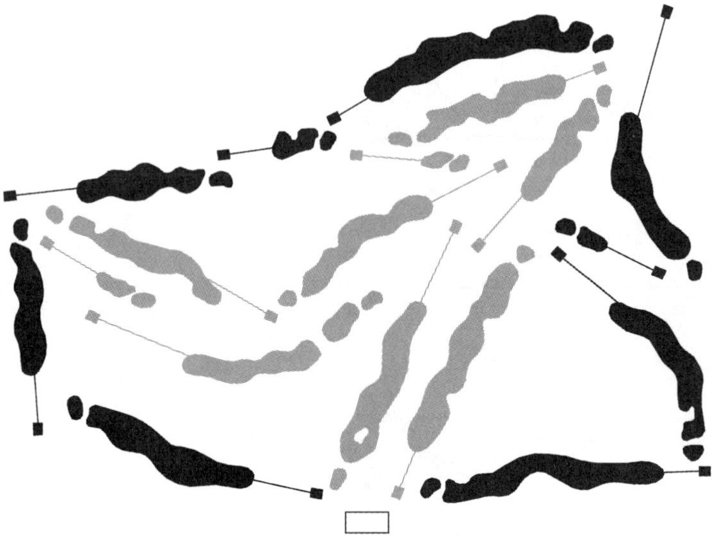

FIGURE 1-7
Muirfield Links was designed by Old Tom Morris. Originally, just 16 holes, built by hand and horse, were opened in 1891. The final two holes of the 18 were added later that year. Muirfield is the first known course routed in two loops of nine holes each. The first nine plays around the perimeter of the property in a clockwise direction, and the second nine is contained inside the first, running counter-clockwise. Note that not more than three successive holes run in the same direction, meaning the wind—no matter which way it blows—enters into play through-out the round.

FIGURE 1-8
Portmarnock Golf Club, situated just north of Dublin, Ireland, is one of the earliest examples of a purposeful routing in which the holes are laid out in two 9-hole loops, each returning to the clubhouse. Of note is that the nines are side by side and not intermingled. On Christmas Eve of 1893, a Scottish insurance broker named W. C. Pickeman and a friend, George Ross, rowed over from England to the peninsula of Portmarnock to scout out land suitable for a golf links. They liked what they found and went to work laying out the course. Only nine holes were built at first, and this is the reason behind the returning nines and, quite possibly the side-by-side configuration that was employed when another nine was added two years after the original.

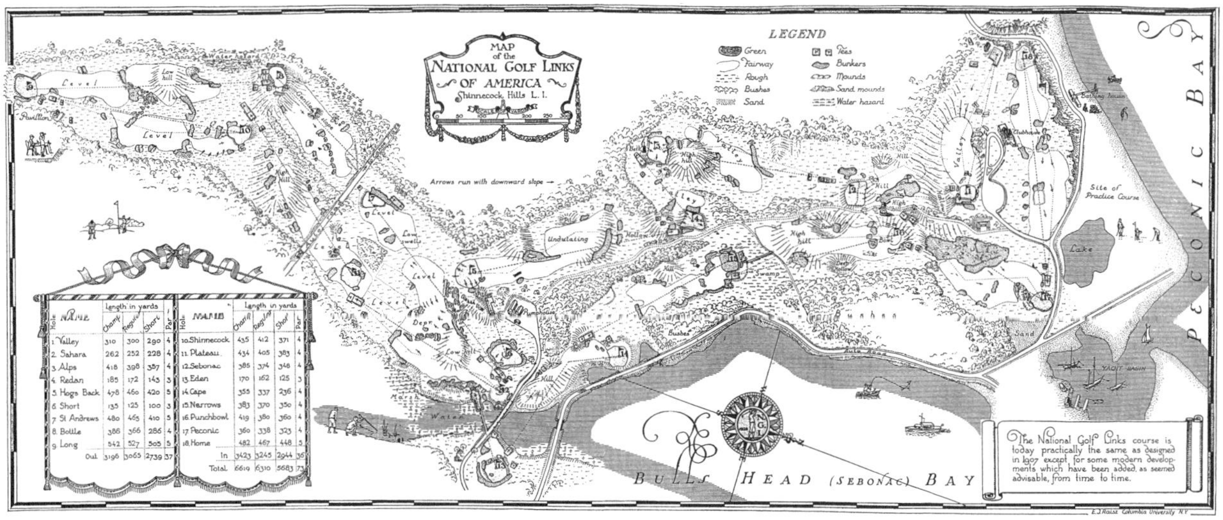

FIGURE 1-9
The National Golf Links, envisioned by Charles Blair Macdonald to be America's first truly classic golf course and a blueprint for growing golf in the States, was established in 1911. During the preceding five years, Macdonald scouted ideal land until settling on affordable but outstanding land along the coast of Long Island, New York. The catalyst for Macdonald's vision was a 1901 survey conducted by a magazine among prominent British golfers. The golfers were asked to put forth their candidates for the best golf holes in the world. Intrigued, Macdonald made visits to see firsthand these "ideal" golf holes. National's third was inspired by the famous Alps at Prestwick, its fourth by North Berwick's Redan, and its seventh by the Road Hole at St. Andrews. Macdonald's idea to take many of the world's great holes and strategies and wrap them into an American course that would have no equal was a defining moment in American golf course design. Indeed, The National lives up to his plan and remains among the best courses in the world. Writing in *Metropolitan* magazine the year prior to its opening, Horace Hutchinson sums up the reality Macdonald so much wanted to create by stating that the course "has no weak point."

Any golfer conversant with golf course abroad and the best we have in America... knows that in America as yet we have no first-class golf course comparable with the classic courses in Great Britain and Ireland. There is no reason why this should be so, and it is the object of this association to build such a course...
—Charles Blair Macdonald

The *end* of this period, again in the opinion of this book, was the creation of the National Golf Links by Charles Blair Macdonald, for it was the ideals and eventual building of the National that gave rise to the game of golf. It was a shot heard around the world, solid proof that courses equally as marvelous as those in Scotland could be realized in faraway and unlikely places. America included.

Macdonald wrote extensively about the "ideal" golf course. His commitment is summed up in an excerpt (see left margin) from a 1904 agreement he penned to attract investors to his concept of building the National Golf Links of America.

The National Golf Links was a wake-up call to the world. Just as good and pristine as it was designed to be in its homeland of Scotland, golf was now underway in busy America.

The Golden Age

Geoff Shackelford, in his aptly titled book *The Golden Age of Golf Design,* declares that golf course design has "never come close" to the impact of all that occurred between Macdonald's completed work at the National (1911) and Perry Maxwell's first work at Prairie Dunes (1937). In this decidedly American period, interest in golf increased, and the appetite of the United States was large. Riding on Macdonald's success in New York, golf course architecture was in full force, and the world would soon see how a Scottish game played across the land would be applied to the new land across the sea.

Although not all courses were carefully laid out, there was an appreciation for those that were. Routing was considered a crucial process. No longer was the act of laying out holes defined by accident. Golf professionals turned architects were now in charge. Their visions were the result of listening to one another, arguing the merits of certain approaches, and, ultimately, setting in the field their dreams of the ideal course.

The significant courses routed in this era are enough to satisfy any golfer's interest in great designs. The architects were defining a new form of golf: that which could literally be built anywhere. Courses were popping up in strange places—not just the linksland of Long Island but inland of the East Coast, the cliffs above the Pacific, and the rolling hills of Georgia. Here is but a short list of some of the significant designs that defined The Golden Era:

- National Golf Links—C. B. Macdonald & Seth Raynor, 1911
- Pebble Beach—Jack Neville & Douglas Grant, 1918
- Pine Valley—H. S. Colt & George Crump, 1918
- Baltusrol—A. W. Tillinghast, 1922
- Merion—Hugh Wilson & William Flynn, 1924
- Bel-Air—George Thomas, 1926
- Riviera—George Thomas, 1927
- Cypress Point—Alister MacKenzie & Robert Hunter, 1928

FIGURE 1-10
Golf course architect Albert W. Tillinghast (1874–1942) was among the most influential of America's designers during the Golden Age of Golf Course Architecture. Here, with a construction foreman, Tillinghast reviews what appears to be a routing plan overlayed to a topographical map. Unlike today's typical set of involved construction plans, courses prior to the 1960s were built almost entirely with just a routing plan and a few details.

SOURCE: *GOLF ILLUSTRATED,* APRIL 1924

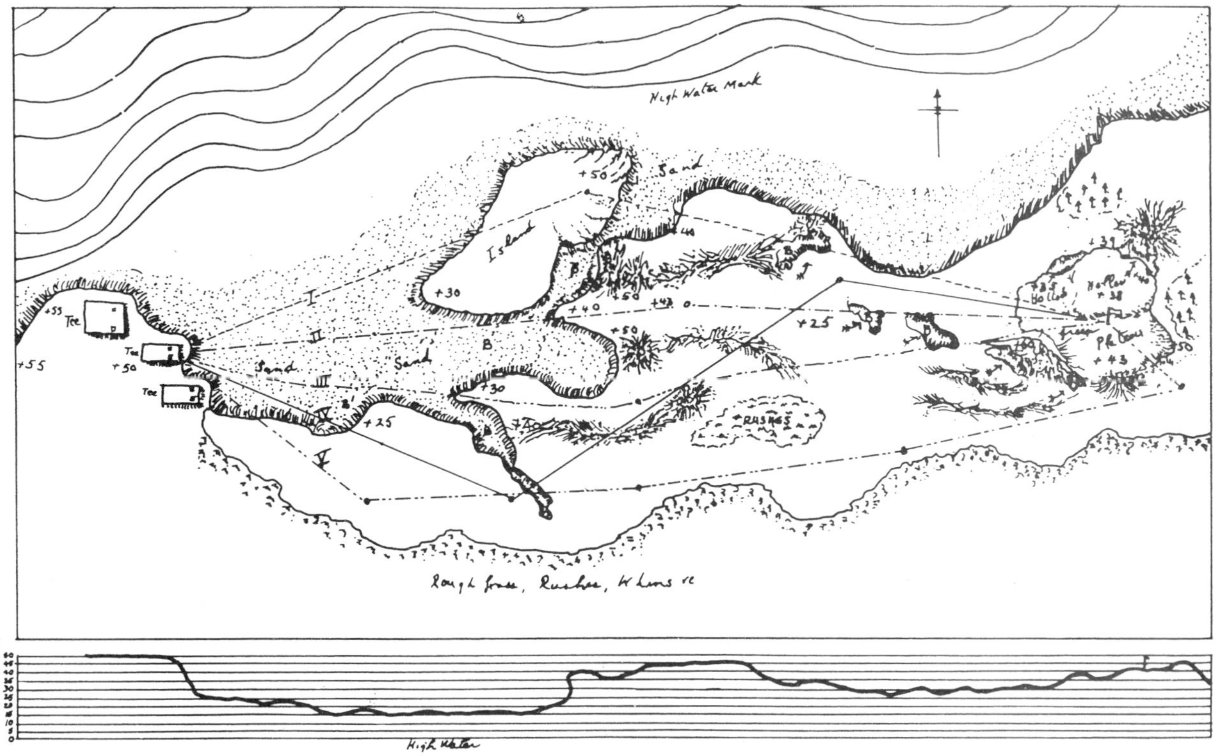

FIGURE 1-11
Alister MacKenzie's winning entry in *Country Life* magazine's 1914 design contest, judged by Bernard Darwin and C. B. Macdonald. MacKenzie called it the "ideal two-shot hole that launched my career." Mackenzie epitomized the Golden Age of Golf Course Architecture, creating some of the most cherished layouts of the era. In MacKenzie's design for this fictitious par 4, he captured the essence of natural linksland designs, which encouraged play from a variety of angles and across multiple routes.

SOURCE: USGA LIBRARY COLLECTION

"The stretching out of holes to their last limit has often not only an evil effect on individual holes, but also on the layout in general..."

—Robert Hunter, from The Links

- Seminole—Donald Ross, 1929
- Pasatiempo—Alister MacKenzie & Robert Hunter, 1929
- Augusta National—Alister MacKenzie & Bobby Jones, 1933
- Prairie Dunes—Perry Maxwell, 1937
- Pinehurst No. 2—Donald Ross, 1903 to 1940s (a work in progress)
- Oakmont—Henry & William Fownes, 1903 to 1940s (a work in progress)

The Modern Era

Infinitely more destructive than a stormy day canceling a long-awaited tee time, the onset of World War II destroyed the Golden Age of Golf Course Design, among other things. Fortunately, when the world had time to partially recover, there were golfers and enthusiasm to pick up where they had left off. Around the world, the first priority, golfwise, was restoring courses that had been neglected or partially destroyed. Then, in the late 1950s, money, leisure time, and a friendly face with the name of Arnold Palmer reenergized golf to the point where there was a call for more course development. The Modern Era of Golf Course Design was officially underway.

New golf courses were being built virtually everywhere. Public courses, vacation destinations, private clubs, and new developments all *had* to have their share of golf. No one—and no place—wanted to be left without emerald fairways and brilliant white sand traps. Golf courses entered the age of consumerism. In February 1971, golf even traveled through space to the moon, where Alan Shepard smacked a 6-iron a distance that even Tiger Woods would envy.

The Modern Golf Hole Not Only Tests The Expert, BUT—Is Pleasurable For Everyone To Play

—Copy from an advertisement run by A. W. Tillinghast, c. 1930s

We have not left this era. Today, courses are routed and configured as much or more based on the influences of the Modern Era as they are the traditions and strategies expressed in the courses of earlier times and eras. The Modern Era was, and is, shaped by several factors. Each plays a crucial part in the evolution of how courses are now expected to be laid out and configured. These include:

- Earth-moving machinery
- The desire for residential golf developments
- Improvements in golf equipment
- The move away from match play formats
- Televised golf
- The advent of professional tours and prize money
- Artificial irrigation technology
- Meticulous manicuring of golf courses
- Advancements in greenkeeping technologies/education
- The popularization of the electric cart
- Environmental awareness
- The push to make golf accessible to the masses

FIGURE 1-12
The Modern Era of Golf Course Design allows courses to be built almost anywhere, not just on the dunes of linksland or the gently rolling land that approximates it. Here, the author (in front at left) discusses progress with his golf course construction superintendent at the 11th tee of The Hideout Golf Club in Monticello, Utah.
PHOTO COURTESY OF DAYLEN, INC. GOLF COURSE BUILDERS

Without question, the single most significant relationship between routing courses and the influences of this Modern Era was the newfound ability to build golf courses *virtually anywhere*. Whereas it had only been practical, for perhaps as long as 700 years previous, to find or mold from the natural land a series of golf holes, it was now possible to attempt to create suitable golf conditions where Mother Nature had obviously not had golf shown on her master plan. Flat land could be turned upside down through the ability to excavate huge loads of soil. Arid regions could be transformed into temporary Seattles. And, last but not least, golf got a lesson in economics, and vice versa. From equipment to television, and from view lots along fairways to Hawaiian resorts, golf became big business. Although routing golf holes will always have roots in the land, there is now a plethora of other influences that routing must consider.

The work of the golf course designer became infinitely more complicated. Golf became more complicated. Routings, once handled by those who just happened to be hanging around, are now the result of a host of professionals. Today, a typical golf course project very likely includes the following professionals just to get the work planned and permitted:

- Land planner
- Golf course architect
- Civil engineer

- Irrigation designer
- Environmental consultants
- Agronomist
- Developer/Project manager

The Death of Peculiarity

As the routing of golf courses has evolved, there has been good change and not-so-good change. Change is, of course, all debatable. Opinions as to what is good will vary depending on who is doing the debating. The topic of peculiarity has been selected to close out this section. Consider it a segue to the nuts and bolts of routing and the nuances that have to be waded through in order to get golfers from A to B. It is good food for thought as we begin to talk about standards, guidelines, and rules.

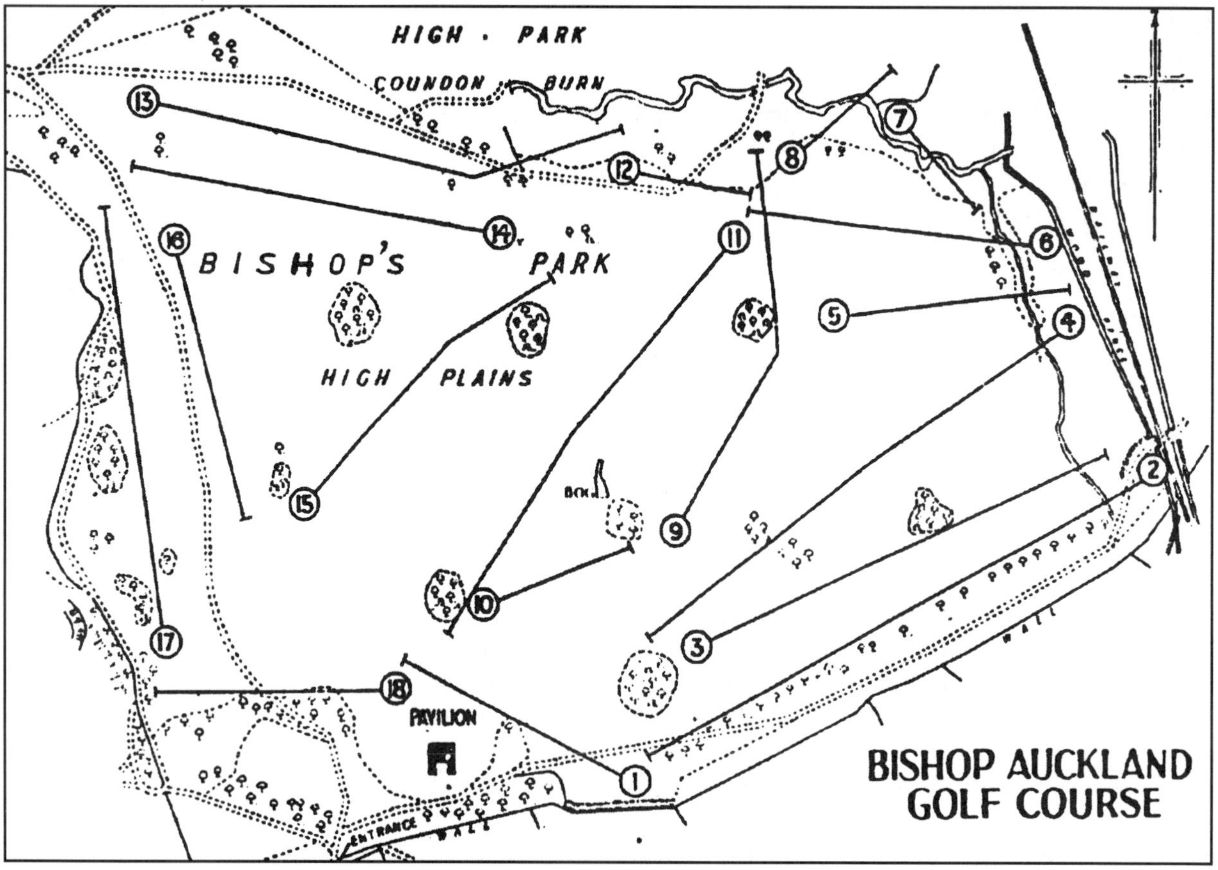

FIGURE 1-13
Bishop Auckland Golf Club near Newscastle upon Tyne, England, has a curious routing that is among the most unusual in the world. Among its oddities are three par 5s in a row, only two par 4s on the front nine, and six par 4s in succession on the back side. Established in 1894 as a 9-hole course, the routing later expanded to 18 holes. It typifies the attitude of early layouts, which had no patience for rules, standards, or the undying need for contrived variation.

COURTESY OF BISHOP AUCKLAND GOLF CLUB

> *Golf evolved in Scotland, and the game—its implements and its rules-adapted itself to those land forms.*
>
> —*Geoffrey S. Cornish, in* News Digest, *May 1988*

The advancements in golf courses and routing have brought about one casualty. It is peculiarity. Another term for this quality is *quirkiness,* one of the few words for which Webster has been unable to trace an origin. *Peculiar* is especially pertinent; its origin relates to a characteristic of distinction, many times intended to define a particular feature of a land or area. Look in your thesaurus and you will see *peculiar* associated with such words as *appropriate, intrinsic,* and *character.*

On early golf courses, the variables that made up the routing were often *quirky.* The order of par and length of holes were not established to follow any idea of good formula, nor was any extreme effort taken to these variables seem perfect. The ideals of ensuring pattern, balance, and symmetry were not as important as allowing the land to unfold the routing. The routing was a product of the land and came to life as places were found to fit holes. Unlike modern times, where routings are very often contrived and purposefully balanced and symmetric, ancient and early designs were whatever they became. There being no concept of par most certainly influenced some of these layouts. Holes were short, long, or somewhere in between. Two examples of courses come to mind that, if routed and designed today, might, unfortunately, get people fired from their jobs.

The first, Bishop Auckland, is a charming 18-hole layout in Northern England. The Bishop, as it is known, sports a most unpredictable order of par. Beginning on the front side, golfers face holes of modern-day par 4, 5, 5, 5, 3, 4, 3, 3, 5 = 37, and, continuing on the back, par 3, 5, 3, 4, 4, 4, 4, 4, 4 = 35. There is simply nothing "usual" about how Bishop Auckland is routed, the order of the pars, or balance between the nines. Amazingly, in the club's centennial book (1894 to 1994), there is zilch about how in the world this design oddity came to be. The rationales, however, can be gleaned by inspecting The Bishop firsthand. Quite simply—and appropriately—this is a course where the land was used to its fullest. Short holes (par 3s) were obviously situated along a meandering creek, and because the creek refused to run uphill to the clubhouse site, these holes are largely bunched in one area, well away from the clubhouse. From there, the puzzle became one of getting away from the clubhouse and back again. The reason there are three par 5s in a row is that the most important thing was not answering to a developer or banker about what would make a good course or whether it would be laughed at by the critics. Rather, the only requirement was that the golf fit—and that it be good and challenging in the process. If you look at the scorecard, it might seem that The Bishop ends on a boring note. How can six par 4s possibly make for a good finish? Well, when you build a course on the sloping moorlands above a valley, you get uphill and downhill and sidehill holes and all sorts of combinations of each. The Bishop's architects realized this. The order of par and everything else unusual about this course is a product of what mattered most. Remember, too, that James Kay, the original designer, and those who followed were not encumbered by the whole idea of par. Bishop Auckland fits, but sadly it would be a difficult task to convince the modern-day developer of this.

THE INHERITANCE OF A GOLF COURSE ROUTING

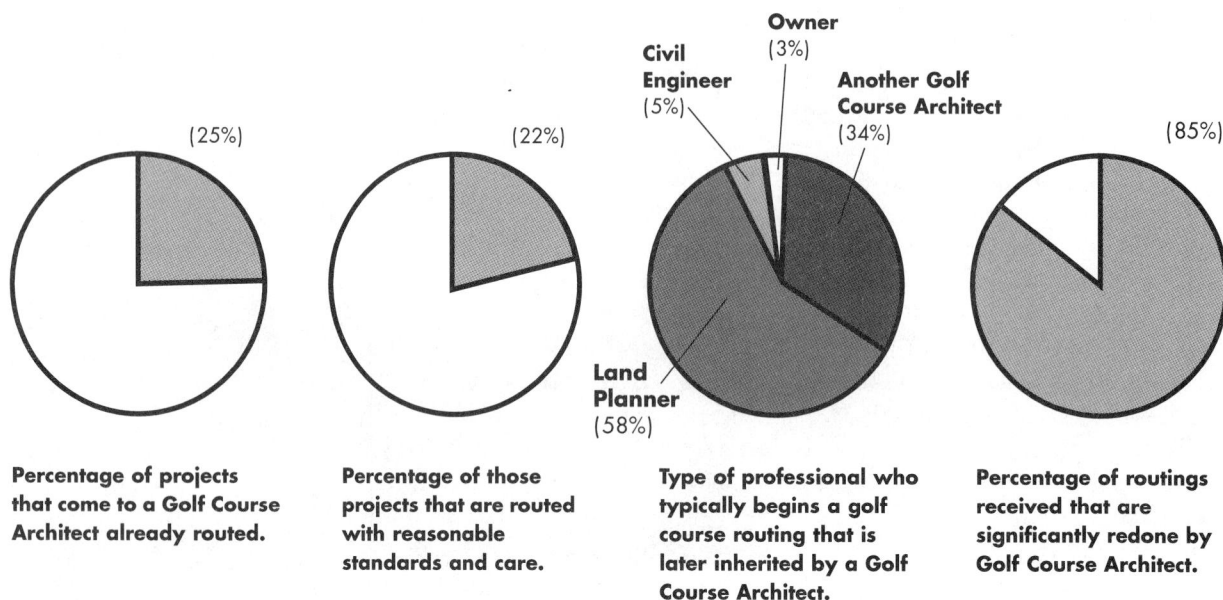

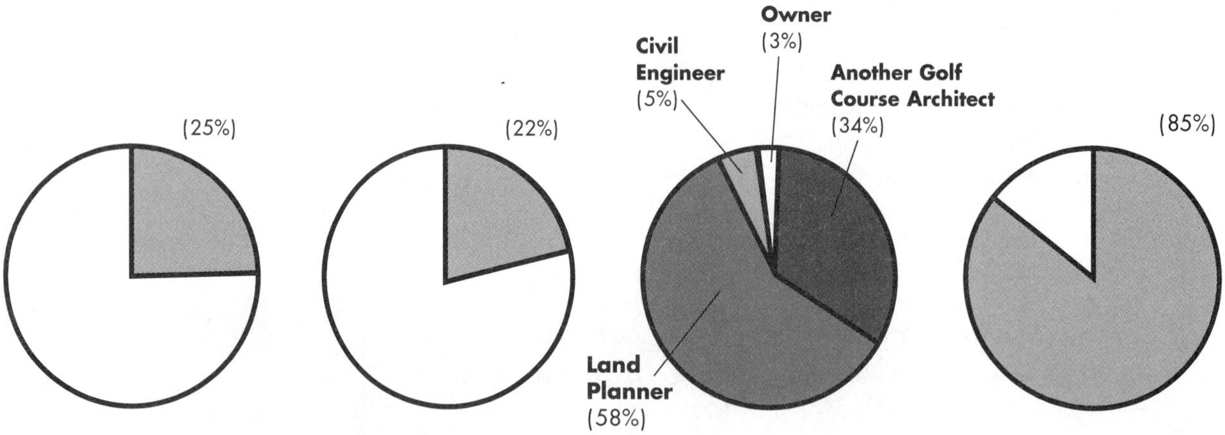

Percentage of projects that come to a Golf Course Architect already routed.

Percentage of those projects that are routed with reasonable standards and care.

Type of professional who typically begins a golf course routing that is later inherited by a Golf Course Architect.

Percentage of routings received that are significantly redone by Golf Course Architect.

FIGURE 1-14
In order to establish a baseline of practice and guidelines in use by those who route golf courses, a survey covering many aspects of routing plans was conducted by the author. The results, culled from 70 golf course architects and planners from throughout North America, Europe and the Pacific, appear periodically throughout this book in chapters appropriate to the survey questions. From the results above, it can be deduced where routing plans are first generated, in what condition they arrive, and to what extent they are modified.

The second poster child of quirkiness is Church Stretton. Founded in 1898 and designed by James Braid, this English course reaches new heights in more ways than one. First, it is essential to know that Church Stretton is built around a mountain. Well, a large hill anyway. When James Braid set foot on the land, he obviously knew that locating the clubhouse on the top would create all sorts of problems, including a congested site and lots of uphill walks. So what to do? Braid ingeniously began with three short holes, all par 3s. They elevate the golfer more than 350-feet to the top of the world, at least in terms of the usually calm land of the south of England. No. 1 is 181 yards, No. 2 is 110, and No. 3 is 165. From the vantage point of the fourth tee, one can see just about 360 degrees. And from here one can also see why Braid did this. How better to ascend the hill in a controlled manner? By using par 3s in succession, he managed to take the golfer from point to point, whereas longer holes would have burdened many a golfer by making the experience laborious and tiring. No matter that these are the opening holes. The balance of the course is almost entirely downgrade. How delightful! *How quirky.*

Peculiarity has gone away mostly because of books like this one. When I played golf at the Bayonette Course at Fort Ord in Monterey, California, it became apparent that Major Robert B. McClure, who laid out the course without any professional design help, had done his homework by reading one of few books about golf course design. Before mobilizing his bulldozers, he made sure to have a "good" and varied order of par, balanced nines, and absolutely nothing quirky.

TRANSCRIPT OF APOLLO 14

On 6 February 1971, Alan Shepard, captain of NASA's Apollo 14 Mission, hit two golf balls on the surface of the moon. The second reportedly stayed aloft for 30 seconds and landed in a distant crater. Following is the transcript of the communications among Shepard; Edgar D. Mitchell, the lunar module pilot; and Houston Control.

SHEPARD: Houston, while you're looking that up, you might recognize what I have in my hand as the handle for the contingency sample return; it just so happens to have a genuine 6-iron on the bottom of it. In my left hand, I have a little white pellet that's familiar to millions of Americans. I'll drop it down. Unfortunately, the suit is so stiff, I can't do this with two hands, but I'm going to try a little sand-trap shot here.

HOUSTON CONTROL: He topped and buried it on the first swing. I assume that the 6-iron was snuck on board.

MITCHELL: You got more dirt than ball that time.

SHEPARD: Got more dirt than ball. Here we go again.

HOUSTON CONTROL: That looked like a slice to me, Al.

SHEPARD: Here we go. Straight as a die; one more. *(significant pause)* Miles and miles and miles.

HOUSTON CONTROL: Very good, Al.

The Apollo 14 space mission allowed astronaut Alan Shepard to hit two golf balls with a specially adapted 6-iron near the area where the lunar module landed on the moon.

NASA PHOTOGRAPH

The Bulletin Board — A Short Story on the Art of Complication

It is a touchy proposition to be critical of the profession from which you make a living, but in architecture, and especially golf architecture, we have managed at times to make what we do either seem very complicated, or to actually be so. Today there are specialized consultants who take care of things that golf architects don't know and subconsultants who specialize in things that the consultants don't know. Each of these entities, by the way, has his own computer systems, printers, and attorneys. It was refreshing—and somewhat alarming—to visit a few years ago with some friends from the United Kingdom who related a tale of a modern-day golf club and how the membership would hear nothing of this overly complicated world of golf architecture.

In the north of England and surrounding a medieval castle was a perfectly charming 18-hole golf course. Its architect unknown, the course was simple, yet elegant because of its simplicity. Built long ago, nothing about it was really fancy, but a surrounding forest and a nearby stream overcame any need for fancy. One day, the local authorities determined that a needed bridge and road project would be best built on a portion of the golf course. A few holes would simply "have to go somewhere else."

What to do? Well, for one, there would be no calling a golf architect, no laborious studies, and certainly no attorneys. Rather, the club appointed a small committee and, within days, a plan was concocted and sent around to the club governors and the head greenkeeper. "Perfect," they concluded. And with that proclamation, a ten-cent copy was made of the roughly drawn plan, and it was stabbed in each of its corners with four ordinary thumbtacks to a bulletin board. This particular bulletin board had been nailed to the wall some 50 years earlier in a narrow hallway between the men's and women's locker rooms, but this had nothing to do with its status. *Everyone* looked there. It was better than sending each member a hand-delivered copy from Prince Charles. In ordinary type at the bottom corner of the plan was a seven-word request: "Please write comments on the sheet below."

And so the story goes. There is really not much more to tell. A few comments were written on the sheet. Most were positive. One asked if the bunkers on the new par 3 might be moved to the left side to compensate for the writer's hooking approach. In the end, the local road-builder helped push some soil around and, within a few months of the bridge being finished, so, too, were four new golf holes. The membership loved the new holes, and the course looks just about the same as it ever did—simple and charming.

In some parts of the world, golf architecture is being approached much as it was 100 years ago. This small project in Northern England is but one example. I find it a good lesson on one hand, but somewhat alarming on the other.

The Influence of St. Andrews

HOLE NO.

2

"If you ever should write anything about St. Andrews Links, begin with the High Hole, for it has given me more bother than all the rest of them put together." So said Old Tom Morris, the most famous among St. Andrews professionals and greenkeepers. In respect for Old Tom, it may be stated that this distant reach of the Links, near to where a flock of golfers may well be making the turn as you read these pages, is every bit as devilish today as it was during his tenure beginning in 1865. This is the beauty of St. Andrews. It has stayed mostly as it always was, at least in form. Our connection to the beginnings of golf is closer because of its stubbornness.

Now might be a good time to point out that the "St. Andrews" here is not that first disciple of Christ believed to have been crucified by the Romans in Southern Greece but rather the *town* of St. Andrews, Scotland, namesake of St. Andrew and affectionately referred to the world over as "The Home of Golf." Even more specifically, Old Tom calls attention to "The Old Course *at* St. Andrews," for it is these 18 holes that have endured as the greatest single influence to golf course routing. They serve as a logical starting point from which the formation of golf courses can be considered.

Before The Old Course, there was a natural and informal approach to golf and courses. Once The Old Course took hold and became the standard, golf courses have taken their components and makeup from her. In the process, what was natural for linksland was replicated in distant reaches on land nowhere like the links and in places a Scotsman could not even pronounce.

You cannot, I submit, consider golf course routing as a topic without exploring St. Andrews. The town, its people, its Old Course, and the other courses there are more than the home of golf; they are golf's *cradle.* Golf, and so much of what we make it to be, is a direct descendant of St. Andrews. Open any book on the game of golf or golf courses and you are sure to find, at the very least, a mention of this amazing place. And in each book, the author has put into words ideas on why this isolated town and its golf mean more to the game than any other corner of the world. Predictable? Perhaps. But oh, so necessary.

THE TOWN

Without the town of St. Andrews and its makeup, there would certainly never have been an Old Course for us to cherish. We know that the original harbor of the town of St. Andrews was located at the estuary of the River Eden, and between this spot and the town was ideal linksland on which golf could be played quite conveniently. It may very well have been as early as the 1100s that stick-and-ball games were played here, perhaps even by Flemish/Dutch traders, visitors to St. Andrews, using clubs designed for their game kolf. But, as we have established, no one knows for sure.

The 'natives' have a pleasure of their own which is as much the staple of the place as old colleges and churches are. This is golfing which is here not a mere pastime, but a business and a passion, and has for ages been so, owning probably to their admirable links. There is a pretty large set who do nothing else, who begin in the morning and stop only for dinner; and who, after practising the game in the sea breeze, discuss it all night. Their talk is of holes.

The influence of St. Andrews on golf is exemplified by an early written account from a student at the University of St. Andrews, James Melville, in 1574. In his diary, Melville described the funds provided by his father for recreation as being enough for "glub an' bals fur goff but nocht a purss for catch pull and tavern." Translated, Melville reports that he has "enough for golf balls, but no money left for tennis or the tavern." This is a city given to golf. Melville understood that, and he put his money toward the one passion that peer pressure would condone—golf.

Perhaps there is no better way to prove the consuming nature of golf at St. Andrews than the words of the well-known scholar, Lord Cockburn, who in 1874 wrote the passage in the left margin.

Geography

The land in and around St. Andrews has been linksland for thousands of years, and it was definitely so in the period when golf was enjoyed to the point of being outlawed, some 500 years ago. Although the land now occupied by The Old Course was most likely covered by water at high tide, St. Andrews had all the necessary makings for golf in the 1500s: linksland, albeit not where it is today, and an active population.

FIGURE 2-1
The Golfers Renaissance St. Andrews, from a historical research series reconstructing medieval and renaissance St. Andrews through illustration. In this view, from around 1540, St. Andrews is seen from the northwest and looking southeast. Golfers are congregating to indulge in their pastime outside the town. Here, on the links, they will be less likely to interfere with the activity of the bustling metropolis.

COURTESY OF JUREK ALEXANDER PUTTER; www.jurekputter.freeserve.co.uk

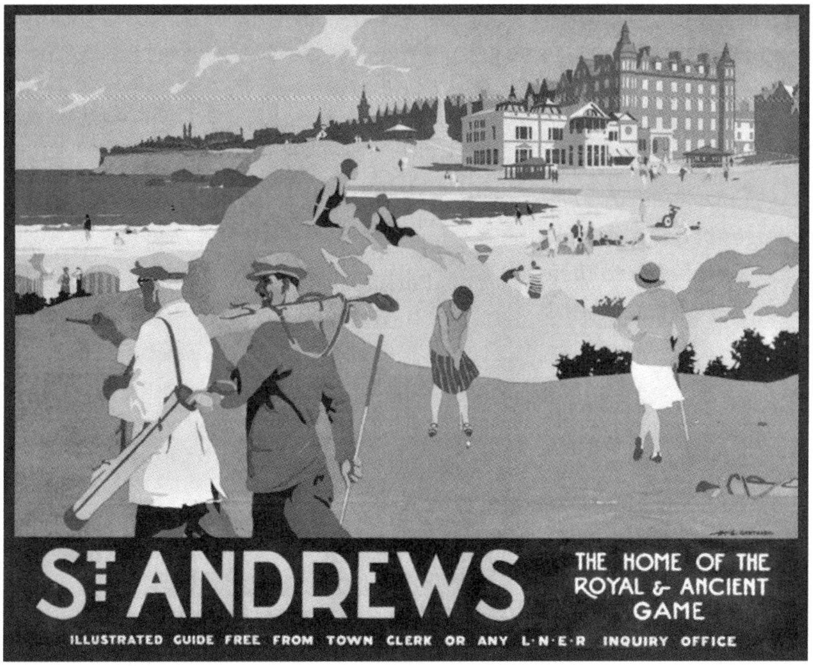

ST ANDREWS
THE HOME OF THE ROYAL & ANCIENT GAME
ILLUSTRATED GUIDE FREE FROM TOWN CLERK OR ANY L·N·E·R INQUIRY OFFICE

FIGURE 2-2
A railway poster celebrating St. Andrews as a golfing metropolis, c. 1923.

COURTESY OF NATIONAL RAIL MUSEUM/SCIENCE AND SOCIETY PICTURE LIBRARY

FIGURE 2-3
St. Andrews Golf Links, circa 1892. By this time, the course is largely as it remains today. The R & A Clubhouse forms the backdrop that has become famous as golfers make their way back to the town from their round out and away.

PHOTOGRAPH BY VALENTINES OF DUNDEE, SCOTLAND; COURTESY OF ST. ANDREWS UNIVERSITY LIBRARY

The blending of the two was a recipe for the development of a game, and, while it will never be known exactly when or where golf was first played, the probability is that it was on terrain very near St. Andrews, if not actually there.

Why St. Andrews?

To be fair, many other places attracted active golfers during the formative years of golf. The Links of Leith, for example, is often regarded as where the first formal golf might have been played, at least under the auspices of a recorded golfing society. This is where The Company of Gentlemen Golfers, established in 1744, played over a five-hole course. Later, this society became the Honourable Company of Edinburgh Golfers, which exists today at Royal Muirfield outside Edinburgh. But as time marched on, golf and St. Andrews became one. This city by the sea, where the land was ideal for golf as it was first conceived, could not be shaken from its municipal pastime. As far back as 1691, St. Andrews was dubbed the "Metropolis of Golfing," and it has never looked back.

As the golfer nears the end of the course, the town returns. By the time he reaches the 17th, he's part of the town.

—Desmond Muirhead, St. Andrews: How to Play the Old Course

A key to St. Andrews' becoming the home of golf lies in its unique orientation. Unlike many other towns where golf was played in the 1800s, St. Andrews is configured with its linksland protruding into the bay—St. Andrews Bay, to be precise. The significance of this pertains to where the medieval city of St. Andrews was constructed in relation to the links. At St. Andrews, you see, it is possible to visit the center of town and never even lay eyes upon the five courses that today are strung together just north of this center. This condition has always been true for St. Andrews. It is blessed with linksland that is isolated yet convenient. It must be appreciated that, before the advent of any organized transportation system, golf was typically played on land near towns. And, in many cases, land for golf was eventually encroached on to make way for expansion of the town and its core. But at St. Andrews, things were different. With the major roads all circulating to the south and west of town, the land to the north—that protrusion into the bay—was unneeded for access and of little use for more than gathering and grazing. The lesson is one we should all remember: good land planning, it seems, was as crucial in medieval times as it is today.

At Leith Links in Edinburgh, for example, things began to crumble in the 1830s, when the growing central city received a higher priority than golf. The golf was apparently not as important as the buildings. Golfers turned to St. Andrews and, with its popularity as a tourist area, the town soon outdistanced all others to become the center of the golfing world.

> *It may be immoral, but it is delightful to see a whole town given up to golf, to see the butcher, the baker and the candlestick maker shouldering his clubs as soon as his day's work is done and making a dash for the links.*
>
> —*Bernard Darwin, describing St. Andrews in* Golf Courses of the British Isles

THE LINKS CHANGE

In the beginning (we are uncertain of the date), the golf links were known to consist of 12 holes. The last hole was near where it sits today, and play went out toward Eden's Mouth of the St. Andrews Bay. Then, after reaching the 11th, golfers turned back and played to the same holes they had just come from, but in reverse order. A round consisted of 22 holes. It was a crude adventure across a wasteland of heather and gorse interrupted only occasionally by grassy areas. The accumulated number of strokes was not important, only that your total was less than your opponent's for a given hole. "Fairways" were very narrow and bordered by thickets of gorse and tall grass. Rabbit holes were everywhere. It seems illogical, but this would one day be the course that all golf course designers would study and that all lovers of golf courses would want to know something about.

FIGURE 2-4
David Anderson ("Auld Daw") with his ginger beer barrow on the Links at St. Andrews (c. 1900). Anderson was a ball-maker, caddie, and then greenkeeper during the mid-1800s. His version of a refreshment stand on the ninth green was a mainstay—a much-needed halfway house for any weary golfer who may have needed to drown some sorrowful shots before heading back in on the return.

COURTESY OF ST. ANDREWS UNIVERSITY LIBRARY

The Old Course is hallowed ground, indeed, worthy of pilgrimage. In such a setting, a golfer can concentrate on his game with a song in his heart. He may sense the myth surrounding the place and the ghosts that resonate through all the centuries since the Old Course and the ancient links first found each other. He might hear, too, echoes of the eager peals of laughter and muttered curses generated so often in this place by the tantalizing, maddening, solitary, exhilarating, fraternal, mortifying, yet rewarding game that gave it birth.

—*Desmond Muirhead,* St. Andrews: The Old Course

The Right to Golf

In 1552 Archbishop John Hamilton gave the people of St. Andrews the right to use the links for golf and, among other things, gathering turf to roof their homes. This is the earliest known documented reference to golf being played at St. Andrews. Its form is a manuscript dated 25 January 1552. A key to the archbishop's graciousness was his retained rights to raise rabbits on the links. In this period, the links at St. Andrews were known as the Links of Pilmoor and described as being "between the Mussil Scaup and the Watter of Edin." Obviously, it was not deemed "The Old Course" back then because it was the *only* course.

Long before, in 1123, the area of the links had been bestowed on the Burgh of St. Andrews, presumably for grazing rabbits and gathering peat for fuel. Rabbits provided food and clothing and did not seem to cause problems until 1797, when the Links were sold and the rabbit industry flourished. Obviously, golf and rabbits do not mix in great quantities—of either one. Golf was becoming more popular, and rabbits—well, rabbits have their own way of becoming popular.

The period during which rabbits played havoc with the increasing seriousness of golf came to be known as The Hundred-Year War. It began with an ill-advised sale of the Links in 1797 and took just less than 100 years to resolve. During this time, rabbit scrapes dotted the links, and one can only imagine how discouraging it was to often find your ball holed out in the wrong kind of hole. A temporary rule was even imposed to allow lifting balls out of rabbit holes without penalty. The right to graze rabbits [was eventually rescinded when it became quite clear that golf was more precious to the people of St. Andrews than the rabbits. A special parliamentary act in 1894 was necessary to reestablish golfing rights and return the links to the golfers.

Amazingly, it was during The Hundred-Year War that golf grew significantly and St. Andrews became a popular tourist destination. Most of the rule changes and modifications to the now-famous Links were also carried out in this time. Not only were the Links transformed from a rather barbaric series of holes dug in the ground to a more manicured golfing ground but almost every significant hallmark of St. Andrews routing came about during this "rabbit time." Perhaps the rabbit should be the symbol of golf's longevity. Golf won the war, and it was the persistence of those caught by its charm and challenge that made it so.

The 18-Hole Standard

The late Fred Hawtree, a golf course architect and an extremely thoughtful man, writes in his book, *Aspects of Golf Course Architecture,* "It is tempting to suggest that the first tiny seed of golf course architecture was sown in October, 1764. A meeting of the Gentlemen Golfers of St. Andrews expressed the view, 'That it would be for the improvement of the links that four first holes should be converted into two.'" The act described by Hawtree seems to have been a matter of convenience to the society. Nowhere does the record mention any grand scheme to the plan. It was not necessarily to make the course a longer length,

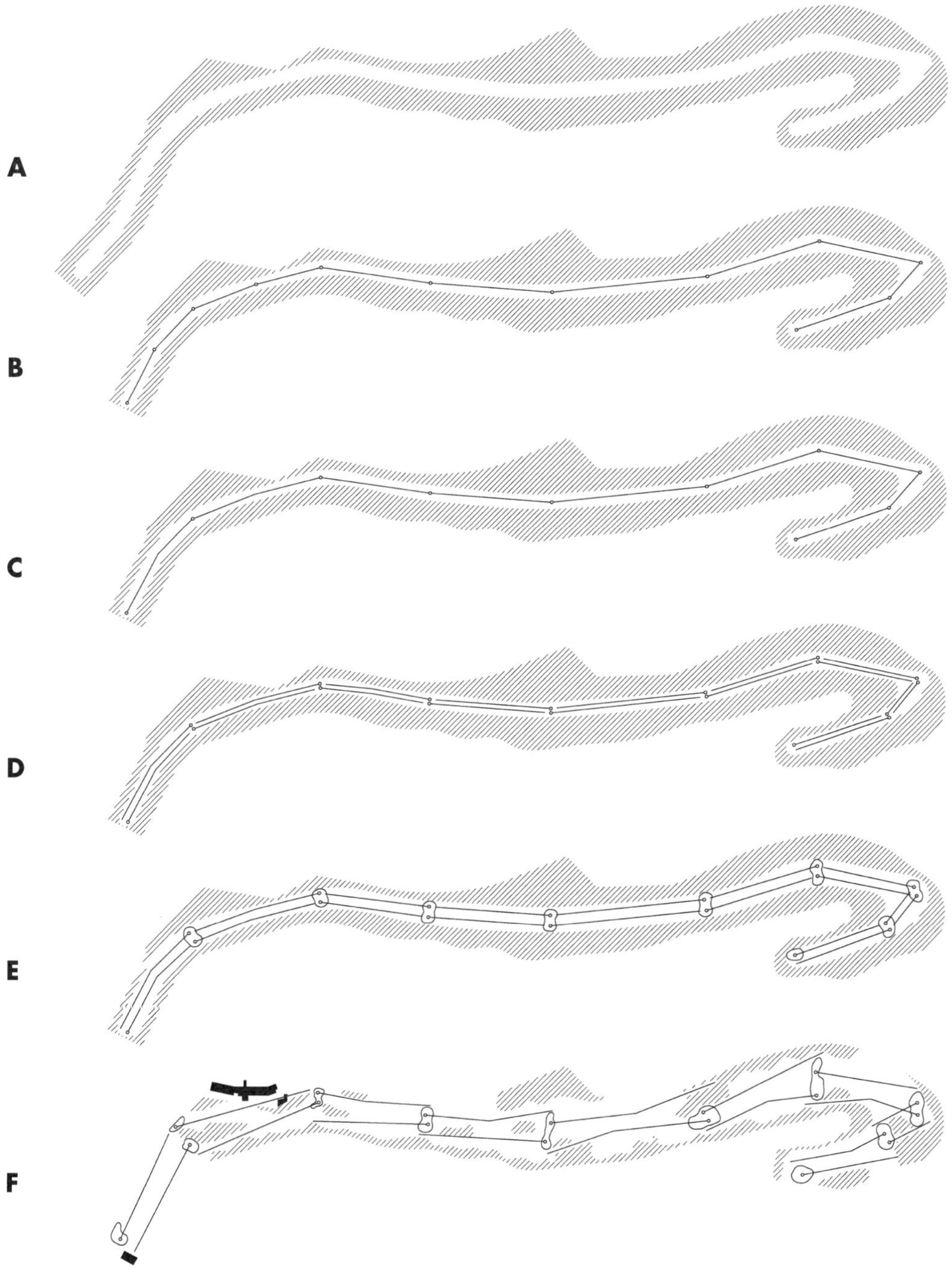

FIGURE 2-5
The gradual changes in the St. Andrews Links, which we call The Old Course in modern times, account for what is perhaps the single most profound affect on golf course routing. In this series of diagrammatic routings, the links are represented from their earliest formal configuration to the present day. (A) — 1600s: The links are as informal as a narrow path worn across the rugged linksland. The starting point was uphill from where it is today, behind the R & A Clubhouse. (B) — Late 1600s: The layout was a 22-hole course made up of 12 actual holes dug in the ground, probably played as an out-and-back round, but golf at this time still had no defined structure as to number of holes or par. (C) — 1764: The first four holes are condensed into two, and the 18-hole course was born! (D) — 1832: Two holes are cut at each green location to simultaneously accommodate outward and inward play. (E) — 1857: The Course corridor is widened, and pairs of holes are cut farther apart. (F) — Today: After considerable widening in the mid- to late 1800s and the advent of formalized tees and greens, the Links at St. Andrews (or as it is now known, The Old Course).

SUNDAY PLAY

Old Tom Morris (1821–1908) is credited with upholding the no-play-on-Sundays tradition at The Old Courses, saying "Nae Sunday play. The course needs a rest if the gowfers don't." Interestingly, a check of records well after his death revealed that no such ban was ever formally adopted for the Old Course. Proof that tradition at St. Andrews is more powerful than anything.

although that was its effect. No drawn plan survived. In fact, we do not know if a formal plan was ever drawn, nor do we know who carried out the work. Rather, in just two short days, the idea was formally adopted, and soon St. Andrews Links consisted of only nine holes (ten holes dug into the ground) where before there had been 11 (12 holes dug into the ground). A round of golf, at least at St. Andrews, was now 18 holes.

It is very likely that there was not much work to be done to physically make this change. With no improved greens, no teeing areas, no fairways (to speak of), and none of the components of modern courses (sprinkler systems, cart paths, drainage, and on and on and on) that we take for granted, it was a simple task of filling in a few holes and changing whatever markers were in use at the time.

Pace-of-play expert Bill Yates, who has studied The Old Course in an effort to keep play moving in the 2000s, theorizes that the change very well could have had something to do with congestion on the links, even way back then. "If I analyze the course as it might have been with extra holes in those parts of the round, the waiting times might have driven the members a bit nutty," he notes. Decongestion is as good of theory as any. And why not? Golf is an experience to be enjoyed. Imagine four short holes to begin a round, about 200 yards each. While it might not have been so bad with the limited length of the balls of the time, this configuration still could have caused players to wait, as short holes seem to beg congestion, especially when bunched together. It may also have provided another distraction in that the closing holes, as the holes were played in reverse on the way in, were of the same short length. Hardly the type of finish one would want on a challenging test. Taking the rough dimension of 800 yards (the approximate total of the original first four holes) and removing two holes raises the yardage of these three opening holes—and three finishing holes—to around 400 yards each. Each of these holes—the first two and the last two—are today all par 4s, and, yes, their yardages are, in fact, just under or slightly over 400 yards apiece. This configuration sounds infinitely better than what we envision to have been there prior to 1764. Even with the first stroke play being mentioned in 1759, match play would have been undoubtedly better suited to this design as well.

But, despite its influential membership of gentlemen and lords, the change to 18 holes did not mean the immediate change of all courses across Britain, as many believe. For three-quarters of a century, courses continued to be laid out with fewer than 18 holes, and occasionally more. Nine-hole layouts were popular, and few of these were configured with holes to be played twice (out and in), as at St. Andrews. Until the 1840s, half of Britain's courses had either nine holes or some other number than 18.

Then, finally, The Old Course began to be taken as a role model. With the 1834 bestowment to royal status, the Royal and Ancient Golf Club began a tradition of rule-making and governing that still pertains. Competitions, along with the new game of playing for the fewest strokes, drove the 18-hole standard until The Old Course *was* the standard. Right or wrong, 18 holes became a part of the vernacular that changed the course of golf history.

In my humble opinion, St. Andrews is the most fascinating golf course I have ever played. There is always a way at St. Andrews, although it is not always the obvious way, and in trying to find it there is more to be learned on this British course than in playing 100 ordinary American courses.

—Bobby Jones

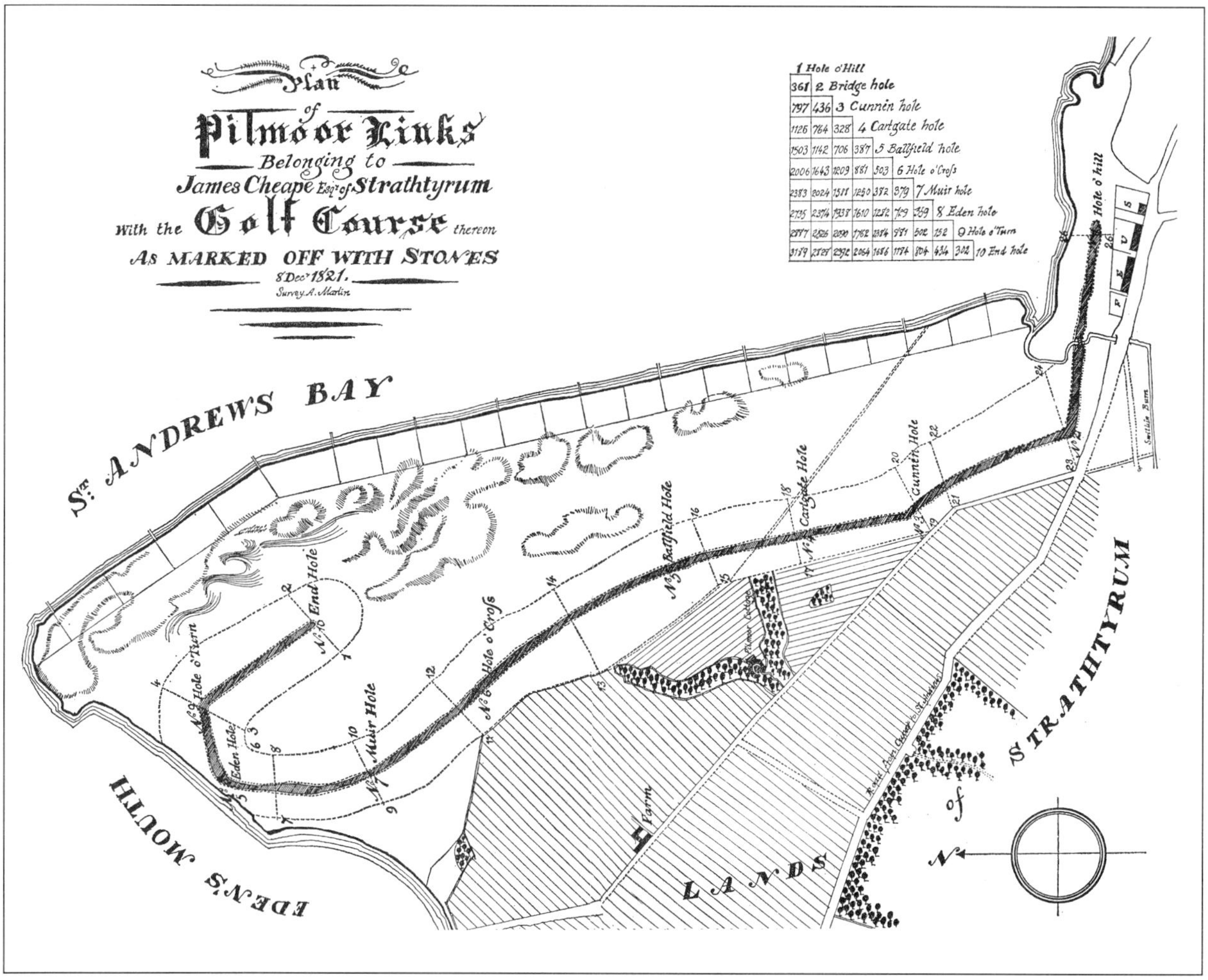

FIGURE 2-6

The Plan of Pilmoor Links, a redrawn version of the original 1821 map by A. Martin, a landscape and topographical painter. Martin's map is the oldest recorded of any golf course. The shepherd's-crook shape of the links is evident, as are the ten holes, identified by name, where the links were played out and back using the same dug holes both ways. A curious aspect of the map is the distance chart included in the upper right-hand corner. Not only do the distances not add up in every instance but also there is no known reason for the chart. It is presumed by many that Martin, perhaps not an avid golfer, was simply responding to the task at hand and providing a surveyor's look at the progression of the golf course so that it might be easy to calculate the distance from beginning to end.

COURTESY OF ILLUSTRATOR JUREK ALEXANDER PUTTER, FROM THE BOOK *ST. ANDREWS—HOME OF GOLF*

The Double Greens

Although modern courses occasionally embrace a double green, the choice is generally for the sake of nostalgia or gimmickry and not, as in the case of The Old Course, for practicality. The St. Andrews of long ago was a true reversible golf course, but as play increased, it became awkward to have outbound players playing to the very same hole in the ground as inbound players. What may have been worse was waiting—*or not waiting!*—for players who just holed out to tee off from a few club lengths beside the previous hole.

In front of us stretches a vast plain, and unless we slice the ball outrageously on to the sea beach, no harm can befall us. At the same time we had much better hit a good shot, because the Swilcan Burn guards the green, and we want to carry it and get a four. It is an inglorious little stream enough: we could easily jump over it were we not afraid of looking foolish if we fell in, and yet it catches an amazing number of balls.

—Bernard Darwin, in The Golf Courses of the British Isles, *referring to the first hole at St. Andrews*

In 1832, improvements to the greens were ordered. The result were greens featuring two separate holes, one for outbound play and one for inbound. This, at least, assisted in organizing the short shots and putts, which could become confusing if two groups reached the same hole. The ninth and 18th, of course, remained with just one hole each, as these marked the end of the line for both the out nine and the in nine. Little is written about this improvement other than the detail of deploying white flags for the out holes and red for the in holes. This standard remains today, even on courses that it would be nearly impossible to get lost upon.

Enter Allan Robertson, a man born into a ball-making family, the oldest known golfing family in St. Andrews history. His father and grandfather had been caddies. Allan was described as "a short, little active man, with a pleasant face and a merry twinkle in his eye." He grew up on the St. Andrews Links. The course was the living room of his life. In 1848, Robertson, St. Andrews' greenkeeper, was responsible for the most significant development in St. Andrews' double greens: he actually *doubled* them. What before had amounted to two holes stuck into a slightly larger area now featured greatly improved green surfaces, some extremely wide, that served golfers much more appropriately. Improvements continued to be made to the greens. In 1857, Robertson again enlarged the surfaces even more.

Left- and Right-Handed Options

Modern wisdom has it that golf courses are best played clockwise, beginning on the left-hand side and playing around, eventually ending up to the right of where you began. Because a predominance of golfers have a tendency to slice, playing in this manner keeps balls inward and minimizes errant balls that might otherwise leave the property. Of course, this wisdom is subject to all sorts of conditions, and it cannot be said that it is a hard and fast rule. St. Andrews, in its original configuration of double greens, went down the left side of the pathway and returned on the opposite side. It went clockwise, just as some prefer modern courses to be oriented.

Old Tom Morris and Allan Robertson are credited with co-creating St. Andrews' first new green: the 17th. Previously a single green had served both the first and the 17th holes. The new green, together with a new tee for No. 2, contributed to the option of playing the course in two ways; the left-hand course, used since double holes were placed on the greens in 1832, and the new right-hand course, now the standard at St. Andrews. This change allowed the first and 17th holes to be among the only four greens that were not double in use. (The other two were, the end of the line, Nos. 9 and 18.) Morris later created a new 18th green, slightly west of its original site.

St. Andrews is no longer played in both directions. The exception is the occasional historical buff who will obtain special permission from the Links. Interestingly, many bunkers from the older right-hand play of the course remain, but go mostly unnoticed to everyday players. Near the twelfth tee, for example, a looming trap sits just 60 yards off the front of the tee for no apparent reason. Originally it was meant to trap balls at the old High Hole, but today it mostly collects an occasional topped ball from No. 12 or a horribly hooked tee shot off No. 7. Such bunkers are common throughout The Old Course. It is amusing to see newly designed golf holes with a sand bunker placed oddly off the front of a tee, most likely in imitation of some areas of The Old Course. But little do people realize this trend is mimicking a leftover condition and not one intentionally created for the way most people experience The Old Course.

Alternate Paths

Prior to 1832, when two holes were placed on each green, the breadth of fairways was unchanged from their rough form as mere pathways to and from each individual hole. The holes were still named individually, even though each green now sported two actual holes.

RULE 1 OF THE ORIGINAL R & A'S RULES

You must tee your ball within a club length of the hole.

Sir Hugh Playfair of St. Andrews is credited with reclaiming land torn away by the forces of the sea, specifically land along the once narrow fairway for Holes No. 1 and 18. Playfair allegedly sank old boats to shore up the coastline, eventually regaining enough land so that play could expand beyond the single-width fairway that formed a pathway for these two holes. His efforts were just part of the groundwork for one of St. Andrews' greatest features, the defining of fairways for each of the 18 golf holes that are now in play.

Old Tom Morris and Allan Robertson were the first to undertake serious clearing of the links to widen what originally amounted to pathways connecting the greens. This development spawned the glorious fields that span out before golfers at each hole. These expansive areas, flanked by roughs and bushes, revealed the undulations and subtle ridges that are now such an integral part of The Old Course. Many have attempted to duplicate their grandeur and intricacy, but there is no equal substitute for the originals.

This improvement to the Links proved highly significant to golf course routing, as it marked the first recorded design of golf holes where alternative routes to the target were encouraged. When the areas of the holes were widened, the interspersed bunkers and contour changes created multiple choices for negotiating each individual hole.

Continual Change

A common statement is that "The Old Course has never changed." Obviously, this is not true. Change has, however, been rather gradual and spaced out. In 1865, Morris continued to improve the links. He built formal tees, but the holes looked much as they do today. R. A. Hull, who today might be called a green architect, redid tees and lengthened the course from 6333 yards to 6533 yards in 1905. He also

If the "Strath" Bunker could recite the words it has heard and tell you of the sights it has seen, there would be much food for fun and philosophy.

—*John L. Low,* Aspects of Golf Course Architecture

I could take out of my life everything except my experience at St. Andrews and I would still have a rich, full life.

—Bobby Jones, addressing the citizens of St. Andrews on his acceptance of the Freedom of the City honor, 1958

plopped down 13 new bunkers. James Braid, as recently as the 1930s, increased the total yardage to 6900 through new championship tees. Despite all this activity, Nos. 1, 9, 17, and 18 have changed very little through the years. In a nutshell, the past 800 years have brought about significant change—otherwise, we would not be spending time on this chapter.

Desmond Muirhead, in *St. Andrews: How to Play the Old Course,* suggests that the influence of the University of St. Andrews very likely played a role in the tremendous attention to strategy that is embodied at The Old Course. What better way to explain the amazing positioning of hazards or the remarkable thinking-man's style that presents itself at each tee. For hundreds of years, the scholars and professors, who were known to be avid golfers, probably pushed their ideas until eventually they caught on or were implemented by others willing to take the credit. St. Andrews was designed by more than the hand of nature; she was given intelligence.

THE LINKS IMMORTALIZED

There has long been discussion about the shape of the links when viewed from the air or in map form. It takes, without question, the form of a shepherd's crook. Whether or not this is significant, the links remain mystical to all who traverse her fairways. Those with a ho-hum attitude to the revelation of the shepherd's crook are no more impressed that the alignment of the holes at the Old Course also resembles a candy cane. You cannot please everybody.

Of all that has been written about The Old Course, not an awful lot has been written about its *routing.* After all, it goes out—and comes back. While much has been penned about its individual holes, their hazards, the ambiance, and even its caddies, the routing and what makes it tick apparently seems so ordinary that few have bothered to discuss it. Thus it gave me great pleasure to literally stumble on an obscure book, *A Round of Courses,* by a poet, Patric Dickinson. In a small shop in Pebble Beach, there it was, half lying on the floor in a stack of books waiting to be cataloged and half begging to be taken home to a shelf full of other obscure golf books. What does a poet know about golf course routing, you ask? Well, in Dickinson's case, you can sense how he is intrigued with the timing and the way St. Andrews unfolds. See for yourself as he shares this insightful description:

ST. ANDREWS UNIVERSITY

No fewer than 12 signers of the American Declaration of Independence received degrees from St. Andrews University. Benjamin Franklin, the great statesman and inventor, could very well have changed history had he had a propensity to design golf courses rather than printing presses.

> But never was a course so like the motions of the sea: the slow, steady start of the first four holes, the sudden stride of the long 'Hole o' Cross', this is just like the movement of the ebb—running quickly now through 'Heathery' to its farthest out, the 7th, the 'High Hole'. Now comes slack water in truth, for here is the loop and 8, 9 and 10 at flat, slack-water holes, to be exploited with all possible power. It is as if here at low water the old wreck shows its ribs, and one has just time to dig for the treasure in its hold before the tide turns again...and now as, just before it turns, the tide seems suddenly to recede a little farther

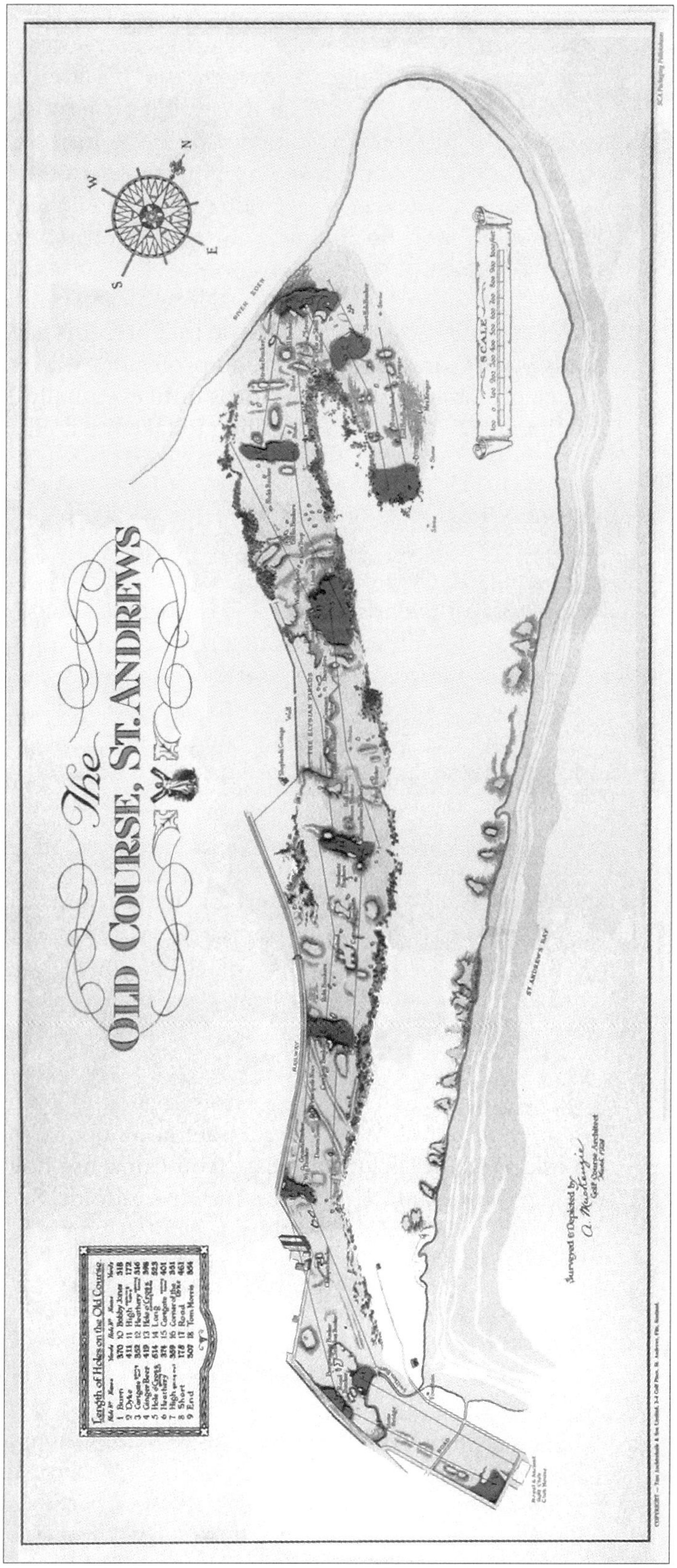

FIGURE 2-7
Alister MacKenzie's famous map of The Old Course, commissioned in 1923 and presented to the links in 1924.
COURTESY OF AUCHTERLONIES OF ST. ANDREWS, www.auchterlonies.com

After one round I thought the Old Course was the worst I had ever known. On my second visit I played three rounds and ended by thinking it was quite a good course, after all. On the third occasion I played there for a week and ended by concluding it was the most wonderful course in the world.

—Bob Gardner, America's 1926 Walker Cup captain

and then begins to ripple inwards, now comes the short 11th. Its green pairs with the 7th but is a little farther out on the very edge of the links, so that a shot over the green seems as if it will drop splash! into the estuary of the Eden... From the twelfth tee to the eighteenth green, in floods the tide, and perhaps you are being lucky enough and playing well enough to come in with it until you reach the 'Road Hole', where the last sandcastle of your golfing pride and hope must stand against the waves until you are safely on the eighteenth tee.

—*Patric Dickinson,* A Round of Golf Courses

The First Map

The first known map of the St. Andrews Links, the original of which hangs in the Royal and Ancient Clubhouse, confuses many. It is titled "Plan of the Pilmoor Links" (Figure 2-6), as the area was known as Pilmoor at this time. The theory is that the map's creator, A. Martin, took a surveyor's rather than a golfer's approach to depicting the routing of the golf course. Nonetheless, his map gives us a terrific perspective of golf in the early 1800s. It is regarded as the first map—routing plan—ever drawn of a golf course. At least it remains the first we have on record.

Significant about the course is its path-like approach. Holes are just that: *holes.* The map pinpoints stone markers, numbered 1 through 26, and defines the supposed boundary of the Links by a broken line. The holes are named in their original form following consolidation from 22 holes to 18.

The 1821 map very likely had to do with housing on the road adjoining the links and was not created for the purpose of one day appearing in a book about golf course routing. To A. Martin, who was a landscape and topographical painter, the task at hand was likely one of recording the tract and its basic mapping details. The links just happened to be the largest subject he had to record.

Subsequent Maps

Following A. Martin's first-ever map of a golf links, two other early maps were made. In 1836, William Chalmers drafted the links and, interestingly, used within the title "Golfing Course" to describe the plan. In 1879, the firm of Little and Boothby drafted the links and the immediate area. Both the Chalmers map and the 1879 update did not show centerlines of holes, only the features and landmarks that dotted the links and its ground.

Centerlines, now a staple of routing plans, first appeared on a map of The New Course in 1894. The New Course was laid out by Tom Morris to a design by W. Hall Blyth, an Edinburgh civil engineer. The costs of design and construction were met by the Royal & Ancient Golf Club. This significant map (Figure 16-5), which also shows features of The

Old Course, was lost for many years until it was rescued in 1976 by Walter Woods, an alert greenkeeper."We had piled a bunch of wood and rubbish on the beech below the Jubilee Course to set a huge bonfire for an annual charity when there on top of the pile I noticed a four-foot long cardboard tube," related Woods. "My assistant, David Kilgour, retrieved it and took it back to the office." Woods and Kilgour never gave the discovery much thought as the events that night had them preoccupied. Above Woods' desk on some dusty rafters the tube sat for nearly twenty years. Just before his retirement Woods rediscovered the tube and cut it apart with the help of his mechanic. Woods reported the find, the R & A deciding that it rightfully belonged to the Links Trust. In 1996 Woods presented it for hanging in the new clubhouse which overlooks both the New and Old Courses.

A second map of the New Course also includes the Old Course. This map, drawn by Blyth two years later, in 1896, is part of the collection of the Royal & Ancient Golf Club. It, along with the 1829, 1836, and 1879 maps, hang in the Clubhouse of the Royal & Ancient Golf Club.

Much later, in 1924, Alister MacKenzie presented St. Andrews with his plan recording The Old Course (Figure 2-7). The MacKenzie plan accurately depicted the features and play of the course and was undoubtedly an effort he enjoyed as much as anything he ever drew.

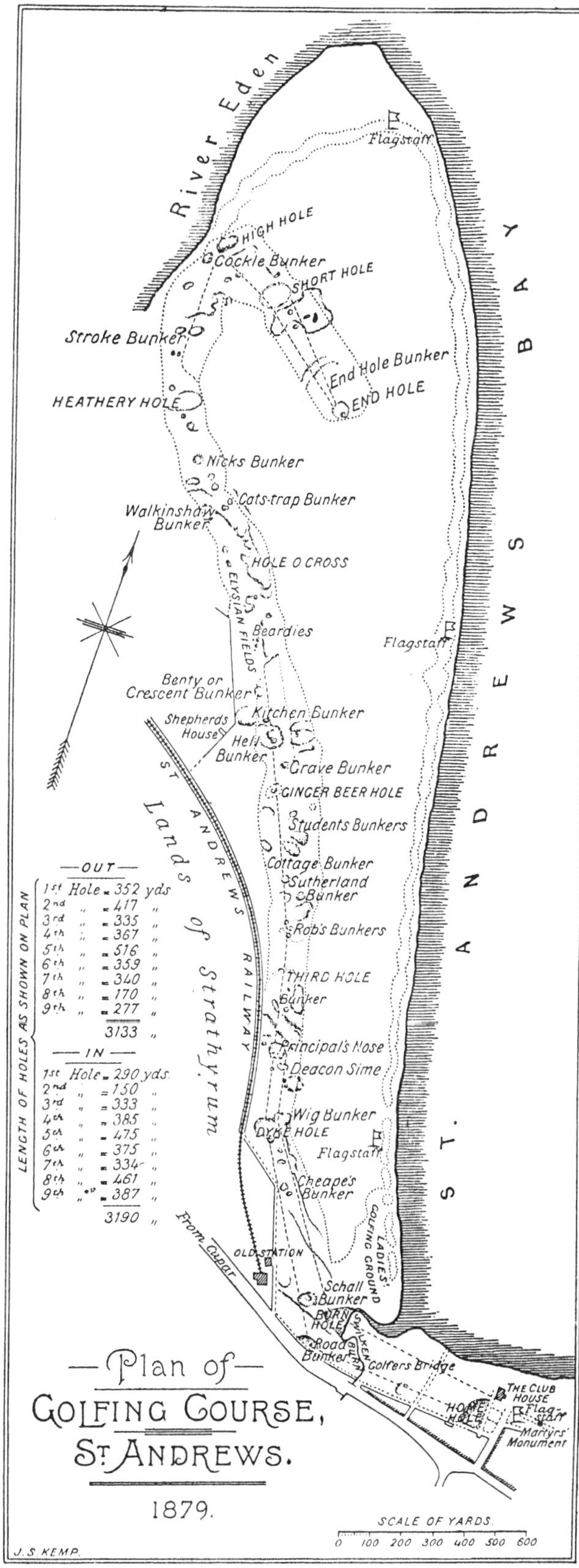

FIGURE 2-8
This map of The Old Course shows its 1879 configuration and is similar to the more famous and elaborate map generated in the same year by the mapping firm of Little and Boothby. This line drawing accompanied an 1894 travel article.
SOURCE: *HARPER'S NEW MONTHLY MAGAZINE*

ST. ANDREWS TODAY

> *There is only one Old Course, and nature built it.*
>
> *—Robert Trent Jones Sr., in* The Complete Golfer

Words are rarely adequate to describe actually being in St. Andrews. The writings of the poets, the golfers, and the architects who have been inspired by this magic place are as good as any. Many of my favorite writings are quoted here. But, to any golfer, golf architect, or golf developer, I recommend a pilgrimage to St. Andrews at your next availability. I have been there in the spring, and enjoyed it. I have been there during the Open, and enjoyed it. And I have been there in the autumn, and enjoyed it.

During my last dinner there, it was hard not to notice, even as late as 11:00 P.M., that the conversation at the pub always crept back to golf. In the morning when we rose to walk down to the first tee, golf was in the air. And when the tees went into the ground and it came time to strike the ball out toward the Swilcan Burn, all the golf energy that had been

What better introduction to explain the magic of St. Andrews than the famous poem by University of St. Andrews student R. F. Murray, who captured the essence of his town in this 1885 poem:

OBSESSION

Would you like to see a city given over
Soul and body to a tyrannising game?
If you would there's little need to be a rover,
For St. Andrews is the abject city's name.
It is surely quite superfluous to mention,
To a person who has been there half-an-hour,
That golf is what engrosses the attention
Of the people, with an all-absorbing power.
Rich and poor alike are smitten by the fever
Their business and religion is to play;
And a man is scarcely deemed a true believer,
Unless he goes at least a round a day.
The city boasts an old and learned college,
Where you'd think the leading industry was Greek;
Even there the favoured instruments of knowledge
Are a driver and a putter and a cleek.
All the natives and the residents are patrons
Of this royal, ancient, irritating sport;
All the old men, all the young men, maids and matrons—
The universal populace in short.

—R. F. Murray, 1885

building inside me was released in one swift moment. It soon returned. It always does in St. Andrews. This is where golf began, and it is where all golfers belong in heart and spirit.

THE OTHER COURSES

Among the many pilgrims to St. Andrews, some leave not being fully aware of the other courses that grace the city. Too bad, for they are fine courses in their own right. There is the tale of the awe-inspired golfer, a foreigner, who after securing a tee time plays his round and is in heaven at the surrounds. It is not until well inside a local tavern that evening that he remarks to a local patron how the famous 17th seemed so tame. "I parred it easily," he says. "I was nearly to the green with a drive and simply pitched up for a two-putt." The conversation eventually revealed that he had not been playing The Old Course but the New. His 17th was a par 3 of not more than 220-yards. Presumably he had a few more drinks.

The Links Trust, established in 1974 by an Act of Parliament, is the body entrusted with the operation and maintenance of the golf courses and facilities on the St. Andrews Links. The nonprofit organization returns all surpluses to the maintenance and development of the courses and their facilities.

The New Course

The second course to be formed at St. Andrews. It is not so new today, having opened in 1895. The course was laid out by W. Hall Blyth, a civil engineer, and the building and nuances carried out by Old Tom Morris and his trusted assistant, David Honeyman. It remains one of the best-kept secrets at St. Andrews, as it is often overshadowed by the popularity of The Old Course and the thousands who vie for tee times each and every week.

The Jubilee Course

An 1897 feasibility study, although no such term then existed, determined that it was possible to build a 12-hole course between the New Course and the sea. This would fill in the remaining land that had so far not been used for golf. The grand idea was to build a course for beginners, women golfers, and those who simply required a shorter course. The original plan was laid out by John Angus Jr. Work to clear fairways and groom the land was completed in just a few short months. In 1902, the course was extended to 18 holes and, in 1946, lengthened to 6200-yards. Golf course architect Donald Steel added more length in 1989. His redesign created the present course of 6800 yards playing to a par 72. Because of its proximity to the sea, the Jubilee offers terrific views and the more-than-occasional winds coming directly across the links with far less protection than any of the other courses of the Links Trust of St. Andrews.

THE ROUTING GETS PROTECTION

In 2001, about 14,000 cubic yards of sand were used to protect the fragile coast beside the golf courses at St. Andrews Links, ultimately protecting The Old Course itself from the eventual erosion that would otherwise occur. The project involved building up the eroded dunes to replicate the natural processes of the estuary.

Nature's master plan has produced 18 holes that all possess their own character and individuality. That plan includes the simplest of ingredients; smooth, close-cropped turf, heather mooreland and dense whin or gorse; a few big sand pits, such as Hell, the Cottage and Shell Bunkers that are far older than the Course.

—*James K. Robertson,*
St. Andrews: Home of Golf

Significant St. Andrews Dates

1411	St. Andrews University, Scotland's first, is founded.
1457	An Act of Scottish Parliament bans golf.
1553	Archbishop Hamilton confirms citizens' rights to play golf on the links.
1598	The town church complains of golf being played during services.
1691	The town is described as a golfing metropolis.
1754	The Society of St. Andrews Golfers is founded.
1764	The links is modified from 22 holes to 18 holes.
1797	The Town Council sells the links for £805, marking the beginning of the Hundred-Year War pitting rabbit breeders against golfers.
1805	A lawsuit is instigated about rabbits infiltrating the links.
1821	The first known map of the links is made by A. Martin and titled "Plan of Pilmoor Links."
1832	The greens are improved to allow for two separate holes to be cut on each (except the ninth and last), creating 18 separate holes as opposed to only nine holes played twice, once going out and again coming in.
1834	The Society of St. Andrews Golfers becomes The Royal & Ancient Golf Club.
1845	A proposed rail line threatening the Burn Hole is rerouted.
1848	Allan Robertson creates large double greens, widens fairways, and creates the new green at the Road Hole.
1855	A second green is built at the High Hole.
1857	The R & A adopts 22 rules, of which one stipulates that a round shall consist of 18 holes (one round of the course).
	The first championship is played at St. Andrews.
1865	Old Tom Morris is appointed the first professional and greenkeeper of the R & A Golf Club.
1870	A new first green is built.
1877	Separate teeing grounds are built to accommodate play.
1888	Robert Lockhart becomes part of the Apple Tree Gang after bringing clubs and balls to the United States from St. Andrews
	Rules of golf are issued to all clubs by the R & A.
1894	The town of St. Andrews regains possession of the links.
	The first known map of a golf course to depict centerlines (The New Course) is drawn by W. Hall Blyth, a civil engineer.
	With the addition of The New Course, the St. Andrews Links is forevermore called The Old Course.
1904	Old Tom Morris retires as greenkeeper at age 83.
1905	Increased distance resulting from new golf balls prompts the addition of more than 100 new bunkers in advance of the Open Championship.
1913	Golf is no longer free on The Old Course.
2000	A Web camera is installed at the first tee of The Old Course, allowing people around the world to see activity there 24 hours per day.

I have played gowf close on eighty years, and that's longer than most folk get living.
—*Old Tom Morris, quoted in W. W. Tulloch,* The Life of Tom Morris

FIGURE 2-9
There is no greater icon to represent St. Andrews and golf than Old Tom Morris (1821–1908). Morris, who was born in St. Andrews, returned there in 1865 to become greenkeeper for the Royal & Ancient Golf Club. It was a position he held until his retirement in 1904, and where he formed his great knowledge of the game. Among the courses he had a hand in creating are Prestwick, Royal Dornoch, Muirfield, and Carnoustie.
PHOTO COURTESY OF THE USGA LIBRARY

The Eden Course

The Eden opened in 1914 and was the work of Harry S. Colt, famous for insights into golf and, especially, his flair for routings. On this property, acquired from the Strathtyrum Estate, Colt set into play 18 holes of shorter length than those of the Old and New courses. Its par-73 routing continues that tradition today, playing shorter and offering one additional stroke to that of the Old and two to that of the New. Colt, coauthor, with C. H. Alison, of *Golf Course Architecture* (1920), was a long-time student of how courses could be better laid out for enjoyment and strategy.

FIGURE 2-10
Kingsbarns Golf Links was established in the year 2000, more than 600 years after golf was first played along the linksland near St. Andrews. Although not a part of the property or courses operated by the St. Andrews Links Trust, Kingsbarns is living proof of the bond between golf and linksland. It is testament to the fact that even when built in the present day, golf can be as dramatic and engaging as the original links. Designed by golf course architect Kyle Phillips, ASGCA.

COURTESY OF KYLE PHILLIPS GOLF COURSE DESIGN

FIGURE 2-11
The author (left) as a young scraper walking over the Swilcan Bridge.

THE SWILCAN BRIDGE
This famous landmark, more than 800 years old, was the access for people to get to the Links, which at the time was entirely situated across the burn from the town. It was also the bridge used by traders bringing goods to town from their landing spots beyond the linksland.

The Strathtyrum Course

The Strathtyrum, which opened in 1993, was the first new course to be built at St. Andrews in nearly 80 years. Like its ancestor, the Eden, it, too, was made possible by the acquisition of new land. Golf course architect Donald Steel created an interesting addition: an even shorter routing than the Eden, but with four fewer par strokes. The Eden plays 88 yards per par stroke, while the Strathtyrum plays 74 yards per par stroke. Not too different mathematically, yet the four-stroke difference in par can make a large difference psychologically.

The Balgove

Opened in February 1972 at an original yardage of 2085 yards, the nine-hole layout was remodeled along with the building of the new Strathtyrum Course. The idea was to build a short course to serve beginners and anyone desiring to play a short course for fun and enjoyment. Today it is a par-30 course measuring 1500 yards. The course has proved so popular with adults as well as children that the management committee had to introduce a special rule: During school summer holidays, adults can play the course only when accompanied by a child. In 1993, the Balgove was completely overhauled by golf course architect Donald Steel.

"Help, I Can't Get Out!"

I have been to St. Andrews three times. My first visit was to play golf and study the links. The second was as a spectator to the 1984 British Open. (A very dear friend, George Farrow of Northern England, makes it an annual custom to inform me that the word *British* is superfluous, as there is only one Open, that being the one played in Britain. The others, of course, all need qualifiers: "U.S.," "Canadian," "French," etc. I print this in hope that George will one day leave me alone with regard to this matter, but I fear he will not.) My third visit was to prepare for the book you are holding or viewing on your monitor.

On this recent visit, I was fortunate to meet the general manager of the Links, Alan McGregor. Alan is responsible to the Links Management Committee and the Trustees for carrying through their policies. The Trustees are responsible for setting policy, for new developments, and for ensuring that the Links, the largest golf complex in Europe, is run in accordance with the Act of Parliament. The Links Trust employs 200 people, including about 70 greenkeeping staff. In addition, about 150 self-employed caddies and bag carriers are licensed by the Trust. Alan told a favorite story, which I have repeated now more times than I can recall, during my visit.

When Alan first came to St. Andrews, he met with some of the local members, and it surprised him a great deal to hear a few complaints about the bunkers on The Old Course. "Some are too deep and we can't get out," they said. Alan was quick to suggest, among other solutions, that perhaps they shouldn't be hitting their balls into the bunkers in the first place. After all, this was The Old Course. Challenge and shot-making are part of the game and its grand design. The discussion continued, and it was not until later in the conversation that one gentleman saw through Alan's view of the situation. "Alan," he said, "You don't understand; they are having trouble *physically getting out* of the bunkers."

It seems The Old Course's bunkers had gradually been getting deeper, due mainly to continual wear and tear. To a senior citizen, the task of getting into a bunker might be far easier than the process of climbing out. One can only imagine the event that led to this discussion. "Say, Bob, where's Lord Mackerel? He was over there by the Spectacles the last I saw him."

A group of St. Andrews golfers will no doubt find Hell Bunker just as menacing today as it always has been. Its presence at the 14th, or the Long Hole, cannot be ignored, c. 1897.

PHOTOGRAPH BY J. PATRICK & SONS, COURTESY OF THE ROYAL AND ANCIENT GOLF CLUB OF ST. ANDREWS

Understanding Land & Climate

HOLE NO. 3

In reality, there are only two types of land in terms of golf: (1) good land, and (2) less-than-good land. Good land is land suitable for golf in its natural form, with little or no intervention. The other variety is that which needs considerable attention in the form of earth-moving, feature-building, and augmentation beyond merely planting the turfgrass.

Now that you are armed with this simplistic viewpoint, allow me to complicate it by noting that a great piece of land may be rendered virtually useless for golf due to influences above or beyond its borders. Examples: a massive freeway towering around its edges, a major international airport and the descending perfume of jet fuel—or how about a pig farm located a few hundred yards upwind? And even though there may be terrific landforms for golf in, let's say, Antarctica, it is doubtful that there are enough designer golf sweaters to combat the hostile climate. And, in reverse, it is good to point out that a so-so site may be made nearly excellent if it comes with views of snow-capped mountain peaks, a babbling brook, or a terrific climate that will attract golfers from around the world.

With each piece of land comes a multitude of attributes, some positive and some negative. It is essential to find out about these attributes. And, although it may be possible to route a golf course without such intimate knowledge of the land in question, this would amount to malpractice, pure and simple. Such practice should not be attempted, although I have personally seen it performed several times. How remarkably awful to see a routing plan with holes going against the natural lay of the land toward views that make no sense, or plowing over intriguing details of nature that could never be duplicated, even in a million years of nature trying it all again. One can only hope that such routings remain where they belong: in a deep drawer or cabinet, far out of the reach and temptation of those naive enough to unroll them and seriously contemplate bringing them to reality.

THE COMPONENTS OF LAND

Land is made up of earth, rock, water, and vegetation. These form the basis of all that occurs physically on any given piece of ground. How each of these components are arranged and the complexities of each determine the specific type of land and, ultimately, how it may be appreciated for future golf use.

These four components of land are the "earth, wind, and fire" of the art of golf course architecture. For it is these ingredients, when artificial shaping and additives are incorporated, that form the features and qualities of a finished course. Our fairways and greens are the earth repositioned; our sand and waste areas are the rock crushed into fine particles; our lakes and ponds are the water redistributed; and our grasses and trees are vegetation painted onto the overall canvas.

Some indifferent holes have many hazards; and some of the best have few. Nearly all great holes have a particular terrain which has made their greatness possible.
—Robert Hunter, The Links

Earth

The earth is the largest of the natural elements of golf course routing. It represents an amazing playground on which most everything begins and to which everything returns. It can obviously be molded, but a far better first step is to get to know the land by uncovering areas that may not require such effort. An important realization in the creation of golf courses is that most things nature has left on the land cannot be duplicated once they are eradicated. Even in those rare instances when a natural element *can* be reproduced, the result is never as interesting or authentic as the real thing.

Generally, land types include:

- Flat land

  Land that is dead flat and also that which is nearly flat, perhaps with only a slight tilt in one or two directions.

- Rolling land

  Land that has gentle changes in contour, with high and low areas abundant across its scope.

- Mountainous land
  Land that has severe elevation changes and steep slopes resulting from the foothills of mountains or mountains themselves.

Areas can comprise a combination of land types. The earth rarely begins and ends according to a survey or property line, so it is not always the case that a land parcel will feature just one of the types above. Also at play is the possibility that a parcel may involve land that is totally or partially not natural. For example, once rolling terrain that has been cultivated for crop fields may now be flat, and land that was flat in a previous life may now be rather mountainous due to the aftermath of an open pit mine.

Among the many influences of natural landforms on golf are:

- Steepness
  Golfers must be able to negotiate a course, and balls travel farther downhill and shorter uphill.
- Strategy
  Elevation changes and the movement of the land introduce strategy and challenge.
- Aesthetics
  The movement of the land can be pleasing and create backdrops, shadows, and interest.
- Features
  Elevation changes can form features that highlight areas of a golf course.
- Vistas
  Views from high elevations look out beyond the golf course; views from lower spots can create secluded views that take in the immediate surroundings.
- Conditions
  The shape of the earth affects the condition of soil and drainage; the ability to sustain growth is also influenced by the orientation of slopes to sunlight and shade, which may be caused by high landforms, tall vegetation, etc.

If one could have a course with sand dunes, with water hazards both as streams and as lakes, with fairways through virgin forests, with long, rolling contours, high plateaus, lovely little valleys to play through and to cross as hazards, one would have the superlative and almost ideal golf country.

—George C. Thomas Jr., Golf Architecture in America

Rock

Rock is important in the context of golf, as it represents an obstacle. On the negative side, it can halt construction and does not support vegetation, except within its voids. On the positive side, rock is a texture that can add to the detail of a golf course by helping to accentuate, frame, and define the golf experience and its journey.

On the surface, when rock is indigenous, it can contribute to the natural qualities of the land. Many great golf holes and courses have earned their place in the golfer's mind through the contrast and timelessness of rock. A serious golfer does not need to go far into the mind's eye to picture the 16th at Cypress Point-the waves crashing against the promontory of rock jutting out into the Pacific; the 18th at Pebble Beach—its tee perched beyond the protected beach, and the endless seawall holding back the tides on one side and the fairway on the other; the par-3 17th

Man could improve on what nature had provided... there would be no stopping it. Sand would appear far from the shore; exotic trees in the endless plain; water where there was no water before. There would be Golf Course Architecture.
—*Fred W. Hawtree,* Aspects of Golf Course Architecture

at PGA West—its dark stone encircling the green like the edges of a dart board positioned too far away; Mauna Lani on the Big Island of Hawaii, where golf holes ribbon their way through hostile lava fields and grow brilliantly on imported soil that was painstakingly trucked in from miles away; or the tiniest of details at St. Andrews, such as its ancient Swilcan Bridge, whose stones are carved from the same rock that made the city it serves.

It must be kept in mind that rock is also an essential component of soil. For golf courses to grow well, they require soils that drain and not become saturated with water. Clearly, rock is both yin and yang in nature. While its presence is many times unwelcome, it can also be a distinct advantage. An appreciation for this is a must.

Influences of rock on golf include:

- Features and landmarks
  Naturally occurring rock, when left in place or positioned in a design, can become a prominent and marketable quality.
- Rock as texture
  Rock and rock products, such as sand, are useful both above and below the ground.
- The contrast of rock
  Rock, whether nearby or in the distance, offers contrast to the smooth surfaces of turfed areas.
- Rock and water
  Stone can set off shorelines and interrupt the flow of water to create pleasing sounds.
- Rock and soil
  Rock, in appropriate sizes and doses, enables soils to drain, and good drainage is essential for turfgrass to flourish.
- Unwanted rock
  Too much large rock can increase costs, for removal and/or for covering it with acceptable imported soils.
- Rock as a surface
  Rock and products made from rock can form surfaces for paths, retaining walls, signage, and structures.

Water

Water is the most free-flowing of land elements. Its shape and movement are defined by the part of the earth that it shares. Low spots with no outlet on the surface form ponds, lakes, bogs, and lagoons. Low areas that are linear and descend form watercourses such as rivers, creeks, sloughs, and channels. Even in its absence, water defines land through its previous travels and the carvings its force has left in the earth and rock. As witnessed in usually dry ravines and sandy washes, the aftermath of water—and the potential for it to flow again—are intriguing conditions.

Water is a feature of land that must be carefully considered in terms of a range of causes and effects. Whether naturally occurring or artifi-

FIGURE 3-1
Rock can be an extremely dramatic feature for golf, providing picturesque backdrops, obstacles, and landmarks.

COURTESY OF THE STONE CANYON GOLF CLUB; JAY MORRISH, ASGCA, GOLF COURSE ARCHITECT

cially created, bodies of water and water-related issues must be given priority consideration in planning golf courses.

Influences of water on routings include:

- The obstacle factor

  Getting around a golf course with bodies of water requires circumventing the water or crossings such as bridges and causeways.
- Water as a hazard

  Water is the most penal of golf hazards, for seldom is there a possible recovery; in the right dose, this can add to the excitement and risk that makes golf challenging and enjoyable.
- The view of water

  When water is integrated with the golf course and viewpoints it may be appreciated and enjoyed.
- The movement of water

  Unlike the earth, when water moves spontaneously, it is pleasing.
- Sound

  The sound of water can be refreshing, soothing, and add intrigue to the golf experience.
- Water for growth

  Almost all golf courses require artificial irrigation; very often, the most convenient source of this water is a pond or lake. Such reservoirs can store water for application at a rate and time that fills in gaps in natural precipitation.
- Natural precipitation

  When it rains, it pours; water must be dealt with in terms of capacity and flows.
- Drainage

  Water may be temporary; under flood conditions, it must be diverted, contained, and drained.

The made course cannot compete with the natural one.
—George C. Thomas Jr., Golf Architecture in America

- Wildlife

  Where there is water, there is often wildlife, and its compatibility with golf uses should be anticipated.

- Environmental aspects of water

  Water quality and conservation is a consideration before it enters the golf course, while it remains there, and after it leaves.

- Maintenance

  Water on golf courses typically involves maintenance of the water areas and shorelines.

To be sure, water represents an oasis. To humans, an oasis represents the most basic elements of life, an essential form of sustenance. It can be comforting in one instance and dramatic in another. It brings up the nature of risk when it interrupts the routing. Whenever and wherever one sees the centerlines of a routing plan cross a body of water, one immediately knows that the shot will require a set of nerves that may be allowed to sleep during less perilous shots. But, like the element of rock, water can be a welcome addition, and it can also be a hassle. It should never be overdone. Eighteen holes with water may be a novelty, but probably no more so than a movie with 18 chase scenes.

Among the most breathtaking bodies of water is our largest supply, the ocean. In golf, the ocean represents the ultimate in all of the qualities noted above. Although only a handful of golf courses get to be rout-

FIGURE 3-2
Flowing water, such as this natural stream, forms natural low points in the land, which in turn create slopes and shadows that add character to the finished golf course.

THE HIDEOUT GOLF CLUB, MONTICELLO, UTAH; ARTHUR JACK SNYDER, ASGCA, & FORREST RICHARDSON, ASGCA, GOLF COURSE ARCHITECTS; PHOTO © MIKE HOUSKA/DOGLEG STUDIOS ed alongside the forces of the sea, those that are generally rank high among our top-rated and best-loved courses. Next in line behind these celebrated links are frequently those with views to the ocean, some well in the distance. The lesson, and one seems to be evident here, is that golf courses evolved from the forces of the sea , having first being enjoyed on the linksland formed at the ocean's edge.

What should be diligently sought for is land which resembles in character and contour links-land.
—*Robert Hunter,* The Links

The power of water, or even a substitute that contains no water at all—perhaps woodlands, a prairie, some dramatic shaping, or a vista to a mountain range—may well constitute an essential element of the layout of a golf course. The word *ocean* may therefore be used as a metaphor for looking at land. Every piece of land has an "ocean," and even on terrain that is on the verge of not having one so obvious, the idea of an ocean may be a good place to begin appreciating a site. Of all land, we might ask the question, "Where is your ocean?"

Vegetation

Plants include those that may be retained on the land and those that may be added to help form the golf course. Vegetation includes grasses, groundcovers, shrubs, brush, trees, and water plants. Like all natural components, leaving what nature has provided is worthwhile where it is practical to do so. In routing a golf course, the variety and extent of existing vegetation should be noted and considered. Approaches to vegetation include dodging plant material, augmenting what is there with indigenous plants, and planting exotic species to create an effect or theme.

The three primary types of land in terms of vegetation are:

- Barren
  Land devoid of virtually all plant material.
- Sparsely vegetated
  Land with only a few areas of vegetation, or vegetation so minimal that it looks sparse.
- Forested
  Land with dense brush and trees.

Influences of vegetation on routings include:

- Backgrounds
  Vegetation-covered hillsides and trees are excellent backdrops to golf holes and views across the land.
- Framing
  Vegetation can frame golf holes and views.
- Strategy
  Vegetation that is high in profile or rugged in texture can persuade shot alignments around areas and bring about choices in shot-making.
- Landmarks
  Prominent vegetation can form landmarks and assist in orientation to holes and direction.

FIGURE 3-3
Natural vegetation, when it can be integrated to form backdrops and definition to golf holes, is an asset that must be carefully identified in the early stages of looking at land parcels.

THE HIDEOUT GOLF CLUB, MONTICELLO, UTAH; ARTHUR JACK SNYDER, ASGCA, & FORREST RICHARDSON, ASGCA, GOLF COURSE ARCHITECTS; PHOTO © MIKE HOUSKA/DOGLEG STUDIOS

- Shade
  Mostly a positive for golfers, but often a negative in terms of getting appropriate sunlight to turfgrass.
- Wildlife
  Vegetation forms habitat and cover for wildlife.
- Environmental
  Appropriate vegetation can help sustain ecosystems.
- Color, accent, and aroma
  Blossoms, leaves, and foliage are most often positives, although occasionally negatives in terms of litter and debris.
- Screening/Safety
  Specific and mass plantings can screen and direct shots.
- Visibility
  The right amount can assist in visibility; too much can inhibit it.
- Maintenance
  Most vegetation requires maintenance in order to remain healthy and pleasing.

CLIMATE TYPES

The abridged definition of climate is "the set of conditions in the atmosphere that defines a region." In routing golf courses, we need to know about the climate of a particular site because its contributing factors will influence the finished golf course. When those who plan golf courses do *not* take climate into account, an interesting phenomenon occurs: The climate conditions go ahead and influence the finished golf course anyway. Climate is a variable in golf course routing that for the most part cannot be changed. Except for artificial irrigation, there is no climatic counterpart to the earth-moving equipment we put to work reshaping some golf courses. Temperature, rainfall, humidity, sunlight, and wind are ours to live with and not to change. Climate is what it is.

DEFINITION OF DIRT
Soil that is misplaced.

Essential climate data for land include:

- Annual rainfall
  Broken down by month.
- Total precipitation
  Rainfall separated from snowfall, month by month.
- Temperature
  Average highs and lows, month by month.
- Humidity
  Average figures, month by month.
- Wind
  Prevailing wind direction and speed, which can change from time of day to time of year.
- Severe weather conditions
  The area's susceptibility to conditions such as hurricanes, frequent lightning, monsoons, windchill, etc.
- Sunlight
  Known cloud cover and sunlight angle (See Figure 3-6).

Seasons

Winter, spring, summer, and fall were all learned long ago, along with sharing and manners. The seasons for golf are even simpler. There are just two: when the weather allows for golf, and when climate conditions are too severe for golf. Once this important information is determined, it is possible to sort through data to find out what the climate conditions are during these two periods. Of course, it is also possible that there is no off season and that the climate above the land in question can support year-round golf.

Understanding weather for an area is the first step in identifying the kind of golf course that may fit the land. A glance at the climate data will begin to suggest variables such as economics, turfgrass types, potential maintenance challenges, and water needs. Also important is a look at the weather during times golf cannot be played. Winter conditions in some areas may necessitate special consideration due to heavy snowfall and the associated runoff from snowmelts. In addition to historical data, existing golf courses in the region may be a useful source of information about operations relative to the climate and any special issues they have discovered.

Temperature & Humidity

Temperature and humidity data are essential clues to how comfortable a climate will be. These are telltale signs of how the overall golf experience will be enjoyed on a piece of land if it were to be developed into a golf course. Beyond the comfort factor, the realities of growing and maintaining turfgrass, the type of plant material that may be practical, and even the quality of water in lakes may be summed up, at least initially, by looking at temperature and humidity data. Such realizations as the evaporation to be expected from reservoirs can also be learned through this data.

Evapotranspiration is a derivative factor that involves temperature and humidity. This is a measure of the amount of water lost from the soil plus the water lost from plants through transpiration, which is the process whereby water is passed through the leaves of a plant to the environment. Environmental factors that influence the evapotranspiration rate (an important rate for greenkeepers to know) include solar radiation, ground surface temperature, humidity, and wind velocity. The typical evapotranspiration rate is known for most areas. This rate, although it may change once a golf course is developed, is crucial in determining the needs for artificial irrigation.

Altitude

A golf ball hit at higher altitudes travels farther than one hit at sea level or below. (Furnace Creek, a layout in Death Valley, California, is, in fact, below sea level.) Altitude also affects growing conditions, the varieties of turfgrass and plants that will thrive, and the maintenance requirements of the finished golf course. It is also a factor in the comfort of golfers. Someone not used to a mile-high elevation may become unusually tired due to the change in oxygen in the air.

Precipitation

Precipitation is the discharge of water, in liquid or frozen state, from the atmosphere onto a land or water surface. It includes drizzle, rainfall, glaze, sleet, snow, graupel, small hail, and hail. Graupel, for those of you (including me) who are not familiar with the term, is granular pellets of snow. Sometimes it is called *soft hail.* Precipitation is an important factor, as it determines the extent of artificial irrigation and affects solutions for adequate drainage.

Wind

Sometimes they say winds are calm. Well, if they're calm, they're not really winds, are they?
—*George Carlin,* Napalm and Silly Putty

Except for the handful of diehard golfers who refuse to quit playing during heavy rainstorms, wind represents the most appreciated—and unappreciated—of the climate variables. Wind has always been a nemesis to golfers. One can hardly picture the early linksland of Scotland devoid of crosswinds and gusty conditions. And it is a sure bet that every golfer on earth recalls windy days by questioning how it was possible that the "wind seemed always in our face and, on only a few holes, at our backs."

Prevailing wind direction is a factor that should be well researched for a piece of land. Golf holes must be laid out taking wind into account,

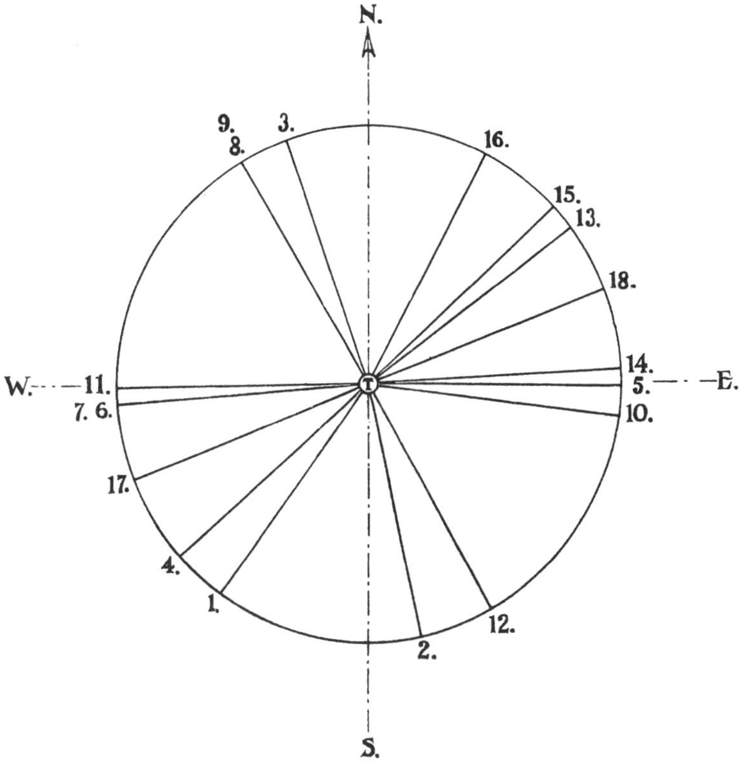

FIGURE 3-4
Reprinted from a 1933 souvenir booklet on the Carnoustie Golf Links in Scotland. This clever chart shows the direction of play of each of Carnoustie's 18-holes. As anyone who has visited Carnoustie will attest, the devilish wind there plays havoc with the golfer. This chart points out how the routing makes frequent changes in direction—something the wind rarely does during the same round.

both for playability reasons and with respect to creating a diversified challenge. Having all holes playing either into or against the wind will not be received well. Neither will having all holes playing crosswise to wind direction. Wind information is usually obtained by contacting the nearest airport, and doing so will yield an accurate description of how the winds behave. I have become very good at finding the phone numbers of local control towers. You will be surprised how many air traffic controllers play golf and will be happy to speak with you.

Wind, however, can be a fickle thing. Mountains, valleys, buildings, and even the unexplained can change wind patterns, sometimes from one ridge to the next. Prevailing winds, which can change from morning to afternoon and season to season, may behave oddly on a piece of land. For some sites, it may be impossible to get accurate information from an airport or the local weather service. Instead, you might consider talking with a local farmer.

As a last resort, for especially remote sites, you can arrange to have an anemometer (wind gauge) erected on the site to record wind direction and speed throughout the year. According to Ben Yapyuco, a renowned expert in weather instruments, having a solar-powered anemometer installed for a year will set you back a few thousand dollars. But, if there is no local farmer, no airport, and no reliable year-round weather data, it may be a worthwhile investment.

U.S. Weather Bureau Wind Scale

The U.S. Weather Bureau uses a graduated scale of 13 levels (0–12) to represent different wind conditions at corresponding wind speeds:

0 = Light (less than 1 mph)
1 = Light (1–3 mph)
2 = Light (4–7 mph)
3 = Gentle (8–12 mph)
4 = Moderate (13–18 mph)
5 = Fresh (19–24 mph)
6 = Strong (25–31 mph)
7 = Strong (32–38 mph)
8 = Gale (39–46 mph)
9 = Gale (47–54 mph)
10 = Whole Gale (55–63 mph)
11 = Whole Gale (64–75 mph)
12 = Hurricane (above 75 mph)

FIGURE 3-5

CLIMATE'S EFFECT ON BALL FLIGHT

WIND'S EFFECTS ON A DRIVE

Tail Wind		Head Wind	
Mph	**Yds. Gained**	**Mph**	**Yds. Lost**
2	2.5	2	3.5
4	3.5	4	8.0
6	4.0	6	13.5

The Three Rules of Wind

1. As head wind velocity increases, the proportional loss of distance increases (if a head wind doubles in velocity, the resultant loss of yardage will more than double)
2. As tail wind velocity increases the proportional gain of distance decreases (if a tail wind doubles in velocity, the resultant gain in yardage will less than double)
3. A head wind hinders more than a tail wind helps (more yardage will be lost to a 10 mph head wind than will be gained by a 10 mph tail wind)

ELEVATION

Altitude (ft.)	**Driving Distance** (yds.)
0	220
1,000	224
5,000	237
10,000	252

Note: At extremely high elevations, the ball will tend to travel shorter distances due to the loss of lift in the thin air.

TEMPERATURE

5º F increase in temperature = 1 extra yard of carry distance due to change in air pressure.

HUMIDITY

Contrary to popular belief, balls will travel further in more humid air.

Sunlight

The basic concern about sunlight is where it comes from, where it goes, and how this will ultimately play with a given piece of land. The most fundamental of concerns is identifying where the sun rises and sets. A familiar rule of routing is that opening holes—the first holes of a course—should not play into a rising sun, and the finishing holes—the holes at the end of a course—should not face into a setting sun. Severe slopes, ridges, and mountain ranges can affect this rule of thumb. Holes that are separated from low sun angles at the beginning and end of the day may not be as negatively affected. Certainly, holes on top of ridges and hills will see considerably more sun at these times of day.

Sunlight is also an indicator of the type of golf experience that might be anticipated on a site. If it is known that there is frequent and considerable cloud cover, the requirements for shade and the nature of backgrounds to golf holes may not be as crucial as they would be in a sunny climate where there are bound to be few reprieves from bright light.

The angle of the sun varies with the season and is determined based on the location of the land. Although this is not a simple matter to comprehend, every effort was made in Figure 3-6 to express how the angle of the rising and setting sun can be determined with a few known site specifics and in a relatively short time.

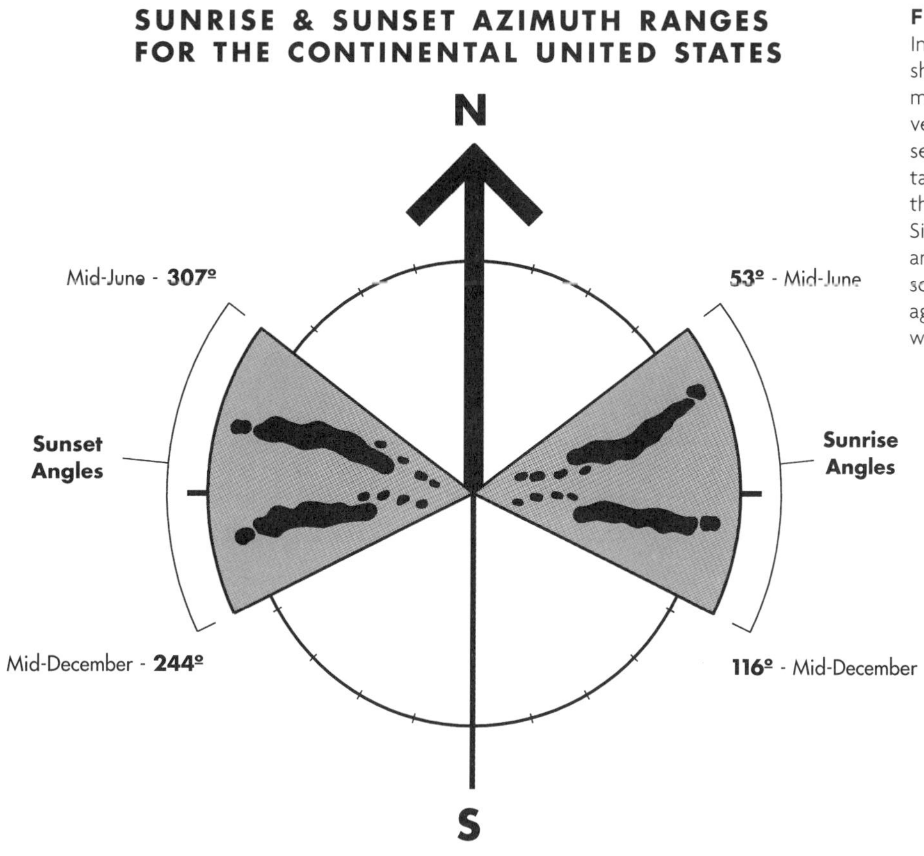

FIGURE 3-6
In this simplified diagram, the shaded areas represent the alignments to avoid in order to prevent conflict with the rising and setting sun. Note that the diagram takes in only the broad range of the continental United States. Similar data can be obtained for any area of the world from local sources, typically governmental agencies that record climate and weather data.

METRIC SCALE

When required, the scale of choice for routing in metric is 1:2000 (1 inch to 166.6 feet), preferably with 1-meter contour intervals. Occasionally, for sheet size or other reasons, golf course architects work at 1:2500 scale (1 inch to 208.3 feet) and sometimes 1:1500 scale (1 inch to 125 feet). For working drawings (grading plans and final plans), the scale is often 1:1000 (1 inch to 83.3 feet).

For slopes of greater than 15 percent (roughly 1 foot of grade difference in each 7 feet of distance), sunlight can change the temperature of the ground considerably. South-facing slopes are most apt to receive sunlight that will warm the ground, and north-facing slopes receive less. This is the fundamental reason that ski slopes are almost always on the north sides of mountain ranges, for these northern exposures retain cold and therefore melt less quickly. For similar reasons, slopes must be considered when evaluating land for golf courses with respect to ground temperature, growing, drainage, and snowmelt conditions.

HOW LAND IS CAPTURED

Surveying, the art of defining land and describing its precise size and shape, has come a long way since markers made of stacked stone were set in place at St. Andrews by archaic means. Today, the most common form of surveying is by way of topographic mapping generated by a combination of analog photography and digital stereography. Topographical maps show the vertical rise and fall of land.

Although it is possible to route golf courses without such topographical information, this is akin to routing in a vacuum. Imagine planning a hike across a wilderness area and having only a map that tells you where things are in a flat, two-dimensional plane. You might set off in a direction that avoids a lake and goes around some woods only to find yourself facing a 10,000-foot-high mountain range. Whoops. A decent topographical map of the area of your planned hike would have shown the mountain range. Your route could have been better engineered.

Although it is possible to set the horizontal geometry of a golf course by considering property boundaries and obstacles on maps with flat information only, myriad vertical factors normally make this a poor idea. The only exception might be an extremely flat site, where it could be argued that routing and preliminary planning can indeed be accomplished without knowing precisely how the site tilts. However, speaking from experience, I have had the honor of attacking several flat sites and can report that none were entirely flat. I believe Columbus first pointed this out, which makes 12 October pertinent to those undertaking the routing of golf courses. No site is, by strict definition, flat.

In fact, knowing which way the minimal gradient is headed can be of extreme importance to the planning and routing of nearly flat sites. At one site in a town called Eloy, Arizona (Figure 3-12), there was a whopping 5 feet of fall across a mile and a half of land. In addition, an interstate highway bordered the site, and I can attest that having an accurate and detailed topographical map—even though it contained only a few broadly spaced contour lines—was of great benefit. It informed our approach to the routing as we began the process of determining how holes would best fit on the site, the best way to drain the course, and the relationship between the height of 18-wheelers traveling down the interstate and golfers just a few hundred feet away.

Those who request consultation on golf course routing without first having good mapping in hand will get only partial service. It may amount to costly advice without much substance.

> *And while we do succeed in approaching nature by artificial means so frequently we are in utter despair in the realization of the utter futility of imitating the primitive contours and sweeps of the dunes.*
>
> *—A. W. Tillinghast, writing for* Golf Illustrated*, February 1935*

CLIENT: I've got a great site for a golf course! Can you fly out here and look at it for me?

GOLF COURSE ARCHITECT: Sure. I'll be right there.

CLIENT: So, what do you think?

GOLF COURSE ARCHITECT: It looks great. Very pretty. Where's the topo map?

CLIENT: We don't have one.

GOLF COURSE ARCHITECT: Well, when you get one, call me, and we'll see if a course will fit, and exactly where and how.

Base maps are just that: maps that form the base for other plans and details to be depicted. Basic characteristics of land parcels that can be captured on base mapping include:

- Property boundaries
  The limits of the available land.
- Easements
  Defined areas crossing or interrupting the parcel that permit access, uses, utilities, or other rights that cannot be ignored.
- Topography
  The rise and fall of the land, usually expressed by contour lines, which represent a constant elevation along a continual path, and/or points that correspond to spot elevations.
- Natural features
  Rock outcroppings, cliffs, caves, ridges, ravines, etc.
- Watercourses and water bodies
  Perennial, annual, and intermittent.
- Vegetation
  Individual trees, canopies of trees, wooded areas, areas of broad coverage, and plantings.
- Utilities
  Existing and future, both above and below ground.
- Built improvements
  All built improvements, including buildings, structures, walls, and, well, anything that has been previously built.
- Roadways, streets, and trails
  Including the limits of the rights-of-way.
- Zoning
  Areas of allowable use, jurisdictions, etc.

Specialized characteristics, which are very often on separate maps altogether, or on layers that can be placed over base maps, can include:

- Aerial photography
  Detailed images of the land can be projected over base maps for added clarity and reference.

Golfers never really lose their awareness of the natural beauties of a golf course — the freshness of the air in the morning when the dew is heavy on the striped greens, the pungent quietness in the evenings when the crickets start up and the setting sun makes the fairways ahead seem lusher than velvet.

—Herbert Warren Wind, Herbert Warren Wind's Golf Book

- Slope analysis

  Depiction of areas where slopes are steeper than a certain threshold.
- Climate mapping

  Wind currents, temperature zones, and other atmospheric conditions above a site.
- Soils analysis

  Typically a map that identifies soils types and may extend to show the depths and areas of topsoil.
- Groundwater

  In essence, a contour map of subsurface water.
- Zoning

  Allowable uses, jurisdictions, etc.
- Adjacent lands and land use maps

  Very often, the land beyond the subject land is not considered adequately; such mapping can show adjacent land parcels, their use, and many of the characteristics noted above.

Rudimentary Methods

Metes and Bounds: The oldest method of capturing land is by metes and bounds. This amounts to nothing more than a description of a piece of land expressed in words and corresponding to a known direction, usually north and the points of a compass. Here is an example: "Start from the northwest corner of Black Bart's barn and go 100 feet north and then 6 feet west for the first corner, then 200 east for the next corner," etc. A metes-and-bounds description requires a known beginning point to which the directions must return. Metes and bounds are important, but their usefulness in routing is primarily evident when they are rendered graphically as a direct plan view representation of the land. A map drawn to a uniform scale that represents the limits of the land in exact ratio to the land itself is an example of such a graphic representation.

Aerial Photography: Photographs of a site can be quite helpful to orient and give a first impression of the land. This is especially true of color photography. Photographs taken from the ground, a.k.a. snapshots, are good to show views from certain points and what the land looks like from the human perspective. They do little to assist in forming the basics of the routing plan, though.

Aerial photography falls into two classifications: (1) oblique photos taken at an angle, and (2) direct vertical photos taken perpendicular to the level ground plane. Oblique shots are not too helpful in that the perspective of the finished print cannot usually be used to draw precise lines and distances. Such images often amount to nothing more than more expensive snapshots. They are gravy to the process — nice to have but not truly needed. The exception is when such perspective shots are digitally captured and can be linked to a database that permits them to be manipulated in the planning process.

What I Know About Helicopters — Advice on Going Up and Coming Back Down

When I first began to design golf courses, it was often the case that my assignments would involve, let's say, some of the work no one else much wanted to do. I felt it important to get experience working in the field and so, too, did others.

One particular assignment involved rendering some golf holes that had already been built. The client wanted reproducible illustrations of the holes, and because the aerial photographs were several years old, it was decided to get some new photographs specifically for this purpose. The cost to have new aerial photography was significant, and we were on a deadline, so a plan was hatched to hire a helicopter and simply take snapshots above the individual holes. From these photos we would trace the fairways and features and get an accurate representation of exactly where the trees were.

My assignment started with getting quotes on helicopter charters. The best quote was from a local service that offered two options: a large Bell Ranger that seated six and a small two-passenger chopper. The better of these was determined to be the smaller, the two-seater. After all, only one person was needed to take the photos. And that would be me.

The morning I headed off to the airport, I was a bit nervous. This would be just my second flight in a helicopter, plus I had to ensure that the photos came out well. A young kid in his late teens or early twenties greeted me and asked if I wanted coffee. "No, I'd better just get going," I replied. "There's work to get done." He was fine with this and motioned me to follow him. I did so, and we went out back of the office, where there sat the smallest helicopter I had ever laid eyes on. It reminded me of a very large radio-controlled toy. The cockpit was about 3 feet across, just large enough for two narrow seats and what looked like a hand brake in between. The young fellow unlocked the wheels and then asked if I would help him lift the helicopter over some gravel to the tarmac. *Lift the helicopter!* What had I gotten myself into?

Well, if discovering that the helicopter—the aircraft—that I would be flying in weighed no more than a Great Dane were not enough, imagine my surprise when the boy I was helping got in and sat down. At first I thought he was just getting it ready, and then HOLY SHOOT-*he was my pilot!*

Well, I'm here, and it's many years later. The photos turned out nice, and once I quit shaking the illustrations of the holes looked nice, too. It all goes to show that general aviation is a relatively safe endeavor, apparently even when you're flying in something that could have been ordered through the mail. Everything worked out fine. But I promised myself that next time I'd remember the following: (1) Professionally taken aerial photos are probably *always* worth the investment; (2) If you ever have to hire a helicopter, ask if it can be lifted by a couple of guys; and (3) My client was probably just as nervous about a young guy like me handling the assignment as I was about my young pilot.scale as it relates to the design process.

Direct vertical aerial shots are useful. If corrected so the scale is accurate, these can be helpful tools and, in some cases, enough subtle detail is evident so one can see how the land falls and rolls. But, without contour information—topographical data—aerial shots amount to guessing games as to the extent of fall and roll. An aerial photo taken at an angle perpendicular to the site can be a helpful tool for field use and to pick up reference points that may not be evident on a base topo map.

Government Surveys: Government surveys include topographical maps such as those available from the United States Geological Survey (USGS). Typically, these maps are at a very small scale with contour lines at large intervals, few and far between. Other government surveys include mining claim maps, flood control maps, maritime maps, and surveys previously commissioned by municipalities for other projects and uses. In situations where not much has changed on a piece of land, such maps can be very useful to initial planning and routing. They do not, however, take the place of accurate topographical mapping. It is wise to remember that land is continually changing. Even in the span of a few years, landforms and contours can change on a site, especially where rivers and drainage courses are prevalent.

Aerial Photography, Base Mapping & Topographical Mapping

Aerial photography is the method most commonly used to generate base maps from which land for golf courses is captured. The maps generated by aerial photography can identify site features, roadways, vegetation, buildings, and, when manipulated by a process called *stereo compilation,* accurate contours of the land. Essential to the process of topographical mapping is taking multiple photographs from strategically planned and precisely calculated locations. From this series of photographs, lab technicians generate highly detailed topographical maps showing a site's contours. It is useful to understand how such maps are created, if not downright interesting.

[T]here is a tranquilizing effect of golf.... Wandering through woods, observing a tormented sea, relaxing near a reflective pool, observing the majesty of a mountain range—all are part of the game.
—Robert Trent Jones Sr.

First of all, the land to be captured by mapping has to be prepared for photographing. In most cases, a uniform grid pattern is surveyed onto the actual property. The corners of the property and occasional intersections of this grid are marked with large white *X*s that can be seen on photographs taken at high altitude. The *X*s typically are about 6 feet in dimension and formed with plastic sheeting pinned to the ground. These points provide a reference that is used throughout the process. On an existing golf course to be photographed for renovation work, the same procedure can be used to mark the locations of existing irrigation heads and other important components on the ground. A common tool to mark irrigation heads and spots is a simple paper plate. (Chinet® buffet size works best, according to an informal survey of aerial companies.) The result from this effort is the same as with the large *X*s; each white spot shows up on the aerial photographs and can be digitized and entered in a database for use in planning and design.

FIGURE 3-7

This historical illustration shows how early aerial photography was used for golf course planning. Images shot from a camera mounted in an airplane were pieced together to form a continuous print of a land parcel. Crude topographical data, often all that was available at the time, was added to the photos to assist in the routing of courses. Major R. D. Newman was the first to employ aerial photography specifically for golf course planning at Fort Riley, Kansas. Although he has somehow escaped identification as a golf course architect, Major Newman planned and built several courses for the U.S. Armed Services using his method of vertical photography combined with oblique shots to show basic contour features. His advice was to take aerial shots in late autumn, when the leaves have fallen and more land features can be detected in the photographs.

SOURCE: *GOLF ILLUSTRATED*, OCTOBER 1929

FIGURE 3-8

Although it seems that an aerial photograph of a site would provide good detail, unless it is combined with a topographical map showing how the land rises and falls, it remains just a pretty picture.

COURTESY OF MCW DEVELOPMENT

The greatest and fairest things are done by nature and the lesser by art.
—*Plato*

Each flight to record a site through aerial photography has a number of variables to be worked out. The scale of a base map is determined by the altitude from which the pictures are taken. If the base map will serve for the design of a residential development, it typically is made at a scale of 1 inch to 15 feet. The contour lines generally are shown at 1-foot intervals. To achieve this scale, the plane must fly between 1500 and 2000 feet above the site. For preliminary golf course planning, the scale typically preferred by golf course architects and planners is 1 inch to 200 feet. When this scale is desired, the altitude of the plane is much higher—between 4000 and 10,000 feet above the site.

For large sites, which most golf course planning demands, multiple passes are necessary to sufficiently cover the property. Each pass represents a separate photograph. Most likely, the pilot will fly along one property boundary, then turn around and fly back across the property at a predetermined distance from the previous pass. This process is repeated in a back-and-forth pattern until the entire site is covered. Each image overlaps the previous image by 60 percent to allow for interpolation of contours.

Aerial photography requires near-perfect weather conditions. Moderate winds can play havoc with the precise execution of a carefully prepared flight plan. Light or even spotty clouds can be problematic also, as clients are usually not interested in expensive pictures and sophisticated contouring of clouds. Once over the site, at the correct speed and altitude, the photographer pulls the trigger and a programmed number of photographs are taken at calculated intervals in one pass, creating a series of pictures. This forms the basis for determining the contour of the land below.

Contour data are determined by taking photographs of the same point from two different angles. A three-dimensional effect is created, which allows the contours to be interpreted and drawn from this pair of flat images. Up to 20 of these carefully planned photos might be necessary to cover one section (1 square mile) of land. These photos, all at slightly different angles, overlap by 60 percent, which eventually allows a technician to see the topography from a three-dimensional perspective and measure the elevations. As the camera takes each of the photographs, it must compensate for the considerable forward motion of the plane. The camera is engineered to slides backward at the exact speed of the plane during the exposure. This feature allows for slower shutter speeds and increased quality in the photographs. Additionally, a high-tech gyromount houses the camera to compensate for the unpredictable turbulence that can be encountered during the flight.

Once the film is developed, the information must then be transformed into a base map format. Single photographs, or "spot shots," of a site can illustrate general two-dimensional site characteristics such as vegetated areas or roadways. To be accurate in terms of scale, such photos must be produced as *digital ortho photos,* which means that they are digitally adjusted so that all areas are at the exact desired scale. If not adjusted, measurements will be off toward the edge of the picture, as these areas were farther away from the camera lens at the time of the shot.

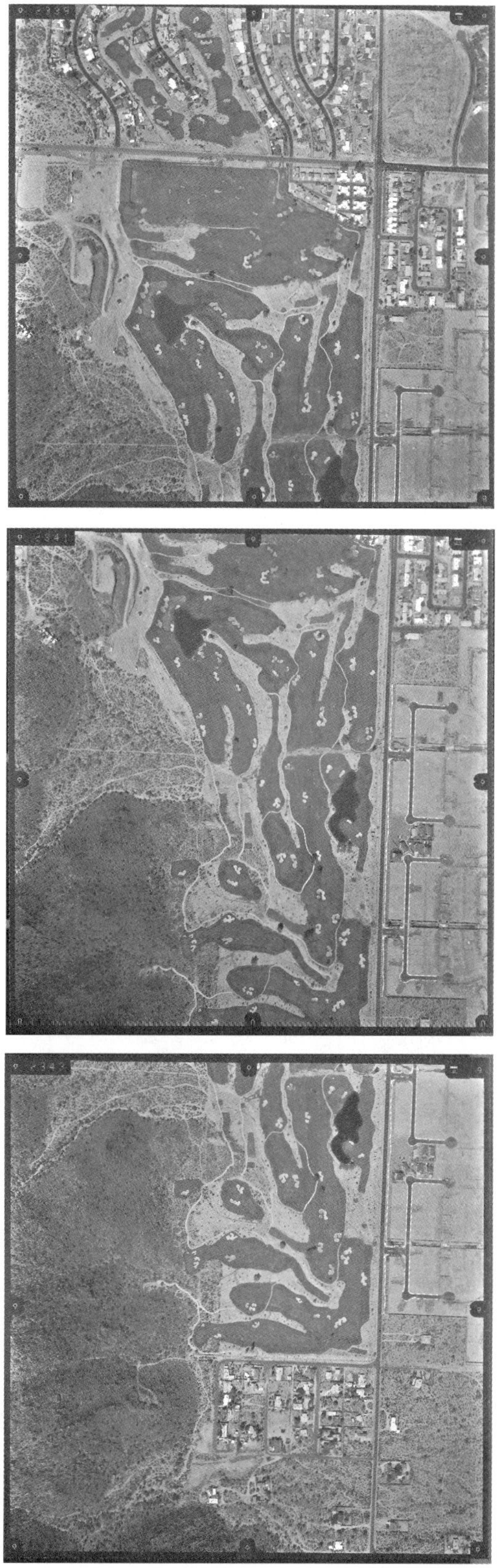

FIGURE 3-9
This trio of aerial images of a completed golf course demonstrates the overlapping shots required for the process known as *stereo compilation.* When the three shots are projected together, points along specific elevations may be seen and traced to form contour lines, which, when combined in a single database, form a topographical map of the area covered by the images.

COURTESY OF KENNEY AERIAL MAPPING, INC., PHOENIX, ARIZONA

Complications can also arise from photos of sites with substantial elevation differentiation. If, for example, the plane flies at a given altitude and parts of the site are considerably closer or farther away from the camera lens due to massive changes in elevation, the scale of those areas will be different.

If a topographical base map is ordered, then a great deal of work has yet to be completed. To begin, two of the many overlapping pairs of photos taken are placed into a stereo plotter. A lab technician looks through an eyepiece that focuses each eye independently on one of the photographs and thus sees the overlapping area in three-dimensional perspective. From this point, the digitizing process begins with tracing items such as roads, existing buildings, tree canopies, and water bodies. Using the surveyed control points and their exact elevations as a reference, elevations along contour lines are found by projecting a reference dot that can be viewed through the stereo plotter and moved up and down until it "touches" the surface of the ground. With the click of a button, the computer notes the elevation and records it for that point of the grid. Spot elevations are also collected along breaklines, or points of major elevation change, such as drainage ways, ridges, and steep drop-offs. Once all of these points are recorded, the computer can calculate and draw in the contour lines automatically. Finally, with the addition of property lines and easements, the digital file is ready for printing, or it may be transferred to a compact disc for use by the golf course architect.

The Digital Age

Before the advent of digital computation, the aerial contour methods described above were even more laborious to record images. The digital world has brought about significant changes in mapping. One of the very first digital plots of a contour map that came across my desk made me quite ill. The detailed

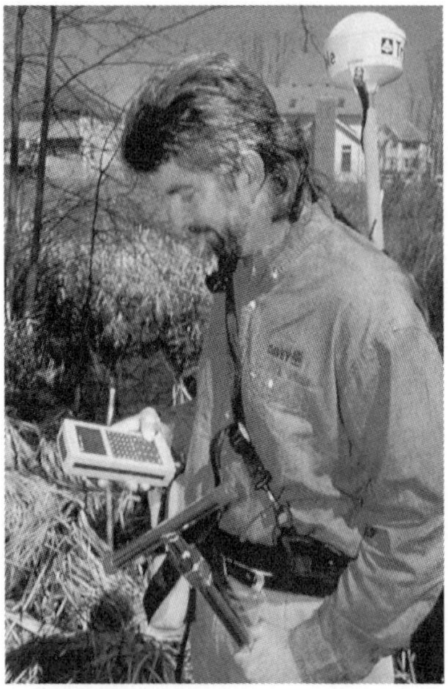

FIGURE 3-10
Actual points in the field are recorded using rebounded signals from orbiting satellites to collect GPS data. Maps are created using the collected database, of which the most common variables are simple coordinates and elevations. Other characteristics that can be collected in the field include vegetation type, soil type, existing structures, stream alignments, and limits of wetland areas. Once golf course routing plans are developed, GPS is invaluable for setting points back into the field so they may be staked for reference during the fine-tuning of the plan and, ultimately, for use during construction.

COURTESY OF DAVEY GOLF

and carefully drawn contours that used to be drawn by hand were all of a sudden jagged straight lines that zigzagged across the map, sometimes in right angles, as if the contours were representing the corners of buildings instead of the naturally flowing land. Thankfully, this has changed. Today the digital world of mapping, commonly referred to as *geographic information systems,* or GIS, is an expanding technology that enables the combination of data from field to desktop—and back again.

GIS technology, an umbrella term, marries the survey process and the planning/design process. It is the thread that holds these data together from the time a survey is made in the field to the point at which construction begins, after all of the planning, routing, and design has taken place. Some of the problems that plagued golf course projects with older technology involved the discrepancies of this in-between period—the data of the design not always matching up to what was surveyed nor to what was built. When properly managed, GIS technology links surveying existing conditions, mapping, design, setting points for construction, actual construction and even the eventual operation.

A great deal of care and thought must be given to the planning of the one-shot holes. Nowhere else, perhaps, should one be so painstaking in valuing the power and angle of the wind.
—Robert Hunter, The Links

GIS can involve each of the previously covered means of mapping, including those labeled *rudimentary.* With GIS, data are entered into digital databases and kept in specific layers, each having reference points that allow the data to match exactly to other layers as they are collected or generated. The best way to think of GIS is as the common depository of data—a magical blender, if you will, that takes all sorts of data and creates useful variations by generating combined layers of the collected information.

Because it is digital in form, the layers collected in this manner need not necessarily conform to a particular standard to be viewed. While we have established that a plan view (a direct perpendicular viewpoint) of land is best for the purpose of routing golf courses, once a routing plan is created and it becomes its own layer of the GIS database, the view of the golf course may be changed at will. Digital imagery allows views to be seen in three dimensions and even in fly-through moving video formats.

The heart of GIS advances is the satellite technology of GPS, which stands for *global positioning system.* Through relatively simple radio receivers, GPS equipment pinpoints locations in the field; these are translated into data that are added to mapping. The data then can make their way back to the field once designs are solidified. For a golf course routing project, the series of events might go like this: (1) Survey points are collected from a site and combined with topographical and other data; (2) A base map is generated that can be used by the design team; (3) Drawings are digitized onto a separate layer that matches the base map; and, (4) Finally, the critical tee, angle, and green points on the routing plan of the golf course are located in the field by the same GPS survey procedure.

Additional aspects of GIS technology include the full complement of satellite-based information that may be available for a land area. Thermal imaging that shows soil temperatures, vegetation coverage, and other climate and land data may be linked to data to create multiple layers of useful information. The key is deciding what information will be *truly* useful. As with all information, the trick is not to be bogged down with too much of the wrong type. Very frequently, the adage "less is more" is useful, as long as data are adequate to get the job done.

I like trees because they seem more resigned to the way they have to live than other things do.
— Will Rogers

The Laser Age

Although laser technology has been known to common surveying for quite some time, mostly for its ability to measure distance and determine elevations, a breakthrough in mapping technology is the capturing of land data via laser *communication.* In a procedure known as *light detection and ranging* (LIDAR), signals from millions of beams of laser light, typically sent from a helicopter, are rebounded from the ground, which permits millions of individual measurements to be computed into a digital model of the terrain below. This invention represents the next era in the laser's influence on land mapping; it goes beyond just making older surveying techniques more convenient and more accurate.

The setup to create such mapping goes like this: Known points are established on the ground and their coordinates entered in a database. These points track the location of the airborne laser unit, which is mounted below a helicopter. The helicopter flies across the property at a variety of angles, altitudes, and routes. The on-board laser beams more than 10,000 shots in each second of flight. Each shot, an individual laser beam, is measured and calculated by the database. At the conclusion of the flight, the massive database is sorted and compared by a software program that arranges the information into a three-dimensional digital model of the subject land. Details as small as 2 to 3 inches, such as a stick on the ground, can be defined if enough information is collected. Natural

FIGURE 3-11
This enhanced photo illustration demonstrates the logistics of the LIDAR system. The millions of beams of laser light are emitted from a helicopter, then rebounded and collected into a massive database of information about the site. The result is a highly accurate computer snapshot of the terrain flown. The output is a digital model of the land, trees, and features that can be used to generate flat topographical maps or very convenient three-dimensional views of the land from virtually any point and perspective.
COURTESY OF DAVEY GOLF

features such as rock outcroppings and the subtleties of slopes can be viewed in amazing detail, as can site improvements such as drainageways and even the trunks of trees. The capturing of land data by laser communication and calculation is advancing rapidly. So, too, are the downstream uses for such systems in the design and construction disciplines.

Scale

The most convenient scale to route golf courses is 1 inch to 200 feet. This places the working scale at 2400 times smaller than the actual land being considered. At this scale, a golf ball is merely a pinpoint that cannot be seen, the cup of a golf hole is about $\frac{1}{1000}$ of an inch in diameter, and the average green is just $\frac{3}{8}$ inch across. Not a whole lot of room for detail, yet a great deal is communicated through routing plans at this scale. The scale of routing plans differs from detailed golf course plans, which are typically larger in scale at 1 inch to 100 feet or greater.

Scale can vary depending on the region. For example, in Mexico and much of Europe, the preferred unit of measurement for planning golf courses is in meters, not feet. The scale most commonly used is a 1:2000 ratio; in metric this means that 1centimeter will equal 20 meters. Interestingly, the preferred unit for golfers remains yards. This brings up the situation where a routing plan is prepared in metric, such as 1:2000 scale (1cm = 20m), yet the scorecard of the course is shown in yards instead of meters.

The philosophy should come from the land.
—Pete Dye

VISUALIZING LAND FOR GOLF

In addition to a solid knowledge of how golf courses are laid out and how to read topographical maps, one more crucial component cannot be forgotten. You need a specific piece of land. While this may sound like advice not worth the paper it's printed on, the cardinal rule—the land should drive the design—begins with a definable chunk of earth. With this component of the problem-solving process, it is 100 percent necessary that you be able to visualize the land. Of that 100 percent, it may be that 50 percent comes from the mapping and the other 50 percent is a process to be worked out in your head. The mapping can, at best, show you something that is at very small scale, not at all charming, and without the occasional bird flying by. An initial step to preparing to route a golf course requires a knack for using your map(s) to gain an impression of the personality of the land being considered.

Reading Topography

Reading contour maps is not difficult, providing your eyesight is good and you follow three simple rules:

1. *Contour lines represent a constant elevation.* Each contour line is assigned a particular height in relation to a known elevation. A contour line is like a continual string laid down on the surface of the land. It simply follows the exact same elevation, wiggling and meandering its way across a site, occasionally the ends of the string meeting.
2. *The ends of contour lines must either meet and connect, or both ends must remain unconnected.* There cannot be an odd number of loose ends when it comes to contours. When the ends of a line meet, it signifies a bump or depression that is contained within the map you are working with. When the ends are unconnected, it signifies that the line continues onto adjacent land. If all contour lines were mapped for the entire earth, eventually they would all meet. Having three contour line ends, all with the same elevation, on a map or drawing is a bad thing. Having five is worse!
3. *Except when showing caves and overhangs, contour lines do not meet or cross each other.* At least not on this planet.

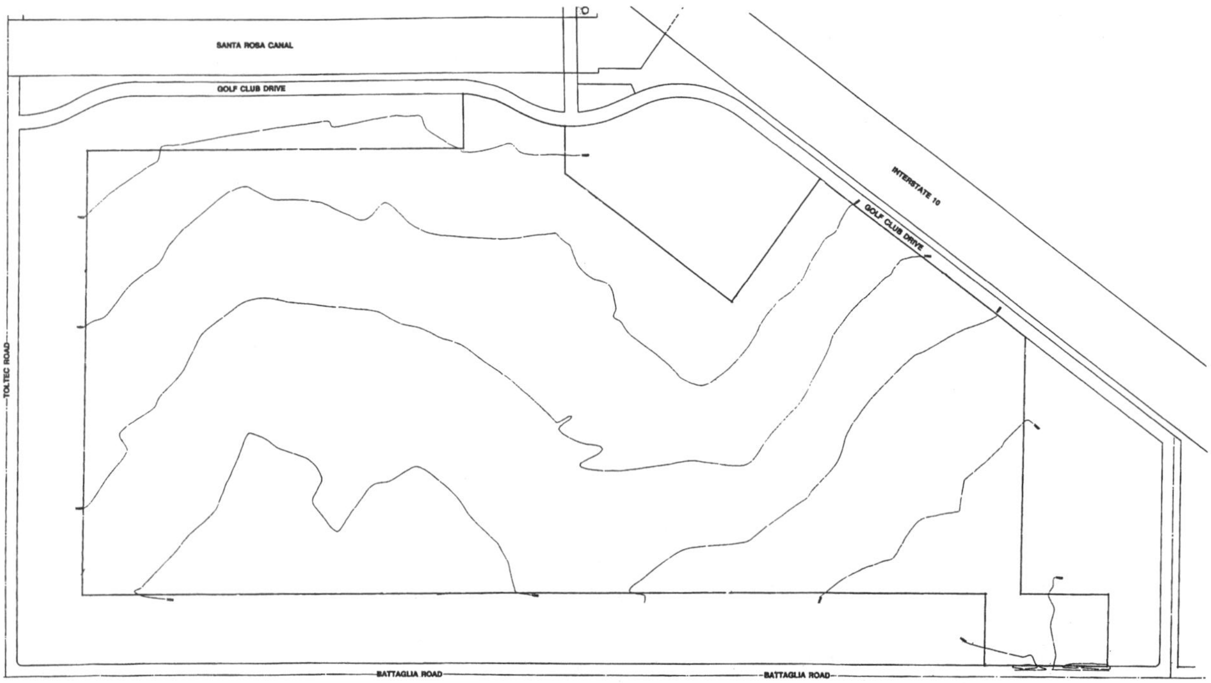

FIGURE 3-12
A topographical map for an extremely flat piece of land where there is just a few feet of fall from one end to the other. Such land requires infinitely more attention to drainage and grading than one with already existing drainage courses and low points.

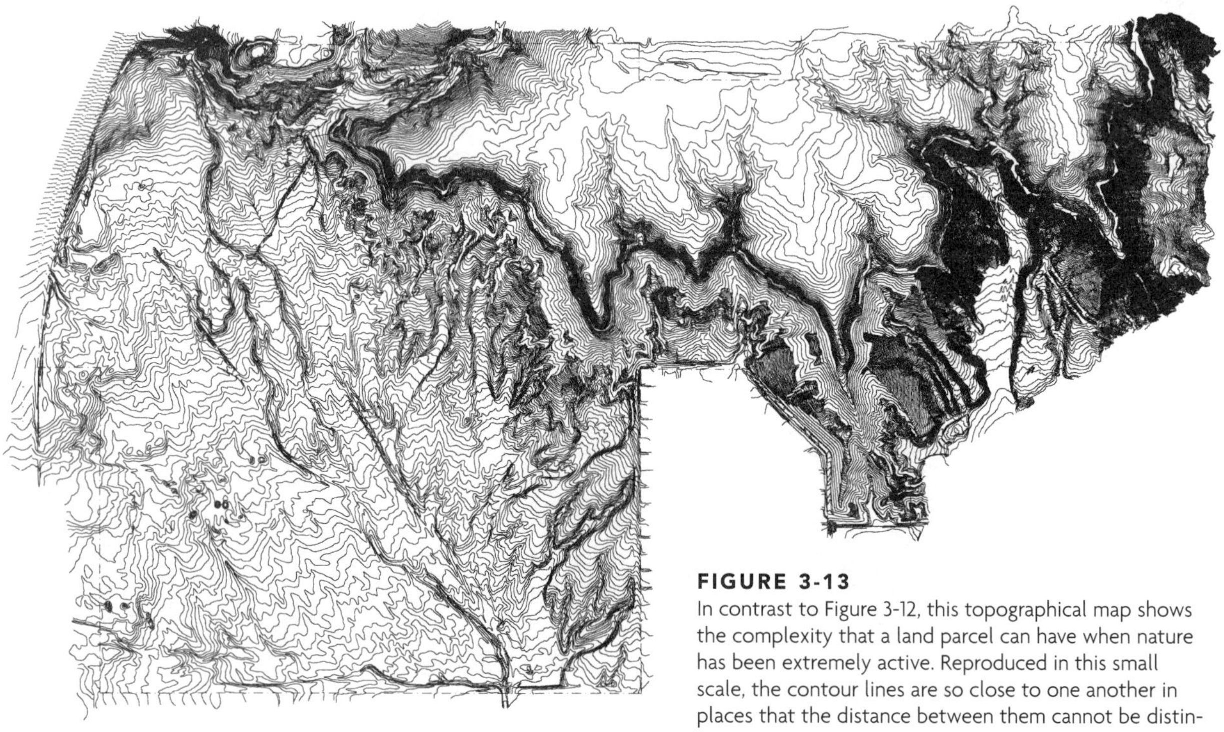

FIGURE 3-13
In contrast to Figure 3-12, this topographical map shows the complexity that a land parcel can have when nature has been extremely active. Reproduced in this small scale, the contour lines are so close to one another in places that the distance between them cannot be distinguished. The dark area that extends across the land is in actuality an 80-foot difference in elevation—a cliff that separates the upper portion from the lower area.

Beyond these three rules, contour maps have subtleties that take practice to appreciate. Most contour lines on topographical mapsrepresent the same incremental difference in elevation. For example: each line might represent 2 feet of vertical difference. Bolder lines are used to represent main contours, such as those for every 10 feet of elevation difference. Intermediate lines might be thinner in pen weight so they may be distinguished from the main lines. Maps vary in this regard. Annoying is the map where all of a sudden intermediate lines are left out as lines crowd closer and closer.

Contour lines tell the story of a piece of land. The valleys, swales, ridges, knobs, cliffs, depressions, high spots, saddles, and crests of a site can be seen by studying its topographical map, Here are some tips about reading topo maps:

- Unless they represent the same elevation, the closer contour lines get to one another, the steeper the grade.
- The alignment of the steepest slope is perpendicular to two adjacent contour lines representing different elevations.
- Depressed contours represent areas that drain inward to a low point and are typically distinguished by tick marks that go toward the low point.
- Spot elevations may appear within topographical maps to pinpoint high points, low points, or any point, for that matter; they are independent data.
- Steep embankments and escarpments can be represented by Y-like symbols that are favored by engineers but are clearly not contour lines.
- A host of other data (drainage paths, streams, lake edges, property lines, etc.) almost always criss-cross over contour lines, and, if not adequately differentiated by line weight or color, they will play havoc with your ability to follow contour lines.

Other useful tools can include scale models and three dimensional images Scale models of sites can be helpful to appreciate land because they are familiar, can be touched, and allow you to take in the whole at once. Three-dimensional computer renderings can be useful but, when viewed on a monitor, are really just elaborate two-dimensional views. Their usefulness depends on the ability to manipulate the view and integrate the data with other site data.

> *A golf course can be reshaped from the land, but it has to be done so with some idea of why.*
> *—Desmond Muirhead*

Good versus Bad

If you are ever fortunate enough to be presented with a piece of land that is "good" without much intervention, congratulations. You will be among the minority of golf course routers. The routing process is usually much easier in these instances. Holes seem to present themselves almost as if by magic. Features need not be created from scratch; instead, they appear out of the ground as if waiting for a golf hole to share their space. And the details, the charm, and the ambiance are there for the taking.

The fact is that most land is somewhere in between all good and all bad. If you were misled by the simplicity of the introduction of this chapter, my apologies. Golf course architect Gary Linn believes there are three primary classifications of land, including the in-between type. According to Linn, the three land types are: (1) dead flat land (or nearly so); (2) mountainous land (mostly steep and on the verge of being too steep); and (3) great, natural rolling land that should come with the warning "DON'T SCREW IT UP!"

The middle-aged golfer is disinclined for mountaineering in the morning... and even less inclined for it in the afternoon.
—*C. H. Alison,* Some Essays on Golf Course Architecture

Many golf courses are now routed and built in spite of the land they occupy, whereas the original relationship between land and golf courses was the other way around. The upside of this change is that we are now able to put golf courses where they are needed, and not only where the land is fully agreeable. The days of golf courses being developed only on linksland or land resembling linksland are gone. Golf course architects have, nonetheless, maintained a link to the past. Many fine designs, even those routed atop the most unwilling land, have a sense of being one with the land. The hurdles nowadays are not only to find a way to get golf to work with the land but to make it appear in the end as if the land was meant for the game of golf. This is no easy task.

Having said this, it is interesting to consider a project being contemplated in the often freezing climate of Central Canada. A developer has floated the idea of individual golf holes in large air-filled domes—18 individual domes, some as large as par 5s, accessed via tunnels, out of the cold and the harsh environment. Rumor has it that Jack Nicklaus might design this "golf course" and stamp his signature on its design. This concept is the ultimate testament to the fact that golf, whose design was once dictated by the land, is now often the designer.

Land Essentials

To seriously contemplate building a golf course you must have enough land, land configured so that a course can physically fit into the property, and land that either has or can be serviced with the required ingredients to support a golf course. These required ingredients include:

- Suitable climate
- Suitable soils
- Suitable access
- Reliable water source (if artificial irrigation is required)
- Positive drainage

Keeping Drainage in Mind

Speaking of drainage. It's never too early to begin thinking about how a site drains—and how it might if a golf course were to be built there. One of the most efficient ways to solve drainage issues, even before they

FIGURE 3-14
At first glance, the feature appears to be an outstanding example of natural landform and an amazing backdrop for golf. The enormous rock formation was actually constructed by The Larson Company of Tucson, Arizona, which specializes in creating artificial environments and features. In this case (and quite an exceptional one), golf architect Tom Fazio, ASGCA, augmented the natural terrain with the likeness of the geology of this coastal site. Actual molds taken from water-worn ocean rock were used to create replica rock outcrops for use as separation, retaining walls, and features.

COURTESY OF THE LARSON COMPANY

come up, is to think of drainage the way the land wants it to work. Another way of putting this is to not try to make water run uphill or do anything else too heroic.

Golf course architect Don Knott has considerable experience working on tough sites, including the mountainous regions of Japan, where entire mountains have been literally reshaped to allow for dramatic golf course development. Knott's approach—to begin solving drainage issues by using the land—is parlayed into eventual efficiency. "If we can solve drainage early on," he notes, "we can usually save a lot of money when it

The Scale of Design—A Short Story

Several years ago, a friend of mine, Michael Cronan, began a talk to a group of architects and designers by discussing what he referred to as the *scale of design.* Cronan began by asking the audience to imagine a horizontal scale where there is a far left end and a far right end. From this point, he began to describe the primary design disciplines and, in relation to the scale, how each is approached.

"At the very left side of the scale," he began, "you have fashion design, for it occurs mostly at the same scale of the finished product; by draping material and fabric over a mannequin or a model, the designer is able to see the results almost as soon as the design is created." He went on to speak of the graphic design profession, which he suggested was just to the right of fashion design on this imaginary scale. In graphic design, the scale at which the designer works is very close to that of the finished product and is maybe only a few weeks away from being brought to reality. Then came product design, interior design, and following these was building architecture. In these design professions, the scale at which the designer works is incrementally smaller relative to the finished product, the building architect relying on plans that may be 48 times smaller than the finished building and with the results being realized in the future by a year or more.

Then—and this is where the story hit home—Michael got to landscape architecture, especially landscape design that involves large sites, such as golf courses. "Finally, at the very far right end of the scale," he said, "is the landscape architect who must envision his designs at a minuscule scale compared to the finished site. What is most dramatic is that the design will very often not be appreciated to its fullest until all of the plants have matured. In some cases, this will be long after the designer is deceased."

Golf course design-especially the routing part—is at the extreme of the design spectrum. While we may play golf courses as soon as they are opened, most get better with age. Trees flourish, areas fill in with growth, and all elements become more seasoned. Augusta National is a prime example of such conditioning. None of those who created it were able to appreciate it in its true finished state, that which we now take for granted as we watch the Masters each and every year.

My friend Michael credits colleague David Meckle, dean of architecture at California College of Arts and Crafts, with this approach to understanding the scale of design work. Meckle, who has a distinguished career in architecture and design—although not golf course design—has worked in a variety of design offices and regularly uses this comparison to point out the importance of appreciating scale as it relates to the design process.

comes to our final grading and drainage requirements." This lesson is cause for the importance in looking at land and being able to visualize it not only for what it is but for what it might become. When it is within your grasp to accomplish both of these, the process of routing will come together much more fluidly.

What Maps Can't Always Show

Maps, as good as they may be, are not always able to give a full accounting of a parcel of land. One reason is that much of the information you need to fully understand a site is not customarily a part of mapping. In some cases, full understanding involves elements other than physical attributes. Examples include:

- Adjacent land
  Overall land planning and uses for the locale.
- Access
  Can people get here?
- Views
  Both those inward to the land and those outward.
- Lore
  All land has a past; very often, this past can help define what should be envisioned there.
- Market conditions
  Will golf be sustainable on this land?

A WORD ABOUT RECLAMATION LANDS

Reclamation lands include those that have been used for one purpose and are being considered for use in serving a different and new purpose. Such land comes with obvious distinctions from regular land in that the site data must be extended to another dimension, one that maps the former uses and identifies areas that may have to be approached in alternative ways in terms of development. Very often, such mapping will identify portions of the land to avoid at all costs. The diversity of types of reclaimed land is so broad that adequately addressing each and every scenario would require a book of its own. Even then, it is likely that with new technologies and methods, previously used land that was judged irreclaimable can now be transformed into sites suitable for golf or other purposes.

Golf is an excellent use of reclaimed land, as it may adjust to the land in a free form way and dodge certain areas. All of this is accomplished through the routing of the course. A key benefit of using reclaimed land for golf is that golf courses are inherently better when they are not perfect. They are lenient with respect to finished surfaces. In contrast to soccer fields, baseball diamonds, and parking lots, golf fairways and features can undulate and move. Very often, reclaimed land, such as an old

FIGURE 3-15
The Old Works Golf Club in Anaconda, Montana, was among the first courses ever planned on a federal Environmental Protection Agency (EPA) Superfund site. In addition to the transformation of a once-blighted site into a sustainable golf course, many historic relics were included in the design, including black slag from the mining operations, which was used in place of sand in the bunkers.

JACK NICKLAUS, ASGCA, GOLF COURSE ARCHITECT; PHOTO © MIKE HOUSKA/DOGLEG STUDIOS

landfill, continually settles and shifts, even if just slightly. A golf course can usually withstand this, as a change of a few inches in grade over the years may not even be noticed. On the other hand, such change to a finely leveled baseball field would be an imperfection and therefore unacceptable.

Reclaimed land for golf uses can include:

- Agricultural lands
  Fields no longer in production of crops
- Brownfields
  Any environmentally impaired property
- Closed solid-waste landfills
- Abandoned open-pit mines
- Former rock quarries
- Former industrial sites
  Factory sites, harbors, industrial yards
- Floodways
  Inundated areas, drainageways, and flood-damaged land

Types of Golf Courses

HOLE NO.

4

Golf courses come in all shapes and sizes. In no other sport or game is one playing field so remarkably different from the next. This quality is one of the many that make golf so rich and diverse. There are short courses—and long courses. There are courses that everyone can play—and some that no one but a select few can play. Without a careful understanding of these various types of courses, the router has no hope of coming up with solutions for how a golf course should be laid out—and, importantly, for holes that make sense and serve the type of golfer who is likely to frequent them.

Despite the great diversity of course types, it is possible to categorize them by their various uses, length, etc. As you will discover, the classification categories are many and the nomenclature almost mind-boggling. But, once armed with a background in course type, you will find it easier to look at routings from the outset and to focus energy on layouts appropriate to the project

A well-designed short course kept to a high standard will often be more popular than many long, tiresome, unkempt courses which boast of championship length.
—Robert Hunter, The Links

CATEGORIES OF COURSES BY USE

Classification of golf courses by general type of use remains one of the most popular categorizations. This is especially true within the golf industry, where individuals concerned with the economics of golf course development throw these terms around in a rather freestyle form. Unfortunately, because this method of classification defines only the type of use that a course will experience, the category names alone do little to describe the physical nature of a golf course. Nonetheless, the approach remains an important means of describing golf courses, if for no other reason than its wide use by developers, bankers, feasibility analysts, and number-crunchers.

Categorization by use gets at the heart of how a golfer either will or will not have access to the course—and, perhaps most telling, how payment is made by a golfer to gain the right to play. You can readily see how these terms became so popular by development and financial concerns, as they cut expeditiously to the chase and imply, in just a few words, the potential for fee collection. Moreover, these classifications hint at what type of clientele can be expected, and this, of course, has a lot to do with what kind of golfer—and, ultimately, what kind of course—will be most suited to the project. It should be noted that these descriptions can apply to many configurations of golf courses and completely ignore the physical differences—length, number of holes, etc.—that a course may comprise.

Public Golf Courses

The term *public golf course* is a catchall expression that can be used to describe any golf course on which the public may play without having to jump through too many hoops. Pebble Beach, as an example, has all the appearances (and price) of a private course, but it is clearly a public golf course because the public has access to play there. The term *public golf course* has a counterpart in type-of-use terminology with the term *private golf course.* When you combine these two with *semiprivate golf course,* you have terms to describe any and all golf course types. Unfortunately, these terms are so broad that they only touch the surface in communicating the nature of golf course use.

Public golf courses can include:

- Daily fee courses
- Municipal courses
- Resort courses
- Development courses
- Semiprivate courses—as policy allows
- Military courses—as policy allows
- University courses—as policy allows

FIGURE 4-1
Military golf courses were established, many informally, to entertain the troops in remote places. In this photo from 1948, a threesome enjoys a makeshift course that is literally no more than a series of wooden poles set out on a flat, unturfed field. Hardly indicative of mainstream military courses, many of which are celebrated layouts with all of the appointments one would expect of a complete golf course.

PHOTO COURTESY OF THE PHOTOGRAPHIC SECTION, NAVAL HISTORICAL CENTER, U.S. NAVY

Private Courses

Simply put, a private golf course is any course not open to play by the general public without a membership or formal guest policy. Private golf courses can include:

- Private golf clubs
- Country club courses
- Members courses
- Military courses
- University courses
- Resort courses—when reserved for guests only
- Company courses
- Personal courses

Semiprivate Golf Courses

The designation *semiprivate* typically means that a course has memberships or offers play to a select group, but the public is permitted to play at certain times or when tee times are available. This category is fairly pointless because it encompasses far too many variations. The term *semiprivate* is most commonly used when a developer wants a course to seem exclusive without actually excluding people from paying a green fee to play the course. It is also used when a course is intended to be private but in the short term has an excess of available tee times. In both scenarios, revenues might be lost if nonmembers were excluded from play.

Daily Fee Courses

The most prevalent type of golf course developed in recent times, a *daily fee* facility is one at which anyone who pays the required fee is allowed to play. The term *daily* often causes confusion, as it implies that paying the fee allows play for the entire day. This is customarily not the case. A daily fee golf course is one on which the public may play for a prescribed green fee *per round.* A better term for this category might be *round fee course.*

Typically, a daily fee course is owned by a concern in the private sector and simply opened to the general public for use. Hybrids run rampant, however, so be aware. Some daily fee courses are built on land owned by municipalities and may be referred to as *municipal golf courses,* even though they are not operated by a municipality and thus do not fit that category. Some resort courses are also daily fee courses. You can see that these terms are often used somewhat interchangeably and often with great liberty. However, a daily fee course is assuredly a *public golf course* by definition and, in some instances, a *semiprivate course.* Most certainly it is never *a private golf course.*

Municipal Courses

To be correctly termed a municipal course, a course must be controlled primarily by a municipality—that is, a public-sector governing body such as a city, town, county, state, or public district. While this sounds

FIGURE 4-2
Municipal courses are often thought of as second-rate. Although they are usually built with more restrictive budgets than courses built by the private sector, this can be overcome with good siting and design. In this example, the setting alone is worth a rating of 10.

THE HIDEOUT GOLF CLUB, MONTICELLO, UTAH; ARTHUR JACK SNYDER, ASGCA, AND FORREST RICHARDSON, ASGCA, GOLF COURSE ARCHITECTS; PHOTO © MIKE HOUSKA/DOGLEG STUDIOS simple, the terms can get fuzzy. Take, for example, a golf course built on municipal land but operated by a private enterprise under a broad lease agreement. In some of these cases the municipality might have little control over the facility. When control of a course by a municipality is negligible it can hardly be termed a municipal course. At most, it is a daily fee course.

A municipal course designation relies on testing for three fundamental qualifiers, of which any two are a must: (1) Is the land municipally controlled or owned? (2) Does the municipality control rates and access? and (3) Is the golf course primarily operated for the general public with great regard for access by all? The underlying principle is that a municipal golf course is one built and operated for the recreation purposes of the general public.

It can be easily argued that all three of these aspects must be present, but there are examples of municipal golf courses where only two are present, yet it would be difficult to argue against their inclusion in the category. If you were to identify the most important qualifier, it would undoubtedly be the issue of rate and access control. Without a legislative body controlling rates and access, it would be easy for a golf course to drift away from municipal orientation, and this is the point where the line must be drawn.

Historically, it might be added, a municipal golf course was one built, owned, *and* run by a municipality. The greenkeeping staff worked for the city, as did the rest of the staff. However, in modern times, it became increasingly tempting for cities to privatize certain elements of their services to residents. Private garbage collection, airport management, and ambulance service are common examples of this trend. Golf courses were an obvious candidate. Who better to build and manage a golf course than a private operation with expertise and a wonderful portfolio of courses? What was once a municipal course is now more liberally defined because of the privatization movement. Typically, municipal courses were run by the parks and recreation departments; even today, when operations may be outsourced, the parks department generally oversees the facility and the contracts that are entered into for management of the operations and/or maintenance.

Resort Golf Courses

This classification is often daily fee in nature, but some resort courses are open for use by guests of a resort only. Resort golf courses are generally available to resort guests on a priority basis and only after remaining tee times have been offered to guests are they sold to the public. Of course, the profit factor may enter into golf course use of this type. Take, for example, the member of the general public who is willing to pay a very high price, considerably more than a resort guest might expect to pay, to play a course of this type. If the gap between green fees is wide enough, it is difficult to turn away the nonguest, even if it means one less tee spot. The main obligation of a resort is to its guests. At Pebble Beach, for example, a resort guest can book tee times well in

FIGURE 4-3
An example of a resort course that is open to the public for daily fee play.

PHOTO COURTESY OF SEAMOUNTAIN GOLF CLUB, BIG ISLAND OF HAWAII; ARTHUR JACK SNYDER, ASGCA, GOLF COURSE ARCHITECT

advance. The golfer off the street is only able to call a day ahead and might not get the opportunity to play when convenient, or at all.

Military Golf Courses

Military golf courses are built to serve the men and women of the armed services and to provide recreation for the families and service personnel assigned to a base or region. The rationale behind their development was to keep the personnel close by and therefore available for active duty. There is also an element of "taking care of our own." How better to recruit and make the military experience a good one than to offer 18 holes of private golf right down the street?

Military golf courses are typically private but, due to their unique circumstance and location on government property, are given this special designation. Military courses are unmistakable in definition. Unlike with almost all other designations, when the term is used, you immediately understand the situation.

Other Use Terminology for Course Types

Our desire to categorize seems never-ending, as new classifications get thrown into the pot quite frequently. Almost all of the above use types may be combined. Although the idea of a resort/military course seems an unlikely hybrid, the notion is not totally without merit; perhaps some Pacific location would lend itself to the development of a military resort with an adjoining golf course for that much-needed R&R.

And keep in mind, we are so far just exploring course *use* types. Even more potential marriages of terms emerge when it comes time to classify golf courses by length, terrain, design, and so on. Other use terminology you may run across includes:

- Country club golf course

  Another name for a private course not generally open to the public.
- Members golf course

  A usually private course at which only members may play.
- Public-private partnership golf course

  A public or semiprivate course in whose development a public-sector body participated, financially or by contributing land, incentives, etc.
- True municipal golf course

  A course owned and operated exclusively by a governmental agency, such as a city parks and recreation department.
- Pseudomunicipal golf course

  A somewhat slang term for a course that meets the definition of a municipal course but is managed by a for-profit enterprise and not by city employees.
- Resort/daily fee golf course

  A resort course that accepts play on a daily fee basis.
- University course

  A course operated by a university for competition and for the recreation of students, alumni, and guests.
- Company golf course

  The private-enterprise equivalent of a military course; a course built primarily to serve employees of a corporation.
- Personal golf course

  A course built for an individual, such as on a private estate; very rare. (Willie Nelson's Perdernales Golf Course located in the Hill Country outside Austin, Texas is one such example.)

> *The game of golf was meant to be fun. Challenging, but not too intimidating. The design must take into account all types of players and must never forget the bottom line.*
> *—Arthur Jack Snyder*

CATEGORIES OF REASONS FOR BUILDING COURSES

There are fundamental reasons to build golf courses. Most have to do with generating revenues and, ultimately, a profit. Unlike use categories, the following course types refer to the primary factor that catalyzes the building of a golf course. Such definitions are important to the golf course architect because they reflect the type of play the course is expected to receive, which necessarily affects certain characteristics of the routing. These characteristics are reviewed in "Types of Golfers versus Types of Courses" and "Quantity of Play Considerations," which appear later in this chapter.

FIGURE 4-4
Real estate golf courses are among the most common in the United States. One reason is that they typically are easy to fund as a result of lot premiums and memberships and because the eventual community will provide the base of players needed to support the course.

PHOTO © MIKE HOUSKA/DOGLEG STUDIOS

A key point to consider in this set of categories is the underlying reliance on financing. Simply put, golf courses cannot be built without funding or, at the very least, a contribution in the form of offsetting a need or condition in or around the proposed site—for example, a municipal course in an area where no courses are available to the general public. In this case, the course serves as a recreation need, and, just like a soccer field or park, might require subsidies to operate.

Real Estate Development Golf Courses

The real estate golf course, or *community golf course,* exists primarily to drive real estate sales of residential lots. Occasionally, such projects involve mixed-use development, such as commercial office space, a resort, or a timeshare facility. Such courses may generate profits as daily fees or through memberships but essentially are planned to extract a premium from lot buyers. They give additional value to the real estate by virtue of their inherent open space, the amenity to the development, and the prestige of having a golf course nearby.

Membership Golf Courses

Such courses are built because it is expected they will command private memberships and dues that will far exceed the cost of developing the golf course. Normally, these courses are combined with residential development, but some courses have been built for no motivation other than exclusive membership.

General For-Profit Golf Courses

This term describes a golf course built in anticipation of its ability to generate revenues that will outpace the costs from play by the general public. Supply and demand are the determining factors—overlaid, of course, by the initial cost of the golf course, interest rates, and so on. An excellent example of a good investment in this category is a course with an average or low cost to build that can generate high green fees in a market where there is a shortage of golf courses, yet plenty of golfers. Take away just one of those ingredients, however, and the economic equation is not nearly as strong.

Recreation-Driven Golf Courses

When a municipality decides to build a golf course and intentionally goes about this with little regard for profit, it is said to be a *recreation-driven golf course.* (Other relevant categories are *municipal* and *true municipal.*)

Military golf courses and university/college courses also belong in this category, as they are built primarily for recreation purposes and not necessarily to generate revenues.

Corporate courses (although few exist) are another in this category. A favorite example of a company course, so very unfortunately now closed, was the Verde Valley Country Club, built by silver miners in the foothills below Jerome, Arizona. Constructed at the beginning of the twentieth century, this nine-hole wonder was as pure and rustic as they come. Most accounts relate that it was largely influenced by transplants from Scotland who were on the job in Jerome to strike it rich. The course was an integral part of the miners' recreation, and company dollars went into its construction and, for years, its upkeep. I cannot begin to do the course justice here, but allow me to whet your appetite for the unusual by saying that it featured an island tee, drives over the tops of hills, and a mining aqueduct bridging high above some of the fairways.

Destination Golf Courses

Any course built primarily to serve a resort, timeshare facility, or tourist area can be categorized as a destination golf course. The key word here is *primarily,* as many courses associated with a resort or tourist area easily meet the criteria of real estate and daily fee golf courses as well.

Another key to defining destination golf courses lies in the determination that the area or development might not be able to attract the required visitations or viability without the golf course. This description extends to courses built to drive economic development to an area—the build-it-and-they-will-come approach. Seldom, however, will you see such golf course projects not begin, at some point, to take on the look and feel of a daily fee golf course—that is, one that can deliver a return on the investment via its ability to pay for itself or better.

Reclamation- & Environment-Driven Golf Courses

Reasons are emerging for building a golf course that have little to do with making a profit, at least as the initial motivation. Environmental problems that can be resolved by constructing a golf course are becoming important instigators to building golf courses. Of course, the long-term viability and consequences of operating a golf course built to recti-

FIGURE 4-5
This daily fee course serves as a flood control drainageway through a residential community.

COYOTE LAKES GOLF CLUB, SURPRISE, ARIZONA; ARTHUR JACK SNYDER, ASGCA, AND FORREST RICHARDSON, ASGCA, GOLF COURSE ARCHITECTS; PHOTOGRAPH BY RICHARD MAACK fy an environmental problem must be carefully weighed. Typically, such courses, by nature of their location, routing, and engineering, solve a problem that might, without the golf course, be even more costly to overcome. You can see the rationale, for example, of deciding to build a $6 million golf course that is likely to generate a profit rather than sinking just as much money into fixing the problem without the associated profitability of a golf operation.

Examples include courses built to mitigate flooding areas, to stabilize ground, or to discharge abundant wastewater; courses built on top of old landfills or mining waste; and courses used to reclaim open-space greenbelts or wetland environments.

Follow this example. At one project, which at the beginning seemed to defy logic, the client asked us how much water a full-length 18-hole course might be expected to use in a day. When the answer came back, the client's response was, "Can't you use more?" In this case, the County of Hawaii was responsible for discharging almost 2 million gallons of treated effluent each day and had virtually no suitable place to accomplish this. The limited soil coverage of this particular part of Hawaii made it impractical to simply allow the treated sewage to run down through the broken lava. A golf course development was the answer(and, in this case, one with plenty of turf areas that could adequately absorb and filter the wastewater and allow it to be used by the grass plants in the natural process of evapotranspiration.

Examples of reasons to build reclamation- and environment-driven golf courses include:

- Flood control

  Courses built to contain floodwaters, stabilize ground, or retain runoff so it cannot damage downstream areas.
- Stabilization

  Courses built primarily to stabilize ground and protect it from erosion.
- Effluent discharge

  Courses built specifically to handle discharge of treated sewage, or effluent.
- Reclamation projects

  Courses built on reclaimed land from mining or industrial operations and integral to the reopening of the land for direct use by people.
- Landfill projects

  Courses built on land once used for interring solid waste or other waste; landfill golf courses are typically built above layers of compacted waste and serve to seal the waste.
- Open space and wetlands environments

  Golf courses can be extremely efficient for returning land once used for other purposes to conditions similar to the original natural ground.
- Buffer projects

  Golf courses have the ability to deaden sound and may serve as a transition zone between land uses; examples of buffer uses are between highways, industrial areas, airports, and designated wilderness areas.

FIGURE 4-6
Only a fraction of golf courses are built specifically to accommodate major tournaments. When this reason is the impetus for a course, all sorts of requirements must be met, as this photo of spectators watching the Phoenix Open proves.

PHOTO COURTESY OF THE PHOENIX THUNDERBIRDS, HOSTS OF THE PHOENIX OPEN; PHOTO BY SCOTT TROYANOS

Tournament Golf Courses

A tournament golf course is one specifically designed to host a major golf tournament, although additional factors drive the decision. Such other considerations can include a nearby resort, housing development, private memberships, and the ability to make a profit from the green fee charged to people who are motivated to play the layout.

The Tournament Players Club (TPC) courses developed by PGA Tour are developed specifically for annual tournament use, although you will find numerous other reasons below the surface. As noted, but worth repeating, *golf courses are almost always built for an economic reason.*

Trophy Golf Courses

There simply is no other category in which to place this very small but honest reason why a golf course might be built. Trophy golf courses are built by an individual with access to huge sums of money who has decided to do so regardless of any economic reason such as most golf course development requires. Look for trophy courses to be off the beaten path and so exclusive that usually only friends of the owner are invited to stop by.

CATEGORIES OF COURSES BY LAND TYPE

Course definitions that reflect the type of land the course is built on include the expected topographical change in the course, the style of play demanded by the course, and the look and feel of the surroundings. This is the oldest means of describing a golf course, as the first courses were judged mostly by the land on which they were built. Why? For starters, the ability to change the land was limited, and therefore what you began with was essentially what you ended up with in terms of the basic terrain. The days of moving millions of cubic yards of soil to create landscapes had not arrived, nor were there the many concepts of use we have classified. This, together with the fact that most people at the time regarded linksland as the most suitable terrain on which to build what is now commonly viewed as a designed golf course, made it chic to build courses near the sea or on any land that approximated linksland. Fundamentally, according to purists, at least, only two kinds of golf course land exist: *linksland* and *nonlinksland.*

Links Courses

The quintessential golf course. A true links is built on linksland, defined as land near an open sea or bay composed of natural sand dunes formed by the wind and the ocean. The primary reason golf courses were built on linksland was its suitability for the purpose—gently rolling land with natural hazards and good drainage—and the fact that no one much cared for this land, certainly not for farming. Deeper theories suggest that the seaports of Scotland were ideal landing points for European travelers, who introduced there some of the many stick-and-ball games played elsewhere.

FIGURE 4-7
Spanish Bay Golf Links is a prime example of a modern-day links course. Built near the famous Pebble Beach Golf Links, Spanish Bay is among the most links-ish of all the courses in the Pebble Beach area.

PHOTO COURTESY OF DON KNOTT, ASGCA

In the strictest sense, a links course cannot be anywhere but by the sea, and on linksland. But today this rule is broken frequently, and the term is often applied to a course by the ocean or a lake, a course built on dunesland or land formed to resemble dunesland, and, quite inappropriately, to any course that plays out for nine holes and then back to the clubhouse regardless of the type of land it occupies. This latter application of the term is deceiving and is therefore advised against. Besides, not *all* true links courses play out nine holes and then back. The configuration of the routing has nothing to do with the term.

Hinterland Courses

Hinterland refers to land located away from coastal areas and in the interior of a region, the *nonlinksland* noted earlier. This catchall historic term embraces all golf courses except those near a coast.

FIGURE 4-8
An example of an inland-, or *hinterland* course with no ties to a shoreline or linksland. The golf experience is focused to the land and the views, not the relationship to water, dunes, and lowlands.

LOST CANYONS GOLF CLUB, THE SHADOW COURSE, SIMI VALLEY, CALIFORNIA; PETE DYE, ASGCA, AND PERRY DYE, ASGCA, GOLF COURSE ARCHITECTS; PHOTOGRAPH BY KEN MAY, www.rollinggreens.com

Other Course Terminology Related to Land Characteristics

In addition to links and hinterland, several other land characteristics are used to describe golf courses. Some refer to the natural land on which the course is built, others to its shaping and style. The following are the most widely used of these terms:

- Parkland course
  Inland course that is either naturally wooded or planted to appear as wooded.
- Wooded course
  Akin to parkland course, but specifically used to describe a course built in a naturally forested area.
- Moorland course
  Course built on open, rolling land.
- Alpine course
  Course located at an altitude generally above 7000 feet and usually wooded.
- Mountain course
  Hilly course built in a mountainous region.
- Mountainside course
  Differentiated from a mountain course in that the course is contained on the slope of a mountainous area, perhaps at a relatively low elevation.
- Hilly course
  Course built on hilly terrain.
- Dunes course
  Course built on inland dunesland or sand hills.
- Riverside course
  Course situated along a river or with a river as its focal point.
- Lakeside course
  Course situated adjacent to a lake.
- Seaside course
  Course located on a seacoast but not necessarily on linksland.
- Desert course
  Course built in a native desert landscape, or one made to appear as such.
- Flatland course
  Course built on relatively flat land.

COURSES CATEGORIZED BY DESIGN & GROUND CHARACTERISTICS

The individual style and theme of a course—those attributes given to the course through the vision of the golf course architect—are often related in the form of descriptive terms. Additionally, the condition of the ground on which a course exists affects how golf balls behave. All of these can be important considerations in understanding course type

FIGURE 4-9
In this example the golf course fits several categories: desert course, target course, hilly and private club.

JAY MORRISH, ASGCA, GOLF COURSE ARCHITECT; PHOTOGRAPH COURTESY OF THE STONE CANYON GOLF CLUB, TUCSON, ARIZONA

and the associated influence on the game. The following terms describe and classify courses along these lines:

- Parkland course

  Also used to describe a course by land type, this term often indicates a design with preexisting or planted trees that takes on the look and feel of a traditional park.

- Core course

  A course contained within a simply shaped parcel of land with no interruptions of housing or fingers of land ownership or use that extend into the area comprising the golf course; a routing term.

- Target course

  A course whose design resulted from its siting on rugged land where the holes are largely isolated and play moves from one improved area to another throughout the round.

- Stadium course

  A course with large mounds or hillsides integrated with the layout for the express purpose of accommodating spectators in large numbers.

- Links-style course

  A course resembling a linksland layout—that is, built to resemble the dunesland of true links courses by the inclusion of hillocks, swales, and vegetation.

- Replica course

  A course designed with holes mimicking famous holes or an entire course.

- Development course

  A course bordered by homes or other development such that the path to be taken is driven by its edges.

- Oasis course

  A course whose design relies heavily on artificial lakes, ponds, or water features.

- Contrived course
  A course whose design is obviously foreign to the natural surroundings of the region or sports an artificial ambiance.
- Natural course
  A course that fits into the natural land or an artificially created course that gives that feeling.
- Classic course
  A course having the design characteristics of courses built prior to 1950.
- Geometrically designed course
  A course featuring a once-popular design theme in which features were straight-edged and abrupt.
- Soft course
  A course conditioned or irrigated such that balls do not roll very far.
- Bump-and-run course
  A course like the early golf courses of the British Isles in that the fairways are hard and balls bounce and bound, requiring players to take this effect into consideration.

FIGURE 4-10
The Tribute Golf Club of Texas was inspired by the great courses of Scotland. This replica course was not meant to duplicate exact golf holes but rather to afford the American golfer an experience similar to the unique strategy and feel of such courses.

TRIPP DAVIS, GOLF COURSE ARCHITECT; PHOTO COURTESY MIKE KLEMME/GOLFOTO

CATEGORIES OF COURSES BY SIZE & LENGTH

In golf, many standards govern how a player will count the score of a hole. Interestingly, nearly all of the official rules of golf have no bearing on the standards of length and par, for these variables are typically set by golf architects as they plan a course and become formally adopted by a committee once the course is finished. The rules are the same regardless of whether a player is playing a very short par 3 course or an 18-hole monster layout.

Until now, our categories have had to do with economics, land, and style. Now we begin to describe courses in terms of size and length—that is, in terms of the game itself.

Number of Holes

Even today, there is no rule that prohibits any number of holes from constituting a course, although the standard that we have adopted is either nine or 18 holes. Quite a shame when one considers the many mediocre layouts that would have been so much better if only a few holes had been left out. Imagine some tight, cramped courses you know with slightly more space.

Golf, as it was originally defined, consisted of "going out" and "coming home." There was never much reason to limit or require a certain number of holes, as this arbitrary condition was irrelevant in the match against another player or bettering one's total score. With each player having the same conditions, who cared if there were 15 holes to play—

FIGURE 4-11
Golf course acreage requirements, while entirely dependent on specific site conditions, are mostly influenced by (1) the number of holes and (2) the overall yardage of the course. These two variables are expressed in the table, which approximates acreage ranges for typical conditions and land types.

ACREAGE REQUIREMENTS

Type of Golf Course		Required Acreage
Regulation:	**9-Hole**	60–90
	18-Hole	120–175
	27-Hole	180–265
	36-Hole	240–350
Non-regulation:	**Executive / Precision**	75–100
	18-Hole Cayman Course	35–55
	18-Hole Par-3	50–80
	9-Hole Par-3	25–40
	Pitch and Putt	< 25

or 24? But we are a species of standardization. Eighteen sounds good; the great St. Andrews cannot be wrong.

The common course and complex configurations are:

- 18-hole courses
- 9-hole courses
- 27-hole complexes—usually made up of three 9-hole loops
- 36-hole complexes
- Multiple course complexes-any combination of courses, course types, and practice facilities

Length and Par of Courses

Golf courses are classified by length and par to indicate the type of play expected of them. Length and par are related by virtue of the standards assumed in determining par (see Hole 5, "Parts of the Puzzle"). By describing golf courses in this way, it is possible to define the challenge that can be expected, at least in terms of play against the widely accepted standard of par.

Length and par are frequently referred to in combination and, very often, are further clarified by a descriptive term such as *regulation, full-length,* or *executive.* For example, you may hear of a 7000-yard, par-72 regulation course, which defines, with little imagination required, what is meant. The following are common descriptive terms associated with length and par.

Categories of Courses by Green Fees

$10 – $25 — affordable
$26 – $50 — mid-tier
$51 – $75 — high end
$76 – $150 — premium
$151 and up — ultra exclusive

Regulation Courses

Regulation courses are courses, usually with 9 or 18 holes, that have a par equivalent to 70 or above for the equivalent of 18 holes and, generally, a minimum average of 340 yards per hole as measured from the farthest set of tees. A course under this definition usually measures above 6000 yards. In the British Isles, the category often extends to courses with a par of 68 or above, as the demand for standardization is not nearly so acute as in the United States. A favorite example of British attitude on this subject is a remote layout near Newcastle upon Tyne in England called Ravensworth. At Ravensworth, the par is a mere 68, but the yardage is 6600. Do the math, and you will discover that this seemingly easy layout is a real bear in disguise. Indeed, Ravensworth will play much more difficult and trying in terms of yardage per par than courses most golfers would consider regulation(somewhere in the 6800-yard range and a par of 71 or 72.

The term *regulation* (or sometimes *full-length*) can be applied to almost any golf course, as evidenced by the "Regulation Par 3 Course" advertised in a travel brochure and referring to a short 9-hole course adjacent to a resort. But, for the most part, *regulation* is the preferred term for describing the quintessential 9- or 18-hole layout that is full-length and has a complement of holes equating to a par of 70 or greater. There is, however, no conclusive definition—its popular use is perhaps our best.

THE SUPPOSED IMPORTANCE OF PAR

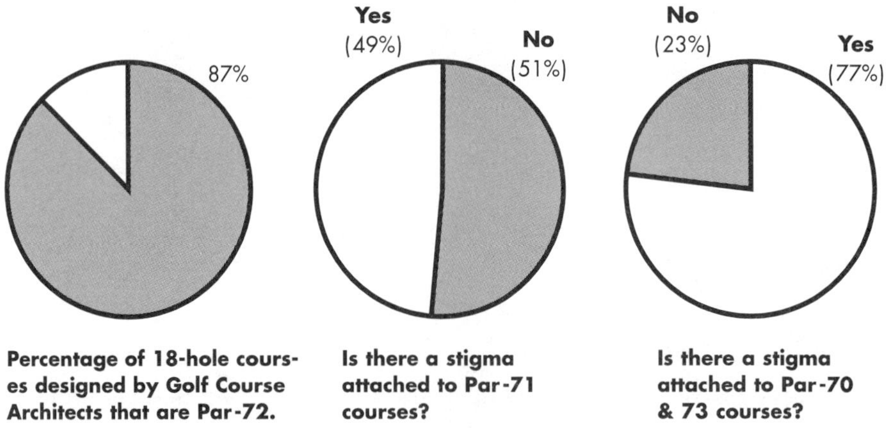
87%
Yes
(49%)
No
(51%)
No
(23%)
Yes
(77%)
Percentage of 18-hole courses designed by Golf Course Architects that are Par-72.
Is there a stigma attached to Par-71 courses?
Is there a stigma attached to Par-70 & 73 courses?

FIGURE 4-12 More results from our survey of golf course architects. It is interesting to note that par-71 layouts are far more accepted, at least according to the golf architects, than are par-70 and par-73 configurations.

Championship Courses

An unofficial but common term that has come to mean an 18-hole regulation course measuring around 6500 yards or more. The term *championship course,* however, technically refers to any course on which a championship is played and, even more so, a course on which a major or national championship is determined. This definition applies to few golf courses, which is probably why copywriters and marketing wordsmiths relish its use. Which would you rather play—a regulation course or a championship course?

The real drawbacks of this term are the widespread misconceptions that surround its meaning. It is not uncommon to learn that some golf developers consider only courses more than 7000-yards in length to fit the definition, while others believe that yardage makes no difference, provided the par is 72. Of course, the notion that a par-71 layout does not constitute a championship course would exclude half or better of the true championship venues in the world, Muirfield, Oakmont, and Pinehurst No. 2 among them. There is not much point in attempting to curtail use of the term; however, the definition to the left receives my vote for the official definition of *championship course,* regardless of whether or not a championship has ever been played on its fairways:

CHAMPIONSHIP COURSE
A regulation course, usually of 18 holes and measuring at least 6500 yards from the back tees, usually with a par value of 70 or greater.

Executive Courses

The term *executive course,* whose coinage is attributed to the late golf course architect William Mitchell, ASGCA, describes a course shorter than a regulation-length layout that also takes less time to play and hence is ideal for executives, who seem to have limited time to enjoy the traditional demands of a round of golf. A better term might be *executive-length,* as the makeup of these courses is suited to a range of golfer types, certainly not just executives.

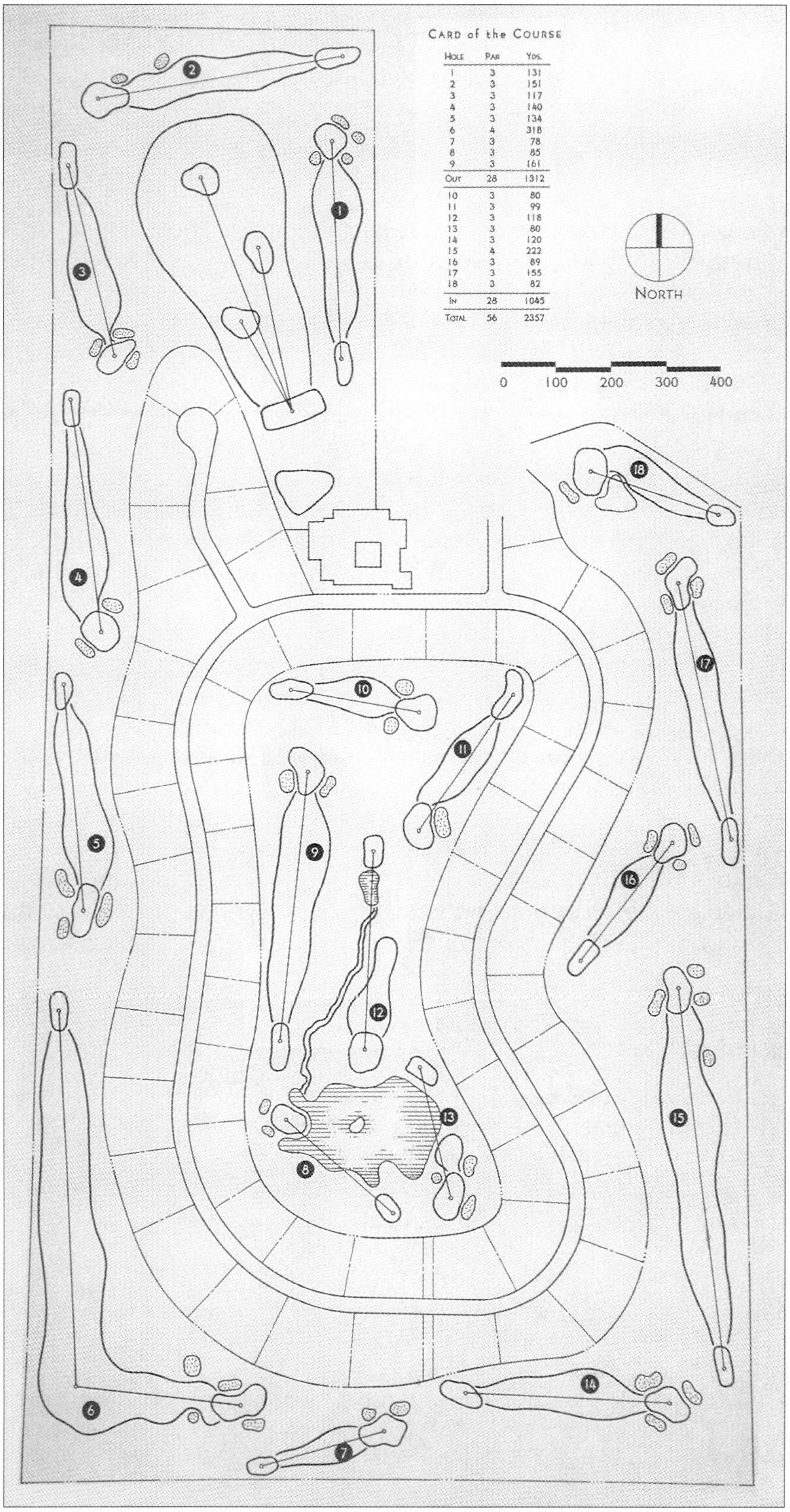

CARD of the COURSE
HOLE PAR YDS.
1 3 131
2 3 151
3 3 117
4 3 140
5 3 134
6 4 318
7 3 78
8 3 85
9 3 161
OUT 28 1312
10 3 80
11 3 99
12 3 118
13 3 80
14 3 120
15 4 222
16 3 89
17 3 155
18 3 82
IN 28 1045
TOTAL 56 2357
NORTH
0 100 200 300 400
1
2
3
4
5
6
7
8
9
10
11
12
13
14
15
16
17
18

FIGURE 4-13
Routing for an extremely efficient executive course. The golf course and modest practice area is just under 50 acres total. This project, Mountain Shadows in Paradise Valley, Arizona, is among the earliest examples of an executive-length course built in a resort setting. The golf course architect, Arthur Jack Snyder, ASGCA, actually created the master plan for the entire site, including the resort area and community.

Technically, an executive course is made up of primarily par-3 holes, with at least one non-par 3 (usually a par 4, but sometimes a par 5) per nine. An 18-hole executive course could therefore range from a par of 56 (eight par 3s and one par 4 per nine) to a par of 62 (five par 3s and four par 4s per nine). Although such courses may be defined by their yardage, par remains a far more accurate method of describing executive courses. In the above examples, for instance, a shortish par-56 executive might measure just 3000 yards, while a par-62 executive might approach 5000 yards. A wonderful aspect of exceutive courses is that they have the widest range of all course types in terms of length: filling the yardage gap between par-3 courses and regulation courses.

With regard to par 5s, there is, of course, no formal rule against their inclusion in an executive layout, although Mitchell was said to have defined an executive as one with "only par 3s and 4s." However, Mitchell also offered the ideal that an executive course should have the goal of forcing the player to "hit every club in the bag," and doing so as you would on a regulation-length layout, at least one par 5 is an excellent idea. A par 5 typically requires the golfer to hit a fairway wood from a non-tee location and thus, as is traditional, execute such a shot within the round.

It is a shame to need to address the stigma associated with executive courses, but such apprehension is a reality. Although there is a demonstrated need for such layouts—less land use, lower maintenance costs, lower demands on time—the willingness to finance and build such courses is far from robust. The many golfers who claim they would support such courses seem to be offset by the movers and shakers in the golf development world, who tend to avoid them, citing their lack of performance, diminished attraction, and poor yields on dollars invested. I liken the problem to that of suspenders. Suspenders are a better means of holding pants up and are far kinder to internal organs than are traditional leather belts, but the reality is that suspenders are simply not as acceptable in our culture.

Precision Courses

The term *precision course* is used to describe a course shorter than a regulation course, much along the lines of an executive-length course. Ron Whitten, the esteemed golf writer, has applied the term to nine-hole layouts with pars between 30 and 34 and executive-length layouts because, as he puts it, "I detest the term executive."

FIGURE 4-14
Routing plan for a precision-length course, an accompanying chip-and-putt course, and a practice range that make up a family-oriented golf center. The precision course was assigned alternative par values for youth players. This allows the course to be played by kids as if they were playing a regulation-length course. The chip-and-putt layout is a series of large greens with teeing areas scattered throughout the landscape.

Hole	Regular Par	Back	Middle	Front	Kids Par
1	3	160	130	100	4
2	4	360	330	280	5
3	3	170	140	120	4
4	3	165	135	105	4
5	3	180	160	110	4
6	3	105	100	80	3
7	3	200	170	150	4
8	3	170	150	120	4
9	3	120	90	70	3
Out	28	1630	1405	1135	35
10	3	220	190	150	4
11	3	180	150	105	4
12	4	375	350	270	5
13	3	205	180	160	4
14	3	140	120	100	3
15	3	190	155	130	4
16	3	155	130	110	4
17	3	110	80	75	3
18	4	360	340	265	5
In	29	1935	1695	1365	36
Total	57	3565	3100	2500	71

I agree, and have encouraged the use of the term *precision course* since reading Cornish and Whitten's book *The Architects of Golf.* The word *precision* communicates the essence of good golf—the demands and realization of accuracy, skill, cleverness, and the pursuit of error-free execution. Unlike *executive, precision* is inclusive of a variety of golfer types, and it sounds infinitely more charming.

Par-3 Courses & Short Courses

Par-3 courses are rather easy to define: regardless of the number of holes, all holes are of par 3 in length. Within the definition are distinctions between types of par 3s. Are most, for example, pitch-and-putt in length? Or are they made up of a variety of lengths, as you might find the par 3s of a regulation layout?

Short courses can often mean a par-3 layout, but the term may also refer to any type of course that is "shorter" than customary. (Refer to the USGA definition of a *short course* in the margin.) For example: a *short executive* is shown in Figure 4-14, but it is not a par-3 course. This example is best defined as an *executive* or *precision* course. Short is simply a descriptive.

Par-3 and short courses include the following:

- Pitch-and-putt course

  Course wherein all of the holes are within pitching length (usually less than 90 yards).
- Pitching course

  Same as pitch-and-putt.
- Kids' course

  Course specifically designed for play by youth, sometimes with miniature par 4s and par 5s that are sized to approximate shots as an adult would play a hole of that par value.
- Youth course

  Same as kids' course.
- Family course

  Course comprising holes on which all age levels can play and enjoy a competitive round together. Usually made up of all par-3 holes and often with separate par values for different age groups.
- Player development course

  Course which has been designed to introduce new players to the game (not exclusively made up of par 3s).
- Mashie course

  Historically, a par-3 layout made up of shots that can be played with irons; a mashie club having the loft of a 5-iron, and a mashie niblick having a loft similar to a 6-iron
- Practice course

  Broadly, a course with other than a regulation-length layout; often, a short par-3 course adjacent to a full-length course or facility of multiple courses. (Practice courses are by no means always par-3 courses, however.)

- First Tee course

  A facility, course, or loop of holes designed for youth to learn to play golf. The First Tee, is an initiative of the PGA in cooperation with many golf organizations, industry manufacturers, and professionals.

OTHER COURSE CLASSIFICATIONS & TYPES

In an effort to round out the various types of courses, it is unavoidable to ignore either the plethora of monikers bestowed to courses by status or the many types of alternative courses that involve variations on the game of golf or formats for play associated with practice.

Words of Status

The people who operate, own, and play golf courses are often looking for distinguishing language to set their course apart from the field. Not good enough are the ordinary terms *golf course* and *country club*. Here are some common descriptives and an attempt to clear up their meaning:

- Royal

  A course so designated by the king or queen of England in order to signify its magnificence; the status is officially attainable only by courses on land the monarch presides over.

- National

  A course on which a national championship has been decided, as recognized by the primary governing body of golf for the country in which the golf course is located.

- World-class

  This term is overused and meaningless in any official capacity.

- Top-ten

  According to whom?

- Signature

  A course designed by a famous golf architect or whose design involved a professional golfer of status; a limitless expression.

- PGA regulation course

  Supposedly, a course of regulation length as defined by the PGA of America, although no such official definition exists.

- USGA regulation course

  Same as PGA course, although perhaps the term is more meaningful, as the USGA does publish guidelines for the lengths of golf holes for certain par values; thus, this unofficial term could be construed as "a course with holes that meet USGA guidelines." However, such a definition would not specify the length of the course, as all holes could be par 3, or the course could be a par-76 layout and still follow the USGA yardage/par guidelines.

- Audubon Cooperative Sanctuary course

  A course that has applied for status with this organization and is working toward full certification under this program.

DEFINITION OF A SHORT COURSE

The United States Golf Association has defined a short course as any set or predetermined number of holes meeting any one of the following criteria:

- 18 holes totaling less than 3000 yards
- Nine holes totaling less than 1500 yards
- Fewer than nine holes that total, when scaled up to an 18-hole layout, less than 3000 yards (for example, a six-hole course less than 1000 yards would scale up to an 18-hole course of less than 3000 yards)

Alternative Golf Courses & Facilities

The pursuit of making golf accessible, affordable, and enjoyable will, hopefully, never falter. Advancement in this area is a work in progress, as witnessed by the many forms of alternative courses and practice facilities that have been developed in recent years. Many interesting ideas have been patented with the U.S. Patent and Trademark Office in the hope that they will catch on and be franchised throughout the world.

An *alternative golf course* is simply a course which breaks the mold of what we consider to be a traditional series of golf holes laid out end-to-end. Examples of alternative course concepts include:

- Practice course

  A series of holes or shots from designated areas, meant to be played in a progression such that the finish is near to the beginning point.
- Cayman course

  A course specifically designed for use with the Cayman golf ball, a lighter-weight golf ball that travels approximately half as far as a regular golf ball.
- Reversible course

  A course whose tees and greens are configured such that it can be played in reverse sequence.
- Dual-teed course

  Typically, a nine-hole layout with two distinct sets of tees so that play the second time around yields a different set of challenges and lengths, the goal being to create the feeling of 18 distinct holes.

An alternative golf facility is defined as any golf facility on which it is not possible to attain an official handicap. Such facilities are not comprised of customary golf holes that can be played in succession against a rating and par standard. An example might be a single green with numerous surrounding tees that may be used for practicing a variety of shots. Only if there were separate greens and tees creating multiple holes would there be a *course* that could be rated. And only with such a rating could a golfer obtain an official handicap. Alternative facilities include putting courses, elaborate practice areas and digital hitting cages. Many interesting alternative ideas to traditional golf courses have been patented with the U.S. Patent and Trademark Office in the hope that they will catch on and be franchised throughout the world.

DEFINITION OF AN ALTERNATIVE FACILITY

An alternative facility is, technically, any golf venue on which a player may not establish a bona-fide handicap such as a golf course would allow. Alternative facilities include such configurations as a series of practice golf holes in which the player does not putt out for a score, areas where tees are arranged for hitting a variety of shots to a common green, and other variations where practice is the emphasis, not traditional golf play. Alternative courses and facilities are a popular trend; they can fit into small acreages and bring new players to the game. Often their purpose is just this: an introduction to golf that avoids the intimidation factor.

FIGURE 4-15
The Cayman golf ball is a specially designed ball that travels approximately half the distance of a traditional golf ball but that behaves much like a regular golf ball on shots from close range and putting. An 18-hole, par-72 Cayman course requires only about 30 percent of the land area required of a similar course played with a traditional golf ball. Cayman balls have also been used on practice ranges where limited length is available.

CAYMAN BALL YARDAGE	
Driver	140 Yards
3-Wood	130 Yards
3-Iron	110 Yards
5-Iron	100 Yards
7-Iron	90 Yards
9-Iron	70 Yards
Sand Iron	50 Yards

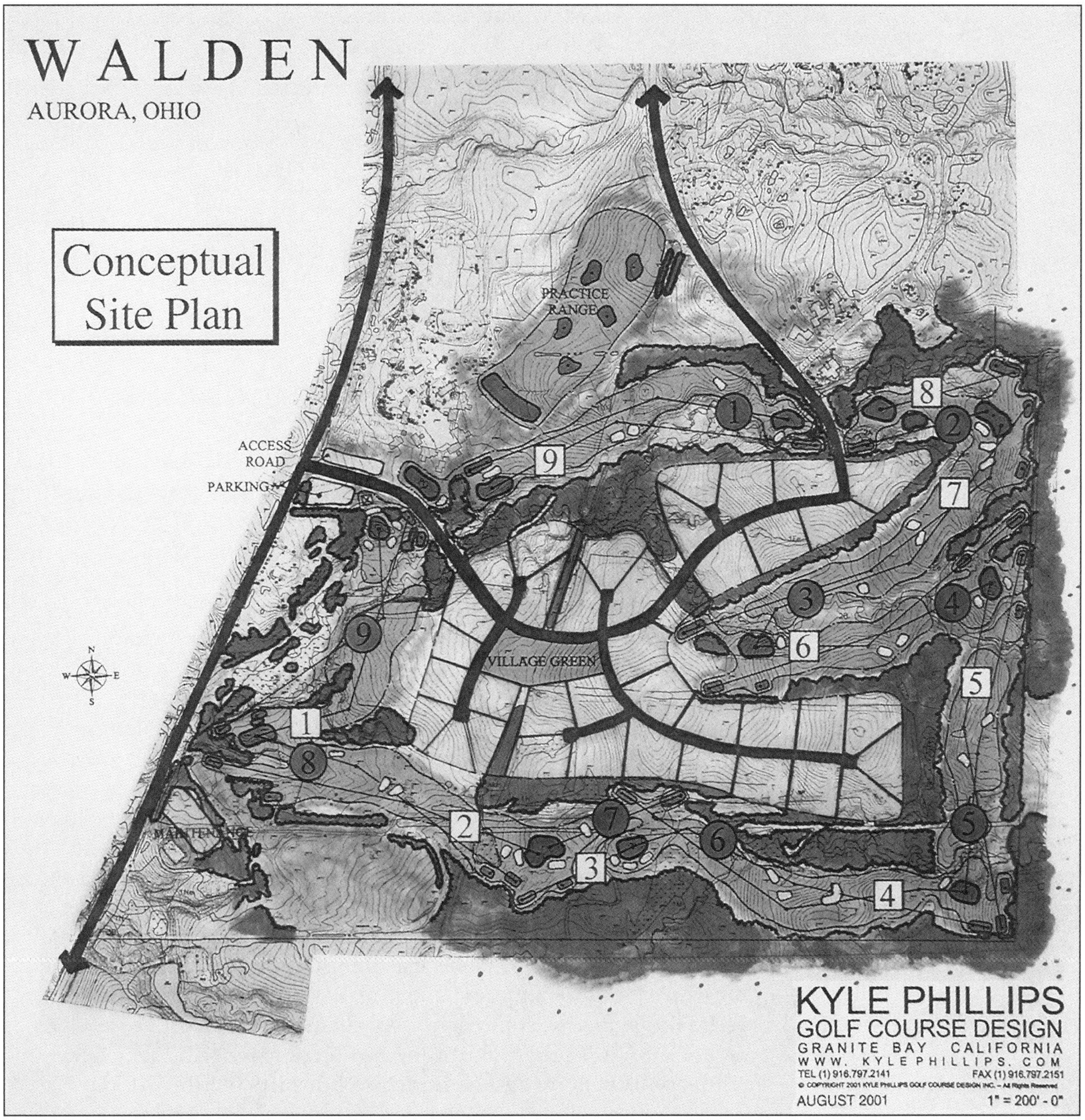

FIGURE 4-16
A creative reversible design by Kyle Phillips, ASGCA. The 9-hole layout is played in one direction and then the other, for a total of 18 holes. Such concepts allow golf development on restricted properties. In many cases, the result is much more appropriate than the standard of 18 holes and a par of 71 or 72.

COURTESY OF KYLE PHILLIPS GOLF COURSE DESIGN

TYPES OF GOLFERS VERSUS TYPES OF COURSES

There are exceptions, of course, to every rule, so it goes without saying that, even with the greatest care, any relationship between a particular type of golfer and a particular type of course will amount to a generalization only. The real value lies in the attempt to make such a connection, which will go a long way toward creating better-suited golf courses. The planning and routing of golf courses demands that the course match the needs of the eventual golfer, yet often, planners are fairways apart from Joe Golfer, who winds up playing the course week after week. Unless you are a glutton for punishment, there is not much point in routing a course for a category of golfers who will be unable, unavailable, or unwilling to grace its fairways.

The best goal is always assumed to be to develop courses that can be played by golfers of a wide range of skill levels and for enjoyment by golfers with a wide range of expectations. While this is mostly a good objective, it is not always possible. The policy should be to *anticipate.* A great balancing act must be performed in meeting the needs of the golfer, the developer, and the land. By understanding course and golfer types, you can draw conclusions that will help create better fits between the two while yielding a proper sense of unpredictability and adventure.

General Playing Ability & Type of Golfers

Golfers come in all forms and, although many subcategories and special classifications exist, it is entirely reasonable to pigeonhole golfers into four broad categories: A, B, C, and D. The A golfer is a scratch player, or nearly so; the B is the good golfer with a handicap from the single digits through to 15; the C is the average golfer with a handicap from 16 through 35; and, finally, the D is the duffer, shooting usually double bogey or more on every hole. By using this classification system, it is possible to translate the ability of a golfer to the physical characteristics of a golf course or type of golf course. The A player will enjoy an executive-length layout for different reasons than a D player, and so on.

Transcending the A, B, C, and D classifications are terms used to describe playing ability or frequency of play. For example, the *occasional golfer* is important to identify. This golfer may venture out onto a course only two or three times per year and is probably a C or D golfer. What is crucial to understand is that the occasional golfer is typically rusty and may take considerable time to negotiate a golf course if it is not conducive to this C or D type of play. In reality, there may not be any golf course that the occasional golfer is able to negotiate with ease, but there are certainly conditions that will aggravate his frustration. A frequent golfer, on the other hand, tends to play much more quickly and is more comfortable with the whole idea of golf regardless of being an A, B C or D.

Golfers are also classified by the type of course they frequent. A country club golfer belongs to a club and plays a particular course the majori-

FIGURE 4-17
A table showing the typical hitting distances expected of A-, B-, C-, and D-type golfers.

TYPES OF GOLFERS & DISTANCES WITH VARIOUS CLUBS

	A	B	C	D
Driver	270	220	200	150
Fairway Wood	240	200	180	140
5-Iron	180	150	130	100
Wedge	130	110	90	70

ty of the time. A resort golfer is typically a visitor who is unfamiliar with the course. The term *municipal golfer* is often used in a derogatory manner. It refers to a golfer accustomed to municipal playing conditions and who—stereotypically—is thought of as unsophisticated. The importance of understanding golfer types is in relating them to course types. Golf courses are nothing without golfers, and the reverse is just as true.

I still remember the short, nine-hole par-3 course where I played as a kid. These memories will always be among my fondest in golf. It is what hooked me on the game.

—Damian Pascuzzo, President, ASGCA

Physiological Limitations

Popular age categories of golfers include seniors (players over 55 years old) and juniors (players under 18 years old). Age is an essential consideration in that both extremes have limitations due to strength, mobility, and endurance. Women golfers are often separately classified, as the swing characteristics and strength of most women who play golf are much different than men's. Disabled golfers earn their own category, as they often need special access and planned course considerations. For similar reasons that A and C players differ on what they enjoy about a particular type of course, so, too, do senior golfers have a different set of likes and dislikes from that of junior golfers who are just learning to play the game.

QUANTITY OF PLAY CONSIDERATIONS

Golf courses receive different amounts of play, typically measured in annual rounds, for reasons that are nearly parallel to the various classifications covered in this chapter. Some factors that emerge after development, such as condition, operating policies, and popularity, cannot always be predicted. The quantity of play that a course receives is dependent on the following factors as well.

Type of Use & Economics

A course open to the public will have more potential customers than a private one to which access is severely restricted. Admittedly, this depends on supply and demand. Economics and general course type will greatly influence the amount of play a course receives, as will marketing, how well the course is designed and cared for, the quality of the management, and the amenities associated with the golf course.

Land Type & Design Characteristics

It stands to reason that a mountainous course with ups and downs and with spans between greens and tees will probably take longer to conquer than one of the same length that is sedate in comparison and has normal distances from one hole to the next. Likewise, a course with abrupt and deep rough bordering every fairway will require more time for searching for lost balls than a course with wide-open roughs where losing a ball is almost impossible. The demands of the terrain and the layout of a course will greatly affect the amount of play possible and practical.

The Sacred Nine—A Short Story

It seems to me that not many people are building nine-hole golf courses anymore. This is quite a shame when you consider that it often happens that 18-hole layouts get forced into a site where nine wonderful holes would have made for a much better finished course. Might nine holes have been more practical? Oh sure, you can find the occasional newly built nine-hole course, but more often than not, there on the clubhouse wall is proudly hanging the plans for the "rest of the course"—the nine that will be built next year, or maybe the year after that... if financing comes through.

My curiosity got the best of me. Although I had heard of Royal Worlington and Newmarket Golf Club, it had never occurred to me that the course was anything but 18 holes. After all, royal courses are *always* 18, otherwise they would not be so royal.

Down a narrow country road just outside Cambridge, England, the shady canopy of great trees suddenly opens to a field of golf flanked by a rather small and quiet-looking clubhouse. Here, finally, is the unassuming home of the Royal Worlington and Newmarket Golf Club. Not just nine great golf holes, I would learn, but a story of golfing contradictions and brilliant proof that the so-called standard of 18 holes can be overcome, providing your heart and attitude are in the right place.

"We don't get too caught up by the fact it's a nine hole course," says Miles Elliott, the club's esteemed captain. The club's position on the matter is one of curiosity as to why visitors seem so preoccupied with the number of holes. At Worlington, you see, what matters are the aspects of golf that have become less and less dear to the hearts of newer clubs and especially, I am sad to relate, the influential Americans who are busily building the game.

Royal Worlington is a social club. The members relish their traditions and respect what is going on in each of their lives. Golf, albeit important, is merely a vehicle for the more cherished routine of arriving, slipping away from the rest of the world, camaraderie, friendly competition, and, certainly not least, celebrating the moment.

Lest I forget, Worlington is made up of nine fascinating and excellent holes. It is, after all, a *golf* club. Although not linksland, the inland site is a rare swath of sandy soil that flows through woodlands and opens onto great fields. One should hardly care how many holes there are on the course characterized by Bernard Darwin as "the sacred nine." That is exactly the point Mr. Elliott was making.

"Our philosophy must just be different," he relates. "There are rituals here that are cherished by the members and it is these which define our club." Among the rituals are the Pink Jug, a club drink—and also the club's icon—that approximates lemonade, but in its own special way. Occasionally, visiting guests are taken aback when told about Worlington's unbreakable rule that all groups play only as *foursomes*—that is, match play between two groups of two where one ball is played by each of the groups. The foursome requirement allows Worlington's nine-hole rounds to be finished in one hour and 20 minutes, or just more than two and a half hours for a twice-around, 18-hole match. Imagine what the feasibility analysis of a modern club would look like if it were to embrace such a format. In essence, Worlington's nine holes is almost twice as efficient as most eighteens. But I seriously doubt that efficiency is the top priority here.

In a day when most people find it difficult to find time to play 18 holes of golf, it is quite odd that golf course architects, developers, and the financing community find it difficult to escape the temptation to build 18-hole courses almost exclusively. Yes, there are alternatives. And they are more real than we would like to admit.

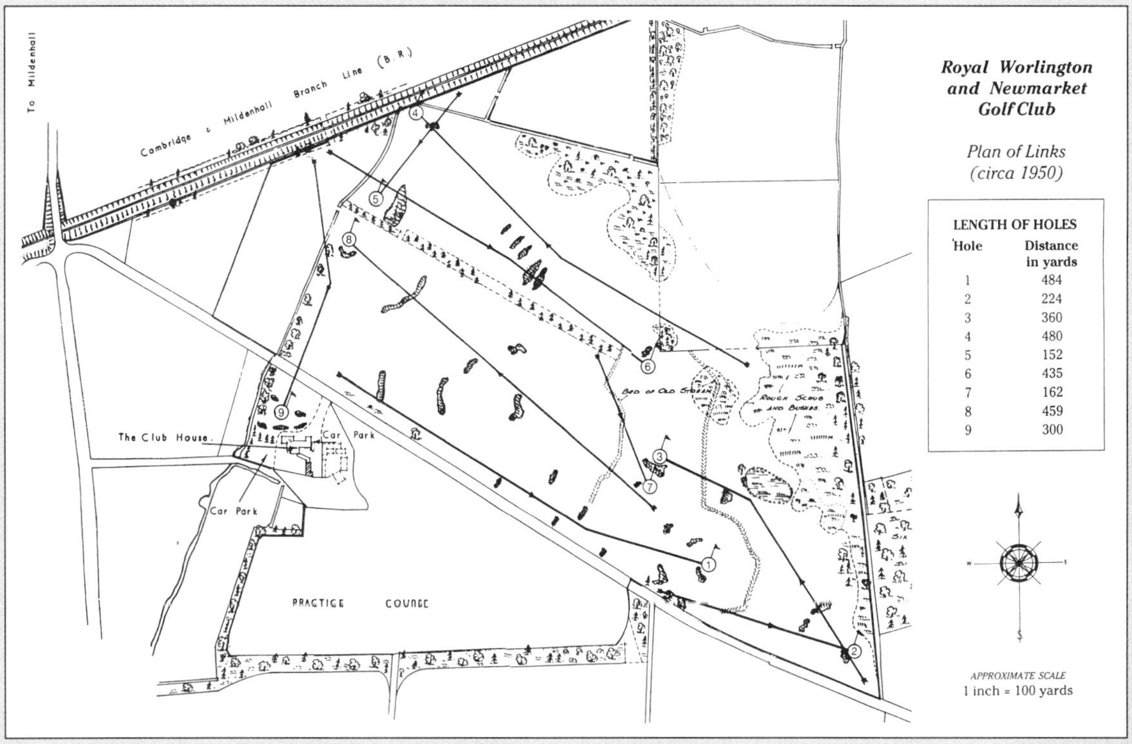

Routing plan of Royal Worlington and Newmarket Golf Club in Newmarket, England, established in 1893. This plan, drawn in 1950, is straightforward, yet it paints an accurate picture of the obstacles that so cleverly attract the golfer to this ideal and unusual royal course.

COURTESY OF ROYAL WORLINGTON AND NEWMARKET GOLF CLUB

Size, Length & Par

These are obvious factors of the number of rounds a course can be expected to sell. Part of the equation lies in the appropriateness of the course within the marketplace, and the other lies in the physical ability of players to complete rounds and therefore give way to golfers who might be waiting to get a tee time. An 18-hole precision course might have an annual capacity of 150,000 rounds at three hours per round, but if this is not what golfers in the area want, they probably won't play there.

Reputation

Reputation is key to the quantity of play, both anticipated and actual. This is often a two-edged sword, as reputation often makes a course so well regarded that players finally attaining a tee time tend to slow down and savor the round to the point that play can be 10 or 20 percent slower than on similar courses with less appeal and status. The Old Course at St. Andrews is among the best examples of this phenomenon. If not for the excellent and relatively recent managing of golfers through an aggressive approach to pace of play, rounds at The Old Course could easily exceed six hours, preventing thousands of golfers annually from playing there. All things considered, an excellent reputation and the associated inconvenience are problems most golf course owners and operators would welcome.

Climate

Seasonal courses and courses with many unplayable days due to weather exhibit conditions that preclude rounds to be played. In some regions, golf courses do not open until late in spring and close as early as October. These courses have less than half the capacity of similar courses in the Sun Belt and probably need to be extremely efficient during operating months in order to make every possible tee time available.

Parts of the Puzzle

HOLE NO.

5

Most people process a golf course one hole at a time. After all, we play courses one hole at a time. When we read in mainstream magazines about golf courses, the descriptions are rarely about the entire course, and almost never about routing. Those who write about courses focus on a particular hole, a series of holes, or even a particular shot required for a hole. Sure, there may be an obligatory description of the course in its entirety, but the adjectives are most always related to its setting, its degree of difficulty, or a common theme such as the undulation of the greens. The routing plan, at least to most, is a far too complicated way to visualize a golf course. Rarely—except in the process of actually laying out a golf course—is it essential to think of golf courses and all their parts as an entire road map.

The first step, in order to create a decent road map, is to gather all of the parts and features that are to be included. There is nothing more frustrating than discovering your map—any map—is missing a prominent feature, a scenic route, or that shortcut to Tipperary. In this chapter, we show how to avoid the awful scene that would result should an important component be left out of a routing plan. This is our checklist of parts. All things should be considered.

Strategy, variety, diverse and rolling terrain, beauty and superlative hazards.
—*Geoff Shackelford,* Masters of the Links, *on the features that a perfect golf course should possess*

THE ARRIVAL

Eventually, people will arrive to play golf. While we cannot choreograph this precisely, we can highlight a sense of arrival. This will contribute to an overall sense of place. When there is a sense of place, memories, connections, and attachment can occur. All of these reflect a good experience, which is desirable regardless of the type of golf course you are planning to create.

Although creating a sense of place is accomplished during the design process, the parts must at least be in inventory. The arrival is made up of key parts. Each must be considered carefully as the components of a golf project are brought together.

The Entry

Golfers are not magically beamed down. They make their way to golf courses. The entry road or drive provides the first impression arriving golfers receive of the facility. The drive can be long or short, and it can offer a glimpse of the course or not. The length will depend on a variety of factors, the most influential of which will be the site planning and access considerations. The shape and configuration of the entry should be carefully weighed in the context of the overall golf course project. It should balance between being functional and engaging. The guest should be exposed to a sense of anticipation, but not one so frustrating as the ketchup bottle that refuses to give up its contents. The laborious entry road that seems never to get anywhere is both costly and annoying.

FIGURE 5-1
A quiet, charming entry road, where islands of pine trees interrupt the path and cause traffic to slow down and admire the landscape.

PHOTO COURTESY OF GOLF GROUP LTD.; PHOTOGRAPH BY RUSTY FLYNN

FIGURE 5-2
A guardhouse provides one of the first impressions, both architecturally and in terms of personal interaction, at a private club. This example is both charming and intriguing, setting the stage for the architecture and experience to come just down the road.

PHOTO COURTESY OF SUPERSTITION MOUNTAIN GOLF AND COUNTRY CLUB; ARCHITECTURE BY OZ ARCHITECTS

Peeks & Hints

When you go to a restaurant, you are not there solely for nourishment. You are there partly to relax, perhaps for companionship, and part of the experience is all of the ancillary sounds, smells, and tastes that go along with good food. Part of this equation is *anticipation*. On your way into a restaurant, it feeds your anticipation if you catch a glimpse of the experience that awaits you.

The restaurant analogy translates well to a golf course, as there are sights, sounds, and smells that can all be taken advantage of in the arrival stage. The arrival to a golf course might involve a full view to the course, a glimpse of one or two holes, or perhaps a shimmering pond visible between the trees. Conversely, arrival can also say, "Not yet, my friend, you don't get to see me until I say you can." In this example, anticipation is prolonged and the promenade allows no peek at all. Maybe your first peek does not materialize until you actually enter the clubhouse, walk a few steps, and are presented with a fabulous view across the finishing holes. Peeks, whether they are early or late in the arrival, are essential. Everyone wants to peek. It's human nature.

The Threshold

All places have a threshold. Thresholds may be overt in their presence, while others may be more integrated with the environment. Regardless of their intensity, thresholds signify, or at least help signify, that you have arrived. In essence, they indicate that you are now someplace, as opposed to still being on your way there.

When I was working on a project in Florida, Wing Chao, Disney's creative and masterful vice president of design and development, explained

FIGURE 5-3
At Disney's Bonnet Creek Golf Club, the golfer is greeted with 11-foot-tall sculptures that signify the arrival and help establish a sense of place.

SCULPTURE DESIGN BY GOLF GROUP LTD.; PHOTOGRAPH BY RUSTY FLYNN

the significance of the drawbridge at Cinderella's Castle. At Disney, the drawbridge is the threshold by which all others are judged. This, of course, is not to say that every threshold at Disney is a drawbridge, for that would not be appropriate. The lesson to be learned is that an intentional crossing over—from one place to another—is a part of the act of arriving. Whether it is turning off the main road at a monument sign, passing a guardhouse, breaking through a tightly landscaped setting, reaching a bag drop area, or literally going across a bridge, a sense of arrival at a golf course is defined by the concept of threshold. Even though it has nothing to do with playing the game, the threshold is part of the arsenal of golf course routing. It needs to be given consideration.

Bag Drop & Parking

I'm often guilty of not thinking outside the box and have to catch myself from falling into the habit of standardization. Please make a note to yourself that there are infinite ways to handle arrival at a golf facility, and all that is written here can be replaced by an ample dose of innovation and creativity. Rules are meant to be broken; this can be a handy loophole to remember.

For example, a place to drop off your bag—usually a circular drive or *U* where an eager young worker takes your clubs and hauls them off while you park your vehicle—has become a standard part of golf courses. Even at the most public of newer municipal courses, where it was once standard practice to sit on the back bumper of your car changing your shoes, then carry your clubs across the asphalt, there is now a bag drop area.

But who says there has to be a bag drop? I have not done the math, but might it be efficient in terms of staffing to simply allow people to park wherever they want and meet them at their car with the very golf cart they will be given to use that day? Regardless, some system must be worked out for dropping people off and getting them and their clubs to the first tee.

Parking has been described as an evil plot to eat up acreage, and this is not far from the truth. In a country where nearly everyone owns a car, we invoke the option of using them and, when we do, we need places to store them. Parking is a component of golf courses and, as such, it is important to make sure in the programming process that the needs are well understood. Trust the warning that if more parking must be added in the future, a portion of the clubhouse will not be torn down to accommodate more spaces; rather, it will be the ninth green, the practice area tee, or that beautiful open area that looks out over the practice green. Parking creates many casualties, some visual, some physical. Plan well. Plan ahead.

Unfortunately, many local standards and ordinances unavoidably lead to ugly parking lots. Concealment may be the only option. At a course I visited in Santa Barbara, Rancho San Marcos, there is the most delightful parking lot that is the antithesis of everything you ever knew about parking. Here, they have no lot at all. Instead, they have an *un*parking lot. No pavement, no lines, and no 30-foot-wide drive aisles. At this peacefully rural setting, parking is accommodated among old oak trees, with intimate parking bays defined with natural stones and the occasional log used to signify where your tire should stop. It is much like driving through a campground with cars parked between old trees and in clusters instead of rows. What a nice departure from the norm. Visually and functionally, this is the nicest parking lot imaginable.

PARKING CALCULATIONS

The number of parking spaces necessary for an 18-hole golf course can be approximated by adding together each of the following line items:

- 2 spaces per hole
- 60 spaces divided by the spacing between tee times (in minutes)
- 2 spaces per designated station of the practice range
- 1 space per 50 square feet of dining area
- 1 space per 300 square feet of retail area
- 1 space per clubhouse staff member
- 1 space per 500 square feet of practice green

CLUBHOUSE & GROUNDS

The clubhouse is a gathering place. It is the village that prepares you for your golf journey by feeding and nurturing you. As golfers leave to play, they say goodbye to comfortable chairs, the indoors, and the ability to purchase embroidered shirts. Routing golf courses necessarily involves careful consideration of all of the possible needs for the clubhouse, including the orientation of the facilities to the layout of the golf course. Do not forget that these needs may go far beyond golf. For instance, a clubhouse may be the perfect place for a wedding or the celebration of the 100th birthday of a great-grandparent. It may serve as a venue for a charity fund-raising event or a corporate shareholder meeting.

Clubhouse Components

Golf clubhouses, once steeped in tradition, are today forming new traditions as tremendous pieces of architecture, at least when done with regard for good planning and as comfortable spaces. The senses are at full alert in the clubhouse. Although architects spend countless hours agonizing over the visual and tactile aspects, these may be swept away in a matter of seconds by the aroma of bacon cooking in the grill. I can

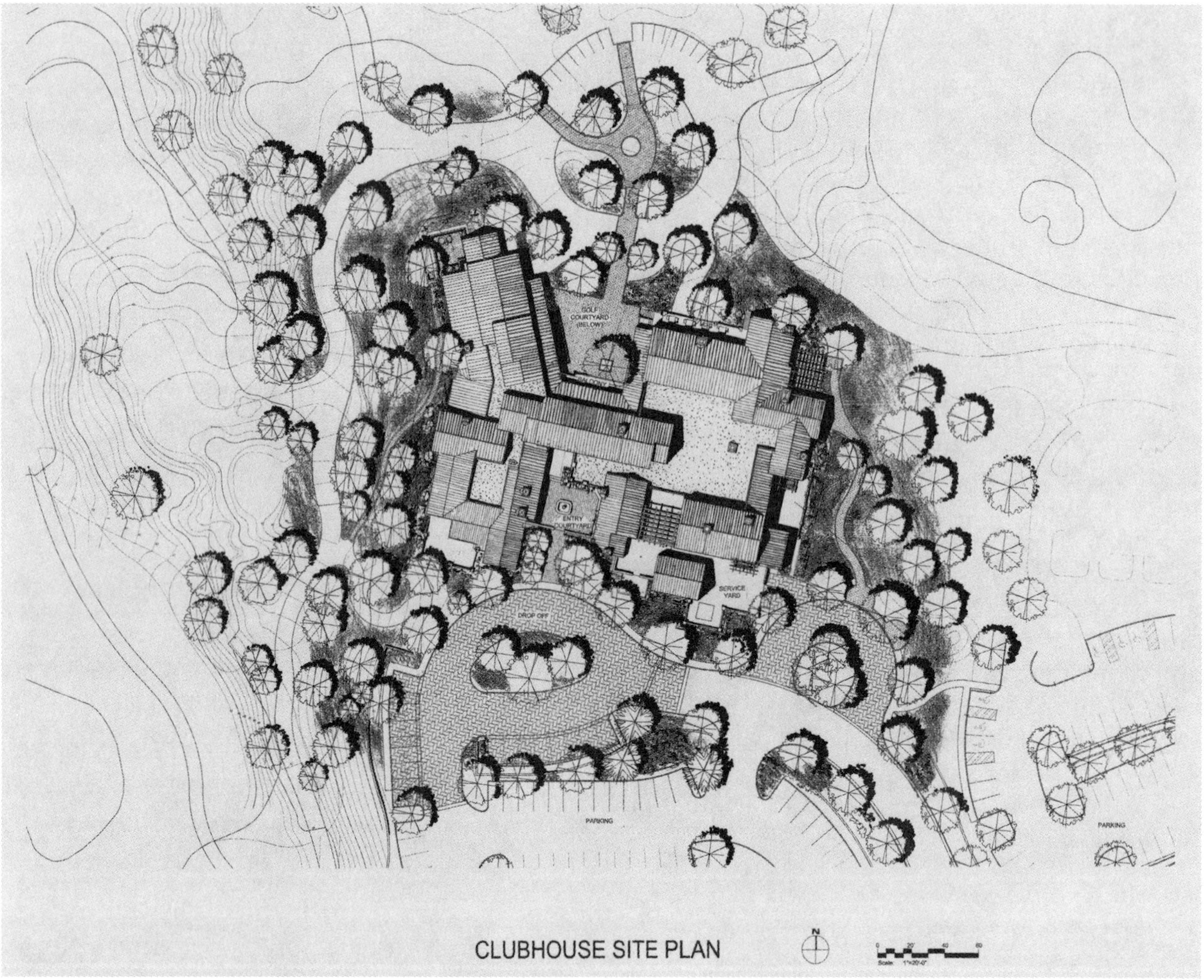

FIGURE 5-4
An example of an extensive clubhouse site plan for a 36-hole private golf club.

SUPERSTITION MOUNTAIN GOLF AND COUNTRY CLUB; COURTESY OF OZ ARCHITECTS

still recall the charming accent and face of the woman who made me breakfast before I teed up at a lovely course near Carnoustie, Scotland, called Panmure. In my mind, I can taste the eggs, the oats, and the strips of thick bacon that Americans would refer to as ham. And this was more than 25 years ago! I am sorry to report, however, that I have absolutely no clue what the clubhouse looked like or how it was laid out. It was not poorly designed, for I would surely have recalled that. It was, I believe, simply overshadowed by things of the moment. This is probably evidence of its excellent design.

It may sound trite, but here goes: Clubhouses come in all shapes and sizes. The best advice is to make sure your team includes a thoughtful clubhouse architect who understands golf. Beyond that, make certain that the programming issues—all of the elements required—are well documented and agreed on in advance. This includes attention to the possibility of future expansion, long-range plans, and even additional uses that may emerge over time. The approximate square footage for the clubhouse should be available so the necessary space can be included on the routing plan. Here is a list of traditional clubhouse components:

- Lobby
  A space to enter.
- Pro shop
  Where golfers go to check in, pay green fees, and buy merchandise.
- Restaurant
  Many times, a combination of casual dining (a grill), a more formal dining area, and an adjoining bar.
- Bar
  A place to imbibe.
- Meeting rooms
  Board rooms, banquet rooms, libraries, etc.
- Snack window
  A quick access point for golfers to get a drink or snack on their way to play or, in the case of returning nines, at the turn.
- Outdoor seating
  A place to absorb the course and remain outdoors.
- Locker rooms and rest rooms
- Behind-the-scenes facilities
  The kitchen, management offices, employee locker rooms, service entrances, etc.

TIME SPENT AT THE CLUBHOUSE

Golfers spend an average of 35 percent of the total time on the course property in or around the clubhouse. This includes time before, during, and after a typical round on an 18-hole regulation course. Therefore, the impressions formed at the clubhouse make up a big part of how golfers remember the overall experience. The ambiance and openness of the clubhouse can often skew one's impression of the entire golf course property. A cramped clubhouse area, for example, even when the course is open and expansive, may give the everlasting feeling that the whole property is crowded.

FIGURE 5-5

The completed clubhouse whose site plan is shown in Figure 5-4. It has all of the elements that make for a terrific experience: views to the finishing holes, territorial views across the valley, water, a feeling of openness, secluded patios and balconies, and an ambiance that fits the overall concept of the development. The golf club, Superstition Mountain (Jack Nicklaus II, ASGCA, golf course architect), sits below the famous Superstition Mountains east of Phoenix, Arizona, where the legend of the Lost Dutchman continues many years after he disappeared after supposedly discovering an amazing gold mine. The architecture looks almost as if the Lost Dutchman himself might have reappeared from the hills and used his once-lost fortune to build an eclectic village at the base of the rugged mountains.

PHOTO COURTESY OF SUPERSTITION MOUNTAIN GOLF AND COUNTRY CLUB; ARCHITECTURE BY OZ ARCHITECTS

It may also be observed that golf, however badly it may be played, seldom brings on a loss of appetite. No one would be so rash as to suggest that potted shrimps or a baron of beef, or even nourishment of a more soluble character, have been responsible for the success of the Royal Liverpool Golf Club. But the visitor who has enjoyed these things will be unlikely to remember any of his bad shots, and may even fail to recollect his good ones.

—*C. H. Alison,* Some Essays on Golf Course Architecture

- Golf cart storage

  Often a stand-alone structure, but just as often integrated into the lower level of the clubhouse itself.

The Grounds

Grounds are the combined areas immediately surrounding a clubhouse. They are the open spaces and reprieves between vertical walls and the areas separating the actual golf course from the buildings. Some are related directly to golf; they may even be for practicing putting or taking a few warm-up swings. Others may be nothing more than landscaped areas of beauty, but to think of them as "nothing" areas would be a mistake. Just as it is rarely advisable to hang pictures on every square inch of wall space, it is unwise to try and cram uses into every square foot of your clubhouse grounds. The following is a list of common uses for grounds in and around clubhouses:

- Putting greens
- Open lawns
- Golf cart staging

  An adequate area to park golf carts and handle shotgun starts during tournaments.
- Starter's shack

  Needed where control of the first tees is remote or requires a designated starter position.
- Scoreboard

  An area to post scores during competitions, perhaps even with a small outdoor venue at which to present awards and trophies.
- Special event area

  An area in which to hold barbecues and other events.
- Other recreation

  Swimming pool, tennis, lawn games, etc.

The needs of clubhouses and grounds are completely dependent on the type of golf course to be built. With this wide variation in potential needs comes a wide variation in the acreage that must be allotted for them. The variations do not necessarily end there. Facilities such as temporary clubhouses, resort operations, and golf schools will have tremendous influence on the space to be earmarked for the overall clubhouse and grounds area.

PRACTICE FACILITIES

Practice facilities are often an afterthought, which is a mistake. Pebble Beach Golf Links was never planned with a decent practice area, and even today when you finally figure out they have one, you have to get there via a shuttle van up the hill. The occasional golfer who attempts to walk there looks lost and probably is. To be fair, of course, the plan-

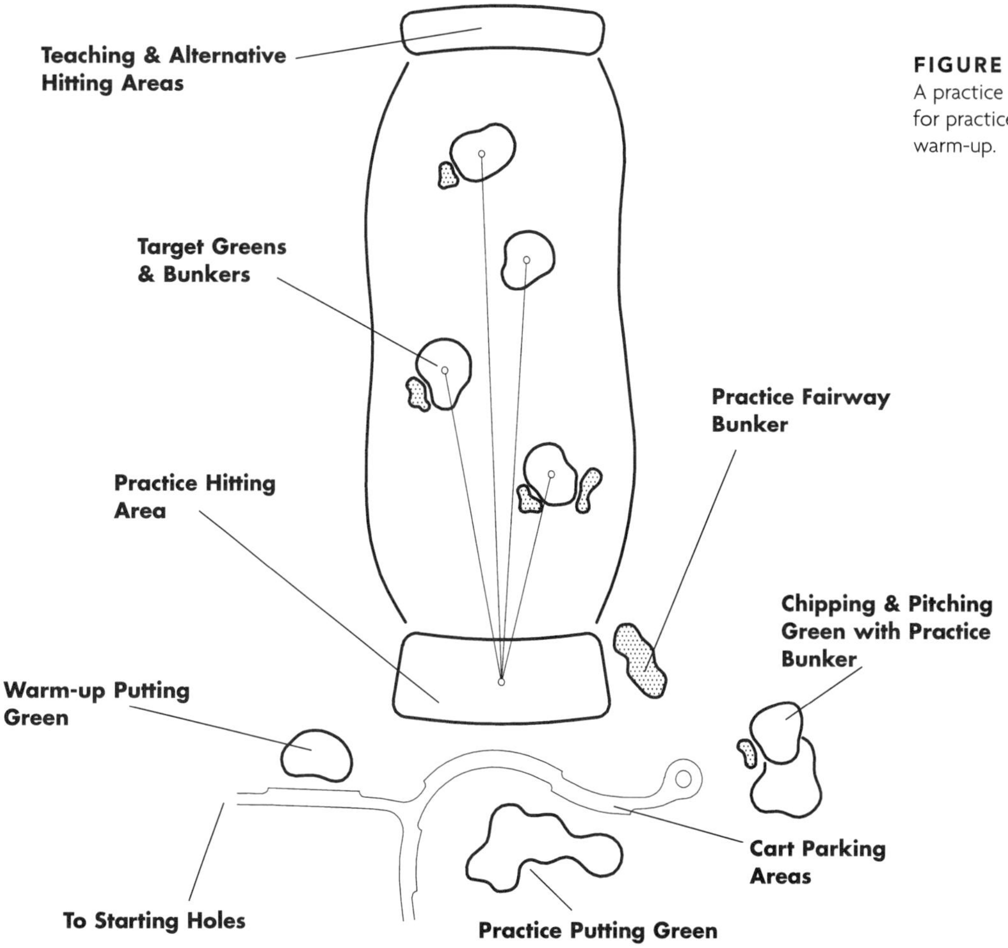

FIGURE 5-6
A practice area featuring facilities for practice, instruction, and warm-up.

ners must perform a balancing act. It does not usually make sense to forego good golfing terrain for a practice facility, especially if you are short of land to begin with. Nevertheless, it also does not make sense to so severely limit practice facilities that they are all but unused.

In today's golf world, practice areas—especially hitting ranges—can be profit centers. An understanding of the objectives and realities of this financial issue often helps decide to how practice areas should be programmed and planned. The type of golf course being planned will drive the intensity and importance of the practice area and its makeup. Or at least it should.

Another aspect of practice facilities at golf courses is how well they approximate the conditions of the course itself. While there are things more annoying than practicing your putting only to find the greens out on the course are nothing at all like the practice green, in terms of the design of practice areas, not much can top this error in planning. In every area of the practice amenities, care should be taken to recreate the shots and conditions—even some of the views—that golfers would experience on the course. This permits a fundamental goal of practice: gaining experience with and preparing for actual course conditions

The Practice Hitting Area

A practice area—or range—may be full-length, which is preferred, or of limited length. A full-length area allows hitting full golf shots from a large tee area and may extend in excess of 300 yards. Width varies but, generally speaking, a minimum of 300 feet is required for the continual length of the area. This does not necessarily account for setbacks to adjoining areas, whether golf holes or uses off the golf course property. Most practice areas are wider than 300 feet to allow more golfers to use the tee at the same time.

Limited-length facilities require logistical consideration. For example, if an area is only 200 yards in length, the clubs and types of balls golfers use will be important to control. This may not always be possible with certainty. Some practice areas of limited length are managed by having golfers use the Cayman golf ball, which travels only about half as far as a traditional modern golf ball.

It is interesting to note that in relation to an 18-hole regulation-length course, a full-length practice range can account for nearly 10 percent of the total acreage of the course, practice facilities, clubhouse, parking, etc. This significant percentage can cause much trouble if not adequately considered. Examples of potential trouble can be in trying to fit a full-length range into too small an area or giving in to the temptation to make the practice range slightly smaller than called for. Neither is likely to yield a good plan.

Good advice is to allow more than enough and proper space for any full-length range, first and foremost. This advice goes for the clubhouse grounds and other non–golf course areas as well. It is generally easier to make up room, if needed, across the expanse of land devoted to the golf holes themselves, which accounts for 85 percent of the total land area. Of course, for all advice, a host of conditions may render it worthless or less viable. Above all, determine the parts that are essential to the practice area and keep them well in mind as the balance of the planning unfolds.

Components of a practice hitting area, some optional, include the following:

- Main teeing area

  Configured in an arc so balls are aimed toward the center.

- Target greens

  Realistic greens flanked by sand bunkers and mounding, positioned at 100, 150, and 200 yards from the tee.

- Practice sand bunker

  With shots aimed out to the range area.

- Uneven lie hitting area

  For practicing hitting from hillsides and swales.

- Teaching/lesson tee

  A separate tee for instruction.

- Double-ended tee

  A tee at the opposite end of the main tee, far enough away that both tees are mutually out of range.

- Cart parking, sitting, and shade areas
- Range attendant counter

  A small shelter or area from which an attendant can dispense balls and assist users of the facility.
- Restrooms

  Especially when the practice area may be distant from the clubhouse

Practice Putting Greens

Putting greens for practice do not take up much space but are essential to any golf course. Bogey golfers, even on days when putting has been performed expertly, will strike 40 percent of their strokes on the surfaces of the greens at an 18-hole regulation course. Practice and warm-up on greens are essential to most golfers.

The total square footage for practice greens should not be too small. A good minimum is 10,000 square feet—ideally, even more. With many

FIGURE 5-7
Plan for a putting course set on three tiered levels defined by natural stone walls. Stone steps and a bridge connect the three distinct greens and allow golfers to play a variety of putts across the 22,000 square feet of putting green area.

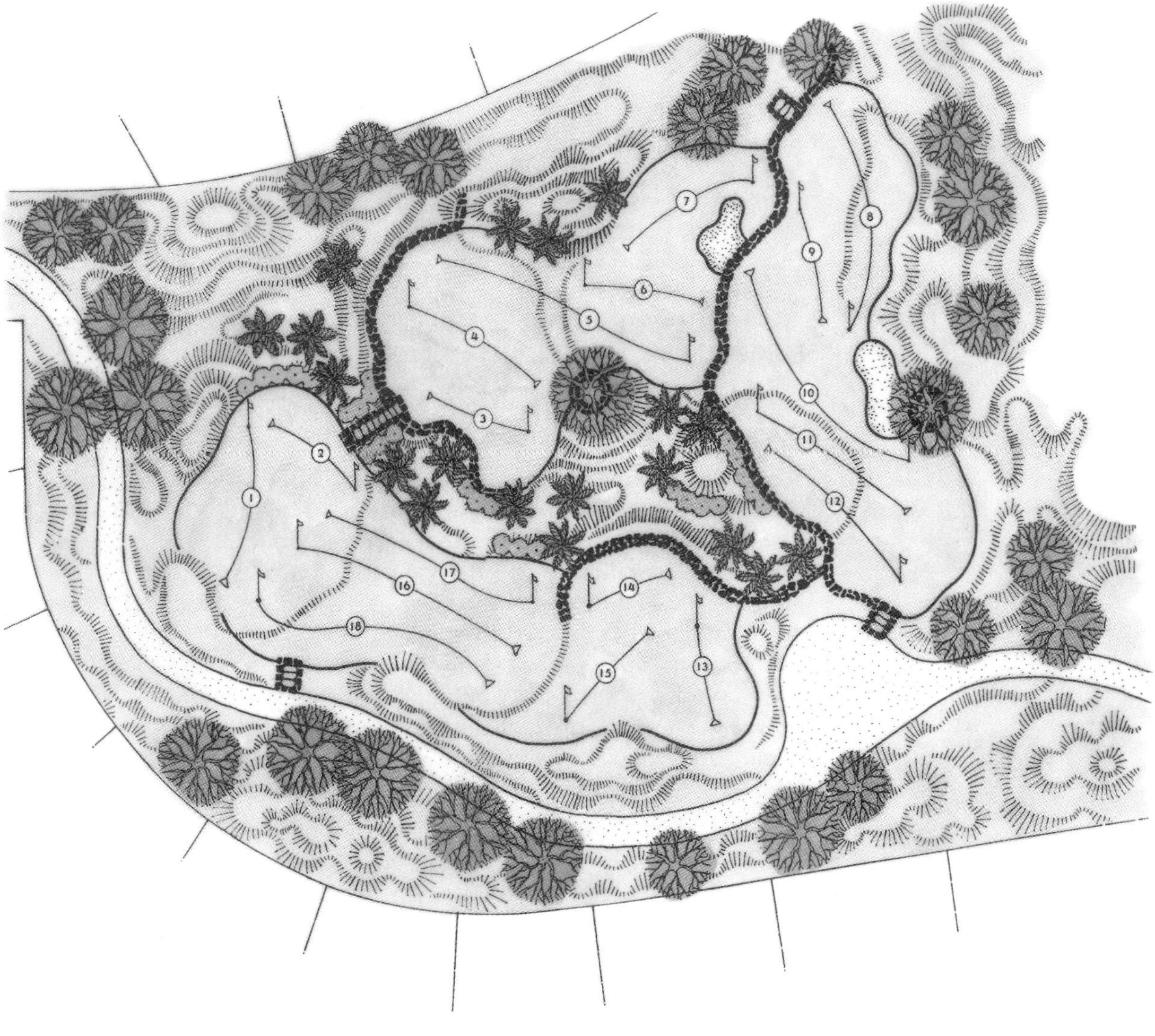

golfers using the greens, they can easily become worn. Having areas that can be closed off to rest is a significant plus. My preference is to see if it is practical to create multiple greens, perhaps two or three. By linking these together with paths and landscaping, it is possible to perform maintenance on one while the other is in use. The slight drawback to having to access separate greens for maintenance is not significant if the total area of the individual greens is approximate to one single large green. Separate, delineated greens open the door to all sorts of flexibility and have value beyond the ability to shut one down for maintenance. The multiple-green configuration also allows for a green to be reserved for putting contests, use by large groups, instruction, and so on.

AQUA RANGES

Aqua or lake ranges are practice hitting areas configured such that players hit from a tee on the shore out over the water of a lake or reservoir. Special floating golf balls are used; these are collected in baskets or nets the way debris and leaves are collected in swimming pool skimmers. Lake ranges make sense where no land is available for traditional practice areas, yet plenty of water surface area can be put to use. It is odd, however, to practice hitting balls into the water. Could this have a psychological effect when the golfer reaches the tee of an actual golf hole that plays out over water? One hopes not.

Short-Game Practice

One of the most frequently forgotten elements of practice at golf courses is a space where golfers can chip, pitch, and hit short shots from the sand. At many courses, due to the lack of room allotted for these uses, such areas are often off limits except for instruction purposes. I attribute this condition to the resemblance of short-game practice to a can of worms. Unlike hitting from a specified area, such as on a range tee, or putting, which is mild in intensity, golfers swinging sand clubs and lob wedges can get out of hand. What looks well thought out on the site and routing plans, if not managed and used properly, can become a crossfire of balls going every which way.

The ideal short-game practice area is configured to meet the needs of the golf course and is carefully positioned. The first step is to make a list of the facilities required and then to fit them in with every consideration practical. A good policy is to make sure adequate protection is afforded the area as well as adjacent areas.

Buffer Areas

Often, areas must be planned that are of no active use but serve to separate and visually define practice areas from other golf holes, the clubhouse, etc. These are important to consider as they take up acreage. Unfortunately, such areas do not magically appear once you begin the routing process—they need to be thought out in advance. Practice areas can be noisy compared to the golf holes of a course. For this reason it is important to achieve as much isolation as possible, yet still locate the practice areas convenient to the clubhouse and first tees. Adequate separation, or buffering with terrain and vegetation, is a requirement, especially from the first tees where concentration is so crucial for a good start.

Other Thoughts

There are always trends in practicing golf. The digital age, for example, has opened many doors to alternative practice routines. Golfers can literally practice indoors, although this hardly approximates real-world condi-

FIGURE 5-8
Putting courses, such as this one at the Angel Park Golf Club in Las Vegas, Nevada, can be intriguing additions to golf facilities. In some instances, a putting course can stand alone, serving resorts, communities, and parks with an amenity that can generate revenues and introduce new golfers to the game.

COURTESY OF ANGEL PARK GOLF CLUB; GARY PANKS, ASGCA, AND ED FRANCESE, GOLF COURSE ARCHITECTS

tions—yet. However, when you consider how much land practice areas consume—10 percent of the total land area of an 18-hole regulation facility—simulation chambers for practicing and diagnosis should not be discounted, especially for projects that become tight as planning progresses.

Additionally, practice areas, warm-up areas, and alternative spaces come in many forms that can be considered in planning a golf course. Your kit-of-parts should include these. Whether the options are ever used depends on your evaluation as you list the parts of a project. Additional, non-conventional, practice components include:

- Putting courses
- Separate tees or areas for golf schools
- Practice holes
  A single hole or small loop of holes.
- Short courses
  Chip and pitch courses, par-3 courses, etc.
- Designated youth areas
- Designated areas for working with golfers with physical disabilities
- Digital practice facilities
  Outdoor video studios, small classroom buildings, netted areas, etc.

THE GOLF HOLES

Finally, we delve into the fundamental part of the puzzle—the golf holes themselves. Golf holes come in a variety of flavors; this is not news. What is surprising is just how many variables golf holes can comprise. An in-depth look at golf holes is a good exercise. It opens your eyes. On an 18-

hole course there should be personality among the holes. Holes should relate to one another, yet be different. Most important, each should have a chance to make a difference. As Arnold Haultain so wisely observed about golf holes in his classic book, *The Mystery of Golf,* "Eighteen dramas, some tragical, some farcical, in every round..."

Desmond Muirhead, to whom I owe a great deal of appreciation for his friendship and colorful insights to the universe of golf course design, has a wonderful way of making complex things seem simple. Desmond points out that golf holes form the bones of the course. When they are put together—routed—they form the skeleton. And when the finished shaping and detail take form and the grass begins to grow, that is the flesh. "Without the bones and the skeleton," he says, "you've got nothing."

Each of the following sections looks at golf holes from a different perspective. The benefit is an appreciation for what makes golf holes tick. Understanding what makes a hole tick is crucial to being able to choose the best combination of parts to make up an entire course. For example, a dramatic hazard may be "king" and tend to sum up a particular golf hole. In another case, the defining feature may be a combination of the severity of length in relation to par and terrain. Still another hole may be defined by its strategy and the choices presented to negotiate its run. In this case, it is not necessarily a hazard or a prescribed number of strokes to match par that the golfer notices. Instead, it is a deeper attraction, one of problem solving, that transcends the physical and demands heightened mental concentration.

The individual parts of a golf hole, regardless of par, are broken down into five key components, the nuts and bolts of golf holes, which are assembled differently depending on a variety of factors. Irrespective of par, length, or orientation, these primary components are a constant:

- Tees
- Fairways and roughs
- Hazards
- Greens
- Miscellaneous parts of a hole

To round out these study areas, we look at fully assembled holes from two perspectives:

- Hole par, length, and orientation
- Shot strategy

[The tee] is one of the few perfectly controlled perspectives in life. We put two tee markers down and we say, stand here, golfer, and nowhere else, and you will look at what we put in front of you.
—Steve Wynn, developer

TEES—THE BEGINNING

"Begin at the beginning," says the King of Hearts in *Alice in Wonderland.* What logical advice, but so often ignored. Although in the process of laying out golf holes on a piece of land it is possible and often advantageous to begin at the green and work backward, it makes more sense to begin at the tee when we go step-by-step to review the components of a golf hole.

Golf play begins at tees, and these starting gates must be positioned with care for a variety of reasons, among them playability, strategy, safety, and convenience. From the tee, a golfer makes decisions that ultimately determine how the hole goes. Like any other point of beginning—the first day of school, the first part of a vacation—the tee of a hole sets its stage. From here, the golfer makes decisions, selects a club, and begins the quest for a decent score, perhaps even with thoughts of a birdie or better. Each tee should present the hole like a picture, with as much visual information as is needed or desired to communicate to the player what he or she must accomplish. The picture presented is often one of beauty, danger, and a little mystery. Course routers must take tee position seriously, as the points that define the tees are among the most important points of any routing plan.

Officially, the teeing ground is the area defined by the tee markers on any given golf hole, specifically the rectangular area bounded by an imaginary line between where the markers are set and extending two club lengths behind this imaginary line. Tees must therefore be made large enough to accommodate the multiple official teeing grounds that will be set at each hole every day.

Tee Characteristics

The following are the key routing considerations with respect to the tees of golf holes:

- Surface area

  Enough area must be planned to handle the use and allow for continual movement of the official teeing ground.
- Alignment

  A crucial aspect, as tees and their edges help guide golfers toward a target or particular pathway.
- Width

  Allows for holes to be played from different angles when markers are moved from side to side of a golf hole. Too much width, however, typically requires extra acreage and setback for safety reasons.
- Length

  Allows for markers to be moved forward or back, thus creating variety from day to day in hole length.
- Visibility

  Golfers need visibility to consider their options and gain an understanding of the hole they are about to play.
- Access

  Golfers need to be able to access tees without undue effort from both cart paths and footpaths.
- Access for golfers with physical disabilities

  Special consideration must be given to access to one or more tees by golfers with physical disabilities.

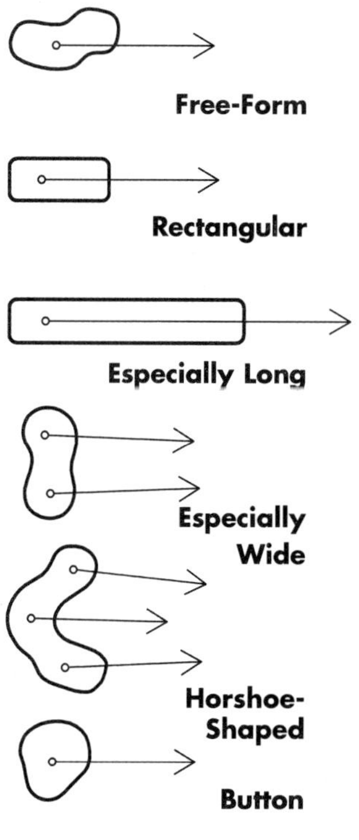

FIGURE 5-9
Tees can take on many shapes. The shape of tees can affect routing, as each tee is the beginning point from which the centerline of the golf hole evolves.

FIGURE 5-10
An example of isolated free-form tees set into the natural landscape and resulting in the least disturbance to the surrounding land. These tees are formed by stone retaining walls.

PHOTO COURTESY OF PHANTOM HORSE GOLF CLUB AT THE POINTE RESORT ON SOUTH MOUNTAIN, PHOENIX, ARIZONA; ARTHUR JACK SNYDER, ASGCA, AND FORREST RICHARDSON, ASGCA, GOLF COURSE ARCHITECTS

- Maintenance
  Tees must be positioned such that they receive ample sunlight and are accessible by maintenance equipment.
- Safety
  Tees must be positioned such that golfers at adjoining holes and non-golfers pursuing adjacent uses are reasonably safe.
- Seclusion
  Tees should not be subjected to noise or distractions.

Multiple Tees

Nowadays, most golf holes are designed with multiple tees. The variety of tees on a hole determines distance variations for holes and courses. The most important aspect of multiple tees is an ability to match golfers to the appropriate lengths and positions from which to play a given hole. Although called by a potpourri of names, the following terms cover the general categories of tee nomenclature. Certainly not all courses have all of these tee designations; here are the most common:

- Back tees
  The farthest tees from which holes can be played.
- Championship tees
  Usually not all the way back, but longer than the regular tees.
- Regular tees
  The tees that most golfers are expected to play from.
- Senior tees
  A more forward set of tees than the regular tees, for shorter-hitting senior golfers.

- Family tees

  A set of tees designed for use by all types of golfers, where youth, adults, and seniors can enjoy playing from common instead of separate tees.
- Forward tees

  The closest tees from which holes can be played.

Forward Tees

A special note is made of forward tees, as these have, until recently, been treated as second-rate in the planning of golf holes. Forward tees are the tees most forward on a given hole. An entire course might feature two or even three tees that are considered forward in the scope of all tees that are part of a hole. The most important reminder is to include them in the consideration of golf holes and to not allow their placement to be an afterthought.

Forward tees serve all golfers who are not able to hit far enough to reach landing areas and greens and, as a result, need an extra advantage in where they begin to play a golf hole. This may include senior players, juniors, and golfers with physical disabilities. Forward tees were once called *womens or ladies tees;* the term now mostly abandoned as the gender of tees is secondary to providing options for where a particular player's skill is best matched to a golf hole.

Tee Position & Alignment

The position of a tee can considerably alter the playing characteristics of a golf hole. Tee position can place hazards in the way or take them out of consideration. In addition to the obvious effect of altering length, tee position can also change the elevation from which a golfer plays a hole and may even subject the golfer to wind and sunlight differences between tees.

Considering the alignment of each tee is essential to guiding golfers toward the center of fairways or landing areas. Even with tees that are free-form in shape, their general alignment can significantly influence the direction that tee shots are played. The alignment of rectangular tees is particularly important. Tees with straight sides and leading edges must be carefully oriented to the intended line of play.

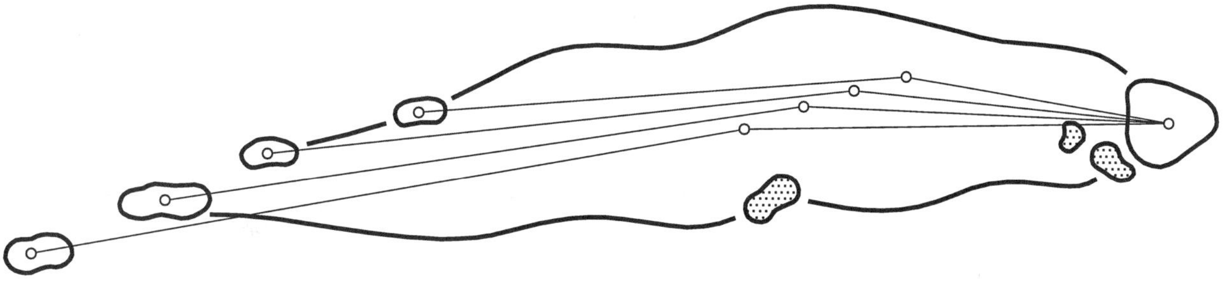

FIGURE 5-11
Regardless of whether or not centerlines are drawn on routing plans, multiple tees establish separate points from which golfers will put balls in play. The anticipated lengths players will hit using each of the various tees are likely to fall at different places on par-4 and par-5 holes. The diagram demonstrates how players of different abilities are likely to place their tee shots in different spots.

Tee Psychology 101

Consider this section a brief introduction to Hole 10, "The Psychology of the Golf Journey." Tees offer two primary psychological influences on the golfer. First is the position of the tee in terms of playing length and in relation to other tees on the same hole. Second is the setting of the tee, which includes a host of conditions such as elevation, seclusion, and landscaping.

With respect to the playing length of the golf hole, obvious intensities are associated with very long holes, while extremely short holes can induce an "oh, this seems easy" feeling. But, physical distance aside, there may be no greater concern than the description of the tee on the scorecard. Forward tees can be taboo to some golfers whose game might well belong there. Championship tees can be a draw to golfers who perhaps lack the skill for such demanding play. It is not uncommon to see average golfers playing the farthest-back tees just to satisfy the macho spirit that lies in their golfing psyche. Even when multiple tees are built into a golf course, so-so golfers often find it thrilling to play from the very, very back. The desire to experience the course "the way the pros would play it" can override common sense. Who cares that it might be too taxing, or that play might be slowed down, or that it might be no fun at all!

As mentioned, the problem of convincing juniors and seniors to play from the forward sets of tees can be perplexing. There is a suggested weakness associated with playing from the very forward set of tees. Men certainly do not want to be seen playing from the "ladies tees," which is what the forward tees historically were called.

So it seems that the only solution, besides creative naming, is to overbuild tees to the point that we wind up with one at the very front, which is seldom used, and one at the very, very back, which is also seldom used. Those in between constitute the core tees. A course with five sets of tee options can feature tournament, championship, regular, club, and family tees. Women golfers might play from any of the tees, but probably more from the club or family tees, depending on their ability. In this setup, gender is not an issue—just options for anyone's taste. In reality, the championship set is where most men will play. This way, they can strike the ball from where it's generally regarded to be tough and challenging. This arrangement is probably acceptable if there are appropriate yardage differences between the tee choices. However, even this approach can backfire, as there will always be golfers who play from the way, way back tees when clearly they have no business doing so.

Keep in mind that golfers strive for control—the golf experience is *their* experience. Ideally, it should be the golfer's own decision as to what tees to play on a given day. Whatever can be done to make the golfer part of the decision and to buy into it will make the experience a better one. The goal is to encourage the decision that will produce the most enjoyable experience.

FIGURE 5-12
Perceived distance can be drastically increased when a large natural feature forms a backdrop to a target seen from the tee or fairway. In this example at the renowned Boulders Resort in Arizona, the green appears much farther away due to the dramatic boulder hill that sits behind the putting surface.

COURTESY OF THE BOULDERS RESORT AND GOLDEN DOOR SPA; JAY MORRISH, ASGCA, GOLF COURSE ARCHITECT

The setting of tees is a broad topic. It is important to consider how tees will relate to the other parts of the golf hole. Will they be secluded or on display? Will one tee among several be sought after because it is higher and therefore more desirable? Has ample space been planned for landscaping and buffering?

Golfers spend a good amount of time on the tee of a hole. An average golfer may spend as much as 33 percent of the time it takes to play an average round, including waiting time, at the tees. Care must be taken in positioning, creating variety and ultimately in naming the tees of golf holes.

In considering the psychology of tees and their settings, consider the following aspects:

- Length
  Perceived length of the shot required (what the golfer sees) versus the actual length of the shot by physical measurement.
- Nomenclature
  How multiple tees are designated.
- Choice
  Find ways to get golfers to play from the appropriate tees.
- Elevation differences
  Higher tees give power; lower tees can make golf shots seem vulnerable.
- Seclusion
  Will the golfer be able to concentrate?
- Views and vistas
- Bordering conditions
  Tees on the edge of a lake or ledge can make the tee shot seem more perilous.

Planning for Golfers with Disabilities

The Americans with Disabilities Act (ADA) has become the standard by which the world has begun changing architectural barriers to allow people with physical disabilities to gain access to public spaces. In general, the intent of the ADA is to increase access not only for people who have trouble walking but also for those with sight and mental impairments.

For golf facilities, this can be a troublesome matter, just as it is for the National Park Service—which has, at least so far, not been able to make the Bright Angel Trail leading to the bottom of the Grand Canyon any less steep or more maneuverable. What the Park Service has done is to make the primary facilities at the Grand Canyon reasonably available to all, and this is the same basic approach that golf courses are taking. The golfing industry has embraced the goal of making facilities more accessible and are leaders in this effort among sports and recreation groups.

Although not official guidelines, the following are considerations in making golf facilities accessible by people with disabilities:

- Motorized carts (assistance vehicles) can be an acceptable means of access in many instances.
- Practice ranges should be planned such that 5 to 10 percent of the hitting areas meet criteria for access.
- At least one practice green and practice bunker of any planned should meet criteria for access.
- Depending on the number of tees per golf hole and the terrain of the area, tees should meet criteria for access by placing an emphasis on forward tees over back tees if a choice must be made which will have access. At least one tee per hole should have access.
- Cart paths with curbs should have openings (curb cuts) every few hundred feet to allow for access.
- Terrain within a golf hole (the fairways, playable hazards, greens, etc.) should be accessible from at least one angle of approach. Note: This may not always be called for in sand bunkers and around steep features, which may be inherently hazardous regardless of access.
- Criteria varies with each locality, jurisdiction, and project. (Refer to the Resources Section for sources of additional information.)

The personal golf cart is among the best ways to provide access to golf facilities and courses by golfers with physical disabilities. Access requirements are similar to those of traditional golf carts, but with considerably less clearance in terms of width. When personal carts are used to achieve access, they must be able to get to tees and greens to the degree possible given the natural conditions of the land.

COURTESY OF SOLORIDER INDUSTRIES; www.solorider.com

FAIRWAYS & ROUGHS—THROUGH THE GREEN

There is no definition in the rules of golf for *fairway* or *rough*. These components are simply "through the green", which is to say that they make up the largest area of golf holes: that portion from the tee all the way to the green. Since they obviously have a lot to do with golf courses (never mind the rules), the subcomponents of these parts are covered in detail.

Landing Areas

Landing areas, which have no specific width, depth, or shape, are simply the improved turfed expanses to which golfers are supposed to hit their balls. Par-4 holes include one intended landing area between the tee and the green where golfers are expected to land their tee shots. Par-5 holes include two intended landing areas, one for the tee shot and one for the second shot. Please note the obvious distinction between "intended" and "actual" landing areas. Actual landing areas are where golfers actually land their shots—which is almost anywhere. Because we cannot control human error or judgment, the routing process considers both, but we make the intended landing area more distinct because this is where golfers *should* hit their shots. In a perfect world, actual landing areas would slide forward and backward along the length of a golf hole as the ability of various golfers result in shorter or longer shots. Actual landing areas, however, wind up being not only shorter and longer, but off to the left and right.

It may be said that fairways are the combination of both intended landing areas and reasonable deviations from what is intended. There is no specific rule or order to fairways, other than their width, surface area, and shape must be commensurate with the design of the hole they serve. A fairway is a target to be hit by the golfer. Each golfer, by way of their own ability, will choose their own spot.

While the term *landing area* is taken to mean that area where balls are intended to come to rest, there is, in essence, a multitude of landing areas defined by the actual shots golfers execute, whether outstanding, typical, or awful. When—not if—a player hits halfway to the intended landing area from a par-4 tee he is, in essence, creating a new landing area, albeit not one we design intentionally; perhaps it is better called *a place where people will hit.* It has never been possible to predict where all golfers on all days in all conditions will hit their balls. We can only attempt to design golf holes with an intended path in mind, with intended landing areas, and with bail-out spaces and opportunities for the poorly hit shots to get out of trouble without undue frustration. The golfer who continually hits well short and right no matter what he does to correct this atrocity will thank us if he does not always find a deep tangle of hazard or brush to hunt through while the rest of his party watches from the more civilized portions of the hole.

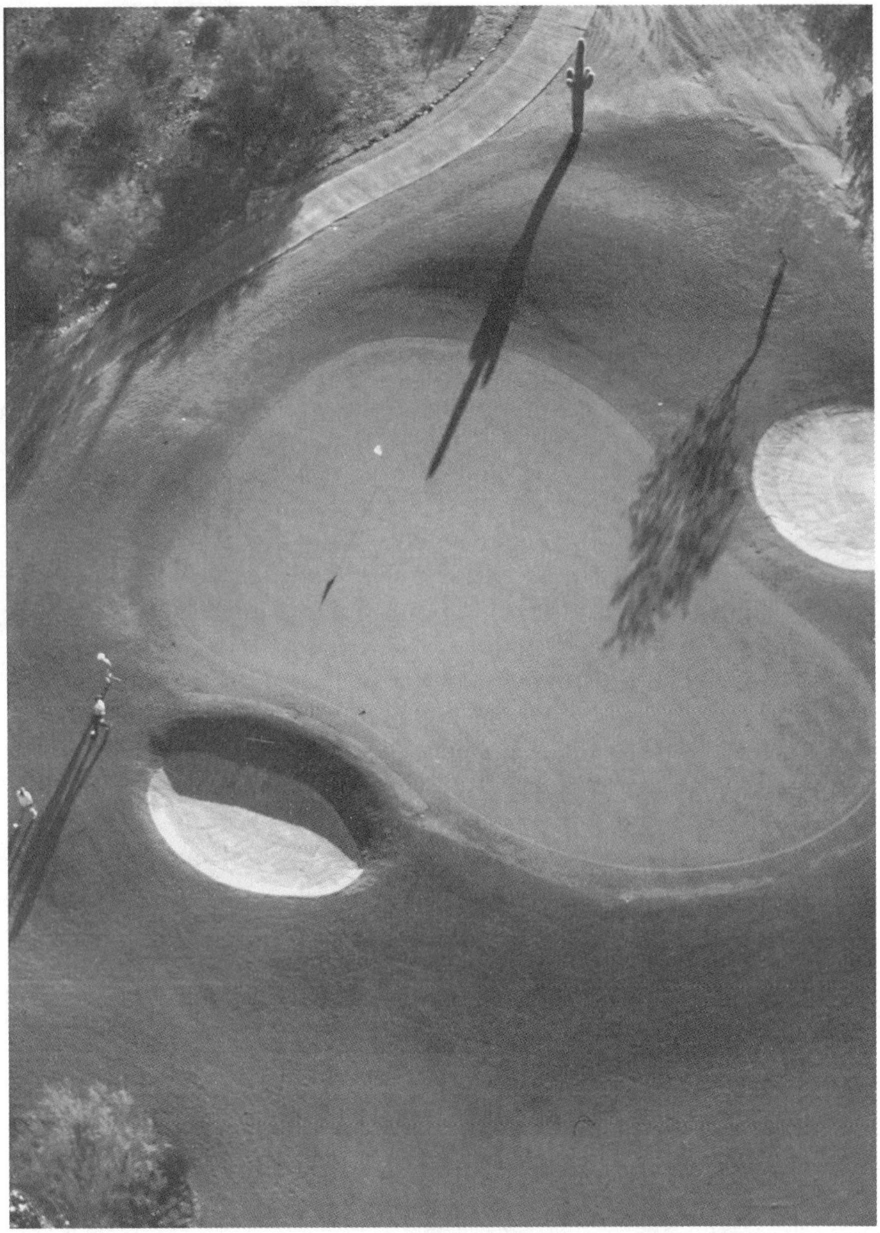

FIGURE 5-13
The green complex of a hole includes the entire area surrounding the putting surface itself. Bunkers, aprons, roughs, and access for the golfer are all part of the makeup of the green area.

PHOTO COURTESY OF LOOKOUT MOUNTAIN GOLF CLUB AT THE POINTE RESORT AT TAPATIO CLIFFS; FORREST RICHARDSON, ASGCA, GOLF COURSE ARCHITECT

Roughs

Roughs are all of the areas of a golf course that can be considered less than ideal to hit from. Roughs are not tees, improved fairways, hazards, or greens. Now more than ever, as courses are being planned with less turf coverage, more natural lands alongside and within, and with all sorts of native grasses sprouting up as borders to their holes, roughs are often an integral part of the routing plan. Their presence may need to be indicated for a variety of reasons, including to demonstrate improved turf acreage and natural areas to be preserved, and to quantify areas that might be artificially created through landscaping.

HAZARDS—THE OBSTACLES OF GOLF HOLES

Hazards are essential to the game of golf. It is against the human nature to go around more than is absolutely necessary. We are not lazy creatures, but we realize that effort saved could lead to more energy when it may be needed. Why go around when you can fly straight through to the destination? The golfer who hits away or even to the side of where the hole is cut goes against this principle. A hazard, then, has a significant psychological impact. The best hazards are somewhere between saying to the golfer, "It's definitely okay to hit straight over or near me, there is no real danger" and "Under no circumstances do you want to come this direction." When a hazard vacillates between appearing not too bothersome and worth going around, it captures the game of golf that lies within each golfer. Risk, reward, chance, effort, betterment, creativity, strength, gamble, and what-the-hell are all potential reactions.

Many great quotes have been collected about hazards, some of which appear in the margins of this book. Natural hazards, which include the natural-looking sand bunkers of linksland courses and all types of naturally occurring water bodies and courses, are the most appreciated in golf. Natural hazards connect the golfer with the land, and the entire sense of playing against nature is intensified when a hazard is natural as opposed to contrived and obviously constructed.

FIGURE 5-14
A spectacular combination of natural rock outcroppings, a constructed water hazard, and a sand bunker, all of which work together to form an exciting and challenging tee shot.

PHOTO COURTESY OF THE STONE CANYON GOLF CLUB, TUCSON, ARIZONA; JAY MORRISH, ASGCA, GOLF COURSE ARCHITECT

The Back Tees of Death

Designing golf courses involves driving your spouse crazy on occasion. Whatever possessed me to lug my golf clubs to a remote Mexican destination back in the 1980s is evidence of how far over the line I was willing to go. Here, for example, I had merely *heard* there was a new golf course just opened and had absolutely no concrete photos or firsthand accounts of whether or not it even existed or, for that matter, was open for play. My first clue that this desire to play golf might be a mistake came at the airline check-in counter when the agent matter-of-factly commented, "Golf clubs? I didn't know there was a golf course there."

At this, my wife eyed me with a look somewhere between "Oh no, did Mr. Golf take another dumb pill?" and "Attention everyone, I'm not really with him." Regardless, off we went, an extra baggage claim ticket in hand and my dreams of playing golf in the depths of Mexico intact.

Upon arrival, and after retrieving our luggage and my golf bag, it became apparent that I might as well have been carrying an enormous harp. Everyone was staring. No one else had brought a harp with them, and no one had golf clubs either.

The next morning, I inquired about playing golf and, after several minutes of loose interpretations, I finally found someone who knew, at least secondhand, of the approximate whereabouts of the golf course. Determined to prove that "where there's a will, there's a way," I dragged my wife along. For the next hour, we entrusted our lives to a taxi driver who kept asking nervously what was in the black bag. Finally, we arrived at a remote entry drive that looked strangely new, yet also like it had been in disrepair for years and years. The same held true for the clubhouse and, it turned out, the entire place. Reportedly only a few months old, this destination golf club had either been under construction for 20 years or its builders had gone to great lengths to disguise its newness by building in tall weeds, cracked concrete, and weathered walls.

Type of Hazards

Besides the technical designations *sand hazard, water hazard,* and *lateral water hazard* (which are defined by the Rules of Golf), hazards for the purposes of discussing routing are assigned to the following categories: sand hazards, wet water hazards, dry water hazards, and pseudo hazards. Each is broken down and explained by example, as follows:

Sand Hazards: A sand hazard is any formal sand bunker, sand trap, sand area, or beach that contains sand or sandy material and is designated as a sand bunker under the Rules of Golf. Sand hazards can appear natural, ragged, tidy, or a combination of these. Recovery is usually possible from sand hazards. In rare instances are they so penal that a stroke is assuredly lost when encountered.

Wet Water Hazards: This category includes lakes, ponds, streams, burns, canals, brooks, oceans, swamps, slues, estuaries, bogs, and so on. Wet hazards are definitive in that they are bodies and channels full of

Now to the topic at hand: *the back tees.* Like a majority of golfers, it was my choice to select the tees I would play on this fine 105-degree day. Joined by another American (Note: This chap had *rented* clubs, and so he cannot be held to the same bonehead classification as I.), we decided mutually, and with great machismo, that the blue tees were for us. After all, we came here to be challenged, not to play the harp!

Along about the eighth hole, my new golf partner inquired if he might borrow some golf balls. It appeared he had lost all but one of the dozen he had purchased. The rough, at 4 to 5 feet high, was a bit much to search through. You know, snakes and all. Of course I obliged, and we somehow managed to finish the round amid sweltering heat, no water, no directional signage, and an up-and-down trek with cavernous ravines and 200-yard carries from the—you guessed it—*back tees.* When we finished the round, we had precisely two balls between us. I was nearly dehydrated, and my partner simply disappeared before I could say good-bye. He may well be there still today. Occasionally I picture him in a thatched hut being tended to by a local doctor who drops by once a month. It's a remote place, you know. Better him than me.

Why do so many golfers choose the back tees? If the truth were known, a majority of the golfers we see every day playing off the tips would be better served at the regular tees or perhaps just slightly farther back. On the fateful day I almost died (the story gets more heroic every year now), my wife pointed this out as she sipped her cool pineapple drink on a shady veranda and listened to me complain about golf in the depths of Mexico, how tough the course was, what an awful time I had, and why she hadn't thought to bring the mosquito spray. Did I mention the mosquitoes? I think they carried off a few Titleists.

When routing, know that your back tees will forever be misused by numbskulls like me. Make the course appealing from all the tees.

water. Recovery is not likely. Most balls hit into such hazards are lost or certainly unplayable 99.9 percent of the time.

Dry Water Hazards: An oxymoron? Perhaps, but not without reason. Dry water hazards are defined under the Rules of Golf as water hazards, yet they are inherently dry as a bone, at least most of the time. Ravines, ditches, dry washes, dry lakebeds, depressions of rugged terrain, dense brush areas, and sinkholes are examples of dry water hazards. Unlike with wet water hazards, recovery may be possible. Dry water hazards may be negotiated more easily by golfers moving from hole to hole. And also that their affect on missed shots is less devastating to the golfer's enjoyment.

Pseudo hazards: Pseudo hazards are obstacles that would not be defined as hazards under the Rules of Golf. Examples include rock outcroppings, waste areas, grassy depressions, grass traps, steep mounds with native grass, old stone walls, trees, deep rough, and severe grades. A popular trend at target-type courses where the surrounding land terrain is especially penal to the golfer is to define any ball hit beyond the

The hazards which distinguish the best golf courses are those which make every hole a new and interesting problem.
—*Robert Hunter,* The Links

turf as subject to the same rule as balls hit into an official hazard. Under this option, the golfer may elect to find the ball and play it as it lies, take an unplayable lie, or replace the ball on the edge of the turf at the point at which it last crossed the turf limits and play with a stroke penalty, just as if he had dunked a ball into a lake or pond.

Quantity of Hazards

The original design of Augusta National is reported to have had just 22 sand bunkers. Imagine that, just 22. Today it is not uncommon for a design to wildly sport as many as 100 sand bunkers. A routing plan can take on the look of a pimpled teenager, especially when the sand is sprinkled throughout and not focused into thoughtful groupings. Plop someone down on such courses, and he may have no idea at what hole he is on. "It all looks the same," he might say. And why? Because the artificial sand bunkers are *everywhere.* Instead of being dished out periodically like excellent desserts, they are throwaway Halloween candy, the kind you dislike after you've seen many, many pieces, each wrapped like the other. After a while, there is nothing special in them, just boredom.

At a course I toured to assist in master-planning a new course nearby, on every side of every hole—all 18 of them—was a natural wetlands. Even if you could see your ball, you were not allowed to enter the water hazard to retrieve it. The pro shop attendant told me they did a great business in ball sales, and no wonder. I suggested that rather than build a new course, they try to make the one they had a bit more forgiving.

The number of hazards is a function of course type, player type, and the theme to be expressed and marketed. Hazards come in all shapes, sizes, and configurations. Using them all is like a movie that uses every cliché. Variety is good. Excess is usually not.

Hazard Logistics in Routing

Hazards can align play to one side or the other. Placing a hazard on one side of a fairway may cause play to favor the opposite side. Or the opposite may be so; a hazard may attract play toward it if the golfer contemplates taking a shorter, more dangerous route. Hazards can also slow play, especially when they cannot be accessed quickly and when recovery may take multiple shots by the average or below-average player. A water hazard where balls are lost will require playing separate shots, and this takes time and can cause frustration. Routing must consider the benefit of a hazard and its potential to undermine both a good time and otherwise good routing. Exciting and intriguing are good; guaranteed frustration and failure are bad.

Large hazards occupy space, so they must be carefully weighed for their benefit, suitability, and efficiency. They do reduce maintenance costs if the space would otherwise be occupied by improved turf. The famous 15th hole at Cypress Point has very little turf to maintain compared to the other par 3s on the course. This does not make it a good hole, but it is, in fact, a positive in the eyes of the greenkeeping crew with respect to turf care.

Hazards can also preserve. Retaining natural areas and wetlands can be an excellent way to integrate golf with sensitive areas. Be sure that access is appropriate and that adjacent golf uses will be a complement and not a detraction.

Reasons for Hazards

The reasons to design a hazard into a routing plan are as follows:

- For intrigue
- To create strategy options
- To penalize non-ideal shots
  Not necessarily bad shots, as the badly struck ball is usually penalty enough.
- As an aid in aiming
  To suggest a direction away from or toward something.
- To aid in depth perception
- Aesthetics
  To add contrast, color differentiation, or texture variation to a landscape.
- To protect adjacent uses
  To influence shots away from adjacent land, other golf uses, etc.
- To stop balls
  Preventing balls from further peril. The sand bunker at the edge of a cliff, such as the long sand trap along Pebble Beach's famous 18th hole, is a blessing compared to the alternative.
- For preservation
  A natural feature may be retained by using it as a hazard and not eliminating it from the landscape. Water, natural drainageways, wetlands, archeological sites, and so on are examples of this impetus.
- For engineering reasons
  Retention and detention basins may be defined hazards, thereby both accommodating a civil engineering need and serving as an obstacle.

GREENS — GOLF'S TARGET

The size of greens will vary depending on the type of course, type of hole, and physical factors, such as the terrain. Although there is great debate that is unlikely to be settled, theories abound on the "proper" size for certain length shots, pars, etc.

When this subject comes up with Jack Snyder present, he reminds me of the time he was watching two famous (very famous) golfers play in one of those classic Shell Oil–sponsored Wonderful World of Golf matches on television. Ruth, Jack's wife, was at the opposite end of the house and heard the loudest exclamation, "NO!" upon which she found Jack arguing with the TV set. Apparently this famous golfer had commented that the shorter the shot, the smaller the green should be. Jack suggested that this was dead opposite prudent thinking because shorter

Like a Rock — A Short Story

As I maneuvered my dusty black truck in 4-wheel low, it crept over the 10-inch-diameter boulders, and we gradually made our way up the side of a desert ravine to the partially cleared fairway for one of the back nine's early par 4s. "Wow, this is spectacular!" commented the golf director, a new face in the crowd, who had recently taken an active role in visiting the site and communicating with the new owners of the soon-to-be-completed golf course. It was almost three o'clock, and by this time the owners had probably already left their Manhattan offices to make their way through a different kind of jungle to their homes in the hills outside the city.

We parked in front of today's main topic: a field of jet-black rocks that were once blown sky-high by the forces of an ancient volcano. They sat quietly now, covered with patches of green and orange lichen that attached themselves despite the harsh desert climate. On any given midsummer day, the surface of the rock heated to nearly 140 degrees. They were in piles, some 4 to 5 feet high, others scattered among the larger ones—all in all, a random sculpture that could never have been duplicated by man or machine. We were staring at nature's work. It was an obstacle discovered almost one year earlier. I had been traversing the site of this new course, and it occurred to me that this pile of rocks was special, that somehow it could—should—be saved and made part of the final routing.

"I think it's in the way," came a comment from one of the consulting golf course architects. This project, you see, had become a collaboration. Whenever new ownership takes hold, anything might happen. And it had. Even though we were in the midst of constructing an 18-hole course, the design team had grown and the rules had changed. With many opinions at hand, the decisions no longer came as easily as they had in the previous months.

By this time, we were out of the truck, and each of the four occupants had taken a position on the fairway-to-be. My—our—client looked thoughtfully at the rock pile. My comments had already been heard. They were expressed in black and white on the sheets of the original design for the golf hole. They needed no repeating. The idea to leave the million-year-old rocks and have the fairway split around them to create a risk-reward detour option from the tee had, until now, been the *only* design. We stood about 220 yards from the main tee. This would be the point of no return. The player would either go right of the rock pile or go for the gusto and play to a narrow patch of fairway beyond and to the left of the ruggedness. There I stood. This point of no return suddenly had two meanings. There was the question that I already envisioned the golfer facing—and there was the decision soon to be made.

After a few minutes of pacing and head turning, the golf director stared toward the site of the eventual green and said, "If we bulldoze them away, we will never know." And so the decision was made. The rocks that could never be recreated and that would have been lost forever had they been destroyed would remain for golfers to anguish over and make their decisions around. This natural hazard, which had lasted an eternity, had stood another test of time. This one, the greatest hurdle, lasted only a few minutes.

shots, in most instances, mean considerably more impact to the green due to their trajectory, so course conditions and maintenance require larger areas so the green can heal. There are so many opinions on this subject that I am inclined to leave you with Jack's reasoning, which is the best I've heard. All the others amount to rules that can always be broken one way or another.

In considering a green site, the important thing is to define ample room for the green (and surrounding area) that will ultimately fit or be fitted to an area. An extremely wide green may require extra area on both sides in order to handle errant shots when the pin is set to the far side. The same holds true for depth and overall area. Additionally, paths leading to and from greens must be planned. Cart paths obviously have a relationship to greens. Too close is bad. So is too far. Good luck.

MISCELLANEOUS PARTS OF A HOLE

Other parts of golf holes do not necessarily fit into the above categories. Giving them due consideration during the routing process is extremely worthwhile. Here is a list for reference:

- Cart paths

  Adequate room, access, and alignment for cart paths must be planned into the layout. Even when a path system is not depicted in the routing plan, it is essential that cart paths (if they are called for) can access the areas of the course, maneuver across terrain, water, roads, etc.

- Drop areas

  Designated tee-like areas associated with water hazards that allow play to continue from an obvious area.

- Buffer areas

  Ample area to separate holes from other holes and land uses.

- Drainage areas

  Areas for drainage retention and/or detention.

- Maintenance access

  Routes to the maintenance area and for maintenance equipment to access all part of the course must be planned.

GOLF HOLES—THEIR PAR, LENGTH & ORIENTATION

Golf holes go right, left, up, down, around, over, through, across, and alongside. Then, just when you thought it had all been done, along comes developer Duane Hagadone with an idea to float a green for a par-3 on a converted barge accessible only by boat. At his Coeur d'Alene Resort in Idaho, No. 14 plays anywhere from 125 yards to 150 yards to this floating contraption, which can be reeled in or out to make the carry over water slightly shorter or slightly longer. This hole does not go right, left, up, down, around, over, through, across, *or* alongside—it just goes out. It is indicative of creative thinking. Living proof that we may not have done it all as yet. More golf holes are to come.

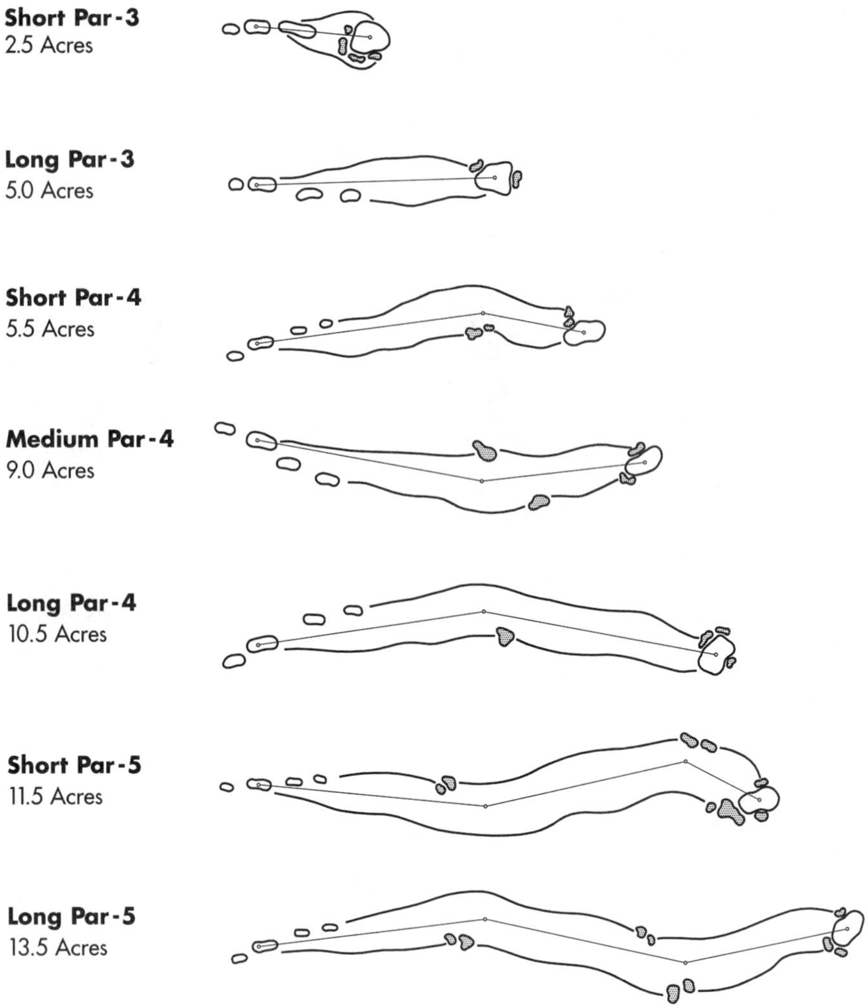

FIGURE 5-15
A range of golf hole types illustrates the relationship of par and length to acreage. The acreages indicated are estimates based on the typical safety envelope that surrounds the hole and defines the space taken up. Note that the short par 3 is roughly four times shorter that the long par 5 but requires less than five times the acreage.

Par

Par is a matter of length, but it also takes into account the playing difficulty of a hole and such conditions as prevailing winds, terrain, and elevation about sea level, which affects atmospheric pressure and, ultimately, the distance a ball will travel. The USGA provides guidelines for determining par (Figure 5-16).

Par determination also, obviously, depends on the type of golf course and, to some degree, the type of golfer who plays it. Variation is essential, but just how much depends on almost every factor described in this book. You can probably find a relevant passage about par—a historical note, a rule, an example, a story, an opinion—in every chapter. A basic refresher on par is helpful to everyone.

Par 4s

We do not typically begin with a par 3, so we will not here, either. It is important to consider that most 18-hole regulation courses with a par of

72 feature ten par-4 holes. Par 4s are the mainstay of the par inventory. The par 4 allows two usually full shots to reach the green under scratch conditions and a standard of two putts for a par of four.

Par 4s must be varied so they are not too much like one another. Whether the par 4 goes right or left, or up or down it should present the golfer with an appropriate dose of contrast to the other par 4 holes on the course. The following are primary types of par 4 holes:

> *Who shall say which par affords the most superlative play? No one will deny the lure, intrigue and importance of the one-shotter.*
>
> *—George C. Thomas,* Game and Gossip *magazine, January 1932*

- Open/mid-length
  Average length and mostly open en route to the hole.
- Bordered
  The hole is flanked along one or both sides by an obstacle or hazard.
- Heroic tee shot
  An expert tee shot which bites off more of an obstacle can lead to a better approach to the green and, likely, less distance.
- Green guarded
  The primary difficulty is at the green; guarded either in penal, heroic, detour, or lay-up fashion.
- Long
  The hole and its primary challenge is defined by its length.
- Gamble reachable
  With an obstacle placed in the way, the hole is reachable by heroic means from the tee.
- Detour tee shot
  The tee shot offers at least two distinct routes that will lead to better or worse positions.
- Lay-up at second
  The second shot is so guarded and of such length that a lay-up has been planned for in the design.
- Lay-up at tee
  The tee shot is interrupted such that hitting a full shot is not worth the risk and the design allows for and encourages a lay-up.
- Open reachable
  The hole is not long, and nothing prevents a long and well-struck ball from getting to the green in one.

Par 3s

The par 3 is the only hole of the top three pars where the golfer is expected to have an opportunity for a hole-in-one at each crack that is taken. Golf architect Les Furber uses this fact to suggest that the green must, at all costs, be visible at the par 3. Otherwise the poor chap who manages an ace is deprived of the thrill of seeing it go in.

The anatomy of a par 3 can be summed up thus: This is the only hole in golf from which play is always to the green from a relatively constant place. Unlike its counterparts at the par 4s and par 5s, where play to the green can—and does—occur from almost anywhere, the par 3 stands as a set-in-place experience that requires the golfer to reach the green from the point at which he put the ball in play. There are supposed to

One-shotters are most important. In these holes one gets a keener interest on the tee than on others.

—George C. Thomas Jr., Golf Architecture in America

be no approaches from through the green here. Doing such is failure, to be sure.

Because the par 3 is intended to be reached in just one stroke, the types of holes mostly follow the types of shots defined later in this chapter ("Golf Holes—Their Shot Strategy"). The primary types of par 3s are listed below:

- Open/mid-length
  Average length and open en route to the hole.
- Heroic
  The green is guarded and reaching it requires a heroic shot; or play may be off this heroic and preferred line resulting in a second shot played laterally toward the heart of the putting surface
- Penal
  The green is guarded and requires play to cross a hazard.
- Long
  The hole and its primary challenge is defined by its length.
- Barely reachable
  With an obstacle placed in the way, the hole is reachable by heroic means only. If the heroic shot fails, a lay-up is in order to a defined position-or else!
- Detour tee shot
  The shot may take two (or more) distinct routes that lead to better or worse positions at the green.

The par-3 hole, because it takes up a relatively small area, can easily be fitted into locations that most other holes cannot. Leftover areas of a site that cannot support any other use may accommodate a par 3. On a project I was working on several years ago, it became obvious that a spectacular par 3 was not going to be allowed in a remote reach of the routing, and we were left with a 17-hole course. A rather square drainage easement near two roads caught my attention, and I asked the civil engineers how much water passed through this area. We also had to find out who actually owned the land! But when all was said and done, a fine—and very short—par 3 was squeezed in this space, and it remains today a picturesque and likeable hole. I believe most people would not even notice that there is a slight walk from the previous green, as we managed to make it seem a natural progression.

The par 3 boasts many advantages in addition to its space and excitement. It is a reprieve to many golfers, not requiring much strength nor the battle to hit more than one full shot before putting. Par 3s have so much to offer the golfer that it is a wonder we do not see a trend for creating more, not fewer, in a round. At a delightful course designed by Robert Trent Jones Jr., Rancho San Marcos near Santa Barbara, California, there are six wonderful par 3s. Although each serves a purpose with regard to terrain, the course is also wonderful in terms of its pace and flow. The par-71 layout would not be as good with any fewer par 3s. The routing works.

At the par 3, there is opportunity for drama from the onset that cannot be matched at the tee of the par 4 or par 5—typically. The best par 3s are those planned around a single feature—a lake, a shoreline, a large and prominent land rise, a valley, or a collection of individual hazards that work as one giant feature. As stated previously, the element of hitting over or beside or partially over a chunk of nature makes the golfer feel that he's pitted against the forces of the land. When hazards or features are just dotted around, the par 3 can get lost, or at least its meaning can. Perhaps this is the best way to define the feeling that a par 3 should inspire: It should give *meaning* to the shot required. Nowhere else is the golfer presented with a shot that, from the first shot struck on a hole, is supposed to go near or in that small elusive hole cut out of the turf at daybreak.

Par 5s

"Three shot holes have fallen out of favor largely perhaps because most of them have no distinctive feature, except length," according to Charles Piper in an article that appeared in *Golf Illustrated* in February 1929. This was not uncommon in the early days of golf. The Old Course had and has only two par 5s and even Tillinghast wrote about the lack of interest in many par 5s and that there were only so many conditions under which a great hazard could form the reason for the three-shotter. Today this opinion is not held by most golfers or golf architects. The par 5 is as exciting as we make it, and it is likely that the lessons learned from seeing the many bad par 5s built in the early days contributed to better ones in modern times. We have also been hitting the ball farther and farther, so it goes without saying that longer holes, such as par 5s, allow the stretch of shots to offer greater reward to those who can hit farther.

The majority of par-5 holes rely on the approach to the green for their primary excitement. To guard against the easy reachable condition in just two strokes, a tendency on par 5s is to emphasize the protection at the green, and this is why we get tight features around the green. Fine and good, but the tee shot and second shots should be exciting and performed with thought, too. Par 5s fit these basic types:

- Open/mid-length

  Average length and mostly open en route to the hole.
- Bordered

  The hole is flanked along one or both sides by obstacles or a combination of hazards.
- Heroic tee shot

  An expert tee shot can lead to a better position for the second shot and less distance to the green.
- Heroic second shot

  Needed to get in position for a good approach.
- Penal green

  The green is guarded in penal fashion, requiring play over a hazard to reach it from any point.
- Continual direction double dogleg

  The hole keeps going to the right (or left) and may buttonhook around a feature.

UNITED STATES GOLF ASSOCIATION'S OFFICIAL YARDAGES FOR USE IN DETERMINING PAR OF HOLES

	Men	Women	Beginning Boys	Interim Boys	Beginning Girls	Interim Girls
Par-3	up to 250	up to 210	up to 100	up to 150	up to 90	up to 140
Par-4	251–470	211–400	101–180	151–270	91–160	141–250
Par-5	471–690	401–590	181–260	271–390	161–230	251–355
Par-6	691 and up	591 and up	261–340	391–510	231–300	356–470
Par-7	—	—	341–420	511 and up	301–370	471 and up
Par-8	—	—	421–500	—	371–440	—
Par-9	—	—	501 and up	—	441 and up	—

FIGURE 5-16
The United States Golf Association (USGA) recognizes par 3s, par 4s, par 5s, and par 6s for men and women. In addition, it has adopted par values based on distances for boys and girls that allow these golfers to play on courses and obtain adjusted handicaps. The USGA recognizes that holes out of the range listed can be assigned par values either lower or higher than shown based on significant conditions that lessen or add difficulty.

- Reverse double dogleg
  The hole goes one way and then the other by way of hazards and/or features placed for the purpose of directing.
- Long
  The hole is defined mainly by its length.
- Gamble reachable at second
  With an obstacle placed in the way, the hole is reachable by heroic means.
- Detour tee shot
  The tee shot offers at least two distinct routes that lead to better or worse positions.
- Detour second shot
  The second shot has distinct routes that lead to a choice of positions for the final approach.
- Detour abundant
  The best type of detour par 5; routes are complex because many choices are available, but the choices add to the fun and excitement.
- Lay-up at second
  The second shot is so guarded and of such length that a lay-up is anticipated and a landing area provided.
- Lay-up at tee
  The tee shot is interrupted such that hitting a full shot is not worth the risk, and the design allows for and encourages a lay-up.
- Open reachable
  Nothing prevents well-struck balls from getting to or near the green in two.

The Other Pars

Par 6s are an oddity, but they are for real. In the day of long, long hitting, holes with enough length to be classified as par 6s might have been an interesting trend. However, it might be pointed out that adding par is by no means a defense against hitting length. In reality, it is the other way around; perhaps par might be lessened and length increased.

Back to the par-6. The best reasons to create a par 6 are to take advantage of a tremendous landform and to appropriately link holes in a routing so that the course makes sense. It might be time to revisit the concept of primitive golf courses where, as you'll recall, there were no pars, no yardage plaques, and no slope ratings. There was a starting point and an ending point, and even these were informal at best. On occasion play could take hours, it has been surmised, to negotiate a single hole. There, perhaps that makes the par 6 easier to digest.

I have been involved in the design of a par 2 and can attest that it is a controversial idea, but one that the smart developer should embrace. A par 2 takes up very little room, not much beyond a third of an acre. I recently sat down to lunch with a well-known developer and explained the par 2 to him.

The par 2 is an interesting concept where a short hole becomes unusually short, perhaps not more than 50 yards. From the regular tees, which are markers set right into or straddling the edge of the putting surface to begin with, the player putts or chips to an ordinary hole with a flagstick. (A local rule allows striking the flagstick on the tee shot.) The forward tees are similar, but the back tees are perhaps just off the green and require a chip, thus making this shot more demanding. The green, ideally, is enormous and allows remarkable diversity in setup and challenge. There could, in cases, be a tedious sand bunker near the edge of the putting surface, but this might be for the most challenging of cup positions only. The advantages are plenty—I can fit it virtually anywhere, there is no setback to the following tee. The next tee can literally be on the edge of the green if necessary. And it is a real conversation piece. It allows for even more variation; we can add a par 5 in place of a par 4 and we will save perhaps 2 acres of land in the process.

I have even proposed a par 2 where the green of the previous hole is extra-large and the double size accommodates the par 2 entirely. I asked the USGA about the par-2 idea and was not given any reason why it might not be considered. The USGA simply stipulates that two putts be allowed at the green, and why not begin right there? If there is a better way to, at least once during a round, discount the importance of the powerful shots and focus all the nerves of the golfer on his delicate game, let it be heard now.

Length

The length of holes has been debated even since golf courses have been planned by "experts." Very often, instead of talking about length relative to the land and the type of course and the variation, designers think of length as a means to thwarting the advances in the technology of golf clubs and balls. There is occasional talk about the rise in the ability of the golfer, but the reference should clearly be to the professional golfer. Average golfers have not become better over the years; they remain fairly constant, as tracked by the handicap system. While they may be hitting the ball farther, it is not necessarily going any straighter. The average golfer still scores relatively high.

> *The short hole should not be long.*
>
> —*John L. Low,* Aspects of Golf Course Architecture

Length must be appropriate—and varied—and provide challenge without being burdensome. I do not buy length for length's sake, in most cases. It has its place every once in a while, but the point of golf is more than crushing a ball. Good and passionate players who are able to crush the ball do not live for this thrill alone. In fact, golf would be a lonely game if that were all there was to it.

Width

The width of golf holes must accommodate their alignment. If the hole bends it will need more room on the side toward the bend—usually. When there are options—detour shots—room will be needed to handle the two or more pathways that a golfer might take. Golf hole width is a function of length, type, features, and many other factors. Figure 5-16 gives the approximate acreage for golf holes of different types; these estimates are almost as much about width as length.

In general, a par 3 requires less width than holes with full tee shots and second shots or approaches from the fairway to the green. This is a function of the length of the par-3 tee shot, which may be a very controlled iron shot and therefore less likely to be as off-line and wide as a driver.

Doglegs

Dogleg holes, besides their amusing name, are amusing in their requirement that we turn as they do and must add the element of a change in direction to our list of things to remember at each shot before the green. Dogleg holes require greater width than straight holes of the same length, at least in most instances. It is efficient to use up the inside of a dogleg with a feature or hazard that must remain. Bending around nothing but home sites or an adjacent golf parcel is a poor idea for obvious reasons. Something of golf value—a valid obstacle—should ideally be present to make the bend seem sensible.

The dogleg can get old to the golfer, especially when used too frequently, too severely, or too often in the same direction. Very few holes are perfectly straight; almost all have slight doglegs. The key is to use doglegs wisely and to make them seem natural, not forced or contrived.

GOLF HOLES—THEIR SHOT STRATEGY

Accuracy, carry, and then length. This, according to golf architect William Flynn (among the youngest—age 19—ever to be asked to design a golf course, as he was in 1909), is the order of importance in designing individual golf holes. It should be noted that Flynn did not say this at 19 but rather when he had a bit more experience in his later years. When you combine these ingredients into different recipes—maybe a little more accuracy here but not so much length, for example—you wind up with holes that play differently. The idea of balancing accuracy and length is a fundamental of golf course design and vital to routing a course.

To have two or more holes identical is a weakness of the layout and the layout-er.

—Charles Piper, in an article appearing in Golf Illustrated, *February 1929*

FIGURE 5-17
This table allows calculation based on adding angle to an otherwise straight golf hole at a point 220 yards from the tee point. When holes are doglegged, length is gained if the tee and green points are kept in their original positions. The column at left gives the dimension if a hole is perfectly straight. Going across the table are incremental angles below which is the yardage to add if the hole bends at 220 yards from the tee, with the original tee point and green point remaining fixed. To arrive at the gained yardage for double dogleg holes the length added from each bend is calculated separately and then added together.

YARDAGE ADDITION RESULTING FROM DOGLEG ANGLE

	ANGLE OF DOGLEG (DEGREES)								
STRAIGHT	**20**	**25**	**30**	**35**	**40**	**45**	**50**	**55**	**60**
260	2.1	3.4	5.1	7.1	9.6	12.8	16.6	21.2	26.9
280	3.0	4.7	7.0	9.7	13.1	17.2	22.2	28.1	35.2
300	3.7	5.8	8.6	12.0	16.0	21.0	26.8	33.7	41.7
320	4.3	6.8	10.0	13.9	18.5	24.1	30.6	38.2	47.1
340	4.8	7.7	11.2	15.5	20.7	26.8	33.9	42.1	51.6
360	5.3	8.4	12.3	16.9	22.5	29.1	36.7	45.5	55.5
380	5.7	9.1	13.2	18.2	24.2	31.1	39.2	48.4	58.8
400	6.1	9.7	14.1	19.4	25.6	32.9	41.4	50.9	61.7
420	6.5	10.2	14.8	20.4	26.9	34.6	43.3	53.2	64.3
440	6.8	10.7	15.5	21.3	28.1	36.0	45.0	55.2	66.6
460	7.1	11.1	16.1	22.1	29.2	37.3	46.6	57.0	68.7

FIGURE 5-18
An illustration of how the chart in Figure 5-17 can be applied to a golf hole. In this example, 31 yards are added to the length of the hole when the tee and green points remain, but the difference in the angle of the centerlines is 45 degrees

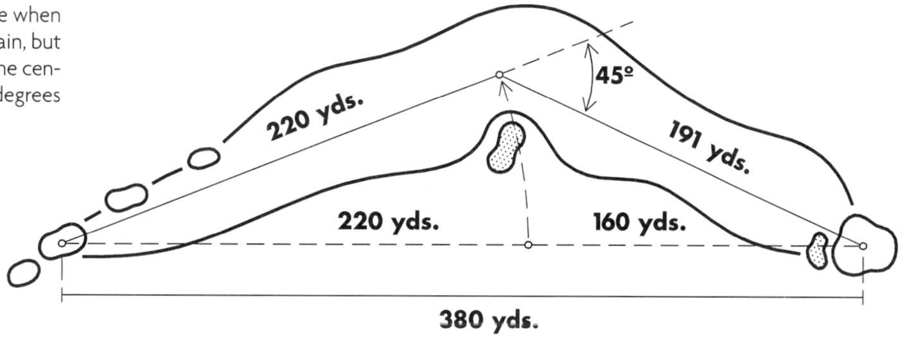

The common classifications of golf holes in terms of their play are penal, strategic, and heroic. This, I believe, is more out of tradition than anything else. Aren't *all* golf holes strategic? Isn't it just that some involve more strategy than others? Strategy can be evident, I submit, even in its absence. In my opinion, *strategic* is no more a good description of a golf hole than it would be of a war. Strategy is a constant. It is part of the game regardless of what lies ahead of the golfer.

Having stated this, I now confess that I have encountered a few golf holes that required, I swear, absolutely no strategy at all. One has a completely open invitation to reach the green in a carefree manner with nary a hazard, bump, or tree in the way. It has always haunted me that it was essentially its fieldlike expanse and landscape devoid of hazards that made the hole so terribly frustrating. Could it be that its lack of strategy

THE PERIODIC TABLE OF THE SHOT STRATEGIES

	Penal	Heroic	Detour	Lay-up	Open
PAR-3 HOLES: Tee Shot	OK	GOOD	GOOD	OK	POOR
PAR-4 HOLES: Tee Shot	OK	GOOD	GOOD	OK	POOR
Second Shot	POOR	GOOD	GOOD	POOR	POOR
PAR-5 HOLES: Tee Shot	POOR	GOOD	GOOD	OK	POOR
Second Shot	POOR	GOOD	GOOD	OK	POOR
Third Shot	OK	GOOD	GOOD	POOR	POOR

FIGURE 5-19
Using the five types of golf shots (penal, heroic, detour, lay-up, open, this Periodic Table of the Shot Strategies cross-references preferred and less preferred uses of the strategy type to hole par and whether the shot is a tee shot, second shot, or third shot. Completely open design is shown as *poor* in all situations, as this design is not generally desirable.

was its strategy? Regardless, understrategized holes are sometimes neither penal nor heroic. So, if subscribing to the traditional method of describing holes, they are admittedly orphans without definitions. I dub such holes *open,* as that is exactly what they are. Open to a golfer's own method of attack... or open for the golfer to fall apart at the relative ease.

Rather than using the traditional classification—penal, strategic, and heroic—a better way to approach golf holes might be to think of the individual strokes that make up their strategy. The following modified terminology permits *golf shots* to be accurately classified, and therefore it enables golf holes to be more accurately labeled with respect to strategy. In my book (I've always wanted to say that), strategy is assumed to be a constant. The types of design strategy refer to the individual shots planned into holes.

Along with this new way of thinking comes the exponential formula that results. By combining the five types of golf shots demanded by golf holes—penal, heroic, detour, lay-up, and open—among par-3, par-4, and par-5 holes, 280 basic variables may be created, not just three types, as many have been told. A tee shot may be *heroic* in nature, an approach may present a *detour,* etc. Infinite possibilities come into play when all of the other variables are added to the equation: alignment, length, hazards, and more.

Penal Design

A golf shot that presents no alternative route to avoid a hazard or feature is said to be penal. The word comes from the Latin *poena,* which means "fine" or "penalty." Penal golf deign is thought to have been a standard of early golf course design, but perhaps this is not so. Only sometimes did hazards completely obscure the path to the hole. In fact, on many natural links courses and even early designed courses, holes defined as penal were played by way of alternate routes devised by golfers who refused to believe there was no way around the impediment. They devised their own routes to the hole and, in the process, invented what has become known as strategic and heroic design—or, in our vernacular; detour, lay-up, or heroic design.

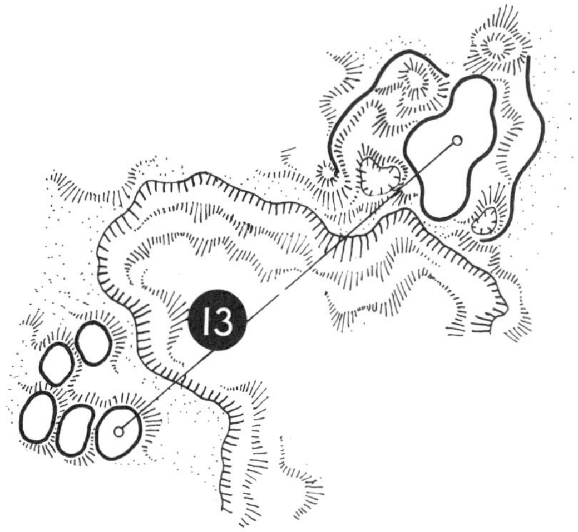

FIGURE 5-20
Example of a par 3 requiring a penal shot over a deep canyon. Although penal, the shot required is only 60 to 70 yards from the regular tees and may be played to the left if the slightly longer carry directly to the center of the green is too much for the golfer. The worst of penal shots are those for which the required carry is in excess of 70 yards from a tee point, or any penal condition beyond the tee shot, as the spot from which a golfer will need to play this shot cannot be predicted. The player who hits just 170 yards off the tee, when faced with a penal shot to the green of a 330-yard par-4, will face a shot he probably cannot negotiate.
FROM THE ROUTING PLAN FOR WHITNEY RANCH MESA; REFER TO FIGURE 7-2 FOR THE COMPLETE ROUTING PLAN

Penal golf holes are not in favor in today's world. The logistics of getting all golfers to the hole is of paramount importance. An obstacle that requires playing across is not as appealing as one where the golfer has choices. Nonetheless, a place remains for penal design, as it provides a change of pace during the golf round.

The most workable condition for penal designs is when the design will not unfairly penalize the higher-handicap golfer. The penal design is also an excellent choice where there is no choice—that is, when a natural hazard presents itself such that routing *must* get across it and the opportunity of drama cannot be ignored. A gorge 150 feet across is a good example. The hole might just lead to the shot of a lifetime and, for most golfers, a carry of this length is a doable feat. Penal design requires careful planning, though. It should only be administered in small doses and when appropriate.

The classic example of a penal shot is the very short par 3 where a range of tees can create a forced carry over water, wasteland, or sand. The actual carry is perhaps no more than 50 or 60 yards for the golfer who plays from the forward tees. It is presumed that nearly all golfers can negotiate a 60-yard carry. This is significantly more palatable than the same forced carry designed short of the green on a par 4. In this instance, the higher-handicap golfer may attempt a long iron or fairway wood to reach the green by virtue of his position off the tee. To necessitate a penal approach in this instance is reason for criticism of the penal school of design.

Note that the designation *O.K.* is given to penal design on the chart in Figure 5-19. The reason is that it is typically more fun to offer choice. The detour, heroic, and lay-up schools are infinitely more interesting. He who decides to play too boldly will, in effect, bring the penal approach into play himself.

> *[I]t is not long driving alone that is sufficient to win a match.*
> —*J. H. Taylor,* Aspects of Golf Course Architecture

Heroic Design

Heroic shots are those that must carry over an obstacle in order to gain a favorable position but where there is ample room to hit around the obstacle. Golfers can incrementally adjust the shot to aim either more

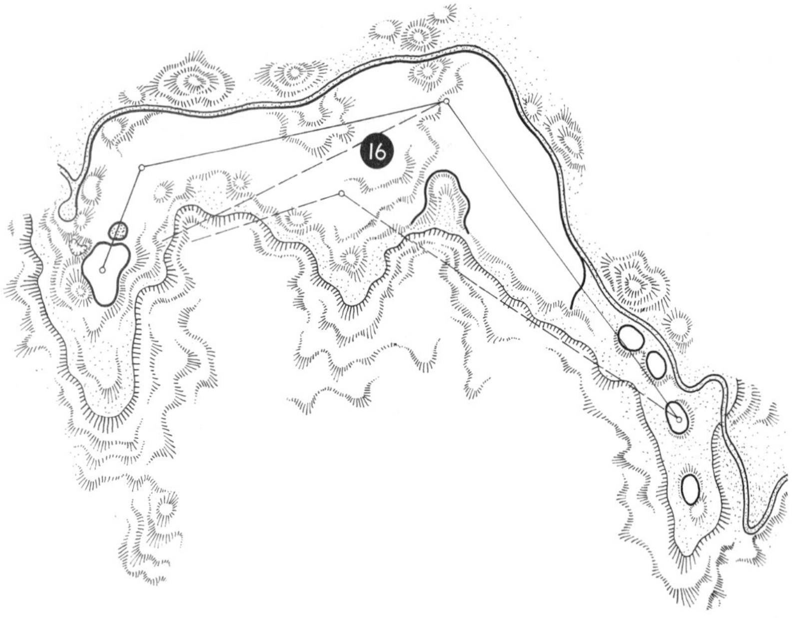

FIGURE 5-21
The heroic shots occur here at the tee and at the second shot, depending on where the tee shot is placed. The entire left of the hole is defined by a steep cliff that meanders from the tee to the green. The green sits out on a point. The successful heroic shot at the tee will put the golfer in position to reach the green in two with a relatively short approach. For the tee shot that is played conservatively, a heroic shot opportunity is afforded at the second shot to reach the green. The conservative shot here sets up a short third-shot approach when played away from the hazard. Many golf holes, especially par 5s, are not generally all heroic or all detour in makeup. Rather, most par-4 and par-5 holes require a combination of strategies that change depending on the ability of the individual golfer.

FROM THE ROUTING PLAN FOR WHITNEY RANCH MESA; REFER TO FIGURE 7-5 FOR THE COMPLETE ROUTING PLAN

over the obstacle or more away from it, depending on the level of excitement desired. A hero is the guy who clears the hazard or obstacle in the greatest dimension. The classic example of heroic design is the shot over a diagonal hazard that extends into the golf hole. The expression "bite off as much as you can chew" is often associated with heroically designed holes and shots. Again: *All holes and shots are strategic.*

Detour Design

Detour shots, unlike heroic shots, offer distinct pathways around obstacles. The choice is to deal with the obstacle or hazard or not. This is not to say that heroic and detour design principles cannot be blended; in many instances, they are. If, for example, a lake presents a heroic opportunity, there may also be a wide and slightly longer fairway route to the hole along which the lake is taken almost completely out of play. In this case, the golfer faces shot options that are both heroic and detour in nature. And, for the mathematicians, you have just added to the 280 variables noted earlier.

The difficulties that make a hole really interesting are usually those in which a great advantage can be gained in sucessfully accomplishing heroic carries over hazards of an impressive appearance....
—Alister MacKenzie, Golf Architecture

Detour shots are shots around. Split fairways and isolated hazards sitting almost in the middle ground of a hole create detour options from which the golfer must choose—and the more the merrier. In golf, detours are good. They prompt thinking and problem solving. They bring out the best in golfers without requiring reliance on length. A drawback, however, is that detour shots often require extra width. Two routes—two fairways—take up more room than just one.

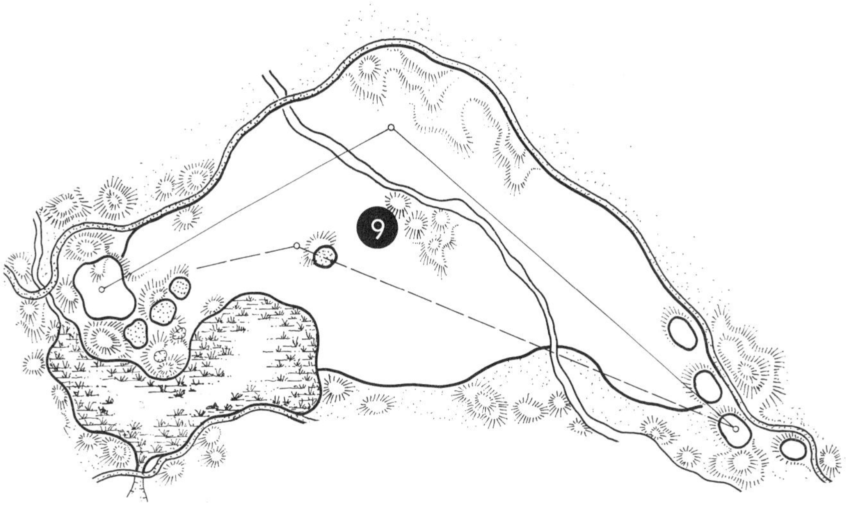

FIGURE 5-22

The detour shot is played from the tee along one of two routes: well right of the stream that bisects the hole, or to the left. The small pot bunker to the left further defines options—detours—that may be taken when playing in that direction. A player may elect to play closer to the wetlands, shortening the approach, or toward the stream, slightly lengthening the approach. This is a classic detour hole in that its shots are clearly optional in nature without approaching the heroic.

FROM THE ROUTING PLAN FOR WHITNEY RANCH MESA; REFER TO FIGURE 7-2 FOR THE COMPLETE ROUTING PLAN

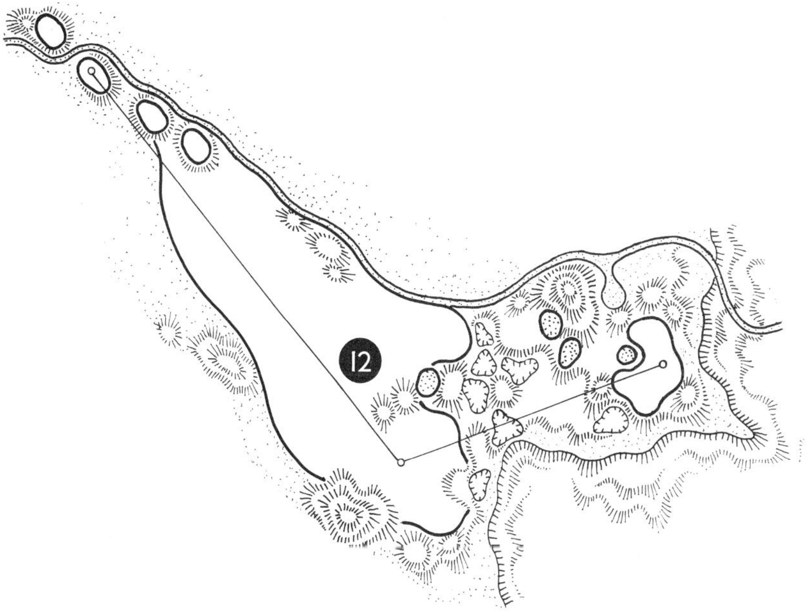

FIGURE 5-23

This par 4 requires a lay-up off the tee for all but the very long player, who may try the Hail Mary shot to the well-guarded green. Options are presented to control the direction and length of the lay-up shot as shown in the wide fairway. The rough ground beyond the landing area is in turf but not an ideal place to position a tee shot. The best lay-up holes require thought beyond just hitting shorter. Without some degree of choice and decision, the forced lay-up shot can be a letdown.

FROM THE ROUTING PLAN FOR WHITNEY RANCH MESA; REFER TO FIGURE 7-2 FOR THE COMPLETE ROUTING PLAN

Lay-up Design

It can be said that a lay-up shot is up to the golfer and may be invoked at any moment in the round, even on penal, heroic, and detour shots. This is true. The hallmark of the true lay-up is *force.* The design condition that *forces* a shot to be played well short of a full shot cannot be considered either heroic or a detour. The lay-up shot is not always liked or appreciated, but it is nonetheless a part of the game. It can be brought about by playing conditions or through the use of a particular set of tees. That extremely penal lake fronting the green can require a lay-up shot when the wind is howling and the tees are back, but this is only a temporary condition. The lake fronting the green is meant to be carried and is therefore penal in nature on any other day.

The reason that lay-up design is not well liked is because it takes the element of gamble out of the golfer's arsenal. If a shot is forced to be hit short, there is no real decision, only restraint. Aside from the possibility of a heroic shot by a skilled golfer to clear the obstacle that has caused the lay-up condition, the element of option is all but eliminated.

A lay-up design is probably best deployed on shortish par 4s at the tee shot. This interruption of brute force, when used sparingly, can be an interesting diversion. The best of all worlds is the lay-up shot that involves a degree of heroic and/or detour playing. Lay-up design, in these cases, brings even more decision making into the picture. Obviously, it has little use at par-3 holes, but great examples of par 3s where a lay-up area has been provided do exist. Merely having a lay-up area, however, does not necessarily constitute lay-up design. The lay-up area is provided as an option, not as a primary landing point. The most famous example of a par 3 embracing this design is the 16th at Cypress Point Club, a MacKenzie masterpiece. In reality the 16th at Cypress is heroic, detour and lay-up all wrapped into one.

A CASE FOR THE LAY-UP

More than 50 percent of the shots taken in golf involve just 14 percent of the clubs a golfer carries. This holds true on an 18-hole course comprising four par 3s, four par 5s, and 10 par 4s, where the golfer is assumed to hit a driver at all of the par 4s and par 5s and putts about 36 strokes. The rest of the clubs, unless they are occasionally put to use on the tee of the par 4s and par 5s, are significantly underused in comparison to the driver and putter.

Open Design

Open design is typically boring, with nothing-to-it fairways that are not encumbered by hazards, twists, obstacles, or anything else. The object is just to get there. That such shots and holes exist in golf is no reason to design more of them. To create abundant shot requirements that are completely open in their design is to go against the origins of golf and its point. Open design strategy should be reserved for appropriate points in a routing. Examples include leading up to a particularly difficult penal shot on a hole or for starting holes of a round. Even then, there should always be some obstacle and choice.

FIGURE 5-24

Both the tee shot and the second shot are relatively open in this example of open design strategy. Although not condoned in a vast majority of instances, open design can be tolerated at the beginning hole of most courses. This one is, in fact, the first hole within a routing. The idea is to allow the golfer room to get away and not be too intimidated. The backdrop to this hole is dramatic, with cliffs towering above the green by 70 to 80 feet. The hole is anything but boring, which is the feeling to avoid. The need for hazards to define the alignment is also minimized by the fact that the fairway is isolated turf bordered by native grasses and terrain.

FROM THE ROUTING PLAN FOR WHITNEY RANCH MESA; REFER TO FIGURE 7-2 FOR THE COMPLETE ROUTING PLAN

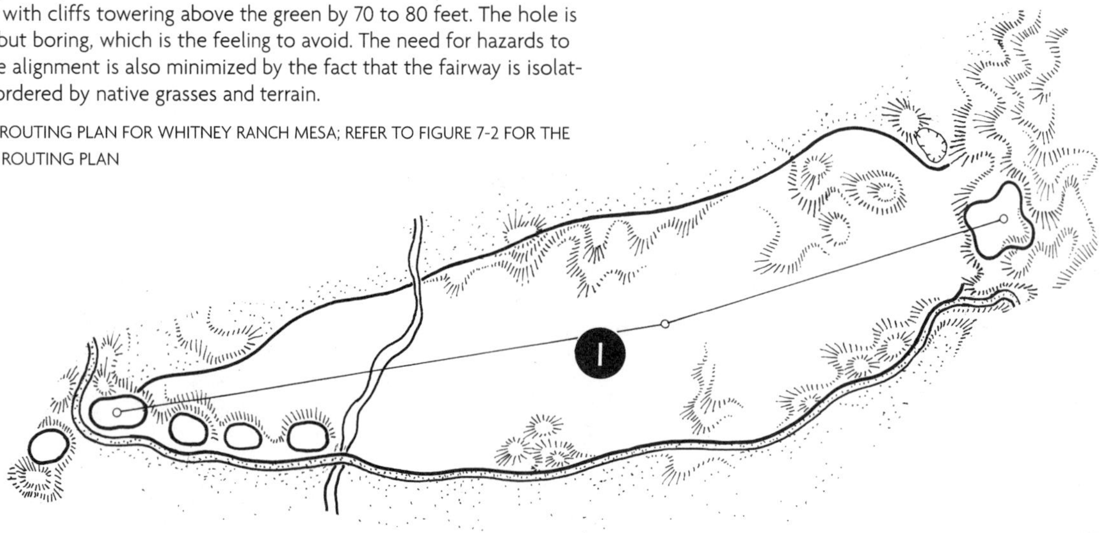

MAINTENANCE NEEDS

The maintenance components of a golf course cannot be forgotten. When maintenance is relegated to an afterthought, the resulting problems can have a lasting negative effect on the conditions of the course. The components of the maintenance operation of a golf course typically includes the following:

- Access and road to facility
- Parking area for employees and visitors
- Maintenance building
- Maintenance yard
  Outdoor storage, fuel tanks, trash receptacle, and wash areas.
- Storage and staging areas
  Satellite areas, sometimes elsewhere on the course property, for storage or staging of seasonal operations such as overseeding.
- Turf nursery
- Practice range service area
  An area designated to house range equipment, ball-washing facilities, etc.
- Golf cart storage building
- Irrigation pump house
- Irrigation supply tank

Obviously, not each of these items is present at all facilities. And rarely are all of the many maintenance-oriented components in one place, all tidy and convenient. Location is a matter of available space, planning and logistics. Certain elements *need* to be in one place. The maintenance building and primary yard, for instance, need to have available parking. But it may not be feasible to locate a turf nursery immediately at this location, which is tolerable. A pump house is likely best located near the main irrigation source, and this very well may not be near the maintenance building. A cart storage building is best situated near the clubhouse, or even part of the clubhouse, so it may be remote from the maintenance area altogether. When maintenance components are spread out it is essential that maintenance access paths connect each component, or at least that the network of paths on the course is suitable for such access.

The size of the components ranges widely and depends on the type of golf course, number of golf holes, practice facilities, amount of play the course will receive, and a host of other factors, the least of which is not budget. Budget for the maintenance operation facilities—which tends to reflect the complexity of the course and how many crew members it requires—will drive their size and extent. The following are average sizes of the primary maintenance operation components for an 18-hole regulation course:

- Parking
  1.5 spaces per full-time employee (a course with 12 full-time employees would require 18 spaces, or roughly 7000 square feet in parking area).
- Maintenance yard
  1.0 to 2.0 acres with an enclosed structure covering approximately 7 percent of the total yard area. This suggests a building footprint between 3000 and 6000 square feet.

- Turf nursery
  12,000 square feet of turf area, including surrounds.
- Practice range service area
  Usually a small structure of no more than 500 to 750 square feet.
- Golf cart storage
  A rough calculation of the enclosed area required may be made by multiplying the number of carts in the fleet by 75 square feet and adding 1000 square feet to this total for a wash and maintenance area. A fleet of 60 carts would calculate as 60 × 75 s.f. + 1000 s.f. = 5500 s.f. This allows for moderate efficiency in parking and provides for drive aisles, maneuvering, etc.
- Irrigation pump house/area
  Typically 200 to 500 square feet. Access must be provided for service and crane parking.

All maintenance areas should be programmed by the greenkeeper, and the project planner and architects should give careful attention to integrating the facilities with the overall look and feel of the golf course and other facilities.

Of special note is the need to make sure that access to the maintenance operations is efficient. Often, a facility is located in an out-of-the-way area, but if a longer access route to this area is required it will be itself a negative. Not only is there associated cost with building, landscaping, and maintaining a long access drive, but there will likely be more impact from the comings and goings to a remote facility. Additionally, the storage of fuel, fertilizers, and application products for the golf course must be carefully considered in determining facility size, and this may, in turn, affect the location decision. Typically, yards cannot be located in flood plains or areas where runoff from the yard would impose on sensitive habitats or drainageways.

OTHER COURSE FACILITIES & USES

Golf courses have other components that sometimes become afterthoughts to the planning and routing effort. This is a shame, as the eventual results reek of poor planning. Examples include:

- Comfort stations
  On-course restrooms
- Rain shelters
- Snack bar
- Starter shack
- Range attendant shelter/building
- Tournament scoreboard area

The list multiplies when the potential needs of golf tournaments are added. In resort operations, the complexities of event areas, outdoor spaces, and similar facilities can be significant. At a course completed long ago, the resort operator wanted to know if we could integrate an amphitheater with the grassy hillside above the second green. A convenient *U*-shaped hillside, 30-feet high, wrapped around behind the green, making an ideal place for outdoor concerts when the weather was nice. By integrating this concept at the second hole, where play would be finished early in the afternoon, we were able to provide the resort with an excellent place to stage evening concerts and programs. The stage was further facilitated by a series of ponds with waterfalls cascading between them, which provided an isolated area on which a platform could be built to accommodate lighting and sound equipment.

I was never completely in favor of this concept until I received a call, many years later, from the superintendent of the course, who suggested I attend an evening event where the venue would be given its greatest test ever. The division of Yamaha that makes jet-skis rented the entire resort to accommodate their annual dealer conference. About 2000 dealers from around the world were there to see the latest in Yamaha jet-skis. The main lake was where the jet-skis were exhibited, and the event included a live band, stunt demonstrations, and late-night fireworks. Here we were on the second green area (covered in plywood to prevent damage), and people were relaxing under the stars and enjoying a golf course that had gone off to sleep several hours earlier. It was an amazing example of overlay use and very likely resulted hundreds of thousands of dollars in revenue for my client.

FUTURE EXPANSION & NEEDS

It is impossible to account up front for everything that might occur in the future. We do not know, for instance, what technological advances and developments will increase needs for acreage or features of golf courses. For that matter, we also do not know what advances and developments might possibly reduce the need for acreage. I have often dreamed of a golf ball that would know when it was too far astray and also the difference between bunkers and breakfast nooks. Obviously, such an invention would significantly minimize the buffers and safeguards we build into golf courses from all perspectives associated with the hitting of the ball.

Remodeling, renovation, restoration, and rebuilding are all part of the future of a golf facility. Planning during routing, or at least taking a look into the crystal ball, can do much to help future undertakings go more smoothly and achieve better results. For this reason, future and possible needs deserve our attention and thought in the routing process. Here is a list to get you thinking—my apologies that it cannot be complete:

- Future road and highway development
- Additional power lines and utility easements
- Golf schools and academies
  Meeting areas, separate practice areas, and related facilities.
- Tournaments
  Parking, staging, and exhibition areas.
- Residential areas
  Future needs and services.
- Resort areas
  Rooms, timeshare units, and grounds.

The Checklist of Golf Course Components

Golf courses are made up of individual pieces. It is up to the designer to put them together so the cracks and grooves between their parts are hardly noticeable. Much like commencing a challenging jigsaw puzzle, the first step is to make sure you have all of the pieces before you begin. Check to be sure none have inadvertently fallen behind the sofa.

THE ARRIVAL:
- ☐ Entry
- ☐ Peeks & Hints
- ☐ The Threshold
- ☐ Bag Drop & Parking

CLUBHOUSE & GROUNDS:

Clubhouse Components
- ☐ Lobby
- ☐ Proshop
- ☐ Restaurant
- ☐ Bar
- ☐ Snack Window
- ☐ Outdoor Seating
- ☐ Locker Rooms
- ☐ Restrooms
- ☐ Behind-the-Scenes Facilities
- ☐ Golf Cart Storage

The Grounds
- ☐ Putting Greens
- ☐ Open Lawns
- ☐ Golf Cart Staging
- ☐ Starter's Shack
- ☐ Scoreboard
- ☐ Special Event Area
- ☐ Swimming Pool

PRACTICE FACILITIES:

Practice Hitting Area
- ☐ Main Teeing Area
- ☐ Target Greens
- ☐ Practice Sand Bunkers
- ☐ Uneven Hitting Areas
- ☐ Teaching / Lesson Tees
- ☐ Double-Ended Tee
- ☐ Cart Parking, Sitting & Shaded Areas
- ☐ Range Attendant Counter

Other Practice Facilities
- ☐ Practice Putting Greens
- ☐ Short Game Practice Green
- ☐ Buffer Areas

PRACTICE FACILITIES— *Continuation*

Alternative Facilities
- ☐ Putting Courses
- ☐ Separate Tees for Golf Schools
- ☐ Practice Holes
- ☐ Short Courses
- ☐ Designated Youth Areas
- ☐ Areas for Working w/Disabled Golfers
- ☐ Digital Practice Facilities

MAINTENANCE NEEDS:
- ☐ Structure
- ☐ Yard
- ☐ Access to Facility
- ☐ Nursery
- ☐ Irrigation Reservoir
- ☐ Pumphouse Locations

THE GOLF HOLES:

Tees
- ☐ Surface Area
- ☐ Alignment
- ☐ Width
- ☐ Length
- ☐ Visibility
- ☐ Access
- ☐ Disabled Access
- ☐ Maintenance
- ☐ Safety
- ☐ Seclusion
- ☐ Back Tees
- ☐ Championship Tees
- ☐ Regular Tees
- ☐ Senior Tees
- ☐ Family Tees
- ☐ Forward Tees

Greens
- ☐ Green Size
- ☐ Features Nearby
- ☐ Green Access
- ☐ Cart Path Relationship

Other Components
- ☐ Fairway & Landing Areas
- ☐ Roughs
- ☐ Cart Paths
- ☐ Drop Areas
- ☐ Buffer Areas
- ☐ Drainage Areas
- ☐ Maintenance Access

GOLF HOLES – PAR, LENGTH & ORIENTATION:

Par
- ☐ Per Hole
- ☐ Per 9 Holes
- ☐ Per 18 Holes

Length
- ☐ Per Hole
- ☐ Per 9 Holes
- ☐ Per 18 Holes

GOLF HOLES – THEIR SHOT STRATEGY:
- ☐ Penal Design
- ☐ Heroic Design
- ☐ Detour Design
- ☐ Lay-Up Design
- ☐ Open Design

OTHER COURSE FACILITIES:
- ☐ Rain Shelters
- ☐ Resort Access
- ☐ Snack Bar
- ☐ Tournament Staging
- ☐ Corporate Area Tents
- ☐ Public Uses
- ☐ Retention

FUTURE EXPANSION NEEDS:
- ☐ Future Road & Highway Development
- ☐ Additional Powerlines & Utility Easements
- ☐ Golf Schools & Academies
- ☐ Tournament Possibilities
- ☐ Residential Areas
- ☐ Resort Areas

A checklist of golf course components that can be used as a guide in programming, planning, and designing.

Real Estate, the Almighty Influence

HOLE NO.

6

by Gil Martinez

And there shall be a golf course, said the developer. Real estate forces, especially related to residential and resort development, impel a high percentage of the golf courses being built today. The perfect amalgamation of a popular recreational activity and project enhancement lies in the fact that golf courses provide magnificent views, offer recreational opportunity for all ages and sexes, make great buffers, preserve view corridors and open space, protect sensitive habitat, make use of otherwise unusable land—and, of course, they can increase land values and increase residential absorption rates.

There is nothing more alluring to a golfer than arriving at the clubhouse, being greeted by friendly faces, smelling the morning air and fresh-cut grass, the sound of trickling water, and the anticipation of a magnificent day as he looks out over a beautiful, serene golf course. This scene is built into a well-designed and well-conceived golf course community, where the resident desires many of the same experiences. All one's senses must be enticed to create a sense of place, a sense of home.

The social elements of design are extremely important—most engineers don't even dream of these.
—Desmond Muirhead

A theme must coalesce the community and weave a fabric of pedestrian-friendly, socially enhancing, active, and passive recreational opportunities and, finally, a sense of community and home (the sense that this is my place, I live here, and it's wonderful).

As a land planner, it is my role to discover in a piece of land its highest and best use that supports the developer's objectives coupled with local and regional goals and socioeconomic needs. A golf course makes sense only if the developer can sell his project to his investors and lenders. And, if a golf course makes sense economically, physically, and politically, we must look at the land not only through the golfer's eyes but also through those of the future resident, the merchant, the golf course operator, the passerby, the guest, the surrounding community, and the politician.

Whether a project is driven by resort, residential, or other real estate forces, we must look to find harmony and balance among all proposed uses. This analysis is done by studying the land from social, economic, political, physical, and even cultural and historical aspects. Once those factors are identified and understood, it is the job of the master planner to create a project that is timeless and successful—and a place people want to be, to live, to visit, and to use for recreation, whether they are golfers, residents, vacationers, visitors, or shoppers.

WILL IT MAKE SENSE?

Before we think about routing a golf course for a community, we must ask ourselves if the addition of a golf course makes economic sense. Detailed and thorough market studies should be conducted in addition to land use studies. Is there enough land? In order to build a successful golf community, you generally need, at minimum, 450 acres. An analysis that compares the demands and rewards of golf and no-golf real estate development is critical to your decision-making process and, ultimately, the success of your venture. This golf versus no-golf real estate and demand analysis should be undertaken early in the process.

Ideally, the addition of a golf course contributes to an increase in land values of 15 to 30 percent—if not more—and stimulates absorption rates by the same factor. If this is not projected, it may not make sense to build the golf course unless other compelling factors drive it. Regardless, golf should enhance the land, not detract from it. After the study is conducted, the developer must ask himself if he is still in the market to build a golf course.

UNDERSTANDING YOUR MARKET

In order to decide whether or not to build a golf course, you must know what questions to ask, and why. Fundamental to the decision and the overall process is the answer to this question: Who will make up the buyers, visitors, etc.? A residential golf course operation should be self-sus-

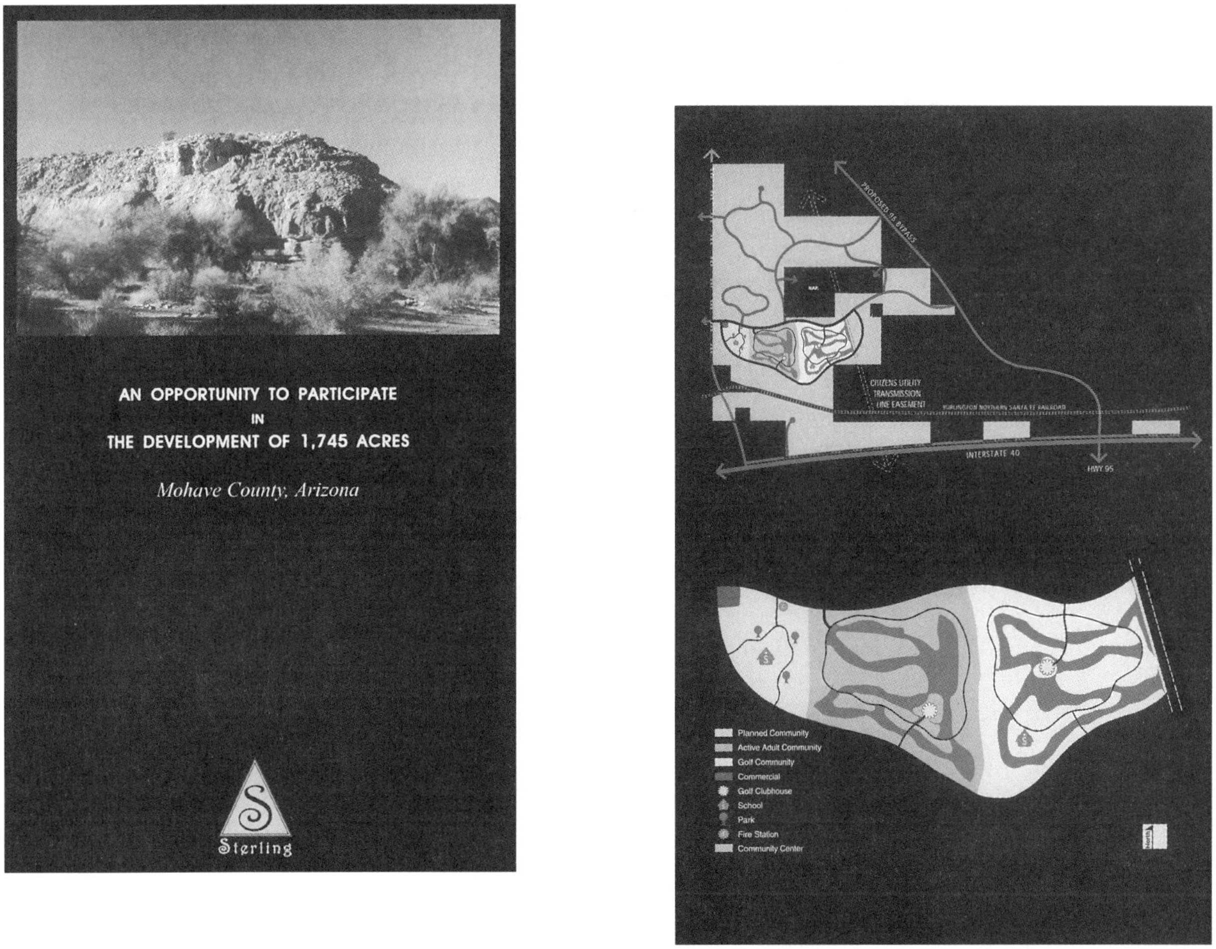

FIGURE 6-1
The process of market research, feasibility study, and initial master planning are often articulated in a presentation format that embodies the overall project strategy and accountability. In this example, a bound booklet, every aspect of a large-scale project is covered, including the land use plan.

COURTESY OF GMA INTERNATIONAL

taining, creating a symbiotic yet independent business endeavor from the real estate. One must also analyze both local and regional demand for both golf and real estate. This analysis quantifies the community buyer.

After the economics are quantified, it is essential to understand the viability of your project with respect to the motivations of potential buyers. Factors might include a look at how baby boomers are inheriting their parents' wealth and coming into their own, looking for a nice place to live and engage in a life sport—how this segment of buyers is leaving behind tennis and skiing for golf. In this analysis, it also makes sense to discover the political viability of building a golf course. As desirable as the financial outcome may appear, an understanding of and familiarity with local political personalities and issues is critical before rendering the final golf/no-golf decision.

To best understand the market in all its aspects, it is advisable to engage a reputable market research firm to work with your land planner and team to discover and identify potential obstacles to the development. Once these obstacles are known, it is possible to create the vision for the highest and best uses for the land. The professional qualifications

I know that many of you remember when houses were built around golf courses. It seems as though today that golf courses are built around houses.
—*Bill Yates, in* Florida Golf News

of your design team should expedite your development process. The credentials of this team will signal to potential lenders the viability of your project.

When the answer is "yes" for golf, based on thorough analysis, your next decision is about the type of facility to plan and ultimately develop. For example, will it be an exclusive private club, a friendly course for play by resort guests, or an age-restricted community that occasionally allows public play? Fine-tuning the precise nature of the development that makes sense in the market is crucial.

THE PHYSICAL PLAN

Now we can look at the physical aspects of routing the community golf course in concert with residential and other land uses. The fundamental features of good community design also drive good golf course routing design—and, as with any good design, the land drives the solution. A good designer looks for features in a piece of land that will be opportunities and those that will be constraints. One must understand the land. After visiting and studying the various aspects of a piece of land, an opportunities and constraints map can be created that shows the topography, severity of slope, significant land features, shorelines, water sources, drainage areas, views, and natural vegetation. This map will serve as a foundation for determining how the land should be planned.

A golf course solution in a residential community can help mitigate constraints by converting them into unique golf course features or can help preserve magnificent neighboring and regional views, making for a great real estate market and lasting impressions.

Locating Access Points & Utilities

Access is a critical component, and it typically involves more than a single point. Knowing how many access points are required—and desired—is a first step. Simultaneously, it is important to minimize the number of street crossings that golfers will encounter as they make their way around the golf course.

In many instances, a golf routing plan can utilize utility easements and other rights of way. This practice can make for efficient land utilization, as many times these parcels cannot be used for any other productive purpose.

Defining Building Pods & Potential Golf Areas

We find that, often, the location of the clubhouse is key in closing real estate sales. For this reason, not to mention the golf experience itself, the clubhouse should be situated to take advantage of spectacular views or a great setting. Intuitively, the clubhouse would be located at the highest location with the best views to the golf course; however, the elevation may expose rooftops or areas beyond the project boundaries

FIGURE 6-2
The initial step in working on a real estate-driven project, especially one of large scale, is to define land uses. This example shows a master land use plan for a large planned community that will be developed to include a range of residential lot sizes. At this stage, only building pods are indicated, and not the details of specific lots or home sites.

COURTESY OF GMA INTERNATIONAL

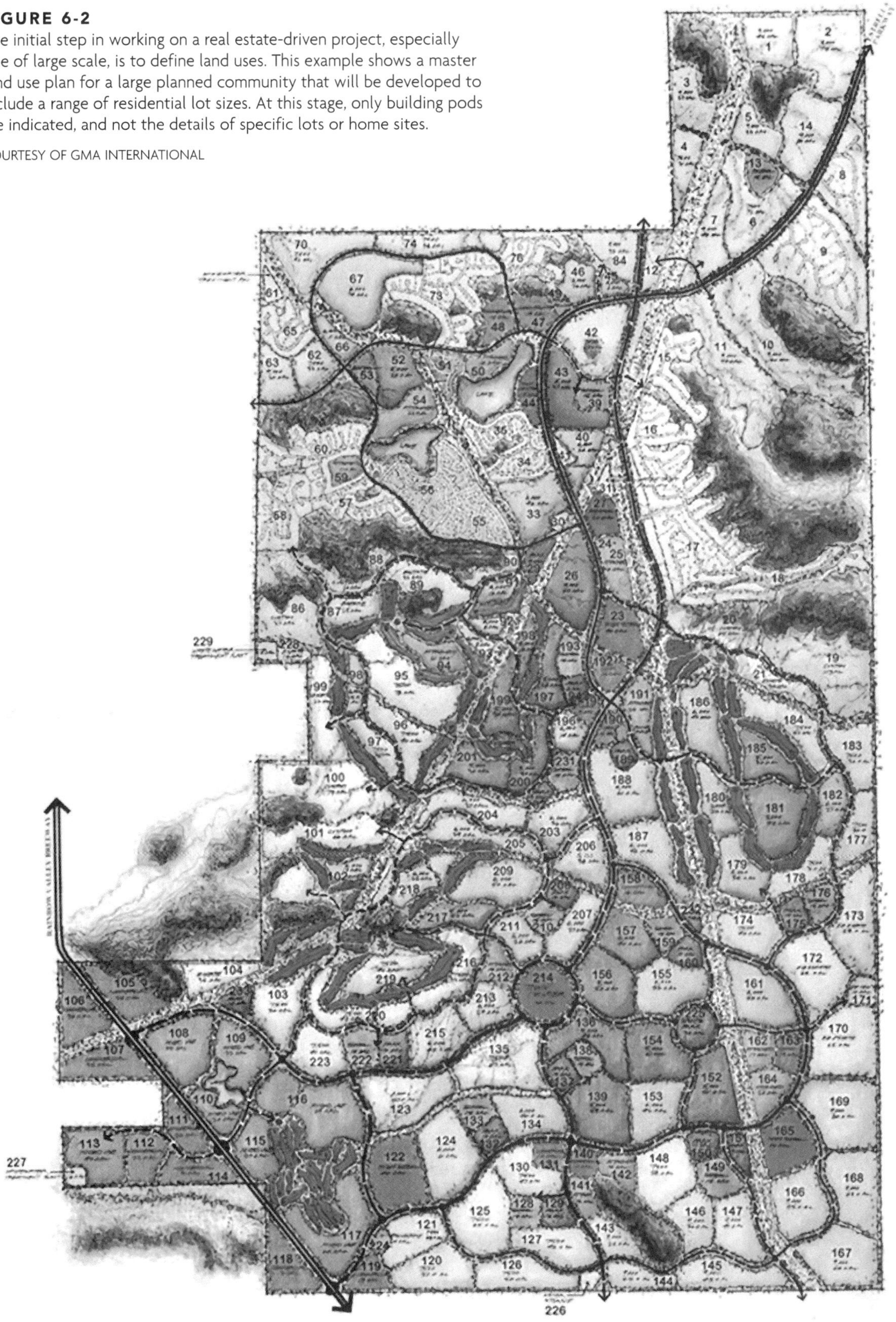

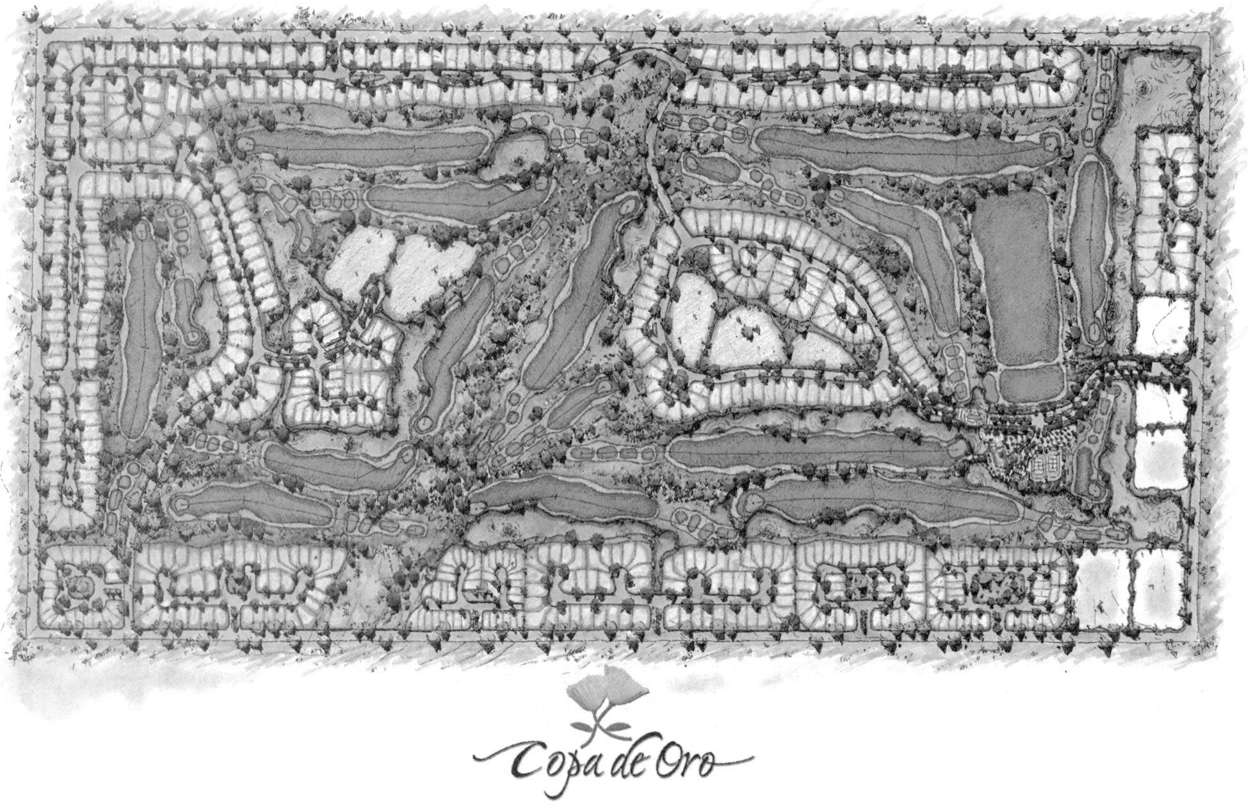

FIGURE 6-3
A compact site such as this one must be kept open in feeling. An excellent way to accomplish this is with a golf routing that keeps at least two holes together. Using this approach, the resident has a sense of expanse that would not be as positive if each of the fairways were lined on both sides by housing.

COURTESY OF GMA INTERNATIONAL

where the developer may not have control over the view impacts of future development. With these factors in mind, the location should also accommodate an area for two returning nine holes and have an area large enough for community events and gatherings.

Several routing scenarios should be developed based on the best clubhouse location. Especially important in real estate developments are view premiums; thus, the designer must evaluate golf course frontage view premiums, keeping in mind that views of the greens and water generate the highest premiums. Corridors should take advantage of the land, providing a great experience for the golfer while maintaining balance with the surrounding real estate and other facets of the land. For instance, long, straight rows of houses detract from a beautiful golf scene. A more natural-looking edge, with homes nestled into the environs and looking like they have been there forever, is a better approach. This can be accomplished in several ways: by varying building setbacks, incorporating cul-de-sacs, and clustering lots around lakes and watercourses to create better and longer views.

Locating the Maintenance Facility

The maintenance facility should be located centrally to the golf course, rather than at an end, whenever possible in order to keep operational costs and maintenance issues to a minimum. This will allow maintenance efforts to be evenly distributed to all areas for day-to-day opera-

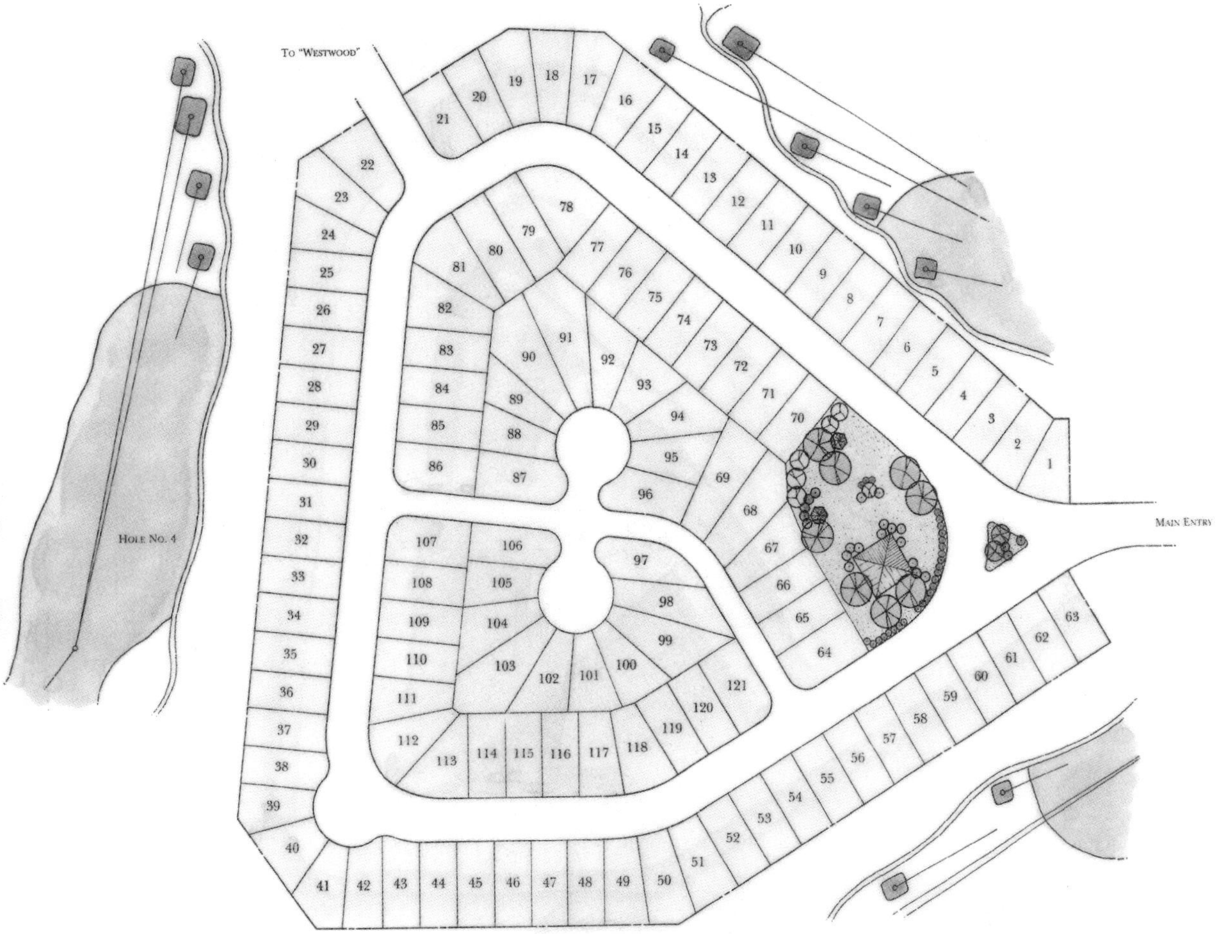

FIGURE 6-4
A relatively small building pod within a golf course routing can be made to have a character of its own. This conceptual plan for a golf village shows small lots that will be developed with attached porch homes, a cross between cabins and patio homes.

COURTESY OF FORREST RICHARDSON & ASSOC.; REFER TO FIGURE 10-4 FOR THE OVERALL ROUTING PLAN THAT INTEGRATES THIS DEVELOPMENT

tions. Unnecessary staff time to respond to areas will be minimized with a central location. Access to the maintenance facility should be carefully planned, and the facility itself should always be architecturally integrated to the community.

TIPS FOR SUCCESSFUL RESIDENTIAL GOLF ROUTINGS

Consider the following a notebook of sorts containing tips and thoughts about the nuances of routing relative to residential golf communities.

1. Golf versus No-Golf

Before you begin, study a golf/no-golf real estate sales analysis. How could the land considered for golf be used if not for golf? Ask yourself these questions: Does golf development make economic sense? How much will it increase land values, and how much will it stimulate absorption/sales? Engage the services of a marketing analyst to help you answer the questions.

2. Topography

Although a complex issue, topographical considerations really boil down to a matter of sorting out what land is appropriate for homes and what land is appropriate for golf. Appropriateness, in this case, depends on several factors: economic, physical, and characteristic. Some might be good for both, which leads to making choices for the betterment of the *overall* project.

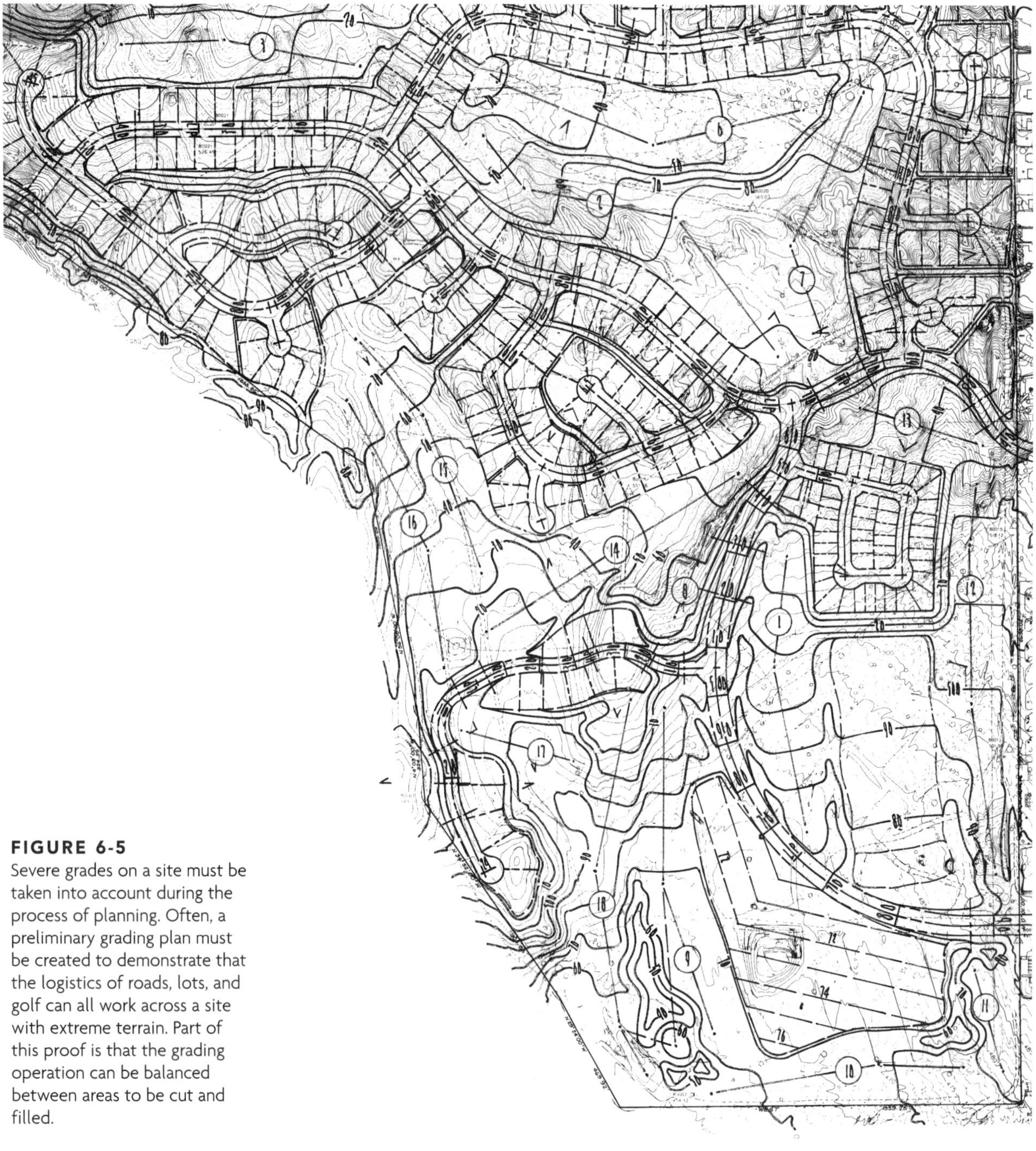

FIGURE 6-5
Severe grades on a site must be taken into account during the process of planning. Often, a preliminary grading plan must be created to demonstrate that the logistics of roads, lots, and golf can all work across a site with extreme terrain. Part of this proof is that the grading operation can be balanced between areas to be cut and filled.

FIGURE 6-6
Natural features include landforms, natural vegetation, ravines, rock outcroppings, and so on. Golf courses, because they are large areas of open space, are excellent vehicles whereby such features can be integrated with a real estate project. The routing can often complement the natural features, at the same time providing interest to both golfers and nongolfers.

COURTESY OF GMA INTERNATIONAL

3. Natural Features

Significant site features consist of boulders, shorelines, water, vegetation, and mature and/or specimen trees. Natural features should be linked together, as this creates a more harmonious and natural experience. Golf, ideally, should be in low areas and home sites kept higher. This helps protect homes from errant balls.

Managing the preservation and enhancement of environmental assets also involves consideration of soils, vegetation, wildlife, climate, wetlands, endangered species, habitat, character, and historic and cultural conditions.

4. Views

Interior views are among the most overlooked aspects of sight considerations. Views to points within the community are just as important as those to distant mountains, panoramas, and valleys beyond. Tees and greens should offer great views and settings. It is always advisable to create long views for lots abutting the golf course. This can be accomplished in many ways: by the orientation of the lot, having a core golf course (instead of a meandering routing through lots), or by mixing open-space uses with golf corridors.

FIGURE 6-7
Views are essential to any golf community. Too much emphasis is often placed on the view to the golf course and not enough on territorial views away from the golf. Here, at Superstition Mountain in Arizona, the golf course enables unrestricted views by providing the unbuilt openness that interrupts home sites and building areas.
COURTESY OF GMA INTERNATIONAL

5. Ongoing Evaluation

After each phase of discovery, it must be determined if the project is still feasible. In the end, the situation may change entirely. This is a part of the process of good land design.

6. Safety & Security

Will the surrounding community and residents be safe? This is a function of access, circulation, and easements. In terms of golf uses, are the setbacks and holes configured appropriately?

7. Multiple Options

Because every piece of land is different and there are many approaches to solving a problem, there are no set formulas or rubber stamps. The land should always drive the solution.

8. Balance

The quality of golf and frontage view lots is an essential ingredient. Might your project have a better outcome with core golf? Do returning nines make sense with respect to the layout of the residential community?

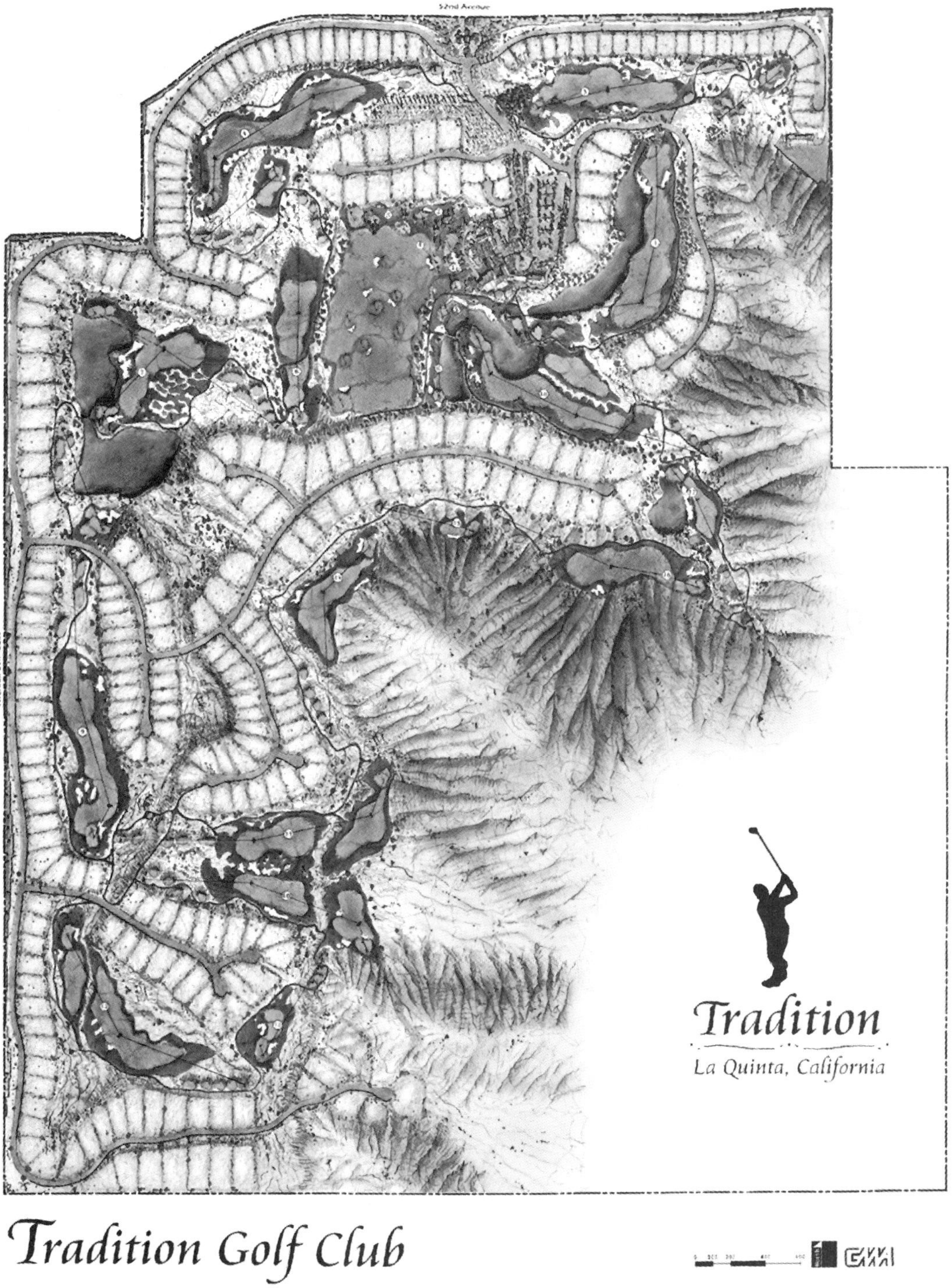

FIGURE 6-8
The main access for a site defines its orientation in terms of security. In this project, a definitive border separates the community from the outside world. A band of homes backs up to the perimeter on two edges, and the steep, mountainous land forms the protection on the opposite edges. Security goes deeper than physical security; a *sense of security* is often more important to the potential buyer than actual security. Projects that feel secure probably are.

COURTESY OF GMA INTERNATIONAL

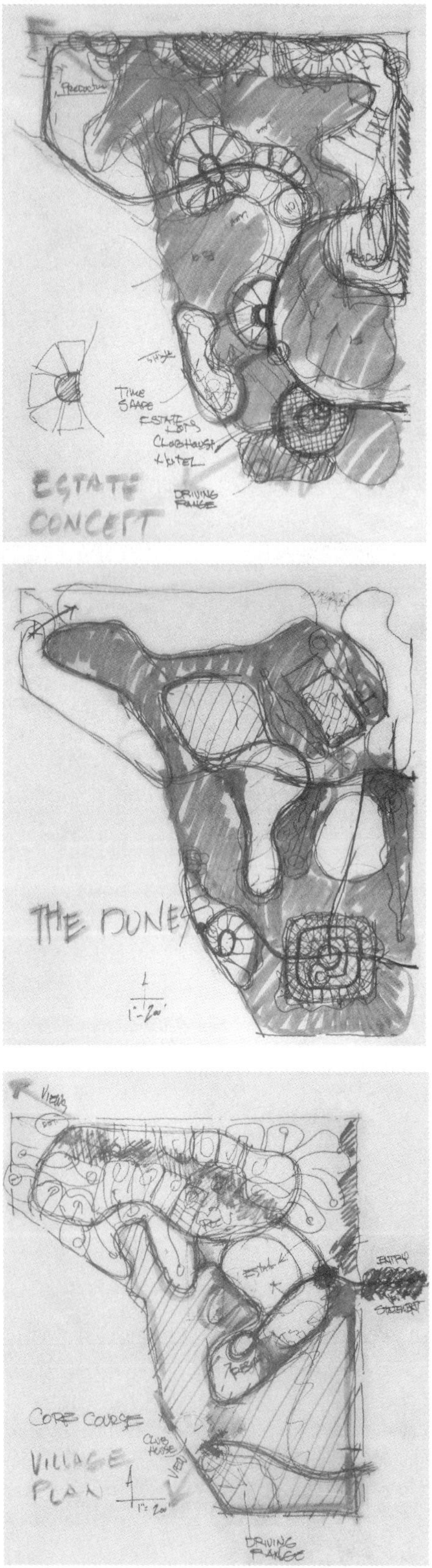

FIGURE 6-9
A progression of sketches shows the thought process of land planning for an 18-hole golf course and mixed-use community.
COURTESY OF FORREST RICHARDSON & ASSOC.

9. Golf Difficulty

Golf should look challenging but play friendly. This typically translates into the use of multiple tees to offer a diverse range of experiences, some with extreme back tees but a contrasting friendly set that can be played by a majority of golfers. Five sets of tees is a good standard, but fewer or even more may be appropriate depending on the course and the type of golfer expected to utilize it.

10. Golf for Nongolfers

Remember: People like to live around golf even if they don't play. The golf course should present every available opportunity for people to enjoy its expanse, vistas, and ambiance. Views to golf should be afforded in various key areas of the project—these are windows to the golf course that enhance the feeling of living in a golf course community. A golf course becomes a part of the "garden" of adjacent property. A 150-acre garden gives one the feeling of living on an estate or estancia. In this way, the golf course becomes part of the home.

11. Trails

Trails enhance marketability and can be integrated with a golf course to create connections between homes, common areas and amenities of a community.

12. Family Orientation

Initially, golf was played primarily by men. Then the game expanded to include women, and now the entire family is playing the game. This change in the popularity of golf is a byproduct of the changing complexion of the active family. Their demands and relationship to golf, as well as their recreational and social needs, will change as demands are met by the golf course and real estate developers. Important aspects of good golf planning in real estate projects are careful attention to developing new golfers, such as with learning areas, practice centers, and, where it can be accommodated, short courses that serve to bring new golfers into the game.

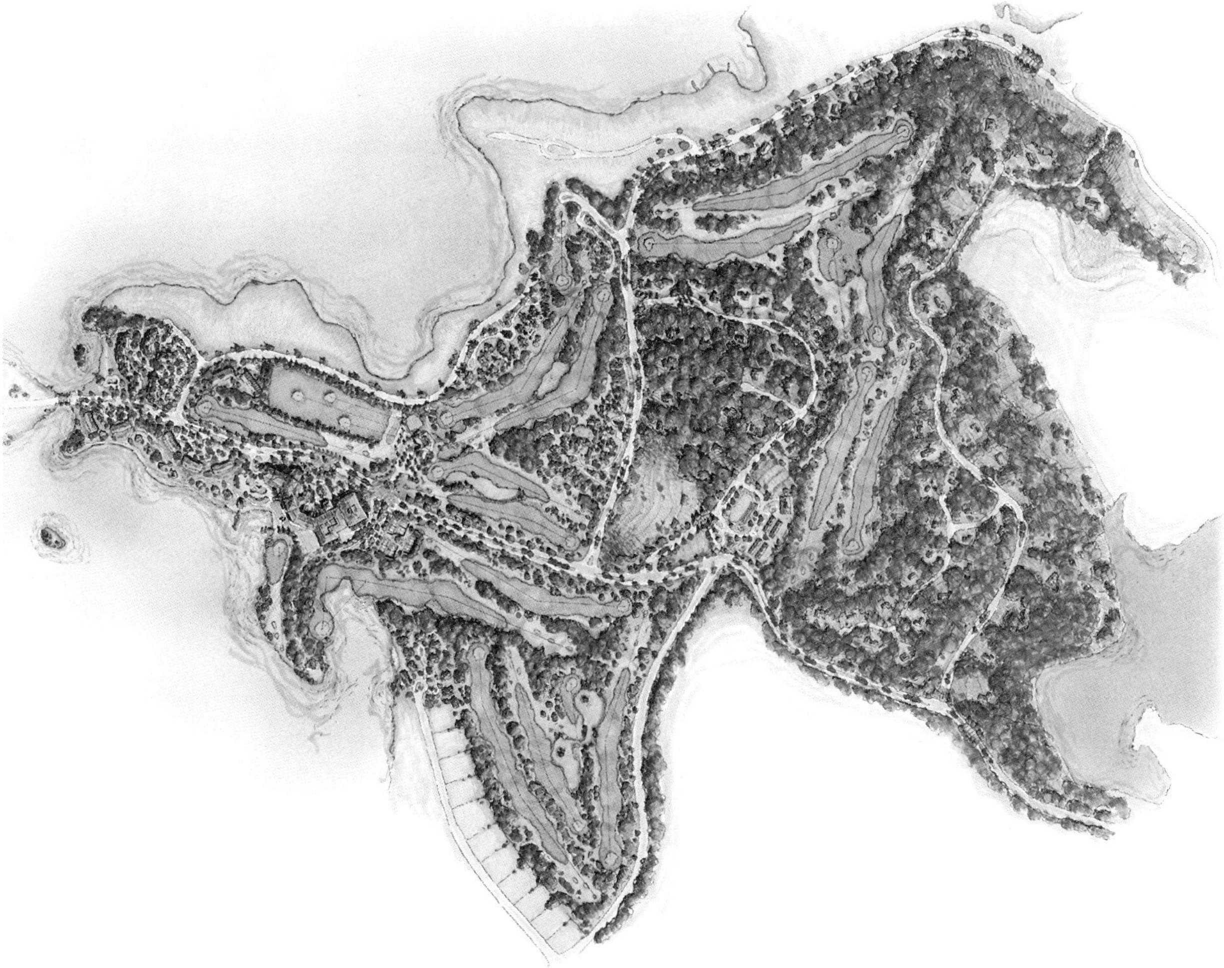

FIGURE 6-10
By taking advantage of a narrow peninsula jutting into a lake for golf holes, all users of the property are able to enjoy the view to the lake and feel as if they are oriented to the water.
COURTESY OF GMA INTERNATIONAL

The golf clubhouse must also be designed for family orientation. No longer is it acceptable to make the facility lopsidedly attractive to one type of user, especially in the true community setting.

13. Symbiotic Relationships

Golf course routing can bring together the areas of a planned community. When it forms connections within the entire land area of a development, the people who live there become related to common spaces, views, and activities. The golf course might radiate from a hub, or it might wind its way around while connecting various places through its open space and aesthetic.

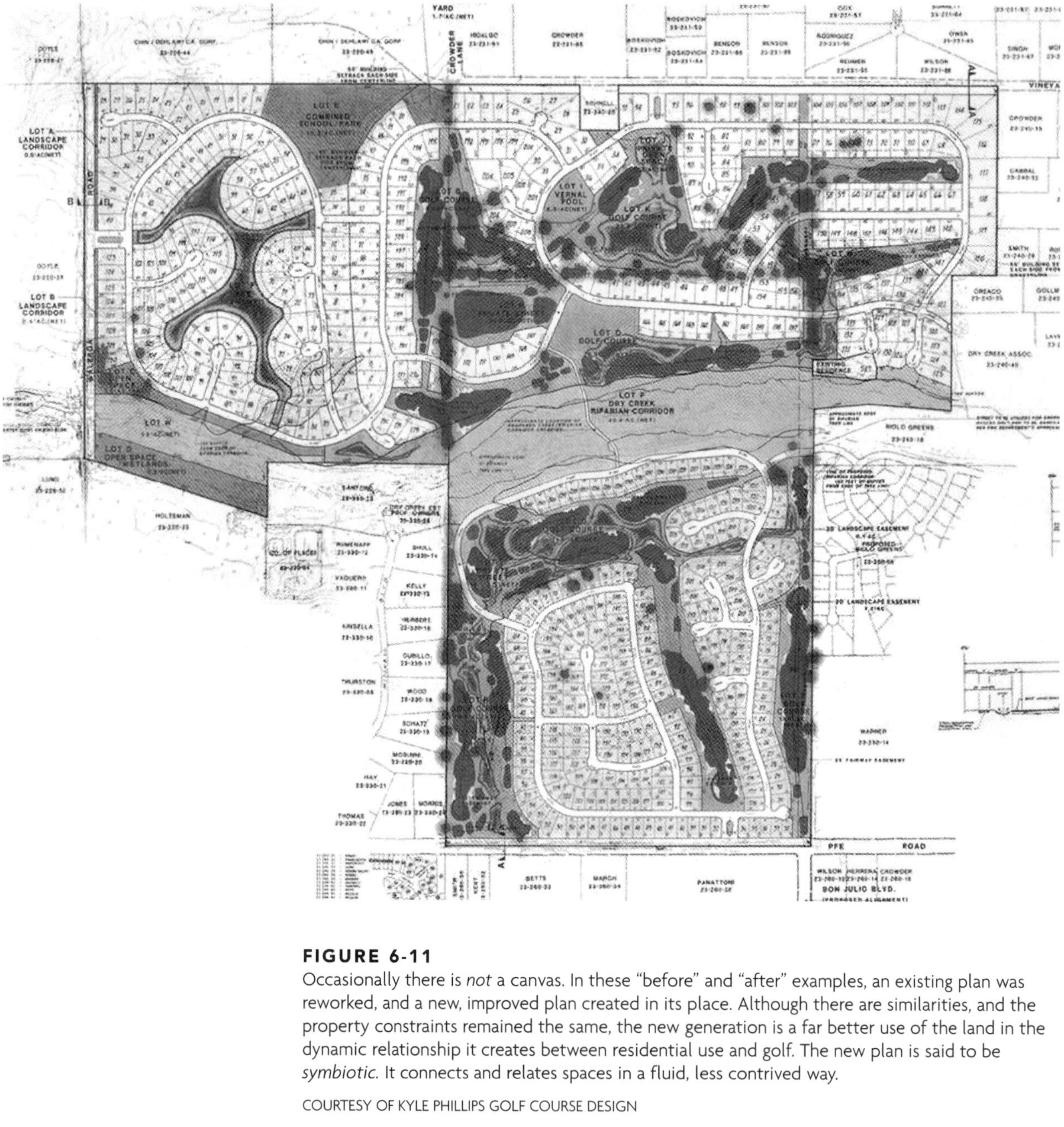

FIGURE 6-11
Occasionally there is *not* a canvas. In these "before" and "after" examples, an existing plan was reworked, and a new, improved plan created in its place. Although there are similarities, and the property constraints remained the same, the new generation is a far better use of the land in the dynamic relationship it creates between residential use and golf. The new plan is said to be *symbiotic*. It connects and relates spaces in a fluid, less contrived way.

COURTESY OF KYLE PHILLIPS GOLF COURSE DESIGN

14. Compromises

Never compromise the golf course and site with such poor design as parallel holes and orienting play into the morning or afternoon sun. These are but a few of the compromises that can work against a golf course plan within a community. Seldom is a plan entirely devoid of compromise—but this should be the goal of every planning effort.

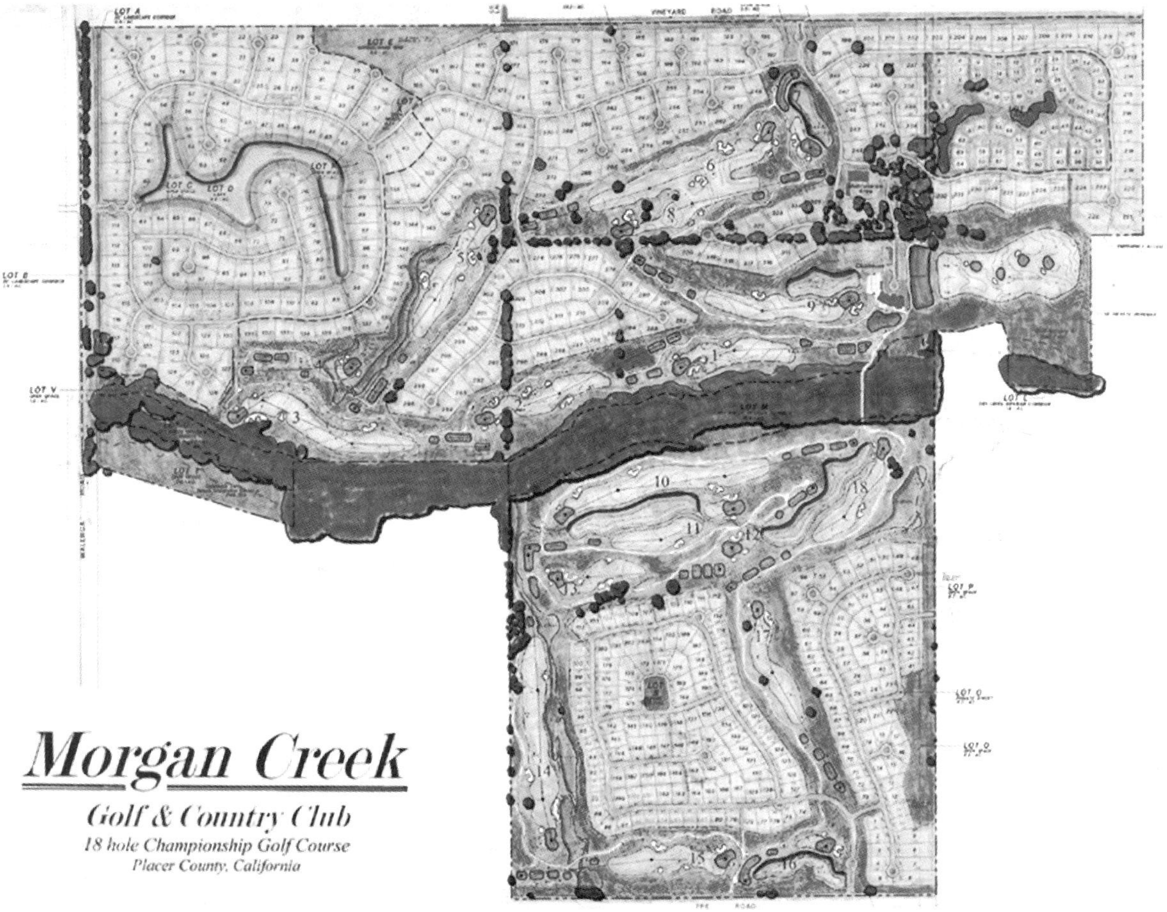

15. Course Flow

The golf course needs to be played in a reasonable time; to create a laborious round of golf is a sure way to create a bad impression on potential buyers of lots and homes. "Reasonable," of course, varies from project to project. There is a science to creating good course flow, and it is not specific to the real estate golf project. Within this book, you will find some excellent references to course flow and a concept known as *pace of play*. I recommend you read them thoroughly. ("Thoughts on the Pace of Play," writing by William Yates, is found within Hole 9 "Fitting Holes Together.")

16. Aesthetics

The routing of a golf course within a community sets up the dynamics of incorporating and connecting both natural and built site features. Taking advantage of natural aesthetics and blending them with embellishments created in the design is at the essence of good planning.

Without good architecture, all effort in planning, no matter how good, is for naught.
—Desmond Muirhead

17. Tournament Needs

A residential golf project may promote its name and reputation via a national or regional tournament. Although this is the exception rather than the rule, potential needs for staging and hosting a tournament should be duly considered. Spaces for galleries and staging areas, as well as areas for food and beverage sources and comfort stations, should be incorporated in the planning stages. When a tournament is in the cards, the tournament areas should be master planned so as not to adversely affect the future residences.

18. Climate

Solar and wind factors not only affect golf, they also affect residential areas and home sites. Again, this book addresses the effects of land and climate—it is simply worth repeating here that the impact of nature on a land parcel goes well beyond the golf aspects of the real estate golf project.

19. Regional & Local Factors

It is generally more difficult, and not nearly as rewarding, to go against the grain by trying to force a style or influence on a region. Authenticity is always more natural and comfortable than designs and styles that seem out of place. It is therefore important to know and understand what makes a region tick—and to capture these influences throughout the creative process.

20. Road Crossings

Road crossings are usually a necessary evil in a golf community—but, with creative planning, design, and landscaping, they can be a distinctive element of the overall design of the community. However, care must be taken to minimize road crossings in the design of the golf course and surrounding land uses. One way this can be accomplished is by keeping the golf course on the interior of a loop road from which islands of property can be accessed, thus obviating any need to cross a road. This is just one example of how crossings can be minimized. Where road crossings are necessary, they should be at intersections where it will be more efficient to direct the golfer safely and easily to the next hole. As a design progresses, thematic signs, special paving, and distinctive landscaping should orient the golfer and serve to warn drivers of the crossing. Wherever feasible, thematic bridges and undercrossings should be incorporated to minimize actual at-grade crossings of roads. This will maintain the flow and the feel of the golf experience as well as add effective design elements to the whole community. Ultimately, road crossings must be safe but should also tie into the overall design and feel of the golf course and community.

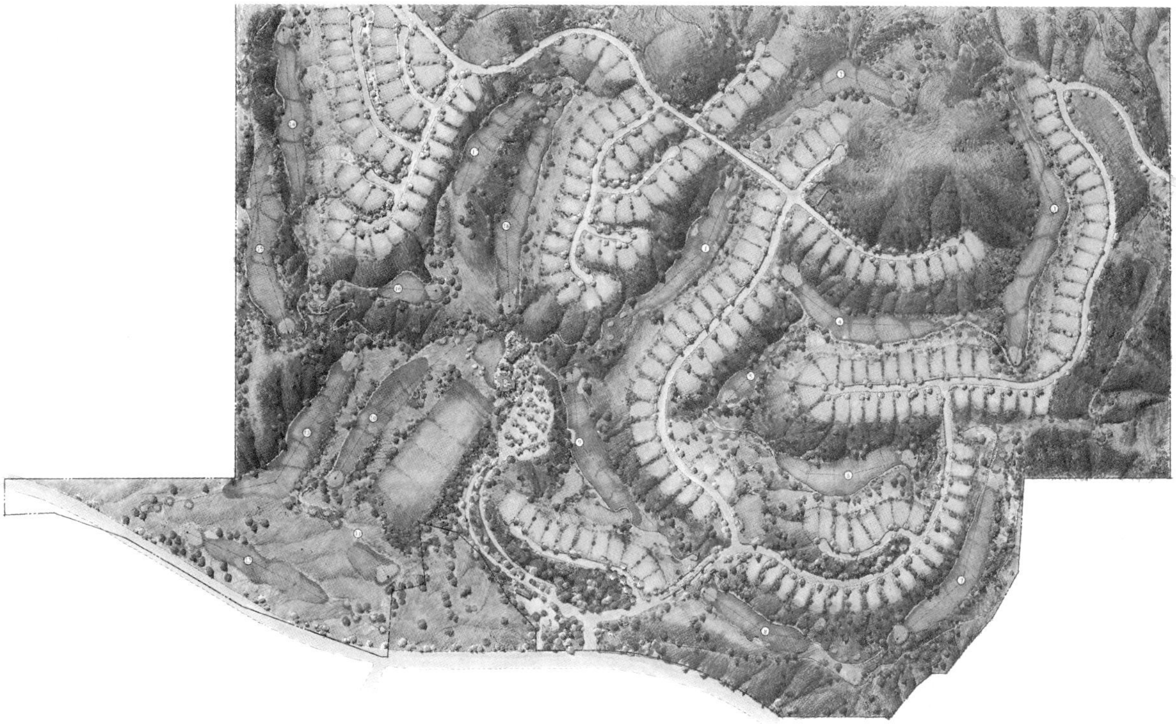

▪OWNER: HASLEY CANYON LAND COMPANY, L.L.C. ▪LAND PLANNERS: GMA

FIGURE 6-12
Occasionally, road crossings are unavoidable. In this example, with significant and steep terrain, the buildable areas were necessarily on the ridges, with the golf course meandering below. This situation made crossings necessary in order to connect the holes while permitting vehicular traffic to access each cluster of lots.

COURTESY OF GMA INTERNATIONAL

21. Maintenance Area

In addition to the general information above, the following tips are provided. The maintenance area is another challenge to the design of a real estate–oriented golf community. A maintenance area (consisting of a building and yard) must not only be functional but also centrally and strategically located to the golf course. It should not be an eyesore. You may be lucky enough to have a piece of land where the maintenance yard can be located in a hidden nook while retaining easy access to all parts of the golf course. Usually this is not the case, and the maintenance space will need to be integrated with the design of the community. This can be done creatively.

One approach is to buffer the yard with landscaping that weaves it into the fabric of the golf course. Walls, fences, and plantings that are thematically consistent with the surrounding uses can be an enhancement rather than a detraction. If the buildings and interior of the maintenance area are highly visible, they can be designed to appear as a home or extension of the clubhouse or other building. Parking should be adequately screened with landscaping, walls, and/or berms. Plantings can add to the oasis look of a maintenance yard if they are well maintained and attractively arranged. Using creative design techniques, the golf maintenance yard can actually be attractive to golfer and resident alike.

The access to a maintenance area may be the most important aspect of all. Direct access to a major road will help eliminate the need for planning for trucks and commercial traffic to and from the facility.

FIGURE 6-13
Planning for a maintenance area can be extensive when the proximity to residential areas is close. In this example, a computer rendering proves that the view to a maintenance facility from future residential areas will be pleasing and compatible with the overall development.

COURTESY OF KITCHEN SINK DESIGNS; www.kitchensinkstudios.com

Additionally, a long access road to a maintenance area will typically mean an equally long ribbon of landscaping buffer. This may be costly and impractical as well as create yet another obstacle to the overall land plan.

22. Continuity

Continuity between the golf course and surrounding community is important to consider in the design of the project. The relationship between the two must be symbiotic. Local and regional factors such as flora and fauna, local character, weather, geography, and history should be considered in the design of the golf course and real estate to maintain continuity with the general area as well. The developer and master planner must know all aspects of the area to be developed. You typically wouldn't build Pinehurst in southern California, and you wouldn't build Tahitian bungalows in the Arizona desert. Maintaining continuity can be accomplished by preparing strong design guidelines that take into account the design goals and objective of the project. If continuity between golf, real estate, and local community is preserved, the project will be a welcome addition to the community and will most likely be successful in terms of its economic contributions.

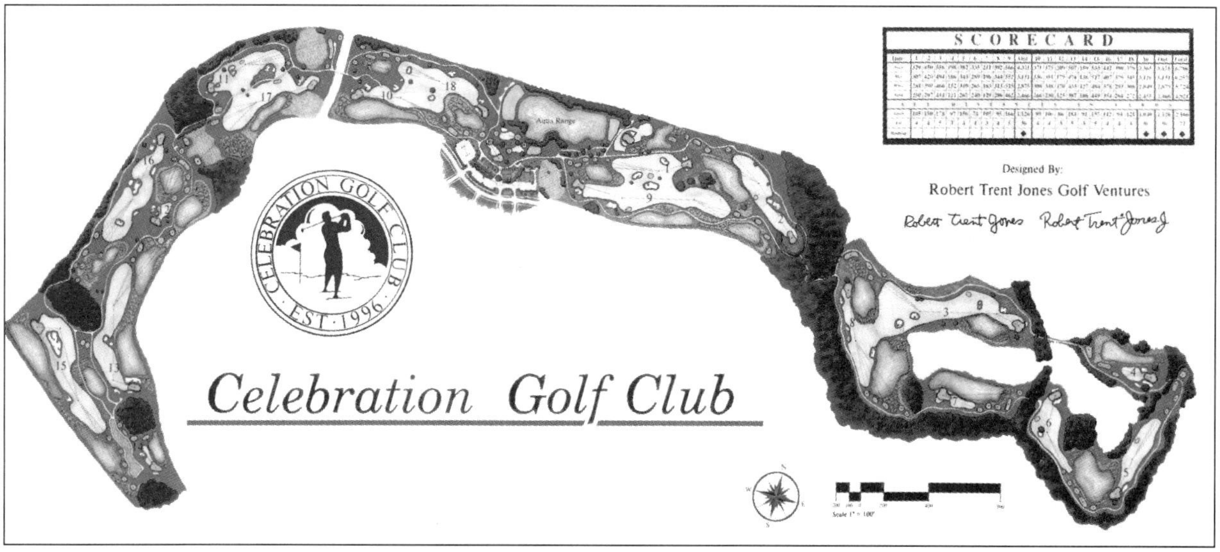

FIGURE 6-14
Celebration, a community in central Florida, embraced a unique relationship between golf and its residential areas. By edging the golf course with ponds and unimproved open space, a linear park was created that completely surrounds the golf areas. The feeling is of a large "Central Park" that all residents, not just golfers, are able to enjoy and use.

ROBERT TRENT JONES, ASGCA, AND ROBERT TRENT JONES II, ASGCA, GOLF COURSE ARCHITECTS; COURTESY OF ROBERT TRENT JONES II

CELEBRATION

Celebration, Florida, is a prototype town created by Disney Development. Remarkable in numerous ways, Celebration has won the hearts of many but also has its share of critics. Any time you create something different, this is bound to happen. The relationship of the community to the golf course at Celebration was a masterpiece in innovation. The routing of the course is illustrated in Figure 6-15. The design of Celebration is layered as follows, beginning with the individual home: house, sidewalk, landscape verge, parking lane, driving lanes, another landscape verge, another sidewalk, lake, and then golf course. Tom Sunnarborg, the project manager for the golf course, admits he was skeptical at first but soon saw the incredible relationship afforded to the resident. "The golf course becomes the 'Central Park' of the community," notes Sunnarborg. "It's magic in how the design reinforces, in so many ways, the pedestrian, public, and community orientation of a community." The integration of golf with urban development has long been handled in just a few ways. The Celebration approach is making waves.

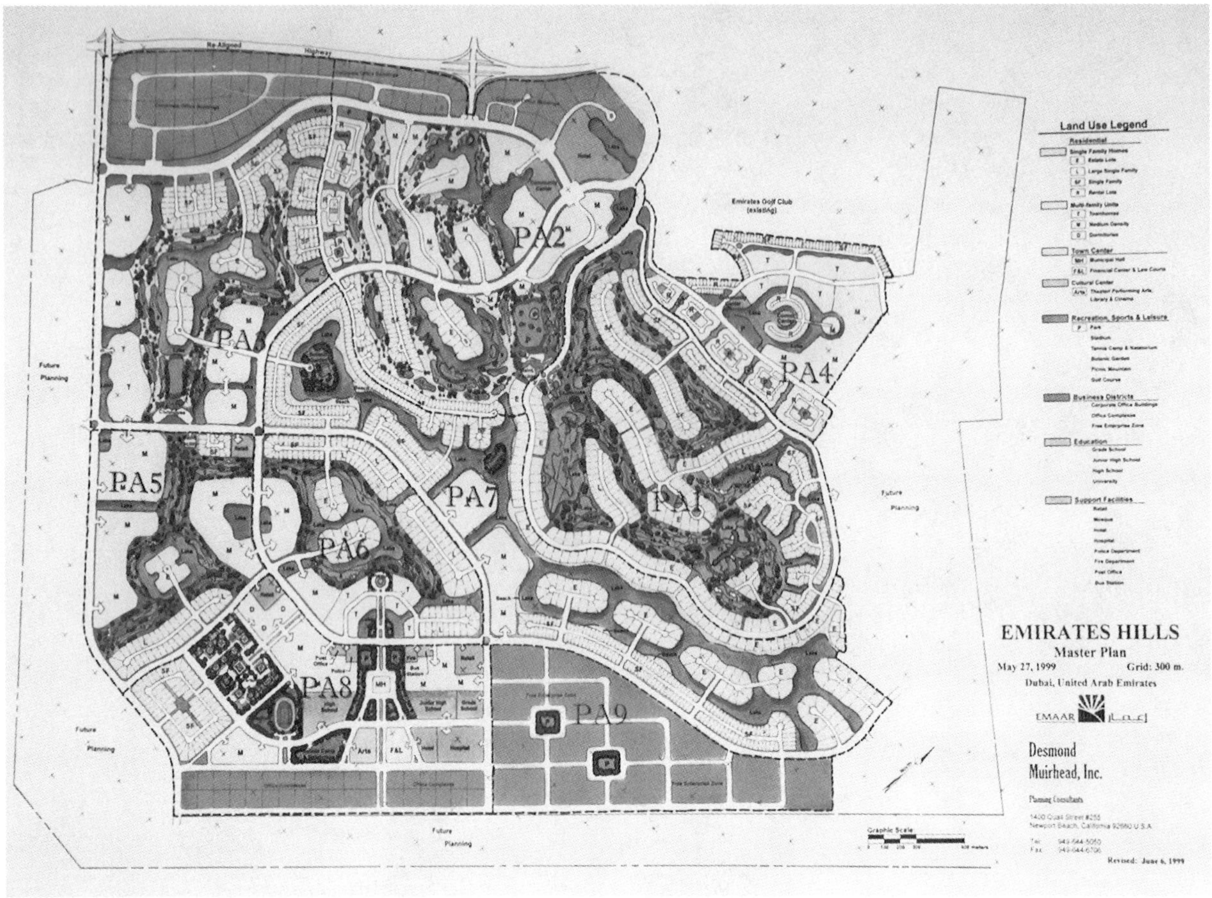

FIGURE 6-15
A fascinating project in Dubai, United Arab Emirates. Clusters of developable areas are creatively situated on islands where the views to golf are across water. These enclaves, with their island orientation, give a feeling of security and create a sense of mystique.

COURTESY OF DESMOND MUIRHEAD, INC.

23. Other Recreation

Pools and tennis courts should be designed and planned as complements to recreational amenities. Many other recreational opportunities can be explored for their ability to attract, serve, and provide revenues. The recreational investment that costs more than it will yield is not inherently a bad investment, just one that must be justified for other reasons, such as attracting buyers or keeping them happy. The same is true of opportunities that may have large yields but may be a long term detriment to life in a community. As an example, a 5000-seat amphitheater may have the potential to get area concerts every weekend, but it may go entirely against the grain of the quiet, laid-back lifestyle created in the land plan.

24. Roads Parallel to Golf

Roads and golf do not mix! A road, especially along the right side of a golf hole, is a bad idea. Adequate corridors are essential wherever roads are present.

25. Core Golf versus Playing Between Houses

Single fairways lined on both sides by houses is rarely an efficient use of land. Not only can it lead to a poor golf experience, it requires numerous access points, which can lead to compromised security in the residential community. When both golf and real estate considerations are balanced, it leads to better golf frontage for homes, less wasted acreage, far fewer safety problems, and overall, a more successful plan. With a core layout, there is less frontage but better quality, as the views are longer and the golf much better suited to a wide-open experience. Additionally, acreage use is lower and safety problems are fewer. The use of double fairways, a compromise between the two trains of thought, is an excellent way to achieve openness while gaining frontage for golf course lots.

In any kind of development you need ideas to strengthen its form.
—Desmond Muirhead

29. Buffers

The type of community being built will affect how buffers will be used. For instance, to buffer an exclusive private golf club community, substantial berming might be used to create a sense of privacy and block

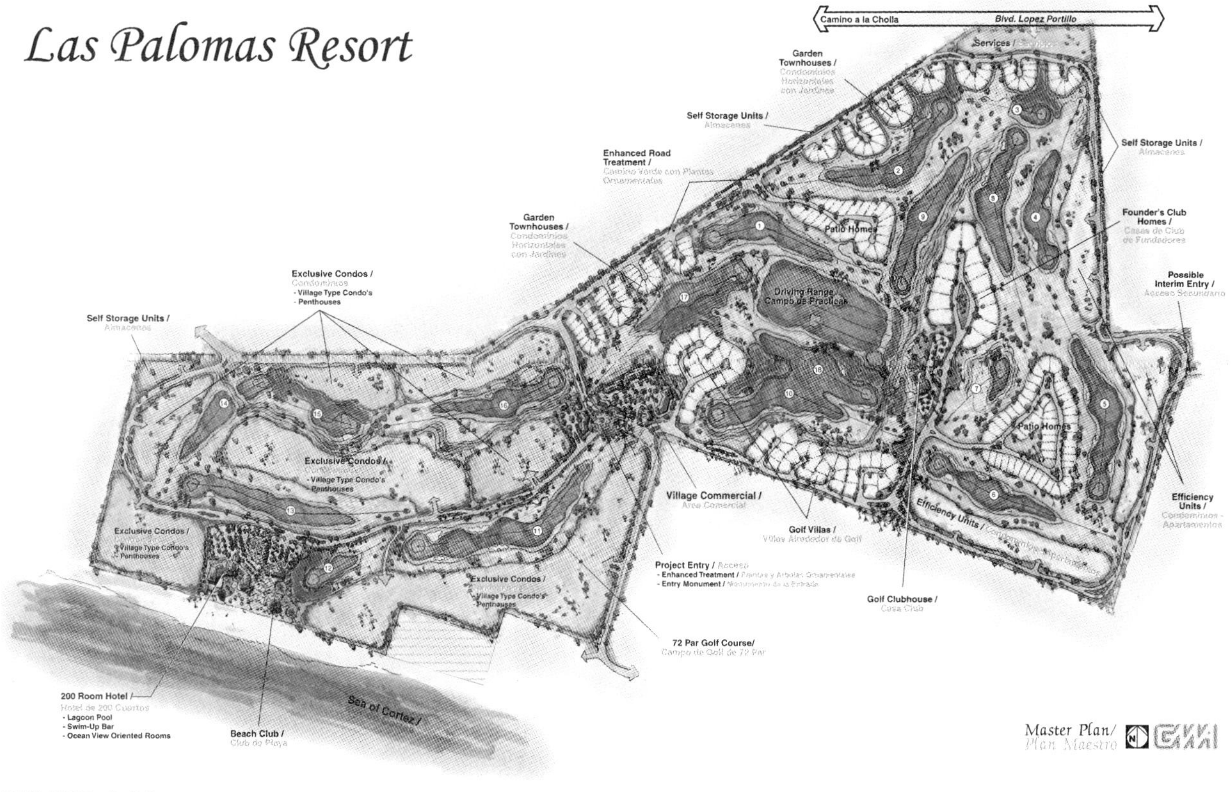

FIGURE 6-16
A plan for a mixed-use property with limited oceanfront acreage. Although it was tempting to situate golf along this stretch, much more economic sense was realized by putting the resort and grounds fronting the beach. This way direct access to the beach is available to guests. By integrating the golf to the resort, both the resort and the golf course take advantage of the orientation.

COURTESY OF GMA INTERNATIONAL

The well-conceived golf property must be designed as a whole.

—George C. Thomas Jr., Golf Architecture in America

outside influences, such as roads and other land uses surrounding the property. Buffers are also used in the transition between land uses, such as between golf and residential areas. Slopes, landscaping, view fencing, and corridors can be used to buffer the golf course.

30. The WOW! Factor

Every project needs a concept, a theme—something that can signal to the buyer and visitor that this is a worthwhile place to be. Such concepts may be woven into the entire experience of a community or restricted to a particular feature or space within the plan. There is no 100 percent right or wrong. Appropriateness is a matter of the vision of the developer and his planning team. As a reminder, however, consider some of the concepts already covered: authenticity, natural features, regional influence, and continuity. A WOW! factor should not go against these principles. The best themes are created by accentuating what is already present and bringing it to the surface, where it can be marketed and, ultimately, appreciated.

GIL MARTINEZ has a remarkable knack for finding the best in land and then magically bringing it to life in the form of engaging and entertaining designs. Even though he refers to himself as a "land planner," I consider his role to be much more. Beyond the issues of planning *and* land, *his vision extends to the economy, the environment, and the experience. Good land planners* plan *land. Great ones bring land to life.*

Gil's work, which begins with a simple walk across unbuilt landscapes, winds up as the platform for someone's back patio. Here, a simple walk can begin all over again, this time across trails, open spaces, and golf courses, all of which form the "Central Parks" of communities and resorts.

For more than 30 years, Gil has been studying land and the relationships of golf and development. He has worked in the deserts of the southwest United States, the tropical regions of Polynesia, and the outbacks of Africa, always—and he stresses this—with an eye to looking at projects from multiple viewpoints. The finished project needs to work well not only physically but also emotionally and economically.

Gil Martinez has a background in engineering, urban planning, and landscape architecture. He holds a masters degree in administration and is a regular contributor to conferences and seminars on the subject of this chapter—how to successfully integrate golf with residential projects.

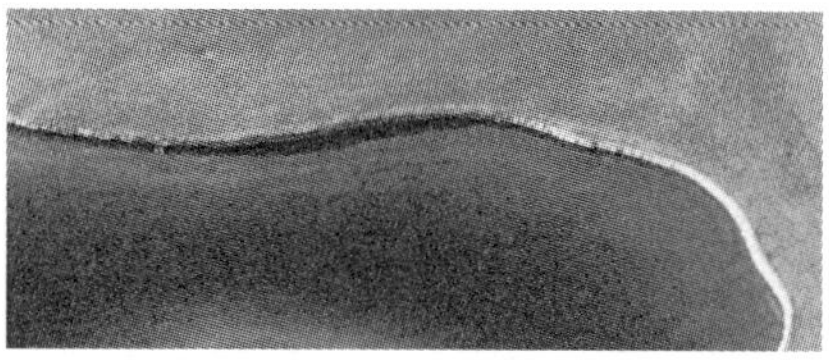

PART TWO

Making the Turn

The "Rules" of Routing

HOLE NO.

7

There is a common saying, "rules are meant to be broken." The logic behind this is that rules are made to prohibit actions that some people find justifiable. Mostly this saying works, although I admit it was useless before the Honorable Judge So-and-so of Mohave County, Arizona, before whom I was contesting a speeding ticket. Judge So-and-so had apparently not carefully studied this rule of rules.

The goal in writing this chapter was to put down on paper a complete collection of the do's and don'ts of golf course routing. You can be assured that each of these rules has been broken, some many times. And you can be assured that each is sure to be broken, for good reason, in times to come. This is part of the nature of routing. While some items are sacred, the game of golf is so unlike other endeavors that the assembly of parts comes with no one-size-fits-all instruction booklet.

I anticipated that some readers might skip directly to this chapter, so those who began at the beginning might recognize a few of the topics. Regardless, the idea here is to provide a routing primer in a checklist format that is as complete as practical.

Americans are given to standardization, but golf courses cannot be turned out of one mould.
—*Robert Hunter,* The Links

THE FINANCIAL RULES

There are 14 financial rules. Financial considerations in routing must be checked off because a golf course plan that is inconsistent with the marketing plan—which defines the customer, the kind of golf he will play, and how much he will spend—will lead to disaster. Other financial aspects include the cost of land, the extent of programming, and environmental issues. A well-conducted feasibility study is typically part of the process that addresses these issues. In lieu of such a study, and even in addition to one, asking questions and getting to the heart of the reasons behind the course are of paramount importance. Trust between the owner and the golf course planning team is a must. Even though an army of people may be involved in planning a golf course, the person or crew doing the actual routing must take a proactive role in the following areas:

- ☐ **Identify the driving force.** What is the driving force behind the course? Why is this course being built?
- ☐ **Identify the market needs.** Compare the driving force to the needs of the area.
- ☐ **Identify the owner and decision makers.** It is occasionally necessary to pinpoint the official owner/developer of a project and, more importantly, the persons who will be making decisions on a day-to-day basis and who will pay the bills.
- ☐ **Identify the owner's goals and objectives.** Clearly understand what is expected of the completed course.
- ☐ **Ask for budgets.** Have any budgets been defined? What is their validity? A final budget must be assigned, or one must be determined by means of the planning, routing, and design.
- ☐ **Identify the golfer type.** What type of player will frequent this course? The answer to this question will shed light on what type of course is required.
- ☐ **Determine the desired round duration.** Has the course been predicated on a set time for a complete round in order to meet expectations?
- ☐ **Determine the desired course capacity.** Based on the region and its climate (season and daylight hours), what is the capacity of the golf course? Is there a targeted capacity that is needed?
- ☐ **Identify the format of play.** Know the format of play anticipated. Will the course support stroke play, match play, or a combination? Will it be the site of tournaments? Will the inevitable shotgun start be at play here?
- ☐ **Research competitive courses.** Research of area courses can yield comparisons covering a wide range of factors including green fees, type of player, condition, access, quality, and length.
- ☐ **Research regional construction approaches.** The type of golf course construction common to the area may influence routing.
- ☐ **Determine the extent of development.** How many holes are projected? What is the extent of amenities? What overall development plans are being considered?
- ☐ **Understand the marketing approach.** How will this course likely be marketed? Do any marketing hooks currently exist? Most important: Why will peo-

ple come here to play golf? If this question can be answered, many problems can be anticipated and avoided. A second way to ask the question is: How will this golf course be differentiated from the next?

☐ **Identify environmental issues.** Will any known environmental conditions affect the financial outlook?

THE ENTITLEMENT RULES

Entitlements are the acquired rights to develop land. These rights infrequently exist without any change or effort. Entitlements include zoning, agency approvals, waivers, property rights, water rights, and the like. Entitlements are necessary because without them, the golf course cannot be developed.

Entitlements may also define conditions, stipulations, and restrictions that will eventually have to be dodged by the cleverness of the golf course plan. These aspects are typically the greatest obstacle to routing. To get complete and final entitlements, it is almost always necessary to route a golf course, at least in a form that establishes where the course will go and what footprint it will consume.

The routing plan created for entitlement purposes is often allowed to be rudimentary in its format—that is, details can be loose. Perhaps golf holes are not shown in a designed form but as embellished stick figures with just enough detail to get by. Providing the plan considers all of the rules of routing—not just those favored by agencies that facilitate approvals—then it is acceptable. The balancing act is to provide enough information based on sound routing principles, but not so much that specific details cannot be changed once the plans are drafted into a set of final design plans and construction documents. In Hole 16, "Presenting Routing Plans," the nature of routing plan detail is covered more thoroughly.

☐ **Determine ownership and control.** Who owns the land, and whether the land is owned outright or leased, is essential information.

☐ **Determine jurisdictions.** Land located within the limits of a municipality will have different permit requirements than land located in a county, state, or province that is outside of city limits. Often, a site is located in two or more jurisdictions, which is almost certainly a precursor to conflict. It is also important to know which individual offices within jurisdictions will have review and approval power.

☐ **List all zoning requirements.** Existing zoning is what is allowed currently on a site; desired zoning is what is required to accomplish the development plans. Zoning districts may also contain a set of standards that can affect golf course development plans.

☐ **List all approvals required.** Which official agencies will have a say in this project? What are their areas of interest? Examples include county offices, state offices, federal offices, coastal commissions, archeological districts, historical commissions, liquor boards and adjacent municipalities. Citizens groups, such as homeowners associations, can often have oversight in the approval process. A list of all of the approvals required will yield a corresponding list of most of the entitlement hurdles that must be cleared in the routing.

☐ **Identify all required easements.** Easements may be required for future utilities (both above and below ground), drainageways, and access through a site; they may also be required to connect separate parcels of land—for example, to allow golfers to cross or pass under a highway. Without being given permission to the crossing, the use of both sides of the highway would be pointless.

☐ **Identify roadways and access points.** How will current and future roads connect? Can the roads handle the traffic to and from the planned development? A traffic study identifying impacts is often forgotten, but should not be; addressing the issues it raises can help avoid substantial challenges later on.

☐ **List all environmental approvals required.** Environmental entitlements extend to three primary areas:

1. Existing natural conditions on land. These may require identification of restricted areas and overall conditions that may affect development. Examples of work that might be required before receiving approvals include habitat assessment, wetlands identification, vegetation analysis, groundwater condition research, and archeological surveys.

2. Existing unnatural conditions on land. These are conditions that may need to be corrected and/or improved before approvals are given. Examples include previous dumping of waste, mining operations, leftovers from previous development, and poor soils from agricultural use.

3. That the proposed development can be harmonious with the land, given the conditions and specific plans, may require documentation. Often, mitigation is a requirement. Mitigation can involve avoidance of restricted areas, creating habitat to compensate for impacted areas, and reclamation of areas compromised by previous activity.

☐ **Understand water logistics and quality issues.** Water is a requirement, usually. So, too, are the rights to water. The water rights of downstream property owners can affect the amount of water that may be dammed, diverted, or taken by an upstream golf course. A full understanding of all water isues is essential; including water availability, delivery, storage, and costs.

☐ **Identify drainage requirements.** Flood plains and drainage issues involve safety of life and property. They cannot be taken lightly. Knowing the easements and approvals needed for drainage coming from both off-site and on-site, and the downstream conditions that will be affected by development, is essential. Equally important are the issues concerning waterways, lakes, and ponds, all of which can be associated with drainage and the entitlement process.

☐ **Identify open space requirements.** Requirements for open space may be a contingency of granting entitlement through zoning.

The entitlement process can be confusing—and time-consuming. For this reason, there are armadas of specialists in these matters. Lawyers, planners, lobbyists, more lawyers, and environmental consultants can all make up teams that sort through these issues from the project's inception to final approval. Rarely, as has been mentioned, does this happen without a degree of routing. The routing of the golf course can actually resolve many entitlement issues. Figuring out how to avoid, circumvent, or creatively use what are considered obstacles is often best done by the router of golf courses.

Among the most frustrating routing projects are those that get stuck somewhere in the entitlement process. It can sometimes fall on the shoulders of the golf course router to try to solve any and all problems. The danger is in making that single compromise that pushes the project over the top of the precipice; what might have been a good project becomes a terrible one. When too much time is spent forcing square pegs into round holes, the result is usually untenable. Far better, as many golf course architects point out, to design shorter and fewer holes than to hold out for length and a full 18 holes.

THE RULES OF GIVEN CONDITIONS

Given conditions are the issues that lie just beyond the sometimes esoteric realms of finance and entitlements. Given conditions are typically things that cannot be changed without great effort and cost. Some cannot be changed at all, such as the climate, unless a higher authority is part of the development team. The rules of given conditions are mostly to do with an actual piece of land. Therefore, they are best sorted through once a piece of land has been identified and it can be determined that each question has been answered with reasonable certainty and comfort.

The following checklist represents the range of information that is ideally noted on the base map for a golf course site prior to routing. Without the disciplined transfer of this information to a map, it can easily be lost. Even though some items are not about a specific point or area on a map, noting the conditions in the margin of a plan or map is an excellent way to keep track of these givens during the routing effort.

- ☐ **Identify the golf season.** In what months is golf played, or can it be played, in this locale? At what intensity—that is, will summer or winter be the busiest time?
- ☐ **Determine precipitation rates.** A month-by-month analysis is important.
- ☐ **Test soil and water.** This is an optional rule, but one worth following. A site with exceptionally poor soils or marginal water availability will undoubtedly require a degree of heroics to overcome the conditions. Bad soils may not be able to sustain turf

TEN RULES *by Charles Piper*

In an article appearing in *Golf Illustrated* in February 1929, Charles Piper, who at the time was the chairman of the Green Committee of the USGA, wrote ten rules about planning and designing courses. They are slightly edited in the following version:

1. A standard golf course of 18 holes should measure 6000 to 6500 yards.
2. Minimum acreage should be 100 acres, not including the clubhouse, practice areas, or extra room between holes.
3. The most desired topography is gently rolling terrain; streams are good; and flat land should be avoided.
4. Sandy loam soil is ideal.
5. Design should harmonize with the existing topography.
6. Lay out holes north and south as much as possible; create equal lengths on both nines; and avoid parallel holes.
7. Visibility of all features is most desirable; blind or half-blind shots should be avoided.
8. Any design that increases the element of luck is open to serious criticism.
9. Roughs should compel the use of mid-iron clubs but not penalize more heavily.
10. Out-of-bounds is not desirable, especially close to the fairway.

and may have to be isolated and covered with imported soils. Or, pockets of soils that are acceptable may have to be excavated, thus creating potential topographical obstacles. A messy problem can occur when it is assumed that soils and water are okay.

- ☐ **Understand the growing conditions.** What types of turfgrass and trees will grow here?
- ☐ **Identify special maintenance requirements.** Will this course require unusual maintenance practices? Will these affect routing? An example is an environmentally sensitive area that cannot be maintained and would therefore interfere with golf holes unless the tees, fairways, and greens were laid out in positions that could be seen appropriately despite the vegetation continuing to grow uncontrolled.
- ☐ **Understand water delivery.** Identify where water will be delivered to the site, where it will be stored, and any overflow mechanisms that will allow water traveling through to do so.
- ☐ **Identify the basic topography.** Identifying whether the site is generally flat, gently rolling, mountainous—or a combination of land types—is of great benefit, albeit obvious. North-facing slopes may be inherently different in terms of growing conditions and drainage than south-facing slopes. A slope analysis may be required to determine what areas can and cannot be used for certain golf features. For sites with multiple land types, a color-coded notation on a map may help in addressing areas with distinct topographical differences.
- ☐ **Determine the elevation.** The elevation above sea level affects the conditions of shots, and thus it affects routing.
- ☐ **Identify natural drainage.** Natural drainage courses are points, areas, or linear paths in which water always, sometimes, or possibly flows. By identifying natural drainage, the routing can take advantage of—or avoid—such areas as appropriate.
- ☐ **Identify land uses.** Even though a plan may not yet exist, any land uses already spoken for must be identified and well delineated. This is typically the job of the land planner in concert with the golf course architect and a host of specialists. In seasonal regions, it is wise to consider what uses the golf course areas may have in the off-season, such as cross-country skiing.
- ☐ **Identify all easements.** Conflicting easements are to be avoided at all cost! Utility easements, air rights (such as airports and helipads), drainageways, and accessways through a site should each be defined. Remember, easements may also connect separate parcels of land and therefore must be noted on the base map.
- ☐ **Identify off-site influences.** Noise, smells, and intense activity are examples of off-site influences that can be degrading to the golf experience. Sources include freeways, wastewater treatment plants, and even agricultural operations. Anyone who has ever stood downwind of a mushroom plant will understand the importance of this rule!
- ☐ **Determine site acreage.** The size of all areas should be calculated.
- ☐ **Determine access points.** All options for access by golfers, by maintenance workers, and for any other uses should be identified.

- ☐ **Identify existing vegetation.** A broad-stroke inventory of trees, wooded areas, and natural brush is valuable. Again, a color-coded map is often helpful when existing vegetation may be incorporated into the routing plan. Remember, too, that some vegetation may be transplantable.
- ☐ **Identify existing features.** Water, rock outcroppings, large trees, and topographical landmarks—anything that could possibly be used and worked into the design of a golf hole should be marked and highlighted.
- ☐ **Identify prevailing winds.** Prevailing winds may change by time of day and by season. Wind velocity is as important as direction. This is often overlooked.
- ☐ **Identify site orientation.** Note the orientation of the site to the north, sunlight conditions, and so on. Solar orientation is an essential consideration; it consists of sunrise, sunset, and sun glare.
- ☐ **Identify major views.** Be sure to include both those within the property and those to vistas off the property. One method is to rate views, such as *A, B,* and *C,* where *A* views are best, etc.
- ☐ **Identify access requirements of people with disabilities.** Depending on a host of factors, the golf course may need to take extra steps to allow for access by golfers with physical disabilities. Terrain, cart paths, and practice facilities are among the key categories that need to be planned appropriately so golfers with mobility challenges can maneuver and get to golf holes and facilities. The need for access in and around clubhouses and their grounds almost goes without saying.

THE RULES OF BEGINNING

The following rules must be considered immediately before golf holes are envisioned on a site. While they are not *the* beginning, such as the first hole or location of the clubhouse, they do represent beginnings in planning. Most of these rules involve verifying that information is in hand. It may seem an impossible task, but the rules dealing with siting and orientation must be considered almost simultaneously as each area and component is addressed.

In looking at the these beginning considerations, the relationships among routing rules become evident. Make a decision over here, and all of a sudden it affects this, or this, or this. What makes for good access and clubhouse sites might be awful for starting holes. Routing can become a vicious cycle of dead ends. In Hole 14, "Blank Canvas to Solution" these relationships are explored in greater depth. When routing a golf course, the rules of routing and the parts of the puzzle all get dumped out on the table. Metaphorically, each individual rule is an instruction for handling the individual parts that will be used to paint the finished picture.

- ☐ **Verify course programming.** Has the extent and type of golf course been determined? Some cases, of course, present a catch-22. You may not always be in a position to know about the type of course, how many holes it will

ILLUSION OF LENGTH

Often, the shorter course wants to *appear* longer. One method of achieving this illusion is to configure the routing with three or four holes of relatively long length, then spread the shorter holes evenly throughout the round. The effect is a course of limited yardage that does not seem short.

have, etc., until the routing process is well underway. Of course, knowing what is desired is helpful, even if you can't know in advance whether it will fit or not.

- ☐ **Verify practice programming.** All of the practice elements, practice greens, chipping areas, range, and so on, must be identified along with their desired sizes and quantity. Lighting is also important, and it may be influenced by financial considerations to extend hours of operation of practice areas.
- ☐ **Verify clubhouse programming.** Consider the building's size, parking requirements, grounds, etc.
- ☐ **Verify maintenance programming.** Consider the size of the facility, the yard, related parking, and access to the course.
- ☐ **Verify amenities.** Question what other structures and features are needed and wanted. Comfort stations, rain shelters, starter shacks, and range storage buildings are examples.
- ☐ **Walking is different than riding.** Walking requires minimal distances between holes, while cart-only courses are not as sensitive to this issue. Cart storage, cart staging, and cart path requirements must be determined as general requirements in this area.
- ☐ **Begin with access.** People have to get to the course, so define where it will be best to make this happen. Access roads can be costly, often involving a balancing act. Note multiple potential access points so they may be evaluated as other components are sited on the plan. Access extends to the public entrance as well as maintenance, employee, and service entrances. Also, in severe winter climates, keep in mind that snow and ice must not be permitted to prevent access. Grades of entry roads, in these cases, must be less steep so that vehicles can negotiate them in winter conditions.
- ☐ **Identify natural golf holes.** The sooner this task is completed, the more chance there will be to protect areas that are ideal for golf holes, tee locations, and green sites.
- ☐ **Practice areas are big.** A full-length practice area (range) is usually the single largest component of a golf course. For this reason, it must be sited early in the process.
- ☐ **Hilltops are not just for clubhouses.** While the views may be spectacular, the uphill treks will take their toll. It is far better that a clubhouse work with the routing and many times more interesting that clubhouses have views from secluded spots, both to areas on the site and off the site.
- ☐ **Clubhouse locations are often predetermined.** For a variety of reasons, including owner discretion, the location for the clubhouse is sometimes set in stone. Routings, unfortunately, must sometimes begin where they least should as a result of this situation.
- ☐ **Starting points are essential.** It is desirable for starting points to be accessible from and visible and convenient to the clubhouse. Starting points include the following:

    1. First tee
    2. Tenth tee
    3. Main tee of a practice range

- ☐ **There is no sacred course configuration.** Although it is desirable, for practical reasons, for an 18-hole course to return at the ninth hole, courses can go out 9 holes—or however many—and return 18 holes later. The advent of carts and their mandatory usage at some facilities has lessened the importance of returning nines for 18-hole layouts. And, as has been established, neither 9 nor 18 is a sacred quantity of holes. However, this is a tough "rule" to break. At least in modern times, there are rare examples at which people can be taken by the hand and shown the benefits of such rule-breaking.
- ☐ **Orientation is key.** Orientation of the beginning points and components are crucial in terms of views, access, aesthetics, and function. When components are laid out, they must be looked at not just for their ability to fit the land but also their ability to fit the spaces they will look out to and the view relationships that they will have to one another. Orientation must also be considered under the previously outlined rules of given conditions.

Do not let certain standards become an obsession. Quality, not length; interest, not the number of holes; distinction, not the size in greens—these things are worth striving for.
—Robert Hunter, The Links

THE RULES OF IRRIGATION

An artificial irrigation system can be one of the costliest components of a golf course. The following rules should be considered during routing.

- ☐ **It costs to deliver water.** The farther water has to be delivered to a location on a site, the more it will typically cost. For this reason, water reservoirs should be kept centrally located on level sites in order to minimize pumping costs. On sloping sites, reservoirs located at the higher elevations may have advantages, as they can provide pressure with less ancillary pumping requirements. Conversely, too much pressure, such as that which might be generated by a large elevation difference on a site, can be a problem in reverse magnitude, as pressure may need to be reduced.
- ☐ **Pressure costs.** Except in rare instances, there is a cost associated with getting water under enough pressure to operate an irrigation system. Most pressure is gained by electricity. Electricity requires utilities infrastructure, upkeep, and energy.
- ☐ **Consider irrigation routing.** As a golf course is planned above the ground, a separate routing unfolds under the ground. How the irrigation main line will get from place to place should be considered in terms of potential topographical and land use constraints.

THE RULES OF BUDGET

Only a few golf courses have been built without a budget, and I suspect much of the hype of these projects is the brainchild of a good public relations consultant who, I also guess, *has* been given a budget to tell us there was no budget. Here are rules that, if attended to, can help keep the real budgets reasonable.

- ☐ **Natural drainage costs less than artificial drainage.**
- ☐ **Artificial earthwork always costs.** It is pricier than undisturbed natural features.
- ☐ **Rock = Cost.** The exception is rock left in place as a feature. Moving, removing, burying, or relocating rock will come with a cost.
- ☐ **Greater detail = Greater cost**
- ☐ **Larger areas = Larger costs**
- ☐ **Greater complexity = Greater cost**
- ☐ **More material = More cost**

THE RULES OF AESTHETICS

The routing plan that does not consider aesthetics is one poorly prepared. Like a scenic highway or a picturesque trail, the aesthetically pleasing golf course cannot be created independently of its route. The entire experience of the course is shaped by careful routing, and that includes orientation, views, and the relationship between components and areas.

- ☐ **Aesthetics last forever.** This is true whether good or bad.
- ☐ **Aesthetics go deep.** Aesthetics are not just about the components of a site but also about how the they relate to the surroundings. Surroundings begin at the minute detail and go as far away as the views across valleys, mountain ranges, and oceans.
- ☐ **The best aesthetics are authentic.** What nature creates cannot be duplicated, only approximated.
- ☐ **Aesthetics are subjective.** What is pleasing to one person may not be to another; the best projects are those created as if by an artist and not a committee that must try to please everyone.

THE RULES OF LENGTH & PAR

Length means nothing without character.
—*George C. Thomas Jr.,* Golf Architecture in America

The rules to do with length and par of holes and courses are among the most definable, yet are the most often broken. This is because of the array of factors that can make holes more difficult or less difficult independent of length or assigned par value. Length can be the root of evil. Trying for too much, which is common, can lead to a domino effect of problems in virtually every area of a golf course. This, quite logically, is why knowing the acreage of available land and having a fundamental understanding of the programming desired are vital.

- ☐ **Length is secondary to interest.** If a golf hole is judged by length alone, it is usually a poorly contrived hole. Aesthetics, challenge, and strategy are infinitely more important than solitary length.
- ☐ **Marketing is obsessed with length and par.** Never mind that many great golf courses are relatively short or that many classic and celebrated 18-hole courses have pars less than the "magical 72". Regardless of whether or not you can do anything about it, this rule is worth knowing. Despite its absurdity, it remains a rule. Keep this in mind: Length and par are the easiest aspects of a golf hole to characterize. It is no wonder, then, how they are often elevated to the highest point in the decision-making process of some developers.
- ☐ **Short does not always play short.** Elevation differences, elevation above sea level, wind conditions, ground conditions, tightness, hazards, and features can make short play longer.
- ☐ **Long does not always play long.** Elevation differences, elevation above sea level, wind conditions, ground conditions, and openness can make long play shorter.
- ☐ **Multiple tees are essential.** They not only create diversity in length but also offer options for changing conditions, allowing play by golfers with different abilities and permitting healing of worn areas.
- ☐ **Par does not always add up.** Although there are standards for attributing par, they are not always appropriate. The type of course, type of golfer, or a particular set of tees can—and should—influence a par value that is appropriate independent of any standard. For example, an extreme uphill hole of 435 yards may be a legitimate par 5 even though it technically does not fall into the standard range for par 5s.
- ☐ **Par 3s are up to 250 yards long.** This is the USGA standard. The average par 3 is about 155 yards from the regular tees.
- ☐ **Par 4s are 251 to 470 yards long.** This is the USGA standard. The average par 4 is about 375 yards from the regular tees.
- ☐ **Par 5s are 471 to 690 yards long.** This is the USGA standard. The average par 5 is about 515 yards from the regular tees.
- ☐ **Par 3s, 4s, and 5s are not exclusive.** The USGA considers lengths that define par 6s for men and women and even goes so far as to establish standards for determining par for youth golfers up to par-9 designations (see Figure 5-16).
- ☐ **Avoid too much long.** It can be monotonous.
- ☐ **Avoid too much short.** Unless, of course, the layout is intended to be a short course by design.
- ☐ **Apply the length rules to courses.** The same rules apply to courses, not just individual golf holes.
- ☐ **Nines should be balanced.** It is better for the two nines of a course to be balanced in terms of length than to have considerable differences. The latter situation can interfere with simultaneous starts on both nines when this format is desired.
- ☐ **Length can be evil.** The last sentence of the introductory paragraph to this section speaks for itself.

THE PAR GAME

Who's to say that a single golf hole must have a single par value? While not commonplace, occasionally a long par 4 on the men's scorecard is assigned a par of 5 on the women's scorecard. Why not the other way around? A short par 5 from the regular tees might reasonably be assigned a par 4 from the championship tees. Par is a great equalizer in the concern that a course might not have enough yardage. Creativity in assigning par is not taken far enough in planning the golf course.

THE RULES OF PACE & FLOW

Pace is how a golf course unfolds. The following are considered the golden rules of pacing. (*Note:* Most of these rules are associated with 18-hole, regulation-length courses.)

Really good golf holes are full of surprises, each one a bit better than the last. Like a first rate dinner, as soon as you have finished one course with beaming satisfaction something even better is placed before you.
— Robert Hunter, The Links

- ☐ **The first hole should be appropriate.** Not much is worse than too difficult an opening hole, or one so complicated or tight as to bring about emotional distress before a golfer really gets going.
- ☐ **Hole 1 should be a par 4.** Although some experts prefer a par 5, the ideal is based on the familiarity of the par 4. The par 4 is simple compared to a one-shot hole where landing a ball on the green from the tee is the preferred attack, or to a three-shot hole where strategy is compounded by three differently played shots before the green instead of just two. A par-5 opening hole means golfers who are able to reach the green may have to wait until it is cleared. This can cause delays right off the bat. A par-3 opening hole has advantages in terms of getting players off and keeping them within view of the starter, but for reasons of intimidation—not to mention tradition—it is not customary. To be sure, this rule is easily tossed aside when land dictates otherwise. Nonetheless, the first hole in most cases should be a par 4 or perhaps a par 5 and, in very limited instances, a par 3.
- ☐ **Opening holes are introductions.** The opening holes of a course should not define it any more than the first chapter of a story should give away the entire plot. It is these first few holes that begin the journey and, as such, they should be kind and considerate, not too demanding, yet by no means unmemorable throwaways. They should offer something to look forward to and just enough to look back upon.
- ☐ **No par 3 until Hole 4.** A par 3 earlier than the fourth hole has the potential to be too demanding at too early a point in the round. Some will argue that at Hole 3 one will pose no challenge, and they may be correct. At the par 3, however, the golfer must execute a relatively accurate shot with considerably more skill than is required of a par 4 or par 5, where a broad and deep fairway usually awaits. Usually, the tee shot of a par 3 requires more decision making in terms of club selection. Par 3s can cause delays, so it is wise to allow a course to flow for a few holes before introducing one. This is especially true on courses that anticipate busy play. Anyone who has played a popular course with a par 3 at the second hole can attest to the value of this consideration.
- ☐ **The tenth hole is another starter.** On courses with returning nines, it may be convenient to start players off both the first and tenth holes. For this reason, the first and opening holes of the back nine may appropriately be held to the same considerations as the first and opening holes of a course.
- ☐ **Balance is best.** Within reason, seeking a balance between difficulty and length of holes, especially between nines, is good practice. Significant differences in length and difficulty can create pacing challenges. Golf course architects disagree as to which nine—if either—might be better as more difficult. One school thinks that the front nine should be more severe, as a golfer may tire as a round progresses. The other school suggests that it is the back nine where more demands should be placed on the golfer's skill and, besides, golfers are well warmed up by this point. Like the rule says, however, balance is best.

- ☐ **There is no perfect order of par.** It is far worse to force an ideal on the land than to allow its conditions to drive the par order. While it may seem odd to have a routing go 4, 5, 5, 3, 4, 3, 4, 3, 4 = 35 and then 5, 5, 5, 4, 4, 3, 3, 4, 4 = 37 for a total of 72, oddness does not mean the course will be bad. In fact, it's kind of interesting. If the routing presents a reason, it will seem natural and not forced to the golfer who experiences it.

- ☐ **The turn should turn.** Or at least it should announce itself. A routing that aimlessly goes on from the ninth to the tenth is missing an important reprieve. Even if no intermission is allowed, golfers need the turn to give them a sense of time and place. Halfway points mark the beginning of the ending. In golf, they will be missed psychologically, if not physically.

- ☐ **Define areas, not just holes.** Golf courses that are made up of nothing more than holes are among the most boring. A primary point of the rules of pace is that a golf course is about moving from one experience to the next. To merely change the scene of the drama from hole to hole is a lame approach. Great golf courses change their pace by taking golfers from one *area* to the next. This is sometimes accomplished by natural land differences (ridges to valleys), occasionally by vegetation (wooded areas to open meadows), and many times through features (waterscapes to more arid landscapes).

- ☐ **Provide two restroom points.** Nature calls approximately five or six holes after drinking liquids. This implies a rest room opportunity should ideally be present near Hole 6 or 7 and, if a drink is taken at this point, again near Hole 12 or 13. Of course, with mobile drink carts and cup holders in golf carts, there is no telling where and when a golfer might actually need to answer the call of nature. Thus, rest rooms can be located based on the pace of holes and by easy accessed from all points in an emergency. Ideally, no more than five or six holes should go by without a rest room. A single rest room location that serves more than one point in the routing is clever. Rest rooms should fall after greens and before tees, not in the middle of a golf hole. They can contribute to slow play by encouraging breaks; thus, they are best located where short waits are anticipated. One more consideration: The noise created by flushing toilets and swinging doors should be taken into account.

- ☐ **Closing holes should offer excitement.** The closing holes of a course should offer more interest relative to scoring in comparison to other holes. They should have the wherewithal to change the nature of the story that has unfolded and to create twists on the ending, whether the competition is between golfers or with oneself.

> *If you followed all the same design philosophies, all courses would look about the same.*
> *— Tom Fazio*

- ☐ **The 18th should be distinctive.** It need not be spectacular, but it should be significant in its ability to be remembered and appreciated. An 18th hole that is not special can be a letdown to the golfer, who expects that the round be completed with a healthy dose of challenge, strategy, and aesthetics. The element of gamble is often a hallmark of 18th holes. To be avoided are holes of such difficulty and penal qualities that the golfer may end up with a terrible experience as his last memory of the round. Heroic and detour are the best types of shots to present.

- ☐ **Keep interruptions minimal.** Road crossings and distances between holes are annoying if frequent. Routing plans should minimize annoyances.

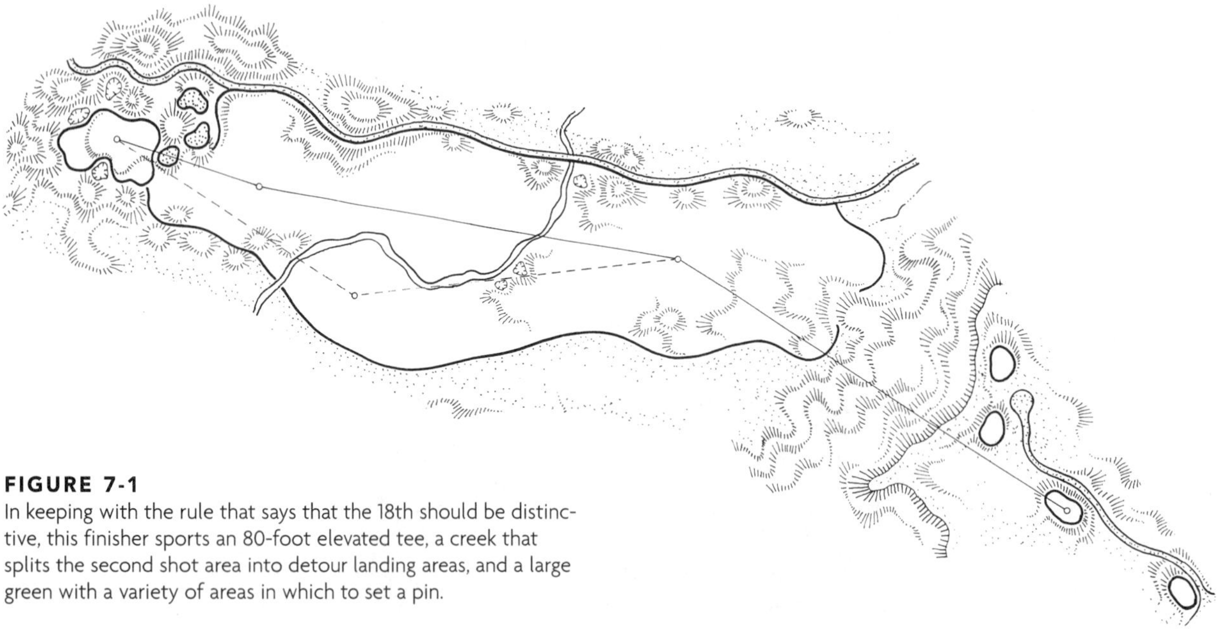

FIGURE 7-1
In keeping with the rule that says that the 18th should be distinctive, this finisher sports an 80-foot elevated tee, a creek that splits the second shot area into detour landing areas, and a large green with a variety of areas in which to set a pin.

THE RULES OF ORIENTATION

Orientation is essential for aesthetic and functional reasons. All components of a golf course get oriented, some better than others. Not all orientation is perfect, and this is okay; one does not expect perfection when it comes to golf. The goals are to eliminate obvious mistakes and to take advantage of the environment in all ways possible.

- ☐ **The clubhouse should have multiple views.** Does the clubhouse look out to interesting vistas? To parts of the course that will entice people to explore and play more golf? Often, a west-facing veranda or porch is desirable, as it permits views to the setting sun. This orientation is also harmonious with outward holes and finishing holes in their preferred orientation.
- ☐ **Provide pro shop visibility.** When possible, the pro shop should be visible from the first and tenth tees, the cart staging area, and practice putting greens. This means the pro shop can double as a place for the starter to conduct starting times, thus eliminating the need for a separate starter shack or starter area. Golfers and staff should be able to find one another easily so that starting times are not delayed.
- ☐ **Make it flow.** The area around the clubhouse, practice areas, and starting and finishing holes should flow with relative ease for the golfer. It should be possible to move from one area to the next without interfering or having to jump through hoops.
- ☐ **Practice area tees should face north.** North light is best for hitting shots and minimizing glare caused by east- or west-facing orientation and by the lower sun angle that can trouble southern-facing tees. Practice areas are most commonly used before rounds are played and therefore their use is typically higher in the morning and early afternoon hours, when there is still enough

time to get in a round before darkness. East-facing tees will be in conflict with the rising sun and therefore are least desirable. When practice areas are regarded as second-rate components of a course, choices that compromise their alignment are often made. Care must be taken to balance the demands of various course elements and to make the best possible decisions for all.

- ☐ **Avoid stages.** Putting people on stage at the first hole can get rounds off to a lousy start. It can be intimidating to be close to the clubhouse or its grounds when on the first tee, which always involves more nerves than the second, third, and so on. The same can be said of practice area tees. Here, many first-time and student golfers must carry out their practice. Golf can be uncomfortable while it is being attempted the first several times. The desirability of privacy and a feeling of partial isolation should be balanced against the rule that suggests visibility from the clubhouse or proshop.
- ☐ **The first holes should not head east.** Again, the rising sun is at play, and therefore we should travel out any direction but east, at least for a few holes. On courses where the tenth hole doubles as a starting hole in the morning hours, the same rules may apply to holes 10 through 12.
- ☐ **The finishing holes should not head west.** Obviously, this avoids playing into the setting sun.
- ☐ **Do not return too early.** Routings that immediately double back toward the first tee are to be avoided, as the sense of getting underway is too soon over; the journey seems held up by this retreat in direction.
- ☐ **Look for north-south holes on east-west sites.** A problem of sites that are longer in the east-west dimension is that golf holes tend to be laid out either east or west. When facing an east-west–oriented site, be sure to work against this tendency from early in the routing process.
- ☐ **Corners restrict.** A clubhouse located in a corner will have half of the potential visibility it would have if located along the edge of a property line. This, of course, does not take into account elevation characteristics, and it may well be that the corner is where a clubhouse belongs. Also to be considered is the activity that occurs around a clubhouse, including the holes going away and coming in, not to mention the space required for parking, cart staging, and so on. Having ample room is a common shortage experienced in routing.

WHERE IS THE FIRST TEE?
In the south of England, the Royston Golf Club operates on leased land where kite flying and weekend picnics are just as allowable as golf. The uses rarely mix, at least well. More curious, however, was the club's decision a few years back to build a new clubhouse on land it owns outright. The result is that the clubhouse is no longer continuous with the first tee or the 18th green. Instead, golfers actually drive across the moors to a remote parking lot where they unload their clubs, play, and then drive back across the moors to have a pint or two. Inconvenient? Perhaps. But it works, and there seems to be no shortage of interest in memberships. This example proves that rules are not always worth the ink used to print them.

THE RULES OF VARIATION

Variation is what makes golf so interesting. The rules of variation demand that holes be varied and that the router pay attention to how the holes fall in order of their play. Variation may imply a degree of randomness, but this is not necessarily called for. For example, irrespective of par, there should be a balance between long and short golf

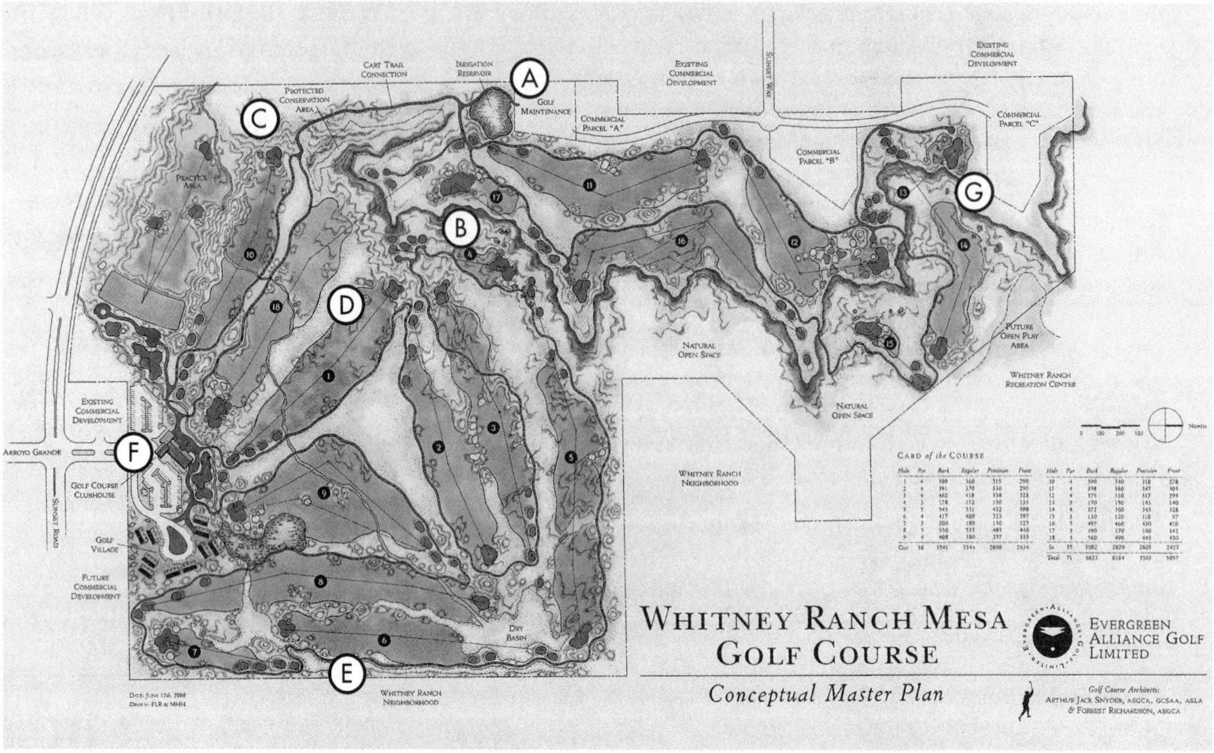

FIGURE 7-2

In this routing plan for an 18-hole regulation course, plenty of rules are broken, but many are also adhered to. This is generally the case. The following points are of interest: (A) The irrigation reservoir, from which the course will get its water, is located on a high point, which permits most areas of the course to be irrigated without electric pumping; (B) Not only do the par 3s vary in direction but also the first falls at the fourth hole, which helps the pace of play; (C) The turn takes players into a new area of the course, the upper mesa (defined by the ridge running across the entire site), which is at times 80 feet above the front nine; (D) The orientation of the opening and closing holes is ideal, as the openers do not play into the rising sun and the closers face away from the setting sun; (E) Holes play clockwise, keeping the slice side inward toward the golf course property; (F) Although it was tempting to situate the clubhouse on the mesa, instead it faces the mesa, which permits finishing holes to sweep downhill; and (G) Natural features are integrated with the design; the deep canyon permits holes to cross one another, as there is no access to the canyon immediately below.

FORREST RICHARDSON, ASGCA, AND ARTHUR JACK SNYDER, ASGCA, GOLF COURSE ARCHITECTS

holes, but it would not be the end of the world if a few short holes fell in one point of the course and about the same number of long holes fell at another point. What matters is that a range of short and long holes—and average-length holes—make up the course. Order does not have to go long, short, medium, long, short, medium. The same logic holds true for all of the other variation rules. Balance should be evident in the end analysis; it matters more than how the holes fall in order.

- ☐ **Vary the direction of par 3s.** Ideally, each par 3 faces a new wind, a new view, and a new orientation.
- ☐ **Vary the direction of par 5s.** The goal is the same as for par 3s.
- ☐ **Vary hole direction frequently.** Especially in early holes, varying the direction will give the golfer a sense of adventure.

- ☐ **Balance dogleg directions.** Dogleg right holes and dogleg left holes should be approximately equal in number. And don't forget relatively straight holes, as they are an important component despite their straitlaced nature. Par-5 holes offer the potential for double-doglegs, where the hole bends one way and then the other.

- ☐ **Consider downhill and uphill shots.** Just as the strategy of holes should be thought of in terms of shots, so should hitting down, up, or level. Downhill shots are generally the most desirable, as the golfer will feel the added power associated with being higher than the point where the shot will land. The balance of downhill, level, and uphill shots cannot be predetermined. Terrain will dictate more than any other factor. Too many uphill shots are to be avoided, especially successive shots and successive holes.

- ☐ **Vary the strategy.** Heroic and detour shots are the most fun and intriguing; they are the essence of golf. Penal shots are essential, at least once in a while. Open shots are necessary for contrast with shots that are not open. Lay-up shots, the oddballs of the bunch, have their place in line. There is no ideal appropriation. Of the 36 nonputting shots required to shoot a par of 72 on an 18-hole course, it is best to look at shot strategy and to write the script, making it fun, exciting, challenging and enjoyable.

- ☐ **Vary hazard type.** Too much of anything is a bad idea. Water, sand, and natural hazards should be placed so they do not come all at once or with more intensity than fits the situation. What makes most ocean courses so engaging is that the ocean holes come and go. An ocean course with almost every hole on the edge of the sea could be very boring indeed.

- ☐ **Vary the difficulty.** Holes should allow for both success and failure. Too many holes at either extreme—difficult or relatively easy—will be perceived as a weakness.

- ☐ **Vary courses, not just holes.** For facilities with multiple courses, it is important to vary them by course type, style, and so on.

> *It is better not to punish the majority of bad shots as they are in themselves sufficient punishment.*
> —*Robert Hunter,* The Links

THE RULES OF TOPOGRAPHY

Golf courses are defined by three schemes: (1) the horizontal scheme, which is where the golf holes go; (2) the psychological scheme, which is the strategy and charm that the holes portray; and (3) the topographical plan, which is how the holes behave. The rules of topography have to do with the up and down of golf courses. Sometimes this is subtle; other times it is bold. Regardless, to ignore topography in the routing might be the worst error possible.

Golfers and golf shots play out differently when the terrain is slightly up, very up, descending, or level. Add in the variables—and combinations—of side hills, terraces, basins, and mounds, and the moonscape of a golf course can become quite complicated. Only through accurate topographical maps or data is it possible to route a course effectively. Merely walking out and poking stakes in the ground based on what you see with your eyes will lead to too many broken rules.

FIGURE 7-3
At the 36-hole Industry Hills Golf Resort in City of Industry, California, a trolleylike funicular transports golfers and golf carts up the steep incline to the clubhouse. This makes the ascent pleasant after the finishing holes of both courses.

PHOTOGRAPH COURTESY OF INDUSTRY HILLS GOLF RESORT; WILLIAM F. BELL, ASGCA, GOLF COURSE ARCHITECT

☐ **Accurate topo is a must.** Aerial photos, old and outdated maps, and hand-drawn property descriptions are fine and useful, but not to plan a golf course with any degree of reliability. An accurate topographical database is essential to make sure the elements of drainage, playability, and safety are properly considered. The term *accurate topo* obviously covers a range of degrees of accuracy. What is suitable for one site may be totally unsuitable for another. Contour intervals of 10 feet may work for early planning, but later work might require 1-foot accuracy.

☐ **Verify sea level.** Topo data must be calibrated to the known elevation above sea level.

☐ **Identify high points.** All high points on a topo map should be marked so they can be seen easily.

☐ **Identify low points and drainage paths.**

☐ **Clubhouses on high points require uphill finishing holes.**

☐ **Uphill practice areas have benefits.** Hitting slightly uphill on a practice range can limit the length of a range and assist in controlling balls. Visibility may also be improved over downhill hitting when the predominant background is open sky.

- ☐ **Uphill holes can be tiresome.** In attaining higher elevations on routings, it is best to do so with longer holes where the rise will be spread out over a greater distance. A 550-yard par 5 can climb almost 100 feet with only a 5 percent uphill grade. The same climb on a 310-yard par 4 requires more than an 8 percent uphill grade and will seem much steeper. Higher elevations can also be attained by using the distances between holes, provided they are maneuverable by cart and walking commensurate with the way the course will be played. Par 3s are excellent for setting into hillsides between grade changes. The par 3, due to its relatively small footprint, can serve as a switchback that allows the course to get uphill faster. When used this way, the par 3 is typically playing along the contour of the land, and the main climbs are to get to its tees and then, on leaving the green, to access the tees of the next hole.

[T]he architect need not be afraid to introduce the occasional blind approach, for he will remember that strokes of this sort are almost always popular, if they do not come too frequently.
—*C. H. Alison,* Some Essays on Golf Course Architecture

- ☐ **Occasional blind shots are acceptable.** Especially when dictated by the terrain and topo, the occasional blind shot can be a stimulating mystery to the golfer. Mysteries are good, providing they can be solved within a reasonable expectation.
- ☐ **Drainage and topo go hand in hand.**
- ☐ **Topo also occurs perpendicular to golf holes.** Golf holes and routing cannot be thought of as matters of uphill and downhill only. Slopes cross hole alignments, an interesting condition that is often unavoidable. Cross-slopes, as they are called, should be carefully limited, as they cannot generally be as steep as downhill or uphill slopes. Straight downhill or uphill slopes do not deflect balls to one side or the other. Cross-slopes occurring in one direction cause shots to move to one side; this is a prime consideration in evaluating the proposed alignment for a hole.
- ☐ **Use depressions to contain.** A depressed feature, such as a grassy hollow, is twice as effective in containing shots as a mound of the same size. The mound can only stop a ball on the side facing the golfer, whereas the depressed area is 100 percent effective. Of course, a depression does not visually separate areas, nor can it deflect low trajectory shots. These traits influence the choice of depression or mound in a given situation.

THE RULES OF SAFETY

The rules of safety are covered thoroughly in the next chapter, Hole 8 "Safety Considerations." The most important safety considerations are listed here for convenience only. It is not an adequate substitute for a complete review of Hole 8.

- ☐ **There is no such thing as 100 percent safe.** Golf has inherent dangers, and even the safest of conditions may be rendered unsafe by the act of an individual, a management policy, faulty equipment, or a fluke condition.
- ☐ **Safety cones are essential.**
- ☐ **Setbacks to nongolf uses are essential.**

- ☐ **Golf holes require adequate separation.**
- ☐ **Tees and greens require protection.**
- ☐ **Proper tee alignment is essential.**
- ☐ **Minimize blind shots.**
- ☐ **Take winds into account.**
- ☐ **Minimize shots into rising and setting sun.**
- ☐ **Place hazards carefully.**
- ☐ **More golfers inadvertently hit right than left.**
- ☐ **Consider elevation changes.**
- ☐ **Consider other uses.** Note practice, clubhouse, parking, maintenance areas, and so on.
- ☐ **Provide ample setbacks to roads.**
- ☐ **Remember: Trees die.**

THE RULES OF THE FUTURE

Planning for the future calls for a review of the following rules. While no one can accurately predict the future, it is the duty of golf course planners to at the very least make sure they ask questions and try to envision needs beyond the current moment.

- ☐ **Plan for future roads.**
- ☐ **Plan for tournament requirements.** If a tournament might be in the cards for a course, spectators, parking, and facilities will have to go somewhere. Where?
- ☐ **Plan for future utilities.** Plan also for expansion of existing utilities.
- ☐ **Identify phasing plans.** Will this project be built all at once? If not, how will future phases affect what is built initially? What can forestall potential conflicts?

THE MOST IMPORTANT RULE OF ALL

- ☐ **Remember: Rules are meant to be broken!**

We Can't Do That—A Short Story About par

One of the great things about golf, and there are many, is that there are really no rules to the layout of courses. However, in today's standardized game, the people who develop golf courses are not apt to take many swings at anything unusual or out of the box. Of course, the box is of virtual construction.

Once, when I was coming up with routing solutions for an 18-hole "championship" course, the terrain was behaving so badly that the prospect of holes longer than 200 yards in one area was bleak. At one point, I fit many excellent par 3s across ravines and canyons in this sector of the property, but perhaps only two decent par 4s and two par 5s. In this rugged area, it was an uphill battle to fit any more longer holes.

Then, after a few late evenings of tinkering, it finally became clear to me that rather than fighting the abundance of par 3s, we should embrace their suitability. The solution was right there on the many sketches I had piled on the floor. Why not allow these holes to come to life? Where the ravines were deep and the land steep, four excellent short holes, each with tremendous character and variation, would fit perfectly, and each without much grading or heroics. The par 3s in this area would fall at holes 9, 11, 14, and 16. Because of limited acreage, we already had two par 3s on the front nine; this made six in total. Then, in order to make up the par 72 (which was a client directive), we easily lengthened two of our par 4s into decent par 5s. The finished par order of this interesting routing plan was as follows: out: 4, 5, 3, 4, 5, 3, 5, 4, 3 = 36; and in: 5, 3, 4, 4, 3, 5, 3, 4, 5 = 36. This was not only a pleasing solution but a smart one.

In presenting this routing plan, I focused on the incredible views and the wonderful way the holes fit the land. A big deal was made about this last point. I recall stressing that the land had dictated what should be done. Even though six par-3 holes was not a customary occurrence, I noted that each would be interesting and distinctive. With regard to the six par-5 holes, they were justified to get us to a par 72, and each was also distinctive.

"We can't do that," said one of the marketing executives. When I asked why, especially when the land begged to be used in this way, he said, "It's just not done." The topic turned to the term championship. Some in the room truly believed that six each of par 3s, 4s, and 5s on an 18-hole course make it unworthy of such a distinction. It mattered not that the term championship has no meaning, or that a crucial element of golf course architecture is creating layouts that aren't square pegs in round holes, or that the land should be in charge.

Ultimately I lost this argument, and we built the course with an ill-advised short par 4 in place of one of the par 3s. To this day, I regret not being able to carry the day. I regret not being more prepared. Had I been, I would have made a great and impassioned speech. I would have cited examples of unusual par order and renowned courses with unusual pars and lengths. But unfortunately, I made no such speech.

If there are golfing gods, I suspect they look down on those decision makers. And when those decision makers arrive at the tee on that "lousy" par 4 hopeful and wishing for a birdie, I am comforted by the thought of the golfing gods, in unison, saying, "We can't do that."

Safety Considerations

HOLE NO.

8

Routing golf courses raises two primary safety issues. The first is associated with the golf course's relationship with land outside of its control. Arthur Jack Snyder, from whom I learned the nuances of the golf design business, is famous for his take on this relationship. When a developer or land planner comments that a golf hole is "interfering" with lots or developable areas, Jack's response is one of simplicity: This "interfering" acreage "was simply never there to begin with." The second safety issue involves the relationship among components of the golf facility itself. Golf holes must be adequately buffered from one to another. The clubhouse, parking, and practice areas must be set back from areas of the golf course that surround or traverse them. The tug of war between necessary acreage for golf and that required for existing, new, and future *non*golf uses is intensified by increasing land costs and, in many cases, a shortage of land in areas that need both golf and nongolf development. Amid these often conflicting objectives, how to address safety issues remains debatable.

Golf may be played anywhere—that is, anywhere where there is room.
—*Garden G. Smith,* Aspects of Golf Course Architecture

This cannot be stressed enough: No hard and fast rules pertain to every instance and condition. Golf is a game of individual and intrinsically different—yes, unique—situations that are infinite in their differences and specific situations. A solution that works at sea level might be inappropriate at 7000 feet, where balls travel farther. A solution that satisfies a small municipality where golfers are laid back and intimately familiar with the layout might be the ultimate boner at a resort course where macho types frequent the tees, each with a Big Bertha® protruding from his golf bag, and each just waiting to inflict a wicked slice on an unsuspecting golf villa.

Here I expand on previous material and share my thoughts on safety—but keep in mind that they are just that: *thoughts.* The ideas presented here are only as valid as the professional attention that goes into using them. No one is advised to plan or, heaven forbid, build a golf course without engaging a professional consultant, such as a golf course architect, to guide and drive the land plan so that the course is as safe as reasonably possible.

SAFETY & GOLF

Golf is no more a safe game than archery is. Both have targets, both involve dangerous projectiles, and both are at the mercy of the shooter, the wind, and all of the distractions that go along with being outdoors. Thankfully, in both sports, we do not have to contend with physical force between players, for this would make the drama a bit too exciting.

A vast majority of golf safety problems are not due to poor golf course layout or design. One needs only to look at the most common areas of damage and injury from golf activity to prove this point. Only in the case of balls hit off line do the routing and design of a golf course potentially contribute to the problem.

The primary categories of injuries to golfers are:

- Injury from swinging clubs
- Fall injuries
- Accidents involving golf carts
- Injuries caused by lightning
- Errant balls hit off line

Swinging Clubs

In the case of accidents involving club swinging, the thinking is that individual golfers must account for their actions. No rule or custom demands that a practice swing be taken or that a shot be executed at a particular moment. These decisions are up to the golfer. Raising a club comes with a level of responsibility for where it comes down, and the course designer cannot be held accountable for actions so far downstream from the physical layout of the course. This does not mean that routing cannot at least assist in preventing club swinging accidents. Ample tee area, pathways far enough from tees, and well-thought-out warm-up areas are all signs of good design practice.

Fall Injuries

Fall injuries on golf courses are primarily the result of poor footing, wet conditions or lack of individual agility. Thankfully, many injuries have been eliminated as a result of metal spikes on golf shoes being phased out. Slippery conditions on hard surfaces did not mix well with the metal spikes.

There are numerous locations and conditions on golf courses where it may not be advisable to walk. This judgement must be left to the golfer. No course could be so closely managed or signed with warnings, personnel or policies to protect against poor judgement or to anticipate the ability of a particular golfer. A golf course is, after all, an outdoor trek across undulating land that is exposed to the elements. In routing courses we can only do our best to anticipate the multiple paths where golfers will need to walk in order to access tees, fairways and greens. But, just as there are options to circumvent hazards during the game, there are also options that the golfer has in his personal maneuvering across a course. Routing is an art performed at very small scale. It can address in a very preliminary way the relationship between likely access points and golf features. It cannot address these in detail. Such detail must be worked out in the process of creating detailed plans and ultimately in the direction of construction work in the field.

Golf Cart Accidents

Accidents involving golf carts are on the rise for the simple reason that more golf carts are being used. On many courses, walking is not even an option. Course routing can take the golf cart into account, but it is impossible to place too much burden of cart safety on this process. If carts are to be used and paths constructed for them, each must be engineered and maintained appropriately. This must be done with regard to the capabilities of the carts to be used and the type of people who will likely drive them. At a private club where cart drivers are familiar with the paths, it might be

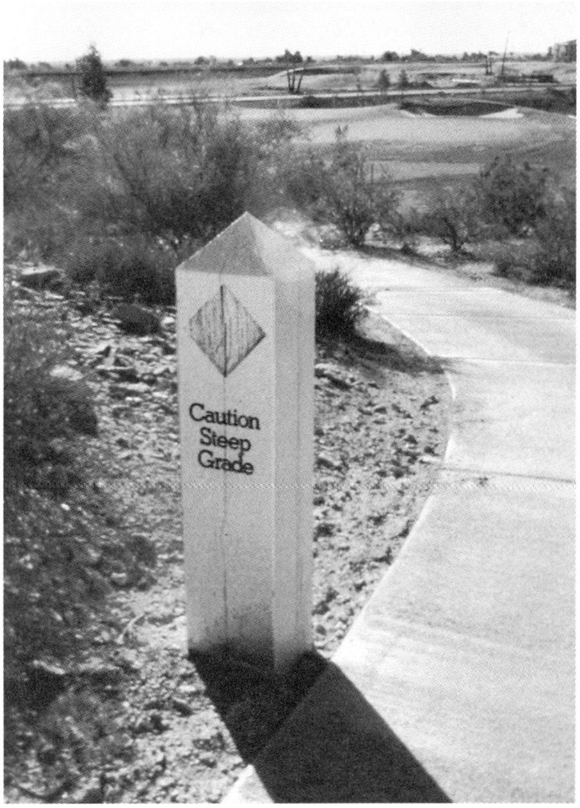

FIGURE 8-1
Golf cart accidents represent problem common to the modern golf course. Routing can take into account the way that golf carts will need get from place to place on the course, which will assist in eventually establishing an efficient path system as final plans are prepared. Signage, such as that pictured, support the notion that cart safety is ultimately one of management and control of the golf course and safe use of carts.

appropriate that paths are more intricate compared to those at a resort courses where the guest will usually be less familiar with the way the paths are laid out.Cart use is almost always the culprit when it comes to cart-related injuries. Two examples of cart accidents come to mind. Both are worth relating, as they sum up what can happen when people get behind the wheel or even take a seat in a golf cart. The first example involves a lawsuit filed by a man who was riding as a passenger in a cart and was dangling his leg out while another fellow drove down the cart path. The leg got tangled in a rope and stake in the ground meant to mark the edge of the path. It followed that everyone and his brother got served with a hefty claim for injury, loss of work, etc. *Read my lips: Don't dangle your leg out of the cart!* And don't sue the land planner, the developer, and the golf course architect if you take it upon yourself to do so. It would please me a great deal to include this gentleman's name, address, and I.Q., but I dare not for fear that it might prompt yet another claim.

The second incident is a classic case of the law of averages at work. At a municipal course that does a remarkable number of annual rounds—

FIGURE 8-2
In addition to the injuries that may result, safety problems at golf courses may lead to legal disputes. In this page from an affidavit prepared by a golf course architect serving as an expert witness in a case, the many variables that can affect safety are pointed out. Even when golf courses are designed with careful regard for safety, they are only as safe as the people using them. No course is immune from errant golf balls.

through the middle of the No. 13 Hole additionally encourages most play to the right of the hole, further away from the practice area.

There are no "blanket" standards by which practice areas are expected to be designed or configured. The individual site conditions, together with the intended use of the the course and practice area, are all influences that will factor into practice area design. At the subject course the practice area has been situated as expected, between golf uses, and has been designed to accommodate a reasonable number of golfers.

It is customary to buffer practice areas by mounding or other topographical features as these land forms will transcend dormancy periods of vegetation, death of vegetation and trimming of vegetation. Topographical buffering, such as mounding, is the preferred method of buffering, as these features are mostly permanent and serve to deflect balls and provide a visual delineation to all golfers. The presence of vegetation may be an aid to buffer areas or limit access, but can be breached and may, in fact, contribute to longer periods of golfers remaining in these buffer areas while searching for lost balls within the vegetation. Vegetation is not a permanent solution and will not deflect golf balls with any measurable consistency.

Line of sight issues involving practice areas must be balanced with the increased buffering that may be afforded via mounding or topographical differences between uses of a practice area and other use. What may offer more protection in one instance may be detrimental in another instance. Each condition is different and therefore presents a unique situation.

over 100,000—a couple of guys missed the approach to a short bridge across a ravine and wound up flipping their cart. This resulted in a back injury to one of the occupants. The resulting action, as filed in Superior Court, claimed that the approach to the bridge was "too severe" and that braking caused the operator to lose control and flip the cart. What the lawsuit did not acknowledge was that this bridge, approach, and path had been used for more than 20 years without the slightest accident or mishap. Even more interesting is that beer is served by a roaming refreshment cart and at the clubhouse of this course, and that it was very likely that the driver had consumed some earlier in the round. Could he have been hot-dogging down the hill? Perhaps we will never know. For some, fessing up to a stupid mistake is much more difficult than taking a trip to the local lawyer's office. While it may be that after 20 years and as many as 1 million cart riders across this same stretch of cart path no one had been injured due to sheer luck...I doubt it.

So, how can routing minimize cart accidents? Obviously it cannot have any appreciable impact when it comes to an error in judgement of the driver. A routing plan can be useful to shed light on areas where extra effort in engineering may be called for as the plans for a golf course progress. However, a routing plan is a view of a course from a relatively high altitude (as high as 10,000 feet as we covered in Hole 3.) This means that its level of detail does not get down to that required to make a final determination on cart paths. On most routing plans the cart paths are not even represented. In the few cases when cart paths are shown, it is the conceptual alignment that is being depicted, not at all the final alignment nor any conclusive aspects. Typically it is an engineer or other consultant that will work out details of path construction, inclines, and barriers. The routing plan establishes a path for the golf holes. The types and the extent of cart paths, if indeed they are to be part of a course, are covered on plans which come much later in the process.

COMMON AREAS USED FOR SET-BACKS

An occasional practice in determining safety setbacks to residential land involves the definition and utilization of common areas that fall between golf course property and land under private ownership. This common area land may be assigned as golf use even though it remains in ownership of a homeowner's association or as a tract of property owned by a community. When this situation is proposed, it is essential that formal legal documents be enacted to protect all parties from liability associated with the use of the common area land. The most prevalent method is to deed-restrict the common land so that no improvements, access, or use is allowable except by the golf course.

Injuries Caused by Lightning

Planning can do little to reduce the potential for golfers to be injured by lightning. If lightning is regionally common, the developers of a course would be prudent to consider including shelters and automatic lightning detectors and warning sirens in their budgets and programming. The best protection is providing golfers with information about how to protect themselves and what to do when lightning is present. This is a management function.

Errant Balls

You can see from the above examples that safety on courses has much less to do with routing than with golf course management and the judg-

It is not always easy to make good dog-leg holes, so much depends on the natural formation of the ground.
—James Braid, Advanced Golf

ment of the individual golfer. The problem of errant balls is also a responsibility shared among many factions: the golfer, to be sure; the managers of a course; and those responsible for the layout and routing.

No golf course is entirely safe. This cannot be disputed, as evidenced by the many factors, including personal judgment, that contribute to a ball's path from one point to the next. The goal is to make golf courses and adjacent areas as safe as they can be under the circumstances and given the conditions.

For an errant ball to do damage, it first must be struck, and this cannot occur spontaneously. A golfer is always at the controls, and it is the golfer who sets in motion the rituals of the address, stance, and final swing at the ball. Golfers hit balls off line and to bad places, and it can be argued that even under the worst of designs and conditions, at the worst of courses with the tightest fairway corridors, it is still the golfer—and not the course—who has broken the window, hit the dog, or dented the passing car.

Those who undertake routing plans can help minimize the incidence of errant balls by applying this list of considerations to site-specific conditions:

- Ample configuration of safety cones from tee points
- Ample width of safety corridors along areas of nongolf use
- Ample separation of golf holes
- Appropriate positioning of tees and greens
- Appropriate alignment of tees to the intended centerline
- Positioning tees so shots are away from adjoining uses
- Minimizing shots hit to areas that cannot be seen
- Taking wind into account
- Minimizing shots into rising and setting sun
- Adequate placement of hazards and rough areas
- Careful consideration of terrain and elevation changes
- Careful consideration of the types of golfers and uses of a course
- Consideration of ancillary activities at courses: practice, clubhouse, parking, maintenance areas, etc.
- Ample setbacks to roadways and drives

SAFETY CONES & ENVELOPES—ESSENTIAL ELEMENTS

The golf course router's best safety tools are the safety cone and the safety envelope. (Figure 8-3) These two essential elements, which vary in size depending on wide variety of factors, are projected over the plan view of the routing. They are used to verify that the routing is sound with respect to each hole's relationship with course boundaries, other golf holes, and course facilities. The method of projecting these shapes varies. Cones and envelopes—which are formed by theoretical limits—

may be visualized by hand-drawn points and lines, through the use of physical templates, or via computer-generated templates. These methods are described in Hole 9, "Fitting Holes Together."

Safety cones and envelopes are part of the process of determining internal checks and balances during the creation of routing plans. Very often they do not get presented or disclosed to those outside the drafting process. Indeed their make-up is technical in nature and amounts to notations that are used by the professional to determine the correct location for setting points, placing features and ultimately linking holes together to form a routing plan.

[M]ake your clearances of a reasonable size—not necessarily of such a size as to preclude grumbling, for grumbling is a part of human golfing nature.

—Horace G. Hutchinson, Aspects of Golf Course Architecture

The Safety Cone

The term *safety cone* is used to describe the imaginary cone shape formed by the point at which a golf shot is hit from a tee and two outward lines projecting from either side of this point. The angle formed by the two outer lines varies depending on the width established on either side of the point at which the center line for the tee shot begins and either ends (for par 3s) or forms an angle point (holes with pars above 3).

At its beginning point a safety cone will fall to either side of the center of a tee or tee area. The width here varies depending on several factors to be discussed within the topic of *safety envelopes.* The ending point of a tee shot determines the angle of the cone. The ending point—which may be the center of a par 3 green or the length of a par 4 or 5 tee shot—is where tee shots will come to rest if hit straight and to an average distance. The two sides of the cone represent the left and right margins between which a majority of golf balls are likely to travel. Although it might be said that each shot intended on a course (putts not included) has a safety cone, the idea is associated with the tee shot of each golf hole because these shots emanate from a predetermined point; the cone is thus most clearly defined by this point.

Important to defining safety cones are establishing the originating point of the cone, the alignment of the tee shot, the length of the tee shot, and the width of the cone at the distance at which the average tee shot is expected to come to rest. Each of these points and dimensions must be determined for the specific condition to which they are applied. To attempt to put forth a one-size-fits-all standard would be of no service due to the multitude of variables that determine these dimensions. The value to determining safety cones is to keep conflicting uses out of this defined area.

The Safety Envelope

In the case of par 3 holes the Safety envelope includes the safety cone extending from the tee area and continues to include an area all around the green. In the case of holes with a par greater than three the safety envelope continues onto the green, defining an imaginary left and right border for each average shot until the centerline of the hole ends at the

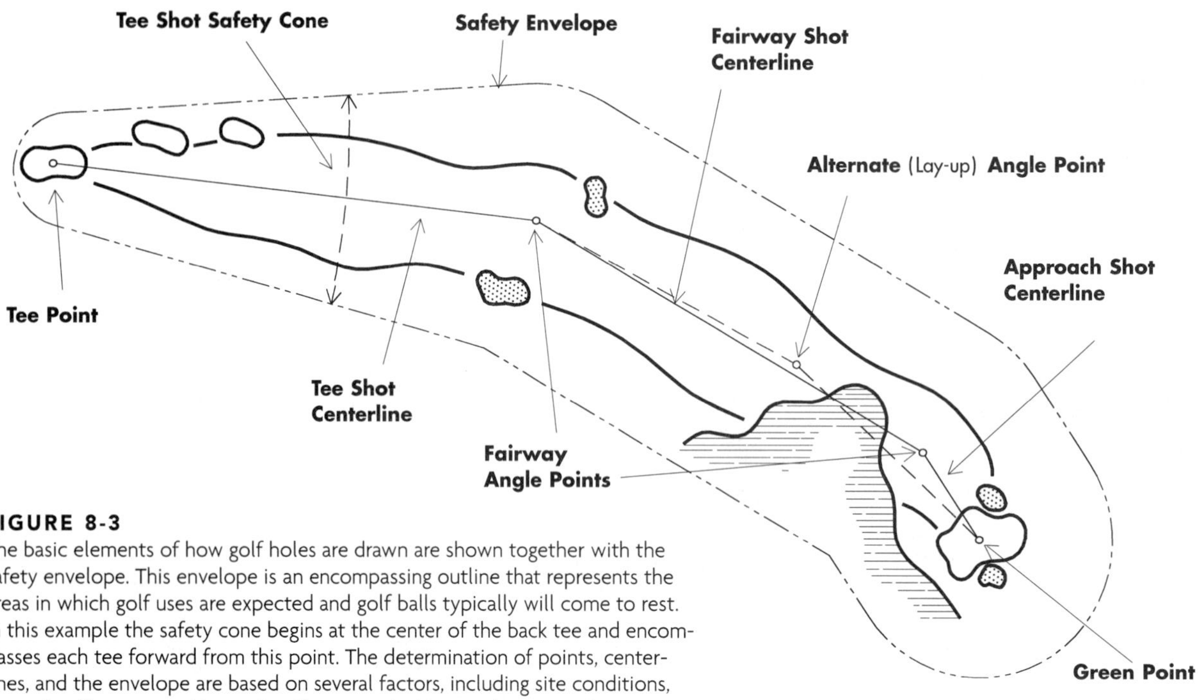

FIGURE 8-3
The basic elements of how golf holes are drawn are shown together with the safety envelope. This envelope is an encompassing outline that represents the areas in which golf uses are expected and golf balls typically will come to rest. In this example the safety cone begins at the center of the back tee and encompasses each tee forward from this point. The determination of points, centerlines, and the envelope are based on several factors, including site conditions, type of golf course, and type of golfers expected to use the course. Just because the term *safety* is commonly used it in no way guarantees that areas outside the envelope are safe. "Safer" would be a more realistic description.

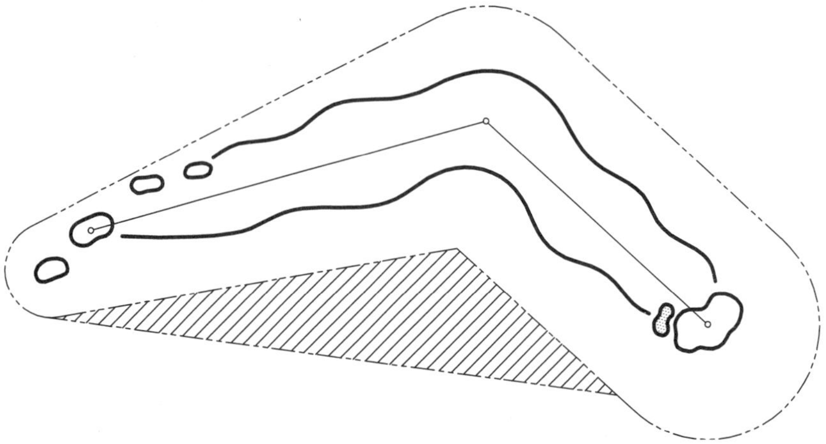

FIGURE 8-4
Occasionally, a sharp dogleg hole may require that additional room be allotted to the safety envelope, especially in situations where no hazard, feature, or terrain forms an obstacle to the inside of the dogleg. The hatched area represents land that must be evaluated to determine whether or not a portion of it should be included in the envelope. Factors that affect the determination include hazards, terrain, vegetation, improved turf areas, and other uses planned for the hatched area.

green. The limits of the safety envelope are the area around the teeing area, the two side margins of the safety cone, the continuing width to the green, and an area all around the green. The envelope suggests the area in which golf balls are most likely to fall and come to rest. The area establishes the zone of impact that a golf hole will have in most instances. It does *not* signify that balls will not, or cannot, go beyond these limits. A safety envelope is nothing more than a reasonable estimation of the area that golfers will require of a golf hole. It is a guide to be breached by the golfer on a bad day, during an awful shot, or following poor judgment.

Necessary Points

Points are necessary to establish safety cones and envelopes. These points, when connected, form the skeleton of a routing plan. Connecting them is much like playing connect-the-dots. An entire golf course routing can be expressed with nothing more than the points of tees, angle points and green points, and the sequential alignments from one hole to the next in order of their play.

Necessary points include the following:

- Tee points
- Fairway angle points
- Alternate angle points
- Lay-up angle points
- Green points
- Practice area points

Tee Points

The points of each tee must be identified, as they establish the beginning of the safety envelope of a golf hole. For exceptionally long tees, it may be wise to consider establishing a point toward the rear of the tee, as this shows more clearly where play could begin.

Many routing plans consider only one tee in defining a safety envelope. There are two schools of thought of the subject of which tee to select. The typical routing plan uses the farthest-back tees to define and plan the course. This is a curious choice, as the back tee is typically not used as frequently as the more forward tees, and thus the golf holes and their safety considerations will be determined from this seldom-used beginning point. The argument in favor of selecting the back tee is that it represents the most distant point at which play can begin on a hole and therefore covers the most ground. The rationale for setting course routings from the set of tees most likely to be used—not the back tees—is that this is where important decisions about routing and safety are most appropriately considered.

Regardless of which tees are used to establish safety envelopes, *all* tees need to be considered to make sure that shots hit from each fall within the overall envelope. It is usually unnecessary to take the intensive step to draft all tee points and alignments, but this might occasionally be necessary. The objective is to verify that each tee point and centerline falls within the safety envelope that is used for planning the golf hole. Occasionally the distance between tees on longer holes will be so significant that tee shots of golfers might need to be drawn to different angle points. This situation calls for a separate centerline to be established from the subject tee and this line will end at a separate angle point.

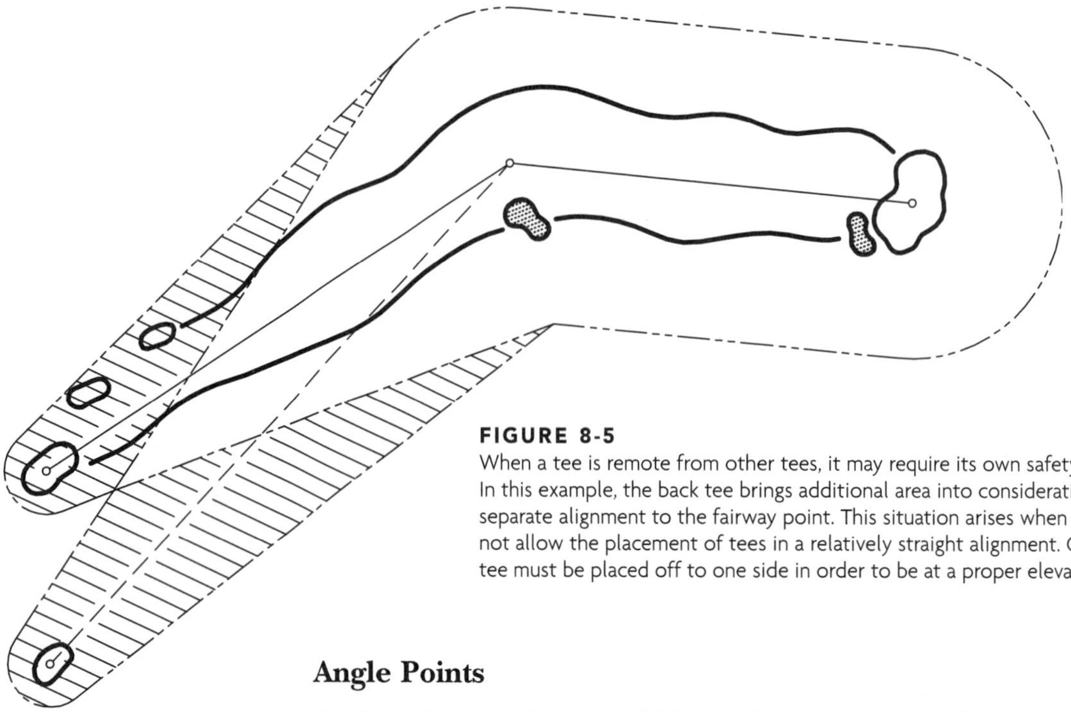

FIGURE 8-5
When a tee is remote from other tees, it may require its own safety envelope. In this example, the back tee brings additional area into consideration due to its separate alignment to the fairway point. This situation arises when terrain does not allow the placement of tees in a relatively straight alignment. Often, a back tee must be placed off to one side in order to be at a proper elevation.

Angle Points

Angle points are those at which tee shots on par-4 and par-5 holes are intended to come to rest under ideal conditions. Angle points are also the points at which second shots on par 5 (or greater) holes are intended to come to rest prior to reaching the green. These imaginary points drawn on routing plans are so named as they are where the centerlines of holes articulate to form angles. The common term for the angles formed is *doglegs.* For perfectly straight par-4 and par-5 holes, the points are still called angle points. It is supposed that this is where they would angle if they could.

In the case of detour and lay-up shots, alternative angle points may be shown on plans to indicate where golf shots might come to rest when the option to play an alternate route is invoked by the golfer.

There is debate on where angle points are drawn—that is, how far from the tee—and indeed which tee?—they should be shown on plans. The results of a survey of golf course architects and planners reveal that the most popular dimension used to indicate tee shot centerlines is 267 yards from the *back tee* to the fairway angle point—this equates to 800 feet. In the same survey, the most popular dimension used to indicate the second shot centerlines on par-5 holes is 200 yards—this equates to 600 feet.

Influences that can affect the distance between tee and angle points are the type of golf course, type of golfer expected to play the course, elevation above sea level, and climate conditions. There are also conditions under which an angle point may be adjusted based on terrain. For example, a severe uphill tee shot might be shown 20 percent shorter than a tee shot on the same routing plan which is carried out across more level land. This makes sense, as the point where shots are *expected* to come to rest should be communicated by the angle point.

Green Points

The defined center of green constitutes the green point. This point marks the end of the golf hole, that often elusive surface where the act of putting takes place. The green point is typically drawn at a point to represent the main area of a green to which a predominant percentage of golf shots are expected to be played. This "center" is often not the measured center from front to back or left to right. Rarely, a green might have two points when the shape of the green is so unusual or large as to require that two centerlines be drawn to communicate the variance in play that will occur when a pin is set on one portion versus another.

That golfers do not always hit their golf balls straight is a matter of common knowledge. This condition is as natural as gravity or ordinary rainfall.

—Justice Charles E. Freeman, Illinois Supreme Court, Larry Geddes v. Mill Creek Country Club, *2001*

Practice Area Points

The teeing area of all practice hitting areas must have a point or points to define where shots will begin. Also important is to identify the true center of the practice range, a common alignment along which shots are generally expected to be hit. It may also be useful to establish points at target greens where an abundance of shots might be played. The points established for practice areas are similar to the points for actual holes, although there may be multiple tee and target points. To cover the widest range of shot length, the distance between the farthest-back point at the tee and the center of the hitting area should be verified to see that this dimension is appropriate for the type of facility and its intended use. (Refer to Figure 8-6)

Centerlines of Shots & Golf Holes

Now, armed with a full complement of points, the router spaces them appropriately and connects them. The lines that connect points on a routing plan are called *centerlines.* Each intended shot is depicted with a centerline segment. The series of shots intended for a golf hole form its centerline. This is often referred to as the *hole centerline.* An understanding of the types of shots represented by centerlines is helpful in determining the length of these lines. The fundamental list of intended shots depicted on routing plans includes the following:

Tee Shot Centerlines: Tee shots are shown for all golf holes from the tee to the center of the green or fairway. For par-3 holes, the tee shot is shown to the green point and can range in length from a short distance (for very short par-3 holes) to whatever maximum might fit site conditions (for very long par-3 holes). Rarely does a par-3 hole feature an alternative lay-up or detour point, but this is acceptable, as evidenced by Cypress Point, where the famous 16th hole, designed by the late Alister Mackenzie, is configured this way. On holes greater than par 3s the alignment from a tee to the point in the fairway at which the shot should come to rest constitutes the tee shot. This distance is generally consistent on a given course and depicted from the same set of tees.

FIGURE 8-6
The safety envelope for a practice hitting area (range) begins by defining a tee center point and a primary hitting direction for the area. The tee should curve slightly to orient those using the area even from the edges of the tee toward this center alignment. In order to direct balls toward this center alignment any features that are intended targets, such as target greens, are best kept toward the middle, as opposed to being far off toward the edges. Where practical, shorter targets are best slightly right of center, medium targets slightly to the left, and longer targets close to the centerline. The length of the envelope will vary depending on altitude, terrain, and type of golfer. Typically, a practice hitting area envelope might be 300 yards long from the front of the tee to the end of the envelope along the main centerline. By pivoting this distance from the tee center point, the limits can be established. Defining the width of the envelope is not always simple. A common method is to take the same length as used to define par 4 and 5 hole centerlines and establish two points, one to either side of the center alignment of the area. The width at this length may be 30 percent wider than the width of the tee, including an appropriate buffer to either side. The result is the safety envelope. Practice bunkers, pitching greens, and other amenities will require additional areas and are not likely to be accommodated within these limits.

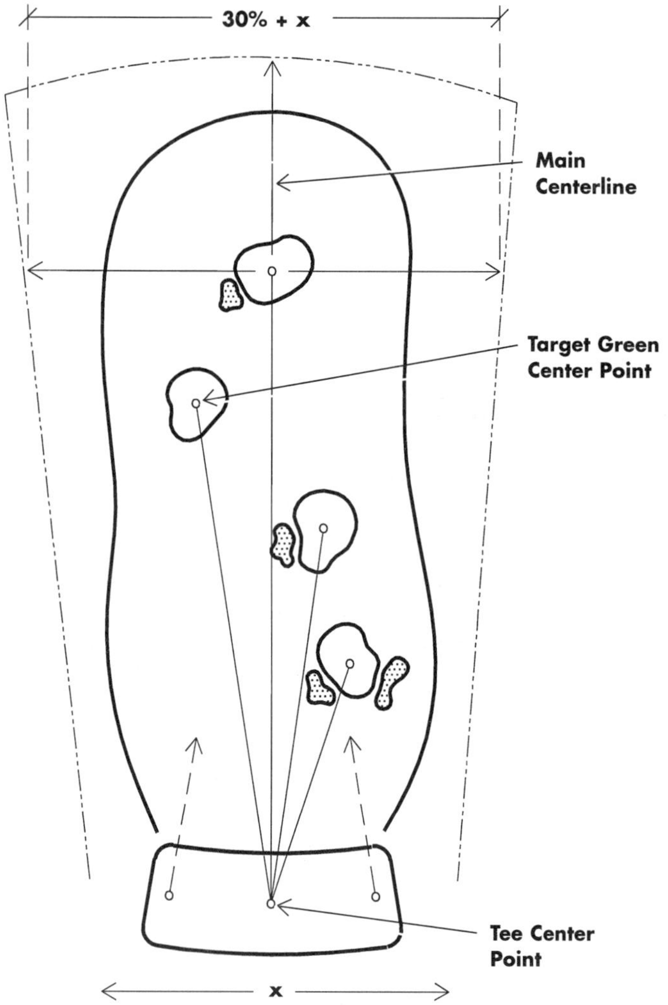

Fairway Shot Centerlines: The alignment from where the tee shot comes to rest to the next point in the fairway on long holes (the par 5 and the seldom-seen par 6) constitutes a full fairway shot. These shots are from one point in the fairway to another. Other fairway shot centerlines include lay-up shot centerlines, centerlines to alternate points, and even aggressive (risk) shots that may be played farther than the typical centerline dimension. Alternative shot centerlines often are shown as dashed lines to distinguish them from the primarily intended path that a golfer will follow if the hole is played as envisioned most often.

Approach Shot Centerlines: The alignment from where any shot from a fairway plays to a green is an approach shot. On par-4 holes, this is the second shot. On par-5 holes, it is the third shot.

CENTERLINE LENGTHS

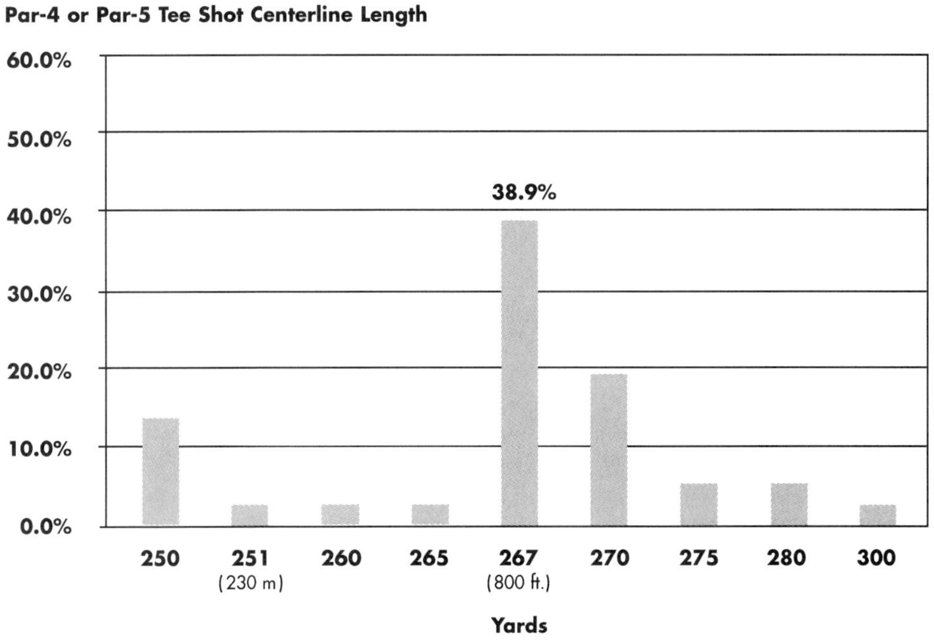

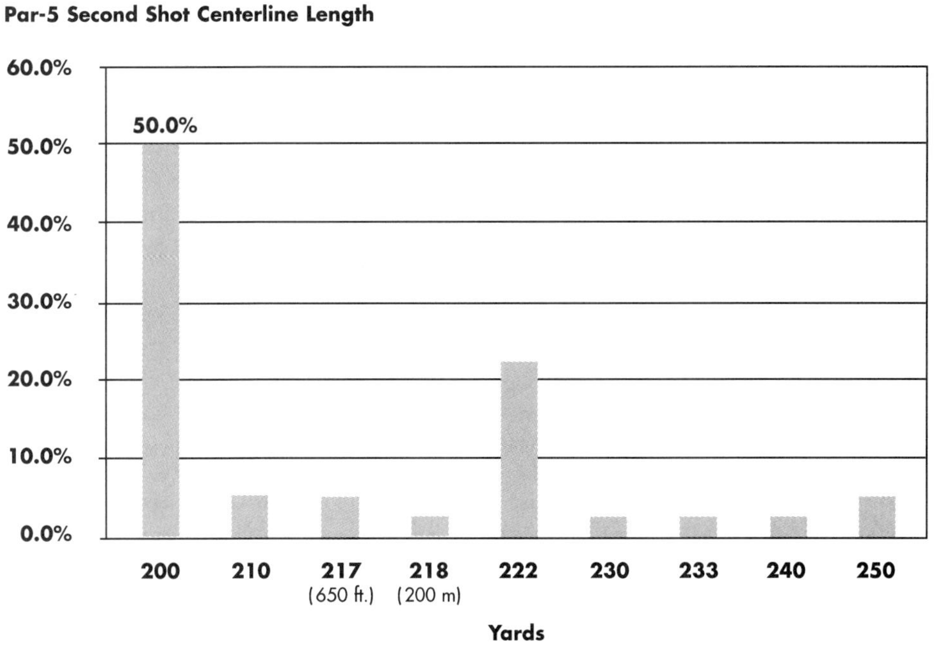

FIGURE 8-7
In a survey of golf course architects and planners, nearly 40 percent indicated that they draft tee shot centerlines 267 yards (800 feet) in length and that the centerline begins at the center point of the farthest-back tee. Fifty percent answered that the second shot centerline on par-5 holes is drawn 200 yards in length. The question pertained to the routing plan for a typical site and not one influenced by extreme conditions such as high altitude or strong winds.

Golf course architects are not magicians. Not so long ago, we positioned fairway bunkers about 240 yards from the back tees, then 260, and now on Sunday I watched the Portuguese Open on television while two young, relatively unknown professionals gave not a second thought about carrying two bunkers at 280 yards.

—Donald Steel, golf course architect, commenting on the need for measures to control length by limiting equipment

The length of centerline segments is predicated by the placement of points. Typically, tee shot centerlines of all non-par-3 holes on a course are shown as consistent distances, as are fairway shot centerlines for full fairway shots. These two consistent distances are determined by the golf course architect and/or planner based on characteristics that vary depending on the type of project and site conditions. Centerline lengths can also be adjusted by originating them at a particular set of tees on the course.

The two most common approaches to establishing centerlines are as follows:

1. The origin of the tee shot is at the farthest-back tee. The line is drawn about 267 yards to the fairway angle point (this equates to 800-feet). Full fairway shots are shown as centerline segments of about 200 yards. *(Source: Survey of golf course architects; see Figure 8-7)*
2. The origin of the tee shot is at the set of tees most commonly used—often the regular tees. The line is drawn about 220 yards to the fairway angle point. (The 220-yard dimension for the tee shot is typical for the average golfer.) Full fairway shots are shown as centerline segments of about 200 yards.

In the first scenario (which is the predominant format of most routing plans), the drawback is that the golf course is planned from the back tee location, even though most play will be from a point more forward, such as the regular tees. Beginning the centerline from the back tee does take the entire golf hole into account, but this is a weak rationale as *all* tees must be taken into account, regardless of where they are or how often they might see play. This includes the tees positioned most forward. So, as is proved many times, the preferred method may not always be the best.

In the second scenario, the tee and angle points represent the shot path and distance most tee shots will travel. This is logical. The angle point in the fairway shows where most tee shots will come to rest when hit ideally. The tees farther back, and those more forward, are secondary —as they should be. Unlike the first approach, drawing centerlines from the most common starting point of holes paints a more accurate picture of how the finished course will play from the standpoint of a majority of golfers. Variables that affect the starting point of centerlines and the lengths of their segments include:

- Type of golf course

  Courses designed for tournament play may call for longer centerline lengths; short, precision-length courses may call for shorter centerline lengths. In both cases, the tee from which centerlines are drawn may be determined by the course type.

- Type of golfer

  Courses to be frequented by average golfers will usually support average-length centerlines.

- Elevation above sea level

  Shots go farther at higher elevations due to lower air density. Thus, centerlines should be shown slightly longer than those for courses at lower elevations.

- Terrain of a particular shot
  Extreme downhill or uphill conditions will result in more or less ball roll and may call for an adjusted centerline length.

SAFETY CONSIDERATIONS TO OUTSIDE LANDS

Outside lands are those areas beyond the property to be used for golf. These lands cover a range of uses, virtually anything imaginable. The most common of these uses, and those to be addressed, include the following:

- Existing and future residential areas
- Roadways, streets, and other transportation corridors
- Public areas
  Parks, schools, trails, etc.
- Commercial activity
- Unknown future activity
- Designated wilderness and perpetual open space

The importance of designing golf facilities with due regard to the uses of adjacent parcels is that people occupying adjacent lands may not be aware of golfers and the potential for balls to exit the golf course. Golfers themselves—those engaged in using or visiting a golf facility—are more likely to be aware of the potential for errant balls. The difference is obvious. Golf courses should be planned carefully to help prevent balls from straying from the property defined for golf uses.

Golf Adjacent to Residential Areas

Although existing and future residential uses are not identical, no real difference exists when it comes to reasonable setbacks from golf holes. Setbacks to housing and residential common space are among the most

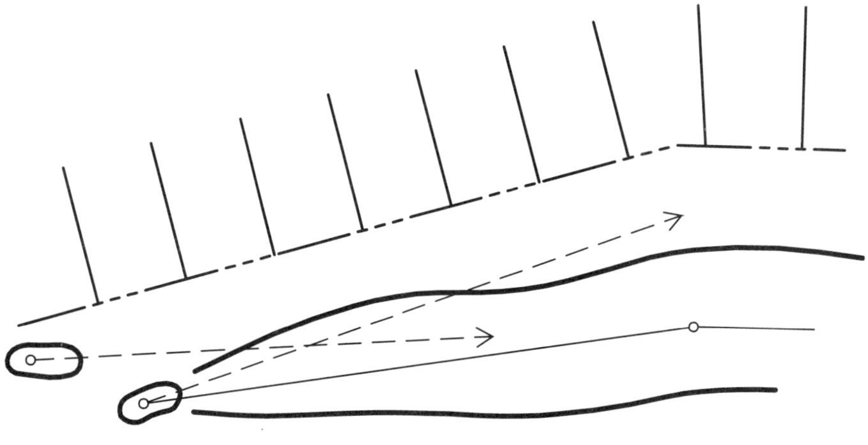

FIGURE 8-8
In most instances, tees should be planned toward the edge of the property in order to encourage play away from adjoining property. When tees are positioned away from the edge of a property, balls may be hit toward that line. In this example, the shorter tee is also misaligned, which is sure to cause problems. Even if aligned correctly, the farther-back tee aligns play away from the left side of the hole while the more forward tee will, due to the geometry, align more toward the left side.

PLANNING & ZONING DEPARTMENT

GOLF COURSE ZONING DISTRICT STANDARDS

PURPOSE & USE:
The purpose of this zone is to permit the development of golf courses while preserving and enhancing water resources, scenic vistas, neighborhoods, property uses and values. All public and private parties acknowledge this article as an instrument to address the paramount concern for safety and the need to design, landscape and re-landscape as necessary to prevent golf balls from striking homes or persons, regardless of impacts to the views from neighboring homes or lots.

Where residential development abuts a golf course, this overlay zone shall extend to, and include, the first tier of lots or homesites adjacent to the golf course. Associated business, commercial and any residential uses which are not directly adjacent to the golf course use shall be excluded from the golf course zone. The associated uses shall be provided for in the base and other overlay zoning districts.

DISTRICT STANDARDS:
1. Sufficient fringe and/or transition areas shall be provided to assure minimum setbacks from adjacent existing and future residential property lines. Golf hole "envelopes" or boundaries shall be created and clearly indicated on the development plan. Envelopes shall observe the following distances to adjoining existing and future residential purposes.
   a. Adjacent to landing areas (150-250 yards from the tee boxes) and all turning points: 200' from the centerline of the fairway.
   b. Adjacent to tees: 100' minimum from the center tee box or 50' from the edge of the nearest tee box, whichever is greater.
   c. Adjacent to the greens: 200' minimum from the center of greens, or 100' from the edge of greens, whichever is greater.
2. Berms, linear hazards, trees, and tall shrubs shall be utilized to assist in defending adjacent property from errant golf balls.
3. As part of purchase agreements of properties adjacent to a golf course, builders or sellers shall have buyers sign golf easements and affidavits which hold the Municipality harmless in the event of personal injury or damage to property associated with golf course activities. A note to this effect shall be added to the golf course development plan and adjacent subdi vision plats. Such documents are in no way intended to relieve golfers from responsibility for their actions.

RESIDENTIAL DESIGN STANDARDS:
The following standards act to provide additional public safety and protection of private property from errant golf balls:
1. In addition to setbacks required by base zoning districts, all buildings intended for residen tial occupancy shall be setback a minimum of 40' from property lines abutting golf holes.
2. Swimming pools and similar residential accessory uses shall be setback a minimum of 20' from property lines abutting golf holes. Walls or other types of screening are encouraged in order to afford additional protection from errant golf balls.

FIGURE 8-9
Page from the golf course zoning standards adopted by a municipality. Although the document contains specific language, it also calls for evaluation by a professional golf course architect for specific site conditions. It is only a guideline.

troublesome of all conditions a golf course routing faces with respect to safety to outlying lands. This is simple to understand when you consider that housing is more valuable facing a golf course. The drive to orient housing along fairways can precipitate conflicts with the golf itself.

There is no hard and fast rule to setbacks from housing, although that has not prevented many from attempting to author one. There are always examples where a generous setback was inadequate and cases where "not enough" has been working fine for 75 years or more. Both situations illustrate the point that you cannot apply one set of standards to a playing board that is inherently different everywhere it exists and on every new day.

Included here is a portion of the development standard of a municipality that adopted specific golf course setbacks to thwart shoddy planning of golf communities. The presumption is that the authors anticipated unscrupulous developers trying to minimize golf course acreage at the expense of safety and appropriate setback space. I applaud the municipality's foresight in adopting such a document but more so its honesty in stating that individual circumstances may require more or less space than outlined. Again, the interpretation must be handled by an expert, preferably an experienced golf course architect, who can sort through the specifics and arrive at conclusions based on his or her knowledge of, and experience with, the game and its playing board.

VARIANCES IN SAFETY SETBACKS

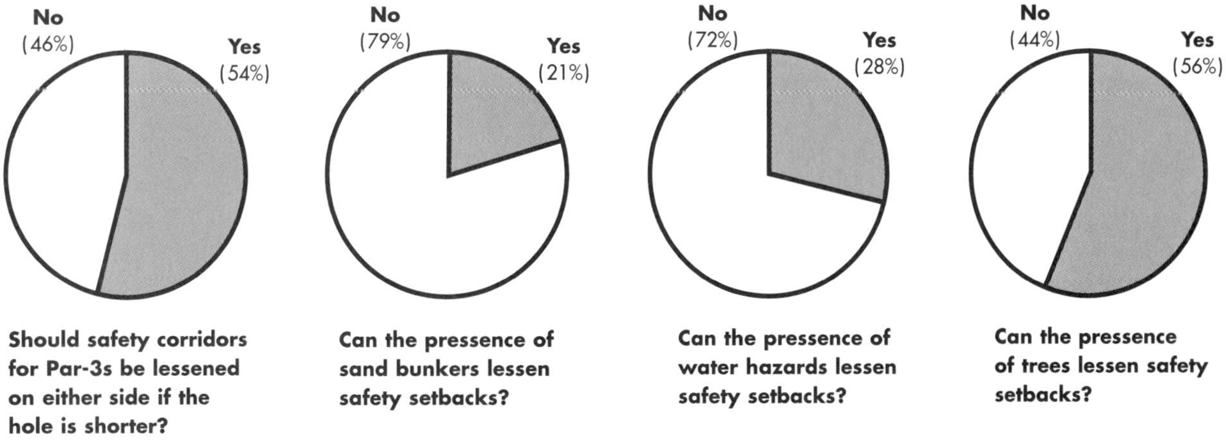
No (46%)
Yes (54%)
Should safety corridors for Par-3s be lessened on either side if the hole is shorter?
No (79%)
Yes (21%)
Can the pressence of sand bunkers lessen safety setbacks?
No (72%)
Yes (28%)
Can the pressence of water hazards lessen safety setbacks?
No (44%)
Yes (56%)
Can the pressence of trees lessen safety setbacks?

FIGURE 8-10
It is interesting to note how golf course architects and planners feel about lessening setbacks based on whether or not a tee shot is for a par 3, when hazards are part of the design, and when trees are present. I agree with the majority in the first two instances—often, it is prudent to lessen setbacks on par-3 holes, especially those less than 160 yards, and the presence of sand bunkers would not generally allow lesser setbacks. With regard to the use of water to lessen setbacks, there is disagreement. Water can, when used effectively, allow lesser setbacks. Trees constituting a reliable means by which setbacks can be lessened depends on their size, quantity, and longevity.

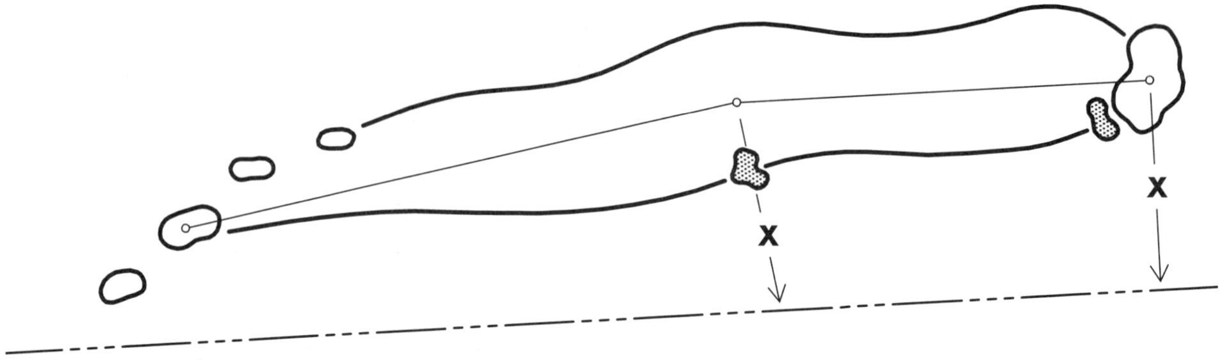

FIGURE 8-11
In most instances, the setback to property lines is consistent at the fairway point and at the green center point. In this example of a par-4 hole, this constant is defined as x and is shown for the right side of a golf hole only. Based on the average responses of golf course architects and planners, x is generally 180 feet to residential areas on par-4 and par-5 holes for typical course types. The same survey results show that x may be as much as 5 percent less to the left side of a fairway point. It is important to realize that there is no set standard—and there cannot be, as conditions vary from site to site. In some instances, based on evaluation by a qualified golf course architect or planner, x may be decreased or increased. Notwithstanding elevation differences, berming, features, or other screening, setbacks to roads may be 30 percent greater than x, and setbacks to parks may be 20 percent greater than x. Where there is perpetual, nonaccess open space adjacent to a golf hole, x may be considerably reduced.

FIGURE 8-12
In determining setbacks for par-3 holes of 200 yards or less, a rule of thumb is to allow a decrease in x of 8/10ths of a foot for every 1-yard decrease in the tee shot that is less than 200 yards. Under this formula, if x were 180 feet on the typical par-4 hole, x might be reduced to 140 feet for a 150-yard, par-3 hole. The basis for a reduction in x is that shots below 200 yards are executed by golfers with clubs generally capable of producing more refined and controlled results. A driver is not as easy to control or as accurate as a 6-iron.

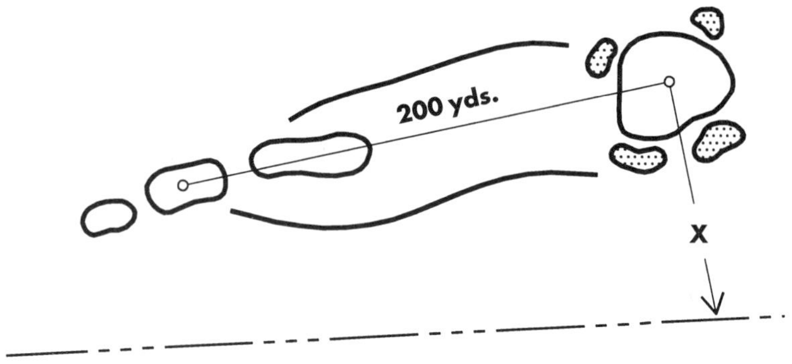

Golf Adjacent to Roadways & Streets

Setbacks from golf uses to roadways and streets is generally about 20 to 30 percent more in distance than from nongolf uses such as home sites, resort areas, and commercial office uses. However, in the case of private drives or minor roadways, which may be well signed to warn drivers to watch for stray golf shots, the setback distance may be the same as to nongolf areas. Generally, people in vehicles or on public roads cannot be expected to be aware of approaching golf balls. An extra buffer between the golf and the right-of-way is generally called for. The goal is to minimize the occurrence of balls leaving the course and possibly striking a car, pedestrian, or cyclist. In the case of pedestrians, a common occurrence is that of non-golfers walking onto course areas. This is a management issue that typically calls for adequate signage warning about golfers and golf balls and, in many cases, a low fence or wall to separate the uses both visually and physically.

Golf course planners should also carefully consider that roads may be widened. It is always best to check the likelihood of future road improvement and to carefully define the existing width of the right-of-way ahead of the routing process. The edge of the right-of-way is the critical line from which a setback should be imposed.

Golf Adjacent to Other Public Areas

The sensitivity associated with golf adjacent to public spaces is similar to that with roadways and streets. The people using these areas are not generally connected to the golf activity and therefore need to be buffered reasonably from golf balls hit off line. Adjacent land, whether used for a park, school, recreational trail, or parking lot, should be identified in the planning process and considered as the golf course is laid out. As in the case of rights-of-way, setbacks to parks, schools, recreational trails, and parking lots are generally greater than to individual homes or businesses.

Trails present a unique set of problems when adjacent to golf courses. The pathways may be used infrequently, or they may be busy thoroughfares. Occasionally, recreational trails deliberately run close to fairways in order to take advantage of the greenbelt created by the golf course. Trails have even been integrated with cart paths and situations designed where various types of trails cross over and intersect with one another. These are exceptions to the general thought that trails should be positioned at or near the same setback distance as residential activity. It is possible to establish controls for walking, hiking, jogging, bike, and equestrian trails through the use of signs that establish who has the right-of-way: golfers or trail users. In this scenario, golfers, whether in carts or walking, use the golf course path system, and people on the adjacent trail use their own designated pathway. Stop, yield, and caution signs can warn and control either or both user groups.

FIGURE 8-13
Multiuse trails can be good neighbors to golf courses, provided both trail user and golfer are aware of each other. An additional provision is that appropriate setbacks be maintained based on the site conditions.

Runs, Hits, & Errors — A Short Story About Cart Paths

At a favorite course outside Los Angeles, there's a relatively long and straight par 4 that runs along the bottom of a hillside. The green is set slightly higher than the fairway, and from this point the next tee is accessed by going up the hill to the right via a series of switchbacks. The cart path extends down the right side of the hole, and one can easily see the difficulty that was faced in laying out the cart path and how it would connect to the path to the next tees.

The cart path alignment is necessarily curious. As the path approaches the green, it extends up along the right of the green, where a cul-de-sac allows carts to turn around and go back against the flow of the hole to where it connects to the path up the hill. Mature trees abound. The plantings obviously were made to frame the hole and probably to conceal the ribbon of concrete path from view.

Having turned our carts around when we arrived at the green, we were facing back toward the tee near the forward pin position. On holing out, our group was refiling clubs in bags when all of a sudden we heard the feared "FORE" from well back in the fairway. Each of us ducked a little, my hands instinctively protecting my head while my body turned away from the sound of the warning. Bam! A well hit but slightly off-line 3-iron came flying in and hit my left hand, which was covering the left side of my noggin. It stung like hell.

The fellow who hit the shot came up and apologized. Within minutes, my hand puffed-up, and I figured something might be broken. Luckily, X rays showed that the area between my thumb and forefinger took the entire blow. The physician asked what the diameter of a golf ball was, then pointed out how there was not more than 1/8 inch extra room before the impact might have shattered any number of bones in my hand.

I could hardly blame the golfer who hit the ball. He told us that he thought we had already started up the hill and only after hitting did he notice our carts peeking out from behind the cluster of trees protecting the cul-de-sac.

Fortunately, the injury was not more serious. The lesson to be learned is not only that golf is inherently dangerous, but also that cart path alignment is an essential consideration. Whether it is defined in the routing or not, there must at least be a notion of where and how golfers will get from place to place. In this case, the problem was a combination of a poor cul-de-sac location and the need for better visibility. Perhaps the extra cost of taking the path the longer way around the left side of the hole and behind the green would have been better.

Golf Adjacent to Commercial Activity

Unlike residential uses, which are more definable, commercial activity is varied and virtually unlimited in scope. A junkyard full of old cars, for example, might be thought of differently than a corporate headquarters with windows facing the golf course, employee lunch areas, and open parking lots. As a general rule, setbacks to commercial lands are the same as to residential areas. Extenuating conditions may increase or decrease this distance as the uses are weighed in the planning process. The setback to the junkyard, for example, may be minimal in comparison to that of a busy parking lot. The busy parking lot may well be regarded as if it were a public roadway with greater setbacks.

Golf Adjacent to Unknown Future Activities

The future is difficult to predict. Golf course routers are encouraged to take into account adjacent land and its defined or likely future use. Adequate care must be taken to document on plans and records the known adjacent uses, especially if the routing plan will be made a part of public record, such as in a zoning or site plan approval process of a municipality. In some legal opinions, golf use that predates another use establishes a right to the golf land that may have to be taken into account by the future developers and users outside the golf property. This, however, does not obviate the need for good planning and reasonable setbacks. Unless agreements with landowners are in writing, it is possible that conflicting uses due to setbacks that are too close may be disputed.

Golf Adjacent to Wilderness & Open Space Areas

Establishing golf uses close to wilderness and open space areas is workable provided that public access is limited to these areas and they are not frequented as parks or gathering spots. "Close" may mean that the improved fairway is directly along the property line of a parcel to be held as open space and not developed. It has even been practice for golf holes to play out and over wilderness, wetlands, and preservation lands that are not under control or ownership of the golf course. This requires agreements and understandings with whomever controls the open space parcels. Additionally, if there is access to these open space areas, it may be advisable to consider signage warning of the golf use.

FIGURE 8-14
Hazards, especially water and other unplayable areas, can be helpful in encouraging shots away from areas outside the course limits. Consider, too, the effect this may have on the opposite side of the fairway where, perhaps, more shots will be directed.

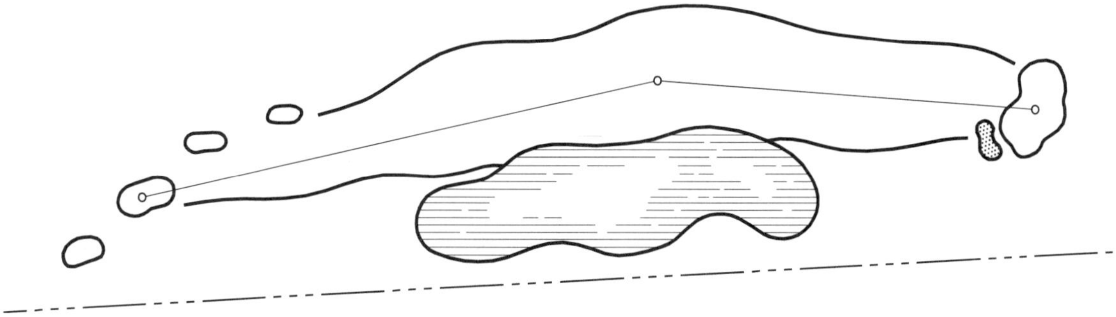

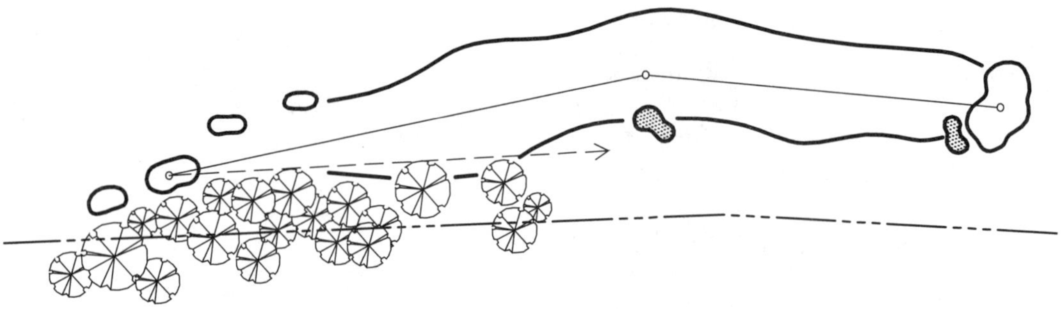

FIGURE 8-15
Natural or planted vegetation immediately adjacent to tees can be an effective tool for preventing shots toward areas outside the golf course boundary, especially when it is dense and tall. The reason has to do with golf ball trajectory. A tee shot has little ability to climb immediately when leaving a tee, and therefore vegetation affects both the aim of the golfer and the resulting flight of the ball at this point of departure. Vegetation located well down the fairway, while it may be a deterrent to the golfer, cannot deflect balls as efficiently. As a golf ball leaves the tees—which are known and controlled spaces—it gains height and travels along one of a multitude of possible paths. The farther away from the tees vegetation is located, the lower the chances that it will have any physical affect on the golf shot.

A Summary of Safety Considerations to Outside Lands

- Perpendicular alignment
  By configuring golf shot alignments perpendicular to (away from or toward) adjacent parcels, it is possible to minimize conflicts.
- Elevation differences
  Golf uses below or separated from adjacent parcels will minimize conflict, whereas golf uses elevated above adjacent uses increases the potential for conflict.
- Favoring the hook side
  Plan golf holes and shots with the left side adjacent to outside lands rather than the right. A majority of golfers will mis-hit golf shots to the right or slice side more than to the left or hook side. (*Note:* This is because an overwhelming majority of golfers plays right-handed. The terms *hook* and *slice* are presumptuous but nonetheless well understood.)
- Angling shot alignments away from adjacent lands
  When a golf hole is to be located along outside lands, it is preferable to position tees close to the property line so that the angle of the centerline in relation to the boundary is increased as much as possible.
- Favoring short holes or shots
  Where possible, short par-3 holes and approaches that involve short shots to greens are preferred over longer shots when adjacent to outside lands. A short par 4 or par 5 may actually encourage risky—and long—shots to the green. This condition is less preferable.
- Consider lay-up shots
  A forced lay-up shot along a property line can establish a more accurate and controlled shot and therefore lessen impacts from errant balls.
- Tandem planning efforts
  Whenever possible, golf course planning should be coordinated with outside land planning so that all uses are taken into account by all property owners and development interests.

- Documentation
  Written documentation, including legends and notes on drawings, is important to support contributing decisions.
- Agreements
  Written agreements can be helpful in defining golf uses and indemnifications that are part of sales agreements of homes and lots.
- Use of water
  Water can be an effective buffer to outside lands, as it is typically permanent. Also, golfers try to avoid water at all costs.
- Waste areas
  Areas of rugged land can offer benefits similar to those of water bodies, but only when they are so rugged that hitting toward them represents a significant penalty or inconvenience.
- Use of hazards
  Hazards can affect the desired alignment of a golf shot and therefore can add to the arsenal of tools that help protect a property boundary.
- Expanded setbacks at landing areas
  Consider increasing setbacks at the areas where a predominance of golfers is expected to hit golf shots.
- Landscaping at tee areas
  Mounding and relatively tall plantings along and off to the immediate sides at the front edges of tees can significantly influence the alignment of golf shots.
- Choice of golf uses
  Positioning practice putting greens, clubhouse grounds, and maintenance areas along property boundaries decreases the potential for errant golf balls but may pose other problems as these areas of a course are often at conflict with residential uses due to their associated activity.
- Practice area concerns
  Practice hitting areas, including practice ranges, must have larger setbacks than other golf uses based on the frequency with which golf balls are hit and therefore the increased likelihood of errant balls.

GOLF SHOTS & AIRPORTS

The potential conflict between golf shots and airports seems to be handled on a case-by-case basis. The typical issue involves improvements such as large mounds, structures, and trees within flight zones — those established at the ends of runways. In addition to the horizontal proximity of golf to airport land, the height of golf shots at least should be considered. The following information, provided by Titleist, gives approximate heights of average golf shots — helpful information whenever golf is near air traffic.

Driver — 80 feet
5-iron — 90 feet
Pitching wedge — 80 feet

SAFETY CONSIDERATIONS WITHIN THE GOLF FACILITY

Those using a golf course are more acutely aware of the potential hazards of golf than those who are off the golf property. This does not mean, however, that thoughtful planning should not be integrated with the routing plan when it comes to protecting one area of the facility from another. Minimizing conflicts within a golf course and its facilities includes appropriate planning of the following:

- Positioning of tees
- Positioning of greens
- Locating angle points
- Spacing between holes
- Buffering around practice areas

- Setbacks to clubhouse areas
  Parking, grounds, and buildings.
- Setbacks to on-course facilities
  Rest rooms, rain shelters, snack huts, maintenance areas, etc.
- Proper sun orientation
  Minimizing glare and maintaining adequate visibility.
- Consideration of site conditions
  Severe slopes may translate to more shot length and different space requirements; wind, altitude, and ground conditions may affect ball travel.

Positioning of Tees

Tees are crucial in that they represent relatively small areas from which a high volume of shots are played. Tees and greens are distinctive in this regard, which represents a convenience to planning in that the defined locations can be taken into account in the routing process. Given the rules and nature of golf, golfers spend a disproportionate amount of time during the round on these relatively small spaces. Specifically, tees are different from the expanse that falls between them and the green. Beyond the tee, it can only be guessed where golf balls might come to rest and from where golfers might find themselves executing shots toward the ultimate target, the green.

The effort must be made to protect the golfer using the tee as well as people on adjacent holes and areas. It is necessary to also consider where golfers waiting for a tee to become available might be staged. Tees must be positioned so that adjoining holes and any practice areas will not be bothered with off-line shots.

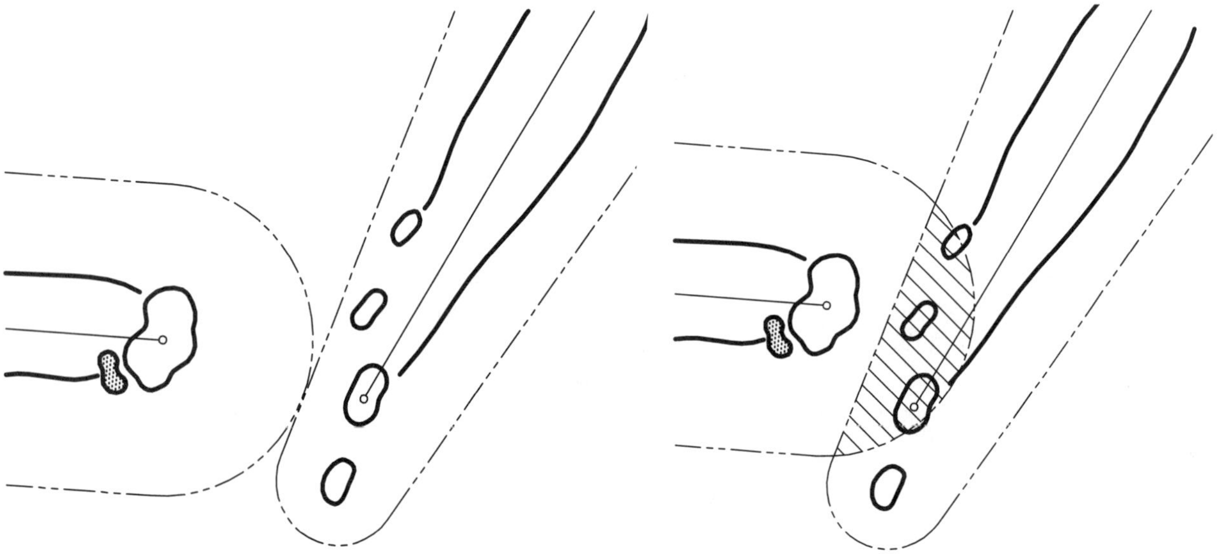

FIGURE 8-16
Locating tees and greens is a matter of keeping them an adequately distance from one another. In this example, the safety envelope of a golf hole is overlaid for both good and poor examples. The area likely to cause conflict is indicated by diagonal hatching.

Because every golfer must begin each hole from a defined teeing ground, which amounts to just a few hundred square feet as defined by the position of the tee markers on a given day, it can be assumed that more full golf shots will be played from tees than from any other area of the course. The centerline from each tee should be carefully considered in terms of its impact on other holes and areas.

Considerations in tee placement include:

- How golfers will approach the tee
- Where golfers will wait their turn to use the tee
- The angle of the shot to the angle point from each tee
- The relationship of the tee shot to other holes and areas of the course
- Dogleg angles
- The relationship of hazards to the tee shot
- The elevation difference between the tee and the landing area
- Mounding, vegetation, and features immediately along the sides of the tee
- Prevailing winds and solar orientation

Locating Angle Points—Landing Areas

Landing areas of a golf hole are the generally open areas around each angle point where good golf shots are accommodated without too much trouble. Landing areas are not typically defined on routing plans—they are simply implied by the position of the angle point. Remember, angle points represent where a majority of play will be to and from. Therefore it follows that they also represent where the subsequent shot will begin.

There is no set size for landing areas. They may take up an area of 100 feet in radius around angle points, or considerably less. A 100 foot radius is, however, a good size to envision landing areas, even if the actual size may be smaller. Landing areas are usually defined by a combination of features, hazards and vegetation. Landing areas must be positioned with respect for other areas of the course, such as tees, neighboring landing areas, greens, practice facilities, and the grounds of the clubhouse. Establishing their location is very often a matter of establishing many other points and required setbacks and then seeing where the angle point falls into place. Of course this may be done in reverse. A landing area can be established and then all other points set based on its location. Safety considerations in angle point (landing area) placement include:

- Minimizing adjacency to areas of other golf holes where golfers may be present
- Maintaining appropriate setbacks to golf and nongolf uses
- Using hazards and buffers to separate adjacent uses in the design
- Defining landing areas with hazards, features and vegetation so that golfers will be able to envision where balls should be hit

How Long to Depict the Tee Shot?

Early golf course architects depicted tee shots on par-4 and par-5 holes under 200 yards, as this was the expected length of an average drive at the time. However, with the advent of ball technology and better-engineered equipment, the average tee shot has lengthened. The increase has meant a wider spread and therefore a wider variance in how long tee shots are drawn on routing plans. Today, tee shots from the back tees are depicted by golf course architects as anywhere from 250 to 300 yards long. The most common uniform length is 267 yards, or 800 feet.

SOURCE: SURVEY OF GOLF COURSE ARCHITECTS AND PLANNERS; SEE FIGURE 8-7

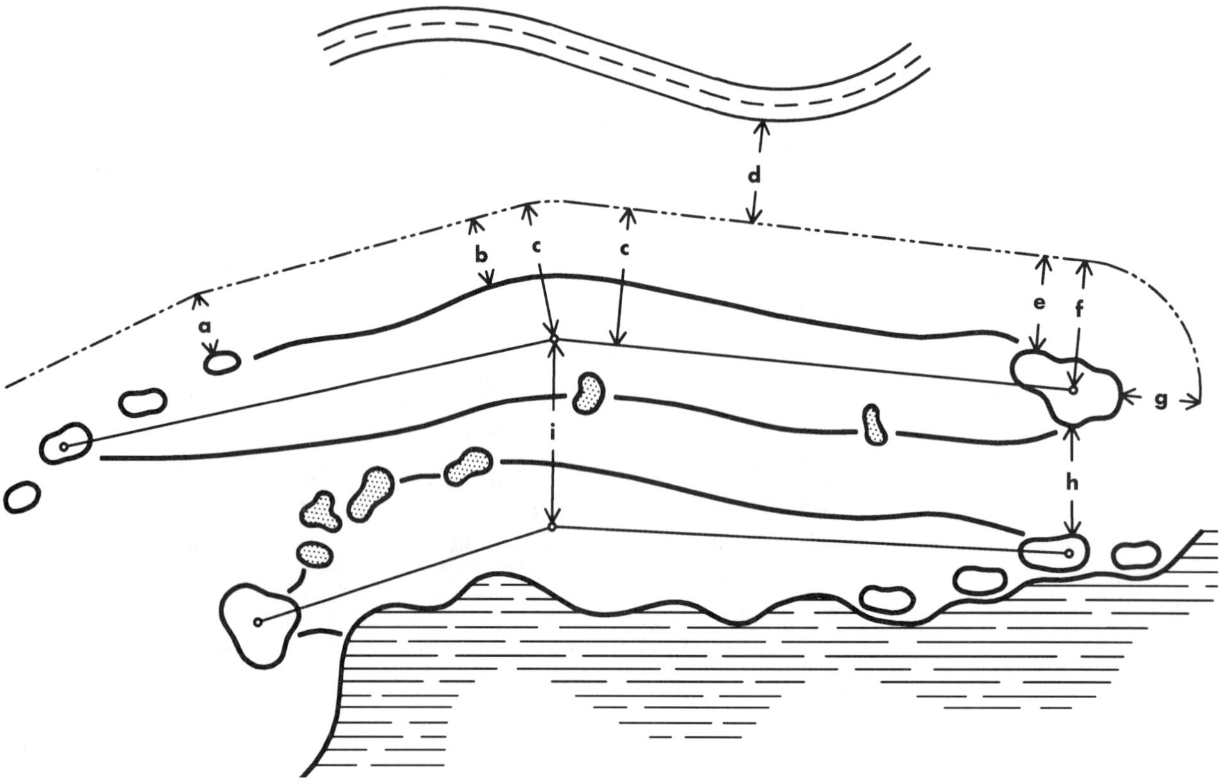

FIGURE 8-17
This diagram shows the results of a survey of golf course architects and planners. The survey asked for the typical dimension used in nine situations involving setbacks to property lines, roads, and other golf areas. The following are the average of the dimensions used by this group of professionals. As with all guidelines used in golf course planning, these should not be universally applied. Site and project conditions vary. This advice is supported by the range of responses given by many respondents. Again, these are averages—useful, but not unilaterally.

(a) An average of 78 feet from the edge of a tee to an adjacent residential property line
(b) An average of 110 feet from any improved fairway area to an adjacent residential property line
(c) 174 feet from a fairway angle point to an adjacent residential property line
(d) An additional 130 feet to the edge of a right-of-way beyond the c dimension
(e) An average of 116 feet from the edge of a green surface to an adjacent residential property line
(f) 164 feet from a green point to an adjacent residential property line
(g) An average of 113 feet from the back edge of a green surface to a residential property line behind a green
(h) An average of 136 feet from the edge of a green surface to any adjacent tee
(i) An average distance of 236 feet between angle points of opposing holes

FIGURE 8-18
Landing areas of holes are determined by where the fairway and green points are set, which are based on tee shots, although this may be done in reverse. The diagram demonstrates good placement of landing areas, as they are not directly adjacent to tees and greens, nor to one another. This example also shows hole configuration such that errant shots hit off the tee to the right will not interfere with adjacent property and will not affect the adjacent golf hole. Certainly it is not always possible to achieve such relationships. Where the locations of landing areas are less than ideal, additional space may be required between areas, and hazards, features, mounding, and other screening may be required.

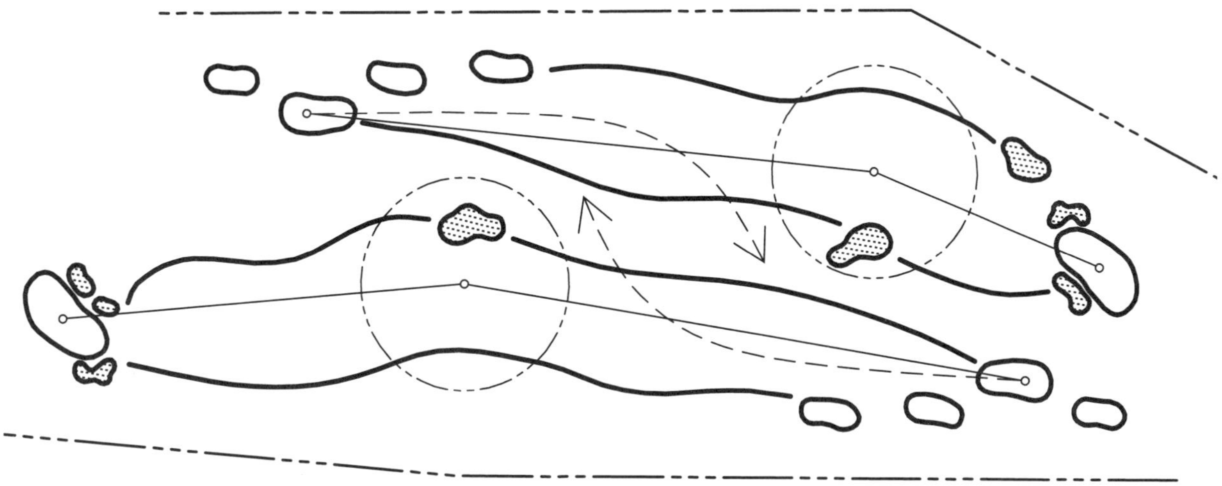

Positioning of Greens

Greens are, essentially, landing areas. They are distinguished in that they represent a more pinpointed target and will ideally receive more accurate play than their counterpart landing areas out in the fairway.

Safety considerations in green placement include:

- The size and shape of the green
- How golfers will approach and exit the green
- The relationship of the approach shot to other holes and areas of the course
- Dogleg angles to the green
- The relationship of hazards to the approach shot
- The elevation difference from the tee or approach shot to the green
- Buffering and separation of the green from intensive uses

A Word About Fitting Holes Together

The next chapter, "Fitting Holes Together," is a must-read for continuing the information about safety. This chapter is about general safety assumptions and thoughts. When holes are strung together, a new set of variables comes into play. The orientation and preferred methods of fitting holes together is not only about safety, but much of it is related.

THE INFLUENCE OF EQUIPMENT, GOLFER & COURSE TYPES

Considerable attention has been paid to the improvement of clubs and balls. This obviously has an important affect on safety considerations, as golf courses cannot easily be adjusted to compensate for new equipment, especially if the equipment facilitates a golf ball traveling 20 yards farther than it did on the day the course was opened. All of a sudden, we have a situation where the landing area of older courses may now be altered. The alignment of centerlines, landing areas, and features (hazards, mounding, etc.) is out of whack when this occurs.

The same situation can occur when a golf course is changed from one type of clientele to another. For example, when a course that was originally designed with tight conditions for above average golfers is transformed into a public-access course for average golfers, it may not match the new type of play. A few elements of the golf course are easy to adjust, such as tee positions and pin positions, but changing the entire course and its physical makeup is usually out of the question due to cost. In planning the golf course, it is reasonable to question the type of play and golfer and take these variables into account. While it would be simple advice to also consider the future of golf equipment, I do not know how to weigh this variable in the routing process. To go overboard and anticipate longer and longer tee shots and greater hitting ability as a result of equipment changes is inadvisable. So, too, is ignoring the likelihood that equipment manufacturers and golfers will continue to push the envelope.

As a last-check before firing, verify that the area is clear and that you are trained to use the firearm in your possession.

—Conventional wisdom excerpted from a police officer's training manual on shooting range safety, also applicable to golfers

I suppose the best advice is to design and route for the conditions that are likeliest—and to remember the essential balance of course design as expressed by the late William Flynn: "Accuracy, carry, and *then* length." My apologies to Flynn if he did not intend the emphasis on *then,* but why else would he have included it? For golf courses to be laid out based entirely on length goes against this essential balance. Accuracy, wherever it is possible, is an asset of routing that transcends the hype surrounding length and the lure of all-out ball-bashing. Applaud accuracy whenever you get the opportunity, for it represents golf far more truthfully than the other two elements Flynn highlights. Although carry and length are part of the game, they are not always developed in golfers. Accuracy can be regardless of the golfer's strength, physical ability, age, stamina, years playing, and so on.

THE EFFECT OF TREES & VEGETATION

It seems a common crutch to rely on trees—both those existing and new ones to be planted—to provide screening and protection from golf play. Well, the fact of the matter is that while trees are helpful and can assist in making golf holes safer, there are far too many variables in the life of a tree to make it a permanent fixture that can be counted on for years to come.

The 90-Degree Dogleg — A Short Story

During high school, I played for the golf team. Our home course had an unusual 17th hole. It was a lay-up par 4 of about 300 yards that went some 150 yards straight out and then turned left for another 150 yards. Interestingly, there was a house right in the crook of this unusual dogleg, and we were always careful about cutting the corner because we did not want to hit anyone or break any windows. Nonetheless, cutting the corner was the concept of this hole, for it is entirely out of the question to ask anyone, let alone high school golfers, to not trim yardage off such a straightforward geometry problem.

Over the years that I played this hole, it became increasingly frustrating to arrive at the tee only to find new measures taken to eliminate the corner-cutters. At first there were O.B. stakes on the left side of the fairway, but these were nothing but imaginary lines, and they could be overcome with ease. Next came a wire screen along the left length of the tee, but golfers would just tee it up high and outhit the damn thing. Later came a row of hedges, but they were of no consequence to a player with a mission. A new, higher screen was added, and while this proved moderately effective, 8-irons were soon leaping over it as if the bar had been raised in a pole vault competition.

One day we arrived to find a new out-of-bounds setup. Now the out-of-bounds continued in a straight line from the left side of the tee all the way to the end of the first straight part of the fairway. Anything hit left of this line on the tee shot, by local rule, was out of bounds. Drat! This, of course, prompted outcry, as the fun of playing the hole had been tossed out in a matter of quickly painted wood stakes. My recollection is that during many practice rounds, the newly contrived O.B. was ignored and the hole was played the way it was loved in its previous life.

The moral of this story is to not create such a hole in the first place, at least not with someone living in such a vulnerable location. The entire point of golf holes is for golfers to discover loopholes that permit them to get to the green quicker and with fewer and better shots. Had the house not been located so inappropriately, this would have been an interesting hole for all the right reasons. As matters stood, this dangerous game thankfully never resulted in an injury, at least that I ever heard about.

A well-conceived routing plan takes existing vegetation into account and utilizes it in a reasonable manner to make the golf course not only more enjoyable but perhaps slightly safer. This said, it is interesting to remember that the earliest golf courses—those carved across linksland—held few trees. The earliest of cross-country links were contrived with no constraints in terms of acreage, they had very little play, and there was certainly no wholesale nursery across town. Although golf course routings are not typically detailed enough to include individual trees, it is good practice to include in the routing plan dense vegetation that is to be retained, key trees in a landscape, and areas where mass plantings might be needed.

The Living, Growing Aspect: All trees eventually die. There is no such thing as the permanent tree. Trees also get bigger. As trees grow, they can change the nature of a golf hole, requiring remodeling, trimming, or a combination of both. Young trees are typically small, and most newly planted trees, which are also usually young, tend to be less influential until they mature and spread out to occupy more space.

The Maintenance Aspect: When trees fall, which they occasionally do, they constitute a safety problem in more ways than one! Also, the routing cannot anticipate whether, when, or to what degree trees and brush will require thinning, nor to what level of competence the task will be undertaken. Usually, trees and vegetation require water and a degree of maintenance to survive and flourish. These concerns are often underestimated.

The Influence of Trees & Vegetation: It usually takes more than one tree to screen an area. For this reason, trees are almost always more useful in mass plantings, especially if the goal is to screen or close off an area or a view to an area. Golfers tend to aim away from trees, especially sizable specimens. The closer the tree is to the origin of the shot, the more impact it will have on the aiming of the shot. Thus, the most effective area in which to plant trees is at the source of golf shots, such as immediately along the front of a tee to either side or both sides. This can have the effect of shifting the golfer's alignment away from the trees or vegetation, as the path of the golf ball during its ascent is likely to be struck down if it strays into the thicket right off the bat. You can see how a tree halfway to the landing area will not have nearly the impact of a nearer tree. The height of the golf shot will probably exceed the height of the tree, which will have little or no effect on aiming. It is typically inefficient to plant trees at the end of a golf shot and expect them to help control or influence shot alignment.

Trees can have the effect of blocking views and also blocking the way. This is sometimes a good thing and occasionally a negative. Visibility should be considered, as should the overall landscape design of all golf course areas. Dense brush, wetlands, and forest areas can also limit access by nature of their density and ruggedness. This can help keep golfers and others away from areas where access should be limited.

THE EFFECT OF TOPOGRAPHY

Elevation differences influence safety by helping control shots in the case of golf holes being depressed into the landscape. When the reverse is true—that is, when golf holes are elevated above the adjacent landscape—there is more potential for golf shots to stray into areas away from the centerlines. The reason for this involves physics. Side mounding, embankments, and the canyon effect they create will prompt balls to be contained in fairways. The opposite occurs when fairways are crowned without the canyon effect.

THE KID & THE BIKE — A SHORT STORY ABOUT RESPONSIBILITY

The golf course architect got the call from the attorney late in the afternoon. "I represent a couple whose son was injured at one of your courses," the conversation began. The details of the injury were reported and, while the boy would be fine, his leg fracture was complicated and school, basketball, and a host of other activities would be on hold for a month or more. "The parents have instructed me to file action against you and the owners of the golf course," the attorney continued.

After a few minutes, the attorney finally got around to suggesting a remedy for the hazard that brought about this awful accident: "A fence should be erected around that thing!" Thinking he meant a fence around the entire golf course, the golf course architect pointed out that the golf course, being part of a resort, was already off limits to 14-year-olds unless they were guests of the hotel and had paid a green fee. It was private property and well marked as such at every customary entrance. "No, I don't mean a fence around the golf course," said the attorney. "I mean a fence around that hole you put out there."

You guessed it—the hole in question was a sand bunker, and the kid, who thought that riding his BMX bike across the undulating mounds would be fun, discovered a pitfall, literally. After going up and over several mounds he came to one that, inconveniently, had a hole cut into its lower side.

Elevation situations that may require extra measures to contain balls include:

- Tees that are extremely elevated above a fairway or green
- Fairways that are extremely elevated above a green
- Routing holes along a ridge
- Golf holes situated above other golf or nongolf uses that are adjacent to the golf hole

SPECIAL CIRCUMSTANCES

Several conditions do not fit the above sections but nevertheless deserve discussion. It seems reasonable to state one last time that golf is a game of individual skill played across an obstacle course that, in today's world, is more often than not between houses or bordering private property. To apply standards to golf course design is not always possible, as its myriad situations cannot be anticipated. The following topics prove that point and drive home the best of all advice: to involve professionals in the design of golf courses and to rely on their experience and knowledge on how courses can be laid out to be reasonably safe for both the golfer and nongolfer.

FIGURE 8-19
Signal bells are common in situations where a blind or partially blind shot is played to an area. Golfers ring the bell as a courtesy when leaving the area. The bell signals to those behind that it will be safe to hit in a few moments.

The Blind Shot: Blind shots are a part of golf, as old as the game itself. To eradicate them, as some have suggested, is not always possible given certain natural terrain and site conditions. In getting from one point to the next, and routing an exciting and interesting golf course in the process, a few blind shots may be required. The important element is to understand clearly the relevant terminology. A *blind shot* is not a *blind hole,* and neither of these is a shot to a green of which not all the putting surface is visible. Often, I hear golfers complain that "the hole is blind," only to discover that it is just the green's surface that cannot be seen from a particular spot in the fairway.

It is not ideal to have a fully blind hole—that is, a hole on which all shots are played to targets that cannot be seen. This is a rarity; I have seen only a handful in my lifetime. The occasional blind shot—that is, a shot played to an area that cannot be fully seen, is more acceptable when the area *can* be seen from a nearly vantage point. Man-made devices that permit this visibility are the platform, the periscope, the closed-circuit video system, and the signal bell. All can work, but each can also fail. The best method is to create terrain—either natural or artificial—that can be used conveniently by the golfer to see ahead. A mound, rise, or cart path is ideal for this purpose when located near a tee or landing area. From the vantage point, the golfer can see what lies ahead even if the view from the center of the fairway is restricted.

Severe Doglegs: Such designs can create safety problems if the hole is not obvious in its intended path. Hazards and other features may help point the way for golfers. Even devices such as cart paths may help the golfer know where the hole is going.

Severe Grades: As has been established, extreme rises in elevation above the landing area can create hazards if not planned for. Severe grades also require movement of golfers, and this requires that paths be located appropriately. Ultimately, well after the routing plan stage, path alignments should be worked out and checked by an engineer for final placement, proper grading plans, and surface specifications.

Screens & Nets: Barriers such as screens and nets are often viewed as an alternative to moving holes farther away or changing courses. This is often an appropriate measure. However, screens and nets can give the appearance of a completely safe situation, which they—or any other measure—simply cannot provide. While a screen may protect a golfer,

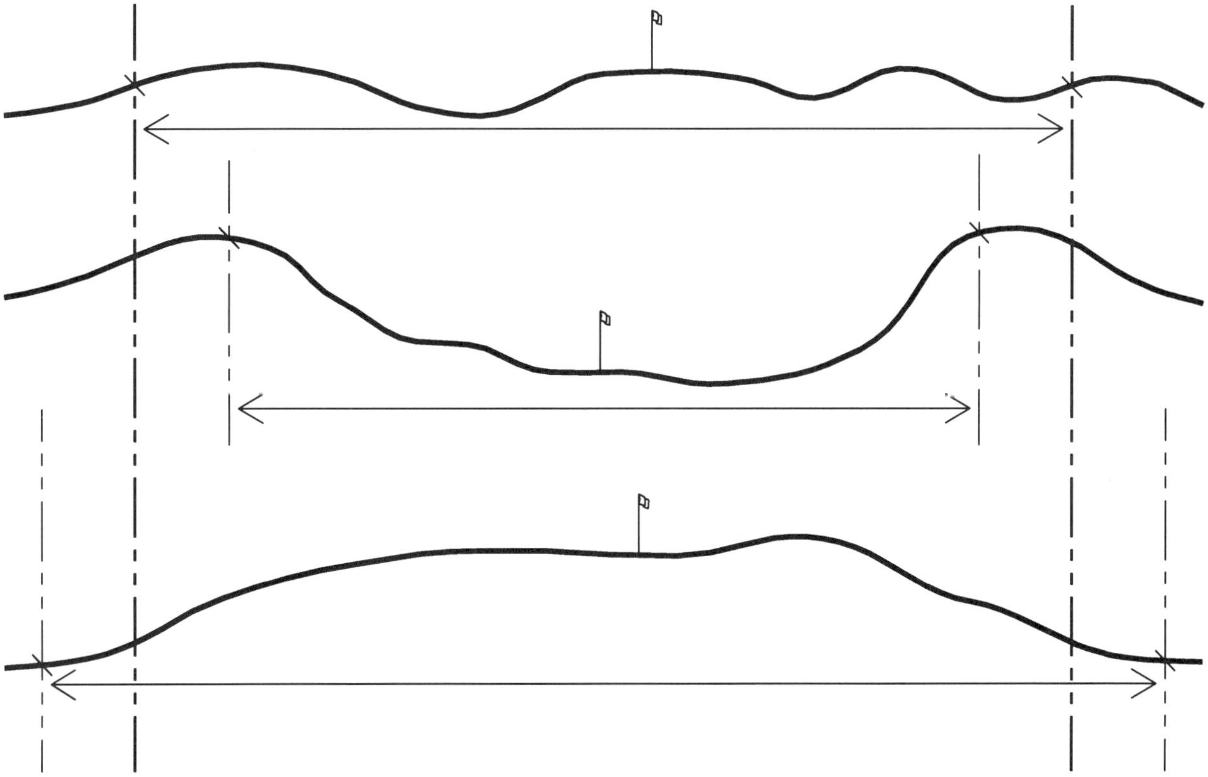

FIGURE 8-20
The effects of elevation differences to the width of a safety envelope are shown in the three examples of a section looking toward the green along the centerline of a golf hole. In the top example, the width required is typical. In the middle example, because the fairway is depressed, the required width may be less. In the bottom example, which shows the fairway being crowned above the edges, greater width may be required.

it may also come loose or be damaged by vandals. In this case, it is perhaps more dangerous than no screen at all. The comfort that both golfer and nongolfer derive from such a device does not go away when a small tear or rip has occurred.

While a screen may be designed to catch balls hit toward a nearby street, it may also give pedestrians cause to be less aware than if no screen were there. As you can see, there is a delicate balance associated with erected structures to keep balls from leaving golf areas. In some instances, the implementation of a screen or net could be an indication that safety conditions are inadequate.

Remodeling: Remodeling typically occurs to courses that were designed many years earlier. At especially old courses it may have been that only a few players per day were anticipated, and it is likely that equipment was much more limiting whenever the course was originally built. The question of how to add safety features to an older layout involves balancing the problem areas against the integrity of the golf course.

It is not necessarily a wise decision to simply take a tight layout and shorten it to gain setbacks. This may cause golfers to risk reaching greens they might not ordinary go for and can create new problem areas. Having said this, it is certainly not wise to do nothing to improve problematic areas. Many times, there is simply no room, and the course must be adjusted—to the degree possible—by a combination of efforts.

The first step in evaluating the existing golf course for routing changes is to identify where problems exist. This should be done in two steps: (1) by determining where safety envelopes may conflict based on existing conditions; and (2) by finding out where golf balls have caused conflict. Armed with this information, the golf course architect can work with the owner to improve safety conditions to the degree possible given the circumstances. This calls for bringing in a qualified golf course architect. As has been said, each situation is different. Older courses are apt to have less room; this is a common fact.

Devices and undertakings in routing that can be used increase safety on existing courses when room is limited include:

- Adjusting tees angles and straightening tees for better alignment
- Creating mounding to separate areas
- Adding and relocating hazards to direct play and create new/improved centerlines for holes
- Shortening holes to better control shots
- Installing nets and screens
- Adding trees and, in some instances, thinning trees to open areas where shots should be encouraged
- Adding signs that warn golfers about areas of potential conflict
- Managing the placement of tee markers and controlling the choice of tee sets by golfers based on their skill level/handicaps

Fitting Holes Together

HOLE NO.

9

My first experience fitting golf holes together was in the desert behind my childhood home. I was eight years old. The tees were small areas raked clean of rocks. The greens were amoeba-shaped dirt areas compacted to a Stimpmeter reading that would have made any greenkeeper envious—or at least curious. The cups were cat food cans. Somehow it all fit together. The summer in which my course, Rolling Rocks, was built there were no plans drawn before I set out to do the work. I simply got up early to beat the 110-degree temperatures, and then, somehow, managed to squeeze 18-holes in the half-acre space, crossing a small ravine twice, and back to the "clubhouse."

It was only after building Rolling Rocks that a plan was drawn. A plan, you know, is important for the scorecard. It was probably not drawn to scale, but it did point out some obvious flaws. I recall distinctly a few areas where players (kids from the neighborhood, my father, brother, etc.) had problems finding their way around. In one area we had more than an isolated incident of balls landing in a neighbor's yard. Fortunately their little squeaky dogs were never in the right place at the wrong time.

[T]he excellence of any good golf course consists of a desirable series of eighteen good golf holes.
—Charles Piper, in an article appearing in Golf Illustrated, *February 1926*

The lessons brought to light by an eight-year-old golf course architect can be applied to many of the issues that crop up on real golf courses: safety, conflicting holes, poor relationship to the land, and situations where the routing seems lost. In this chapter, the basics of working holes into a layout are explored. Do not read this chapter only. Each chapter accrues greater meaning when it is understood relative to the others.

TYPES OF ROUTINGS

Independent of the number of holes or length of a course, routings fall into broad but definable descriptions. Many configurations have been pictured, which helps in identifying them. It has been observed that routings of golf courses, especially when they are small and not full of detail, can look like sausage links (a favorite description of Jim Connelly, an agronomist consultant) or like drawings of pickles (a favorite description of Mike Yukon, a golf course construction superintendent with whom I have worked). Whether sausages or pickles, the individual holes form a series of individual parts, each chained together. The beginning of the chain is usually at the same point or near the end. These qualities are among the most consistent in routings. The rest, all of the many variables that affect the chain, are as varied as one can imagine.

Land Influences on Routing Type

Golf course routings fall into six primary types, of which many hybrid varieties can be defined. These classifications have to do with the general footprint of the course and how the holes relate to one another.

The six types of routing layouts as influenced by the configuration of the land are:

- Block or core routings
  Holes contained within a whole shape that is not broken by other parcels or large land uses.
- Development-driven strip routings
  Usually single or double holes that are bordered by development.
- Drainageway-driven routings
  Routings that primarily follow drainage alignments or establish them.
- Topo-driven routings
  Designs influenced by the terrain to the degree that the routing is a matter of following the only practical route based on the topographical givens.
- Large feature–driven routings
  Designs almost entirely oriented to a massive feature such as an ocean shoreline, lake, river, or mountain.
- Remnant land routings
  Designs configured on awkwardly shaped land parcels that are remnant in nature and often pooled to provide acreage on which the routing must go; therefore, the routing must follow a path implied by the shape of the land.

FIGURE 9-1
Core routing—The holes are contained within a whole parcel of land and not broken up by other land uses. Core routings are also characterized by having all fairways grouped together without any narrow bands of property where just one or two holes are routed.

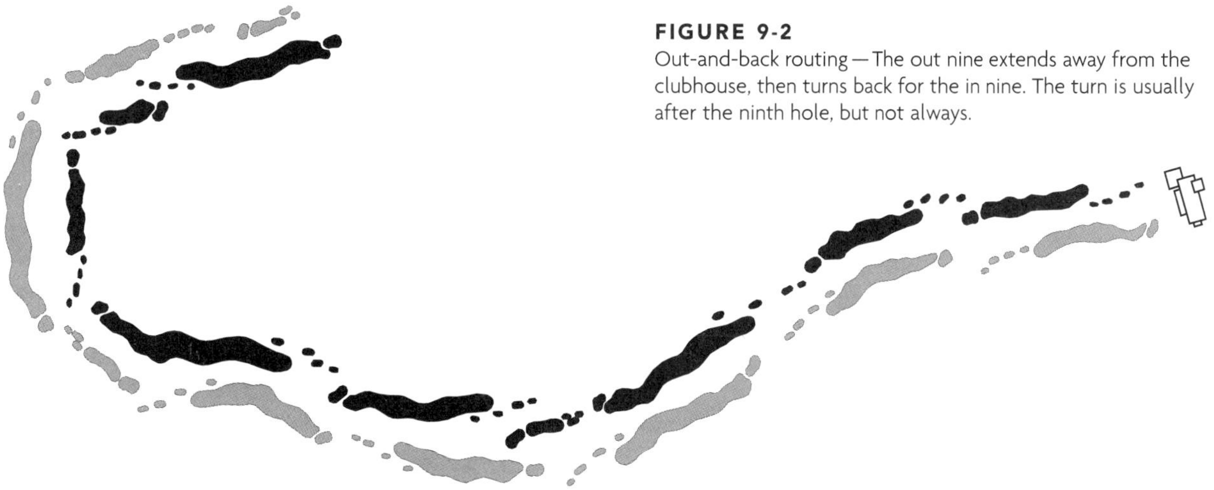

FIGURE 9-2
Out-and-back routing—The out nine extends away from the clubhouse, then turns back for the in nine. The turn is usually after the ninth hole, but not always.

Routing Configurations

The many types of routings of 18-hole courses can be divided into five basic types. Each revolves around the number of times the course returns to the point of origin and at what point (or points) in the round these returns take place. For courses made up of other than 18 holes, the same basic types may be roughly translated, although the need to return to the beginning point before the finishing hole is significantly diminished when fewer than 18 holes are involved.

The five primary routing configurations are:

- Out and back

    Where the routing goes out and does not return until the last hole (Figure 9-2).

Routing is the bones, everything else is flesh.
—Desmond Muirhead

- Returning nines

  Routings that return at the ninth hole and then go out again, not returning until the last hole.

- Multiple loops

  Usually a returning nine configuration that includes one or more additional points at which the routing returns to the point of origin. Such configurations can also sport two or more returning points at other than the ninth hole, such as with three loops of six holes each. Multiple loops are useful when it is beneficial that the clubhouse area be accessed more often than once in the round. Multiple loop layouts can provide more flexibility in playing options, allowing golfers to return after fewer than nine holes or more than nine but less than the full 18.

- Non-ninth returning point

  A course that returns once at a hole other than the traditional ninth; unusual, but occasionally used where conditions dictate.

- Nonreturning courses

  Certainly an anomaly, but occasionally this situation is unavoidable or the right thing to do based on given conditions (See "Way-Out Routings" on p. 269).

FIGURE 9-3
Returning nines routing — Both nines begin at and return to the clubhouse, regardless of their path.

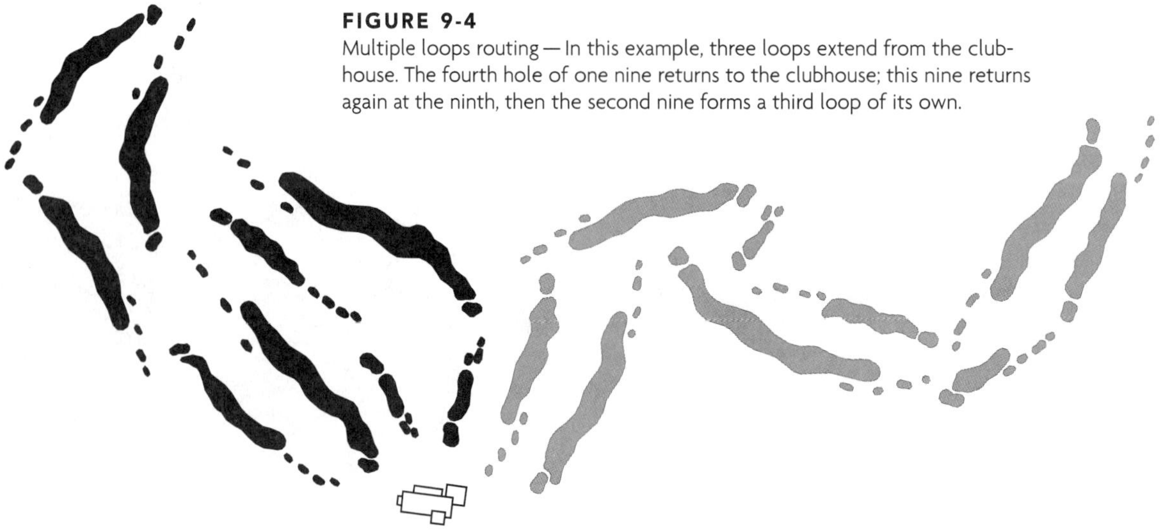

FIGURE 9-4
Multiple loops routing — In this example, three loops extend from the clubhouse. The fourth hole of one nine returns to the clubhouse; this nine returns again at the ninth, then the second nine forms a third loop of its own.

FIGURE 9-5
Non-ninth returning point routing — Here, the course returns at just one point, after the fifth or the 13th hole, depending on which nine is played first. Such routings are rare and are usually devised due to unavoidable situations. Among the drawbacks is the complexity of organizing simultaneous starts from two holes at the clubhouse.

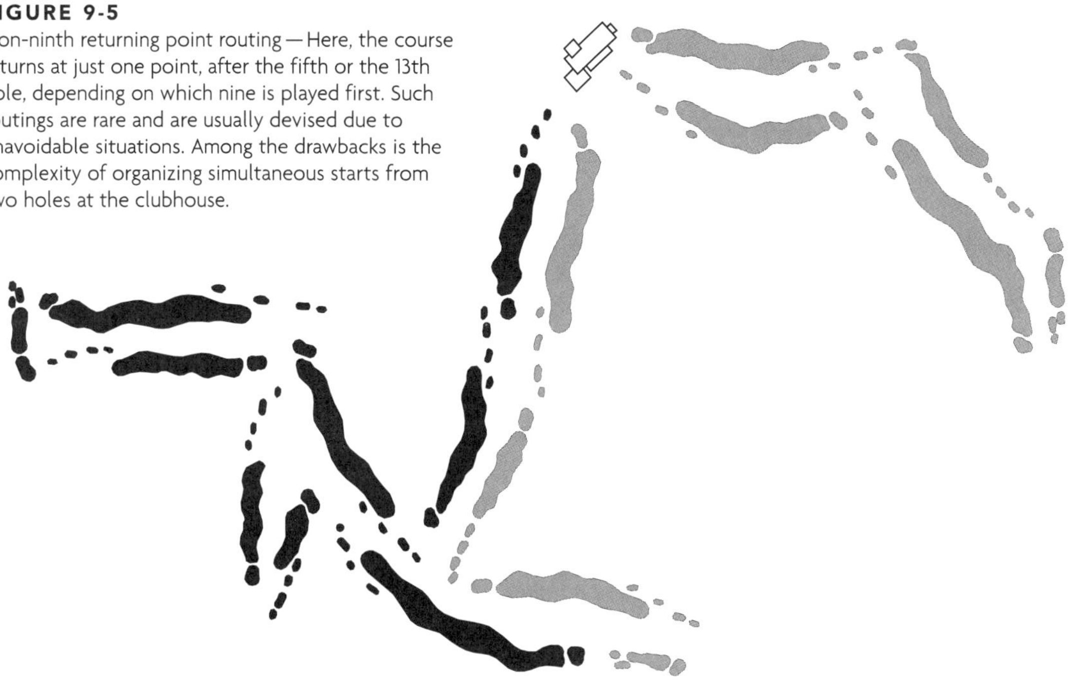

FIGURE 9-6
Nonreturning course routing — In this example, the actual routing for the Black Forest Course at Wilderness Valley Golf Resort in Gaylord, Michigan, the 18th hole finishes well away from the clubhouse. The course, designed by Tom Doak, was configured to take advantage of the best land for golf. The resulting trip back to the clubhouse is a minor inconvenience.

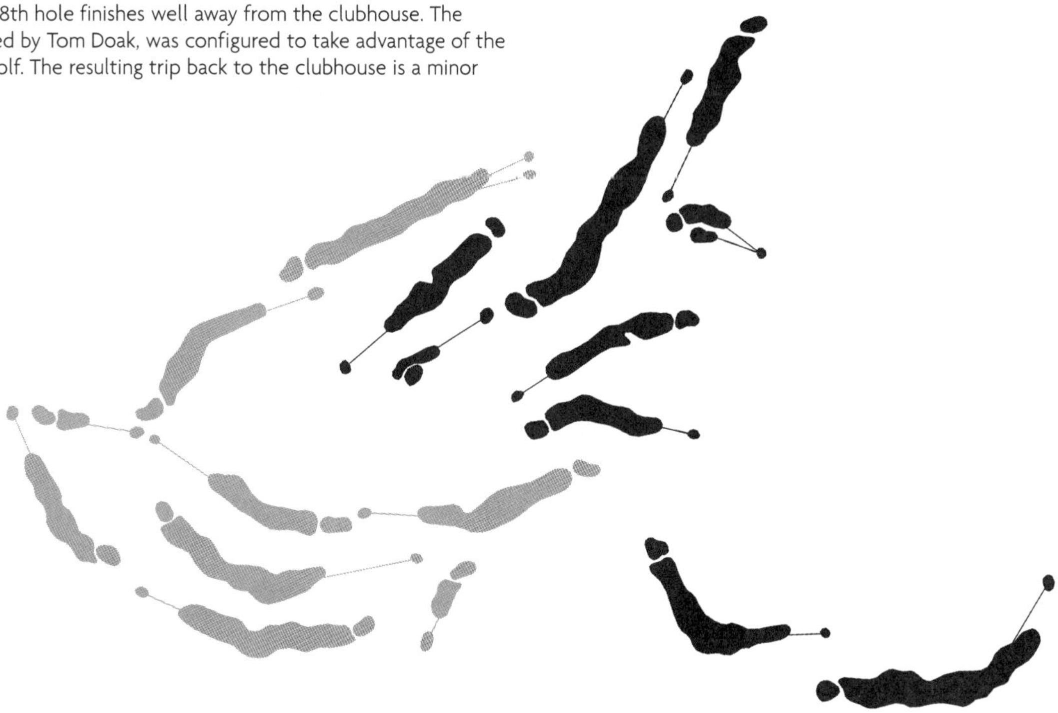

The type of routing for a particular project is mostly influenced by the land conditions that are present. Only in rare instances, where acreage is abundant and primarily flat, is the canvas truly blank. Even in this instance, the driving forces behind the course and the need to make it function from a drainage and grading perspective will likely influence the course's configuration.

The late Desmond Muirhead, an acclaimed planner and golf course architect, pointed out that "it is mentally impossible to think of 18 holes at one go. You simply cannot get each individual thing in your head all at one time." One looks at a routing from a distance. The holes are there, but each individual one is not at the forefront of thought simultaneously. When you zoom in on a routing, your mind is only considering certain parts of the routing (a hole here or there, a series of holes, or how two holes relate to one another.

Fitting holes together goes hand in hand with land planning. Muirhead, however, did not like the term; he reminded golf course routers that "we do not *plan* land. Land is a given. When we route and plan, it is a form of design." If Muirhead had his say, the professionals we know as land planners would be called land *designers*.

THE GEOMETRY OF ROUTINGS

The primary perspective, when viewing a routing, is directly down from above. This is the plan view and the vantage point with which we are most familiar. How the holes fit together is most apparent from this angle. The direct plan view is not the only one, however. The element of vertical relationship between holes and areas is of essential importance. The following topics address both the horizontal and vertical considerations of fitting holes to one another and in relation to the routing as a whole.

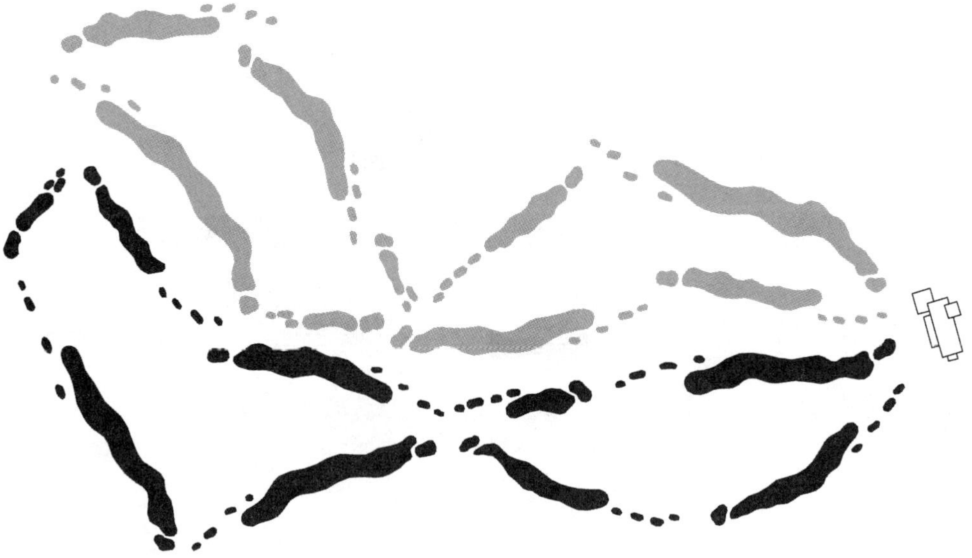

FIGURE 9-7
Side-by-side configuration — Among the most common returning nine routings for an 18-hole course. Each nine is adjacent to but not integrated with the other. This is the most common routing when nines of an 18-hole layout are built at different times.

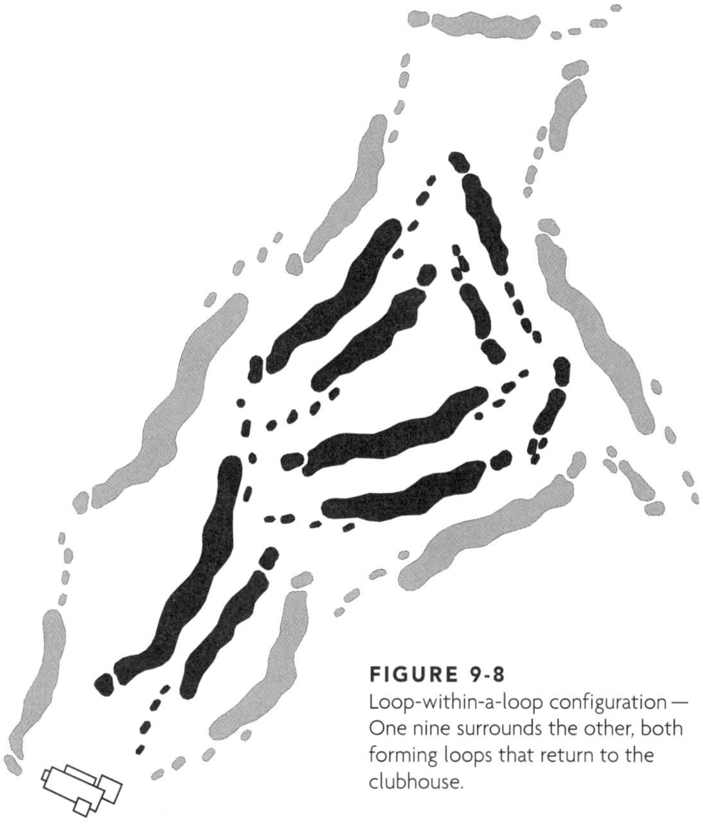

FIGURE 9-8
Loop-within-a-loop configuration — One nine surrounds the other, both forming loops that return to the clubhouse.

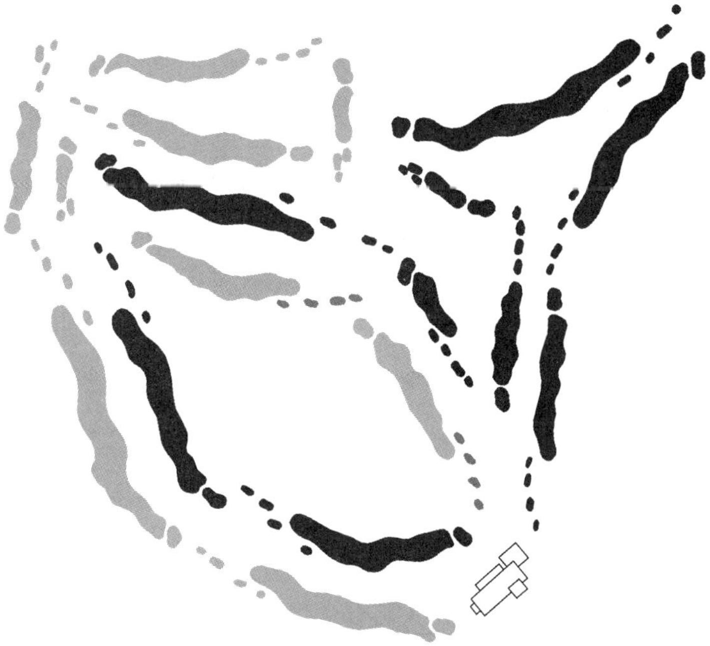

FIGURE 9-9
Interlocking configuration — Each nine intersects with the other, often at multiple points.

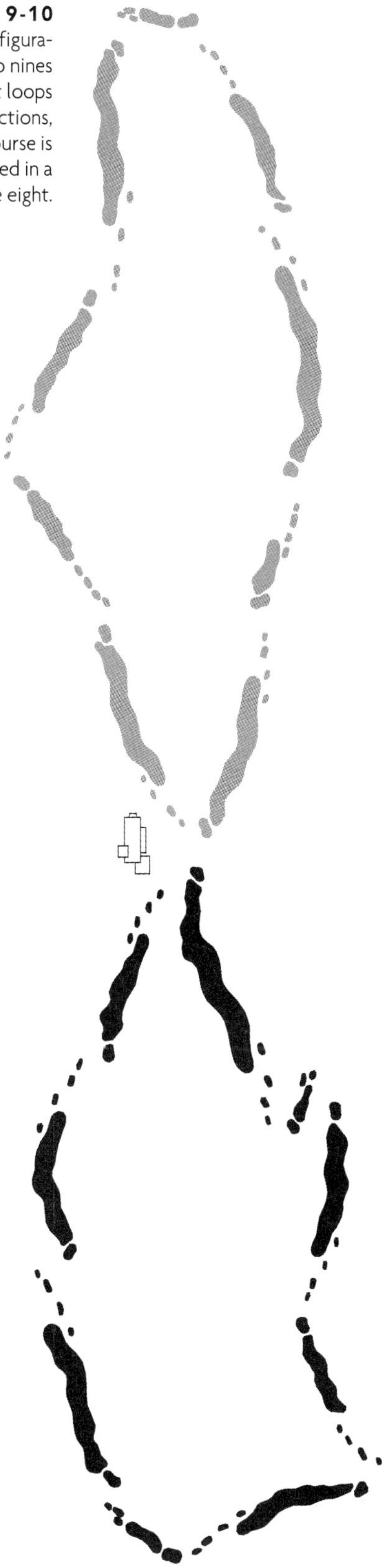

FIGURE 9-10
Figure-eight configuration — When two nines form two distinct loops in opposite directions, the entire course is said to be routed in a figure eight.

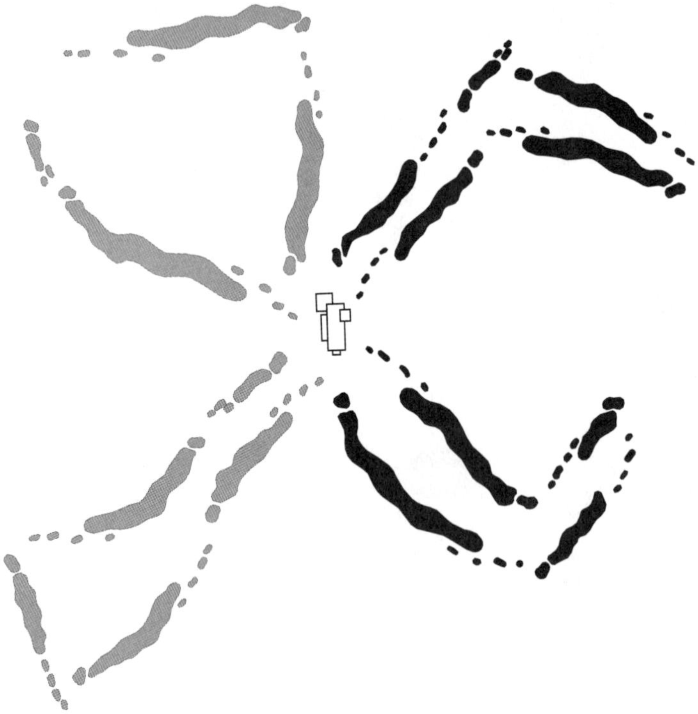

FIGURE 9-11
Quadruple loop configuration — This routing returns to the clubhouse almost as often as possible. Note that ample space for four separate tee complexes and four separate green complexes must be available. This configuration virtually surrounds the clubhouse, leaving little room for access or a practice area.

FIGURE 9-12
Spiral configuration — In this layout, the routing revolves around itself. It is essentially composed of two intertwined loops.

ACREAGES FOR TYPES OF ROUTING	
Core Golf Course	100–130
Residential Course with Double-loaded Fairways	130–160
Residential Course with Single-loaded Fairways	160–190

FIGURE 9-13
The table shows approximate acreage requirements for an 18-hole regulation-length course of three primary types relative to development intensity mixed with the golf. A nominal practice hitting area and clubhouse may be configured into the higher end of the acreage range providing that the course length is kept average or below.

Available Space

The configuration of the space allotted for a golf course will drive many aspects of how holes are laid out. The numerous routings reproduced in this book demonstrate the spectrum of routing types. In every case, the availability of land—usable land, that is—affected the way the holes string out and return. Usable land may be restricted when land is needed for residential development, for maintaining natural areas, or for future uses. This is not to suggest that the land needs of the golf course are not of crucial importance. Often, the golf course's needs are foremost. After all, golf courses usually constitute the largest single area of an overall development. Their parts can be much more difficult to fit into the land than the smaller components of roads, individual home sites, and so on.

At more than 300 feet in width, a single fairway corridor for a golf hole, plus the requirements of length, landing areas, and conditions of sunlight and orientation, must be given priority in placement. Considering that each of these fairway corridors must connect to the others points out even more clearly why the golf course routing is often the crux of solving an entire land planning effort.

Do not strive for length where you sacrifice character. Your yardage is the less valuable of the two considerations.

—*George C. Thomas Jr.,* Golf Architecture in America

Relationship of Greens to Tees

When golfers finish a green, they make their way to the next tee. This fundamental step in the travels of a golfer forms a major portion of the art of fitting holes together. Connecting holes together not only represents a link in the chain but also establishes the change in direction

IDEAL GOLF COURSE YARDAGE RANGES

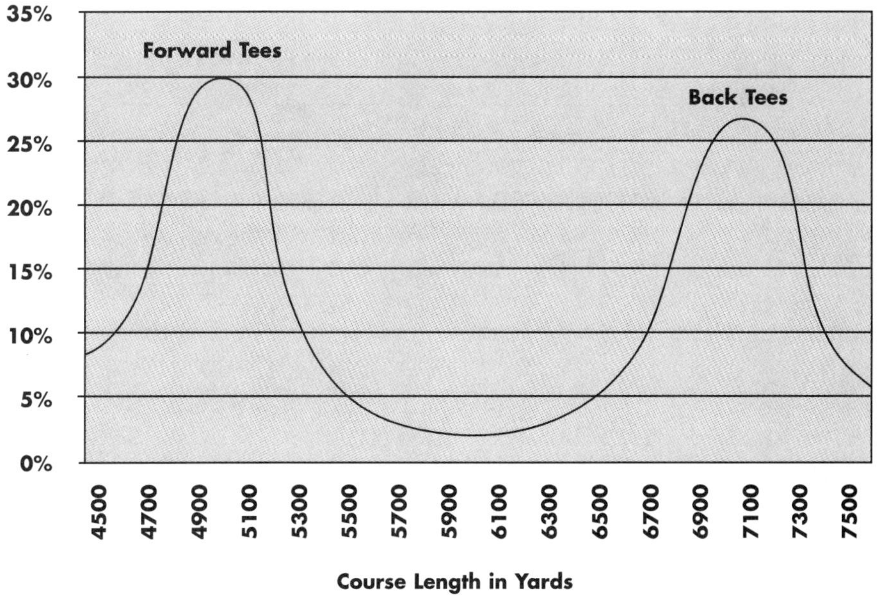

FIGURE 9-14
According to the results of a 2001 survey of golf course architects and planners, the ideal length for an 18-hole, regulation-length, par-72 course is 5000 yards at the forward tees to just more than 7000 yards at the back tees. However, golf course architect Alice Dye, ASGCA, calculates that the average woman golfer enjoys a course that measures slightly less than 5000 yards, at 4800 yards. Golf courses that hope to foster new player development, perhaps through family tees, are wise to consider forward tee length that is even less, perhaps in the 4500-yard range.

that a golfer will follow as the course is played. The determining factor in how a routing is put together is this change in direction between holes.

The link between two holes is a necessary part of the golf journey and should not be treated as an afterthought. Excellent routing envisions the path from the green of a hole to the next tees and makes it as efficient, attractive, and safe as possible. The average or worse routing ignores simple guidelines, thus causing discord in the layout.

Often, a cart path defines how players get from the finish of one hole to the start of the next. This is true even at courses where both cart riding and walking are permitted. Walkers tend to follow cart paths, at least partially. If a specific walking path is provided, it might be used by walkers, but not necessarily at all times. At courses without defined cart paths there will be a path of some type, whether an improved surface or a path established by the wear and tear of traffic.

The tees being played by a golfer will significantly influence the route taken to the next hole. Back tees that are difficult to access can be problematic. So can extreme forward tees, where the distance to be traveled from the previous green seems long. Another potential problem occurs when tees are scattered laterally within an area. In this case, either the pathway must bend and turn so it accesses each tee or the golfer must

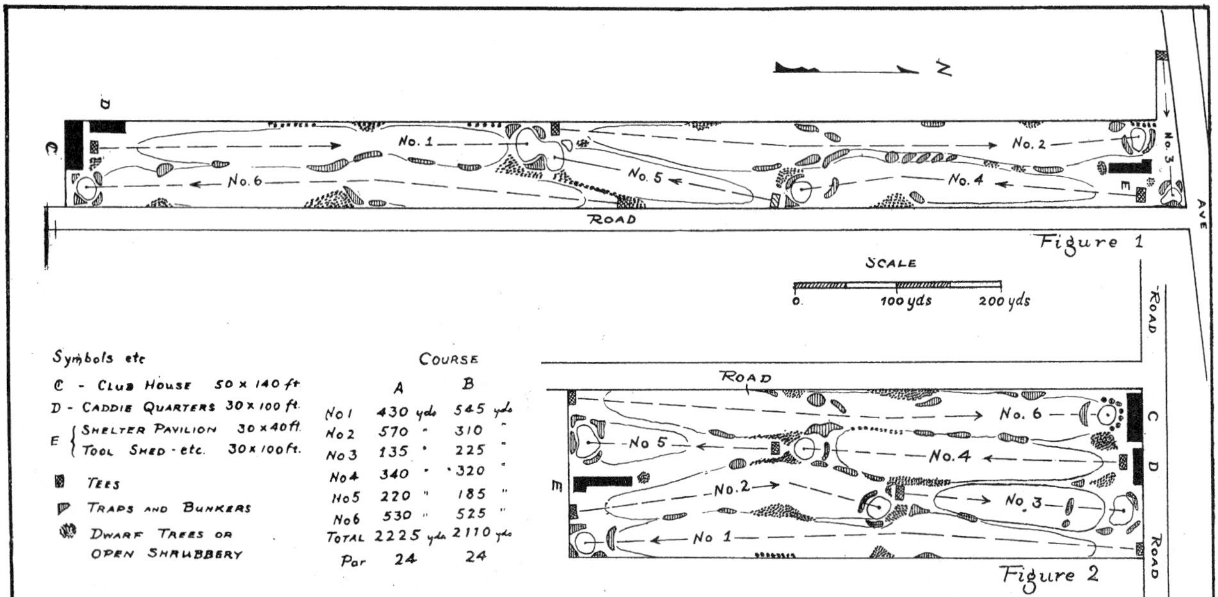

FIGURE 9-15

F. L. O. Wadsworth, an engineer, in 1927 devised the hexaplex grouping concept in response to his own claim that "Modern golf courses are being built on way too much land." His concept demonstrates how six-hole loops "can be 18.51 acres each and create an 18-hole course on just 60 acres." Unfortunately, Wadsworth assumed hole envelopes only 120 feet wide, with no areas between them. He also concluded that greens should be no more than 2800 square feet each. Golf architect A. W. Tillinghast disagreed with the whole idea, pointing out Wadsworth's miscalculations and his overall lack of knowledge of golf course architecture. Fortunately, Wadsworth's concept remained just that.

SOURCE: *GOLF ILLUSTRATED*, DECEMBER 1927

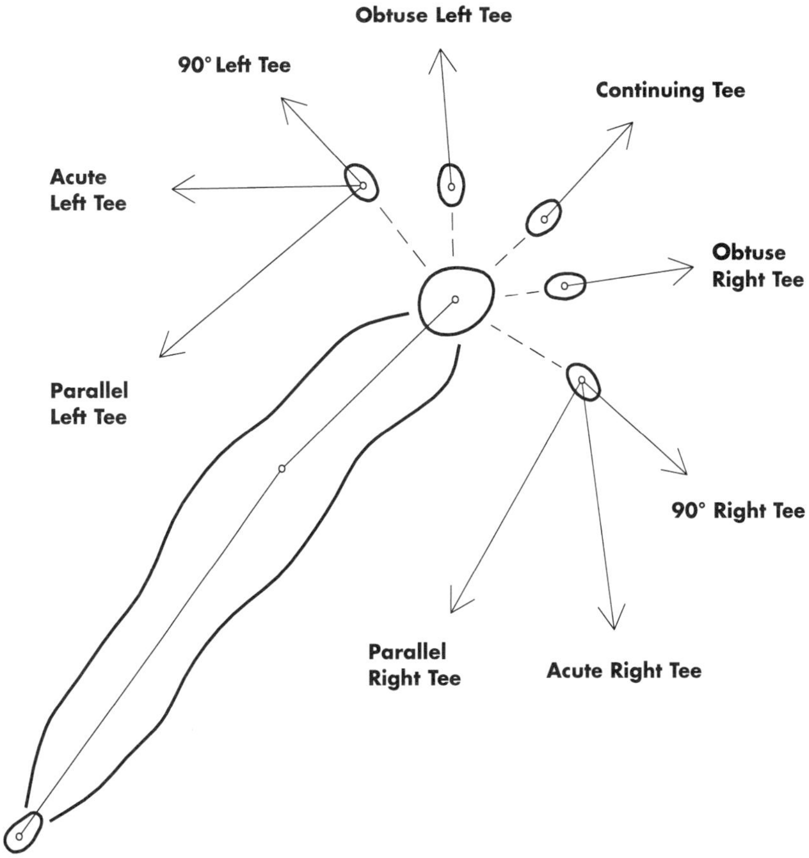

FIGURE 9-16
The direction a golfer heads after leaving a green determines the routing of a golf course. The location of the next tee is a matter not only of accessing the next hole but also of good pace, continuation, and safety. Tees that are acute or parallel must be situated such that they are not in conflict with the hole just finished. Parallel tee positions, while often efficient in terms of land use, are among the least desirable because they take a golfer backward. Acute tee positions create unusable land areas due to the acute angles formed by the outer limits of the safety envelopes of both holes.

spend time making his or her own path to get to a tee located away from the main path.

Considerations in establishing the connection between successive holes include the following:

- Approach to green

  For example, if the tees of the next hole are to the right of the green on the hole being played, keep the intended path to the right so distance is minimized.

- Proximity of primary tee

  The primary tee should be kept as close as practical to the exit point of a green to minimize time in reaching the next tee.

- Forward progress

  It is preferable that tees for the next hole give a sense of forward movement whenever possible; requiring golfers to backtrack too often can have the effect of making the round seem less adventurous and more a matter of covering ground already visited.

- Visibility

  Careful attention should be paid to areas near the green where golfers will park carts and leave golf bags; these areas should be reasonably visible from the hole being played but secluded from the tees of the next hole.

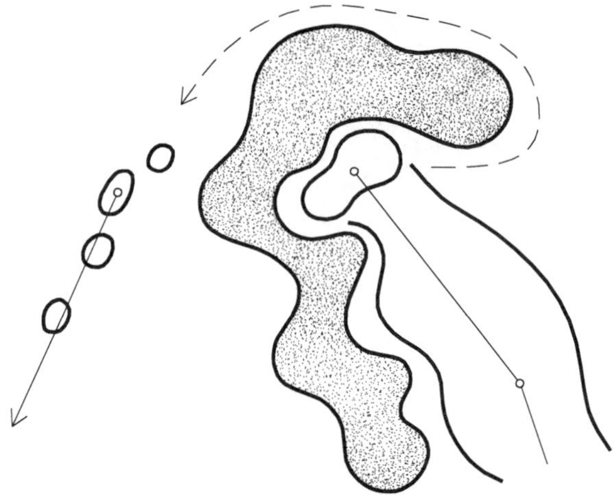

FIGURE 9-17
Hazards and other impassable areas must be well thought out in order that the path to the next tee is not interrupted unnecessarily. In this example, time will be consumed getting from the green to the next tee unless a causeway or bridge is built to overcome the hazard.

- Safety

  No tee should be positioned closer to a preceding green than is reasonable for the given circumstances. Take into account the impact tees might have on the preceding green area, including the space where golfers will park or leave golf bags.

- Distance

  The distance from the green to the next tees should be far enough away for safety yet minimized so as not to delay the golf round unnecessarily. *Note:* For walking golfers, a distance of more than 300 feet from the edge of a green to the primary tee of the next hole is usually considered excessive; when longer distances are unavoidable they should be spread out within a routing and their occurrences minimized.

- Hazards

  Large hazards or inaccessible areas obstructing the link between successive holes can be inefficient.

- Regard the walker

  If a course might allow walking, be sure that the distances between greens and tees are conducive to walking.

- Intrusion

  Tee areas can be noisy, as there may often be golfers there waiting to hit. The area will not be perfectly quiet. Greens and tees should be separated with features, grade differences, and/or vegetation.

- Aesthetics

  Consider the quality of the journey between the green completed and the next tee. On a typical 18-hole course, the total of these spans can amount to 800 yards, which is more than 10 percent of the total distance of the routing from beginning to end.

Intersections in Routings

Intersections are points within the routing where a span between a green and the next tee meets the span between two other holes. This can be a positive or a negative. From a positive perspective, such intersections allow for services such as rest rooms and drinking fountains to be located in a single location. Other positives may be flexibility in how the course is played, the ability to access areas more easily in shotgun starts, and easier movement of spectators during tournaments.

From a negative perspective, intersections may be areas where activity is intense and confusing. In my opinion such situations can be engaging and, if properly handled with screening and separation, can make the overall trek of the golfer seem more like a game and less like a straight out-and-back path. The unpredictability of intersections can make the golf course more interesting and enticing. "Wow, that must be the 16th. I guess we come back this way later on." Of course, multiple intersections where a routing crosses over itself many times can be a drag.

Intersections can also occur between separate courses. This, in my view, should be carefully weighed, as it can be confusing when separate courses meet up and the golfer is presented with multiple choices. We are now faced with getting them to the *correct next* hole, not just the next hole. Also, courses, in most situations, should have their own character and feel. Multiple-course intersections may dilute distinct characteristics or cause strong characteristics to clash. Appropriate signage and wayfinding is essential when different courses meet up. Fortunately, the conditions that lead to such routing situations are rare.

Relationships of Opposing Holes

Opposing holes are two or more adjacent holes at any point or angle. The two situations in which this occurs are: (1) holes that are parallel or nearly parallel to one another, and (2) holes that come together at greater angles. Such relationships are important for a variety of reasons, safety and separation being among the most crucial.

The following list helps in planning opposing holes:

- Efficiency of space

  Dead areas between golf holes are areas not necessary for the use of the hole but valuable aesthetically as open spaces and as a way to separate holes and areas. Such areas will, however, consume space; their appropriateness must be considered in the context of total available acreage.

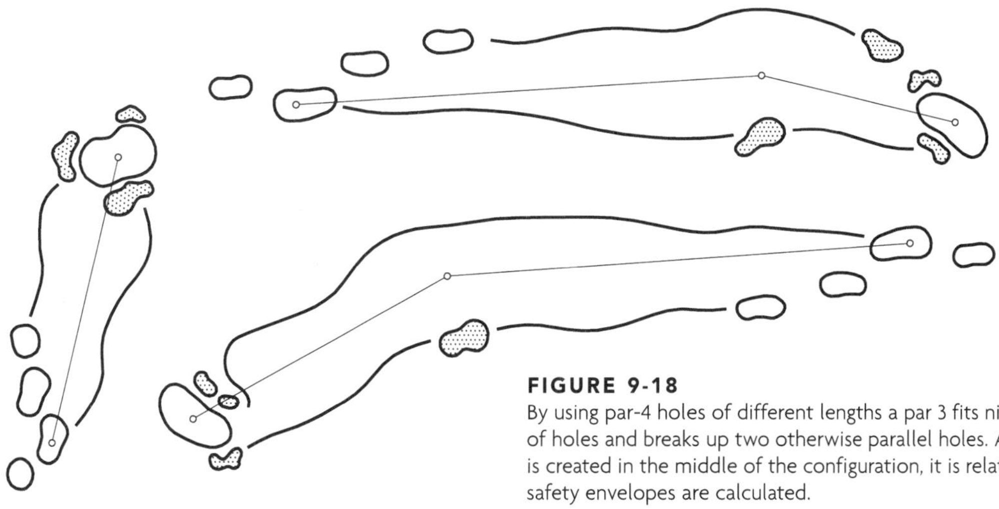

FIGURE 9-18
By using par-4 holes of different lengths a par 3 fits nicely into this stretch of holes and breaks up two otherwise parallel holes. Although a dead area is created in the middle of the configuration, it is relatively small when the safety envelopes are calculated.

> *One shot holes are the most interesting and there is no real reason why there should be not five one shotters.*
> — *William Flynn,* USGA Green Section Record *(1927)*

- Parallel holes

  Precisely parallel holes are generally not desirable, as they go against the idea of variation in alignment. Although often unavoidable, parallel relationships can be minimized by planning doglegs, changing the angle between holes, varying the character of the holes, and using holes of different lengths (an example is the use of a par 4 and par 3 alongside a par 5).
- Separation of tees and greens

  Tees and greens should be separated from other areas as much as possible and when appropriate.
- Landing areas

  The areas where golf shots are expected to land and come to rest should be separated from the landing areas of other holes, from tees, and from greens.
- Hazards

  Hazards, because they represent an obstacle to the golfer, can help separate holes and areas; a single water hazard may add strategy effects to multiple holes if placed appropriately.
- Natural features

  Natural features between holes can be an excellent method of separating and creating interest.

Applying Safety Cones & Envelopes

When fitting holes together it is essential that the safety envelope as described in the previous chapter be adequately visualized. Although the emphasis here is on the combining of holes to form a progression-eventually a course-the act can lead to all sorts of trouble if safety is not considered in the process. As holes are linked together the structure of the routing takes form. Tee points, angle points and green points are set in place. The safety envelopes of holes become evident when offsets are calculated from these points and the centerlines that connect them. As previously covered, the setback to outside property, non-golf uses and other golf holes must be adequate.

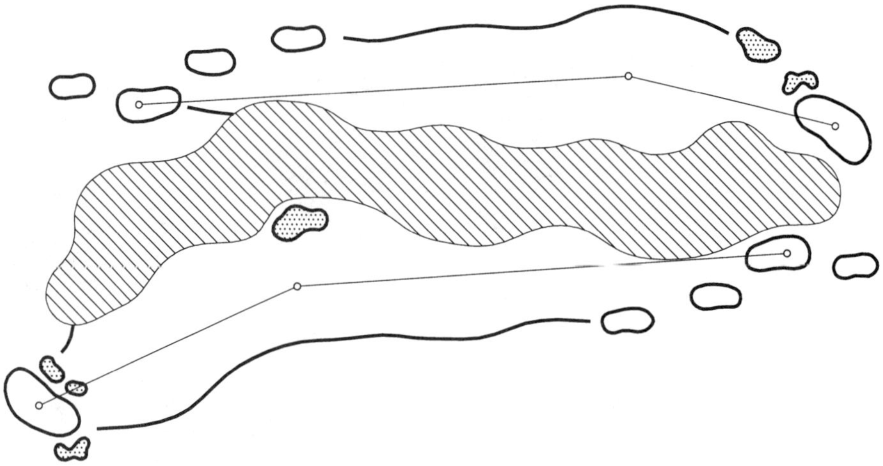

FIGURE 9-19
Hazards can be an excellent buffer between golf holes, giving a feeling of separation while allowing them to be adjacent or even parallel to one another.

The importance of keeping safety envelopes in mind is obvious: to truly fit holes together they must indeed *fit*. There are several methods of visualizing safety envelopes while the fitting of holes is carried out. As the stick figure-like map of a routing plan takes form (that is, the centerlines of holes are laid out on the plan) appropriate setbacks become known by measuring from the points and centerlines to other holes and uses. Measuring with a scale is but one method. The template method is easier for some. With templates the entirety of the golf hole-points, centerlines and envelope-are all in one handy device than can be moved, articulated and positioned over and over, and over again. In Hole 14, "Blank Canvas to Solution," the process of beginning a routing plan is explored and taken through to the point of arriving at solutions. Different methods of building a plan are explained.

The following are aspects of fitting holes together that are driven by the safety envelope of individual golf holes:

- Green to tee gaps

  There must be an adequate separation distance provided.
- Dovetailing

  The nesting of safety cones with one another to form efficiencies between adjacent holes is called dovetailing. Of importance is to make sure that the many other considerations and guidelines are checked whenever dovetailing is practiced.
- Parallel holes

  Appropriate distances between points and centerlines are a must.
- Angle efficiency

  Fitting holes together creates angles which are formed by the outer limits of each hole's safety envelope; these angles can form efficient and inefficient conditions for neighboring land uses and the layout of other golf holes.
- Overall use of land

  When all holes are fitted together to form a routing plan, and the safety envelopes nestled together or overlapped to appropriate degrees, the area encompassed by the outermost limits of the combination of envelopes comprises the total required area for the golf holes.

Fitting Holes Around Practice Areas

Many more shots are played on practice ranges than on bordering holes. Practice ranges are generally marked as out-of-bounds, and venturing into a practice area is known to be a poor idea. Practice areas, because they are so large, are easily identified by golfers even if they are newcomers to the facility. Routers are rarely concerned that a golf hole will negatively intrude on a practice area. Rather, separation is needed to help keep balls hit on a practice area away from adjacent or nearby holes.

When holes must be configured alongside practice areas, they should angle away from the practice area, especially the tee shot alignment of the hole. It is also preferable to have the left side of holes against practice areas, as the potential for an errant shot to the left is less than to the right. An important consideration beyond providing space between holes and ranges is providing a visible means of separation between them. Practice areas should be separated so that people moving toward them will notice berming, vegetation, rough, or unimproved turf. Elevation differences are extremely effective in stopping low-trajectory golf balls and tend to contain the activity of a practice range.

Visibility from the adjacent golf hole to the practice area must be weighed against appropriate separation. The need for separation almost always takes precedence.

Considerations in fitting holes near practice areas include safety guidelines and the following:

- Angle of holes

  Adjacent holes should angle away from practice areas.

- Position of tees, landing areas, and greens

  Whenever possible, tees, landing areas, and greens should be kept away from the sides of practice ranges in the midspan of the length of the range; this reduces the opportunity for golfers to approach the practice area.

- Buffers

  Nonturf areas and mounding are good treatments to consider between practice areas and golf holes.

- Cart path alignment

  While cart path alignments may not be worked out in the routing stage, it is important to plan so that carts will have access on the far side of holes flanking a practice range. Water features and other obstacles should be positioned so they do not cause paths to be aligned immediately adjacent to ranges, especially in the midspan area.

- Type of practice use

  A private club whose practice facilities may be lightly used will have significantly less potential conflict than a heavily used municipal facility where golfer types are unknown and varied.

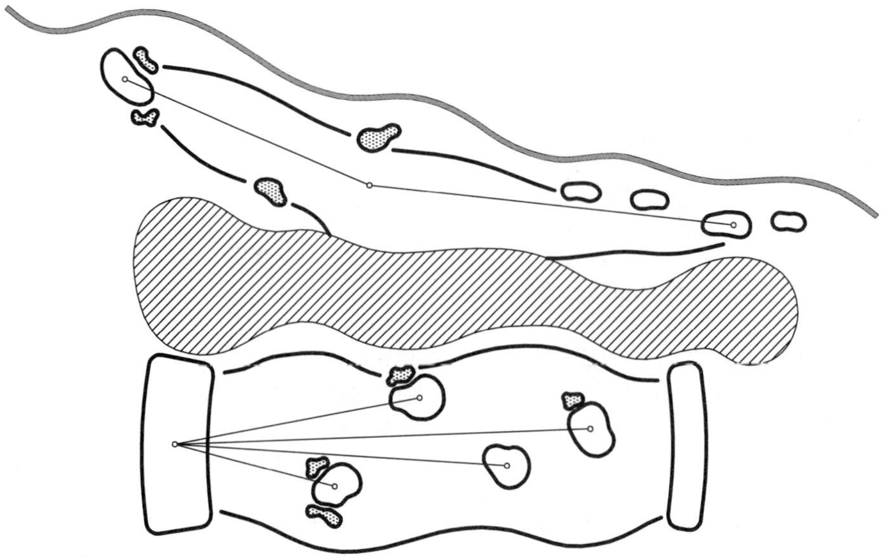

FIGURE 9-20
The example shows the common situation of a hole returning alongside a practice area. Note that the angle of the hole is away from the practice area, and the cart path is aligned on the far side of the hole. These are usually preferable configurations when a hole must border a practice area. The hatched area represents a buffer of nonturf or rough terrain that further separates the uses.

- Intensity of practice use
  A practice range opens early and continues past dark with lighting may have increased impact.
- Type of practice balls
  The use of limited-length balls, including the Cayman ball, will make practice range intrusion to adjacent areas less problematic.
- Golf schools and events
  Ranges can see heavy use in a short time due to golf schools, clinics, and tournament warm-up. Such uses, when they are identified, shouldbe considered in the routing, and ample room allowed for them.
- Screens and nets
  These are useful in many situations, but they can create a false sense of security, and their condition is subject to decline. Appropriate setbacks and areas that buffer the uses both physically and visually are more permanent solutions.

In nine instances out of ten the committee already has a preconceived idea of the proper building site, and in as many cases that site is on a little hilltop at the very greatest elevation on the tract.

—A. W. Tillinghast, writing about clubhouse location in The Architectural Forum, *March 1925*

The Out-of-Bounds Factor

Out-of-bounds is a golfer's nightmare. It is not a hazard but an artificial condition from which there is no recovery. If out-of-bounds is thought of as a hazard by the golfer contemplating a shot, the design is probably poor. While a golfer might notice an out-of-bounds condition along a fairway, it should not dictate strategic play. In general, out-of-bounds should be well out of the normal execution of shots and breached only by the most wild and errant of golf balls.

Designers fitting holes together should employ out-of-bounds as a limit to the golf area. While most routing plans have a boundary along a hole, attention should be paid so that OB does not become a hazardlike influence. Even more obnoxious is the condition where an OB line falls within a golf course, between golf holes. How immoral! The routing might as well say, "I'm confused." This does not mean that OB lines cannot be defined along practice areas, which are part of the facility, but not technically a part of the golf course. And, I suppose, for the unusual situation where two holes conflict in an older routing that cannot be changed, placing an OB condition along one hole as protection is much better than doing nothing at all. Still, it is not ideal.

Elevation Relationships

Nearly all who look at routing plans will understand the horizontal relationship between holes, but few-even when contour lines are present-are able to fully understand the vertical relationships that will exist when the course is finally built. The vertical relationships between golf holes and course components cannot be ignored. It is the role of the golf course architect to be certain that the holes fit well as the land rises and falls.

Elevation relationships are a result of two conditions: (1) natural terrain that is retained in the routing, and (2) grading features that are manufactured through construction efforts.

It might also be argued that vegetation, especially large trees, constitute vertical relationships. Vegetation is not permanent, however, and therefore it is of only secondary interest to the routing plan. The importance of vegetation is intensified when it is so abundant naturally that leaving it will likely constitute a condition that even the most chainsaw-happy crew could not change in a lifetime of trying.

Aspects of elevation relationships between holes include:

- Interest

  Golf holes are interesting when there are elevation differences between them.

- Screening and separation

  Golf holes are defined through mounding and grade changes.

- Containment

  Balls are contained when areas are depressed in relation to other holes and uses.

- Intrusion

  Higher areas can intrude on off-site uses if not considered.

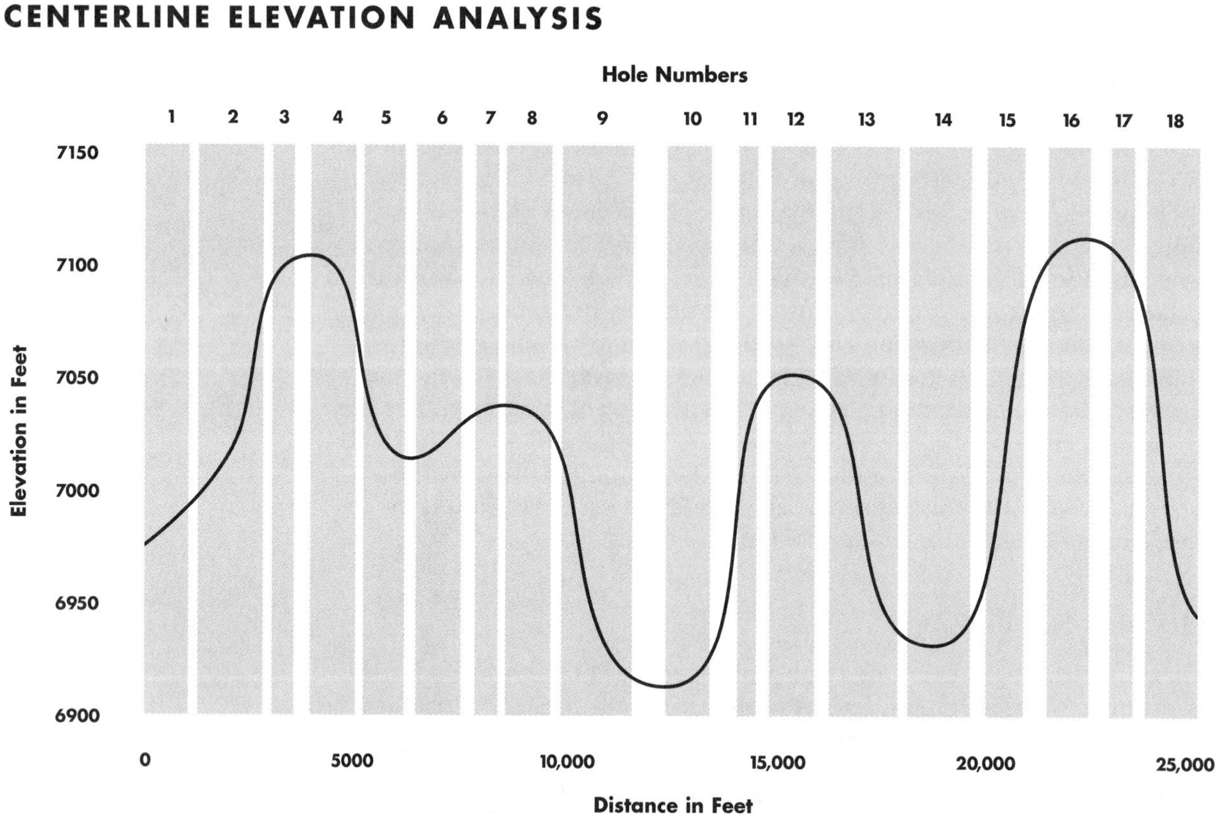

FIGURE 9-21

A graph showing the rise and fall of a routing plan over the span of 18 holes. The elevation difference is almost 200 feet across the course. From the data, you can see that the course makes three noticeable climbs: the first during the first two holes; the second between the tenth and 11th holes; and the third during the length of the par-4, 15th hole. Breaking up the climbs in this way gives the golfer a rest and takes away the monotony that might come if all of the climbs were grouped together. Note that the downhill segments of the routing occur in four stretches and include six holes, or one-third of the course. (Refer to Figure 10-5 for the routing plan that this graph depicts.)

- Views

  Views may be restricted, directed, or opened by paying attention to existing and planned differences in grade.

- Blind shots and holes

  Elevation can create blind and partially blind conditions that are sometimes appropriate. The occasional and well-designed blind shot can be of interest; but conditions must be as safe as practical given the circumstances. *Note:* A hole is not blind if there is visibility to the green but just its surface cannot be seen, nor is a hole blind based on the misplaced shot of a golfer who is blocked from seeing the next target or hole itself.

Construction, Irrigation & Operation Considerations

My friends in construction, irrigation, and operations would chastise me if I did not mention that fitting holes together must take into account the realities of infrastructure, maintenance, and management. Getting irrigation water from hole to hole is just as important as moving golfers around the course. Water can be moved by multiple routes; sometimes it can even take a straight line under areas outside the golf course parcel. This obviously requires easements and engineering. The logistics of irrigating a course, including how the water will enter the property and where it will be stored, should be given adequate attention.

Maintenance personnel will need to access all areas of the golf course. A routing needs to consider the pathways that course personnel will use and how this might affect the daily play, or vice versa.

BLIND SHOT ASSISTANCE

Creative devices have been deployed to assist in playing shots that are truly blind. At Lahinch Golf Club on the west coast of Ireland, a simple stone painted white is moved daily at the Dell Hole (the sixth) to signify where the pin has been placed in this nearly hidden green flanked by steep dunes on all but one sliver of an edge. Bells have been used for ages as a way that golfers completing a green can signal to golfers back in the fairway or on a tee that the coast is clear. Periscopes and video monitors have been installed so golfers can see ahead to areas hidden from view. Perhaps the simplest of inventions is the platform or mound that allows golfers to hike up a few steps to see the terrain beyond. Modern GPS systems, such as those installed in carts, can be set up to provide another layer of information in areas where blind holes are present.

UNUSUAL CONSIDERATIONS

Fitting holes to one another occasionally involves throwing curve balls. Unusual situations can be both worthwhile and viable in the process of routing courses. However, they should not be overused. This would, among other things, make them *not* unusual.

Double Greens

In certain circumstances, it may be practical to combine greens to form one large green surface that accommodates two (or even more) golf holes. (Of interest is Hole 17, "Never Assume Anything!" by Arthur Jack Snyder, in which he discusses, among other points, the design of a quadruple green.) The Old Course at St. Andrews, which is well known for its seven extremely large double greens, is an interesting case study in that the routing plays counterclockwise. Each of the approach shots to her double greens—no matter which hole is being played—is played with the shared hole to the left side. This makes the double greens ideal in that the left is the less likely side for potential conflict due to mis-hit shots.

The Old Course used to be played clockwise, and play was altered between the left-hand and right-hand routings until the current layout was adopted. It is supposed that one reason for deciding on the right-hand circulation of play was to minimize conflict between users of the large two-hole greens. Of interest is the story of an American journalist who in 1994 set off to play the course in its former right-hand format. According to local officials, even though he was provided a map to help him find the old tee areas, he had trouble staying on track. One wonders if he met up with any oncoming golfers and what conversations ensued.

Double greens must be large enough to accommodate play from different holes. Ideally, features should define the greens as if they are really two greens connected by an isthmus of putting surface. These features should not block visibility, as golfers playing into their portion of the green should have an opportunity to see any players occupying the por-

FIGURE 9-22
An excellent example of a double green that serves the ninth and 18th holes of a course. The design has several positive attributes. There is good access to and from the greens, well-thought-out hole alignments that do not conflict, and an engaging view from the clubhouse looking across the long and narrow green that is set below the dining and seating areas.

COURTESY OF GREG NASH DESIGNS, GREG NASH, ASGCA, GOLF COURSE ARCHITECT; ANTHEM COUNTRY CLUB, PHOENIX, ARIZONA tion used by the other incoming hole. Holes coming from opposite directions are candidates for double greens, as are holes playing at angles from which their approach shots are not likely to conflict.

Access to double greens as well as the pathways leading to the green area are essential logistics to work out. Additionally, it is imperative to consider how the players using the green, if there at the same time, might be affected by each other's play. My advice on double greens is to use them when conditions are clearly acceptable and the relationship seems both natural and appropriate.

Combining greens with practice putting greens has been practiced for many years. Many classic clubs have this condition. The typical makeup involves an expansive green that extends down from a stately clubhouse to either the ninth or 18th finishing holes. The Oakmont Country Club near Pittsburgh, Pennsylvania, is one such example. Jack Snyder, who contributed to this book, was superintendent of grounds at Oakmont in the early 1950s. He recalls the occasional long-hit ball that interrupted golfers practicing on the green. "But more annoying," Jack notes, "was the activity of those hitting practice putts, which was quite a distraction to players hitting approach shots to number nine, even if only a few people were using the practice green." Again, when and if this situation seems warranted, a reasonable amount of definition between the practice green and the incoming hole is advisable.

On broken ground, hilly ground or terrain with natural hazards, the golf architect must place his holes so that proper strategy is obtained from the natural topography. On flat, or fairly flat courses, he must place his hazards to take the place of natural ones.

—George C. Thomas Jr., Golf Architecture in America

Alternate Greens

Alternate greens can be used for strategic interest and for maintenance reasons. An alternate green is exactly what its name implies: a separate and additional green serving an individual golf hole. An excellent example is at the Virginia Country Club in Long Beach, California, originally designed by William P. Bell. One green of a par 4 is notched into a hillside to serve the hole in its dogleg right format. The other green sits below and to the left, guarded by a large tree. This green serves the hole in its dogleg left format. Depending on which green is in play, the tee shot must be played completely differently in order to set up an open approach to this par-4 masterpiece. Having played the dogleg right version of the hole to a green that seems no bigger than a small hotel room, one can easily see it takes a beating and would probably not be able to sustain itself if used exclusively. In this case, the alternate green approach was likely adopted for both strategic and practical reasons. Alternate greens must be evaluated in light of the extra cost, upkeep, and acreage required. Also, be sure that the greens are well separated so play is not bothersome to the green not in use.

Alternate Holes

An alternate hole is one played in lieu of another during a round. Not a bonus hole, which is a golf hole added to a routing, an alternate hole is generally alongside its brother. Either of the two can be designated by the green committee, or it may be up to the golfer to choose which to play. At Haig Point on Daufauskie Island, South Carolina, which was designed by golf architect Rees Jones, the situation presents at the last two holes of each nine. By reconfiguring the choices, a variety of courses may be played, which adds interest and a change of pace. Alternate holes are the ultimate in terms of cost, acreage, and maintenance, but they can offer a valuable strategy in the right situation and where the positives outweigh the extra cost.

Extra Holes

An extra hole is a hole injected into a routing that is typically not played to be counted in the round but is there for any of the following reasons: (1) to settle bets, ideally a par 3 after the 18th hole; (2) to provide a hole to be used in the round when one of the regular holes is closed for maintenance; and (3) for no particular reason. Other names for these holes are *bonus hole, gamble hole, bye hole,* and *settle-the-bet hole.*

Mark Leslie, a golf writer, devoted an entire article to extra holes. Among his findings in researching the topic was that Alister MacKenzie had one in mind for Augusta, but it was scrapped, and that extra holes are becoming popular among modern golf course architects. Most such holes are par 3s, and they are usually quite short.

Crossing Holes

Crossing holes occur at The Old Course where the alignment of the par-4 seventh crosses that of the par-3 11th. Quite simply, crossing holes cross each other. The practice began long ago and was not seen as a problem because courses were less intensely used than they are today. Also, golf, in its early years, was often played in crowds where people would band together and set out over the terrain both to play and be a spectator to play. This condition in itself was very likely dangerous, so the occasional crossing holes were of no consequence in comparison.

Keep in mind also that holes that crossed in old layouts were on open linksland. There were few, if any, trees to prevent visibility, and no grade differences that would render a tee or fairway completely invisible to golfers playing either hole. A study of crossing holes in old layouts shows that most of these intersections were positioned at or near the tee of one of the holes, and often of both holes. The tee, being the point of the safety cone of a golf hole (although no such thing was defined back then!) is the ideal place for a crossing to occur. At the tee, the pulse of golf holes is established by the golfer from known and controlled points. Visibility is generally open to the fairway or green and, where crossings were near the tee areas of two holes, one can picture a right-of-way situation where the golfers of one hole allow players on the other hole to play first if there was reason to alternate play. Having said this, most crossings do not conflict during the hitting but rather during the movement of players across the alignment of the intersecting hole.

Holes that cross are rarely seen in modern golf courses. The intensity of use simply does not allow for players having to yield the right of way to

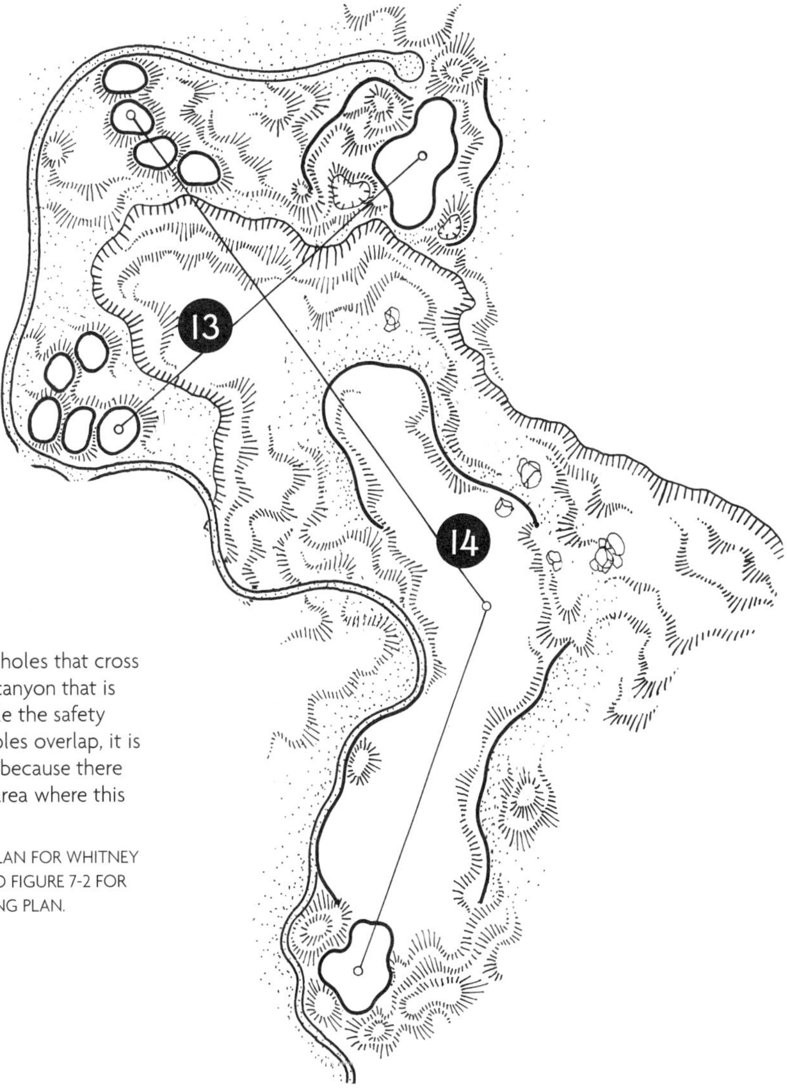

FIGURE 9-23
An example of two holes that cross high above a deep canyon that is not accessible. While the safety envelopes of the holes overlap, it is of no consequence because there is no access in the area where this overlap occurs.

FROM THE ROUTING PLAN FOR WHITNEY RANCH MESA; REFER TO FIGURE 7-2 FOR THE COMPLETE ROUTING PLAN.

another group. The problems associated with crossing holes are more than most golf course owners are willing to accept. Of course, a significant number of golfers play The Old Course each year, and numbers 7 and 11 do not seem to experience unusual delays or conflict. In fact, play out there at the far end of the course is just as civilized as you would expect.

There *are* crossing holes on modern courses. Obviously, the design can be employed on mostly level terrain, as it is at St. Andrews, but this is rare. Two examples of modern designs that use crossing holes are the Karsten Course at Arizona State University, where the tees of holes 9 and 18 cross each other en route to greens on the opposite shore of a long and narrow lake. Management at the Karsten Course, which was designed by Pete Dye, reports that players rarely arrive to the tees at the same instant and, even when they do, nothing prevents them from hitting simultaneously. The path for golfers is routed behind each corresponding tee, so there is no need to physically cross in front of the other hole.

The stretching out of holes to their last limit has often not only an evil effect on individual holes, but also on the layout in general.
—*Robert Hunter,* The Links

The second example (see Figure 9-23) involves a crossing situation on a routing plan where a par 3 and a par 4 cross at the tee shots over a natural canyon to which golfers do not have access. In essence, the safety cones of the two holes are at right angles to one another, and all areas where golfers will be—the tees and landing areas—are outside of the area where balls will be traveling. The design is no less safe than that of holes whose safety cones are side by side. The only conflict may be that once-in-a-lifetime occurrence when two balls struck at the same moment collide in midair. Note the cart paths of these two holes, which swing wide of each tee.

A final word about crossing holes: Do not entirely discount them in layouts, but realize that either the ideal terrain (like the canyon example) or the ideal type of course and play is absolutely essential. The holes must be made safe, and it must be made clear to golfers how to handle them. This is true, however, of all golf holes. Crossing holes are by no means the oddest of oddities. A golf hole can be confusing without crossing another one.

Reversible Holes

A reversible hole is one that can be played backward. Again, The Old Course was set up to be played out and then back in reverse order in its very early times. This arrangement became a problem, and the routing eventually widened to accommodate play on separate out and in holes.

There are excellent variations of this concept. Most remain in conceptual form. Management is a key to such double uses of fairways, which also come with extra work. It must be clear to the golfer which direction is in play on a given day. Such designs will involve extra costs to construct tees, greens, features, and so on.

Shared Tees

A shared tee is one which serves two or more golf holes. Generally this is bad practice due to the conflicts of having players from one hole hitting away while players from another hole are nearby. The workable situation is one where a back tee is shared with the back tee of a hole going in an opposite or nearly opposite direction. In this case the back tees will only prompt conflict on the rare instance when the groups from both holes show up and both groups happen to be playing from the back set of tees. (The routing plan in Figure 10-4 shows a workable shared tee situation at the back tees of holes 9 and 15.)

FIGURE 9-24
An entry from the popular *Golf Digest* Armchair Architect contest sponsored by the American Society of Golf Course Architects and *Golf Digest.* This finalist, entitled "Hooker's Loop," shows a loop of three holes that can be played forward or backward using extra tees and greens. Depending on how play is set up, the loop is played as a par 3, 4, and 4—or 4, 4, and 3.

COURTESY OF MIKE HOPKINS, C. 2000

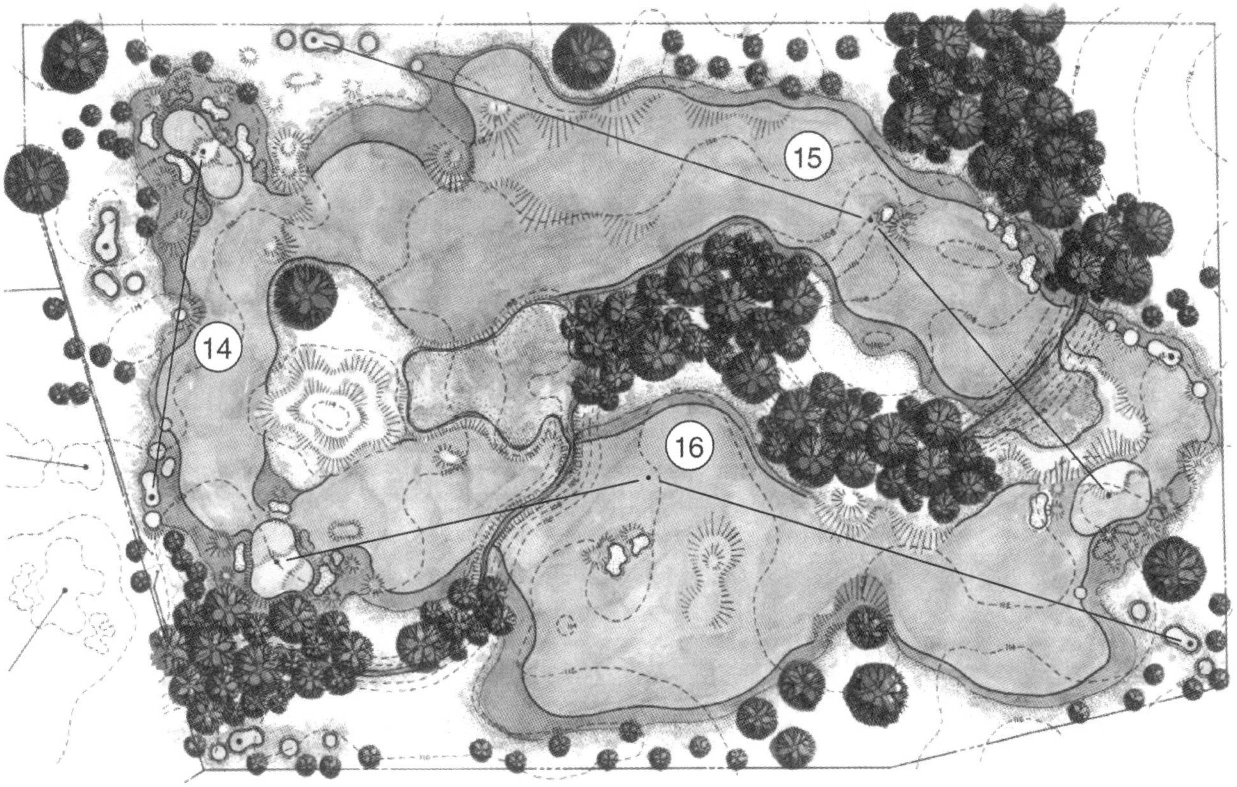
15
14
16

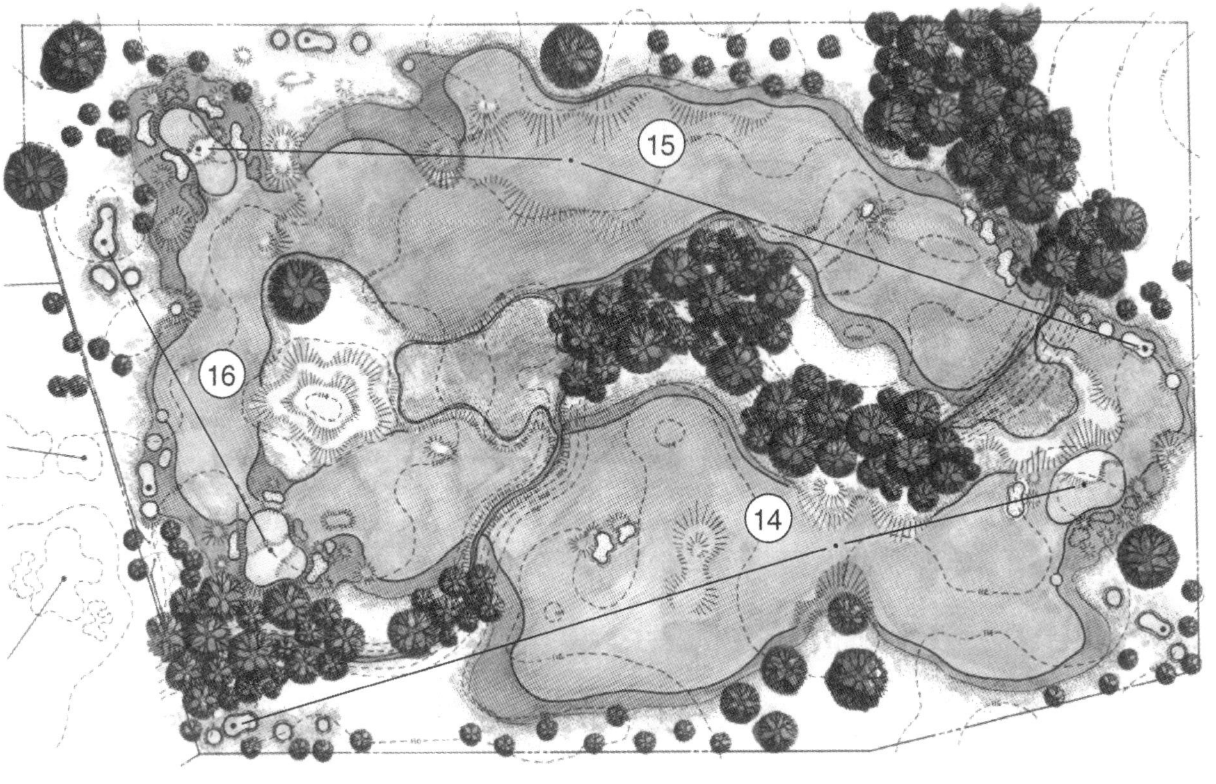
15
16
14

THE FLOW OF COURSES

Rhythm. Balance. Sequence. A routing plan must give careful attention to each. Without these qualities, the golf course might as well be an ordinary maze and the golfer a rat looking for cheese. The idea of rhythm, balance, and sequence was articulated by golf architect Desmond Muirhead while I was writing this book. Muirhead had a distinguished career which began in urban planning and migrated to golf course design. Out of necessity, he began having to solve golf course routing assignments. Although many golf course architects are involved

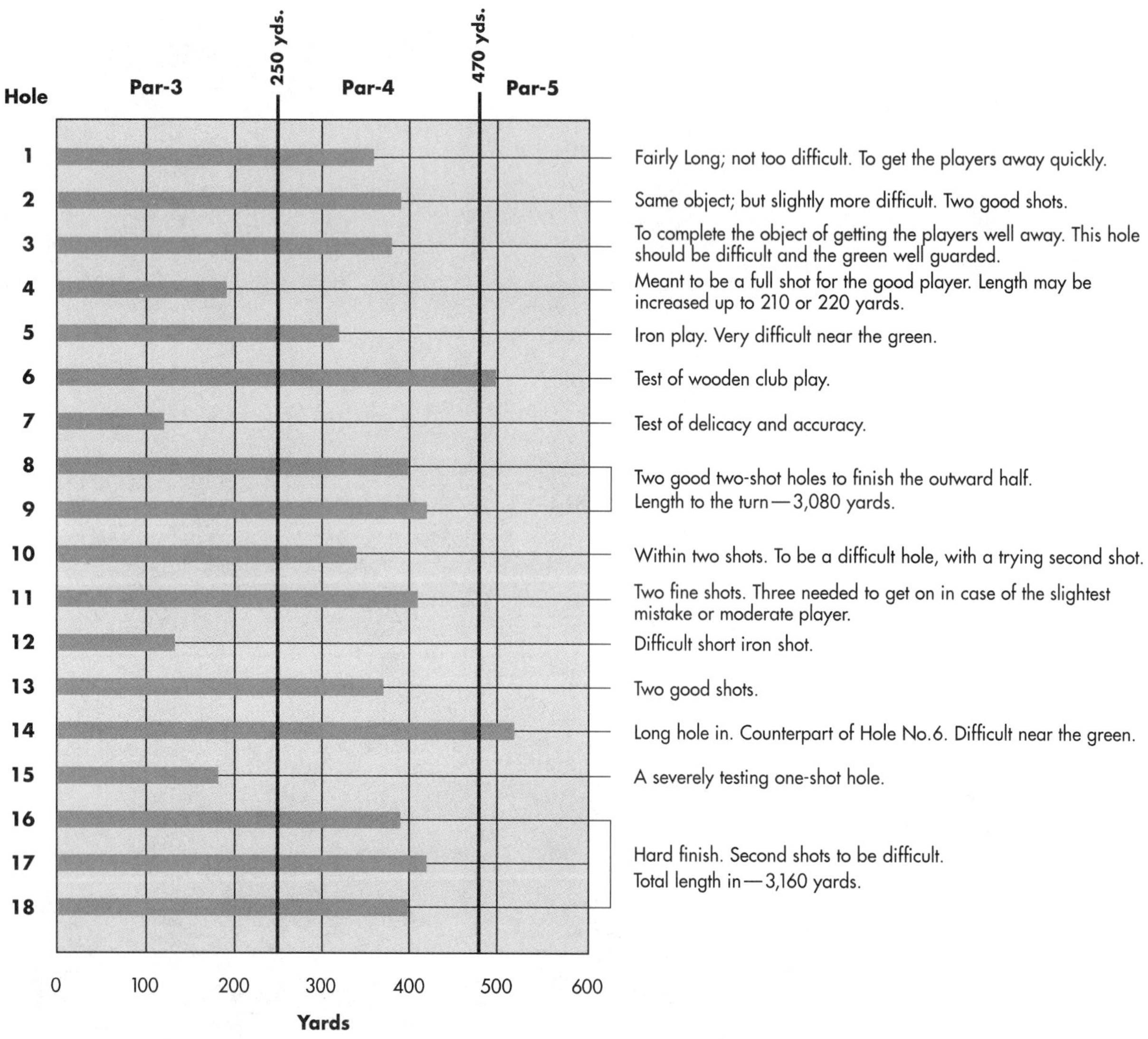

Hole
Par-3
250 yds.
Par-4
470 yds.
Par-5
1
2
3
4
5
6
7
8
9
10
11
12
13
14
15
16
17
18
0
100
200
300
400
500
600
Yards
Fairly Long; not too difficult. To get the players away quickly.
Same object; but slightly more difficult. Two good shots.
To complete the object of getting the players well away. This hole should be difficult and the green well guarded.
Meant to be a full shot for the good player. Length may be increased up to 210 or 220 yards.
Iron play. Very difficult near the green.
Test of wooden club play.
Test of delicacy and accuracy.
Two good two-shot holes to finish the outward half.
Length to the turn—3,080 yards.
Within two shots. To be a difficult hole, with a trying second shot.
Two fine shots. Three needed to get on in case of the slightest mistake or moderate player.
Difficult short iron shot.
Two good shots.
Long hole in. Counterpart of Hole No.6. Difficult near the green.
A severely testing one-shot hole.
Hard finish. Second shots to be difficult.
Total length in—3,160 yards.

FIGURE 9-25
James Braid (1870–1950) first won the British Open at the age of 31. This title opened the door for him to consult on the design of courses, which he did with John R. Stutt, who is credited with coordinating and building a majority of Braid's designs. Braid wrote extensively about golf architecture. In this recreated chart, he articulates his vision for the "Ideal Course of 18 Holes."

RECREATED FROM THE BOOK *ADVANCED GOLF*, BY JAMES BRAID

in site planning issues, none had the portfolio of Muirhead, who had designed entire towns in virtually every corner of the globe.

Rhythm, according to Muirhead, is the relationship between difficulty and surprise; it has to do with the pattern whereby these qualities are presented to the golfer. One way to capture the rhythm of a piece of land is through geomorphism. "Geomorphism is the art of lowering natural low points and raising the natural high points which already exist on the land," Muirhead explained. "Nature knows rhythm best. It's difficult to outdo nature when it comes to rhythm."

What goes out must come in.
— William Amick, golf course architect, commenting on routing

Balance is the relationship between nines and among the par 3s, 4s, and 5s. Muirhead pointed to Pebble Beach as a lesson in nearly perfect balance. "You have these great, thrilling, and fantastic holes along the ocean that occur up front and then at the end of the round. And then these rather mundane holes back away from the ocean. But you wouldn't want it any other way. It makes for perfect balance."

Sequence is the order of par, the speed at which the course unfolds as the round is underway. "Sequence is all about comfort," according to Muirhead. But sequence should not mean that surprise becomes calculated. "There has to be some spontaneous generation to design," he reminded us.

Muirhead lambasted a great many modern courses for their lack of spontaneity. "Ideas add up like crazy," he noted. Muirhead was passionate about this point, taking exception with the predictability that makes many modern courses look artificial instead of natural. "If you think of a river, the current creates effects on the banks and bottom. Now, if you take away the water, the effects are still there. A good routing appears natural like this. It has a natural flow." That all-important flow may be partly rigid in its structure, but it also must be partly left to chance in order to have an engaging sequence. Muirhead was not alone in his feeling that "the intellectual capacity of many golf courses is lacking." It is easy to find example after example of me-too designs that golfers can hardly tell apart.

Routings are made up of the opening, the turn, the heart, and finish. Coincidentally, this is the same flow established for the content of this book and its 19 chapters. The following sections discuss how these elements are handled in golf course design. As we make the turn, contributor Dr. Ed Sadalla adds many insightful thoughts on course psychology as he explores the journey from the human perspective. His chapter, following this one, expands on the thoughts expressed by those of us who are not trained in psychology but are licensed to practice it through our designs.

The Story Unfolds

Golf begins the night before a round, in anticipation of the day to come, and it may not end until many years later, when the golfer finally loses his memory of the experience, his companions, and the details of the round. The way that the routing actually begins is akin to opening the cover of the book and beginning to read.

There is debate on how best to start off a golf course. A majority of golf course architects feel that the relatively easy-going par 4 is best, and

STARTING & FINISHING HOLES

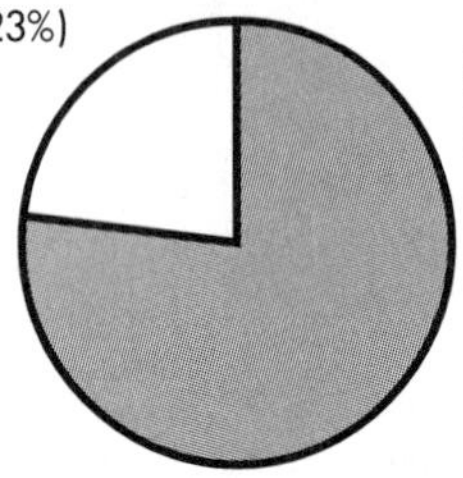

Which makes for a better starting hole: a Par-4 or a Par-5?

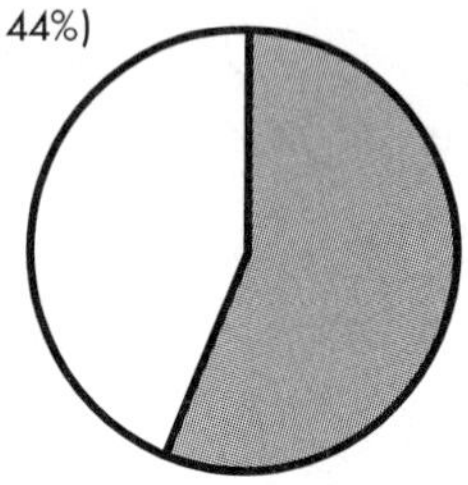

Which makes for a better finishing hole: a Par-4 or a Par-5?

FIGURE 9-26
The results of two questions asked in a survey of golf course architects and planners.

in fact, most courses do begin with a par 4. But this is not a rule, nor should it be. George Thomas subscribed to the idea that a par-5 first hole of shorter length was best. He then followed this with a long par 4. His feeling was that getting started required length to span out the golfers and give them plenty of room in which to whale away at the ball. The argument against the Thomas theory is that the shortish par 5 is bound to leave some groups waiting to reach the green with their second shots. The long par-4 second presents the same problem. Some golfers will reach it in two easily, while others will play it as if it were a short par 5. The best advice is to read the opinions and advice of Bill Yates, an expert in the pace of play. My money is with Yates, who has spent a lifetime studying these issues.

The beginning of a golf course should feel like a beginning. Think of music. There are all sorts of beginnings, but the best presents the beginning in a way that sets the mood and allows the listener to adjust and get comfortable.

Golf as a Story

A game of golf is a story written each day by those who seek recreation, companionship, and competition on a stage defined partially by the golf course routing and always by nature. It is the perfect improvisational theater. Although an actor can get to know the stage like the back of his hand, he cannot be quite sure what will be demanded of him next. His only choice is to take what is given and do his best to overcome the difficulty.

Golf has its introduction, characters, chapters, occasional chase scene, climax, and ending. Good stories have unpredictable twists, sometimes with surprising realizations or even humorous outcomes. Bad stories have not much of any of this. Bad golf courses are like bad stories.

Unpredictability

Often, the best way to call attention to an especially important thought is to give its own heading. So I did.

Interest & Variation

William Flynn, whose writings on golf course architecture are not nearly as well known as many more recognized golf architects, put it this way:

> The principal consideration of the architect is to design his course in such a way as to hold the interest of the player from the first tee to the last green and to present the problems of the various holes in such a way that they register in the player's mind as he stands on the tee or the fairway for the shot to the green.

I would add to Flynn's concise and eloquent words only that the golf course architect must also consider, especially today, with our global emphasis on marketing, that a course should grab the attention before a golfer ever lays eyes on it, and that the measure of an excellent course is how long it stays with the golfer after play has finished. Does the golfer want to visit the course? After he plays, does he want to return? Far too often, I am in meetings where the discussion about attracting play is confined to how much people will be willing to pay, if there are enough people in the area to support golf, and similar topics. I am usually the one raising his hand to suggest once again that making the course exciting will act as a magnet that will attract play. The market analysis of golf courses is important. Interesting and varied design, however, cannot be overlooked, for it represents the lowest cost of all the commodities that go into a golf course.

Way-out Routings

Not all routings go out and come back. The Black Forest Course at the Wilderness Valley Resort in Gaylord, Michigan, plays out to a distant point at the end of Hole 12, then returns only halfway back from that point to the clubhouse. This puts the 18th green about two par-5s away from the first tee. Due to site conditions, golf course architect Tom Doak simply did the right thing — he made the golf fit the land. The drive back to the clubhouse is a minor inconvenience in exchange for superb golf. At another routing, Boyne Mountain Resort (also in Michigan), the Alpine Course, designed by Bill Newcomb, plays down the hillside of a ski resort, the holes literally switchbacking their way downhill. Who says you can't have an all-downhill routing?

Intermissions, Lulls & Interruptions

All stories need breaks. Lulls in golf courses are important because not every hole or area of a course should be so dramatic that no contrast is offered.

The turn is an opportune moment to give the golfer a short rest or break, or at least a point in time to judge the progression of the round. The sequential numbering of golf holes, while obvious, represents a golf clock that strikes nine when the round is half up. Regardless of whether a break or time-out is offered, the routing and landscape should uphold the idea of the turn and give every indication that it has arrived. A snack bar, a scenic overlook, or even a lone wooden bench set into a flower bed can signal that our golf clock has struck nine.

Interruptions are different in that they constitute a break in the chain of a routing. They are discussed here, as they are often confused with planned lulls and breaks. Examples of interruptions are road crossings, long distances between holes, and passages through debilitating areas of a course — below low-flying aircraft, between noisy freeways, and so on. Interruptions can be made to blend. Attractive tunnels can be used as passages from one place to the next. Landscaping can define a road crossing and make it interesting, at least more so than without. Covering a distance between holes can be a wonderful experience providing the trail is aesthetically pleasing and constitutes an adventure of its own. As for the low-flying aircraft, I have no advice.

Contour Map of Emotions

Dr. Ed Sadalla once asked me to think of a course I was completing as if a contour map of its emotions had been drawn. At first this did not register, and then it made perfect sense. Just like there are high and low points in the landforms, there are high and low points in the golfer's experience as he makes the journey around a course. High points might be beautiful views, picturesque holes, dramatic shots, and extraordinary water features. These areas are given high contour lines. Low points are easy to identify. Contour lines are simply connected as they would be for land elevations. The resulting picture—a contour map—is one of tremendous revelation. Sadalla's technique can point out how a course will unfold and where its story might conjure a particular emotion.

The Ending

The best endings leave some imagination flowing. They are definitely not downers. Very difficult golf holes can be downers. I once played a well-regarded golf course that ended on a green where I recall the only five-putt in my life when seriously trying to score well. Technically it was a 6-putt, as the first putt went sailing off the green, and my return was from at least 10 feet back into the fairway. I relate this story whenever the course comes up, and I am amazed at how many people have also experienced awful trouble at this green. The conversations, instead of being about the course, are about the horrible finishing hole experience. Is that how it should be? I think not. Endings are an opportunity —not to punish, but to encourage a return. After five or six putts, I am not sure I want to face such a fate again.

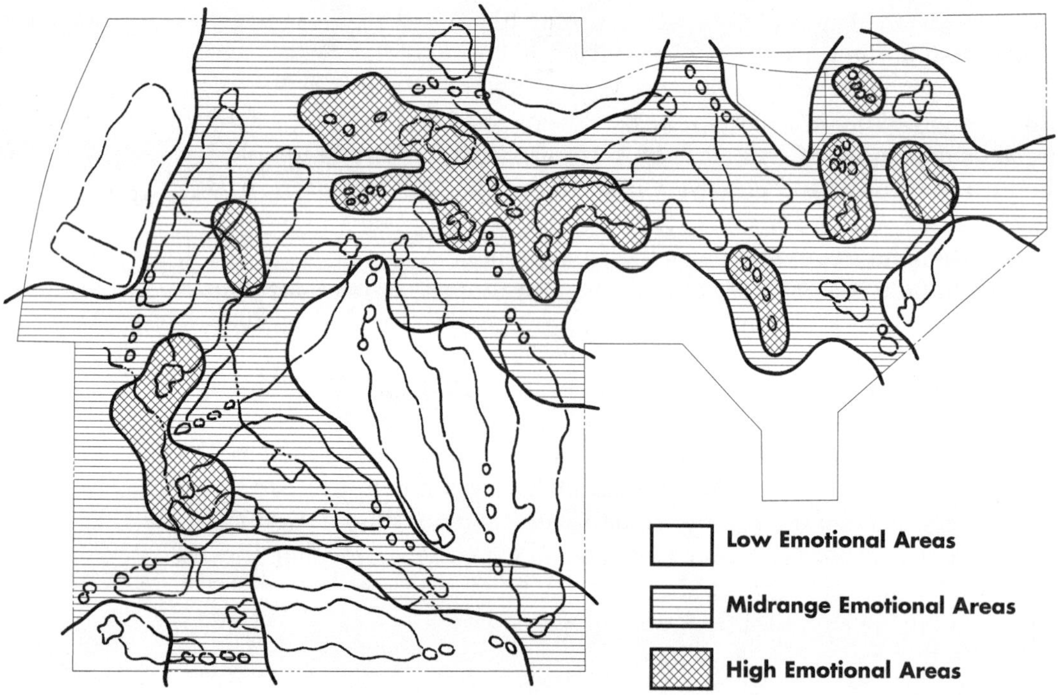

FIGURE 9-27

A contour map showing the emotional rises and falls on a golf course routing plan. This map was created by walking the site and noting views, terrain, hole strategy, elevated tees, etc. Rises occur where holes are exciting, views are breathtaking, and the challenge strong. Low areas represent areas in the plan where there is a lull; views may be restricted, neighboring development close to the golfer, and the challenge less intense. The midrange areas represent areas that fall between the highs and lows. This type of map is used to show how the golf course presents itself to the golfer. By following the routing plan it can be seen where in the round the rises and falls will occur, at what change of pace, and at what frequency.

FROM THE ROUTING PLAN FOR WHITNEY RANCH MESA; REFER TO FIGURE 7-2 FOR THE GOLF COURSE ROUTING PLAN ITSELF.

THOUGHTS ON THE PACE OF PLAY *by William Yates*

BILL YATES is a process engineer. By this it is meant that he engineers the process of how things get put together. If you've ever seen a group of people folding invitations, stuffing envelopes, and preparing a mailing, you have seen the job done efficiently, inefficiently, or somewhere in between. For such projects, people could use Bill's help, not necessarily to fold and stuff but to set up the folding and stuffing system. His job would be to make sure everything is within convenient reach, all items ordered to minimize unpacking time, and so on. Of course, hiring him to consult on getting your daughter's wedding invitations mailed on time might be overkill, but consider the design of a golf course. How much might efficient design be worth? Is it possible to get people more efficiently around a golf course? What would an extra four groups per day be worth in terms of annual revenue? Well, at $50 a round in green fees, it would be worth as much as $365,000 per year in extra revenue at a course open all year.

Bill is the creator of the Pace Designer™ System computer simulation software program. With it, pace of play issues can be studied long before courses are built and the problem areas a major job to change. The Tournament Committee of the Royal & Ancient Golf Club of St. Andrews uses this system to manage pace of play during tournaments, and the St. Andrews Links Trust has been able to better pace tee times at The Old Course itself. Bill's insight into how holes fit together to affect a round of golf is tremendously interesting. I invited Bill to write on this topic rather than do it myself. At all costs, I did not want to follow an inefficient path with his information. I am grateful he agreed to contribute.

Quite simply stated, the routing is the essence of the golf course. Not only does the routing determine the physical journey that lies ahead for any player, it holds the keys to the value of the playing experience as well.

Beyond striving to find the ultimate locations for 18 green sites, then mapping the route of play to those sites that best utilize the topography and natural features of the land, the routing of a course must also consider two major consequences: (1) The routing sets the bar for how long it will take to play the course, and (2) The routing determines how difficult or how easy it will be to manage the pace and flow of play on the course (a significant factor in providing experiential value to the players and financial value to the owners) on a day-to-day basis.

Players value their golfing experience on more than their score. Along with requiring an outstanding design that is in Augusta-like condition, players are hypersensitive about the condition they call "slow play." Much more than taking what they believe to be an excessive amount of time to play, golfers really object to the feeling that they are waiting to play every shot. Standing around on a golf course and walking around on a course

Adjacent fairways do not appear in true Championship layouts. Each hole should be a thing alone.
—*George C. Thomas Jr.*, Golf Architecture in America

are two very different things. The questions are: How long should it take to play? What really causes players to wait to play every shot?

In 1995, the USGA published the *USGA Pace Rating System Manual*, which I had the honor to co-author. The manual described the new Pace Rating System the USGA developed to determine how long it should take to play a course when the course is full. Data from hundreds of observations were the basis for constructing mathematical formulae that could be used to objectively determine the time it should take to play each hole (the hole's time par) and their total (the course's *pace rating*). The key elements that affect the time it should take to play, which are included in the pace rating formulae, are the playing length of each hole, whether or not carts have access to the fairways, the difficulty and frequency of individual obstacles on each hole, and the distances players must travel between holes (greens to tees). As you might recognize, only one of these key elements (the policy regarding carts) is under the control of course managers, none of these elements are influenced by the players, and all of the remaining elements are determined by the golf course architect. That is why the course routing and design have such a significant impact on the time it should take to play 18 holes. However, course design has absolutely no impact on what we typically call slow play. In other words, the course routing and design sets the bar for determining how long it will take to play. How long it actually does take to play is another matter. Let me explain.

Two courses might have the exact same playing yardage of 6500 yards, and because of differences in obstacle difficulty and travel distances between greens and tees, one course might have a pace rating of 4:05 and the pace rating for the other course could well be 4:30. With this new pace rating tool, we can prove three important points: (1) All courses do not take the same amount of time to play; (2) The design and routing of a golf course determine the time it should take to play the course; and (3) Taking more than 4 hours to play golf is not necessarily a result or a symptom of slow play; the time that it *should take* to play (determined by the architect) and the time that it *does take* to play (determined by course managers and the players) are two completely different issues.

Length & Variation for Flow

When calculating a *pace rating*, we always measure from the most frequently used tees. Typically, these are middle tees whose playing yardage is in the neighborhood of 6500. In fact, I was surprised to discover that the average playing yardage of the more than 60 courses I measured in the United States and Canada was 6316, and the yardage of the eight courses I measured in England and Scotland was 6344. I thought that because players in the U.K. played faster than Americans do, British courses would be shorter. Not so.

Does the playing length have a large effect on the time to play? Yes, it does. And, as courses are stretched longer and longer, the time it takes to play will follow.

Pace Manager™ Systems
Pace Rating Summary

Conditions: **Carts Have Access to Fairways on Most Holes** William Yates and Associates

Tees: **Blue**

	Time (Min)	Playing		Distance (Yds) Green to Tee		Total	
Front Nine	137	3047		2887		5934	
Back Nine	132	3259		2335		5594	
Total	**269**	**6306**	3.6 Miles	**5222**	3.0 Miles	**11528**	6.6 Miles

Unofficial 18 Hole Pace Rating

4 Hours 29 Minutes

Pace Manager™ Systems
Pace Rating Summary

Conditions: **Carts Restricted to Cart Paths** William Yates and Associates

Tees: **Blue**

	Time (Min)	Playing		Distance (Yds) Green to Tee		Total	
Front Nine	141	3047		2887		5934	
Back Nine	140	3259		2335		5594	
Total	**281**	**6306**	3.6 Miles	**5222**	3.0 Miles	**11528**	6.6 Miles

Unofficial 18 Hole Pace Rating

4 Hours 41 Minutes

FIGURE 9-28
Examples of *pace rating summaries* for the same routing plan. The top example shows the summary if carts are given access to fairways. The lower shows an increase in round time of 12 minutes if carts are restricted to cart paths at all times. Common to both is the extremely long distance eaten up between greens and tees—a whopping 3 miles! Armed with this rating it is possible, through a series of design and management evaluations, to find ways to improve the round time, creating a better golf experience with less waiting time.

COURTESY OF PACE MANAGER SYSTEMS; www.pacemanager.com

Obstacles, Hazards & the Time to Play

While I do not have objective, definitive data to support my theory, only hundreds of hours of on-course observations, I will make the following statement anyway: "Golf course architects, go ahead and add all of the sand and water you want. These obstacles will not appreciably add to the phenomenon we call slow play. What you must do, however, is avoid building courses with blind landing areas and using extreme rough (deep grasses, trees, and underbrush) in the wrong places." That's it!

Believe it or not, players of varying abilities typically negotiate a well-designed or even diabolical golf holes in a reasonable amount of time, typically within the calculated *time par* of the hole. They seem to do this regardless of the number of bunkers or lakes on the hole. What really slows down play is looking for balls. Therefore, to minimize that time-consuming behavior, course designers and superintendents must take great care to build courses featuring challenges other than deep rough and blind landing areas that are in play for both the scratch and the bogey golfer. Having deep grass in the wrong locations can really slow players down. The most typical wrong locations are on the inside of a dogleg, near blind landing areas, on the banks of streams and lakes that are in play, and closely bordering fairways between 160 to 200 yards from the middle tees.

The Effect of Distance Between Holes

What really affects both the time to play and how golfers play—that is, with or without mandatory carts—is the distance players must travel between holes. This distance can be as short as 20 to 30 yards (in Great Britain, the average distance I measured was 46 yards), or over 700 yards (the average distance between holes on the U.S. courses I measured was 180 yards). As a point of comparison, during an 18-hole round, U.S. players travel more than 1.3 miles farther than their British counterparts.

A drive and a pitch followed by a drive and a pitch is a good deal like serving a watery pudding after a watery soup. Separate them sufficiently and each may be approached with some interest.
—Robert Hunter, The Links

During a consulting assignment, I measured a course that had a spectacular routing laid out over a vast amount of land. The total distance between the holes on that course was an incredible 5222 yards. As a result, the players travel a total of 2.9 miles and spend 32 minutes riding in a cart not playing golf. Players on this course spend over half an hour just to go from one hole to another.

Par Order, Distribution & Rhythm

There are certain effects of the sequence of holes and the rhythm of playing groups on a course that we have for many years incorrectly called slow play. But this kind of slow play is not caused by players playing slowly. When, for example, a par-5 hole is followed by a par-3 hole, there will inevitably be a backup on the par 3 because of the difference in capacity of the two holes. What we typically experience on courses all around the country, and what we find so infuriating, is the subtle effect of the sequencing of holes. Hole sequencing establishes the capacity and the pattern of flow on the golf course. In many cases, we incorrectly blame the players for slow play when the problem is in reality a combination of hole length and sequencing (a capacity issue that is a result of the routing and individual hole design) and course overcrowding (resulting from management practices).

It is amazing how much impact the sequencing of holes, their length, and their relationship to one another have on the ebb and flow—the rhythm, if you will—of play on the golf course. While the course itself remains static, much of the movement of the players is determined by the design and routing of the course. This too, is predictable. When I work with course management teams and golf course architects and have the opportunity to analyze their course and explain the complex dynamics of the intertwined effects of players, management practices, and course design, we make tremendous and immediate progress in conquering what seems to most people to be an impossible battle against slow play.

The standardization of our golf courses has gone on apace in recent years. It has brought us so much of value that few of us have thought to question its utility in all cases. The length of courses, the types of bunkers, the moulding of the greens, the placing of hazards, the sequence of holes, etc., are made to follow certain models. That a course must be either of nine or eighteen holes is one of the most ancient of these standards, and the person who questioned its wisdom in all cases would, I fear, be looked upon as one demented. And yet why should every club, regardless of its membership, its funds, and the land available, feel that it must have either nine or eighteen holes? If a club is able to find land only in the hills, where the play must be very tiring, why should it not have twelve, fourteen or sixteen holes?

—Robert Hunter, The Links

Preventing Slow Play Before It Begins

Given today's new tools, we can determine what the pace of play will be on a golf course that has not yet been built. We can pinpoint specifically where player backups and delays will be and roughly how long each foursome will be standing there waiting to play.

This revolutionary capability enables golf course architects and developers to quantify and determine the length of the round of golf under various routing and management policy options. Through a proprietary computer simulation program, we can assist the architect in preparing an owner's manual of sorts for the new course. Today, for the first time, there is no reason for a new course to open and, in only a few weeks, have a reputation for slow play. We now have the objective tools that enable course designers and managers to carefully determine the best management practices that will optimize the use of their new course and raise the quality and value of the golfing experience to the highest level possible.

Getting Around the Course—Allowing Circulation

If slow play is a traffic problem, then a routing that provides for the smooth ebb and flow of the game will go a long way to winning the battle over slow play. Interestingly, the design and management of the flow of players must begin at the parking lot. From the moment the players arrive on the property until the moment they leave, the design of the parking lot, bag drop, clubhouse, and route to the first tee should promote the smooth, direct, and uncongested movement of players. Moving smoothly through the check-in process and arriving at the first tee on time is as important as moving smoothly through the 18 holes. A sound clubhouse design and player traffic routing plan around the clubhouse will set the tone for a day free of congestion and waiting, and it will make the course far easier to manage from day to day.

The 13-Hole Course — A Lesson in Putting the Cart Before the Course

It is no secret that routing plans are not final plans. Some projects require many iterations of routing in order to arrive at the configuration that satisfies as many concerns and considerations as possible. No routing plan can satisfy all of the issues. The best advice on this subject, and the point of this story, is that all of the routing plan options should be created, drawn up, and approved *before* one begins building a golf course.

At a terribly complex project involving land use issues that still make my head hurt almost 20 years later, a situation arose where the developer was given preliminary entitlement approval to build a golf course. Even the land ownership issues were complex. One parcel was owned by a flood control district, another by a consortium of utility companies. The most problematic was a piece of land owned by the city that issued the approval after a few years' worth of public hearings and decisions. This land was the main problem.

A group of naysayers was against the golf course and made their position known at every step of the process. At one point, routing plans were being generated nearly every morning following protracted meetings with this group, all in an effort to appease them and obtain their support. This went on for months. In all, 45 routings were generated, and this does not include minor variations that were done as quick sketches. It boiled down to five golf holes of concern: holes 14, 15, 16, 17, and a portion of 18. These holes were shifted, shortened, realigned and moved until it seemed that every possible combination had been attempted. Par 4s were turned into par 3s. One par 5 was made into two holes, a par 3 and a par 4. A par 3 was tossed aside and squeezed in elsewhere. This went on for three full years.

When our plans were finally approved, it was a joyous occasion. The next day, a grading permit was secured, and waiting bulldozers began clearing the front nine. Surveyors hurriedly staked points for construction on the back nine even though the final design plans were still being drafted. Work progressed on holes 1 through 13. Then, about a month later, just after blueprints of the controversial holes had been distributed to the golf course builder, a call came that a lawsuit had been filed and, unbelievably, a judge had issued an injunction preventing construction of the last five holes.

In an amazing show of confidence, my client ordered construction to continue on the holes already in progress. If construction were to stop altogether, there would be no way to stay on schedule and meet the summer planting window. The heavy equipment that had been poised to move into hole 14 and 15 moved backward and concentrated on what was now being built as a 13-hole golf course.

The court case dragged on. Finally, a decision was reached that was favorable to the golf course. There were no grounds, said the judge, for not allowing the five holes to be built. His decision was based on the ample public comment and right of the city to lease its land based on the economic and recreation benefits that a golf course would bring.

Work had now been going on for six months, and grass was growing nicely on the first 13 holes. From the air, the golf course had a curious look. Because it was an out-and-back routing, the footprint of the complete holes looked like a series of single fairways beginning but very strangely going nowhere.

Then a bomb was dropped; the group opposing the use of the land took their case to the state supreme court. In an unprecedented move, the work was stopped once again. Only after several months, well after the planting window was lost, did the court issue a ruling allowing the course to be built.

No one expects entitlements to drag on, and certainly not that the project will wind up in front of a supreme court. I never was able to find a solutionthat would have completed the 13-hole course we had managed to build. Without the land in question, there was simply no way to complete the routing. We would have wound up with an interesting course of fewer holes than expected, or perhaps found a way to shoehorn holes off in another direction. Either way, the finishing hole would have been almost a mile and a half away from the first hole.

REMODELING

Fitting holes together as part of remodeling follows the same basic principles as outlines for new routings. Homage must be paid to the existing routing. Often, the givens of an existing routing cannot be changed to the degree that modern safety guidelines suggest.

Almost any routing changes to an existing routing will cause dominos to fall—that is, changing one area will cause another to need changing, and so on. One hopes this will stop, but it doesn't always. I find it amusing when those who do not route golf courses casually gesture at existing courses and suggest change—usually a new road, clubhouse, or development. At a public meeting at which we were asking for approval to move a maintenance facility to a new site, one of the opposing attorneys (there were four opposing attorneys, each representing a different opposing entity) casually waved his hand and noted that there was plenty of room to change things around so the maintenance area would not have to move. My reaction was to point out that I did not practice law and he should refrain from designing golf courses.

Some thoughts on fitting holes and golf components in a remodeling situation include:

- Perfection

  It may not be attainable in terms of setbacks and separation of golf holes due to the more relaxed standards in place when the course was originally built.

- Additional land

  Holes may have to be shortened if additional land cannot be acquired and there is no room to shift holes to accommodate realignment.

- Clubhouse areas

  When clubhouses are relocated, they must be positioned to serve the golf course and have appropriate relationships to access, parking, and practice areas.

- Maintenance areas

  Maintenance areas that must be moved on existing courses should (1) be centrally located, (2) be screened from adjacent land uses, (3) have efficient and direct access, and, (4) preserve the integrity of the course. On courses with limited acreage, the issue of access is infinitely more important than screening, as the facility itself can always be screened, but it is not always practical to screen an access road leading to a facility.

The Psychology of the Golf Journey

HOLE NO.

10

by Edward Sadalla, Ph.D.

What does it mean to say that routing the course has psychological implications? It does not mean that psychological factors can uniquely specify or determine how a golf course should be routed. It does, however, suggest that when routing the course, you are simultaneously designing a set of experiences for the golfer. Among other things, you can influence the golfer's emotions, aesthetic responses, the tempo or pace of the round, and the degree to which the golfer is required to think or solve problems while playing. These factors will, in turn, influence the golfer's ability to swing the club and strike the ball.

Whether the context is a tournament or a recreational event, golf is an emotional game. Like other forms of athletic competition, it tests temperament and character and offers unlimited opportunities for elation, embarrassment, and failure. Bobby Jones described golf as "… a game of considerable passion either of the explosive type, or that which burns inwardly and sears the soul." A round of golf has the capacity to produce the following feelings in a golfer: appreciation of nature, anger, anxiety, confusion, control, elation, embarrassment, experience of beauty, fear, frustration, power, precision, relaxation, and satisfaction. Clearly, some of these emotions are positive and desirable, while others the golfer strives to avoid.

Golf is an invention, not, as some would have it, a divine gift, and while we may celebrate the pleasure it brings us, it's best to remember that we are singing of ourselves when we do so.
—*Desmond Muirhead,* St. Andrews: How to Play the Old Course

The choices made among routing alternatives will influence which emotions are experienced as well as the frequency and intensity of those experiences. The golfer's emotional responses will, in turn, influence his or her physical ability. One of the fascinating aspects of the game is that strong emotions, especially negative emotions, can overwhelm the golfer's ability to play effectively. As Tiger Woods remarked as a U.S. Open Golf Championship was drawing to a dramatic close, "I think the guys who are really controlling their emotions are going to win." The relationship between emotion and performance is no less true for the recreational golfer.

Course routing can be guided by a set of psychological and behavioral objectives. These can include the following:

- The course should be playable by and enjoyable to golfers of varying ability levels while remaining challenging to better players.
- The course should be routed so that the flow of play is not excessively slow.
- The course should be designed to be memorable or to contain memorable holes, and should engage the physical, intellectual, and emotional abilities of the golfer.
- The course should generate more positive than negative emotions for a wide range of golfers.
- The course should have the highest possible aesthetic value.

Why does the game of golf produce such interest and fascination in the people who attempt to play it? Part of the answer to this question can be found by considering the origins of the game from a psychological point of view.

HUMAN ORIGINS & GOLF

Humans evolved on the savannas of Africa, and modern humans have inherited an apparently universal attraction to savannalike environments (expanses of grass dotted with trees). For 95 percent of human history, food was acquired by hunting and gathering. Daily life consisted of hunting for food, and success ensured both survival and status within the group. When not searching for food, hunter-gatherers spent time refining their tools and practicing the skills that underlie successful subsistence. The games of ancestral humans, like the games of contemporary hunter-gatherers, probably involved demonstrations of skills that were central to hunting. These skills remain the most common elements in modern sports.

Golf, like its early contemporaries from Europe (jeu de mail, chole, and kolf), is a stick-and-ball game. The objective is to strike a ball so that it travels from point A to point B. The game is one of a set of games in which a person demonstrates skill at accurately delivering a ball to either a stationary or a moving target. Most commonly, games require the player to aim the ball with the hand or foot. Golf requires the use of a variety of tools. As Winston Churchill famously remarked, "Golf is a game whose aim it is to hit a very small ball into an even smaller hole with weapons singularly ill-designed for the purpose."

All projectile-target games make use of the ability of humans to accurately throw a missile. Evolution designed humans to be able to throw various types of objects. Throwing is a uniquely human skill—other primates cannot throw with any accuracy whatsoever—and is central to our ability to hunt and kill prey. As evolution favored humans with the perceptual and cognitive skills that enable successful hunting, it also produced the ability to play golf. In a sense, a round of golf may be regarded as the metaphorical equivalent of the hunt.

Both hunting and golf involve heightened awareness of terrain and the ability to imagine the outcome of a series of actions. Both fully engage the imagination and the senses. Both require a kind of relaxed concentration for optimal performance. Note how well the words of Rick Bass, a modern hunter, apply also to the experience of golf:

> One sets out after one's quarry with senses fully engaged, wildly alert: entranced, nearly hypnotized. . . . Each year during such pursuits, I am struck more and more by the conceit that people in a hunter-gatherer culture might have richer imaginations than those who dwell more fully in an agricultural or even post-agricultural environment. What else is the hunt but a stirring of the imagination, with the quarry, or goal, or treasure lying just around the corner or over the next rise?

The origins of the game provide clues about how to route a golf course. Because hunting was a universal activity of ancestral humans and because humans have always competed at the skills involved in hunting, the modern golfer has inherited a set of universal perceptual, cognitive, and emotional reactions. By regarding a round of golf as a type of hunting game, it is possible to understand a golfer's aesthetic reactions, emotions, experience of space, perception of hazards, and performance on the course.

WHAT MAKES UP THE GAME OF GOLF?

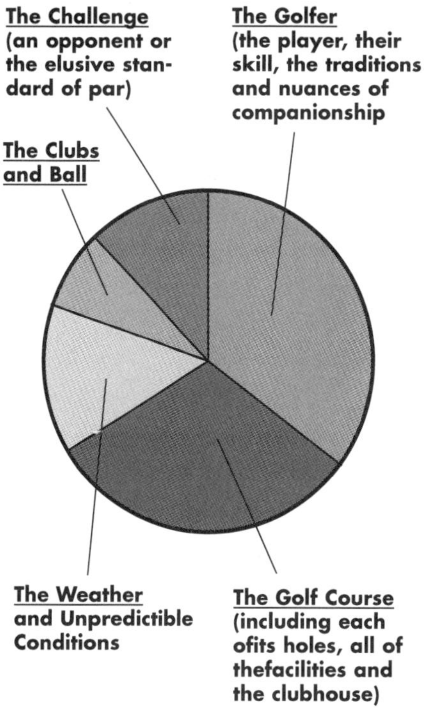

FIGURE 10-1
A game of golf is an interaction between three elements: the golfer, the course, and the influence of weather, equipment and competition. The game of golf is unique among sports in that there is more variation in the playing field than is common in other forms of competition. The result is that the playing field for golf is far more influential to one's experience and performance than in most games.

PSYCHOLOGICAL CONSIDERATIONS IN COURSE ROUTING

The following are the primary components and conditions to golf courses most influenced by psychological factors. This is not to say that there are not many more situations that can be influenced by how the design may play out psychologically. Every area—literally every nook and cranny—of a golf facility can affect a golfer and modify his impression of the experience. The impact of a design is not only in the broad-stroke decisions but also in every detail.

Practice Areas

Golf should be a game in which we get away from it all, not in which life gets busier and busier.
—Lorne Rubenstein, in The Globe & Mail *newspaper*

In contrast to the lifestyle of traditional humans, modern urban life is typified by a sense of time urgency. For the average person, life is rushed, overscheduled, and lived at an excessively fast pace. The average golfer arrives at the course with residual tension from daily life and needs both time and a place to slow down, warm up, and practice various facets of the game. An optimally routed course will have a driving range, short game area, and putting green. For reasons discussed below, these elements should not be located in direct proximity to the first tee. The driving range, of course, should be oriented to the north or south so as not to face golfers into the rising or setting sun. If a north-south orientation is impossible, a course that faces east is preferable to one that faces west. Golfers who begin their round at daybreak will rarely have time to use the range. Further, many golfers want to use practice facilities in the late afternoon on days when they do not intend to use the course.

The First Tee

Location of the first tee has considerable psychological significance. The first shot of the day can set the tone of the whole round. A bad first drive—a poor score on the first hole—can diminish enthusiasm and have a contagious effect on the entire round. For this reason, most first and second holes are not the number-one handicap hole, a tradition we are all thankful for. For the recreational golfer, one of the most important factors concerns the degree to which action on the first tee is visible to bystanders. On some courses, the first tee is located near the clubhouse or a practice area, affording bystanders a clear view of the group beginning the round. Under these circumstances, the first shot of the day must be performed in front of an audience. For most golfers, this magnifies the difficulty of the shot.

For example, Lincoln Park Golf Course in San Francisco, California, has a first tee located between the practice putting green and the pro shop. Benches behind the tee are provided for patrons who have purchased food from the snack bar and who wish to eat outside. A foursome teeing off at Lincoln Park is typically aware of the eyes of other golfers. In contrast, the first tee at the Tournament Players Club Desert Course in Scottsdale, Arizona, is located some distance from the clubhouse, completely out of sight of casual spectators. Perhaps the most extreme example of teeing off in the presence of an audience occurs at the first tee at St. Andrews in Scotland, where a camera linked to the World Wide Web ensures that the golfer's first shot is witnessed by a worldwide audience.

Experimental psychologists have studied the effect of an audience on the performance of complex skills for more than five decades. The literature is remarkably consistent—an audience will impair the performance of the average golfer. Because humans are instinctively aware of being watched, an audience is a potent source of distraction. The golfer tries to pay simultaneous attention both to the audience and to the task of swinging the club. Because the mind can focus on only one thing at a

FIGURE 10-2
In this historic photo of the first tee at the St. Augustine Country Club (c. 1899), this golfer has quite a gallery on hand to scrutinize his opening tee shot. Care must be taken in orienting the first tee. Ideally, separation and seclusion is preferred. The grandstands in the background of this photo are quite curious. Probably they were for polo matches — at least we hope so.

SOURCE: *OUTING* MAGAZINE, 1899

time, trying to do two things at once impairs concentration on the swing. Further, an audience is likely to increase evaluation apprehension. Being watched implies that one's performance is being evaluated, which in turn causes an increase in tension and physiological arousal.

Excessive physical tension inevitably disrupts a golf swing. Tension causes a subjective change in the way the body is experienced. The club is gripped tighter. Heart rate and blood pressure increase measurably. The palms may begin to sweat. The breath becomes shallower and more rapid. Normal feedback from the muscles of the body, which is essential to the golf swing, is disrupted. Swinging with a sense of rhythm becomes increasingly difficult.

Tension and arousal are especially disruptive when skills are not well learned and where high levels of concentration are required. On the other hand, tension and arousal can actually improve performance if skills are habitual and automatic. For this reason, professionals and skilled amateurs might actually improve when performing in front of an audience. Their golf skills are more automatic and are less subject to disruption. Because the golf swing is a simpler task for the skilled golfer, the arousal produced by an audience tends to increase concentration and motivation to perform. Further, tournament players are likely to have played in front of an audience and have learned to eliminate spectators as a source of distraction.

Golf ball: A sphere made of rubber bands wound up about half as tensely as the person trying to hit it.

— From a wall plaque in a pro shop, author unknown

The Elevated Tee

Why is the elevated tee a source of such great pleasure to the golfer? The best holes are likely to be those with elevation changes, especially from higher elevations to lower. Natural tee sites are those with an

A good golf course makes you want to play so badly you hardly have time to change your shoes.
—Ben Crenshaw

impressive view. Books that depict great golf holes are invariably filled with vistas from elevated tees.

Relatively few classic holes have significantly elevated greens or holes where the tee box is at a lower elevation than the rest of the hole. Interestingly, studies of human reactions to paintings and photographs of landscapes reveal similar preferences. There is a strong human tendency to prefer landscapes that contain a prominent elevated place where one or more people could stand.

British geographer Jay Appleton proposed that humans are born with an innate preference for places that offer both prospect and refuge. *Prospect* refers to a clear, unobstructed view of the landscape. *Refuge* means a safe place where one is secure from threatening or dangerous parts of the environment. Environments with both of these features historically offered the opportunity to see without being seen and to eat without being eaten.

Humans have excellent vision but a poor sense of smell and only average hearing. Our ability to locate both prey and predators depends largely on vision. It is suggested that we therefore automatically prefer places that offer a good view of the surrounding terrain. Historically,

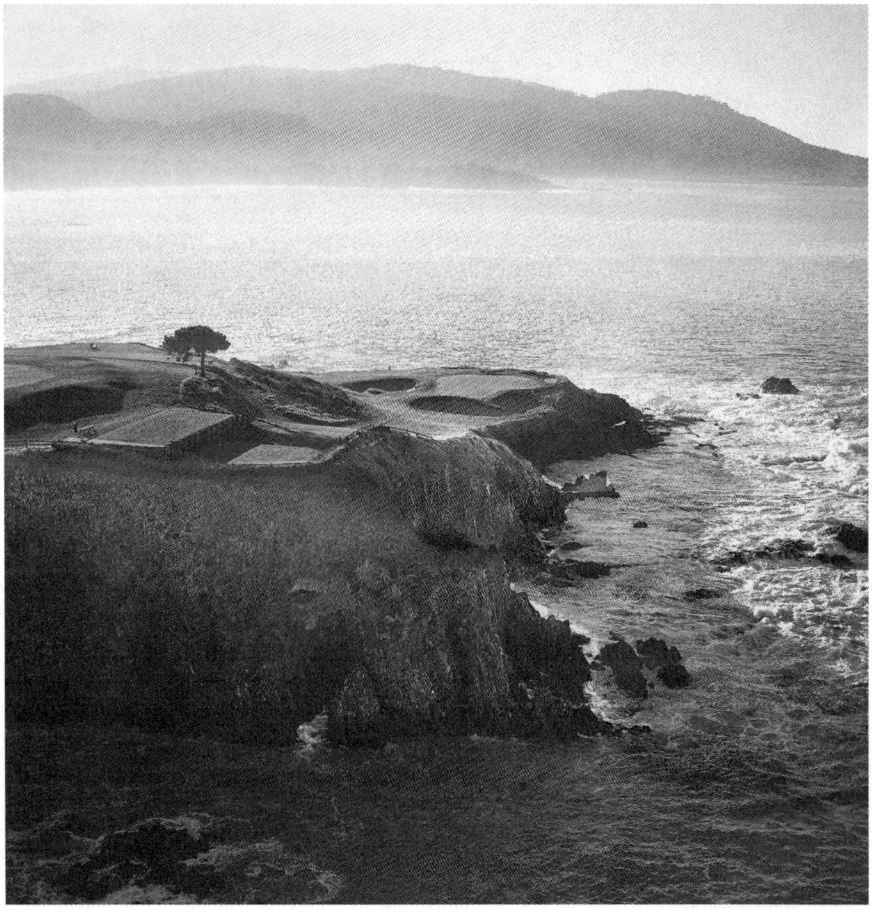

FIGURE 10-3
The famous seventh hole at the equally famous Pebble Beach Golf Links is perhaps the ultimate elevated tee. Not only is the green well below but also the backdrop of the ocean is an endless reminder of what encircles the green.

COURTESY OF PEBBLE BEACH GOLF LINKS; PHOTOGRAPH ©JOANN DOST; JACK NEVILLE AND DOUGLAS GRANT, GOLF COURSE ARCHITECTS humans have also had to be concerned with refuge from predators or from other hostile humans. Elevated places are more easily defended and hence offer refuge. Projectiles such as rocks and sticks can be rained down on an enemy from an elevated place with less effort and over larger distances. The elevated tee is therefore a place where the golfer feels a sense of power, peace, and security. The shot will carry farther, increasing the sense of personal power.

[G]olf is played mainly in a five-and-a-half inch course, the space between your ears.
—Bobby Jones

Tee Orientation

A profusion of level tee sites allows for the construction of multiple tee boxes. Multiple tee boxes combined with variations in pin placement allow for great flexibility in course difficulty. Length is, of course, most influential to difficulty, but the angles created by the tee box and landing areas in the fairway will also influence the golfer's strategy in playing the hole. Multiple tee boxes make the course playable by the widest range of golfers, but it should not be anticipated that golfers will automatically select the tee box that is appropriate for their level of skill.

A design feature that causes difficulty for the average golfer but that might not be much noticed is the alignment of the tee box. A tee box is usually rectangular in shape and oriented in a given direction. The orientation of the tee box refers to the direction of a line perpendicular to a line drawn between the tee blocks. At first glance, such alignments seem of minimal importance because all golf shots played require the golfer to orient the body in relation to the target line. However, humans typically are field dependent; they derive their orientation from their immediate surroundings and have difficulty disengaging from the visual impact of those surroundings. If a tee box is oriented obliquely to the landing area, the recreational golfer will have trouble compensating. If the tee box is oriented so that it points at a hazard such as water or a bunker, the perceptual effect of the hazard will be enhanced, and shots will tend to land in the hazard. Better golfers are more practiced at being field independent and can gauge the direction of the target in relation to their body and the plane of their swing.

Green Sites

Green sites typically require level ground with sufficient square footage for a putting surface. Elevated greens do not produce the same positive emotional responses as to elevated tees. Attacking any target on higher ground is more challenging and less likely to be successful. The green is analogous to the place where the quarry is captured. On the tee, the golfer surveys the surrounding terrain. On the green, the golfer's attention is more narrowly focused on the space immediately surrounding the hole. Further, elevated greens are like fortresses; they are difficult to approach, and they magnify errors. Elevated greens appeal primarily to advanced golfers who are looking for an extra challenge. Few golfers are capable of attacking an elevated green with a fairway wood or long

FIGURE 10-4
A green may be secluded or out in the open. Secluded settings are best when there are no views to take advantage of, or for variation on open sites where it seems there is no place to hide. In this example, the green is virtually a stage that can be seen from other areas of the course.

© PHOTO COURTESY OF MIKE HOUSKA/DOGLEG STUDIOS; COURSE DESIGN BY PALMER COURSE DESIGNS; RUNNING Y RANCH GOLF CLUB, OREGON

iron. The fortress green and the small contoured green are best designed in relation to a short iron or pitch shot. Larger greens or greens located in a depression or contained by mounding may be best suited for a long approach shot.

SPATIAL CONFIGURATION OF ROUTING

Golfers are tremendously influenced by how golf holes and features are set into the environment. This begins with the fundamental routing of holes and fairways. The directions and pathways established in the planning stages will define the journey required of the golfer. There is no turning back from these decisions-they are cast in the earth, unchangeable without significant cost and ordeal.

Orientation of the Route

Human vision is poorly adapted for looking directly into the sun. For this reason, as has been advised elsewhere in this book, courses should not have initial holes facing east or finishing holes facing west. A hole facing into the sun has a number of distinct disadvantages. The ball will be difficult to follow, and play will be slowed as golfers search for errant shots. The aesthetics of the hole will be degraded because the sun will eliminate contrast and color. The ability to judge distance will be diminished. Finally, the tendency to squint while looking into the sun will cause increased facial tension, which leads to increased bodily tension. Hunters do not hunt while looking into the sun, and a golfer's enjoyment will be diminished on holes that play into a low sun.

Turns & Landmarks—Their Effect on Perceived Distance & Orientation

Humans use landmarks and path systems to navigate through space and are notoriously bad at recalling changes in direction along a path. Studies of maps show that curved routes are straightened when they are drawn and that angles greater than 45 degrees are distorted in the direction of 90 degrees. Turns of greater than 45 degrees have an effect on the perceived length of a route. If the designer routes a series of holes with a tortuous or squiggly path, the course will seem subjectively longer to the golfer. Conversely, a relatively straight path system with fewer turns will seem subjectively shorter. In routing, this spatial illusion can be used to expand or contract the perceived length of a course. If the area available for the course is small in size, necessitating a short course, a path system with many turns will tend to expand the subjective length of the course in the player's mind.

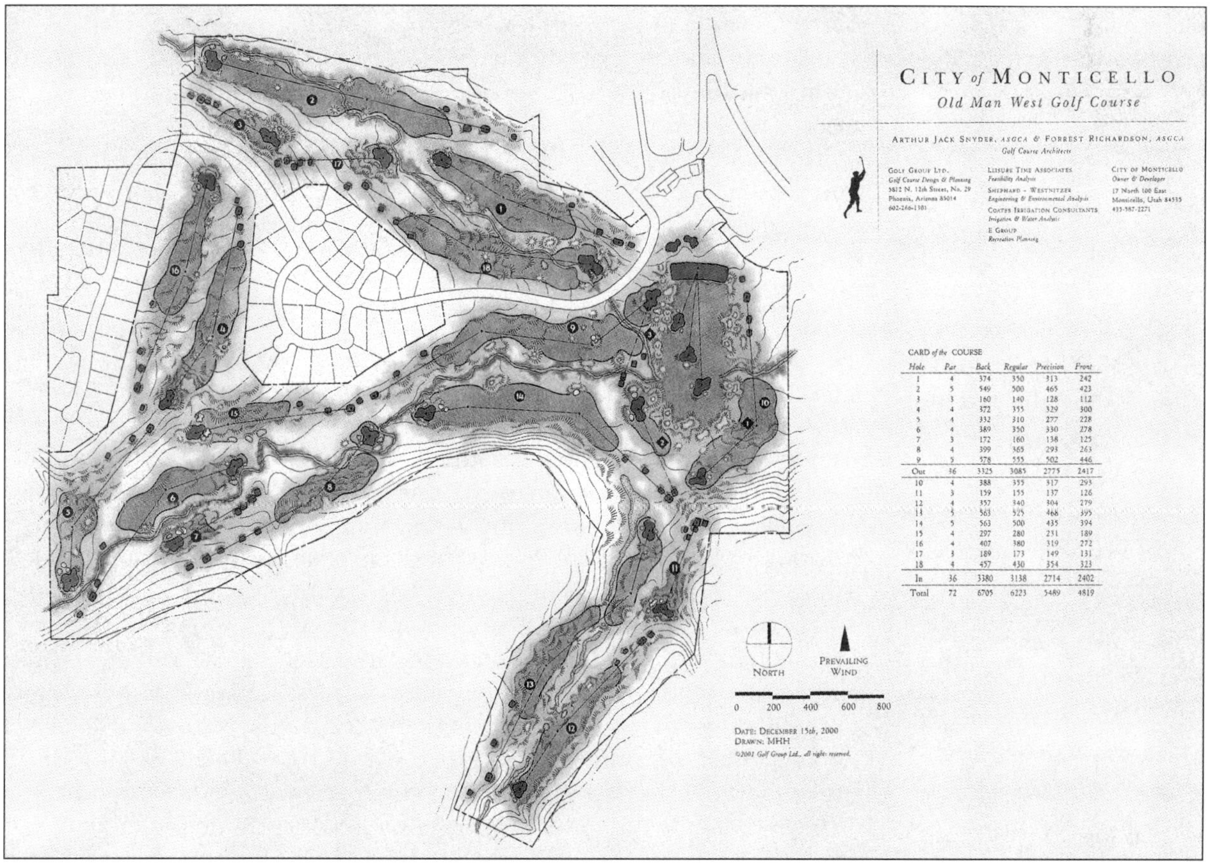

FIGURE 10-5

This routing for an 18-hole course crosses over itself along a ridge and again near a natural creek. The interlocking nines give the golfer a taste of what's to come and a review later in the round of places visited. Although the design turns frequently, it does so in response to the land and offers many vistas of the surrounding valley and often snow-capped mountains of this alpine location. When twists and turns are the result of natural terrain or built terrain made to look natural, the routing is likely to seem more comfortable to the golfer.

THE HIDEOUT GOLF CLUB, MONTICELLO, UTAH, ARTHUR JACK SNYDER, ASGCA, AND FORREST RICHARDSON, ASGCA, GOLF COURSE ARCHITECTS

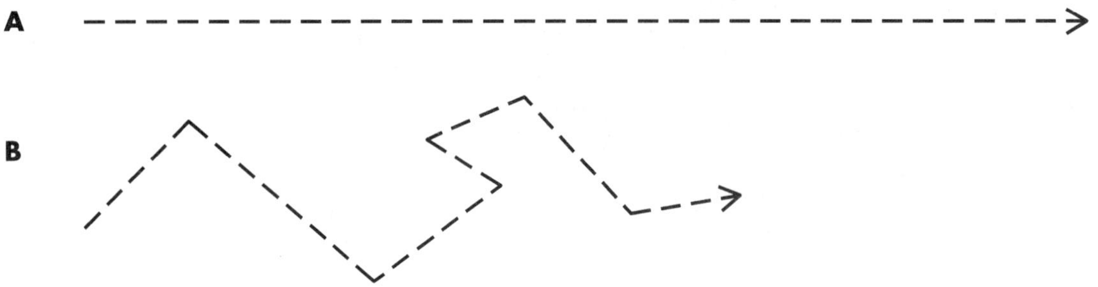

FIGURE 10-6
Both of these paths are the same length. However, study participants who walked the routing overwhelmingly estimated the length of B as 25 percent longer than A.

Consider the two path systems (Figure 10-6) that were employed in a study of spatial memory. After walking each path, participants were asked to estimate its length. Although both paths were identical in length, participants estimated path B as 25 percent longer than path A.

Path effects occur when no obvious landmarks are visible throughout the course. Humans commonly maintain their sense of direction and distance in relation to external landmarks. When trees or other visual obstacles surround and enclose a path, a corridor effect is created. In such instances, internal landmarks such as water, bunkers, and other hazards influence the ability to judge distance. Generally, adding landmarks along a path promotes perceptual accuracy. Landmarks serve as intermediate reference points, allowing a golfer to better judge the distance and elevation of a target. Homogeneous expanses of fairway make distance and elevation estimation more difficult.

Sequencing & Course Character

COURSE PERSONALITY
Perhaps the all-time greatest description of a golf course was penned by Jim Murray, a columnist for the *Los Angeles Times,* when he wrote this about Spyglass Hill:

> *If it were human, Spyglass would have a knife in its teeth, a patch on its eye, a ring in its ear, tobacco in its beard, and a blunderbuss in its hands. It's a privateer plundering the golfing main, an amphibious creature, half ocean, half forest.*

The order of difficulty in a route is a powerful psychological manipulation. It affects the flow of play, the level of excitement, and the golfer's stress level and self-confidence. The sequence of difficulty defines the character of a course almost as much as do course aesthetics. Generally, the first few holes of a course are designed with comparatively low difficulty levels in order to build the average golfer's confidence. As noted, it is rare to find the number-one handicap hole early in a course. Therefore, because golf courses that begin with high levels of difficulty and become easier are the exception instead of the rule, a golfer will assume that if the first few holes are hard, the entire day will be a difficult challenge. The idea that early holes are less difficult was ingrained to the game of golf by early routings and the designs of early courses. To go against this tradition changes the golfer's expectations and will most assuredly yield a different type of experience.

In many contexts, it is appropriate for a course routing to be nothing more than a sequence of easy holes with wide landing areas where hazards can be easily avoided. Such designs, after all, would speed the flow of play and present difficulty levels that are likely to be appropriate for the majority of players. Golf is an intrinsically difficult game to master. Less than 10 percent of golfers develop any real consistency at striking the ball. But entirely easy routes are also not entirely fun. The challenge of negotiating through and around hazards, which is such a vital part of the game, is missing from such routings. Even on short courses or par-3 layouts, the sequence must offer an appropriate challenge, for without challenge we have made the hunt too easy and therefore not exciting.

The spirit of golf is to dare a hazard, and by negotiating it reap a reward.

—George C. Thomas Jr., Golf Architecture in America

The opposite of the consistently easy route is the consistently difficult route. Such courses are generally limited to the highest levels of tournament play and are designed to discriminate between the ability of highly skilled players. Like all difficult tests, they are primarily enjoyed by players who are looking for difficult challenges. This type of routing is seen as threatening and frustrating by the average golfer if he can find no way around the peril. Consistently difficult routes maximally impede the flow of play.

The use of contrasting difficulty levels is a way to make specific holes more salient and more memorable. A few average holes may be needed to bookend or accentuate a truly great hole.

The tournament finish is where the holes get progressively more difficult toward the end of the course. This type of finish has a number of psychological consequences. In actual tournament situations, it tends to encourage conservative play among leaders. Among good players, play on such finishing holes is characterized by caution and low risk taking so as to avoid a bogey. In contrast, a relative easy 18th hole that offers the chance for a finishing birdie to win encourages risk taking.

The tournament finish has an entirely different impact on the average recreational golfer, for whom it can be associated with high levels of failure and consequent frustration. Because human memory seems designed to remember the beginning and end of a sequence (known as *primacy* and *recency* effects), frustration at the end of a course is especially memorable.

TORREY PINES — SOUTH COURSE
CHART OF HOLE DIFFICULTY

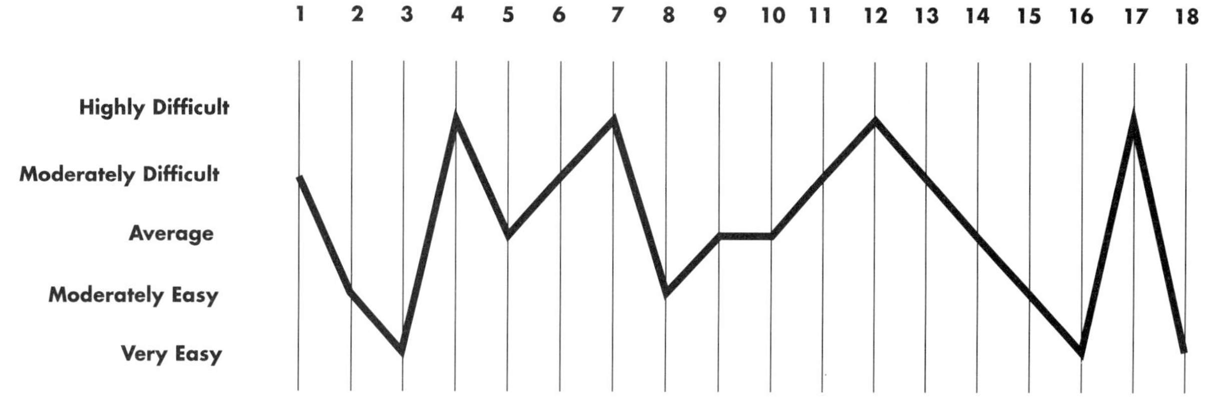

FIGURE 10-7
This chart shows the relative difficulty of the 18 holes of the famous Torrey Pines South Course in San Diego, California. The routing varies until the 12th hole, where the difficulty level becomes easier and easier until the 17th, which is more difficult. By ending on an easy note at the 18th, the finishing holes allow a stream of successes with just one interruption.

THE TOUGHEST HOLE IN THE WORLD

A British publication once wired James Braid for a comment on what he thought the toughest hole in the world was. The message was handed to him on the course while he was in the midst of an important match and at a time when he had found trouble off the tee. He was generally annoyed at the interruption and, after reading the telegram, scribbled the following reply: "The one I am now playing."

Psychological Aspects of Hazards

We traditionally distinguish three categories of golf holes—penal, strategic, and heroic—but this book goes a step better by suggesting five categories—penal, detour, heroic, lay-up, and open. Using this improved classification, we can safely state that penal, detour, and heroic holes are the most prevalent in golf course design. Each is mostly dependent on the nature and location of hazards.

Penal Holes: Penal holes penalize deviations from the optimal shot. A short drive may land in a fairway bunker. A drive that strays from the fairway lands behind an obstacle, in the water, or in deep vegetation. The island green is a prototype for the penal hole; there is no way around the trouble. Penal holes have a primarily emotional impact on the golfer. Apprehension or excitement precedes the shot; elation or despair follows the shot. Difficult penal holes tend to have a disproportionately frustrating effect on high-handicap golfers who lack the requisite distance or accuracy to avoid hazards. A course made up of difficult penal holes is a dispiriting experience for most golfers, although an occasional difficult hole may add spice to an otherwise easy round. Penal holes are not to be avoided; it's just that their use and frequency must be carefully considered.

Detour Holes: Detour holes are designed to allow the golfer a variety of options or choices in shot selection. A detour hole rewards the player for planning a sequence of shots. On par-4 and par-5 holes, one side of the fairway is usually optimal for landing a drive. Hazards are arranged so that greens may be defended from one angle and are perhaps open from another. Where a penal approach will defend the entire front of the green, a detour approach will allow the golfer the option of flying the ball to the target or playing a low pitch-and-run shot off to one side or the other.

If penal holes appeal to the golfer's emotions, detour holes appeal to the golfer's imagination. Detour holes are more likely to be appreciated by golfers whose shot-making skills are good enough to make planning and problem solving reasonable activities. The distinction between penal and detour holes may be lost on golfers whose shot patterns are more random.

Heroic Holes: The heroic school of course routing, discussed and defined extensively by the late Robert Trent Jones Sr., contains a combination of penal and detour elements. A heroic route places hazards so that the sequence of shots is important but the optimal shot always entails a greater degree or risk and a higher penalty. Each hole is designed to have a risk-reward ratio such that the shot with the greatest reward also entails the highest risk. The architect George C. Thomas put it thus: "The strategy of the golf course is the soul of the game. The spirit of golf is to dare a hazard, and by negotiating it reap a reward."

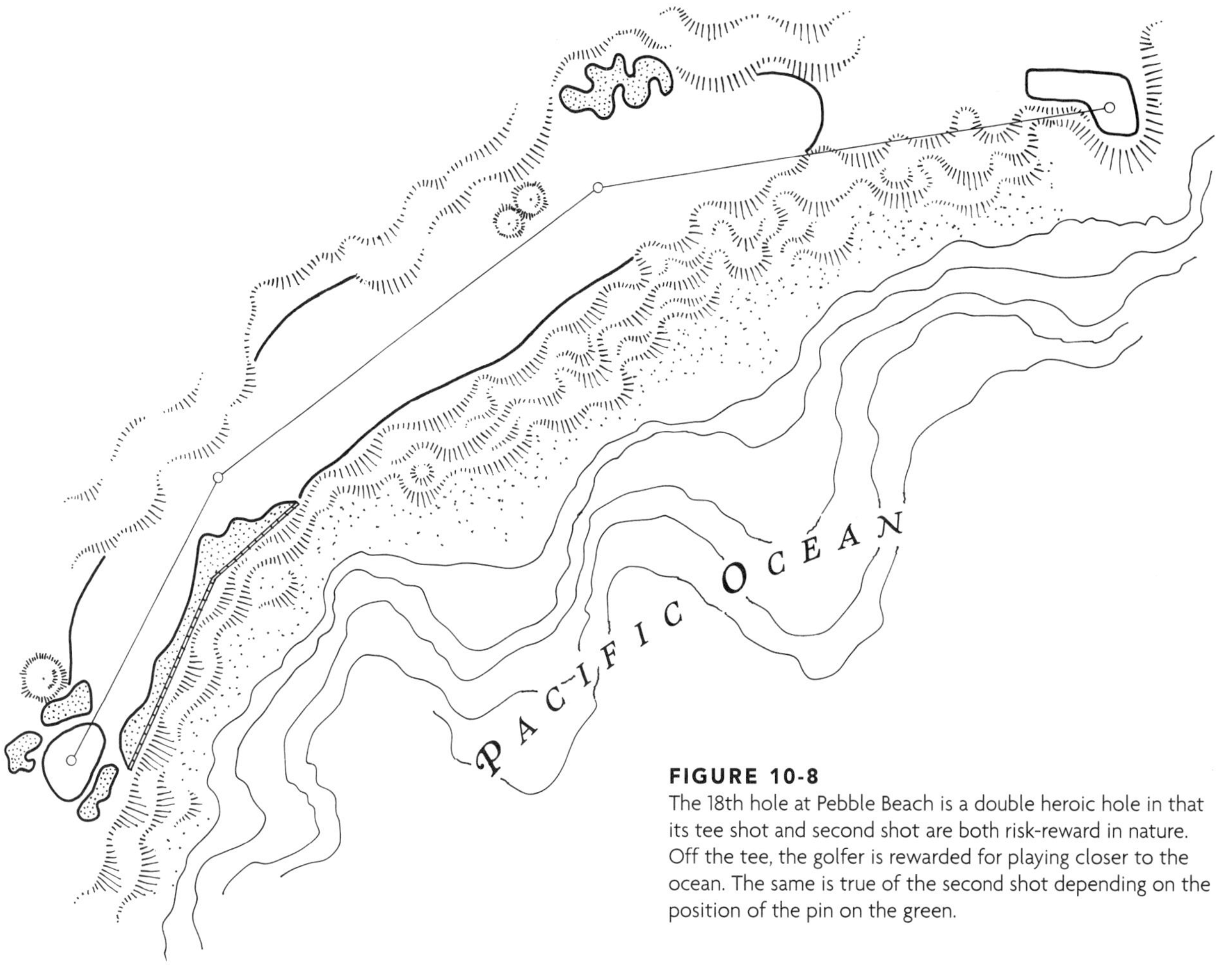

FIGURE 10-8
The 18th hole at Pebble Beach is a double heroic hole in that its tee shot and second shot are both risk-reward in nature. Off the tee, the golfer is rewarded for playing closer to the ocean. The same is true of the second shot depending on the position of the pin on the green.

The 18th hole at Pebble Beach is a prototypical heroic hole. The Pacific Ocean cuts diagonally across the direct route from tee to green. The golfer may elect to play more toward the green but in doing so must carry a long shot over the breadth of the hazard. An errant shot results in a ball into the ocean and a resultant penalty. Playing away from the hazard also means playing away from the green, making par increasingly more difficult. The heroic golf hole makes demands on both the golfer's imagination and emotions. The golfer is required to assess his shot-making ability and degree of emotional control. Fear is the dominant emotion when contemplating a high-risk shot, and it must be overcome if the shot is to be played successfully.

Hazards make golf dramatic; and the thrills that come to one who ventures wisely and succeeds are truly delectable.
—Robert Hunter, The Links

A well-routed golf course includes penal, detour, and heroic holes. The two remaining categories not specifically discussed here, lay-up and open, are certainly not to be omitted from designs. They are, however, odd occurrences that are not widely deployed. The essence of a good routing remains playability. The goal is a course that is playable by the high-handicap golfer and challenging to the low-handicap golfer. The

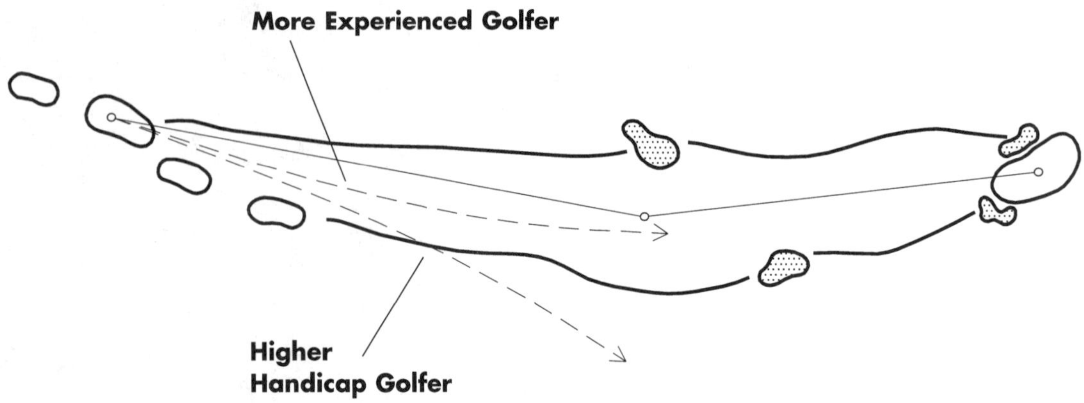

FIGURE 10-9
The diagram illustrates how the combination of a misaligned tee and a hazard close to the landing area can affect the high-handicap golfer more than the experienced player. Even though the sand bunker to the left is not a terribly penal hazard, the higher-handicap golfer will view it as more threatening than the good golfer will. The good golfer tends to use such targets as aids in aiming and depth perception. The same is true of tee alignment. The experienced golfer is less affected by this and usually aims based on the realities of the hole, not the direction in which the tee points.

placement of hazards on a course is analogous to the use of spices when cooking. The good cook is aware of the preferences of the guests but tries to prepare a dish that is neither too spicy nor too bland.

Perceived versus Actual Difficulty

It is important to note that difficulty of a hazard and the excitement it generates do not always go hand in hand. Many of the difficulties in golf are mental, not physical—subjective, not objective. One can distinguish between the actual difficulty of a hazard and the perceived difficulty of the hazard. Hazards with high perceived difficulty catch the golfer's attention, stimulate the imagination, and produce an emotional response. Water is an example of a hazard with high perceived difficulty, even on holes where it is easily avoided. Water often compels fantasies of failure in the average golfer. Peter Dobrineiner, a British writer, put it succinctly: "Water creates a neurosis in golfers, the very thought of this harmless fluid robs them of their normal powers of thought, turns their legs to jelly and produces a palsy of the upper limbs."

The true hazard should draw the play towards it, should invite the golfer to come as near as he dare to the fire without burning his fingers.
—*John L. Low,* Aspects of Golf Course Architecture

On many occasions, however, hazards with high actual difficulty have low perceived difficulty. For example, deep rough is a more difficult problem for most players than is a shallow sand trap. However, a green with prominent bunkers tends to attract more attention and elicits more apprehension than a green surrounded by rough. The former is more visually interesting, more exciting, and tends to be perceived as more hazardous, although the green surrounded by deep rough is likely to add relatively more strokes to the scorecard.

Cursed be the hand that makes these fatal holes.
— *William Shakespeare,* Richard III

Generally, golfers are likely to notice and emotionally respond to any hazard that a human would have difficulty walking through. Water, sand, trees, shrubs, and desert all constitute a challenge to human movement and hence are visually engaging. Subtle difficulties, such as those that cause an uneven stance and those that cause a ball to roll off the fairway, may not catch the attention of the recreational golfer but surely add to the difficulty of the course. The recreational golfer benefits from fairway landing areas that are relatively flat. If the fairway is canted to one side, the high side should be to the right because the average golfer is right-handed and tends to slice the ball. While golfers are likely to notice prominent hazards to the right of the fairway, they may miss subtle tilting of the landing area. In such cases, the hazard penalizes the golfer and slows play without adding much excitement or interest to the round.

It is also important to recognize that as the skill level of a player progresses, the perceptual effect of different types of hazards changes. For the average golfer, hazards should be well placed and salient but not especially difficult. Driving over rough not as exciting as driving over a bunker. The better golfer is more likely to notice hazards with high actual difficulty and to play to avoid them. Further, more advanced players tend to focus on the target while less advanced players tend to focus on hazards. For the advanced player, hazards may function as landmarks, allowing more precise distance estimation and more precise calculations of where to land the ball.

Rating versus Slope

The *rating* of a course is the score a scratch player would be expected to shoot from a particular set of tees if the round were played perfectly. It is expressed to the nearest tenth of a stroke. The *slope rating*, which identifies the relative difficulty of golf courses for players who are not scratch golfers, is a calculated rating from 55 to 155 expressed in whole numbers. The process, now an accepted standard, was first tested in Colorado in 1982 and put into practice the following year. The slope rating is calculated by subtracting the USGA course rating from the *bogey course rating* and multiplying by 5.381 for men or 4.24 for women. The bogey course rating is determined by an evaluation of the overall difficulty of the golf course under normal course and weather conditions for the bogey golfer—that is, a golfer with a handicap of 17.5 to 22.4 strokes for men and 21.5 to 26.4 for women. A course's *slope rating* is determined by the effective playing length combined with the obstacle stroke value of each hole in relation to the scratch golfer and the bogey golfer. The length aspect takes into account elevation, roll, forced lay-ups, wind, and altitude. The obstacle aspect is a numerical evaluation of ten categories: topography, fairway, green target, recovery and rough, bunkers, out-of-bounds, water, trees, green sur-

DIMENSIONS OF BEAUTY

Water is a mirror and kaleidoscope. Looking down, the golfer can see everything reflected—the sky, the trees, the green, himself. Water is the universal substance.
—Desmond Muirhead

Most great golf courses rely on great natural terrain. When a course is located in a region of natural beauty, the routing problem is to create a sequence that strings together the most beautiful features of the landscape into an agreeable challenge for the golfer. A more difficult routing challenge occurs when the course is planned for an area with little natural beauty or with disagreeable surroundings. In such cases, the designer is faced with either a blank canvas or a canvas that already has disagreeable imagery on it. When the canvas is essentially blank, visual interest must be created rather than simply exploited, and the creativity of the architect is directly challenged. In cases where the course is in the midst of unattractive surroundings, the route may be designed to insulate the golfer from the adjacent terrain, much like an urban park is designed to psychologically remove its visitors from the urban landscape.

Although the features of terrain that have high scenic value are usually intuitively obvious to the golf course architect, scientists have studied the attributes of landscapes that have high scenic value. The three primary dimensions of landscapes preferred by viewers are:

- Complexity
- Legibility
- Mystery

Complexity

Complexity refers to the number and variety of elements in a scene. Within limits, the greater the complexity, the greater the scenic value. Elements that add to complexity along a route include (1) elevation changes, (2) waterscapes, and (3) landform diversity.

1. Elevation change and undulation add interest to a route, both visually and in terms of the angles, problems, and shot options created for the golfer. As noted, most great golf holes involve perceptible elevation changes. As landscapes become flatter, they tend to decline in complexity and lose visual interest. If a designer is faced with a predominantly flat site, aesthetic value must be created through the shape of the route and by the forms, colors, and elements located along a route.
2. Water is a dominant visual landscape resource and almost always increases scenic value. Many of the greatest golf holes in the world derive their greatness from water. As Jimmy Demaret, a U.S. Masters champion, noted, “If you moved Pebble Beach fifty miles inland, no one would have heard of it.” Almost any route, whether undulating or predominantly flat, can benefit aesthetically from the incorporation of water. The way in which water is incorporated into the scene, however, may increase or decrease its potency. The impact of water has been shown to depend on the following factors:

- Land-water contrast

  The amount of visual edge between land and water is a potent source of complexity. The land-water edge should be visually salient.
- Shoreline complexity

  The complexity of the edge of a body of water refers to the variety of shapes produced by the land and water. Because the visual edge between land and water attracts the eye, the designer can add complexity by varying the shape of these contours. Natural lakes, rivers, and seascapes almost always have a high degree of edge complexity. Artificial bodies of water tend to have less complexity at their edges.
- Size of the water body

  Water body size may be manipulated to increase complexity. A diversity of sizes tends to add interest.

FIGURE 10-10
This pond has a complex shoreline, interrupted by aqueous vegetation, that meanders along the fairway of this golf hole. The hill in the distance contrasts with the flat surface of the water. All of these elements make for a pleasing view to the golfer and contribute to the positive feeling that water can add to the golf experience.

CONCHO VALLEY GOLF CLUB, ARIZONA; ARTHUR JACK SNYDER, ASGCA, & FORREST RICHARDSON, ASGCA, GOLF COURSE ARCHITECTS

It's the only game outside of solitaire where you play alone.
—Will Rogers, from his Weekly Article #163, January 24, 1926

- Internal contrast

  Internal wetland contrast refers to the height and texture of vegetative elements within a water feature. Water elements that have plants, shrubs, trees, or flowers along the border, or within the water itself, tend to be more interesting. Such elements tend to be present in natural watercourses and wetlands but they are less prevalent, or indeed absent, in artificial water bodies. The passage of time and the action of natural forces produce the evolution of wetland-edge ecosystems and the internal ecosystems of bodies of water. Newer artificial lakes and streams tend to lack complexity unless such elements are specifically created.

3. Landform diversity refers to the amount of contrast generated by vegetative elements, hazards, and color contrast. Water and elevation are not always options in routing a course. Beautiful golf holes and aesthetically pleasing golf routes can be developed by increasing both the complexity of visual elements and the complexity of the route itself. For example, the color contrast between natural desert vegetation and the green of a well-maintained fairway always adds visual interest. A distinctive tree can provide a focal point for a hole and add complexity to an otherwise homogeneous setting. As such, routing should take trees, views, and landform diversity into account. Also, routes that contain a number of turns or distinctive fairway hazards are more complex and hence more interesting than routes that are straighter or less differentiated.

Legibility

Legibility refers to the degree to which a route hangs together or has organization. In essence, it is a measurement of coherence. The more legible the route, the easier it is for the golfer to stay oriented in space. After a round is completed, the golf course exists as a memory in the mind of the golfer. The more legible the route, the easier it is for the golfer to remember its features.

Generally, humans prefer routes that are organized and coherent. This preference is another remnant of our hunter-gatherer ancestry. Comprehension of large areas was vital for early humans. It was necessary to locate prey, to find and return to edible plants, and to find the way back home.

Well-defined fairways with clear boundaries increase the coherence of an individual hole and also increase the coherence of a route. One can contrast a course where each fairway is bordered by trees, shrubs, water, or other visual obstacles with a course where the boundaries between fairways are ill defined. In the former case, the route is visually coherent and legible. Each hole is visually isolated from adjacent holes, and the golfer has the sensation of moving along a well-defined path system.

In some cases, the architect may consciously choose to design a route with little organization or coherence. Frederick Law Olmstead, designer of Central Park in New York City and Prospect Park in Brooklyn, tried to create environments that psychologically remove the park visitor from the city. He employed routing plans that disrupted the ability to main-

FIGURE 10-11
Aspects of water involve its size relationship to its bordering land, the complexity of its shoreline, its overall size, and contrasts that occur within it and around it.

PHOTO COURTESY OF LOOKOUT MOUNTAIN GOLF CLUB AT THE POINTE RESORT AT TAPATIO CLIFFS; FORREST RICHARDSON, ASGCA, GOLF COURSE ARCHITECT

tain a sense of orientation. One of the most famous sections of Central Park is "the ramble." This section begins at approximately 79th Street and spans north for about 15 blocks. It is a series of paths through the woods that twist their way in and out of trees. The path structure is indecipherable, and after a short walk the visitor loses all sense of orientation. The ramble was created so that one could get lost in the trees and experience a sense of great distance from the surrounding urban environment. This is a great lesson for laying out a golf course. Sometimes it is good to be lost, at least temporarily.

It is not the love of something easy which has drawn men like a magnet for hundreds of years to this royal and ancient pastime; on the contrary, it is the maddening difficulty of it.
—*Robert Hunter,* The Links

FIGURE 10-12
Even though the perceived danger is greater than the actual, this short par 5 is memorable partially as a result of its risk. The dramatic hazard that confronts the golfer appears almost impassable, yet it is easily overcome. This gives a sense of accomplishment that adds to the memorability of the hole.

PHOTO COURTESY OF PHANTOM HORSE GOLF CLUB/POINTE SOUTH MOUNTAIN RESORT; FORREST RICHARDSON, ASGCA, GOLF COURSE ARCHITECT

Mystery

Mystery is a recurrent element of preferred landscapes. Mystery involves the idea of entering a scene to gain information. Information is suggested but hidden from view. Mystery is the promise that proceeding along the route will reveal new or additional information.

For example, paths that proceed straight for a while and then turn and disappear from view tend to be preferred over paths that can be clearly seen. The change of direction adds visual interest. Mystery is involved whenever a component of a scene is partially hidden. An example of a scene that is often highly rated in research studies is a brightly lit field partially obscured by nearby foliage. In a description of the design principles of the Japanese garden, Sima Eliovson discusses the element of mystery:

> The obscured view is used to enhance distance as well as to create mystery. The garden viewed through a partially obscuring leafy branch or group of slim tree trunks will not only seem to be farther away, but will become more alluring. The partially concealed view attracts the interest more than that which can be seen at a glance. The visitor is prompted to look more carefully through a half-screen of trunks or branches in order to discover what is beyond. The fact that it is vaguely seen makes it more elusive, distant, and intriguing.

Similar principles are often incorporated into great golf holes. The common dogleg design of golf holes is a prototypical manipulation of mystery, as are holes where parts of the landing area are obscured by trees, water, or hazards. Of course, the ultimate manipulation of mystery is the totally blind shot. Blind shots have a history in classic links courses. They can, on occasion, add to the enjoyment of a hole; however, they do have several disadvantages. The most obvious is that they deprive the golfer of the pleasure of seeing the shot finish. Further, blind shots tend to slow play because errant shots are more difficult to locate. This is especially true in modern times, when we do not rely on the caddy or forecaddy to go ahead and scout shots hit beyond a blind. Blind shots to fairway landing areas should be associated with greater enjoyment than blind shots to the green. The blind fairway shot may still be followed with the eye for some distance, and its precise finish is less important. The shot to the green is a test of precision rather than distance; seeing a shot finish close to the hole is analogous to a hunter seeing his missile actually strike the prey.

If you play a golf course and know everything about it the first time out, then the designer has failed.
—Desmond Muirhead

MEMORABILITY AS A GOAL

What causes elements of a golf course to become etched in memory? In some cases, it is the sheer beauty of vistas encountered along the route; in others, it is the unique configuration of the hole. Anything that adds emotion to an experience tends to increase memory of the experience. Golf holes that contain elements of risk or difficulty are likely to be memorable. Holes that elicit a feeling of danger are likely to be memorable. The same factors that elicit attention also produce strong memo-

FIGURE 10-13
Hole plan of the hole pictured in Figure 10-12. The hole is a combination of heroic, lay-up, and penal shot strategy depending on the skill—and nerve—level of the player.

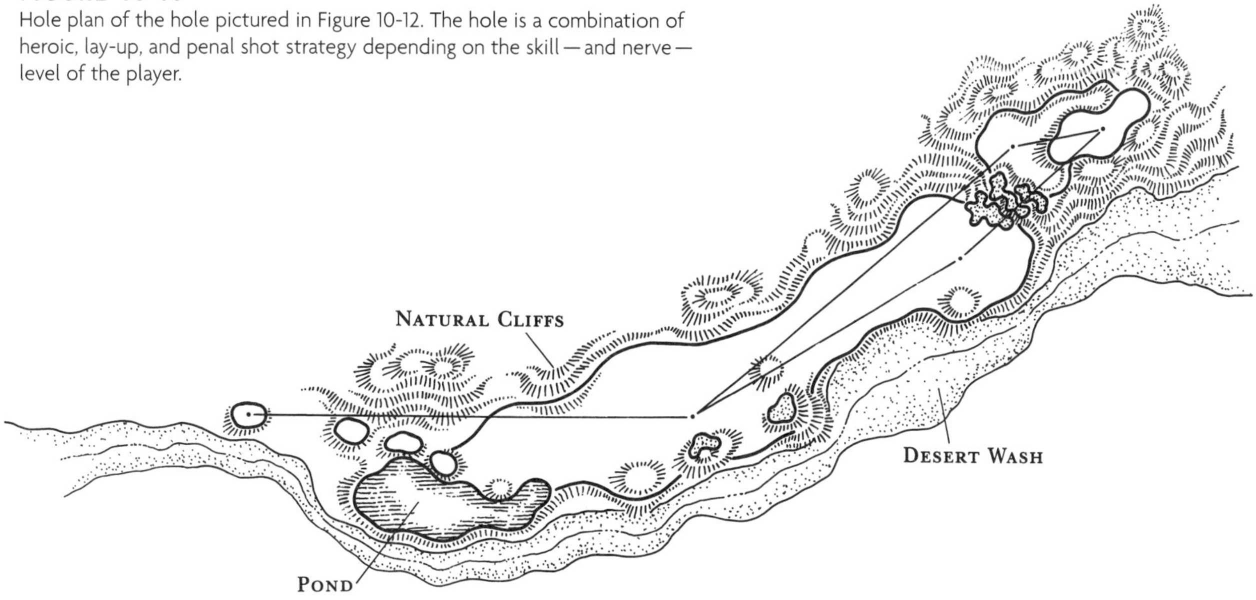

ries. It follows that holes that combine breathtaking scenery with heroic or penal shot choices are likely to be the most memorable.

A route with memorable elements does not, however, have to consist of a series of dramatic vistas or daring shots. Some courses have a subtle beauty that upon repeated encounters insinuates itself into memory. As course architect Alister McKenzie remarked, "A good golf course is like good music. It does not necessarily appear the first time one plays it."

I ENJOY CALLING ED SADALLA "DR. ED," but I'm not sure he enjoys this as much as I do. To me, whenever someone has earned the right to be called doctor and they are not in the business of ordering injections, asking you to say "ahhh," or visiting you in the hospital, I am immediately interested, my curiosity at full alert. There is something impressive about this, although I can't put my finger on it. Anyway, when I first met Ed, which was during some volunteer consulting work for a new exhibit at the Phoenix Zoo, we got to talking about golf and our mutual fascination with how drastically golf course design can change the experience one has on any given day. We casually spoke of writing a book, and there the idea rested until I called and asked for his help on this project.

Dr. Sadalla received his Ph.D. in psychology at Stanford University. For the past 20 years, he has been the director of the environmental psychology doctoral program at Arizona State University (ASU) in Tempe. During this period he has taught courses in environmental psychology at both the undergraduate and graduate level. Environmental psychology, a rather obscure specialty, involves the study of human behavior in relation to the large-scale environment. Specifically, it is the study of the impact of the built environment (at architectural and urban scales) on human behavior. What possibly could be more appropriate to golf and its unique charm?

PART THREE

The Heart of the Course

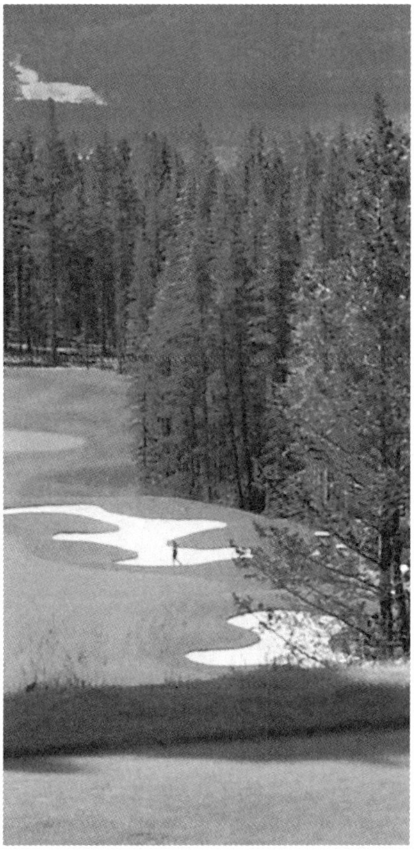

Programming & Site Evaluation

Hole No.

11

You can learn a lot about programming and site evaluation by watching Martha Stewart plan a meal. I once sat transfixed by Martha cooking a Thanksgiving meal, and what I learned is that she spends a great deal of time planning and figuringthings out and not all that much time actually cooking. How many people are coming? Will there be any vegetarians? Is the table big enough? Will we need the table leaf? Who's left-handed? Where should I seat them? By the time she is ready for guests, Martha has everything planned down to the organic cornstalk wreath at the front door, the cornucopia nametags, the CD of Bulgarian folk music, and appetizers of grilled albino pumpkin and ground acorn. Without her expert planning, I'm convinced that a meal at Martha Stewart's would be nothing to write home about.

Eventually golf courses are built in the physical world. They make the leap from ideas and plans to occupy sites made up of land and all that goes with the land. The components we mix to form golf courses are the ingredients. These ingredients can be simple, complex, or somewhere in between.

[I]n selecting the land for your course always look for diversity on different types of ground to be played over.
—*George C. Thomas Jr.*, Golf Architecture in America

In this section, I explore the finer points of programming and site evaluation. By *programming* we mean the complete list of everything that will be carried out on the land. This includes all of the components and how they will be used. By *site evaluation* we mean the process by which land is examined to see what activities it is capable of supporting and what activities might be hampered by its configuration or conditions.

Programming and site evaluation are often at odds, perhaps to keep one another honest. Desired programs can uncover faults with sites—and desired sites can find ways to change programs. It is the nature of golf course routing that these two initial activities produce interesting discoveries. Seldom are circumstances so perfect that what is wanted is completely doable. If that is your goal, go design and build tennis courts. They are infinitely easier to work out.

PROGRAMMING FOR GOLF

Tom Fazio points out that he started doing his best work when, instead of just being interviewed by clients, he started interviewing them. "You need to ask the right questions to understand the programming," he says. And how very true this is.

Understanding the programming of a golf course is to look into the future and envision what parts of the puzzle will be built there. The topics covered up to this point have involved looks at what these puzzle parts consist of, the conditions that can be encountered, and the rules that must be followed when assembling a golf facility. Programming is a process. It is like writing the outline of a script. Not only must the dialog be written but also attention must be paid to the scope of the performance, how many parts will be played, and the extent of sets, costumes, and the like. Think of that school play you attended. You were handed a program upon entering the auditorium. It told what you were going to see, in what order, the number of scenes, and so on.

Who Does Programming?

Programming is often determined by a developer. In this case, the developer knows what he wants, and he describes the program by comparing it to another project, perhaps one he has built before. Regardless, a program is always created by listening, whether to an owner explaining what he wants, to the land telling you what it can offer, or a combination of each. This is a valid way to start; in fact, it is really the only way to begin the programming process. By listening, you will eventually be able to itemize the various components intended for a site. Whether they can be accommodated is a matter yet to be determined.

Interestingly, programming is a moving target until the routing plan has been accepted and the project is in the final design stages. Even then, in many more cases than developers would like to admit, programs change for a variety of reasons.

> *The real test of a golf course:* is it going to live?
> —*H. S. Colt, from* Some Essays on Golf Course Architecture

At the project represented on the cover of this book, the Phantom Horse Golf Club in Phoenix, Arizona, the original program called for building a short 9-hole course in a small flood control basin next to a freeway. Then along came some adjacent property owners, and all of a sudden the developer, Bob Gosnell, had a tiger by the tail, and it was growing almost every day. What had begun as a relatively small boutique resort property was transformed into one of the largest destination resorts in the southwest United States. With this change came a realization that the course as originally planned would not be a compatible golf amenity. The program changed. Even before any serious routing could take place, there were new constraints and new ingredients to fit into the increasing site acreage that was growing because landowners wanted in on the action. A larger course, now 18 holes and regulation in length, meant a larger clubhouse, a full-size maintenance area and yard, and all of the activities associated with a resort hotel and golf destination. Programming was an evolutionary process. In the end, it worked tremendously well, and Bob Gosnell, to whom I owe my career, hit a home run by allowing his program to expand and morph to the requirements of the market and the project. Having said this, it is always best to *try* to plan ahead. Scurrying to change in the midst of a design is seldom pleasant.

Land planners, architects, engineers, and marketing experts also play a role in programming golf courses. Practitioners of these disciplines ideally are joined by the golf course architect in working out what type of golf course and related facilities are called for. The goal is to determine whether they will all fit onto a piece of land and, if not, what should be changed: the program or the land itself.

The following professionals are regularly involved in the process of programming a golf course:

- Owner/developer
- Land planner
- Golf course architect
- Civil engineer
- Feasibility study specialist
- Marketing consultant
- Clubhouse architect
- Golf course management consultant
- Golf course greenkeeper

The Feasibility Study

Another approach to programming is to solicit the expertise of a qualified golf course feasibility consultant. When properly executed, a feasibility study can yield a wealth of information on what type of development can be sustained in the region and the extent to which the golf facility will need to be developed in order to be a good investment. The feasibility study also considers the recommendation *against* golf development. For this reason, it is essential that whenever a feasibility study is commissioned, the potential results are clearly understood. The developer who will move forward no matter what the study advises may need the weight of a study solely for funding purposes. Unfortunately, studies churned out for this purpose go by the same name, *feasibility*, when their true role is that of approval stamp to a particular dream.

It is possible that a worthwhile feasibility study can be commissioned for a client who does not have a specific piece of land. In this case, the feasibility study usually contains an outline of the program. The document represents a snapshot of what could reasonably occur in the market where a course may be considered. Such a study may compare a series of sites and make a recommendation for one above the other. Assuredly, such a feasibility study must be revisited if and when a specific site is chosen.

Budgets, Costs & Viability

Programming outlines can be used to establish budgets, or they may be used to prove established budgets are right or wrong. Either way, the need to arrive at budgets, at least for a vast majority of projects, is essential.

The viability of a project is determined when the budget is held up to the light and a realistic return on the investment is calculated. There are as many ways to make this comparison as there are to hit a sand shot. One of the best approaches is to use what is called the *warranted investment approach.* This approach establishes a threshold of investment cost for the project based on a specific return of profit. It is common for a feasibility study to provide multiple scenarios for a warranted investment. One might show spending $3.7 million to build an 18-hole course as the limit of warranted investment if the money is to be recouped within five years. Another might show that $4.9 million could be spent if the developer could justify a payback in eight years. Yet another scenario might show a warranted investment of $5.2 million if 27 holes were built all at one time.

It is imperative to realize that costs are not restricted to the initial costs to design and build. The true cost of a project extends to the costs of operation, both initial start-up costs and those projected each year that the study covers. The magic term used to bring the worlds of investment, debt service, operations, and profits together in one happy place is *pro forma,* Latin for "the appearance as seen from in front." The job of the pro forma is to see into the future—to establish, realistically, what will be if the development plan is carried out as it has been described.

Nor should one always be sure that the ideal—which means, after all, my ideal or your ideal—is so very desirable as to warrant the laying out of a huge sum.
—*Robert Hunter,* The Links

The warranted investment approach, because it offers a threshold, can be used as a baseline by the planning team. Regardless of whether the figure is generated before routing or based on a specific routing plan, the dollar amount can serve as a balancing point from which spending less will translate into better profits and higher return and spending more will very likely make someone's day unpleasant.

A derivative of the programming process is the *probable cost.* Teams of people generate cost estimates for the golf course and all of its facilities, infrastructure, and details. This probable cost—or costs, if there are multiple options and programs—gets wrapped into the feasibility study or pro forma.

Wide differences are possible in determining project viability depending on the type of owner and developer behind the project. A private, for-profit owner/developer whose only stake lies in the ability of the golf course to return a profit will not be able to lose money and must answer to the bottom line at all costs. On the other hand, the homebuilder or resort developer can often justify a loss on golf development if the positives outweigh the negatives. A homebuilder can build golf courses all day long if the premium on lots exceeds the cost of the investment in building the course. A resort developer may find it reasonable to experience a modest loss on the golf investment if the course serves to attract guests to book rooms and extend their stay. A municipality can justify golf development for the good of the community and in the name of public recreation. This may be true even when it may take a significant period for the municipality to recoup the investment, or when a slight loss may be associated with the course.

Usually the sites are easy; it's the owners that are more challenging.
—Tom Fazio

A Reason for Being

Among the most crucial aspects of determining programming is defining why building a golf course is being considered. In Hole 7 "The Rules of Routing," this task is referred to as *identifying the driving force.* This calls for sorting through the owner's goals and objectives, then mixing in the answers to questions about whether or not the proposed locale can support a new golf course. When all of these data have been digested, it is possible to state—usually in one succinct sentence—the fundamental *reason for being* that the golf course will have when completed.

Primary Golf Ingredients

Despite the fact that numerous and detailed parts were outlined in Hole 5, "Parts of the Puzzle," in reality, just six primary ingredients must be considered before beginning to draft a program. They are somewhat different from the master list of puzzle parts, for they represent the essential elements that *support* a golf course and not necessarily the many improvements that will be installed or shaped during construction. Without each of the following, there can be no golf course:

- Acreage
  The land on which a course is to be built.
- Soil
  The basis from which turfgrass will grow.
- Water
  The lifeblood of turfgrass, whether natural or artificial.
- Suitable conditions
  Appropriate for turfgrass and the game of golf.
- Money
  A simple enough concept.

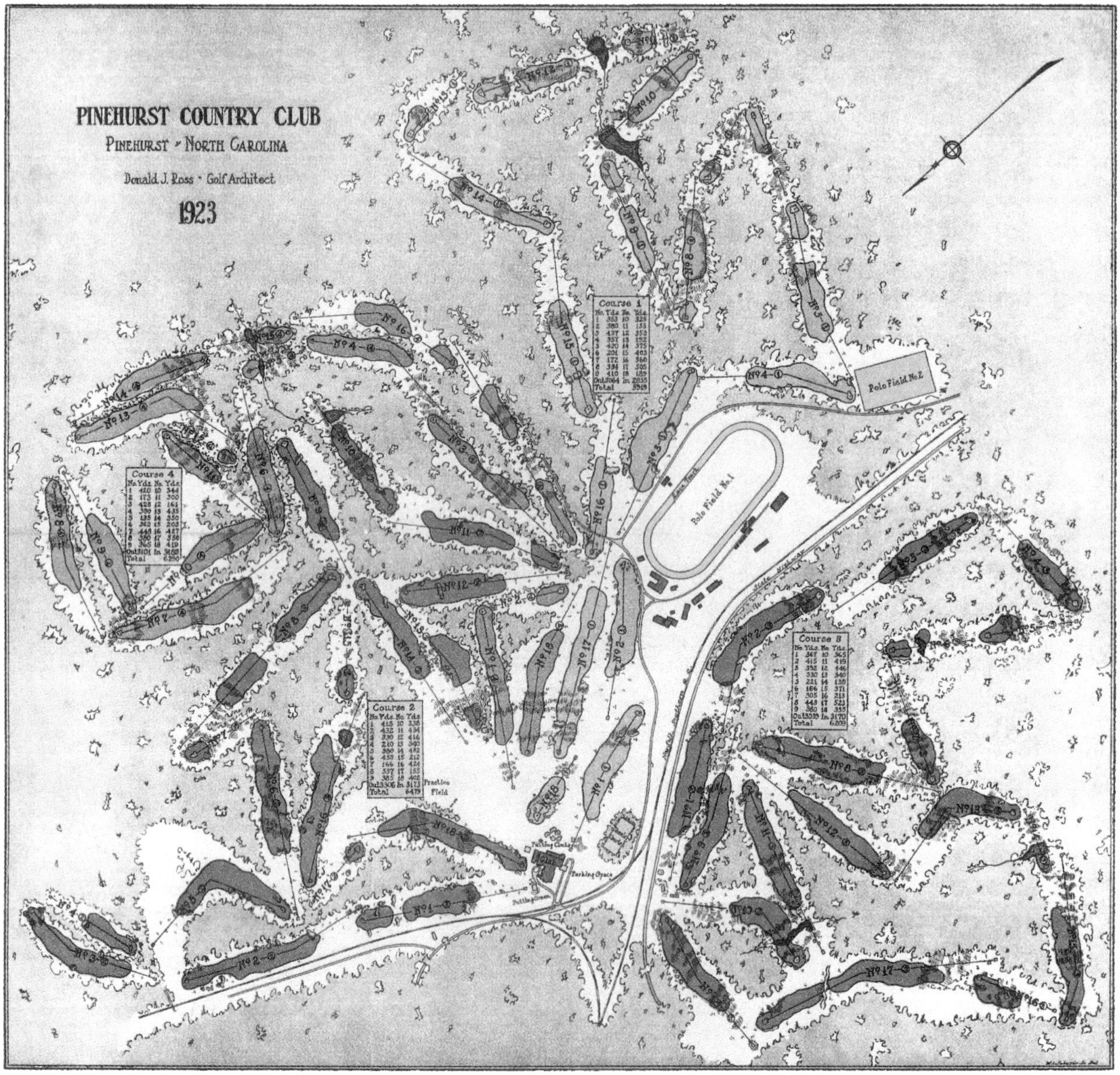

FIGURE 11-1
Planning a property for multiple courses can exponentially increase the number of steps in the site evaluation process. Clubhouse, parking, and practice facilities must all be taken into account, as must the issues of beginning and ending golf holes. In this 1923 master plan of the Pinehurst Resort in North Carolina, the complexities of beginning and ending four courses can be appreciated. Shown are the first four of Pinehurst's renowned courses, as configured by the late Donald Ross, ASGCA. Note that only one of the four courses, the No. 3 Course, returns after the ninth hole. Today, Pinehurst consists of eight 18-hole courses (144 holes in all) served by four practice ranges and four separate clubhouses. Another two courses are on the drawing board.

COURTESY OF THE TUFTS ARCHIVES, PINEHURST, NORTH CAROLINA

- Golfers

  Without whom a golf course is rather pointless; the population must be interested.

Now, in anticipation of the clever chap who will argue that you can still build golf courses on dirt tracts with sand greens, or ones with artificial turf and no need for water or good soil, or that there is nothing to prevent an eccentric rock star from building a course just to look at, I list his points here to save him the trouble. But for the practical golf course, the type that 99.9 percent of the world can relate to, you need the above or you are sunk right off the bat.

The Framework of Programming

If you dissect most of the programming documents for golf courses, you will see a pattern of headings. Each heading must be thoroughly researched and defined in terms of size, scope, length, quantity, and quality. The four primary areas of golf course programming are:

- Clubhouse and area
- Practice facilities
- Golf course configuration and components
- Maintenance facilities

Building the Program

The verb *building* is used intentionally. The best way to think of the process of creating a program is to imagine it as if the golf course and its support facilities were already built. The outline will describe what the eventual project will be. Imagining what will take place at the golf course allows each area to be described, and each necessary improvement can be defined in terms of size, scope, length, quantity, and quality.

The reason for such detail can be illustrated by a clubhouse that is described based on what is desired of a project. Let's assume that a large group event facility is needed to accommodate special events. When programmers visualize this facility, they realize it will entail extra parking, perhaps a more striking entryway, a larger drop-off point, and ancillary improvements such as lighting of the clubhouse grounds and the visible area of the golf course so they may be appreciated at night. Before you know it, a 5-acre clubhouse site has grown to 8 acres or more.

Similar visualizations can be made of the golf course itself. Will there be cart paths or not? Must the practice area accommodate a few players at a time or a hundred golfers prior to a shotgun start?

The finished product, when developing a program, is a verbal description and a quantification of each component of the project. Quantification is key. It does little good to report that "practice greens will be provided." A program document is a set of instructions—a recipe—and therefore it is necessary to be specific. Here is a more appropriate description: "Two practice putting greens of 8000 square feet each and one practice green for chipping of 4500 square feet will be provided."

FIGURE 11-2
Establishing a program for the golf clubhouse is an essential starting point in determining the size and requirements for all its usable areas. This example shows the four primary components: food and beverage, cart facilities, golf facilities (pro shop, locker rooms, etc.), and function areas.

COURTESY OF OZ ARCHITECTS, INC.

	Program Space	Public	Back of House	Cov. Ext.	Ext.
1	**RESTAURANT / ADMINISTRATION**				
	Entry				
	Entry Breezeway			974	
	Courtyard				2,571
	Entry Foyer	260			
	Recep./Living Room	674			
	Concierge/"Den"	149			
	Circulation	0			
	Administration				
	Reception	135			
	Member Services	103			
	Circulation	74			
	Accounting		206		
	General Manager		130		
	Copy / Storage		115		
	Office		91		
	Food & Beverage				
	Dining	1,664			
	Pvt. Dining Foyer	266			
	Pvt. Dining Terrace				596
	Pvt. Dining	409			
	Dining Terrace			766	1,437
	Bar	648			
	Bar Terrace			834	
	Bar Storage		120		
	Bar Dining	748			
	Restrooms	479			
	Phones	72			
	Kitchen		2,159		
	Mech. & Elec.		112		
	Refrigerated Trash		0		
	Receiving/Trash				1,203
	Food & Bev. Office		101		
	Circulation	483			
	TOTAL	**6,164**	**3,034**	**2,574**	**5,807**
	TOTAL INT.	**9,198 sq. ft.**			
2	**CART FACILITIES & SUPPORT**				
	Cart storage, charging and wash		5,657		
	Ice machines		34		
	Range balls		0		
	Employee Lounge		338		
	Employee Restrooms		170		
	Bag storage		587		
	Grill		610		
	Laundry		80		
	Members Restrooms	426			
	Mech./Elec./Plumbing		631		
	General Storage		1,117		
	Golf Cart Staging			200	1,000
	Circulation		568	95	
	TOTAL	**426**	**9,792**	**295**	**1,000**
	TOTAL INT.	**10,218 sq. ft.**			

PROGRAM SPACE	PUBLIC	BACK OF HOUSE	COV. EXT.	EXT.
3 **GOLF FACILITIES**				
GOLF OPERATIONS				
Covered Arcade			1,307	
Pro Shop	1,426			
Pro Shop Terrace				927
Retail Storage		169		
Dressing Room	61			
Director of Golf		108		
Work area		184		
Circulation	188	140		
Valet/Bags		154		
MEN'S LOCKER ROOM				
Foyer & Phones	505			
Attendant		97		
Shoe storage		95		
Lounge	871			
Lounge Terrace				500
Lockers	2,994			
Wet area	1,499			
Circulation	249			
Terrace				437
Storage		75		
WOMEN'S LOCKER ROOM				
Foyer & Phones	96			
Attendant		98		
Shoe storage		93		
Lockers	1,812			
Lounge	643			
Wet area	1,167			
Women's Terrace				475
SPA				
Office/Storage	127			
Spa Waiting	168			
Treatment Rooms	306			
Circulation	306			
Fitness	540			
Fitness Court				1,013
Storage	20			
TOTAL	**5,185**	**1,213**	**0**	**1,488**
TOTAL INT.	**6,398 sq. ft.**			
4 **FUNCTION AREA**				
Entry and Breezeway			466	
Restrooms	709			
Function Storage		422		
TOTAL	**709**	**422**	**466**	
TOTAL INT.	**1,131 sq. ft.**			
SUMMARY				
1 **RSTRNT/ADMIN**	**6,164**	**3,034**	**2,574**	**5,807**
2 **CART FACILITIES**	**426**	**9,792**	**295**	**1,000**
3 **GOLF FACILITIES**	**11,303**	**458**	**0**	**2,425**
4 **FUNCTION AREA**	**709**	**422**	**466**	**0**
TOTAL SQ. FT.	**18,602**	**13,706**	**3,335**	**9,232**
TOTAL INT.	**32,308 sq. ft.**			

Now, armed with information at this level of detail, what is required is clear.

The steps to creating a programming document for a new golf course generally follow this sequence:

1. Determine the type of course.
2. Determine the types of golfers who will use the course.
3. Verify climate and conditions.
4. Describe the clubhouse and area (parking requirements, meeting rooms, seating capacity, retail space, food/beverage areas, cart storage, cart staging, landscaping, outdoor event staging, etc., and the square footage associated with each component or area).
5. Describe the practice facility needs (range, greens, teaching area, etc., and the targeted acreage associated with each).
6. Describe the basics of the golf course (number of holes, length, par, configuration, amenities, and the targeted acreages/quantities associated with each).
7. Describe any special management and maintenance issues (desired capacity, duration of rounds, cart usage, environmental limitations, turf area limitations, type of water usage, etc.).
8. Determine water requirements (quantity of water needed, source of water, storage needs, type of irrigation system, etc.).
9. Describe the maintenance facilities (building, yard, storage areas, and the square footage of each component).
10. Describe any site and utility infrastructure that will be required (flood control, drainage, power, natural gas, communications, and potable water, for example).

This guide establishes the typical sequence for creating an overall program for a golf course. Each item usually is authored by the members of the team with which it is most closely aligned. For example, a clubhouse architect typically puts together the program components for the clubhouse with assistance from a management consultant and perhaps even a food/beverage consultant. The maintenance area description is assembled by a greenkeeper, who devises the list of components and square footage requirements for the entire maintenance operation.

Moving Forward with a Program

It is refreshing now and then to find a club which has ignored the race for length and gone in for quality.
—Robert Hunter, The Links

Programming can occur before, during, or after site evaluation. It may even take place during all three of these periods. At the least, the programming should be reviewed during all three to ensure that what is being projected for a project is still viable as the site is evaluated and planning progresses. Programs, as noted, often change depending on market conditions, complexities of the site, and the determination of probable costs. Environmental, engineering, entitlement, water, and drainage issues can throw curves at programming that require conclusions to be recalculated to see how budgets, costs, and validity are affected.

PROJECTED REVENUE ANALYSIS GILBERT FAMILY GOLF CENTER/Hetchler Site 18-HOLE 'PRECISION' COURSE + 18-HOLE 'PITCH & PUTT'	2004	2005	2006	2007	2008
GOLF REVENUES:					
Green Fees	$470,000	$567,000	$650,700	$719,000	$769,800
Driving Range Fees	150,000	180,960	207,667	229,472	245,670
Cart Fees	140,600	169,700	194,700	215,100	230,300
Other (Lessons, rentals, etc.)	100,000	120,640	138,445	152,982	163,780
TOTAL GOLF REVENUES	**$860,600**	**$1,038,300**	**$1,191,512**	**$1,316,554**	**$1,409,550**
GOLF REVENUE/ROUND	$17.21	$17.90	$18.62	$19.36	$20.14
OTHER REVENUES					
Total Merchandise	$25,000	$30,200	$96,000	$106,100	$113,600
Total Food and Beverage	62,500	75,400	160,000	176,800	189,300
TOTAL OTHER REVENUE	**$87,500**	**$105,600**	**$256,000**	**$282,900**	**$302,900**
TOTAL GROSS REVENUE	**$948,100**	**$1,143,900**	**$1,447,500**	**$1,599,500**	**$1,712,500**
Less: Direct Costs					
Merchandise	$15,000	$18,100	$57,600	$63,700	$68,200
Food & Beverage	25,000	30,200	64,000	70,700	75,700
TOTAL NET REVENUES	**$908,100**	**$1,095,600**	**$1,325,900**	**$1,465,100**	**$1,568,600**
EXPENSES:					
Golf Course Maintenance	$400,000	$416,000	$432,600	$449,900	$467,900
Golf Administration	265,000	275,600	286,600	298,100	310,000
Golf Cart Expense	35,200	42,400	48,700	53,800	57,600
Driving Range Expenses	45,000	54,300	62,300	68,800	73,700
Fixed Food & Beverage	15,000	15,600	25,000	26,000	27,000
Lessons Commission	50,000	60,300	69,200	76,500	81,900
Capital Improvement	5,000	5,000	5,000	5,000	5,000
Contingency	71,500	75,000	79,300	82,800	86,300
TOTAL EXPENSES	$886,700	$944,200	$1,008,700	$1,060,900	$1,109,400
ANNUAL PROFIT	**$21,400**	**$151,400**	**$317,200**	**$404,200**	**$459,200**
GROSS MARGIN	2.3%	13.2%	21.9%	25.3%	26.8%
WARRANTED INVESTMENT ANALYSIS					
Maximum Sustainable Debt Service Using 90% of 3rd Year Cash Flow at 8.5% interest for 20 years			**$2,701,593**		

FIGURE 11-3
A pro forma (Latin for "the appearance as seen from in front") is the crucial means whereby the financial viability of a golf course is determined. The pro forma shows how much the course will cost and projects returns on the investment.

The routing plan of a golf course, while it may be created based on a program, is just as often the catalyst that establishes the basics of a program. Both are acceptable methods, which is evidence that the process of routing is closely tied to programming. In fact, they are virtually inseparable. Sure, you can create a routing plan without a program first. The program, in this case, is a matter of listing all that was drawn on the plan. You also can do the opposite—create a program, then simply try to draw on a particular site all of the program's components. The usefulness of each method is brought to the surface when the program and the plan are in harmony—and it can be proved through numbers that the project as a whole is possible from a financial standpoint.

SITE EVALUATION

It used to be that golf courses were built only on land obviously conducive to golf holes. This was generally linksland or land that approximated linksland by virtue of its sandy soils and gently undulating landscape. Then came the migration of golf to inland parts of the countryside, to forests and hilltops—and, from there, the sky was the limit. Now, no land can automatically be written off for its golf potential. Construction techniques and abilities, together with the will of the developer, have taken seemingly impossible sites and turned them into golf courses. Add to this reality the desire of the golfing public to experience golf where they live and where they travel, and you have summed up the growth of golf into areas and terrains that were previously too complicated to consider.

The enthusiastic golf course designer cannot stop evaluating sites. On many occasions, I find myself looking at the landscape while traveling and picturing a golf course nestled into it. In a fleeting moment, while passing at 70 miles per hour, I have often programmed and evaluated a site, forming an impression of what it would cost and how breathtaking the results would be. Perhaps this daydreaming is what got me the audience with Judge So-and-so described in Hole 7.

Site evaluation is the first physical step toward an actual golf course routing on a specific piece of land. The history, background, details, rules, and considerations up to this point have led to this moment. The opportunity to look at the ground that may become home to a golf course awaits!

GOLF COURSE SITE ANALYSIS

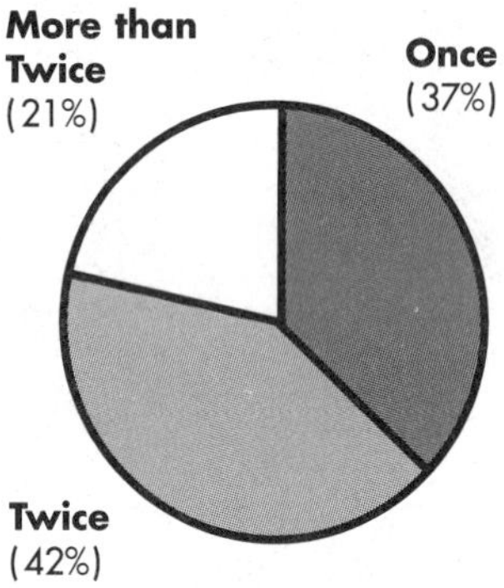

How many times is a Golf Course Architect likely to visit a site before the routing process is completed?

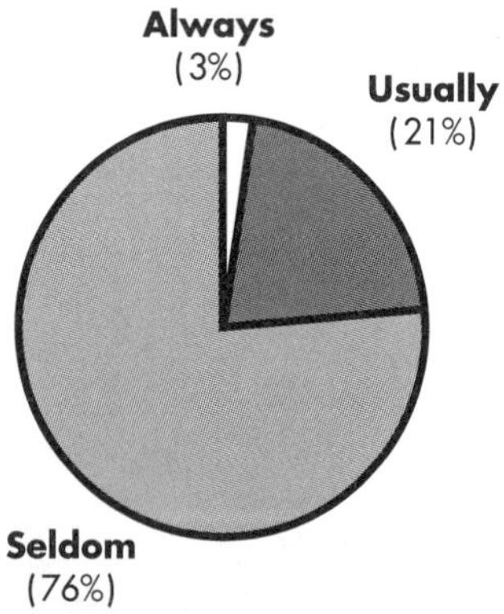

How often do Golf Course Architects conduct soil surveys before a routing is accomplished?

FIGURE 11-4
Results of questions asked of golf course architects and planners in a survey.

Ground Work

Collecting data about a given site constitutes the groundwork of the evaluation. It is never a good idea to make rash judgments about sites for two reasons: (1) the judgment may favor a particular development approach that winds up being impractical, and (2) the judgment can unfairly conclude that a certain approach—or even the entire idea—is not practical at all.

Besides the obvious importance of having good maps and topographical information, aerial photography and maps showing the land use and roadways in the neighborhood of the site are always useful. In addition, one must have a firm understanding of overall project objectives and site-specific conditions that must eventually be dealt with. Without this knowledge, site evaluation cannot be effective.

Important information to have at hand includes:

- Known development objectives
- Topographical mapping
- Property boundaries and easements
- Climate conditions for the area
- Existing permissible land uses
- Complete list of required entitlements and approvals

- Logistics of water availability and delivery
- Soil and water quality reports

Knowing the Limits

Property boundaries seem final, but they come with the occasional hidden zinger. Just because a property line exists does not mean that the land is 100 percent usable up to that point. Setbacks, requirements for open space, safety considerations, nuisances of adjacent land uses, oddly shaped parcels, and easements may play a role in further defining the actual area of usable land.

When evaluating a site, it is a good idea to physically draw on the site map the actual areas that can be used based on these and other constraints. What emerges is a secondary set of boundaries that define the areas actually available for use. While this may sound simple, it is not necessarily so. Utility easements, for instance, may be used for golf, but at the risk of allowing interruptions for the few days per year that the utility company that owns the right to traverse the easement may need access. A base map at this stage of evaluation may look like a colored mess, which I suppose it is. But identifying all of the off-limits areas and the corresponding conditions of use is of vital importance. The result is not a confusing base map but a clear idea of the acreage available for the golf course and all that goes along with it.

Over and above being concerned with the available acreage, evaluation requires that the shape and configuration of the land be considered. A narrow strip of land 100 feet wide and 2200 feet long amounts to more than 5 acres, but none of it is usable for golf holes. About all you could muster there would be a series of putting greens. Width of an area is a critical attribute. So, too, are the angles of corners. The more acute the corner angles, the less useful they are. Even though actual acreage may prove adequate, it can begin to slip away when widths and angles are carefully studied.

Additional questions to ask at this stage are about future use, phasing, and nearby development. Each can affect the site, negatively or positively. Depending on the ownership of the land and whether it has already been purchased or is being considered for purchase, a title report can be of value in determining the exact property lines, easements, and restrictions on new development.

At a project we built and opened a few years back, a power company truck drove onto the newly finished course one afternoon, and workers began staking locations for some new and quite large utility poles. The golf course owner thought it was a practical joke at first, but the utility

TYPICAL ACREAGE ALLOTMENT FOR AN 18-HOLE REGULATION COURSE

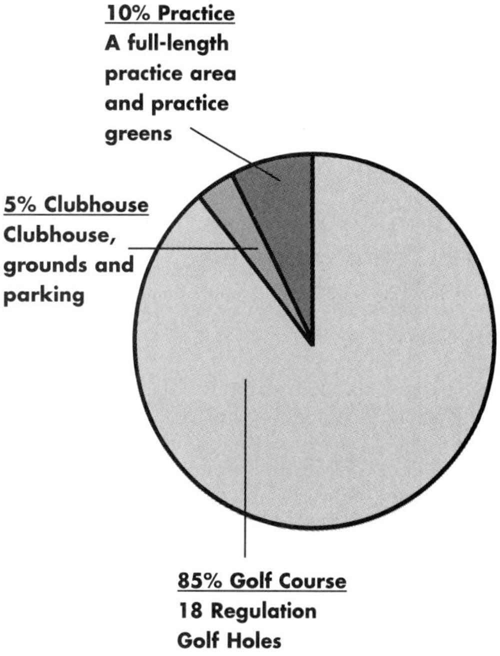

FIGURE 11-5
This chart points out the importance of finding a place for a practice range if one is to be part of a project. The practice range accounts for more acreage than two golf holes, and its width and length are not easily negotiable. The customary elements in and around the clubhouse area account for about 15 percent of the total acreage to be allocated to the golf course.

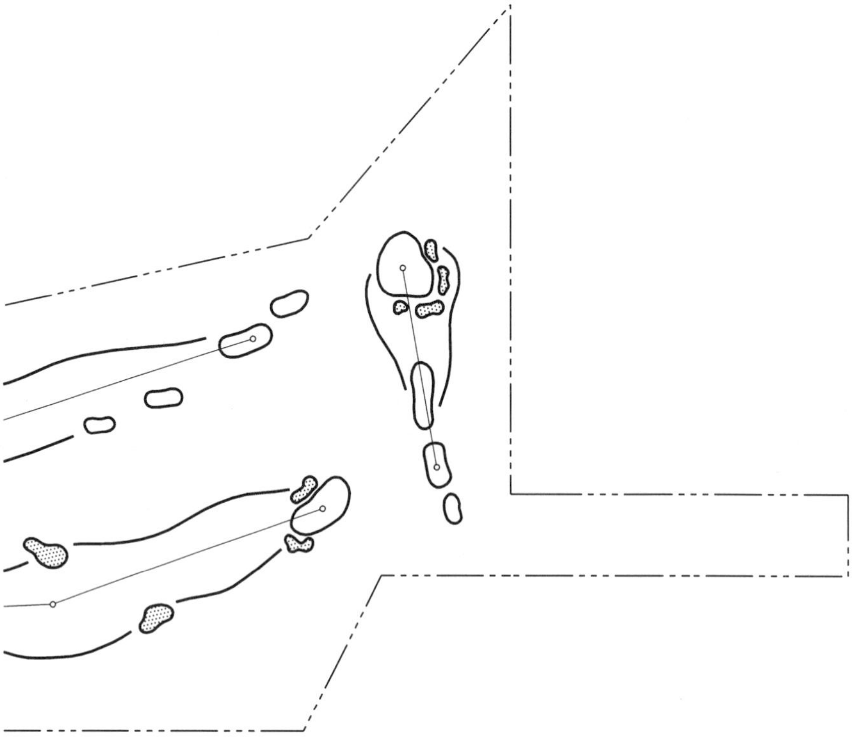

FIGURE 11-6
As this corner of a routing plan demonstrates, some areas of a parcel are simply not usable for golf holes. Narrow strips of land and acute angled corners are among the most worthless. Unfortunately, these problem areas are often seen as part of the land available, making it hard to explain why more acreage is needed. Identification of such areas is a key step in evaluating land for golf.

workers, it turned out, were authentic. What had occurred was an error of enormous proportions. Although a title search had been performed, a 40-foot-wide utility easement had been overlooked by the title company. The result, now that the course was already built and being enjoyed by golfers, was to suggest the acquisition of more land to move a hole and stay clear of the large, looming poles. Damages were consequential. Not only was there the cost of the land and cost to rebuild the golf hole, revenue would also be lost while the course was closed, and the aesthetics were ruined by the power poles. If this story doesn't make you a believer in title insurance, surely nothing will.

Site Logistics

Logistical considerations for a site include the source for water to irrigate the course, how it will arrive at the site, and, if necessary, where it will be stored. In addition, access points, required road crossings (or underpasses), potential need for bridges, and other obstacles must be identified. Such matters can add significantly to the cost of projects. In the span of a short meeting, information that can lead to the expenditure or savings of hundreds of thousands of dollars can be passed from one side of the table to the other. Decisions that must be made depend on this information. Not knowing the logistics of a site is like working in a partial vacuum.

Evaluating Site Topography

Appraising the topography may be the fastest way to ascertain whether a site is viable for golf, at least in terms of the physical issues and independent of other factors such as zoning, finance, and having enough golfers to play once a course is built. Certain terrain poses constraints to golf. Evaluation of the topography is the litmus test of viability. Can a golf course be built here? At what cost? Of what quality?

Land for golf falls into three basic categories—flat, gently rolling (great for golf), and mountainous. The first poses few problems, the second is quite agreeable, and generally only the last raises red flags. This classification of land is, of course, simplistic, as land can be somewhere between these broad types, and there is always the parcel that contains elements of all three. A review of the three land types and what to look for in site evaluation is covered below:

1. Flat land

   Flat land can pose problems for drainage and may require excavated low points that allow water to pond and be pumped or returned to the ground. Flat land, especially without trees or significant vegetation, can be bland and therefore requires significant augmentation to become

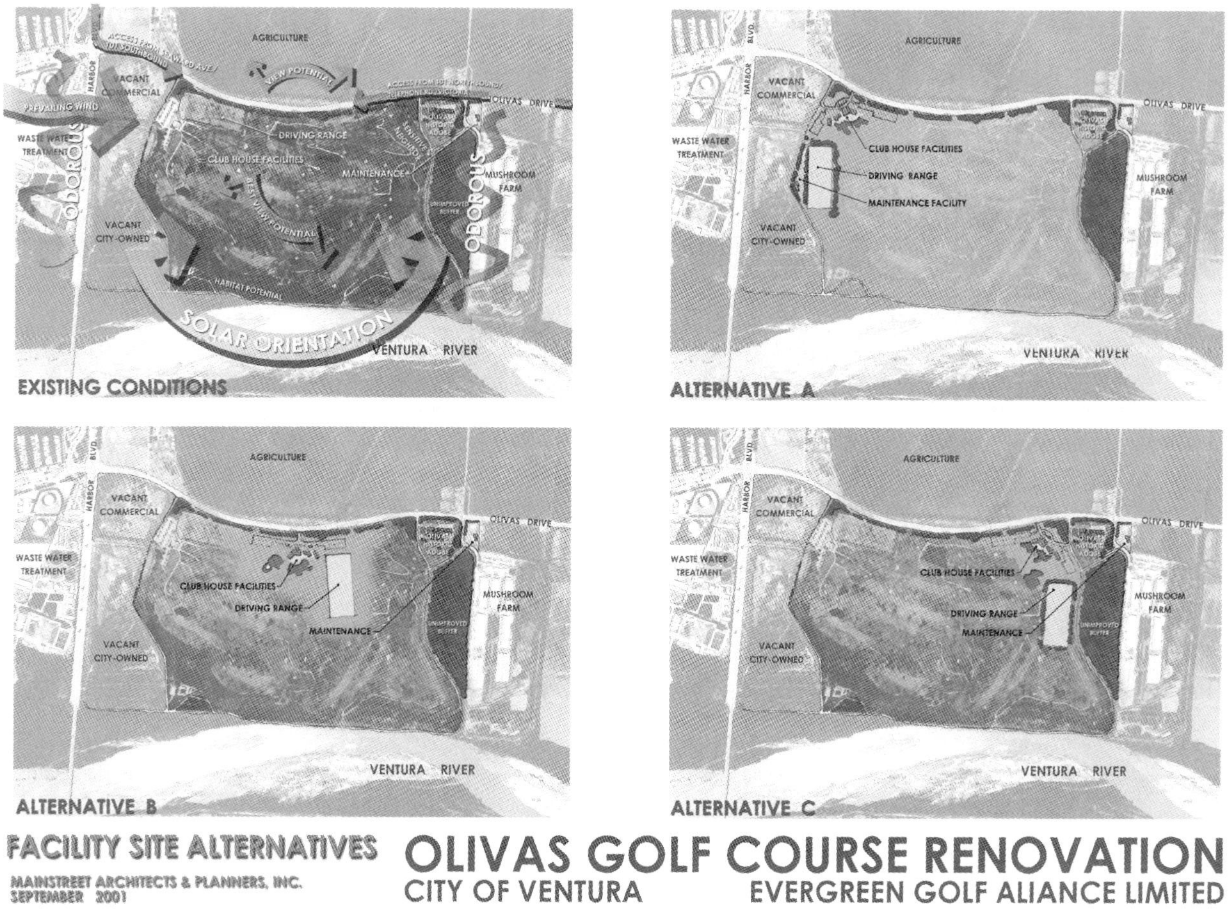

FIGURE 11-7
An aerial photo of an older golf course being evaluated for remodeling. Superimposing the existing conditions on the photo allows for greater understanding of the site. This permits proposed designs to be checked against the conditions.

COURTESY OF MAIN STREET ARCHITECTS, VENTURA, CALIFORNIA

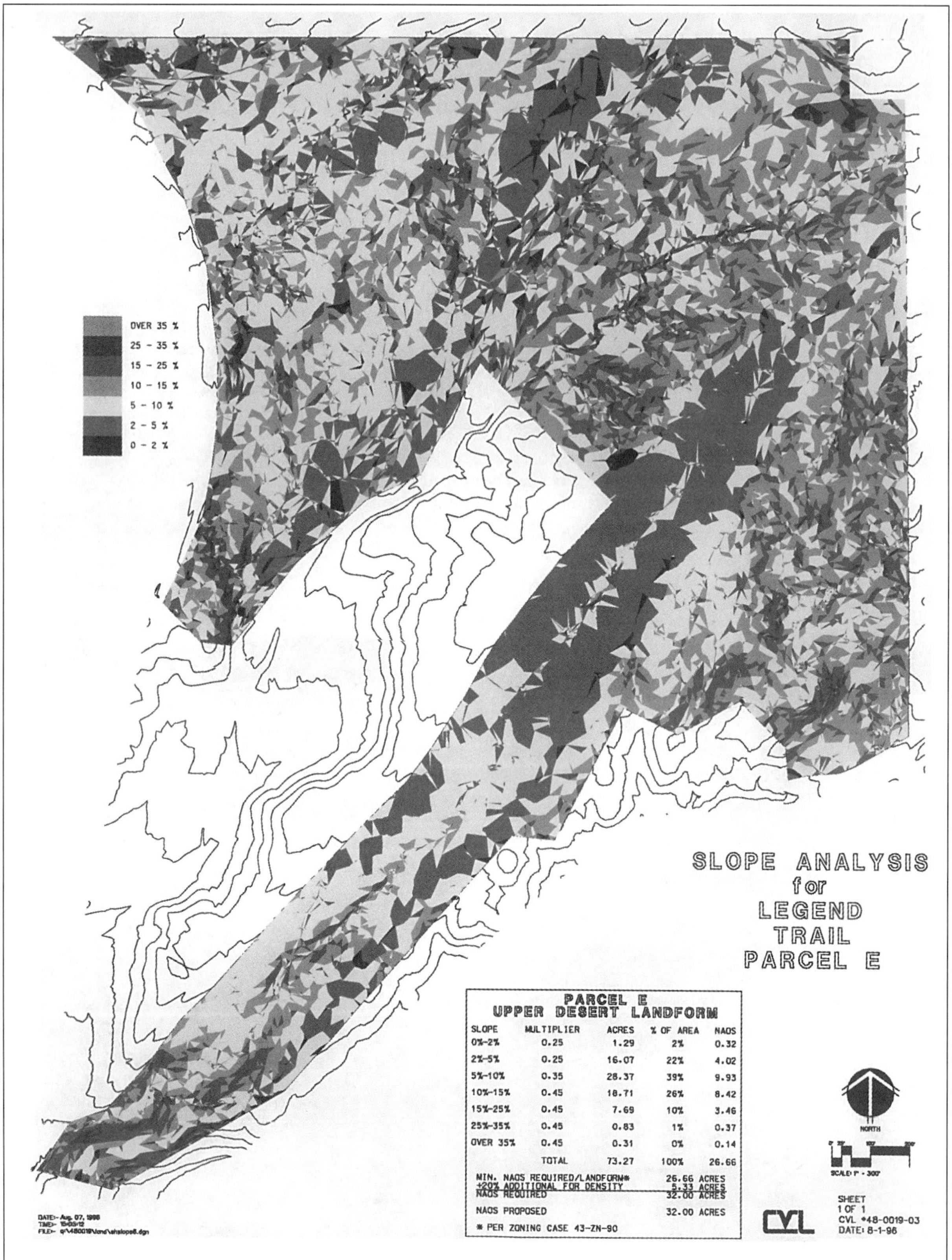
OVER 35 %
25 - 35 %
15 - 25 %
10 - 15 %
5 - 10 %
2 - 5 %
0 - 2 %
SLOPE ANALYSIS
for
LEGEND
TRAIL
PARCEL E
PARCEL E
UPPER DESERT LANDFORM
SLOPE | MULTIPLIER | ACRES | % OF AREA | NAOS
0%-2% | 0.25 | 1.29 | 2% | 0.32
2%-5% | 0.25 | 16.07 | 22% | 4.02
5%-10% | 0.35 | 28.37 | 39% | 9.93
10%-15% | 0.45 | 18.71 | 26% | 8.42
15%-25% | 0.45 | 7.69 | 10% | 3.46
25%-35% | 0.45 | 0.83 | 1% | 0.37
OVER 35% | 0.45 | 0.31 | 0% | 0.14
TOTAL | 73.27 | 100% | 26.66
MIN. NAOS REQUIRED/LANDFORM* 26.66 ACRES
+20% ADDITIONAL FOR DENSITY 5.33 ACRES
NAOS REQUIRED 32.00 ACRES
NAOS PROPOSED 32.00 ACRES
* PER ZONING CASE 43-ZN-90
NORTH
SCALE: 1" = 300'
CVL
SHEET
1 OF 1
CVL #48-0019-03
DATE: 8-1-96

interesting. This can be achieved with golf features, plantings, and alignments to take advantage of views—if there are any!—to distant mountains or valleys. Most land is not entirely flat; even the flattest-appearing land is bound to have a gradient. Still, the effort to overcome such land can be extensive.

2. Gently rolling land

   Ideal for golf. Not too flat, yet not too steep. Interesting dips, rises, and swales that seem ideal—as if a golf course would fit in without much work. What more could one ask for?

3. Mountainous land

   A better term might be *land steeper than is comfortable.* The term *mountainous* implies mountains, which are not necessary for the land to be too steep for comfort. Land that fits this category must be evaluated for the largest of uses in mind. For an 18-hole, regulation-length course, if it is possible to fit the practice area, clubhouse parking, and 10 to 12 par-4 and par-5 fairways on the site, then it is usually possible to find spaces for the other necessary areas, such as tees, greens, and par-3 holes. The consequences of routing golf courses on mountainous land may include: (a) substantial grading requirements; (b) higher construction costs; (c) increased maintenance costs; (d) implementation of a no-walking policy due to the terrain and distances between holes; (e) potential shortening of course length in order to fit components or to compensate for difficult holes; (f) potential reduction in the number of holes, such as a 9-hole course instead of 18; (g) elimination of a full-length practice range due to land constraints.

'How close can we put the golf course to the airport?' —Developers have pondered this question for years, recognizing that screaming jet engines on takeoff can help mask the chirping of birds that so irritates golfers.

—*John Garrity,* America's Worst Golf Courses

Finding Places for Golf

Up until now, the work was all about collection of site mapping, data, and information. Visiting the site, while useful for context, was not entirely essential. This changes when the work shifts to the realities of how and if golf will fit, and where. Although it is possible to partially evaluate a site without actually visiting the land, it will remain just that—a partial job. Better to visit the site and see for yourself. Very little can take the place of using all your senses. To see and touch the land that is being evaluated is second to none. To see beyond the limits of the property boundaries, firsthand, cannot be approximated by two-dimensional photos e-mailed from someone's desktop. To smell the air, to hear the locals talk about their area, and to taste the excitement of what golf may bring, all this is priceless, too.

FIGURE 11-8

A slope analysis shows the areas of severity on a site. Now a matter of running site data through a computer program, the old method involved laborious measurement of the distance between contour lines and lots of colored pencils to shade areas over 15 percent in grade, over 10 percent, and so on. In this computer-generated map, steeper slopes, slopes below 10 percent and intermediate slopes are distinguished by contrasts in shading. Such maps assist in determining the best placement of the various components of a site—roads, lots, and golf.

COURTESY OF COE & VAN LOO ENGINEERS, PHOENIX, ARIZONA

So Many Routings, Not Enough Rubles — A Lesson in Site Economics

I could probably fill a book with stories about my time in the Soviet Union working with a team of planners, construction executives, and resort architects trying to figure out the master concept and plan for a 30,000-acre peninsula. It is difficult to choose among the stories. There was the crab leg dinner I ate in the sauna at Brezhnev's mansion. (Brezhnev was not there.) There was the enormous helicopter that ran on diesel fuel and its three pilots who sat and smoked just a few feet away from the fuel tank. There was the loyal worker who followed our contingent and Russian hosts literally wherever we went, continually pouring vodka into small glasses. That story I cannot seem to recall as well as the others.

This story—or lesson—is about the site we worked on: an amazing 30,000-acre peninsula jutting into the Sea of Japan and lapped by blue waters to the south and the calm ripples of a bay to the north. We were there, as our client pointed out, "to plan the Pebble Beach of Asia." And so we eventually did.

Our approach was to create a destination that would serve the golfing population of Japan, a mere hour's plane ride away. This amazing land was in Asiatic Russia near the maritime submarine port of Vladivostok. The chief planner was Vernon Swaback, an acclaimed architect, visionary, and author who had worked with the legendary Frank Lloyd Wright. Swaback started his own practice in the desert of Arizona, where he has planned several large resorts and communities, each something to behold in the creativity and comfort they reflect. Swaback pointed out how we needed more than golf at what became known as The Peninsula. He noted that the concept of *destination* was going to require activities that would keep guests there for longer stays, especially when the weather was not conducive to golf.

As the plan unfolded, the team had sketched a fishing marina, a recreational boat marina, three resort lodges, a major spa, hunting grounds, and as many as 108 holes of golf spread over seven miles. Courses were clustered, some sharing a clubhouse and others as stand-alone 18-hole layouts with individual themes. There were as many as 20 credible ocean holes among the courses. Two in particular, I profoundly remarked, would be nearly as special as anything Seventeen-Mile Drive had to offer.

It was a breathtaking—and ambitious—plan, and everybody was enthusiastic about taking it to the next step. As the plan progressed, it became clear to us that the absence of infrastructure was perhaps an insurmountable obstacle. It had been noted that the site would require a nearby airport, a desalination plant (for drinking and irrigation water), and the construction of a new road, if not for access by guests, at least for the purposes of delivering goods from Vladivostok, some three hours away by truck. All told, the bill—even before development—might exceed $2 billion.

Eventually, the Soviet Union became the Russian Federation. The iron curtain was lifted, and what little was left of the economy took an even greater beating. Not only would there be no help from the Russians, but the uncertainty of doing expensive business in such a political and economic climate was unappealing to investors.

Through planning and site evaluation, we concluded exactly what a good planning team is supposed to conclude: whether the project is viable or not. It was a painful realization, but it may one day pay off. After all, the land is still there—and so are the plans.

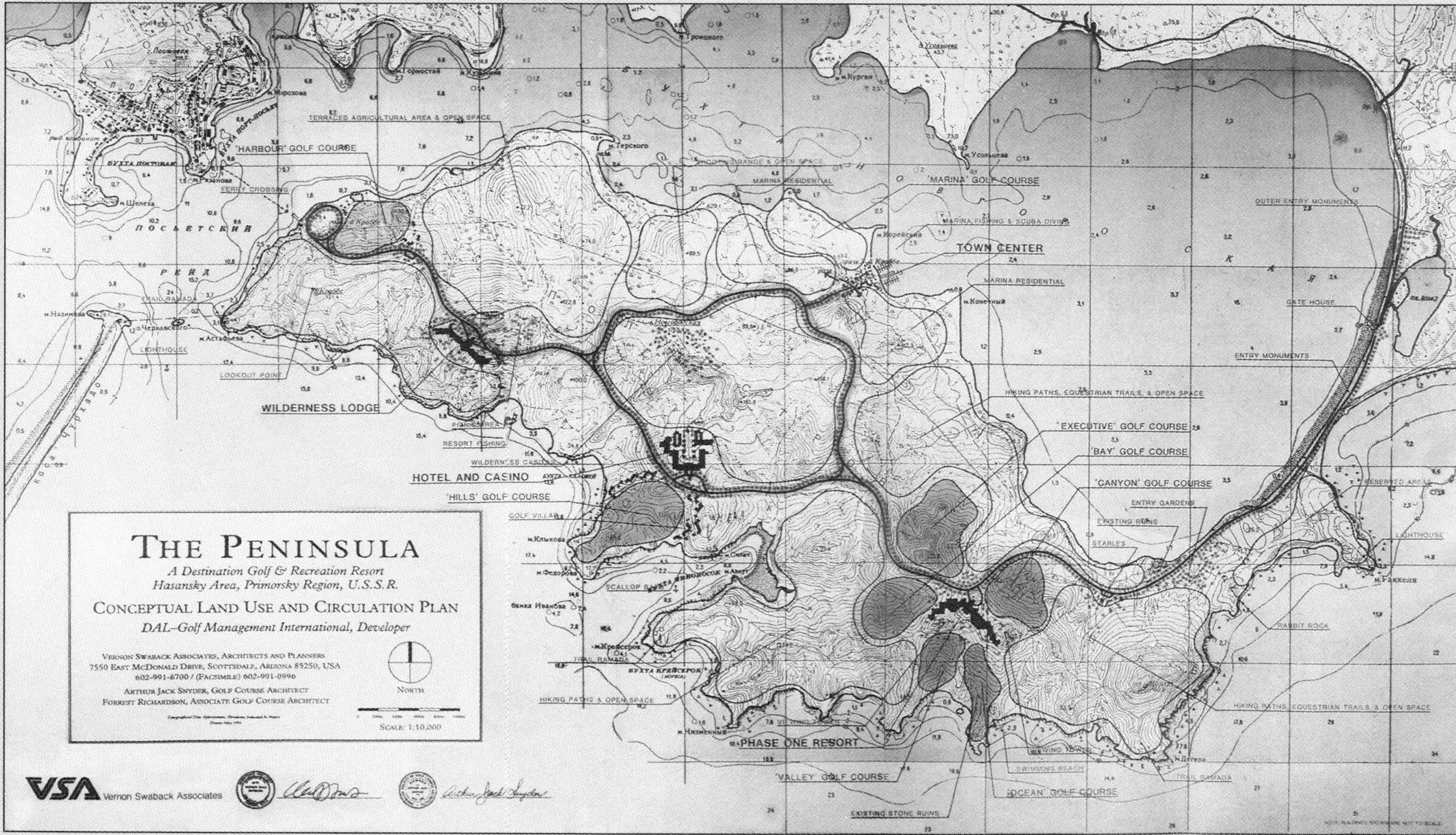

The conceptual master plan of The Peninsula was a result of painstaking site evaluation (see “The Secret Topo” in Hole 13). The plan features areas for 108 holes of golf, many set high above the Sea of Japan on the Russian coastline.

The primary concerns in finding places for golf are:

- Appraising natural land features

  What does the land have to offer?
- Appraising views

  This includes views not only to distant landmarks and scenes but also to areas inside the property.
- Defining the usable acreage

  Knowing how much is usable and for what purposes immediately paints a picture of what, generally, is going to be possible.
- Establishing potential access points
- Appraising potential beginning points

  It is important to realize that clubhouse locations lead to locating starting holes, which lead to finishing holes, which establish practice area locations, and so on. Of course, the order in which these beginning points are viewed has a lot to do with project priorities. Finishing holes may be most important to a particular project and, if so, can actually drive everything else.
- Identification of areas for large uses

  Parking, practice ranges, and resort sites consume sizable acreage, and therefore the evaluation must determine whether or not they can be accommodated.
- Identification of topographical limitations

  Complex sites with steep slopes are good candidates for a slope analysis showing what areas are more severe than a threshold appropriate for the site. This may be 15 percent or even greater. Slopes above 15 percent can pose many problems for golf use. If they cannot be avoided or used creatively, they may require significant earthmoving.
- Identification of natural golf holes

  Does the site feature natural golf holes—that is, areas and settings that seem as if they were destined for golf?
- Appraisal of land for interesting golf

  Will this land make for an interesting golf course?

Creative Problem Solving

Financial analysis may indicate that a site is simply too difficult for golf. Developments have limitations, and their staying power will quickly go away when probable costs rise beyond the return. Some of the amazing mountainous courses of Japan are examples of how human drive and ambition can be unstoppable providing enough money and time are allotted for excavation and earthmoving. Mountains literally have been moved to make way for golf courses, and new, smaller mountains created in their place and positioned off to either side, allowing just enough room for golf to creep past and descend to the next level, where the heroic grading operation has been repeated all over again. Such sites, which are not exclusive to Japan, involve tremendous creativity in finding ways to get golf courses to fit, let alone to get them to begin and end near the same spot.

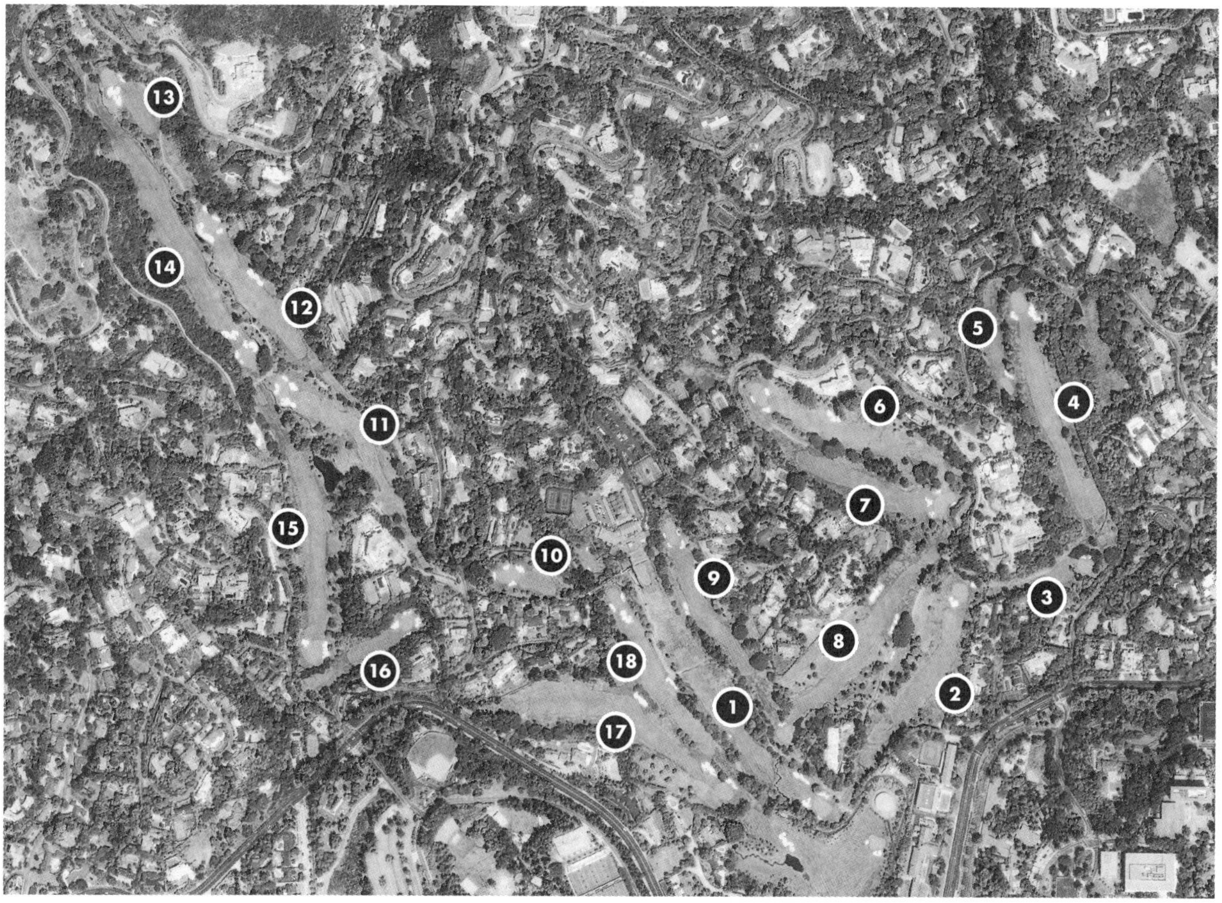

FIGURE 11-9
In this aerial photo of the Bel-Air Country Club in Los Angeles, California, it appears that the golf course is hemmed-in by intruding homes and streets. In actuality, the routing by George C. Thomas Jr. (1873–1932) uses a series of canyons for the golf holes, and the homes are well above the fairways. To get from one canyon to the other, four tunnels and one suspension bridge were cleverly engineered based on Thomas's vision. The tunnels occur between holes 5 and 6, 9 and 10, 10 and 11, and 16 and 17. The suspension bridge takes golfers from the tee at the tenth above the 18th green and across a canyon. Together, the tunnels and bridge allow golfers to get from one hole to the next without climbing over the ridges that separate the canyons.

COURTESY OF BEL-AIR COUNTRY CLUB

FIGURE 11-10
One of the narrow tunnels connecting holes at the creatively routed Bel-Air Country Club in Los Angeles.

It's kind of fun to do the impossible.
— Walt Disney

Perhaps the most celebrated example of overcoming a difficult and steep site is the acclaimed Bel-Air Country Club in Los Angeles, California. While the tremendous earthmoving efforts in Japan reflect good ideas made possible by advances in excavation equipment; Bel-Air is a beautiful example of ingenuity that overcomes the need for such intensive construction effort. In 1925, golf course architect George C. Thomas had the vision—and outright guts—to propose tunnels at Bel-Air after he and collaborator Jack Neville (credited as the primary designer of Pebble Beach) hit test shots across a canyon previously thought too severe for golf.

In his book, *Golf Architecture in America,* Thomas describes the configuration of tunnels at Bel-Air:

> [T]he clubhouse was placed high on the ridge dividing two little valleys, and the ninth green was placed in one of them, and the eighteenth green in the other, at the narrow ends of these little canyons. From the center of the clubhouse above, a shaft was sunk to the level of the greens, and tunnels run from this shaft to the valley close to each green.... [A]n elevator in the shaft takes players upward to the clubhouse itself, which is near No. 1 and No. 10 tees.

Each of Bel-Air's tunnels has the effect of sidestepping the steep ridges above the canyons that make up its masterful 18-hole layout. As golfers leave greens tucked against the steep canyon edges, they are whisked deep through the mountain. At the end of the tunnel they are let out to the next tee, all with very little climb and no annoying switchback trail going way up and then way down. Added to this is a suspension bridge erected high above the ninth green. It carries golfers from the tenth tees across the canyon to the green beyond.

Thomas admitted that his tunnels and bridge were the exception rather than the rule for utilizing hilly terrain for golf. Regardless, his routing at Bel-Air is among the cleverest ever created. The lesson to be learned from its story is one of overcoming a difficult site by seeking a solution beyond what has been tried before.

Another common challenge is not having enough land area. This problem is difficult to overcome, especially for the project that absolutely will not permit a shorter course or fewer golf holes. Well, something has to give, so what will it be? Tight sites are, unfortunately, commonplace. The long-term problems can be deep and troublesome; safety, playability, and pace of play are the top three when an unsuitable program is forced into a tight site.

Not all site obstacles can be overcome. The best advice, besides to be creative, is to pay careful attention to the rules of routing described in Hole 7. What may seem impossible and unworthy should always be given a chance to be proved otherwise. Before the notion that something cannot be done gets your blood boiling, it should first get your creative juices flowing. Routing a golf course requires simultaneous problem solving, a healthy dose of practicality, and plenty of stubbornness.

SPECIAL PROGRAMMING & SITE CIRCUMSTANCES

Not all golf course sites are created equal. That is what makes the job of routing them so much fun. Indeed, if all projects were alike, the job would hardly exist. The following sections address some unusual issues in programming and site analysis. *Note:* There are more where these came from, but these constitute those that crop up frequently.

Evaluation of Multiple Sites

Evaluating two or more sites for comparison purposes requires the same steps and thought processes for each. The comparison can be made in spreadsheet format, where attributes and conditions are compared like apples to apples. This situation arises when a developer is looking at multiple land parcels and is torn between which one to purchase.

A similar situation is when an extremely large acreage must be evaluated for the ideal area in which to site a course. The difference is that there may be many more potential sites and parts of sites to consider. Mathematically, the options are much greater because the course can be confined to one area or spread across the site in a variety of ways. Often, one must create multiple routing plans so options can be studied and compared. Another method is to create land use plans that, instead of showing the detailed routing of holes, show large masses for golf use and smaller bubbles for ancillary uses such as the clubhouse, maintenance, etc. Even in this format, the plan suggests a routing for the course. The bubbles drawn to indicate golf must be sized, shaped and linked to be workable when it comes time to lay in individual holes and course components.

Reclamation Sites

Environmental considerations are important on all golf course sites, not just those with heightened awareness because they have been earmarked for clean-up from previous use as landfill, dumping ground, or mining operation. Land reclamation for golf has become a popular consideration.Not only is land compromised by waste or mining usually acquired at no cost but also there is often funding available for cleanup and rejuvenation. Any available pot of money for such projects depends largely on the type of site to be reclaimed, where it is located, and under what jurisdiction it resides. Sites near residential areas are typically given highest priority for reclamation, as are sites that potentially intrude on nearby natural habitats. Communities are committed to reclaiming such sites and returning them to productive use for recreation, including golf. Obviously, if a land parcel were public to begin with, restrictions on its use might require any recreation facility built on it to be public as well.

The projects described above are termed *reclamation projects*. They cover a range of land types from partially compromised lands to complex Superfund sites. In terms of programming and site evaluation, such land and the projects it might accommodate involve special vision on the part of the planning team.

FIGURE 11-11
A bubble plan depicts land use in broad-stroke form. In this example, the uses of a site are shown based on their density of use, each in a different shade. The land planned for the golf course shows only where the golf course will go, not any detail of its design. This does not mean that no routing has taken place, for such exhibits cannot be created without some degree of routing and an understanding of where such key components as the clubhouse, practice areas, and beginning and ending holes can be located.

COURTESY OF COE & VAN LOO ENGINEERING, PHOENIX, ARIZONA

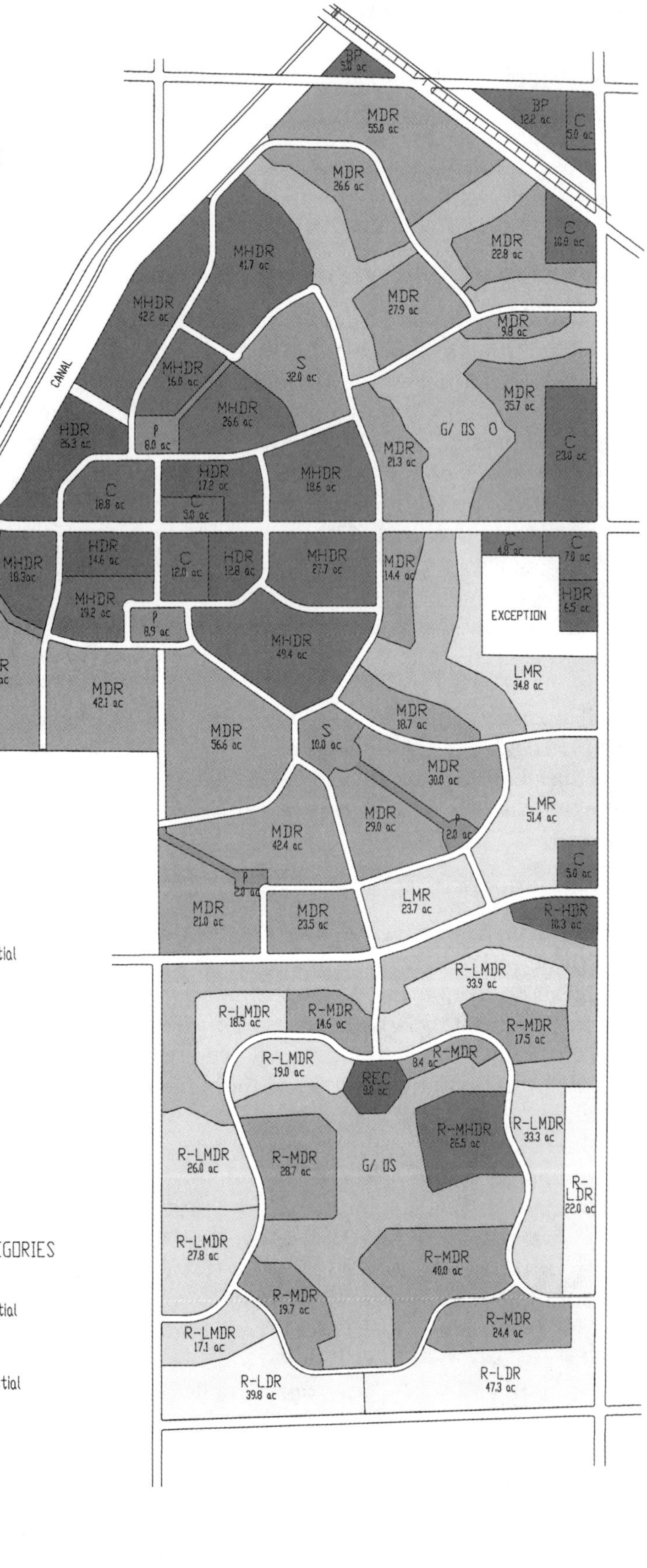

Special attention must be paid to the following tasks in order to program and evaluate reclamation projects:

- Obtain a complete site background

  An understanding of the site and its past use is essential; specialists must be consulted on how the site was cleaned up or what future cleanup is required.

- Determine funding potential

  Some sites are so environmentally compromised that future uses may not be funded without special indemnification; lawyers and experts are needed to sort out these logistics.

- Define the limits of impact

  The exact location of compromised areas and the depth and content of any problem soils must be mapped so that proper evaluation can be made. Often, this information will constitute a separate layer to the GIS database of a project.

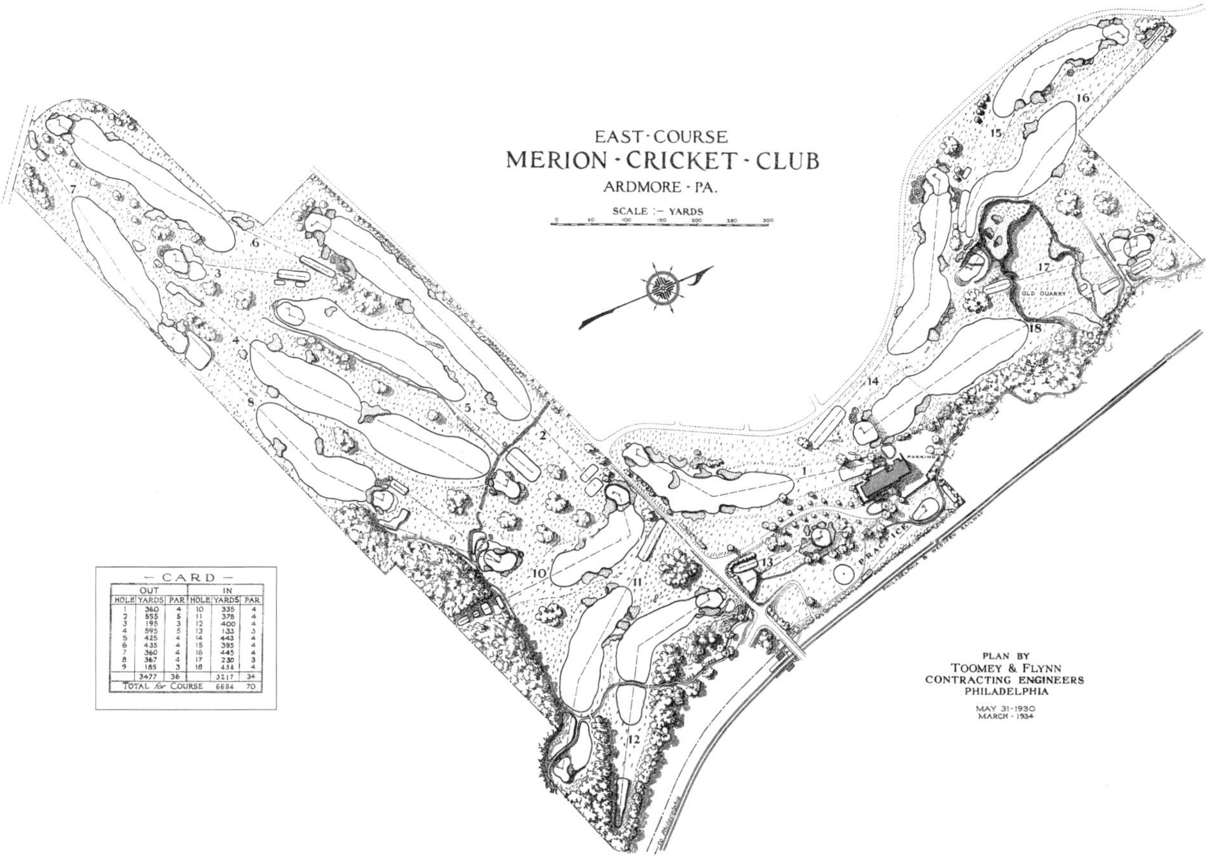

FIGURE 11-12

The East Course at Merion in Ardmore, Pennsylvania, is one of the earliest examples of a course built on reclamation land. On just 125 acres, golf course architect Hugh Wilson was able to create an outstanding course with a routing that utilizes an old quarry to form a strategic corner. Wilson, who made his living in the insurance business, became interested in golf architecture when the Merion Cricket Club decided to build a new course. He studied the courses of Great Britain and the National Golf Links, where C. B. Macdonald was about to open his "ideal American links." This plan, drawn by William Flynn, who supervised construction of the new course, is a prime example of an early routing plan.

COURTESY OF THE USGA LIBRARY

- Understand the long-term consequences

  For example, solid waste landfills (dumps) can produce methane gases for decades after they are closed, and building a golf course on top does nothing to stop the gases from being generated. Settling of the interred waste, the introduction of irrigation water, and the collection of gases are important considerations that must be dealt with for the duration of the use of the land.

- List the required entitlements

  Entitlements can be complex for projects involving reclaimed land. The good news is that there are usually entities committed to transforming the damaged land into a positive state of use; these entities are the saviors of such projects.

- Assess project viability

  Is it worth the effort? Is it possible to overcome the costs and mitigation necessary to make the project interesting and financially sound?

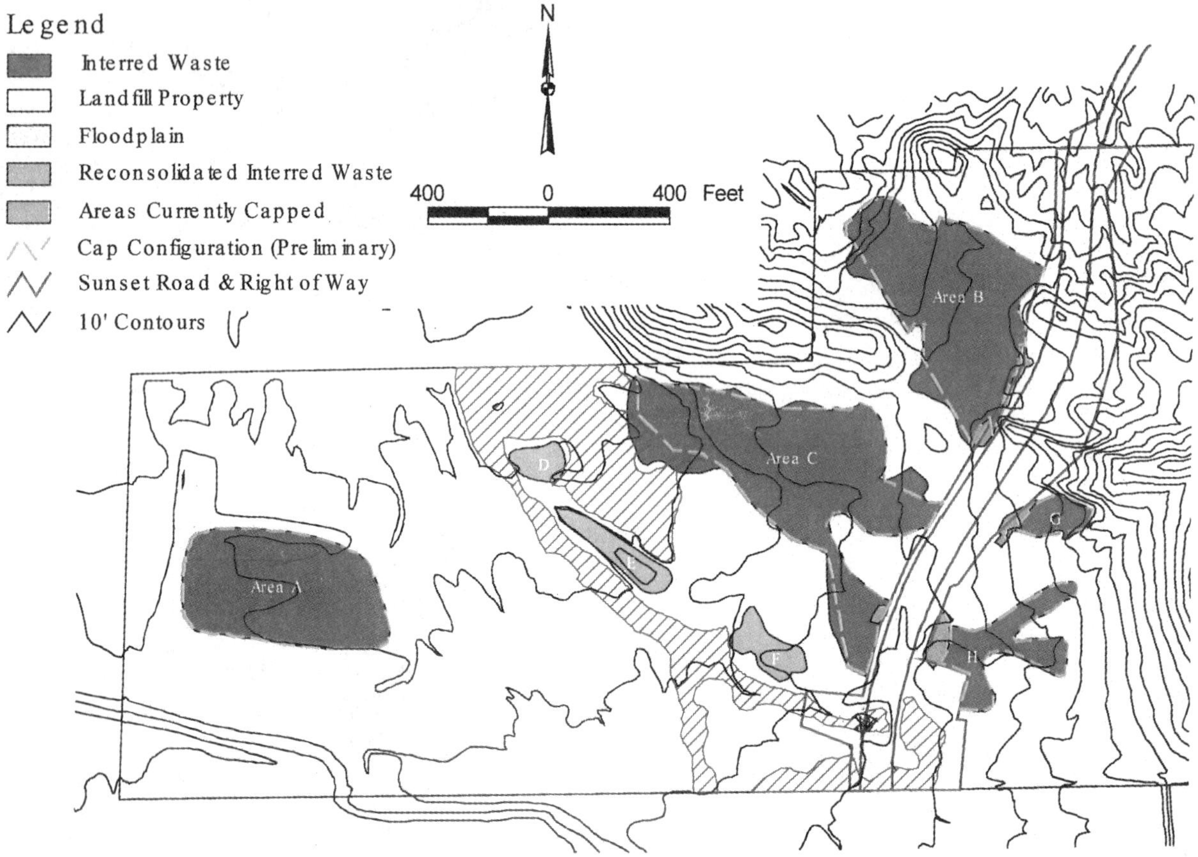

FIGURE 11-13
This map of a solid waste landfill shows where pockets of waste are located. Armed with this information, the golf course router can dodge the pockets or route holes so shots play over them to avoid costly mitigation that might come with impacting them directly.

Entitlements for Environmentally Sensitive Land

All land can be classified as environmentally sensitive. The differentiating factor from one parcel to the next is usually seen in the entitlements required before development can take place. Although all land must be approached with awareness and appreciation of the environment, some land brings with it requirements that must be evaluated and considered in the programming and site inspection phases. There are two categories of entitlements: (1) required entitlements and (2) needed entitlements. The difference is that required entitlements are essential for their black-and-white nature—that is, without them you cannot move forward and with them you can. Needed entitlements are those you can legally do without, but the consequences may be just as detrimental as not having a required entitlement. An example of a needed entitlement might be the favorable opinion of a citizen's group that monitors activity along a river valley. While the group may have no legal authority, their voice may well be the strongest and most influential heard in the region. To not seek their input and support is likely a mistake.

At a complicated project (see "The 13-Hole Course" in Hole 9) in a desert setting, we had numerous required entitlements—a seemingly endless list of approvals from government agencies and offices. We also had to acquire the other type of entitlement—the nod of approval from the property owners who lived along one edge of the course's routing. These residents had no formal approval rights; they could not outright stop the project on any legal basis. What they did possess was political influence, and their weight in obtaining the approvals of the various jurisdictions was formidable. I recall spending more time and energy to work with this group than on any other project. There were walks in the desert, meetings, and public hearings refereed by city officials. In the end, I believe we made them happy and all parties "won," even though it was no one's intent to have winners and losers. Many years later, a nice woman with whom I had crossed words on many occasions saw me walking along the golf course, and we struck up a friendly conversation. Since the golf course had been built she had lowered her fence to get a better view to the course, and she was very complimentary of the way things turned out. She had only one complaint: The wild javelina were so prevalent in the evenings that she had to transplant some of the tomatoes and peppers she had been growing just outside her back fence. Not long after saying goodbye, it dawned on me that this was the same woman who had once vehemently opposed the golf course because it would drive all the wildlife away from the area.

Naysayers will always be present. Their voices must be heard, but their opinions must be tempered by reason and science. The programming and evaluation process should anticipate the challenges associated with a project. Once these are defined, the right course of action can be planned and then implemented.

Conservation Easements

A conservation easement is a parcel of land, usually owned by a nonprofit land trust, designated to be left in a condition that maintains its open space, passive use, or cultural attributes. Conservation easements may be used to entirely protect land, preventing any development whatsoever, or they may be used less restrictively to keep land as open space while allowing limited but sustaining uses. Conservation easements, which are typically set up by landowners, have been used to protect agricultural land from development, protect environmentally sensitive lands, and even to overlay land with golf courses. Land trusts may acquire land through donation or purchase, hold negotiated conservation easements (permanent deed restrictions that prevent harmful land uses), use partial development to finance the protection of the rest of the land, or utilize life estates that allow the owner to live on the land for their lifetime, after which the land reverts to the land trust.

The Moundbuilders — How a Routing Plan Saved an Archaeological Treasure

Located not far outside of Columbus, Ohio, is a golf course I became intrigued with on reading an article, written in 1930, that I came across at the USGA's Golf House Library. It was a travelog from *Golf Illustrated* written by Chalmers Pancoast, who played golf all around the country and reported on the courses he visited.

The Moundbuilders Country Club sits in a glen surrounded by woods. It was founded in 1910 and is one of America's oldest continually operating golf courses. It's both charming and challenging, but it was not these attributes that lured me to visit. Rather, it was the incredible story of an ancient civilization and how this unassuming rural golf club had unknowingly preserved a piece of its history.

Some 3000 years ago, a group referred to as the Hopewell Indians inhabited what is now the geographic center of the state of Ohio. Known as the Moundbuilders, these artful and enterprising people —for reasons still not fully known—took to building mounds in large-scale patterns. They worked all across the land bordering the Ohio River. Their earthen mounds were of two types; the first was linear in nature and perfectly shaped into straight lines and hollow circles and hexagons, and the second was abrupt piles with symmetric slopes.

Nearly all of the Moundbuilders' work was trashed in the nineteenth century as Ohio grew and a new civilization moved in. Where elaborate relics of the Moundbuilders' unexplained triumphs once stood, grew railroads, cities, roads, and farms. Today, in fact, only a handful of remnants of the elaborate mound complexes remain. Perhaps if air travel had been invented at the time enough people would have seen and appreciated the spectacular patterns and shapes. Perhaps our new civilization would not have been so quick to discard the work of these great land artists.

My tour guide at the club was Harland Fargo, a past president and longtime member. I asked the same questions he heard many times before: Why did the Moundbuilders build the mounds? (Here's the flippant answer members can't wait to use on unsuspecting first-time visitors: "What else would you expect Moundbuilders to build?") Whose idea was it to put a golf course right over the mounds and use them in the design? Don't you find all this a bit weird? Fargo was full of stories and, as we made our way around the course, he not only answered my questions but also gave me some perspective on what it means to play golf on ground which was considered sacred by those who created the ancient mounds.

"Honestly, no one knows why the mounds were built," Fargo said. "Even the archeologists don't know for sure." When I asked how the archeologists feel about having fairways and golf holes playing over the ancient mounds, he said, "Well, they do know that the Moundbuilders conducted ceremonies in and around the mounds. We tell them we're just continuing the tradition."

In fact, once each year at a certain date and exact time, the sunrise comes chasing precisely down the ninth fairway and between its two 10-foot-high parallel mounds. Although not for several years now, a few members used to gather with Bloody Marys in hand and experience the same phenomenon of light that the ancients did. Of course, the members then went and did what they enjoyed most of all: They played golf. We have no clue what the Moundbuilders did afterward.

The Moundbuilders Country Club from the air.
COURTESY OF THE CLUB

The first nine of the Moundbuilders Club was laid out by Thomas Bendelow with tremendous respect for the mounds. The second nine, laid out by the legendary golf course architect Jack Kidwell, is not among the mounds themselves, though they are nearby. It is a wonderful complement to the older nine, whose holes are strategically tucked behind, to the side of, and over the mounds. Each linear mound is from 8 to 10 feet in height above the otherwise flat site. There are no fewer than five blind shots on the original nine. Each, however, can be negotiated by standing on the back of your cart or relying on the extra-tall flagsticks. At No. 3, the green is entirely encircled by a perfectly circular mound. It was here, while I putted for a bogey, that my sense of the absurdity of the place was replaced by the feeling that this was not a golf course just built some*where*—it was a course built some*place*.

The idea to use the mounds instead of disrespecting them was brilliant. Sure, perhaps the choice was made because moving them would be too much work. But I give Bendelow more credit than that. This golf course could only be duplicated in form. The metaphysical, the fact that it is an authentic place of ceremony and gathering that goes back thousands of years, is unique.

"If they had not built a golf course here, the work of these people would have been lost forever," Fargo noted as we completed our tour. Indeed, this is another aspect that makes the Moundbuilders Club so wonderful. Perhaps it was a fluke. Who knows? The important thing is that mounds once covered by prairie grasses are now covered in turfgrass. The work of these ancient people was preserved. Today, next to the tee at the ninth is a 10-foot-high wooden platform which visitors can climb to look out over the golf course. The question is, do they see a golf course or the work of the Moundbuilders?

My time at the Moundbuilders was eerie. The mounds present obstacles that challenge the mind more than any hazard or golf feature could. The lesson to be learned is that the land we work on has more to teach us than just what is there, for all land has stories about its past that is too often lost in our quest to create the new. And, once we uncover the soul of a site, we are able to consider much more than just what can be put there. The story of the Moundbuilders teaches the value of preservation and how golf can coexist with even the most unlikely of special sites.

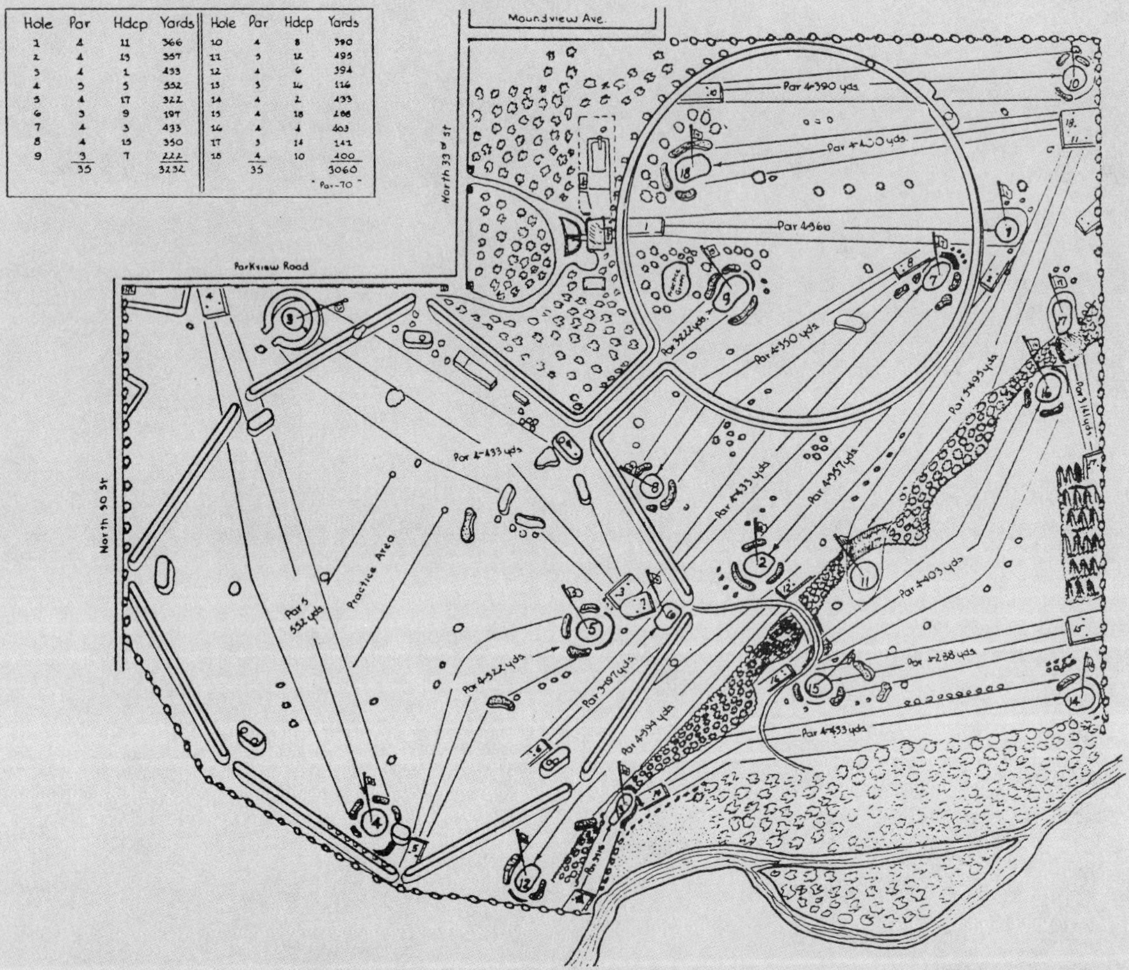

Routing plan of the Moundbuilders Country Club, one of the most interesting and distinctive golf courses ever created.

COURTESY OF THE CLUB

Remodeling Projects

Remodeling projects are so different from new golf course projects that they rarely can be worked out using the same processes. Numerous special circumstances apply to programming and site evaluation. The most important distinction between new and remodeling projects is the limits to which each of the course components is allowed to expand. In a new project, components can go pretty much anywhere as long as the plan follows the project's rules and standards. In a remodeling project, the limits are considerably narrower and more restrictive.

For starters, it is helpful to understand the four *R*s of remodeling projects. They are:

- Remodeling
  These projects involve existing golf courses that will undergo significant changes to their features, alignments, and, often, routing.
- Renovation
  These projects are limited to upgrading the components of the existing golf course with little or no change to its structure and design.
- Restoration
  These projects are undertaken to bring back features, subtleties, and qualities of a golf course that have been lost or changed over the years.
- Rebuilding
  These projects are essentially new golf courses built in place of old ones with little or no regard to the original routing.

The four *R*s are not always distinguishable. *Remodeling*, for example, is used both as defined above and as a catchall phrase that encompasses all four *R*s. A project may call for some renovation but a lot of remodeling. A hybrid project may involve both remodeling an existing 9-hole course and adding a new second nine.

Programming and site evaluation for remodeling projects (renovation, restoration, and rebuilding included) may require the following considerations:

- Historical background
  What was the driving force behind the original design? Is there significant reason to retain some of the history and charm of this golf facility in the new program?
- Detailed site mapping
  All improvements and features need to be detailed on site mapping so each is considered in terms of its value if retained and its cost if replaced or removed.
- Changes to area conditions
  Especially with older layouts, drainage and nearby land uses may require new measures to be taken on the golf course land; these must be defined and verified in the programming/evaluation process. [11-14]
- Entitlements and approvals
  These may be very different from those of a new project on bare land.

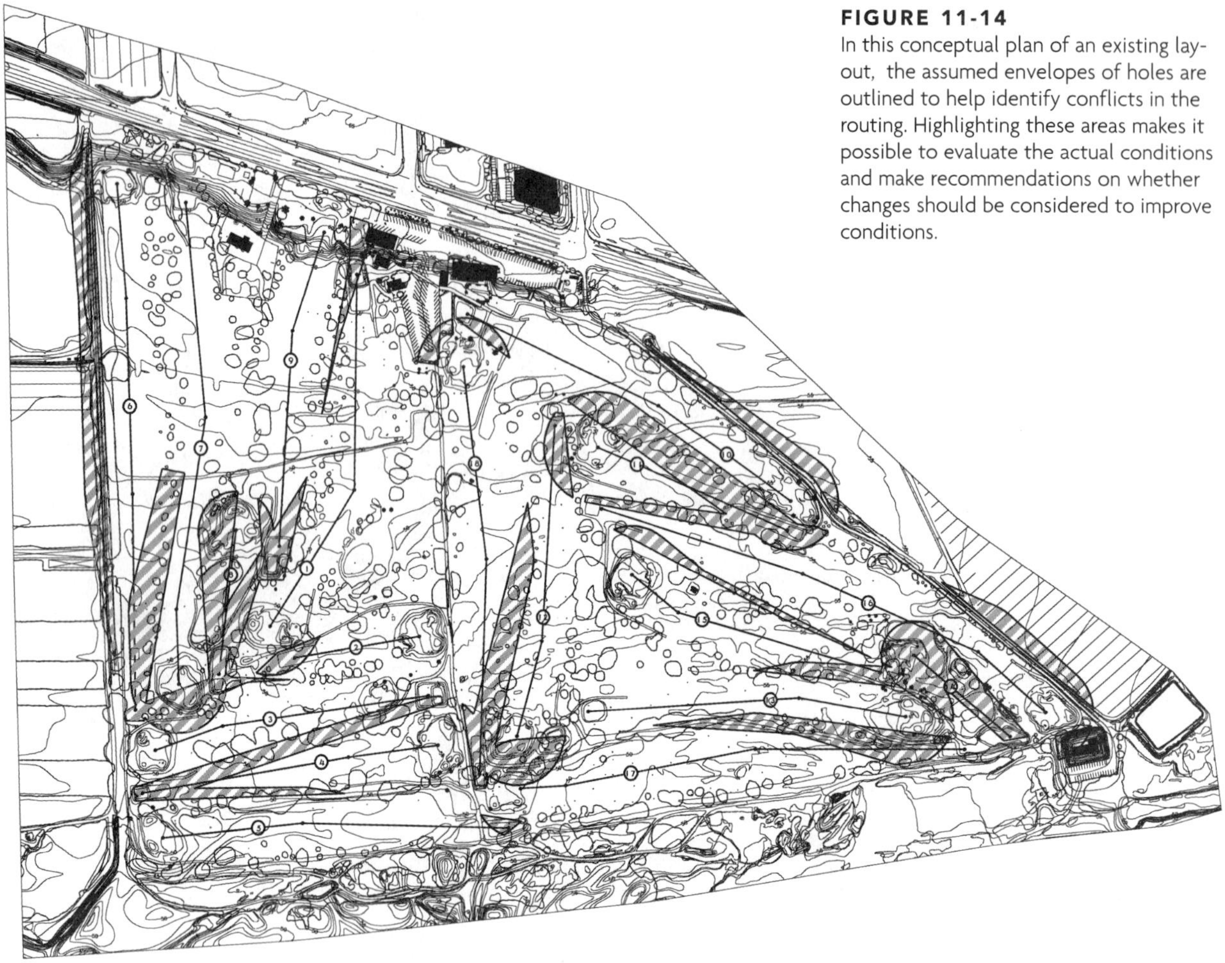

FIGURE 11-14
In this conceptual plan of an existing layout, the assumed envelopes of holes are outlined to help identify conflicts in the routing. Highlighting these areas makes it possible to evaluate the actual conditions and make recommendations on whether changes should be considered to improve conditions.

- Analysis of safety

  Existing safety conditions may have to be compared to guidelines that would apply if the course were being built new. The program and evaluation cannot expect all new work to meet current guidelines, but could outline steps in the eventual design that would eliminate significant areas of concern in the existing layout.

- Study of neighboring uses

  Changes to the golf course should not negatively affect existing uses that border the land. A study of uses will call attention to areas to consider in the final program and plan.

- Existing program

  The existing program can be defined and these data compared to a newly crafted program. The result is one way of determining the extent of changes necessary to the golf course, as each area of change will likely involve site considerations that must be integrated with the eventual plan.

- Irrigation and drainage systems

  All underground systems must be weighed for their viability and potential to be replaced, repaired, or updated.

The Extinct Tree — A Short Story about Bureaucracy

"Hello, this is Professor Glückinspell. Is this Forrest?" Professor Glückinspell had only called once before, and it was a strange time for him to call. It was considerably earlier in Hawaii. The professor said that up near the sixth hole, off to the left of the green near an outcropping of lava, he had found some plants that needed further study.

This addition brought the total of protected species of plants to three at this mountainside site undergoing planning. We had previously agreed to protect species by installing irrigation heads all around a single tree in case the lava-covered slopes above the ocean ever caught fire. I recalled sitting in a meeting several months earlier when the representative of a state agency pointed out that the state would approve the routing plan only if we installed this irrigation protection and oh, by the way, he knew we could use only treated effluent to water the course, which would probably not be good for the tree. When asked if it might not be better to run a separate line of potable water to provide emergency water should the lava rock catch fire, he said that it would violate such-and-such an agreement to use only effluent on the parcel designated as golf course. The second tree species we had to protect was off to the side and would not be affected by the proposed 27-hole golf complex.

"I am not sure," the Professor continued, "but this may very well be a new species! None of us has ever seen it before." I shared in the professor's enthusiasm. It is not every day that a new plant is discovered, at least not on the projects I work on. I asked Glückinspell what the discovery meant in terms of delays. I was not trying to be callous, just practical. The Professor explained that new species would not necessarily precipitate a delay but that we would have to protect the small trees and possibly shift the green away from the area to avoid impact. I was disappointed, but the effort seemed worthwhile. A new plant was indeed worthy of protection, as are all plants, whenever it is practical.

I called Jack Snyder, with whom I'd been working on the project, and told him the news. We decided to adjust the entire hole. Our duty was obvious: The tree, no matter how small and insignificant, needed to be left alone. And so we left it, even creating a better hole by taking advantage of a higher tee point and a sharper angle to the new green site, now farther right and past the site of the unknown tree.

Several days later, Glückinspell called again. "Hello, this is Professor Glückinspell, and I have good news for you." And that's when I received the greatest lesson in bureaucracy idiocy I could ever hope to get. The Professor explained that before sending leaf samples and DNA evidence to claim a new species, he and his staff made one final check of records at the University of Hawaii for some historical reference to the thin-leafed, spindly half-bush, half-tree plant—and they found, on a page numbered beyond 500 in an old dusty book, a perfect illustration of the tree. Personally, I was disappointed; I thought the

Professor deserved a tree. But, as the Professor explained, the tree had been declared extinct in 1934—so its protection was no longer an issue.

Shocking but true. Extinct species are not protected. If we someday find a dodo bird wandering outside Springfield, Ohio, there will be no reason to call the Environmental Protection Agency because it won't care.

Glückinspell appreciated our efforts and said he would begin the tedious process of having the tree removed from the extinct list. Maybe, if he could convince the government he was not crazy, it would someday be added to the endangered list. In the meanwhile, however, none of us working on the plan cared about it. After all, it didn't exist.

(*Note:* I have deliberately avoided naming the tree, and those of you who do not believe Professor Glückinspell is real are correct. The story, however, is true, and it is a fact that there is no official protection for extinct species.)

What Makes a Great Golf Course

HOLE NO.

12

An Interview with Peter Oosterhuis

PETER OOSTERHUIS has very likely been exposed to more golf in more places than just about anyone. He first played competitive golf in Great Britain, then went on to claim 19 international events, among them the French, Italian, and Canadian opens. Twice he went the distance at The *Open, finishing as runner-up and ever so close to victory. (*The *Open, of course, is the one that needs no precursor such as "U.S."). He was appointed to six Ryder Cup teams, handily beating some of the best players in the world. Nowadays, to anyone who tunes in to televised golf, Peter is known as the level-headed voice that has occupied the 17th—sometimes 18th—tower for CBS. His broadcasting career is also international, as he provides commentary for The Golf Channel and other networks around the world. His interest in architecture is evident in his thoughtful comments about the golf courses and holes he covers for television audiences. My favorite barb is to suggest that any comments he may have about my designs for new courses had best be restricted to the 17th or 18th hole. After all, I reason, those are the only holes he ever gets to see. Of course, this is just a friendlytease. Peter is a well of ideas and thoughts, and they indeed extend to holes other than the last two, as you will discover below.*

I am indebted to Peter for his friendship and time. During our first discussion about the foreword of this book I realized he has a special perspective on golf courses and how they are laid out. To not tap into that would be a shame. So I spent a few hours talking to him about golf and golf courses.

FIGURE 12-1
Peter Oosterhuis on his usual perch above the 17th or 18th hole of a televised golf event.
COURTESY OF PETER OOSTERHUIS

INFLUENCES

Where did you start playing golf?

I grew up in southeast London and began playing golf at a very small course called Dulwich and Sydenham Hill. It wasn't a great course, but it was tricky. I was only 12 years old and remember that there were blackberry bushes out on the golf course. I went there a couple of times to collect blackberries with my mother and she eventually said, "You're eating too many blackberries. Why don't you hit a ball around instead?" So that's how I started playing. My mother and father both played.

How have your early golf experiences affected you?

Well, I still like blackberries. I think your first golf experience has a lot to do with how you look at golf—and courses. I played for Great Britain in the World Team Championship in 1968, on a four-man team of amateurs, when I was 20 years old. It was played at Royal Melbourne in Australia. The other three members of the British team were Michael Bonallack, who went on to become secretary of the R&A; Ronnie Shade, who was a tremendous amateur and has since passed away; and a great gentleman named Gordon Cosh. So here we were, chosen as the four best amateurs in Britain to represent Great Britain in the World Team Championship. In talking, we discovered that each one of us had grown up on small, unpretentious golf courses where you could shoot low scores if you were a good player. This has always been interesting to me. With all the great courses available—the links courses of Scotland and all the great courses around southeast England—you'd think one of the four would have grown up on a classic course that might have been difficult and more of a challenge. But we all grew up on shortish courses that were relatively easy for a good player.

Is there a lesson to be learned here?

Yes, I think golf should be enjoyable. I think it's possible to ruin the spirit of a beginner if you expose him to golf on too difficult a layout. The four of us played enjoyable courses on which we could relish shooting low scores. Today I sense a pressure on developers—and ultimately designers—to design courses that are challenging before they are fun. I understand the need to market a championship course, but the ultimate goal must be enjoyment. The key is to make courses challenging and yet provide a way for people to play from a set of tees that matches their game. We can learn a lot from the type of course I grew up playing.

Do you believe fun and challenge can coexist?

Yes, I do. I feel that courses where people can score well and make a few birdies give confidence. And confidence can bring more players back to the game—and back to courses to attempt even better scores. This is good for golf. In my opinion, we need to provide realistic sets of tees and make sure courses are set up right after the architect has finished his job. The only thing worse than playing too tough a course is having to spend five hours or more playing that same course!

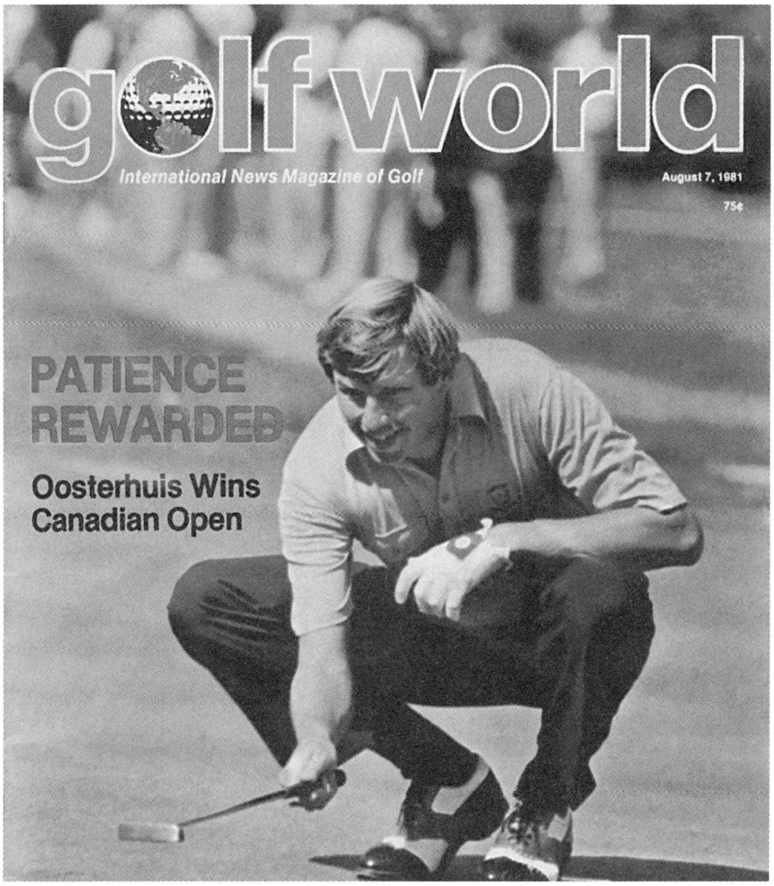

FIGURE 12-2
Oosterhuis on the cover of *GolfWorld* following his victory at the Canadian Open in 1981.

THE GOLF SETTING

What is the primary component of a great course?

I believe the overall setting is key to any great course. Riviera Country Club, where I was director of golf for two years, was always one of my favorite places to play. When I was interviewed for the job, I recall talking about the setting and my fond memories from playing in the Los Angeles Open. Whether they believed it or thought I was just trying to get the job, it certainly was the truth. The location of the clubhouse on the edge of the canyon looking down over the course was important. Setting adds to the aura of a course, whether you're playing a tournament there or playing a casual round.

To be great, does a course always need a spectacular setting?

Certainly not all golf courses can be built along the ocean or a lake, and not all will have remarkable canyons like Riviera. But a course needs to have a certain atmosphere. When there is little in the way of natural setting, it's up to the designer to find whatever about that site is special and highlight it for the golfer. Great courses all have a sense of place, and it's not always about the land.

FIGURE 12-3
View from the 18th fairway at the Riviera Country Club in Los Angeles, California. Oosterhuis was director of golf here in early 1990s.

COURTESY OF RIVIERA COUNTRY CLUB

FIGURE 12-4
Pinehurst in North Carolina is among Peter Oosterhuis's favorite golf places.

BROCHURE COVER FOR PINEHURST, C. EARLY 1930s; COURTESY OF PINEHURST RESORT

How can a great course not have great land?

A great atmosphere can overcome a not-so-good site. Creating a great atmosphere has as much to do with the management and the people as it does the physical land. When I mentioned the aura of a course, I was speaking to this idea; a golf course is a combination of its setting and its ambiance. While I think it's important that the nature of the trees and the land be as good as possible, we have to face the reality that there will need to be golf courses built in settings that are less than desirable from a natural point of view. This is where creativity and imagination come into play.

What are your favorite settings?

Pinehurst in the North Carolina Sandhills is one of my all-time favorite places. The overall feel, the driving through the pine trees, the nature of the course—it all fits. And even in the more mundane corners of the property, it is all held together by a well-thought-out atmosphere. Pinehurst is just as much about a management style as it is about a setting.

It may well be contended that an 'ideal' golf course is an illusion which can never be reached. Perhaps an acceptable definition of an 'ideal' golf course is that it be a severe test for the expert, but perfectly fair to the mediocre player, and withal a thing of landscape art where none of the features jar one's sense of the beautiful.
—*Charles Piper, in* Golf Illustrated, *February 1929*

What should people expect from a great golf course?

I think fun should come first. Golfers might want a challenge, but that's where balance enters the equation. If they choose tees that are too far back and too tough a test, it won't be very much fun. Of course, the course needs to offer some challenge. The result when golfers hit a good shot as opposed to a mediocre shot needs to be worth the effort. If the course is not a challenge, it can become boring. Beyond that, people should expect to be in a nice place. A golf course should be expected to be a thing of beauty with respect to the landscape and detail.

How can we improve the golf experience?

Some golf courses seem more interested in getting people on the course, getting their green fees, and they don't really care about the experience beyond the golf course. They say, "Buy your tee time, play your golf, and disappear." Improvement boils down to changing that attitude. It requires a commitment to better planning and more creativity. Giving people the opportunity to take a little time is part of the outing—and, I think, good business.

Having played throughout the world, was there a place that surprised you in terms of great courses?

I was surprised by the great golf courses in the Sand Belt of Australia, near Melbourne. The Victoria Golf Club, for instance, which is close to Royal Melbourne, is not nearly as famous, but a tremendous place. And there's Yarra Yarra, a terrific course. I guess it should be no surprise that Australian courses, with their British and links-style influence, would be great, but I wasn't expecting it. I have some great memories from Australia, both as an amateur and as a professional.

When did you first take notice of golf architecture?

Well, I wasn't that conscious of golf course architecture, really, until I got away from the Tour and became director of golf at Forsgate Country Club in New Jersey. One of its two courses was designed by Charles Banks. So all of a sudden I was conscious of Charles Banks, and that led to finding out about Seth Raynor and Charles Blair Macdonald. Just a few of the eastern courses those gentlemen did were enough to intrigue me. When you're playing as a touring pro trying to earn money, you tend to just try to figure out the best way to shoot a score. But an appreciation of course design helps you to look at the architect's design strategy and what's behind that strategy.

Where are your favorite memories of courses?

That's a tough one, because as a professional, a favorite course usually has something to do with how you played there. St. Andrews is one of my favorite places—and yes, I played well there twice, although the Open

FIGURE 12-5
St. Andrews, Scotland, is a town built of golfing memories. "There is simply no place in golf where the feeling is as rich and inspiring," says Peter Oosterhuis.
COURTESY OF ST. ANDREWS UNIVERSITY LIBRARY

title somehow managed to escape me! I had a good chance in 1978 when Jack Nicklaus had his second Open win at St. Andrews. There is simply no place in golf where the feeling is as rich and inspiring.

What about St. Andrews makes it a great place?

Going out—all the way out—and then coming back into the town. There's a special atmosphere there, and it has remained basically unchanged over the years. Maybe you wish there was still a railroad line instead of an old course hotel, but the feeling is probably the same to golfers playing there today as 200 years ago.

What about the United States—any favorites?

Pebble Beach and Cypress Point are right up there. Pinehurst No. 2 and Harbour Town would be next.

Because of their setting?

Again, it's the fantastic atmosphere—the whole experience. And that is the great lesson. Not everyone will have the opportunity to play Cypress Point, but the challenge for the designer is to embrace the ideals that made these places great. Each great course has some areas that are less than desirable, even the great places I've mentioned. But the coming into the property; the atmosphere as you're finishing the round, and most everything in between fits together. The architect's goal is to get golfers to say, "Hey, I had a great time. I enjoyed playing this course."

What is the main difference between British and American courses?

Apart from links courses, which are different from other styles and settings, I have to say that British courses tend to have less money available for golf course maintenance—certainly much less than in the United States. So many American courses are manicured beyond belief. They seem to be trying to prove a point that the more money they spend, the more perfect the turf, bunkers, or whatever. At some courses, the goal of perfect conditions has become the most important aspect—more important than good routing, design, and setting.

Is variety good between the continents?

There's nothing wrong with a bit of variety, but the standards at some courses are so high. Developers try to attain it, but it's not realistic. Golfers begin to expect it, but it's not practical.

ON ROUTING

What is your philosophy about starting holes?

You need a hole that is not too difficult but also not too easy—just something to get the round underway and get it moving. The practicalities of getting players onto the course must be taken into account. At Royal Lithum & St. Annes, we see a par 3 in an opening hole—in a major championship, no less—and it works just fine.

What par makes for the best opening hole?

Regardless, it has to fit into the character of the course. The first hole makes you aware of the nature of the course. From a touring pro mentality, I would say a par 5 doesn't make as good an opening hole because all of a sudden you've got all kinds of problems in pace due to people waiting until the green is cleared for their second shots. I have to say par-4s are really the best choice for getting players off the tee and on their way.

What length should the opening hole be?

Medium length, just enough to get the round underway. But again, it needs to fit the land and the character. On a course where length is a key component, you might want an opening hole that gives a hint of what's to come by making the hole a bit on the long side.

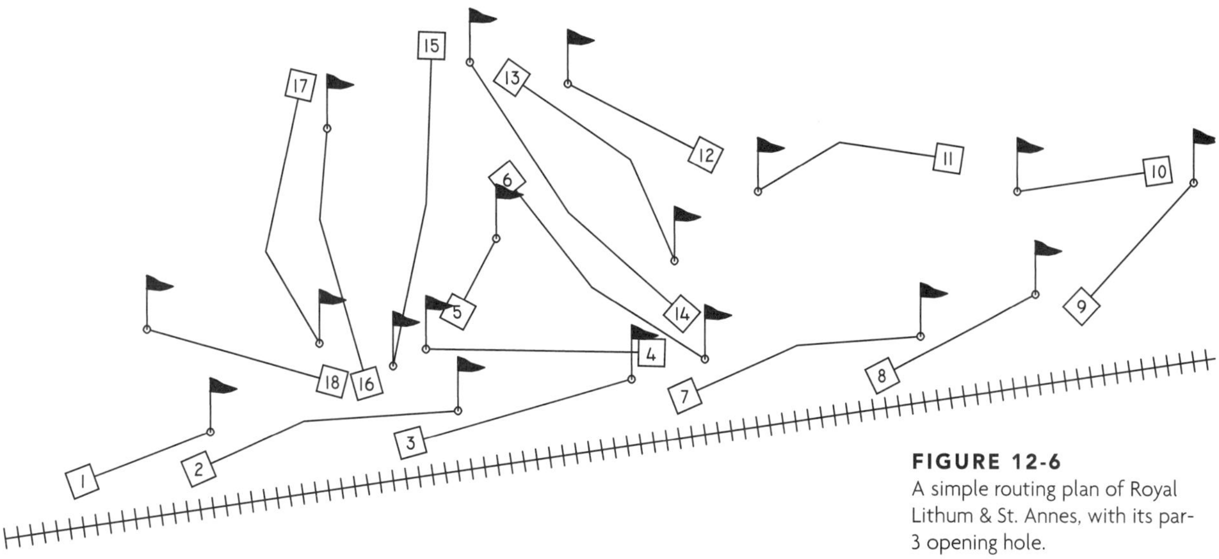

FIGURE 12-6
A simple routing plan of Royal Lithum & St. Annes, with its par-3 opening hole.

COURTESY OF THE CLUB

What about the series of opening holes—what makes sense?

The beginning of any course should be pleasant. I don't think it's right to have particularly difficult opening holes. You're not trying to prove a point; you're just trying to get the play moving, get people into the atmosphere of the course. Ideally, I like to have some time before reaching a par-3, maybe no earlier than the third or fourth. Of course, the par-3 at Royal Lithum & St. Annes at No. 1 is part of the drama, and that's one aspect that sets it apart from most courses.

What about par 5s?

At par 5s, the golfer has more decisions to make. That's one reason I'm not a fan of them for the first hole. But after Hole 1, they can happen any time.

Are finishing holes more important than starting holes?

Definitely, especially if you're going to encourage people to come back, remember the course, and enjoy a little post-round. Golfers should come in off the 18th and think, "Wow! What a great hole that was!" They feel good even if there were some indifferent holes during the round. If they enjoy the finishers, it will probably be a good experience in terms of the golf.

What do you like to see in finishing holes?

My career in television has made me appreciate the power of drama in golf. On TV, we intensify this, of course, but it's a good lesson to follow. The excitement of a round is shaped by the finishing holes—let's say from 15 on home. You kid me about the 17th, so I'll start there. I've

FIGURE 12-7
Desert Mountain's Geronimo Course features a tricky par-3 finishing hole playing from hilltop to ridge. Peter Oosterhuis considers the hole a wonderful finish, and the clubhouse, which sits above the green, to be one of the most comfortable environments and best clubhouse designs anywhere.

COURTESY OF DESERT MOUNTAIN PROPERTIES—COCHISE; JACK NICKLAUS, ASGCA, GOLF COURSE ARCHITECT; BOB BACON, CLUBHOUSE ARCHITECT

always liked a par 5 at 17 because it allows a swing in scores just before the finish but still leaves a fighting chance at the 18th. The 18th should always be a challenging hole, maybe a stern par 4. Perhaps it is better not to have water at the 18th because a bad shot could take away any chance of recovery. We don't want people coming in saying, "I hate this course." Hopefully, the experience of all 18 holes is going to outweigh a bad shot at the last hole, but a lot of water can ruin that possibility.

Can a par 3 make a good finish?

I'm probably used to having the 16th or 17th hole as a par 3, but that doesn't mean the last hole can't be a par 3. What matters is great atmosphere, and if it's a real challenge right in front of the clubhouse, why not?

What would you say to developers of golf courses who are reading this going, "A par 3 on the 18th. He's crazy."?

I would explain the setting, the atmosphere, the excitement of the players, and the enjoyment of the players. If the players walk off the green and say, "Hey, that was really a neat hole," then that speaks well to the overall experience. It couldn't be an ordinary par 3. I'd also point out how the hole fits into the rest of the design. If the setting is right, the routing is right. I'd tell them that golf isn't about standards or necessarily following the norm. At my home club, Desert Mountain in Scottsdale, Arizona, the 18th hole of the Geronimo Course is an excellent par 3; it works really well and creates a setting in front of the clubhouse that is hard to beat.

No game depends so much as golf on its arena for success: on an interesting course an interesting game will be played.

—*John L. Low,* Some Essays on Golf Course Architecture

Has standardization been good for golf?

It's the same as the goal to make all greens an 11 on the Stimpmeter. People feel they need to do certain things because it's the way it's done on tournament courses or because every other owner and developer is doing it. But they're very selective in their emulation. We don't see too many back-to-back par 3s or par 5s, yet one of the greatest courses in the world, Cypress Point, has both. I think golf was not meant to be standardized to the degree it is today.

What is your philosophy about par 3s?

I feel it's important having variety in length. Now, maybe we're falling into the trap of saying, "We have to have four par 3s, one's got to be shorter, so we're going to have two sort of medium length and one longer." That's standardization. I like to see good one-shot holes that fit the land—and the routing. If the opportunity presents itself, let's see five par 3s. If it works out even better, maybe there are only three.

And short par 3s?

You have to encourage precision. It can be short, but it's probably far from easy. A short par 3 can create all sorts of havoc. Most of the trouble lies in the contradictions going on inside the golfer's mind. "Gosh, it's only a 9-iron, should be a piece of cake." Of course, we all know the shortish shots can go astray. On the short par 3 a missed shot is also a missed golden opportunity.

And long par 3s?

I don't think golfers should necessarily be required to hit a fairway wood at a par 3, at least in a calm wind. For the most part, a par 3 should be reachable by golfers with a long iron. Of course, you're talking to a guy who was pretty good with a long iron, so maybe I'm biased. At Riveria's fourth, you have 235 yards, and I always found myself trying to play a 1-iron even in the wind when maybe I should have been playing a soft driver. Again, the hole should fit the land and the layout. That should come first and foremost.

Is there room for new innovations in par 3s—new famous holes?

You have to be careful not to be seen as being too new or different, but if it fits, or seems to fit, then yes. I think there is something to be said

Undoubtedly, special strategy with originality is more interesting than more simple propositions.
—*George C. Thomas Jr.,* Golf Architecture in America

for the island holes. From a dramatic point of view, the 17th at Sawgrass probably has no equal. If it's a windy day, the players are thinking about that hole a long time before they get there. They know the round can be ruined. The pressure builds up on the preceding holes!

What is your philosophy about par 5s?

Well, it's certainly becoming difficult to build a three-shot par 5 for a touring pro. We've seen them reach 642 yards at Southern Hills. The trick is to intensify the risk reward, even for the average player. Players should have to make a weighty decision if they are playing their second shot to the green.

What about par 4s?

Personally, I've always enjoyed the short par 4s; they tempt the player to be aggressive, but the penalty for missing the shot is significant. Variety in par 4s is essential—after all, there are more of them. A long par 4 where the challenge is only in the length is boring. Golfers just don't want to pound the ball and then hit a 3-iron. There needs to be an exciting or fun element.

What are your thoughts on water features?

Some of the classic sites involve water. Many times, just a view of the water can help define the atmosphere of the course. Out on the course, it doesn't take much water to make a statement. A burn just a few feet across can be quite a factor—a real hazard when well placed. Water can add to the beauty of a course, but it should fit in.

Should courses have forced carries?

The routing has to be realistic. We need to make something that's fun for every standard of player, and most often that means there should be a way for the average player to play around a penal hazard. If it's only a short carry, then the rules are different. Every once in a while, it's exciting to be required to play over something. That's part of golf.

How important is balance between the nines?

What's important is treating the routing as 18 holes rather than two nines. It's the 18-hole experience that counts. That usually means balance, but there are exceptions to every rule. If one nine turns out to be par 34 and the other 37, it doesn't matter if it all makes sense and the land is used to its best advantage.

What are your thoughts on the total par of courses?

We're back to standardization and the pros and cons. It's unfortunate that a great par-70 course, which might be more fun to play than an

FIGURE 12-8
A short par 3 of not much over 100 yards is engulfed by water. Peter Oosterhuis believes that, where it makes sense, water is a positive attribute.

COLDWATER GOLF CLUB, AVONDALE, ARIZONA; FORREST RICHARDSON, ASGCA, GOLF COURSE ARCHITECT; © PHOTO COURTESY OF MIKE HOUSKA/DOGLEG STUDIOS

average par-72 course, isn't regarded as well by many golfers. If you use the land properly and have capitalized on the best aspects of the property, you will always come out ahead of trying to fit a certain mould. Overall, I think people are more excited by par 3s and 5s. For that reason, I'd be inclined to attempt three par 5s and five par 3s before just two par 5s and four par 3s. Same par, but a different perspective for the player.

What about the length of courses?

Today it's all about the ability to sell a golf course, whether it's to members or to a resort or whatever. If someone's obliged to create a so-called championship course at 7000 yards, with all kinds of tough hazards, it will be even more crucial to have many tee options. If the play is too difficult, it's just going to be a frustrating experience. I understand the need for the 7000-yard or longer course, but building options into the design has never been more important.

And how do we get players to use the right tees?

That takes clever management. You can set up a course with the appearance of length without having to push players to the back tees. On some holes, length doesn't matter that much, but on others it can cause ten minutes of grief and extra time for everyone on the course to get finished. Architects should probably take a more active role in writing a script for courses—how they are to be set up. At Riviera, I had to guess what George Thomas envisioned. But wouldn't it have been great to have his thoughts written down firsthand in a handbook?

How do you feel about returning nines as opposed to nonreturning nines?

I prefer the going out and coming back.

Why is that?

I think maybe it's the feeling of the continuity—that it's an 18-hole round rather than two 9-hole rounds. When a course goes out and comes back, the transition from the ninth to the tenth is a state of mind, not a physical state. You're out in the wilderness, away from the clubhouse, enjoying the experience of the course. It's part of the round as opposed to an interruption.

ON CLUBHOUSES

You've been to hundreds of clubhouses. What makes a great clubhouse?

The arrival at a golf course needs to create a good first impression. That's part of the atmosphere I spoke about. With respect to clubhouses, they are the "village" that a golfer begins from and will later return to. We underestimate the fact that golf is a social event. It's too bad that people are rushed and they are trying to do so many things in their lives that they can't spend the time to sit down and go over the scorecard and have a drink after their round. A good clubhouse setting and design can help slow people down. Golf is much more of an experience than just hitting shots from tee to green.

Any favorite clubhouses?

If you've shot well, any clubhouse can be a favorite. What makes the historic clubhouses great, of course, is all the history and charm that they've absorbed throughout the years. But in terms of relatively modern clubhouses, I love the clubhouse at my home course, at Desert Mountain's Cochise and Geronimo Courses. It is the design combined with the setting that is special. A clubhouse should entice players to spend time—to complete the golf experience with a drink and good conversation.

ON PRACTICE FACILITIES

What can make practice areas better?

Good targets are essential. There's not much to be gained in striking golf balls without having something to aim at. Targets on ranges should be more than a few flags spaced out every 50-yards. They should look like real golf problems.

What's missing from practice facilities?

I think everybody is delighted when there is a good short game practice area. Every course should also have a decent practice bunker. More shots get taken from within 20 or 30 yards of a green than anywhere else on the course, yet most players neglect their short game practice. A good facility that encourages short game shots is essential.

AREAS FOR IMPROVEMENT

What's your biggest criticism of course design today?

There's too much trying to create a course that's going to challenge the best players in the world when so few courses need to be built that way. If marketing needs say you need to show a tough course, then fine, highlight the toughest holes or shots. But to allow a marketing need to completely take precedence over designing and building the right course for the property, that's crazy.

Should the ball be limited in distance?

I think so. I think if you're talking to the top players, they are all saying that some of the new golf balls not only go farther but they now can be controlled into the greens. So now all of a sudden they've managed to gain extra length with control. There's no denying we've seen extra distance in the last couple of years.

Do you think golfers should be encouraged to walk more often?

I enjoy golf more when I walk. That may be because I grew up walking. The rhythm of the game seems so much better when you walk. You have more of a chance to enjoy the surroundings and appreciate the design features than just going along at 12 miles per hour to the ball.

How can golfers be encouraged to walk?

That's a question better asked of golf course owners. It's a shame that so many places won't even allow golfers to walk. Bringing back caddies would be a good thing because now you've got youngsters involved in golf. I caddied when I was in school. It provided a bit of pocket money, but mostly I was exposed to golf and all the great lessons that can be learned by watching people play the game.

Is the TV influence good for golf?

Well, I would hope so. I would hope that people get excited seeing great shots played on great courses. Hopefully, TV encourages people to go out and play golf, trying to hit the best shots they can. And even though most are never going to hit the ball 280 yards with their 3-wood, hopefully their course can offer up the same challenge on a slightly shorter layout.

Is TV responsible for slowing the game?

Not all on its own. Golf is a drama. The life of golfers out on the course is bound to mimic how they see themselves in relation to the famous and celebrated. Televised golf has a duty to report what's going on. If somebody's playing slower than he should, we should stress how extra time can take away from the rhythm of the game. I feel that good rhythm usually allows players to hit good shots.

What are your thoughts on touring pros and golf course architecture?

Unfortunately, I don't think most touring pros know what the average player wants. But that's not to say there is no value to their involvement. They are hired by the developer, so naturally that's where their marching orders come from. Far too often, the expectation goes back to creating tough courses worthy of play by great professional golfers. That's not necessarily what's best for the customer. I would like to see the touring pros who get involved in course design convincing developers to make the game more fun. [12-9]

What are your feelings about remodeling classic layouts?

Well, there have been good jobs and bad jobs. Sometimes it's not practical to lengthen a course; it just can't be done. It's just a fact of life that the players today play a different game than the players of the 1930s did. The game has changed, so a lot of classic courses don't test the best players the way they were designed to. I do think there's a place for golf courses where the driver isn't the automatic. The trick is providing an option. You can hit the driver if you want to, but the player has to factor in the risk and may want to play more conservatively. The older courses that can't—or shouldn't—be changed might just need to be set up tougher. That's a better policy than redoing them.

Are lay-up shots as much fun as full drives?

They can be. The lay-up shot is a strategic play. Whether you're watching TV or playing, I think people generally want to see the more aggres-

FIGURE 12-9
Peter Oosterhuis (right) looks over a course under construction with author and golf architect Forrest Richardson, ASGCA (center), and Arthur Jack Snyder, ASGCA (left).

sive shot played. However, there is also a satisfaction in seeing a hole played well with good thinking and clever execution. Lay-up shots can definitely be somewhat demanding on their own!

FINAL THOUGHTS

What advice would you give architects today?

Stressing the values—the core values—of the golf course. To use land in the best way possible to create good golf holes. I'd point out that if this is done, it will create a much more marketable course than one built by a formula taken from somewhere else.

What advice would you give developers?

The ambitious developer still thinks he needs a course that off the back tees is over 7000 yards. He feels obliged to be able to say that. But that may not be the best course for his customer. He winds up using extra land, and pretty soon everything starts to cost more. As I said, few courses need to be built to this length or toughness. That's what developers need to hear.

Anything else?

If we do golf right and courses are laid out with care, people can take away from this game a lifetime of great experiences. Not all of them are about hitting the ball or scoring. There is the outdoors, the nature and the beauty of the course. For young people, there are valuable lessons that go along with an individual game such as golf. There are memories of all types. Like the blackberries on the course where I was first introduced to golf—I suppose my mother did the right thing 40 years ago by sending me off to hit a ball about.

Walking the Land

HOLE NO. 13

A clever anesthesiologist was knocking me out for a minor operation. While he prepped the IV, we got to talking and soon discovered our mutual passion for golf. "Have you ever walked out on a golf course early in the morning, before anyone has been there?" he asked. "Have you ever experienced being the first person to walk down a fairway and leave your footprints in the fresh dew, the smell of the golf course all around you—but nothing else?" He continued with this operating room poetry, but that's all I am able to recall. When I woke up, the thought in my mind was exactly as he had left it.

Although there are different ways to appreciate a piece of land, none is as appropriate as walking. I believe this is true of playing golf, just as it is true of getting to know a piece of land that is being considered for golf. Although it is possible to study and ponder land from afar, the situation is like that of my daughter's pediatrician trying to figure out what to do for an awful sore throat over the telephone. Without seeing the patient, an educated guess is the only answer.

PREPARING TO WALK THE LAND

In addition to getting to the site, a host of other preparations may be worthwhile. Too much preparation is not a problem. Just ask Jack Snyder, who accompanied me to a rugged site in the desert east of Scottsdale, Arizona. He was recovering from an appendectomy and had the sense to bring a pillow to hold over the affected area as a way to ease the four-wheel-drive adventure.

Reason for Site Visit

It is imperative that the reason behind the site visit is well understood. Is it to evaluate a piece of land initially, with no immediate expectation of a routing plan? Or is it to verify site conditions, views, and nuances of the land in order to draft a routing plan—or multiple plans as options? Is it to follow up on ideas that have been drafted for a routing plan, to verify specific options and alignments that are about to be committed to a presentation? The reason for the site trip boils down to the point in the process to which the project has matured.

The fundamental reason to visit any project is to see the property firsthand, to solidify impressions, to meet people, and to make endless notes on maps about what is possible and what is not. Routing in the absence of a personal visit to a site can and does occur. Mostly, however, this is poor practice. The investment in a golf course, not to mention all of the planning that goes into one, is significant in terms of effort, costs, and fees, at least usually. To not opt for a site visit by the golf course architect—and, for that matter, other members of the team with responsibility for the routing plan(s)—sends a very early signal about the approach to the project. To elaborate on advice given earlier, it is always best for the doctor to see the patient before making a diagnosis.

FIGURE 13-1 A weary group poses in front of their vehicle, a large transport helicopter that was provided by Soviet officials. (I, delighted to be on the ground, am second from right.)

A situation where it may be acceptable to make a site evaluation from afar—without a visit—is the case where only a general opinion is needed on the viability of a site for golf. Once a review of the available data is made, it can be determined whether or not a trip to the site is warranted. In the instance of such a remote evaluation, data can be gleaned from maps and an opinion rendered by phone or a written report. Still, there may be—in fact, there *will* be—good, bad, and evil that cannot be seen until more research is conducted. An essential part of this research is an actual visit to the site.

You are the routing plan—the wider your education and experiences the better it will be.
—Desmond Muirhead

There is also a difference between flying over a site and actually setting foot on the ground. True, you can get a good look at the land from the air, but the details and subtleties relevant to golf should come from the perspective from which golf is played. Golf is not played from helicopters or low-flying aircraft. Very large sites may be reconnoitered from the air, but the finer points of routing are unlikely to be worked out from this vantage.

Getting There

Another image that comes to mind is the film *Planes, Trains, and Automobiles* with the late funnyman John Candy. Because golf course sites are often remote, it can be quite interesting (and entertaining) to make the journey. This is perfectly acceptable, and golf course architects and planners tell many good stories about jumping in helicopters, small planes, boats, and beat-up trucks to access the top of a mesa or floor of a valley. Upon arrival, occasionally, there isn't much to see.

The best advice about accessing sites is to plan ahead and leave plenty of buffer in the schedule for finding your way into and out of the brush while still leaving time to catch the flight back to civilization. Projects located in urban areas are more a matter of getting good directions, not to mention parking where no one will steal your car or briefcase.

Advance Arrangements

Locked gates, the Weather Channel, cattle, bears, mountain lions, four-wheel drive, deer-hunting season, snake species identification book, language interpreters, and maps with a standard scale—you can draw your own conclusions about this list of What You May Find or Need. Every site is different, so arrangements will fluctuate depending on the where, when, and who of the site visit.

One of the most important preparations is a study of the site by way of maps, aerial photos, and site snapshots. These tools allow areas of the site to rise to the top of the interest meter, resulting in better use of the time allotted for visiting the site.

Additionally, if programming for the project has already been considered or formulated, related data and documents should be reviewed in advance. This goes for other commissioned and existing site research. Examples are soils tests, environmental assessments, and water quality reports. Climate information, regional land plans, and entitlement issues

The Secret Topo — A Short Story

The trip to Vladivostok, Soviet Union, involved nine Americans: a planner, two developers, two golf course management executives, a construction executive, two golf course architects, and an interpreter. Our charge was to investigate a large uninhabited peninsula, really an island, and determine the viability of turning it into a destination resort with multiple golf courses.

Before we left home, we asked the Russians to send us a copy of the topo for the land. The idea was for us to study the site and form general opinions before getting there. But no topo arrived before we left.

When we arrived in Russia, one of the first questions asked was about the topo. "Topo is coming soon," came the reply. We believed this and spent the next 24 hours adjusting to the time change a world away.

The next day arrived, but no topo. And then the second day. The third. And a fourth. We had eaten plenty of Russian cuisine. Drank plenty of Russian "mystery juice." And sipped plenty of Russian vodka. Each of these was a precious commodity. Topo, apparently, was even more precious. So, too, was the ability to actually visit the site. Our hosts took us to virtually every corner of Vladivostok and the surrounding countryside except the focus of our visit, the site itself.

That we were in Russia trying to design such a major project and had neither visited the site nor been given topographical maps began to disturb us. While the developers met behind closed doors to discuss financial issues, the architectural and design contingency toured buildings, fisheries, and technical schools. When we inquired when we would visit the site, we were told the weather was not right for the helicopter. When we asked about the maps, we were told they would be ready soon.

The requests for maps were beginning to get old, both for us and for the Russians. Finally, in the context of a financial discussion, one of the developers made a strong request that we all really needed to get to the site and "by the way, topo maps would be helpful." This seemed to work, likely because developers tend to talk finances and finances tend to mean business. That evening we were informed that we would visit the site in the morning, by helicopter. The anticipation mounted. After being in the Soviet Union for almost five days, we had not even visited the site, where there was much work to be done, nor had we any idea beyond a road map what the land really looked like. In fact, a map of North Korea that I had purchased back in Phoenix actually showed the peninsula land—it was just under 1/4 inch long and, if you really tried, you could make out the way the ocean and bay formed the protrusion of land. This had been our only reference. A dot on the map which had been pointed to by pencils, pens, and fingers.

As it happened, we did take off in the morning but could not land due to windy conditions. Our helicopter was a massive beast that could hold 45 soldiers. On this day there were just nine of us and an equal number of local officials. We did manage a great flyover of the property. It was absolutely breathtaking. Still, we needed maps!

That night—the end of our fifth day in Russia—we conspired how to get maps. It was like a secret meeting of the nine Americans, plotting about who to ask next...and wondering why it was so damned hard to get a topo map. True, placing a phone call to the United States involved five or six Russians, and even then you might reach Ohio, perhaps northern California, or occasionally New York. The economy and infrastructure were crumbling. We could see this, yet it still seemed odd that no topo map had been presented.

The topo map appears! I study the long-awaited map as Russian officials look on with watchful eyes.

That night, we cooked pasta for our hosts; we had brought it from the States complete with meat sauce. They had never had any such a delicacy and were grateful for the cultural enlightenment. It must have worked. We were told that the next morning we would *drive* to the site and that — they promised — "topo will be in morning for you." Translated: Topo will be available tomorrow.

This indeed did happen. The drive itself is another story altogether. Arriving at last was a magical experience. Finally, we were at the site and not hovering in a military helicopter at 1000 feet. Our motorcade made its way across dirt trails, and for the next several hours we absorbed the site and its tremendous potential. Toward the end of the afternoon, we arrived at an old mansion that had been used for bombing practice. As we explored the ruins, we noticed a man in a trench coat unfolding a small map. Alas! Topo.

We learned later that the topo was government property and, as such, was closely guarded. In fact, it was stamped CEKPEm (SECRET). On the way back home a few days later, I had the terrifying realization that contained in my briefcase was a secret Russian document. The thought crossed my mind that I might be detained by the Russians and accused of spying. That, too, is another story.

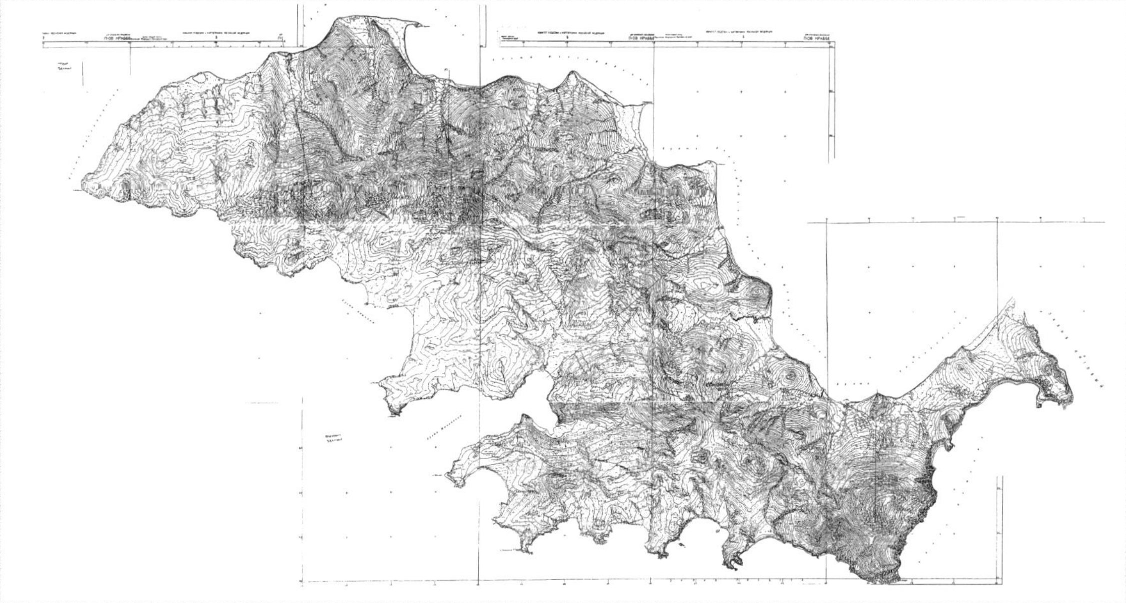

One of the actual — and elusive — topo maps for The Peninsula project in Asiatic Russia. Along the edges of the map was the word "SECRET" in Russian. Luckily for me, although I carried the map back through customs and immigration checkpoints, the map did not raise any suspicions.

must be known. These reports and documents should be among the materials rounded up and forwarded for review prior to the initial site visit.

Other useful thoughts on advance arrangements:

- Check weather forecasts
- Schedule appointments

  It may be useful to coordinate meetings with local representatives, adjacent property users, local golf course construction resources, etc.
- Schedule times

  Sites and lighting look different at different times of the day and from different vantage points. For this reason, it may be good to visit early and later in the day to experience the diversity of sunlight and glare conditions.
- Obtain topographical and base mapping

  Including all property boundaries, utilities, and restricted areas (see Hole 11, "Programming & Site Evaluation," for complete lists of useful data for mapping).
- Verify map availability

  It is common for people at or near the site to promise maps when you arrive; this not only diminishes the opportunity to study maps and land in advance but, often, for one reason or another, the maps never show up. Insist, if you can, on receiving maps in advance.
- Verify map scale

  Until you have been in the field with a map that has been "conveniently" sized on a Xerox machine and at a scale of 1 inch to 315 feet, you have not experienced a true mathematical crisis. Accurate scale is important, preferably 1 inch to 200 feet, which works nicely for normal-size sites, and perhaps 1 inch to 400 feet for very large sites.
- Obtain any previous routings

  Often, previous planning and feasibility studies were made of the site; acquire these documents for reference if appropriate and available.
- Obtain any environmental assessments

  These may include full environmental assessments, wetlands reports, and hazardous materials reports.
- Obtain any soils and water reports

  Existing soils reports and surface water and groundwater reports are often useful in determining present conditions at the site. Even reports from neighboring land of a similar type and configuration can be used as a gauge in understanding regional conditions.
- Drainage data

  Drainage reports and studies are useful as they can paint the picture of what happens to the land during heavy precipitation. Often, an engineer can supply data indicating the CFS (cubic feet per second) of existing drainageways, streams, and ravines, both for normal flows and flows during flood conditions.
- Advance survey points

  It is sometimes warranted to have survey points placed in the field to assist in getting your bearings, to identify where property begins and ends, and to identify any other important location not apparent on maps or survey plans.

What to Bring

Here are notes on what is appropriate to take along when you venture into the field to look at a site (obviously, not all sites require all items):

- Maps, aerials, land plans
- Existing routing plans
- Rain gear

  Rain jacket and umbrella.
- Insect repellent

  This might not work for chiggers and ticks but does for most insects.
- Sunscreen and hat
- Camera

  To take snapshots of features, views, etc. Video also can be useful as it captures more of the experience, including that of your voice and panting when going uphill.
- Scale

  For measurement and scaling plan dimensions.
- Pens, pencils, and highlighting pens

  Highlighting pens can be useful for marking plans in different colors to distinguish areas, features, green sites, etc.
- Compass
- Hand site level

  An excellent tool for checking grades across nominal areas. A hand site level is a small, hand-held telescope with an internal bubble level. When you look through the tube, you see the level and can zero in on a reference point, such as a person's beltline or a point on the ground that is level with your eyesight. Through a simple calculation, you can see if land a considerable distance away is lower or higher than your position, and by approximately what differential.
- Tape measure

  A 300-foot tape is often useful to check distances, especially in difficult terrain, where it may be hard to pace accurately to determine an approximate distance.
- Flagging ribbon

  Useful to mark your way in heavy brush and woodland sites.
- Change of clothes

  Socks and shoes especially.
- Water and trail snacks
- Cell phone and two-way radios

  Two-way radios are great for communicating across a site when someone goes ahead to see if there are any good green sites, or bears.
- Club and balls

  If you feel compelled to bring a club and balls, try a 6-iron; it works best to approximate most lousy tee shots and can be used to duplicate virtually any approach shot you may want to try hitting.

The Universal Laws of Maps

1. Any two or more maps that must be matched together will meet along a line that passes through the most important point or points to be studied.
2. Gusts of wind occur only when maps are unrolled and being held by the slightest of grasping pressure.
3. It takes 12 minutes to find a map that has been set down in a field no matter how large the site or how much brush is present.

Who to Bring

There may be reasons to bring a civil engineer, a representative of the developer, and various other people who will have great influence of the routing. Ideally, the golf course architect and land planner should have some private time to absorb and experience the site. Whether this is entirely alone will depend on the makeup of the team preparing the routing. To see the site at different times of the day it is good advice to plan your day so this can occur. I very often will walk with a group, but then by myself or with only a few people. It is generally easier to work out solutions when alone than it is in a group.

At a project that shall remain nameless, a land planner who was responsible for the entire planning process never managed to find time to personally visit the site, although his staff made visits, as did I. At more than one meeting, our mutual client inquired what the planner felt about the site, only to find that he had not yet been there. This planning group was eventually replaced on the project, and I suspect that the lack of a personal visit was the reason.

GPS Control

GPS (global positioning system) equipment can be effective in locating points in the field and in recording points found. Such equipment, because of its increased affordability, is now an excellent and efficient method of finding your way—and working on routing specific concepts—while in the field. GPS equipment can be calibrated to a specific site, or off-the-shelf equipment can be used to record reasonably accurate bearings. Such bearings may be calibrated later by an engineer and transferred to a specific site plan. This is a valuable way to record and define interesting spots.

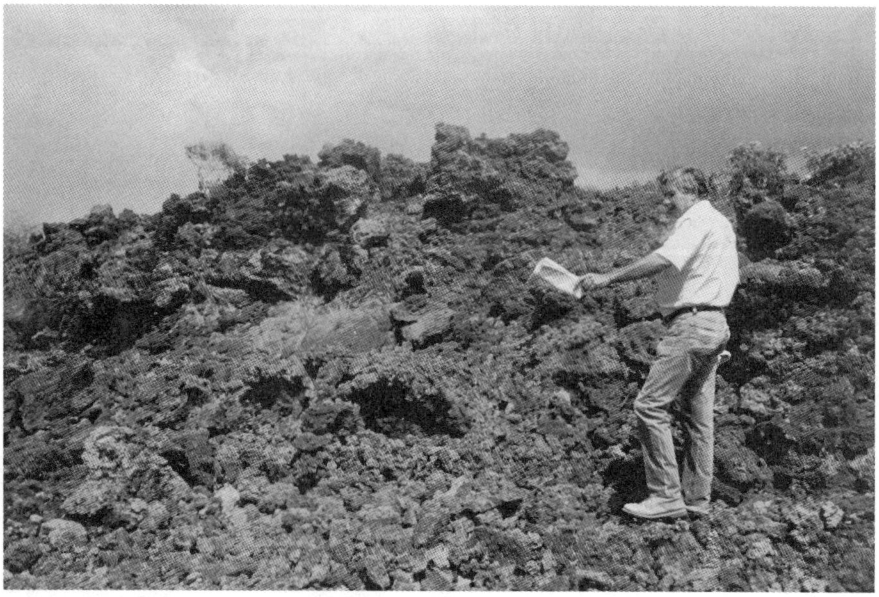

FIGURE 13-2
This Hawaiian site, completely covered in crunchy lava known locally as a'a, was an especially rough walk. It is often smart to have a golf course construction expert on hand to render an opinions on how a project might be built — indeed, *if* it can be built! The late George Biersdorf, my friend and a veteran of building golf courses in Hawaii on extremely tough sites, is pictured here.

FIGURE 13-3
Dramatic features, such as this natural rock ledge, may not show up on topographical maps. Without visiting a site personally, the nuances of such features cannot be appreciated. The golf course architect may miss a wonderful opportunity.

© PHOTO COURTESY OF MIKE HOUSKA/DOGLEG STUDIOS; BROKEN TOP GOLF CLUB; JAY MORRISH, ASGCA, AND TOM WEISKOPF, GOLF COURSE ARCHITECTS

Portable laptop computers and hand-held displays can also be used in the field. Site maps can be loaded in advance and referred to as a field visit takes place. Technology is changing rapidly, and the latest equipment is bound to be months old. This requires the golf course router to stay up to speed on the newest advancements in satellite technology and the world of GPS and GIS (geographic information systems) tools. Timeless in tradition and known for its remarkable ability not to crash or lose battery power, the old-fashioned map printed on cheap paper should not necessarily be discarded in favor of the technology of the moment.

THE WALK ITSELF

Rarely is a site visit a walk in the park, unless it is an actual park. Even when the terrain is relatively easy, hot days, cold days, rainy days, snowy days, and days when Murphy's Law is in effect can complicate an otherwise simple walk. The advance logistics of obtaining permission, getting keys necessary to open gates, and knowing what dangers may lurk in the bulrushes should be worked out in detail. The adventure awaits.

The pitfalls of a site visit can be amusing. Private property can be a problem if no one knows you are coming. Getting stuck, as yours truly did miles from civilization in a four-wheel-drive Chevrolet Suburban, can

Let those who are designing the links walk slowly and meditatively over nearly every square yard of the land at least two or three times before coming to any final decision as to where to place a single tee, bunker or hole.
—*Harry Vardon,* Aspects of Golf Course Architecture

be both embarrassing and expensive. Hostile transients living in the wild can account for quite a surprise. Add to this the occasional volcano, swamp, or wild dog, and you might as well be in an episode of *Survivor.*

At one site, I was hiking all by myself and came face to face with what I have described since as a mountain man. Not Bigfoot, mind you, but a definite human making unfriendly grunts. At his side was a dog, and I can still feel the rush of adrenaline that came over me as we stared at each other wondering what to do. I turned around and walked back down the hill. When I got to the bottom, I scratched out the idea of a tee up there. Didn't seem like a good place.

Getting Oriented

Orientation can be attained in a variety of ways. Site variation means differences in the reference points and methods used to gain bearings. The following are common features and methods that can be used for this purpose:

- Fence alignments

  Note that fences do not always follow property lines.
- Utility poles

  Poles show up excellently on aerial photos due to the shadows they cast, but they do not always appear on base mapping.
- Prominent topographical features
- Drainage courses

  These are usually evident in the field and on topographical maps, as they are low areas of linear proportions.
- Ridges and high points

  They are often easier to detect than low points because they are defined by obvious locales or ridge lines that seem to standout across a site.
- Prominent trees

  If denoted on mapping data, they can be used for reference; if not, they should be integrated into the data for a site.
- Buildings
  - Roads and trails
- Water

  Ponds, springs, streams, etc.
- Survey points

  Occasionally some nice fellow has left a survey point in the field; it may be a benchmark, monument, or other marking (just make sure it's accurate).
- GPS

  A surefire way to know where you are at all times; infinitely more useful when your mapping is calibrated to your GPS device.

What to Look For

When on a site, no matter how flat, uninteresting, or far opposite these conditions, the order of the day is to record what you see and find interesting. Chances are that the things you determine are interesting

FIGURE 13-4
Prominent features are excellent points for orienting oneself in the field. Pictured is golf course architect Arthur Jack Snyder, ASGCA.

at a virgin site will also be interesting, if they can be retained, on a finished golf course. All golf courses have features—tees, fairways, greens, bunkers—this goes without saying. These features can usually be envisioned as they are familiar to those who know golf. It is the things we cannot necessarily walk across, or perhaps things we might not ordinarily consider, that need scrutiny in walking the land. The trick is to think beyond that of a golfer. When your perspective is versatile you begin to appreciate qualities that can take a good plan and make it a great plan. From the viewpoint of an ant you appreciate the detail and the make up of soil. From the viewpoint of the bird you appreciate how the land unfolds across an entire region. The perspective of the golfer, albeit crucial, is not exclusive. The subtleties of the land, the views, natural features, and unique land relationships that are most often there to begin with need only be discovered. Here is a list of what to look for and record as you evaluate a site during a field visit:

- Drainage conditions

  Look upstream of low points to see the conditions of the drainageway leading to the low point.

- Sunlight conditions

  View angles and distant land features, such as mountain ranges, that might contribute to loss of sunlight at certain times of the day or year.

- Views

  Views are always best appreciated in person and, when possible, at different times of the day. Remember: views include those to other parts of a site and those away from a site to distant landmarks.

[H]e who cannot see such natural features and take full advantage of them is ill fitted for work in this field.
—*Robert Hunter,* The Links

- Soils

  Have a general awareness of soil types and differences from area to area.
- False topo

  Trees in gulches can conceal significant topographical features, especially on preliminary topographical mapping that has not been verified in the field. Additionally, outdated topographical data may not reflect recent erosion, excavation of materials from the site, dumping, and flooding.
- Trees and vegetation

  Note areas of interest, diversity, and intensity.
- Damaged areas

  Identify areas scarred from brush fires, clearing, or dumping of debris.
- Features not identified

  Anything prominent should be identified for placement on a base map and the finished routing plan.

Finding & Determining the Golf Areas

Golf areas are all of the areas where golf improvements may eventually be built. They comprise all of the parts of the puzzle that make up the golf facility. Finding golf areas involves paying attention to these puzzle parts and project programming, together with the many considerations discussed in previous chapters. It also requires knowledge of how holes are fit together and insight into how the routing plan will eventually shift from a bunch of notes and impressions to an actual routing plan. The same understanding applies to determining golf areas. The distinction between *finding* and *determining* deserves explanation.

Finding is as implied. The role of the router is to dig deep into the makeup of the land and *find* the opportunities, if any, for placing golf holes and features into naturally conducive areas that will yield an interesting and pleasing result. An example of this is a hilltop and gently winding swale measuring about 1200 feet in length. From the hilltop you might have an excellent view to a valley far away. The swale joins another swale at its end. From the description, without benefit of other data, you can appreciate that this might make a terrific and natural par 4, with the tees atop the hill and the fairway winding along the swale to a point just before it meets the other swale. In this case not much effort is required to make the golf hole. Finding it was about all that is required. The same approach holds true at a rock quarry where a par 5 is routed along the cliff above the quarry itself. Although not a natural feature, the quarry is a *found* feature and it does nicely to create the basis for a golf hole.

Determining is the act of solidifying what has been found, or envisioning what may be built to improve on the found conditions. When a golf area or component is *determined,* artificial grading may be needed to make it work. A general concept of routing is that determining found features is usually much better than determining ones that require artificial efforts. Exceptions abound. At Shadow Creek in Nevada, barren, flat land was transformed by Tom Fazio into a grotto of trees, streams, ponds, and lush landscaping—at the cost of many millions of dollars beyond that spent on any golf course up to that point. As at many barren

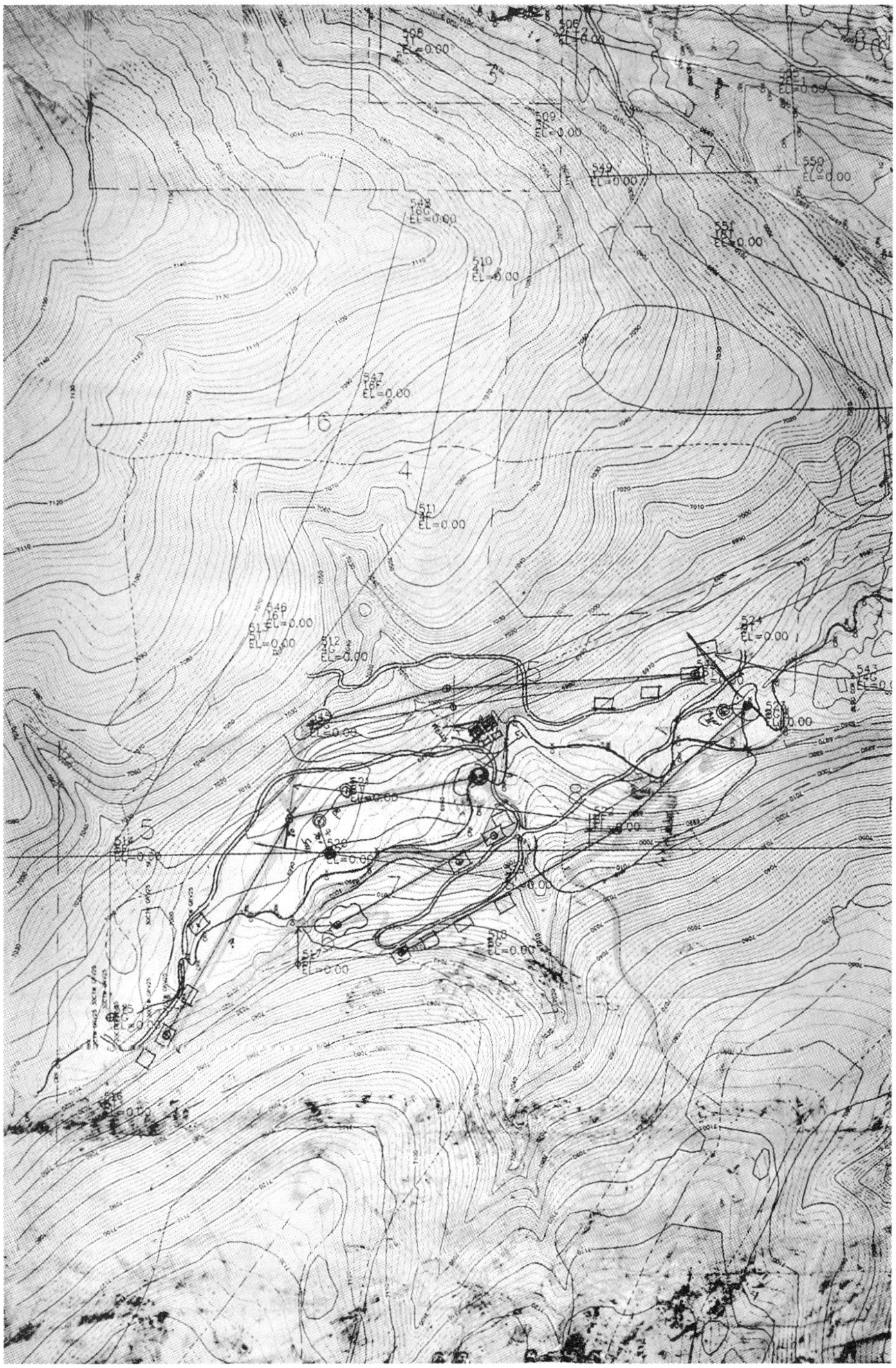

FIGURE 13-5

Determining golf areas is accomplished in a multitude of ways. Often, the alignments for holes are roughly penciled in on the topographical map and then these areas verified in the field by comparing the alignment of holes to actual conditions. In this example, holes have been drawn on a map while in the field. Note that the cart path alignment has also been sketched. This prevents the situation where access to a golf hole is unplanned and therefore poorly executed as an afterthought.

FROM THE HIDEOUT GOLF CLUB, MONTICELLO, UTAH; REFER TO FIGURE 10-5 FOR THE FINAL ROUTING PLAN OF THIS AREA: HOLES 6, 7, 8, AND 15.

SCAFFOLDING IS CHEAP
Relatively speaking. An accurate way to assess the exact view from an unbuilt clubhouse veranda is to have scaffolding erected on the intended site. If a 6-foot fill is expected and the second story planned to 10 feet above the grade, then 16 feet of scaffolding height is required. *(Courtesy of Gil Martinez, land planner)*

sites, not much could be found. The only approach was to find ways to make it work. In the case of Shadow Creek, the effort was taken to the extreme.

The following golf areas constitute the puzzle parts most important to identify when walking a site:

- Access points
- Clubhouse location
  Parking, grounds, cart staging, practice putting greens, etc.
- Beginning points
  First hole, tenth hole, practice tees, etc.
- Tee sites
  Places at which golf holes can begin.
- Green sites
  Places at which golf holes can end.
- Natural features
  For use as hazards, landmarks, points of interest, and visual aesthetics.
- Maintenance area access and location

The impetus to find golf areas is overridden by the need to find features that cannot be duplicated, if any exist. At almost all costs, such features should be given the utmost consideration in becoming part of the routing plan. Sometimes it may, at first, seem crazy to save a particular feature. The point to keep in mind is that once abandoned, such features cannot, probably, be recreated. It is always best to argue for saving natural or special features, at least initially.

On a course completed several years ago, an old stone cistern measuring about 20 feet by 20 feet was integrated with the routing plan on the fairway of a hole. The idea was to consider actually filling it with water. With berms around, it was felt that any inconvenience to the golfer would be not much different than that of a small pond in the same location. But what a conversation piece. A historic structure made of natural stone that was once used to hold well water for cattle would become part of the course. Although the idea stayed on the routing plan, it was nixed during the phase when we prepared final construction documents. "Too different" was the justification made by the client and management team. The cistern hazard bit the dust. Today there remains just a plaque describing it. It is doubtful that many bother to read it.

What to Watch For

Besides the warnings made previously, both outright and implied, you would do well to be careful and aware of the following:

- Barbed wire
- Leaving gates open
  The only thing more embarrassing than letting cattle roam onto an interstate highway is having to show up for the resulting court hearing.
- High altitude effects

- Accidental fires

  Catalytic converters under vehicles can easily ignite standing brush.
- Crossing highways
- Flash floods
- Bees

  I enjoy honey; I do not enjoy swarms of angry bees.
- Unstable land

  Abandoned mines and lava tubes (naturally formed caves under lava that cooled quickly) come to mind; both can be unexpected and outright dangerous.
- Setting plans down

  And forgetting where you put them.
- Hazardous areas

  Pay attention to the warnings that come with landfill projects and reclamation sites; they pertain to access and the potential dangers prior to removal or cleanup of hazardous materials.
- Existing golf uses

  Flying golf balls do not necessarily stop when the golf course architect is wandering around the site of an expansion or remodeling project; always stay alert and remember, "fore" means business.

BALLOONS AS SITE REFERENCE

At a site in Phoenix, we used ordinary colored helium balloons to mark the tees, angle points, and greens of holes along an existing development. They were easier to set than stakes and were less permanent, which we felt was a better choice. It was also amusing to picture the surveying crew purchasing 40 balloons at the local party store and getting them to the site.

THE SECOND SITE VISIT

The follow-up site visit can be, and usually is, an important aspect of walking the land. To adequately complete a routing plan, typically more than one visit to the site is needed. The second (or third, fourth, etc.) visits are used to verify assumptions made after the initial visit and to further set points and angle points. This is when the routing is solidified in terms of its usefulness. Changes and site visits beyond this point are usually performed in the green-light phase of the project and when design plans and construction documents are moving toward completion. The same suggestions and warnings pertain to subsequent site visits.

Setting Center Points & Angle Points

A valid survey is undertaken following an initial visit to set tee, angle, and green points so they can be inspected by the golf course architect. The most common way of setting such points is by driving a property stake into the ground and placing a length of plastic PVC pipe over the stake so it can be seen from a distance. The length of pipe can be from 10 to 15 feet or more depending on the amount of brush, height of trees, and blind conditions created by the terrain. The PVC pipe sleeves are painted in "official" colors used for such purposes: red for tees, blue for angle points, and green for greens. It is essential to recommend that the PVC pipe is long enough to be effective and that paint colors are fluorescent so they can be seen across long distances. Also, colors must be adjusted for terrain. In dense, bright green foliage, it may be best to use bright pink instead of green for greens.

Those Are Not Sand Fleas — A Short Story

Finally, the plane took off; the thunderstorm was behind us. It had been quite a day. We had arrived in San Antonio early that morning and were driven to the site, where we spent the day wandering around in the brush and making notes on the topo map we'd been sent earlier in the week. It was a fine site for a golf course. Our job was to put some early routing concepts on paper and see what could be done with the balance of the land. Our client was looking to purchase the property. As yet, no firm decision had been made to buy the 400 acres across the highway from the Sea World amusement park.

I was glad to be leaving. The next morning I had to be up early for a flight to Honolulu. There were supposed to be a few hours between the two trips. Now I'd be lucky to have half a night's sleep.

Before I knew it, blue waters were beneath me, and the plane was on its final approach to my favorite islands. This trip was to be part work and part R&R. Thankfully, the first part would be the R&R.

After only one day on the beach, I noticed something new. Sand fleas seemed attracted to my ankles. I did not remember sand fleas in Hawaii before. It seemed odd. After a few more days, the sand fleas continued. Interestingly, my wife, the person in our family who usually is an attractive target for annoying insects, seemed totally immune. That seemed odd, too.

After ten days in Hawaii, I returned home. It was great to be back at the work I love. While the trip was worthwhile, there's no place like home. One of the first calls I made was to my mentor, Jack Snyder. And one of the first things Jack asked me was "So, how are your chiggers?" *"Chiggers?"* I said. "What do you mean?" Jack explained that everyone who had accompanied us on our hike in San Antonio, including him, had brought back chiggers. "Well, I *have* been bothered by sand fleas," I told him. Laughing, Jack said, "Those are not sand fleas!"

And so began my education about one of the worst nightmares walking land has to offer—chiggers. What an awful animal!

> *The insertion of the small fangs into the skin is painless, and is merely intended to puncture the skin so that the feeding process can begin. Once fixed, the larva injects into the wound a fluid which breaks down the cells underlying the outer layers of the skin. The liquid food resulting from the process is sucked back into the digestive system of the larva. The alternation of injecting and sucking then continues for two or three days until the larvae is fully fed and has increased in size three or four fold. During the whole period of feeding, the chigger does not change its position on the host. The popular belief that it burrows into the skin to feed and lay eggs is quite erroneous. Studies reveal no trace of a tunnel and since the larva is sexually immature it cannot lay eggs. The irritant effect of the fluid injected by the larva causes a skin reaction characterized by small inflamed pimples and intense irritation. Once the larva has finished feeding it drops to the ground to complete its life-cycle. It descends into the soil and, after a period of five or six weeks, changes into an eight-legged nymph.*

That, my friends, is the description of a chigger, compliments of an agricultural extension office of a leading university. A small reddish insect no bigger than the head of a large pin. Even many years later, it gives me the heebie-jeebies.

FIGURE 13-6
Establishing cleared paths along the centerlines of golf holes is often necessary in order to verify that routing plans will work and are practical. This is true mostly of sites with dense brush and vegetation. In this example, a preliminary routing plan was created, and the golf architects are clearing a path to better access the site and make final adjustments to the plan in advance of the final entitlement process. Care is taken to clear around large trees and to avoid unnecessary disturbance of natural features.

A funny story told by golf course architect Bill Coore involved the staking of points at his Talking Stick layout in Scottsdale, Arizona. The land was completely flat before he began, with little vegetation taller than a large dog in the way; nevertheless, the staking process was carried out the way he and partner Ben Crenshaw had always done it: Set property stakes and put 15-foot PVC pipe over them, etc. According to Coore, the result looked like a project by the landscape artist Christo. "You could see every single one of the stakes from any vantage point," Coore admitted. "Even we were confused when we got on site."

The point of setting points is obvious: It establishes exact points with exact distances between them, and this allows verification of whether or not the conditions work in the real world like they seem to on the small-scale plans. Points are often changed on site evaluation. Changes are defined by noting the offset based on compass directions or may be done by GPS/GIS. While Coore and Crenshaw might have benefited from lower profile staking, the effort was still worthwhile. Without staking, nothing can be proved to work.

Site Visits as Tours

It is not good form to take dignitaries to a site before you know what might go where. This includes CEOs, mayors, and investors. Too many initial comments can be made that can immediately preclude good design from seeing the light of day. Although casual visits may be acceptable, "guided tour" visits are best kept until a decent routing plan is conjured and can be articulated well by its creator.

As part of the entitlement process, or the process leading up to the entitlement process, it is useful to invite representatives from jurisdictional agencies to the site to look at specific areas and provide in-person input on areas over which they have approval power or oversight. Participation is key. By involving people in the process, you gain their trust and, you hope, their assistance in getting problems worked out if they arise.

Two examples come to mind. The first involved the city council of a major U.S. city whose approval was needed for the development of a golf course on environmentally sensitive land to be leased from the city. The developer took a calculated risk by nearly strong-arming the council members into spending one of their many meetings on the controversial project in the field. "How else can you make an effective decision?" he reasoned. The council agreed, and it became my job to lead a contingent across acres of wilderness to show them, firsthand, the existing condition of the land and what we were planning to do to improve areas and make way for a world-class golf course. (*Note:* Yes, even though I am usually critical of this term, I felt compelled to use it due to the political nature of the situation. My apologies to anyone of whom I was critical for using the term.) The meeting paid off nicely, with the council members acknowledging that they had been hearing a bunch of nonsense about the awful things that would befall the city if the golf course were to be built. We also videotaped the tour. I believe this made its mood more formal and decreased the chance of a free-for-all in terms of opinion and conjecture. After all, there was record of the tour, and no one could deny what was seen or discussed.

The second situation involved realigning a stream back to where it was before being diverted to make way for a road. Our design called for the stream to be put back in the low swale of a part of the site, yet this was not allowed without the approval of several agencies, including the U.S. Army Corps of Engineers. We decided to invite the Corps to the site and show them the environmental benefits of what we were planning. Again, it was a calculated risk. What if the representative said, "Absolutely no way"? Well, that didn't happen. We didn't let it. By having our ducks in a row, we came across professionally, and it was obvious we had done our homework and knew the issues. The site visit went extremely well, and so did the eventual project.

Blank Canvas to Solution

HOLE NO.

14

Golf course architects are frequently asked this question: "How do you begin laying out golf holes on a piece of property?" Answering in just a few sentences amounts to boiling down all of the previous 13 chapters to a few passing thoughts. Although we can make those thoughts sound pretty good, the effort trivializes what we do. People want to know about the magic that happens when a blank piece of paper turns into a routing plan—all of the other stuff is not nearly as exciting or romantic. Occasionally, this same discriminatory interest leads to the demise of a routing plan. When the person doing the routing cuts to the chase and begins transforming the blank canvas without proper respect for the process, the resulting routing plan is often no better than a pretty picture. In transforming the blank canvas, our energy is spent sorting through what is functional and efficient, and, hopefully, we try not to forget the absolute need to be interesting and creative at the same time. This is a juggling act.

An open mind is the best to begin with.
—*Harry Vardon,* Aspects of Golf Course Architecture

Up in the air are hundreds of considerations, rules, opinions, needs, wants, realities, dangers, and objectives. More seem to come out of nowhere. What we thought would work will not. What we thought would not work will. Creating a routing plan is like playing Pickup-Sticks. A bunch of sticks are dumped into a pile and, carefully, the players begin removing them one by one, being cautious not to disrupt the pieces that are still piled up. In routing a golf course, the "sticks" are the givens of the site and all of the parts of the program—the number of holes, extent of the clubhouse, and so on. If an individual stick is handled incorrectly, the pile comes crashing down.

BEGINNING THE PLAN

The only way to begin is by spreading out a base sheet. On it will be the topographical information, each of the constraints discussed in previous chapters, and any highlighted areas of interest or concern. Have at hand the complete list of components that must go onto the land and the overall objectives of the project. The following topics address the last-minute details before pencil is committed to paper or, in the instance of computer-generated plans, before clicks of the mouse are committed to digital files.

Purpose of Routing

Why is this routing being prepared? The answer to this question is quite important. If the routing is to prove a piece of land is workable, it might be done in rough schematic form. If it is to attract investors, it might be lavish and full of detail. The purpose of the routing plan leads to the type of plan to create and this, in turn, will answer many other questions about how to proceed.

One vital question is the appropriate number of routing plans to create in a given situation. For example, does the project require the designer to create several rough plans, two or three to be selected for presentation? Or is it more appropriate to create just one final plan? To complicate matters there is often a need to prepare diverse plans for a single site. Example: A site may be suitable for a 27-hole regulation course, an 18-hole regulation course and an 18-hole precision-length course, or just one 18-hole course with much more separation between holes. Which is best? Should all three options be studied and presented? Why? Why not? It is best to answer these questions up front. Of course, some answers will pop up as the process unfolds. Maybe a particular configuration was not considered up front but the idea emerges while a plan is being created. Example: an 18-hole layout has returning nines, but it becomes interesting to look at nonreturning nines to overcome an awkward point in the routing. Perhaps two routings are created. Both have positives and negatives that can be weighed.

The quintessential purpose of a routing plan is to demonstrate how a golf course will flow on a given piece of land. While other variables and goals may pertain, this remains the simplest of all. The routing plan establishes the golf course. Everything a golf course might become hinges on the foundation of the routing plan. This is true whether the plan is loosely sketched or detailed to the hilt.

Routing plans are used for the following purposes, none of which are necessarily exclusive:

- Determining land suitability

  Will a particular type of course fit onto a particular piece of land? The two primary aspects of determination are land acreage and the topographical nature of the land.
- Siting evaluation

  Determining where on a large land area it is best to place a golf course.
- Budget determination

  Estimating construction costs for a golf course and facilities on a specific site.
- Land planning

  Routing plans are crucial to the overall effort of land planning, in many cases to determine how much land is residual after the needs of a golf course are met and in some cases to figure out if residual land can be used for golf.
- Client approval

  To obtain the approval of a group or individual.
- Proposal process

  Often, in competing for the rights to develop a golf course on a specific site, developers present routing plans along with their proposal to invest in, build, and operate a golf course facility.
- Obtaining entitlements

  Routing plans are used as exhibits to present when applying for zoning changes and similar processes of approval.
- Environmental compatibility

  For determining compatibility with habitats and in seeking the approval of agencies with oversight of environmental matters.
- Land marketing

  To sell a piece of property on which a golf course is thought to be a good idea and worthwhile use.
- Project marketing

  To sell a project and the concept for a golf course.
- Funding

  To obtain funding from banks, investors, and other sources of money.
- Remodeling

  Routing plans for remodeling and addition projects have unique characteristics and uses.

REMODELING IS NO BLANK CANVAS

Remodeling projects are an animal of their own. Not only is each different, but each comes with an already painted canvas that might be touched up, restored, or completed. One of the best resources for remodeling project information is the American Society of Golf Course Architect's (ASGCA) Remodeling University, an educational program and database of important procedures and remodeling case studies. Contact the ASGCA at www.asgca.org.

In laying out a golf course one should make every effort to take advantage of those natural features which will increase the interest of the play. Now and then one finds a hole of real distinction which nature herself has modelled, and to add anything artificial would be a crime.
—Robert Hunter, The Links

Gathering the Givens

This process relies on the discussions of previous chapters, the basics being topographical mapping, programming, and the constraints of the land. A thorough review of all of the programming and site evaluation needs should be conducted prior to routing. Equally important is that the notes collected from field visits to the site are in hand and well marked on the base sheet that will be used to create the routing plan.

Highlighting contour lines on topographical maps is an excellent practice, especially when terrain is complex or subtle details in the land are abundant. By marking up a base map it will be easier to find your way, especially after long hours when the contour lines can be easily lost by a weary designer. The easiest way to mark a map is simply to highlight contour lines with a bright colored marker every 5 or 10 feet so that the lay of the land is evident. High points and low points can be colored between contours in a separate color. The resulting map will be much easier to absorb when it comes to placing holes into the landforms. Obviously, for relatively flat sites, this step is less important.

Developing a Project Concept

It was established early on that *all* golf holes are strategic, some more obviously than others. The same can be stated with regard to the concept of a golf course. Even when the concept may be weak, a golf course will eventually communicate some degree of personality by the nature of its location, its management, and its maintained condition. Before being built, the personality of a golf course project begins to be determined by all of the influences at play—the owners, the designers, the climate, and the land. Routing is a starting point to begin defining this personality.

The land itself typically has the most influence on forming the concept for a golf course, and this is why a majority of the most celebrated courses in the world are reflections of the tremendous land they occupy. Routing cannot ignore marvelous land, and what reason would it have to do so? When the land has something obvious to offer, the smart golf course architect will embrace this and make it the bragging point of the project. An old quarry, a placid lake, a mountain backdrop, a deep ravine, a dry lake—all are examples of land features that can lead to strong and exciting concepts.

You may deduce, therefore, that without land that is rich in character, a golf course will need more added concept than one with such richness. Correct. A golf course that lacks in one area would be wise to compensate in another. Great land alone does not guarantee prestige. Conversely, because a course will be highly prestigious, perhaps by being part of a five-star resort operation, is no excuse for it to lack interesting land or design. Again, the areas from which a project gets its personality—or concept—should not necessarily be thought of in tandem.

Golf course concepts are sometimes difficult to put a finger on. Certainly, not all golf courses need themes along the lines that a theme

FIGURE 14-1
Project concepts can be driven by a variety of influences. At this site, it was decided to embrace the tranquil woods, with holes leading to and from a diamond in the rough—a contrasting clubhouse that seems to rise out of the landscape.

PHOTO BY RUSTY FLYNN

park would dream up. Yet, why not? Golf is the ultimate example of an experience economy. This idea, developed by Joseph Pine II and James H. Gilmore, describes the latest in a series of economies based on how goods and services are brought to the consumer. Early on, our economy was built on agriculture; raw goods were purchased by consumers and turned into things to eat and live by. Then came the processed economy; consumers bought ready-to-cook products and packaged goods that were already mixed and blended. Then came the service economy; someone else did the work, and food and goods were ready to pick up at the drive-through window. Finally, we have the experience economy—the themed experience that dunks the visitor into an entire environment. The common denominator in this progression of economies is the ability to charge incrementally more for each level. A pound of flour costs less than a pound of cake mix, which costs less than a baked and decorated cake, which costs far less than a birthday party—including the cake—following first-time parachuting lessons above an active volcano.

Golf, because it involves products and services and time spent by the consumer, is the model way to take advantage of the experience economy. The concept for a golf course can be a matter of intrinsic need—if not to attract players, then to differentiate. It may also be a matter of marketing, or of carving a niche in anticipation of future

Every person who has ever designed a golf course has had his or her ideas as to how it should be done. Golfers should cherish that fact for the endless variety of golf courses has added immeasurably to the charm and interest of the game.

—*Geoffrey Cornish,* Some Essays on Golf Course Architecture

competition. The most successful golf courses in the world—not just those included on someone's list of the top 100—are those with purposeful concepts.

To establish a project concept for a golf course, the following characteristics should be considered:

- Voice

  If the course could talk, what would it be saying? Would it be comparing itself to another course, setting a new standard, or being different? Would it tell the golfer that it is simple, traditional, or feisty? Voice may be an odd way to think of a golf course, but it is an essential form of expression that comes through loud and clear once a course is finished.

- Aesthetics

  The visual appeal (or turnoff) of a golf course communicates a lot; the routing plan begins to establish the aesthetics, whether good, bad, or indifferent.

- Prestige

  Is the course one that welcomes, limits, or prohibits? Often, prestige is a matter of who will play there, who can play there, or who has played there.

- Common or uncommon

  Common, at one end of the scale, signifies a course that is typical or very much like many other courses. *Uncommon* is the opposite. Sometimes the goal is to be common, and sometimes it is to be uncommon; how familiar a course seems is a strong personality trait and one that can be tapped for marketing.

How does one develop a concept? In the routing plan stage, the concept of a course can be brought to life, or it may come to life on its own. The decision is based on the specifics of the project. Important, too, is whether the concept is authentic or contrived. Both types can succeed. A concept based on the natural land and its features may be more authentic than that of a course in Iowa that embraces a landscape theme mimicking the linksland of Ireland, but neither is necessarily better. Both, however, are better than the project that does not embrace the slightest concept, for such a project is destined to be lost in the shuffle. Appropriateness is a matter of meeting the objectives and setting a standard that matches the project.

To bring concepts to life, the individual golf holes of a routing plan may take on a variety of traits and qualities. A concept may begin at the details of a hole, such as in a particular type of hazard or design feature, and it may be articulated through the routing as a whole. There may be predominant low areas, or high points, across a routing. The plan might align holes to a prime view or landmark. Or it might orient the golfer to a large body of water, with holes playing toward, alongside and away from the shoreline. The best routing plans are those that embrace the idea of concept at the onset. The objective need not be wild or crazy, but those remain options. The objective is to have the plan lay the groundwork for creating a path for the golfer that will provide discovery, challenge and enjoyment. A routing plan should not be thought of as a superhighway to move golfers from beginning to end. Rather, it must be a scenic highway, one that is fun to drive with twists and turns that are appropriate to the design.

A Table Big Enough
Routing plans, especially for very large sites, can take up a lot of table space. Many golf course architects are adept at Ping-Pong simply because these tables make excellent work surfaces for large plans that are being attacked by hand-drawn methods.

METHODS OF ROUTING

Three methods of routing surfaced in the research for this book. Variations on each are abundant. The most common method seems to be ordinary hand-sketching on tracing paper placed over base sheets. The router goes through iteration after iteration of possibilities and eventually sketches a final plan. Templates are common, although many routers I spoke with pooh-poohed their use. They either love them or hate them. I suspect this has to do with the quality of templates; maybe the reproductions of my own templates will make a few believers out of those not yet convinced. Computers are becoming popular tools used in routing, yet few architects are using them exclusively. The computer screen, which is no larger than a slightly oversized sheet of paper, limits the ability to see the entire course at once. This is being improved by projection tools and larger screens.

One of the more interesting variables in the routing process is the people involved in the project—how many of them, and who they are. At some golf course architectural offices, routing assignments are given to multiple designers and the results discussed in groups. At other firms, a single designer secludes himself in a room and spends a day or longer coming up with variations and options. At other organizations, including mine, a few people gather to discuss solutions, working together and challenging each other along the way.

Regardless of the method of placing holes in a plan, the objective is the same. The plan should be everything it can be. Although simple in its form, the plan represents an effort, magnitude, scale, and cost leaps and bounds greater than the sheet it occupies when ready to be presented.

The Sketching & Drawing Method

Sketching and drawing are quite simple. Typically at a scale of 1 inch to 200 feet, translucent tracing paper is placed over a base sheet and the routing begins, usually in pencil. Beginning points are defined, holes are laid into the land, and distances are worked out—all by hand and through trial and error. As sheets become messy or cluttered with ideas they are discarded, and new, fresh sheets are unrolled across the same base sheet. As ideas are refined, the plan may be traced from previous tissue sheet overlays. Eventually, a complete plan is drawn that depicts all of the holes and areas.

Occasionally, creating routings by the hand-drawing method involves penciling hole alignments directly on the base maps, with no tracing paper overlay. This method can be effective if the contrast is evident between the base sheet and the pencil or pen used to draw the alignments, holes, and features.

FIGURE 14-2

In this series of routing plan sketches, a project begins to take shape. Not only are the golf holes being worked out but so too are the streets and residential areas. The beginning point is an enlargement of the site map on which general ideas have been roughed out. The thought process can be traced through the series as it progresses.

COURTESY OF DESMOND MUIRHEAD, INC.; SEE FIGURE 16-21 FOR THE FINISHED PLAN OF THIS SITE.

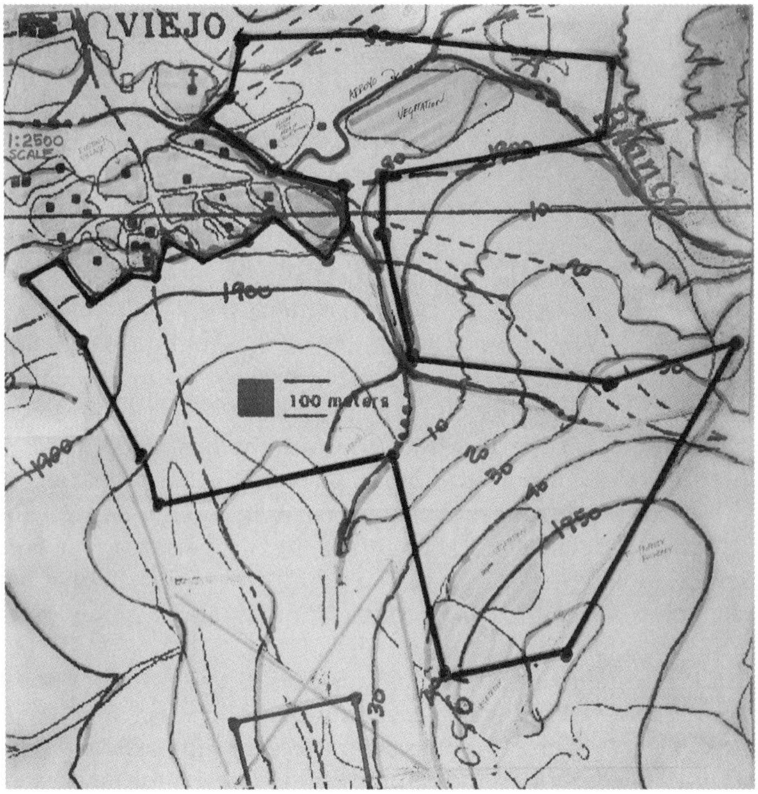

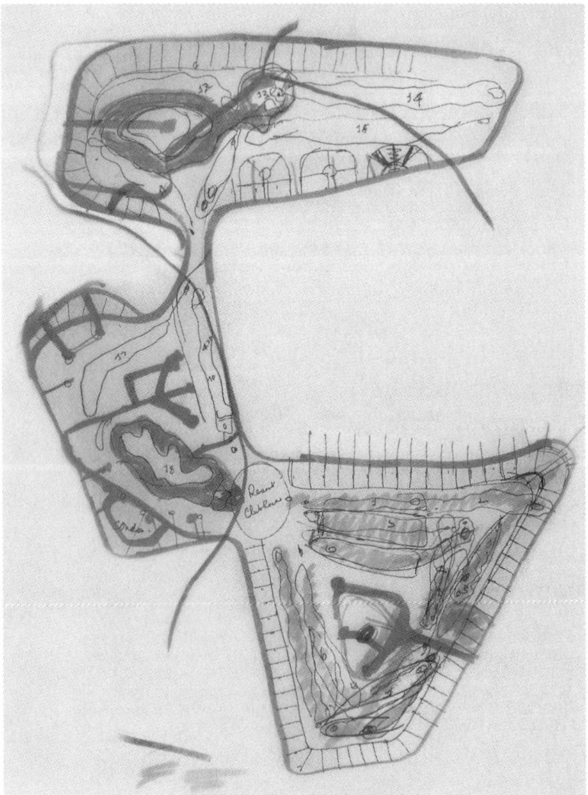

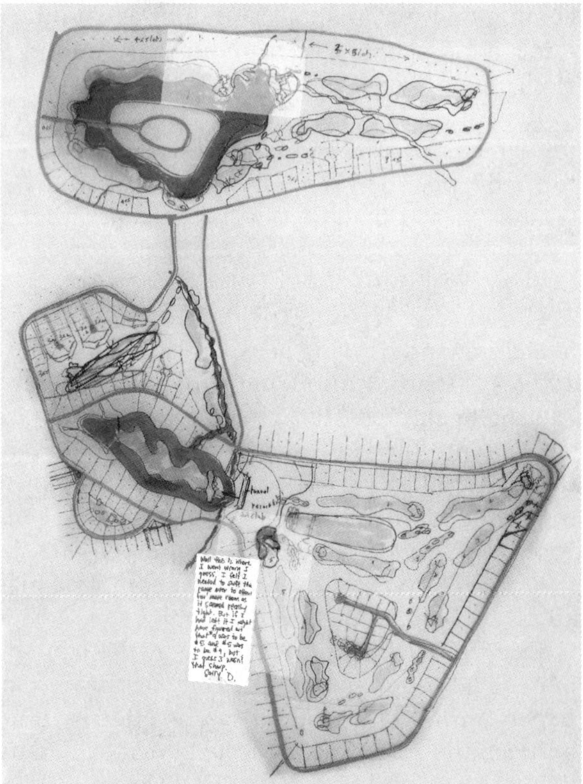

The Template Method

Templates have been used since the early 1900s, when the first formal routings were crafted by golf architects. In *Golf Course Architecture in America,* George C. Thomas writes about his introduction to templates:

> [Y]ou will soon be marking up maps at a great rate, and a little trick taught me by Willie Tuckie, Jr., is a wonderful aid. Your map is, of course, contoured to scale, and you cut out of blotting paper miniature fairways, making them also to the same scale as the map; it is easy to place them on your contour map with thumb tacks, first having your map on a board. You will find that by hinging these little fairways at or about the 200-yard mark, you can make them follow the contours on the map as dog-legs or straight holes. You can play with them just as if they were picture puzzle units; and by making them of different lengths, all to scale, with their width corresponding to that of fairways...you will find them of the utmost help.

Thomas nearly describes the templates used by many golf course architects today. The primary difference is the use of transparent or translucent mylars and acetates not yet invented in Thomas's time.

The templates of templates included in this book have been expertly reproduced so you can scan or copy them and print them out on sheets of plastic such as those used for overhead transparencies. Once the copying is done, trim each part around the edges and punch holes in the templates so they can be hinged together with simple brads. If you are lucky, you will find such brads at your local office supply store. Please note that these copyrighted templates may be copied at will by purchasers of this book provided the copies are used in practice and not offered for resale. You may show this passage to any copy shop that is so astute as to notice the copyright notice and request a document of permission.

I ask that those who do copy the templates to make a contribution to the American Society of Golf Course Architects Foundation. Even a nominal amount will go to good use. The ASGCA Foundation is dedicated to the advancement of research on golf courses and their design. It is dedicated to attracting new players to the game and enhancing the beauty and virtues of golf. Send donations to:

ASGCA Foundation
221 North LaSalle Street
Chicago, Illinois USA 60601
www.asgca.org

The templates we use are identical to those in this book and were printed on colored acetate so that nines of a common project may be distinguished. I recommend some such color-coding method, or at least a bright mark or decal.This will help distinguish between nines, or courses in the case of routing large complexes of 36 or more holes.

ADDING UP PAR

A clever way to quickly add up the par of a routing is to think in terms of 4s (4 x 9 = 36 is a standard that's easy to keep in mind). When looking at a series of pars for nine holes, such as 4, 4, 5, 3, 4, 3, 5, 3, 4, it is relatively easy to think in terms of how many under or over the constant of 4 each par represents. Rather than adding all of the pars in the par order, you would simply think as follows: "even, even, one over, back to even, even, one under, back to even, one under, one under = one less than 36, which is 35." Quite simple and quick.

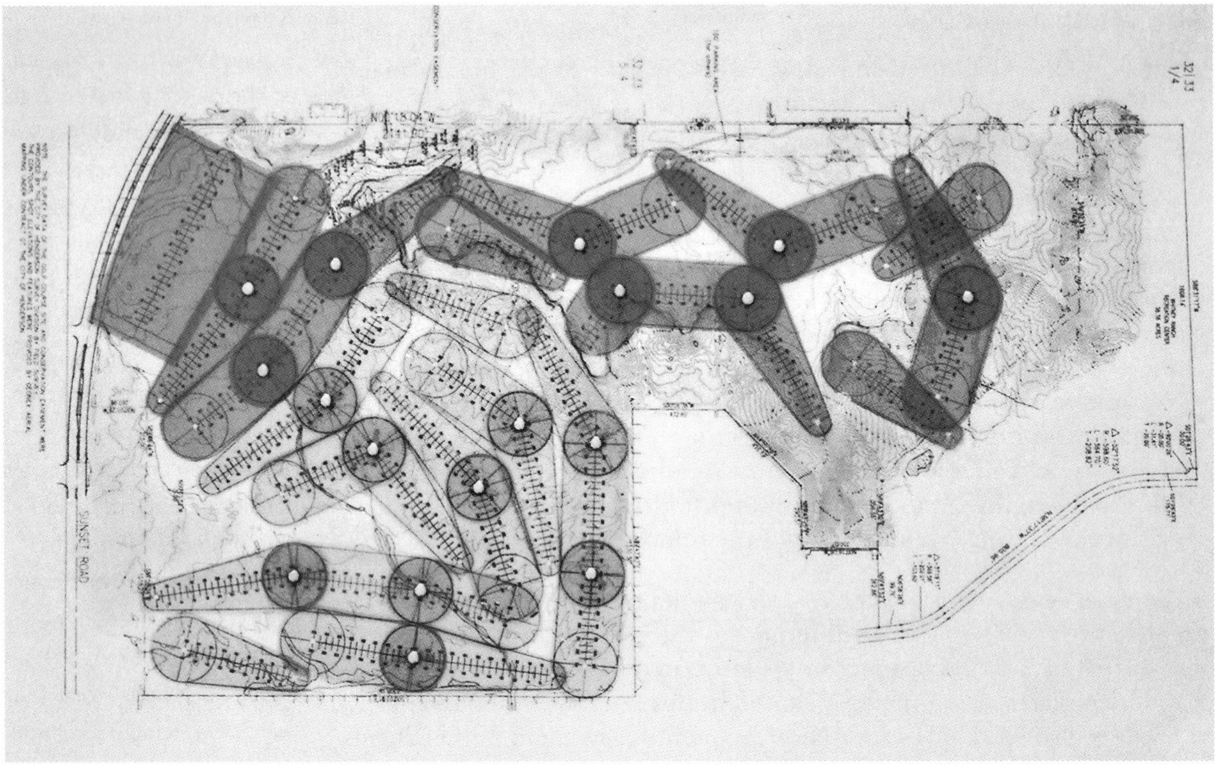

FIGURE 14-3
Templates over a base map consisting of topographical data. Working with see-through templates allows many configurations to be tried and tested. Potential keepers can be traced onto paper or snapshots can be taken with a Polaroid or digital camera. Many plans can then be compared and evaluated before beginning the sketching process. (Refer to Figure 7-2 for the finished routing plan shown here in template form.)

TEMPLATE SET

The templates on the following pages may be reproduced onto clear or translucent material, such as copier-compatible films made for overhead projection. Once copied at the exact same scale as these originals (1"=200') each template can be trimmed out by hand.

By punching holes in the positions of the small circles the templates may be hinged together with brads available at most stationery stores. The punched holes at tee points and green points will allow reference marks to be transferred onto plans. Reproducing four sets of these originals will yield enough templates for most regulation length 18 hole routings. By copying multiple sets onto films of different colors (translucent yellow, green, etc.) it will be possible to distinguish between nines when used for routing.

These templates represent typical conditions, safety cones and hole envelopes. They cannot be applied to all conditions or routings. Specific site conditions will require additional set-backs and in some cases may permit less space to be allocated. Templates are a guide only. Their use for routing plans must be combined with a professional who has the skills and experience necessary to carry out a safe and efficient golf course plan.

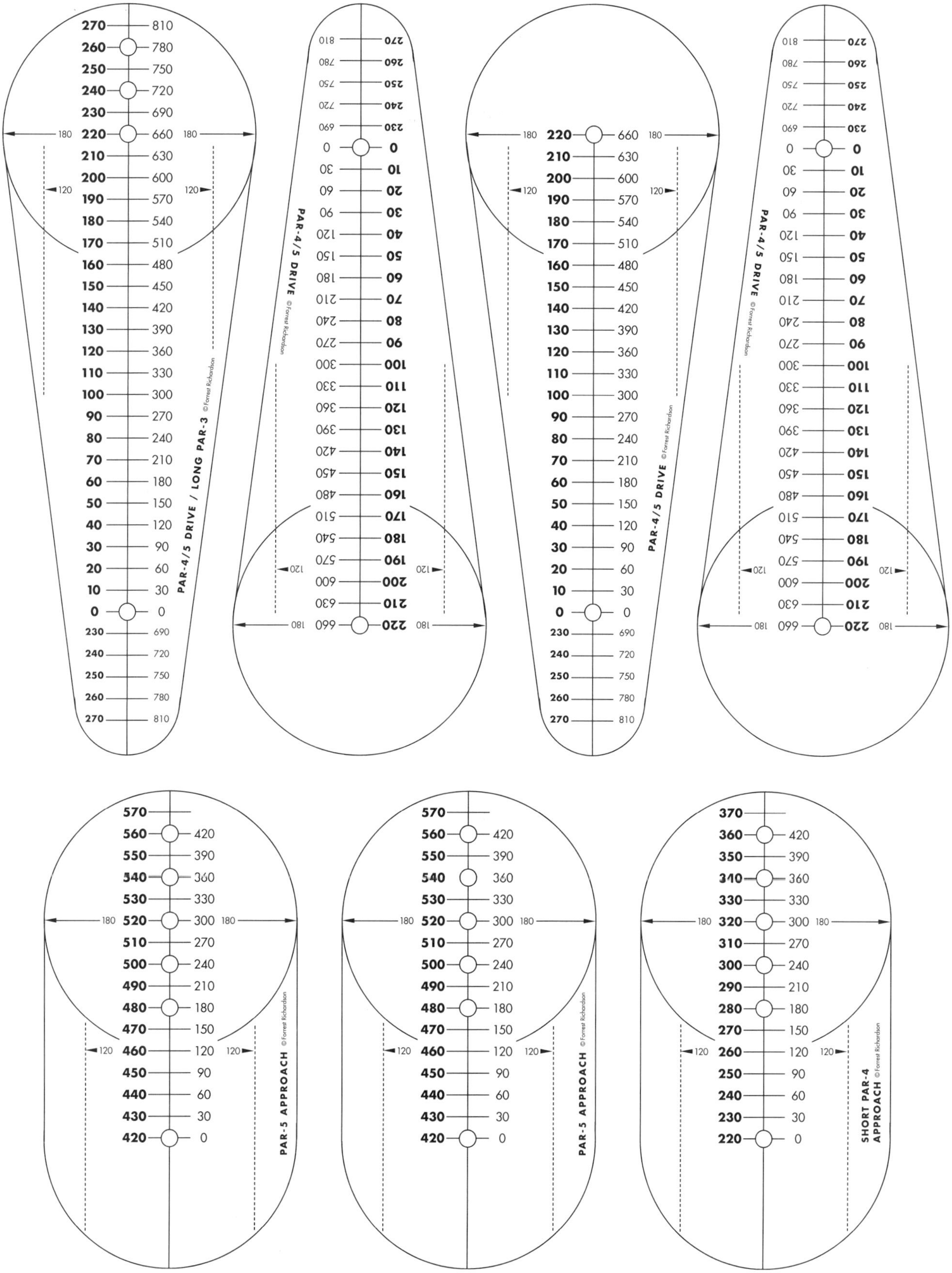
PAR-4/5 DRIVE / LONG PAR-3
PAR-4/5 DRIVE
PAR-4/5 DRIVE
PAR-4/5 DRIVE
PAR-5 APPROACH
PAR-5 APPROACH
SHORT PAR-4 APPROACH
© Forrest Richardson

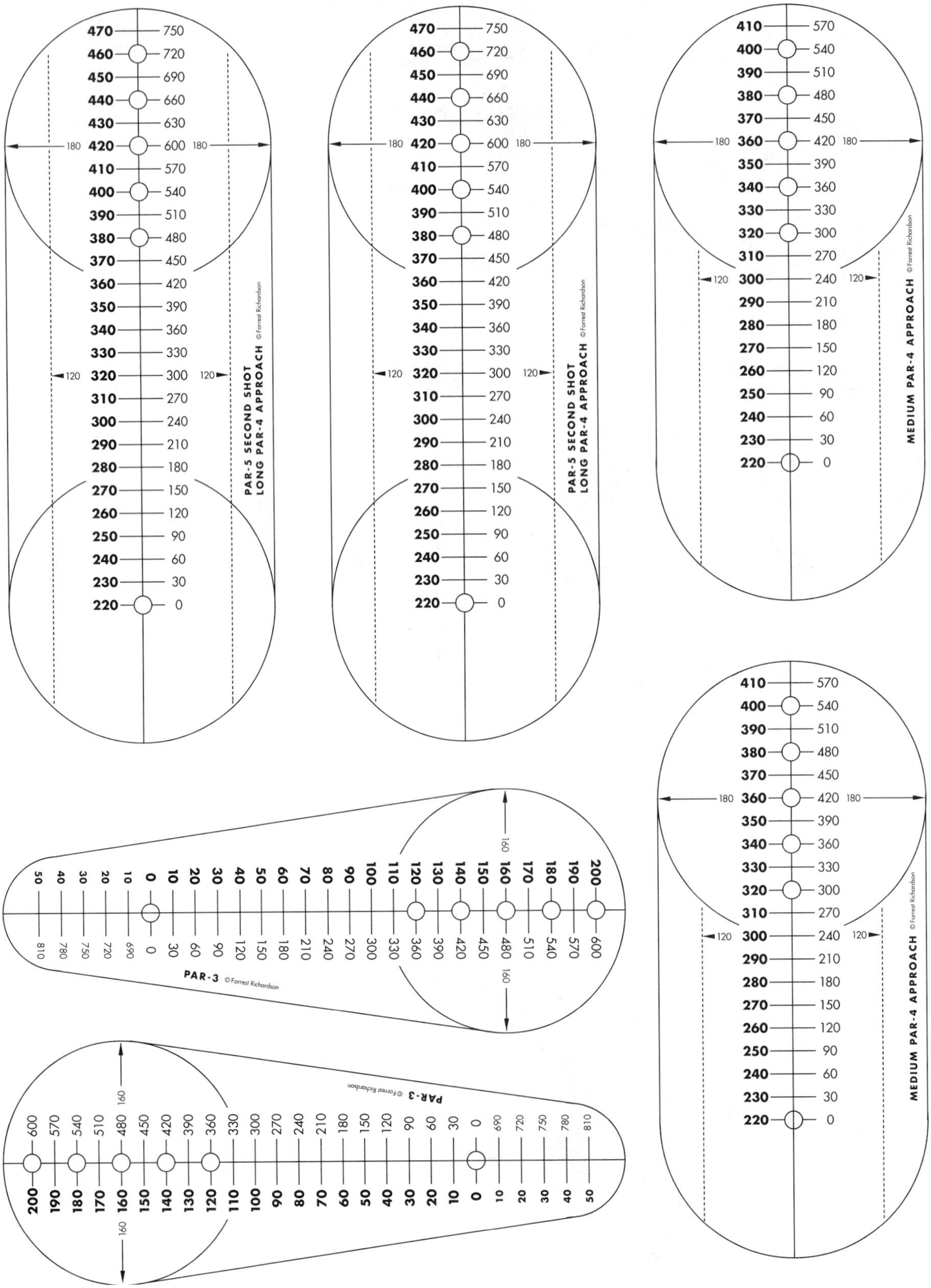

TEMPLATE SET continued

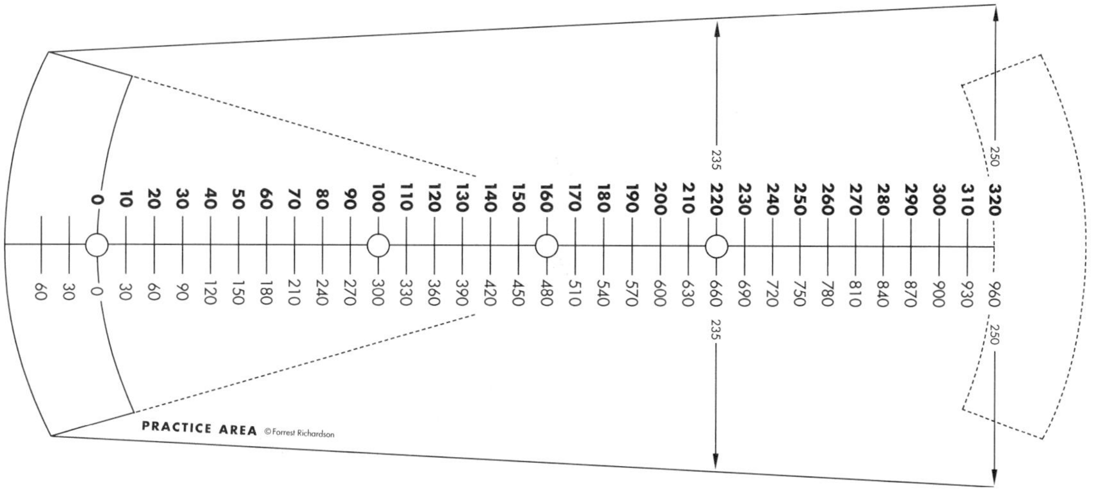

PRACTICE AREA TEMPLATE
The provided practice area template represents a typical practice hitting area requiring approximately 10 acres of space. The arced tee is shown at a width of 400 feet. The distance to the outer limit is shown at 300 yards (900 feet). The width is shown at 470 feet at a point 200 yards from the center of the tee area. The template is intended as a planning guide only and cannot be assumed to fit all sites and conditions. Practice area design will need to be adjusted based on specific site constraints, uses and conditions.

The use of templates cannot be better explained than in Thomas's description above. You simply place the templates on top of your base map and try various options and layouts. Obviously, with see-through templates the results are much easier to appreciate, as you can see below to the contours and map layer. The thumbtacks Thomas mentions are obviously a throwback to the days when you could find them at your corner dime store. I have not been able to find either—dime stores or thumbtacks—in several years.

Templates, when placed on a level table, pose no problems so long as you record your efforts as you go along. This can be done by placing a tracing sheet over the templates and quickly tracing their centerlines. Another effective method is to take a snapshot of the templates with a digital or other instant camera. This approach offers the benefits of recording multiple options for later comparison. Once a few finalists are selected from the photos, the templates can be laid out again and a tracing made that can be used to create a final routing plan.

A variation of the template method is the use of ordinary single-conductor electrical wire such as that used in commercial wiring. The best gauge is the heavy stuff—12-gauge. Cut the wire to standard hole lengths; they can be bent to form doglegs. Marking the ends and dogleg hinge points with nail polish or permanent marker is good practice. The drawback of this approach is that the wires denote only the centerline of golf holes. If you can visualize the safety envelopes of hole and allow enough distance between these wire centerlines, the wire method works fine. I used this method when I first worked with Jack Snyder, then made proper templates for him back in the early 1980s.

The Computer Method

The use of computers is evident in almost all routing plans, even if just in the creation of base maps and topographical data. Some software programs specifically support golf course design and land planning of the golf community. The first such computer-generated plan I saw, sev-

FIGURE 14-4
Computers can be used to lay out golf holes. Software programs created expressly for the golf course architect and planner, such as the proprietary software designed and utilized by Nicklaus Design, make the task much easier.

COURTESY OF © NICKLAUS DESIGN

eral years ago, was an awful mess. It obviously was created by plopping on-screen templates into place and then clicking around the screen, zooming in and then out, until components "fit." Obviously, more time had been spent learning the software than understanding the art of routing. As I said, it was awful. Things fit, but not well. Tees were far from greens, and landing areas were bending around other greens.

Today's computer-generated routing plans are improved because monitor displays are now at greater resolution, in color, and larger. The computer-aided drafting (CAD) professional is immensely more adept, and all of these variables pave the way for plans to have a greater degree of success in being created entirely on the computer.

Still, the ability to think in a physical space—a room—has its merits when routing. A plan flat on the table being worked on with ordinary pencils and pens conveys a reality that cannot always be appreciated on a computer screen. The quickness and ease with which surrounding land can be visualized in a room is decreased when the base map is on a screen. In a room, the table lamp can serve as Mt. Whatever and a pile of books can take the place of the nearby shopping village. Of course, these things can be seen on a computer screen, but far less intuitively. A computer monitor is typically vertical to the user and sites are not.

Working on a level table orients the person doing the routing to the golf course and its land. Working on a traditional computer monitor, no matter how sharp and high-tech, is less intuitive.

An individual hole can be modified at relatively small expense, but to change the layout is a formidable task, and one that is rarely undertaken. The highest service that a golf architect can render to a club is a really good layout.

—Charles Piper, in Golf Illustrated, *February 1926*

THE ROUTING PROCESS

Regardless of the method used, transforming the blank canvas is achieved in the same sequence. Hole 15, "Different Approaches," describes the individual procedures and methods used by celebrated veterans of this business. There is little variability in the process of translating a routing from thought to visual form. One begins, as with assembling a jigsaw puzzle, by locating the "corner pieces" and figuring out where these key parts must be positioned. By corner pieces it is not literally meant *the corners* of a golf course site, but rather the key parts that are obvious beginning points aimed at a solution. Of course the actual corners of a site can account for a beginning point. Considerable attention has been paid to the geometry of actual corners in our look at land, sites and the process of fitting. This is especially so in number 4, below, The Clubhouse, Starting & Ending Points. Very often it is a corner of a site where a clubhouse is destined to be positioned. Beware, as the pitfalls of such a locale can, well, literally back you into a corner.

Prior to handling the corner pieces (whether they are actual corners or not), it is important to figure out how many routings might be required. This may seem a silly question, as everyone knows that only one layout is needed for the final building of a golf course. But the nature of presenting plans is not nearly so cut and dried. The client may expect (even demand) multiple plans. Also, considering that sites can be sliced up in multiple ways, sharing optional layouts is often good practice. The decision as to how many plans to create may change. A requirement for three may yield only two worth talking about. On the other hand, it may be that four or more good and worthwhile schemes are generated and *should* be presented even though just one is expected. The more holes involved in a site, the more complex multiple and optional plans can become. It can get out of hand.

The following sequence is a step-by-step account of the fundamental tasks required to create a routing plan. Within each task is a series of subtasks. Collecting these smaller tasks within the broader task simplifies the organization. When each step is followed, the process of routing is not only seems more manageable but actually is.

1. The Givens

This advice has been given in previous chapters. You cannot begin to lay out a golf course without knowing, understanding, and defining the many obstacles, conditions, and allotments that are inherent in a piece of land and its surroundings. The givens must be at hand and accurate. Ideally, they are clearly marked on the base sheet. They include the topographical subtleties of the site together with each and every note recorded when walking the land.

2. The Access

By now it may have been determined how people will get to the site. If not, this decision will soon be made. Access is essential, unless you plan to helicopter people to the site. Maintenance access should not be forgotten, and while you're at it, you may as well decide on good spots to house the maintenance activity. A central location is good. Direct access is usually more crucial as a yard and building can be screened but a long drive cannot.

Optional access points should be well noted and the pros and cons for each well understood. It is awful, while presenting a routing plan, to find that a single piece of information about a particular access point was not well communicated and therefore the beautiful plans hanging on the wall are useless.

3. The Natural Points

Natural features, tees sites, green sites, fairways paths, water features, low points, and high points should be well known and highlighted on the base map. These are often expressed by some means of rating. A truly amazing spot may be given the highest priority, such as with a hand-noted red star; a worthwhile green location may be marked with a yellow check mark, and so on until all of the identified spots are documented and there for the taking—or potential bypassing.

The Fire Station Approach to Maintenance Area Locations

Locating maintenance facilities can be a troublesome endeavor. For a variety of reasons, central locations often are not workable, and a discussion ensues about whether or not a central location is indeed essential. The answer is "no, it is not *essential,* but it does have merit." A lesson can be learned from the method used in locating fire stations. Fire stations are located in what are known as *first-due areas.* This means that the station is located in the geographic center of the area that the engine is responsible for serving, adjusted for road configurations, obstacles, and so on. The issue is not entirely whether or not the annual trips by the fire engine will take an *average* amount of time but rather whether or not they will take the *lowest average* amount of time. It might be easy to locate a fire station on the edge of an area, and one could argue that some calls will be answered slowly and some, because they come from near the same edge as the station, will be answered quickly. This, of course, is a bad argument, as some calls for service will have to endure longer waits, and service will be compromised. It is not as fair and equitable as a central location. The same holds true of maintenance areas, at least to the degree possible and practical on a given site.

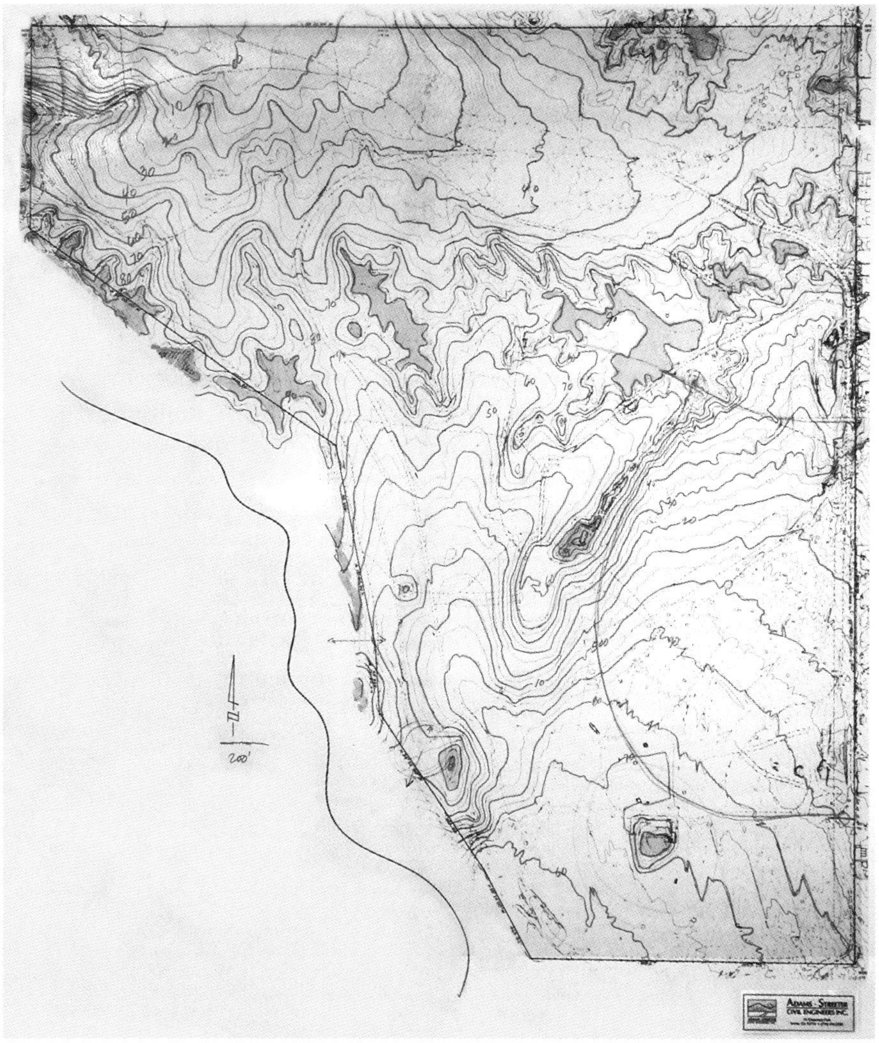

FIGURE 14-5
This base sheet, which was used in the field while walking the site, has been highlighted to show the high points of the land. Hilly sites with lots of contour should be handled this way before any routing takes place.

4. The Clubhouse, Starting & Ending Points

The clubhouse, as has been discussed, is often the first component to be located. This is because many developers can more easily understand a clubhouse than the complexities of an entire golf course. A clubhouse is just one thing. It is familiar and has known quantities that most people grasp immediately and can picture in their mind's eye. A golf course, on the contrary, is many things. Each is different, with no standard that can be applied. In any case, if a clubhouse location seems most important to those involved, it probably is.

An essential consideration in clubhouse location is looking at the geometry of the site in the immediate area of where a clubhouse is being considered. If your plan for an 18-hole course is to have two outbound holes (Nos. 1 and 10) and two inbound holes (Nos. 9 and 18), and a practice range tee playing out from the clubhouse area, then a certain scope of available corridors leading to and from the clubhouse site is

The proper solution is much on the order of a chess problem; the first effort is generally not the best.

—George C. Thomas Jr., Golf Architecture in America

required to get all this accomplished. The best way to think of this is in terms of an arc. Envision the clubhouse as a point on the plan. From this point a large enough radius is drawn to encompass the area of a clubhouse and its grounds. Along this arc you will need enough linear distance—width—to position the two tees (Nos. 1 and 10), the two greens (Nos. 9 and 18), and the practice range tee. This probably amounts to 1100 feet. Add to this the requirements for an entrance drive, practice putting greens and anything else, and you can see how the distance along this arc is quickly used up. The larger the diameter of the circle that defines the clubhouse area will result in more span to accomplish your task. Of course a larger circle (radius) will also consume more space. When you grasp the arc approach it becomes a geometry problem to apply the arc to a site. When the clubhouse circle is somewhere in the middle of a site you, in essence, have the entire circumference of the circle to use for your beginning and ending holes, and practice tee. In the case of a clubhouse along an edge of a property the available arc is usually 180 degrees or more. Ah, but when the clubhouse is crammed into a corner look what happens. At best you have only 90 degrees of the circle to support all of these tees and greens. Unless the circle gets very large you will quickly run out of space to accomplish what is needed.

Often, a land planning process preceded the routing, and it is too late to do much to change access or clubhouse points. This is a shame, as

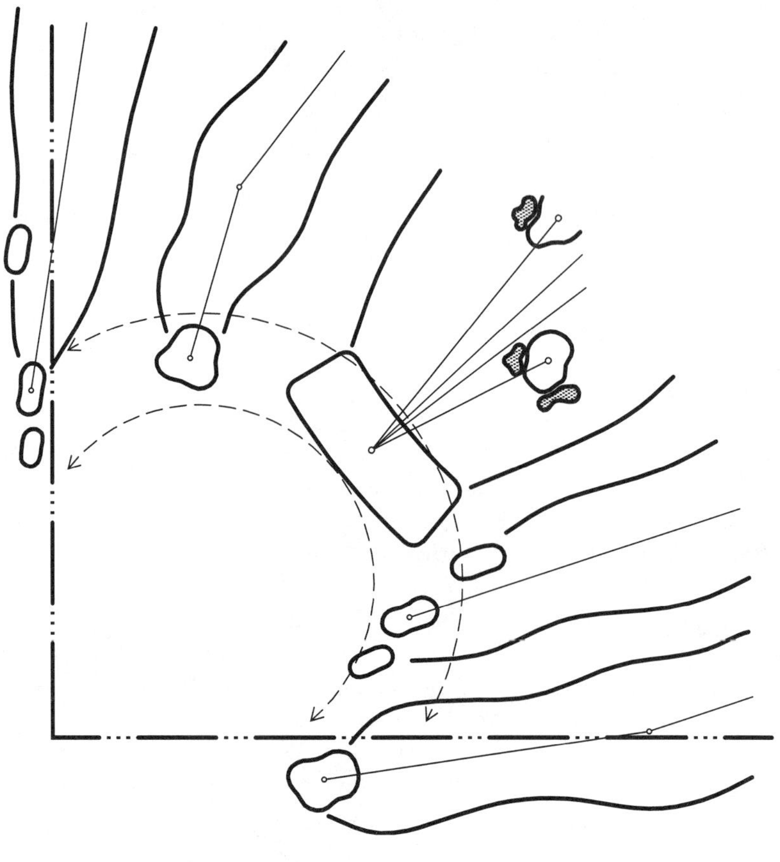

FIGURE 14-6
The importance of establishing corridors leading to and from the clubhouse area are shown. This diagram illustrates a corner location, one of the most troublesome spots to position a clubhouse. Arc "a" represents the area of a clubhouse and its grounds that comprise about 5 acres. This arc measures about 650 feet and is clearly not enough to accommodate two beginning holes, two ending holes and a practice area tee in the corner location. By making the arc larger, "b", you can see how the tees and greens would fit better as they would be further out into the land parcel. The larger arc, however, means more acreage will be created for the clubhouse.

there may be good cause to put a clubhouse here instead of there. Determine the importance of any predetermined clubhouse locations early on. You may devise a routing plan that *proves* a layout with a different clubhouse location is better. Such an option, if not investigated, might lead to a poor routing plan and, hence, a poor golf experience.

The clubhouse location—or multiple options for one—must be identified. Together with the givens of programming for parking, square footage, grounds, and so on, the clubhouse leads to the beginning and ending points of the course itself. If, on an 18-hole layout, the course is to return at the ninth hole, then the clubhouse will lead to both the ninth and tenth holes as well. These opening holes—that is, the tee locations for the outbound holes and the green locations for the inbound holes, must be located to allow ample room. Also, consider: Will the starting hole be acceptable? too difficult? Will it be too long? Will the 18th hole provide enough drama? too much? Will it be long enough? You know the routine—but it cannot be overemphasized. The clubhouse and the points where the course begins and ends are of primary concern.

To illustrate the above importance, think of that great course you played where the finishing hole seemed lacking, or maybe it was out of character. I have played numerous courses—some famous and celebrated—where the finishing hole was a throwaway, obviously set into the routing to do what? To get the golfer back to the clubhouse, and not much else. A finishing hole should be impressive—although not overly difficult or annoyingly spectacular. Whatever it should be, it should not be primarily a way to get back to the clubhouse. Again, golf is not a game played on an interstate highway system made of grass where the path is primarily intended to get one from place to place. Sure, that is the effect. But it should not be apparent to the golfer.

The interest of wrestling with the difficulties of unsuitable conditions is no doubt one of the many charms of this occupation.

—*H. S. Colt,* Some Essays on Golf Course Architecture

5. The Large Areas

I have been guilty of beginning to route a course only to discover that there is no room for a practice area, a large event staging area casually mentioned by a guy with red hair—and, unfortunately, I could go on. Identify large use areas. You may even consider doing this a bit earlier in the routing process. But at the expense of an excellent clubhouse location, natural features, and starting and finishing holes, a practice facility is probably not top priority. Routing is always a balancing act. Tip too far in one direction, and you may lose an outstanding golf experience—too far in the other direction, and the practice area becomes a messed-up afterthought. Decisions, decisions.

6. The Concept

If the golf course does not get its concept from the routing effort, it will get it somewhere else. As with any design, concepts integrated with functional aspects are the most successful. In rare instances does it seem okay to route independently of a big idea. Perhaps when determining whether or not a golf course can fit on a land parcel it may be tolerable, but even

Conversation with a Bartender — A Lesson in Getting Inspiration

Chris Ursino is a bartender at Pebble Beach Golf Links. I met him for the first time in the spring of 2001, when I went to look at the new fifth hole, now set along the ocean. Chris is a friendly man, slight, bearded, and with an obvious passion for golf—and life. Without much prying, you can learn about his love for family, his general kindness, and his awareness of others. Of course, I suppose most of these traits are his qualifications for being bartender at Pebble Beach, but it's my guess that Chris would stand apart even when lined up with the best of the best.

At the time we met, I was working on a few routing plans and had been sketching in a small book I often carry when traveling. I was also working on this book. Chris asked what I was working on, and for the next hour or more I had the opportunity to visit with this Korean War veteran, former caddy, and gentleman who has served umpteen million drinks to golfers from around the world. Here is what I learned from him:

1. What makes Pebble Beach so appealing is the coastline and the movement of the sea. The coastline *is* the routing. People love Pebble Beach because it speaks to them in a way that not many other golf courses can.
2. Returning nines disrupt play. Golf courses should play out and then come back.
3. There should be a halfway house on or near the ninth hole where golfers can get refreshments. This can be a small stone house, a nice place, where drinks and snacks are served. It shouldn't be an afterthought.
4. Golf course architects should *not* locate restrooms at the tees of par-3 holes. Too much is going on there: club selection, extra time checking exact yardages, bets, etc.
5. More courses should provide on-course caddies, such as at greens where the putting can be tricky. This is especially helpful during tournaments, when play can become slow. The use of just a few on-course caddies could speed play considerably.
6. Having multiple sets of tees is a great design trend, but a way is needed to qualify golfers for a particular set of tees. Golf architects may be doing their job, but course managers need to step up to the plate and do theirs.
7. If there is no room for a practice area, then there at least needs to be a warm-up area. Otherwise, the first few holes will be slow.
8. There is way too much emphasis on length in modern golf. The game was born from an emphasis on accuracy, and everyone who influences the way golf is played should keep that in mind.
9. The average golfer suffers on most long courses.
10. A round of golf is divided into three acts. Act I is what happens before a round, Act II is what happens during the round, and Act III is what happens after the round. They are all important. The routing of a golf course must consider all three acts.

in this case it seems like the proverbial cart-before-the-horse situation. "Yes sir, Bob, we can fit 18 holes on this here land, but truthfully we have no darn clue what would make it a desirable golf course." The best chefs expertly combine ingredients to make a unified dish. What makes the chefs great is that they do it for a purpose. The result is worthwhile and fulfilling because the components are brought together to form something that is greater than the sum of the individual parts. Do not discount the need for a concept—a recipe. Far too many courses have been routed this way, and it is depressing to consider how or why this has happened.

7. The Golf Holes

Whether by hand-drawn lines, templates, or computer programs, golf holes are laid out by aligning their centerlines and making sure the necessary safety envelopes are there in space. This is done by keeping centerlines apart as appropriate to the terrain and conditions.

A review of the variables discussed in earlier chapters and the need for randomness, order, pace, flow, and surprise indicate why routing plans can never be identical from course to course. Length and par—and the order in which they fall—are matters to be worked with, pondered, and attempted.

8. The Final Test

Elevation sections may need to be drawn to prove that a hole can physically work and is not too severe or blind. What is the final yardage? Is the variation of holes as expected? Whoops, then maybe it needs a touch of surprise. The final test of a routing plan is looking at it from every conceivable angle—from that of the golfer, the owner, the environment, adjacent landowners, high-priced personal injury attorneys, passers-by on the highway, the greenkeeper, the marketing executive, the travel agent, the golf writer... and it almost never stops.

ROUTING ANOMALIES

Moving from a blank canvas to a finished plan is an ability that takes information and practice. The more you are exposed to routing the easier it will seem to come. All of the variables explained in this book, when combined, form a very complicated network of ifs and thens. As a routing plan comes to life we learn to do this *if* this occurs. This repeats over and over as the plan is looked at and solutions pondered by the designer. Sometimes it is a vicious cycle. When we fix one area to meet an objective or rule, we might create another problem in a new area. This has been previously discussed. But what happens when the routing begins with some special circumstance? Or when we look to inflict some special circumstance to a routing? The following are thoughts about transforming the blank canvas for such routings and circumstances.

When you play a course and remember each hole, it has individuality and change. If your mind cannot recall the exact sequence of the holes, that course lacks the great assets of originality and diversity.

—George C. Thomas Jr., Golf Architecture in America

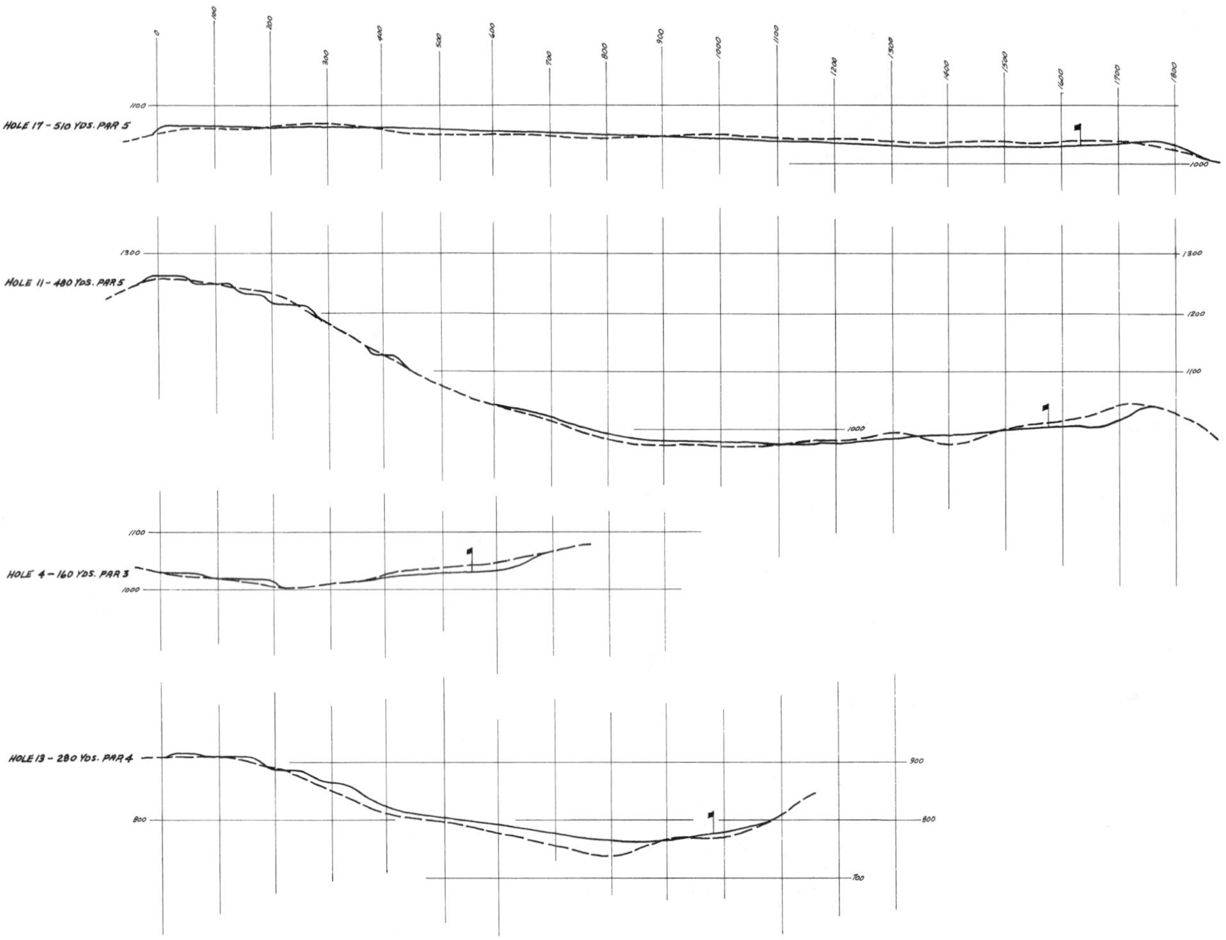

FIGURE 14-7
Sectional studies of holes are used to compare existing contours along proposed centerlines with the extent of grading that may be required for golfers to see from point to point. Such plans are primarily reserved for hilly sites where some effort in grading will be required to fit holes into the terrain. Sectional studies can be appropriate to have before venturing into the field, especially where a preliminary sketch of hole alignments has already been prepared.

Precision (Executive-length) Courses

Courses of this type represent the widest variation in length and par flexibility of any type of golf course. Between the span from par-3 courses to shortish regulation courses there are diverse options. The 18-hole precision course may have just a few par-4 holes, or it may have several. In approaching routing plans for courses of this length there are abundant rules to be broken. For example, you might begin with a par-3 hole, or end on one. Because there are many par-3 holes on such courses, it is not at all uncommon for several par 3s to be in sequence.

The precision (executive) course must still follow the basics principals of routing. Beyond this, the holes must be varied, perhaps more so than on a regulation course where par 3s, 4s and 5s intermingle and provide a variation on their own. On the precision layout there will likely be par 3s in a row. This means that their lengths, shot strategies and features should be significantly different lest the golfer will feel a sense of boredom. Although it is commonly seen, all holes on a precision layout should not be short in length. The ideal course of this type should force the use of all of the clubs in the bag. The monotony of short irons to par 3s and short iron approaches to par 4s is not warranted. Holes should be varied so players will feel like a full complement of shots has been demanded. I have always been a fan of trying to work in a par 5 on precision layouts—not only are you interrupting the sequence of par 3s and 4s, you are introducing a new challenge, perhaps one not expected. The par 5 is also a means to force the player to hit at least one full shot from the fairway, a demand not likely without the length of a par 5.

Varying the hole design feeds our natural curiosity and satisfies that itch of anticipation. Variety is more than the spice of life; it's the life of golf.
—Tom Fazio

Par-3 Courses

The same advice applies as stated above regarding par 3s within a precision layout: vary their length, shot strategies and features. Take exceptional care to alter the tees. Some should be lower than the green, some level and some elevated. Hazards must be varied in their placement—right, left and perhaps some which are penal. The notion that detour shots cannot be offered on the par 3 is nonsense. Greens can be planned wide with hazards in front that make the golfer choose his route carefully. Do not leave behind the idea to consider options tees and, if you dare, an optional green. The par-3 course can be an exciting routing, but it requires careful attention to make the holes different and distinct.

Special Design Circumstances

This book has explored many ideas about routing that are not standard practice. They are the clever, unusual, different and, many times, fun designs that golfers remember fondly. Some of these might even serve as an attraction to the course. Here is a list, categorized by features and attributes, of ideas you do not want to overuse, but are always worth considering if the application is appropriate:

- Tees

  Optional tees in terms of length and elevation, but also optional tees in terms of the alignment to the fairway or green.

- Fairways

  The detour shot is among the most beloved in golf; optional fairways, different paths and choices will be forever enjoyed. Landing areas can be multiple. Perhaps one requires a lay-up shot.

- Greens

  Double greens; alternate greens that are in play based on how the course is set up on a given day; and optional greens that a golfer can choose as the target.

The only thing great courses have in common is that each possesses a character all its own.
—Tom Doak

- Par

  Par can exceed 5 and the argument in favor of the par 2 has been presented. It should not be forgotten that par can also be altered dependent on the tees played: At the very long par 4 the par value for the forward tees might be set at five. And why can't this be done in reverse? For the short par 5 can't we envision par from those championship markers at four?
- Hazards and obstacles

  Besides the customary, the world of golf has seen archeological relics, stone walls, and rock quarries introduced to golf holes as unusual obstacles. Water and sand are not the only crayons that can color the routing plan.
- Holes

  Reversible holes, optional holes, and bonus holes.

WHERE TO LOOK FOR SOLUTIONS & INSPIRATION

Problem solving is what routing golf courses is essentially about. It cannot be described more simply. Judith and Richard Wilde, who have written extensively about how design professionals go about problem solving, wrote a memorable book entitled *Visual Literacy* in which they showcased the results of class assignments given to design students. These assignments, which I describe in a moment, addressed the following areas connected with teaching the art of problem solving:

- Reevaluating a problem in personal terms
- Creating conditions for self-questioning

  by moving from the known to the unknown
- Encouraging the use of concepts to dictate technique

  instead of the other way around
- Discovering design principles

  rather than memorizing them
- Discovering personal methods of problem solving

To teach design students of varying disciplines, Richard Wilde has built a system of forcing students to solve problems by thinking beyond the box. How fitting that he employs literal boxes (squares) to accomplish this. His standard assignment begins easily enough as a written problem, but below the written task on a single sheet of white paper are as many as 20 empty squares that the student is *required* to fill with a completely different solution. Most of the time, the requirements are for completely different solutions—occasionally, a progression of solutions. The forced multiple attempts bring the creative and beyond-the-box thinking to the surface.

"By dedicating themselves to creating, say, twenty solutions to a single problem, rather than just one or two, students come to realize that the potential number of successful solutions is infinite," the Wildes note. "The idea of *unlearning* comes into play as well, prodding students to go beyond the habitual."

The assignment is not perfect for routing a golf course. One cannot draw optional routing solutions in the space of small squares on a single sheet of letter-size paper. But this does not prevent the multiple routing solutions to be forced onto tracing paper during the routing process. I cannot think of better advice, and I am grateful to the Wildes for reminding me of this great lesson.

In coming up with solutions to a routing plan, you may feel there is simply no solution other that that which has been staring you in the eyes for the better part of three hours. But how important it is to try new thinking, to expand your thought process beyond what you "know to be true" because you read it in a book about routing golf courses. Frankly, I am suggesting that you toss out all you know and at least ask the question "Why not?"

Inspiration is problem solving in disguise. When in a quandary about what to do or where to proceed, you can choose among several avenues. The following section outlines some useful paths to take.

Back to the Land

I have boarded planes to fly more than 500 miles just to stand on a piece of land that I've already spent the equivalent of four days hiking over and studying. Sometimes you have to see the land one more time.

Back to the Concept

Perhaps the concept you have is wrong. Perhaps you don't really have one at all. Maybe it is a false concept. Look for authenticity. What about this site can rise to the surface and survive the cold reality of becoming a viable golf course? Often, the most obvious thing *should* be the concept. Unfortunately, it is not easy to see the obvious, even when looking in all the right places.

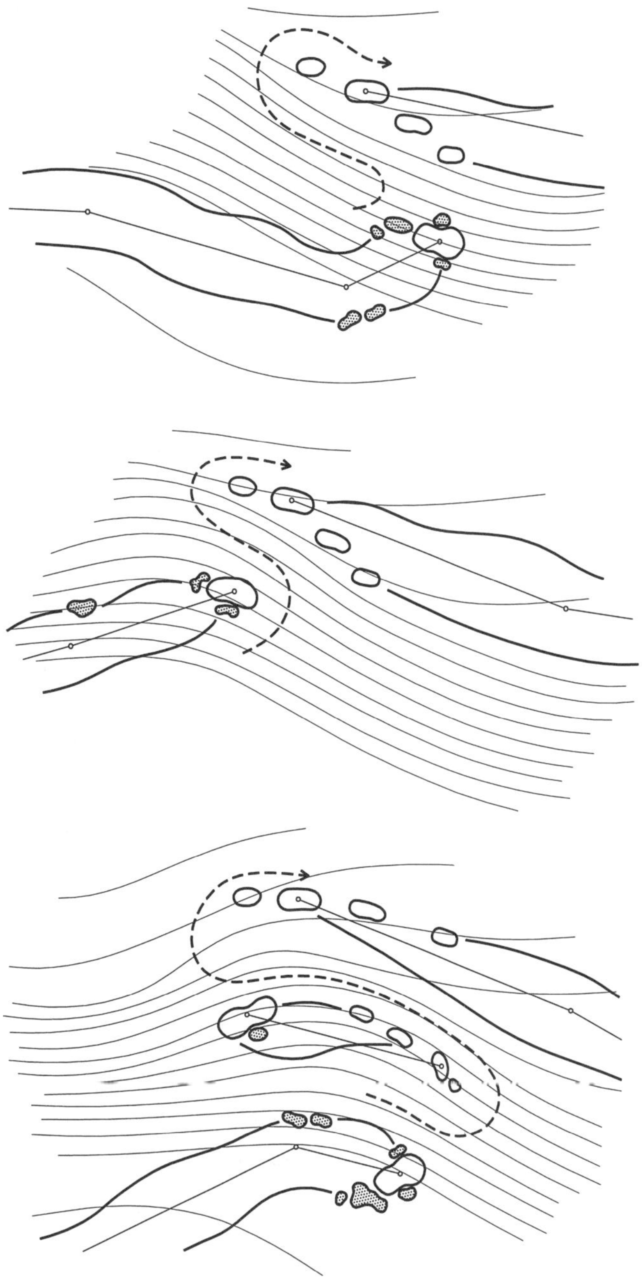

FIGURE 14-8
Routing holes down severe slopes is not nearly as troublesome as routing holes up them. In going down, tees can be set at the top or within the hillside and play to distant fairways or greens below. These examples show clever methods of getting up a steep slope. *At top:* The green of a par-5 hole is cut into the hillside, which results in only one uphill shot; the distance to the next hole accounts for most of the uphill terrain. *At center:* A significant amount of the steep terrain is taken up by the second shot of a par-4 hole, which must be kept short in order to avoid too difficult an approach for the majority of golfers. *At bottom:* A par-3 hole is benched into the hillside and serves as a sort of switchback from the previous hole to the tees for the next hole.

Back to the Drawing Board

Never say never. Great golf holes have been made out of bad situations. Some of the most creative, breathtaking, and spectacular routings have come from land that said "no"—from land that was first passed by due to the obstacles inherent in its hills and valleys. From dead flat land have risen great triumphs and soft-spoken wonders that take their design bows from sensible attention to detail. It is in how you look at problems that solutions are found. Don't be afraid to return again and again, if necessary, to the drawing board.

WHEN TO STOP

Routings are influenced by a number of goals, objectives, conditions, and limitations. They are also influenced by the spirit of good design, the creation of an exciting adventure, and an aesthetic setting. One way to approach a routing is to separate the objective from the subjective among the goals, objectives, conditions, and limitations. This can be done on a single sheet of paper. The list will help separate what parts of the plan are likely to be judged as pure right or wrong and which parts are subjective and therefore not likely to be judged 100 percent either way. The value of making such comparisons will be realized when the plan is presented and discussed. For most people, solutions which satisfy objectives of a project are much easier to judge than solutions which are subjectively based.

Finished routing plans can be subjected to a litmus test of sorts. The following test comprises a good set of questions to ask about the character of the plan. Interestingly, a routing plan can be a winner regardless of whether the answers are "yes" or "no." Why? Because that is the unique nature of routing golf courses. Except with respect to safety and land conditions, there is seldom a full right or wrong.

- Is the course interesting?
- Is the course memorable?
- Is the layout efficient?
- Will building the course be an uphill battle?
- Am I nervous about presenting the routing plan?

Different Approaches

HOLE NO.

15

Just as there are many ways to play a golf course, there are many ways to lay one out. Developing routing plans is a process that keeps the mind highly active. Moving one piece in one corner can precipitate a cascade of other changes.

Along the road of bringing together the various sections of this book, I spoke with my fellow golf course architects about how they go about their work. I not only learned new methods but also opened my eyes to the tremendous reliance this business has on the human mind. Appreciate for a moment all of the many considerations, influences, and subtleties that must join—almost simultaneously—to arrive at routing decisions.

The following is the result of ten separate interviews at which the same eight questions were asked in the same sequence. Some interviews took place over a cup of coffee, in clubhouse grills, and, when there was no other choice, over the phone. The goal was to see how different individuals approached routing and what advice they might have. What I learned here, and I hope you will too, is that there is no right or wrong when it comes to the process. The right or wrong parts reside in the rules. The individual, as you will see, chooses how to abide by them.

The golf course architects and designers interviewed are a diverse group, but the questions asked each were the same. Each has been numbered, which makes it possible to read through the answers for each architect, or you may skip through each and refer to the answers for a particular number all at once. While the latter approach requires more page-turning, it may prove entertaining, as the answers can be compared. Either way is quite interesting.

THE QUESTIONS

1. Where do you begin a routing plan?
2. What is your process for routing a course?
3. How do you get holes set in place?
4. Do you follow a formal checklist?
5. What mistakes have you made?
6. What pet peeves do you have about routing plans?
7. Name some of your favorite routings.
8. What is the most humorous routing story you recall?

THE INTERVIEWS

Bob Graves

Bob Graves is a soft-spoken man, unless he needs to be otherwise. We finally met, after corresponding for almost 30 years, in a restful corner of the Alaska Airlines lounge at the San Francisco airport. Bob is coauthor of *Golf Course Design* (John Wiley & Sons, 1998), has practiced golf course architecture for more than 40 years, and is a past president of the American Society of Golf Course Architects (ASGCA). He has designed and redesigned more than 800 courses. He is the only person I interviewed who keeps a dark green golf pencil tucked behind his left ear.

1. "I begin at the clubhouse, at least 99 percent of the time. We look for a place that has good access and will fit well to the site. Occasionally, we get to help plan the roads and access. That, of course, means we have more latitude to place the clubhouse."
2. "First, I assume enough space is available and will usually start by looking for two nine-hole loops. But later, it's quite possible that I may find nine holes out and back. I'm definitely not opposed to that but always try for the returning nines if possible." Bob thinks, as he puts it, "longitudinally and latitudinally." He tends to split the site diagonally to see where this might take him. He looks for a clockwise routing, where possible. "The goal is to give maximum variety in shot direction. In the first five or six holes, we're looking to accomplish three things: The first is variation in direction, the second is a variety of length of holes, and the third is an appropriate place for the par

It is best, if possible, to create an atmosphere of large and unrestricted space, which is the most delightful contrast to the cramped and restricted streets and offices of a large town.

—*C. H. Alison,* Some Essays on Golf Course Architecture

3s and 5s. This is the basis of our process in the beginning, besides constantly relating things to the topography and looking for holes that cry out to be golf holes. I circle these on the topo map."

3. "I sketch my routings on tracing paper placed right over the topo. I don't like templates because once you move them the idea is lost." Bob explains that once he begins to like a hole or series of holes, he uses heavier and heavier lines until they become somewhat permanent. Using the tracing paper method, he is able to develop several options a day. He also travels to the site, often several times, to verify his assumptions.
4. "Just in my head—but this may vary from project to project."
5. "We had a topo map once that was so poor due to heavy tree cover that it was basically useless. Our first mistake was not getting a better map before going ahead with the routing and design. This led to an awful mess. I think every hole had to be moved during construction. And one thing wrong would cause another; it was a domino effect that involved roads and other infrastructure. It was a real mess." According to Bob, this experience is why he has made sure his mapping is as good as can be ever since.
6. "Disregarding the site. I see plans done all the time where people simply blow through the site and lay in 18 holes irrespective of the topo. A routing plan must absolutely follow the lay of the land; otherwise, it's just a bunch of pretty lines." For the past several years, Graves has cotaught a class in golf course design at Harvard. There he sees students make this mistake more often than any other. "'Look at the damn topo!' I tell the students. You can't lay out a golf course and pretend the land goes where you want it to go. The design and the routing needs to flow with the land." Among Bob's other pet peeves are tees you can't find when leaving a green, long walks between holes that he terms "forced interludes," and clients who are unwilling to even consider nonreturning nines. "Balls, Band-Aids, and Beer: Those are the Three *B*s that created this whole business of making courses return after nine holes."
7. "I especially like figure-eight routings because they give you the maximum variety of direction and every orientation in a round." People don't typically pay accolades to a course and relate their feeling to the routing. But if a course feels good and is comfortable, the chances are good that the routing plan has been done with care.
8. "I visited a project once where some civil engineers had created the routing plan and this poor guy actually had it built. There was a dogleg par 3—I mean a real golf hole of about 180 yards that bent around some trees. As far as I know, it's still there today."

FIGURE 15-1
The Three Ps, according to Graves and coauthor Geoffrey Cornish in their book *Golf Course Design*, are essential to all routing plans: *playability*, to uphold the fun nature of golf; *practicality*, for long-term maintenance considerations; and—a favorite word of Graves's—*pulchritude* (aesthetics), for beauty's sake. All three revolve around the environment, a constant and driving force.

Gary Linn & Don Knott

Gary and Don are partners in Knott Brooks Linn, a California-based golf course design firm. Both Gary and Don worked for Robert Trent Jones Jr. and have practiced in virtually every corner of the world. Knott

FIGURE 15-2
Hole No. 12 of the Kinojo Golf Club in Japan. Gary Linn, ASGCA, and Don Knott, ASGCA, golf course architects.

PHOTO COURTESY OF KNOTT BROOKS LINN

is a past president of ASGCA. Their office is immediately above an East Indian restaurant. Just before lunch, it begins to fill with all sorts of scents and aromas.

1. "Often, we get development envelopes that have been created by others, usually land planners," says Linn. "But regardless, we almost always begin with the clubhouse. We have to find a place that has good access and where we can make the course come and go."
2. "We start with the topo," says Linn. "The topo enables us to size up a site before we go into the field. Very often, we will do a few sketches on the topo, and then we visit the site. There have even been cases where we have worked out some preliminary grading concepts for especially mountainous sites well before seeing the land. Having the topo up front saves everyone a lot of time by making it possible to figure out whether a golf course is even possible on a site." Both archi-

tects have worked in Japan, where it is not uncommon to move massive quantities of dirt just to run a few holes along a steep slope. Linn boils it down to a three-step process, at least most of the time. The topo comes first, followed by understanding the obstacles (including environmental constraints), and, finally, by making necessary site visits to appreciate the land. "It's a bad idea to route before doing some investigation," he warns.

3. The firm does not use templates, relying on lots of tracing paper. "I use a light blue pencil at first," says Knott. "This way, I'm putting my thoughts down without committing them to a darker line." Using an assumed clubhouse location, Knott routes holes out and back and may go through numerous attempts before landing on one that has promise. "While there are rules, there are also infinite possibilities. We simply work until the various elements come together. It's a juggling act."
4. Like so many others, these guys point to their head when asked about a specific checklist. Don, who has been given the nickname "Mr. 71" in reference to his propensity to come up with par-71 routings, adds, "One rule I always push is the idea of routing a hole into the land without grading and to avoid changing the drainage pattern. If you can accomplish this, you solve two problems: one is less grading work and the other is a potential drainage hassle that gets avoided."
5. Nearly in unison, "Too many road crossings, too many long walks between holes, and too many water hazards." Knott adds, "Another thing we've done that we now know isn't so bright is to run holes down the bottom of valleys. If you use one side or the other, it allows that natural drainage to stay where it is, and that saves cost and trouble." "I've gone to more gentle doglegs," says Linn, who apparently was once a fan of much stronger angles for par 4s and 5s.
6. "We've seen doglegs around houses and corridors that are only 300 feet wide because somebody thought that was a cardinal rule," says Linn. "Real estate is at the heart of a lot of bad routing plans," comments Knott. "The United States invented real estate golf courses, and this often prompts the question, 'What is the minimum space for a golf course?' The standards for how much space a golf course takes up never came from great courses; they came from other real estate courses. One of my pet peeves is the lack of priority that the golf course architect is sometimes given in laying out a course. In routing a golf course, you have to be able to see 300 yards down a view. But for streets and houses, this distance is much less. When a golf course is being planned through a real estate project, the routing of the course is the first thing that should be considered. Unfortunately, it is real estate

Top Ten Routing Considerations

Besides safety considerations, the most crucial aspects of golf course routings are listed in order of importance:

1. Varying the length of holes
2. Varying the direction of holes
3. Selecting a good clubhouse location
4. Varying the par of holes (good par distribution)
5. Ensuring returning nines
6. Orienting opening and finishing holes away from the sun
7. Finding predominantly north-south hole alignments
8. Creating minimal travel distance between holes
9. Balancing uphill and downhill holes
10. Making sure the 18th hole is not a par 3

(Source: Survey of golf course architects and planners conducted in 2001)

that can push the influences away from good golf. You have to beware."

7. For Gary Linn, it's Cypress Point. "It has three different landscapes, and each fits the land." "The routings people remember are always associated with great pieces of land," says Knott. "The course needs to feel right. The more space you have, the better I think you can get the course to feel."
8. "Once we had done our third or fourth project in Asia, we realized that no matter how many options you show, the clients over there are really not interested in anything except standard par-72 layouts," notes Linn. "It was quite amusing once to show up with a whole slew of options that had all sorts of different configurations and to be able to anticipate without any question which plan they would approve. It was, of course, the par-36, par-36 standard layout with four par 5s and four par 3s. We might as well have left the others at the office, and we sure could have saved a lot of time."

A final word from Linn is worth repeating to anyone interested in studying golf course routings: "Window seats on airplanes can be very useful."

Dr. Michael Hurdzan

In 1997, Dr. Michael Hurdzan was named Golf Course Architect of the Year by *Golf World* magazine. His study of turf management began at Ohio State University, after which he went on to earn a masters degree in landscape architecture and a Ph.D. in environmental plant physiology at the University of Vermont. Besides being an internationally recognized authority on golf course design and environmental issues, he is a super-nice guy. He is a partner in the firm Hurdzan-Fry. Dr. Hurdzan's office is like a museum of golf memorabilia. Before visiting him, I had considered my library moderately impressive. I now know that I have a collection of books; Hurdzan has a *library*.

1. "My first step is to gather as much information as possible about the site. Once we have everything from the property lines to topographical data, and all of the environmental issues, entitlement processes, and other approvals, we then create what we call a constraints map. This map is essentially everything that has to be considered on the site." From this point, Dr. Hurdzan typically looks to access points. "Sometimes there are many options, but usually there will be one or two that drive where we place the clubhouse," he says.
2. "We prioritize our client's objectives." Hurdzan notes that this approach allows his team to look at routings with an eye to saving costs and to getting at the heart of what decisions must be made. "We don't begin putting any lines on paper until we go through this process. Only with the constraints map and priorities in hand do we start the schematic routing work."
3. Hurdzan-Fry doesn't use templates. Instead, their process relies on ordinary colored pencils—the erasable kind. Triangles are sketched to represent back tee locations, dots at angle points, and circles for

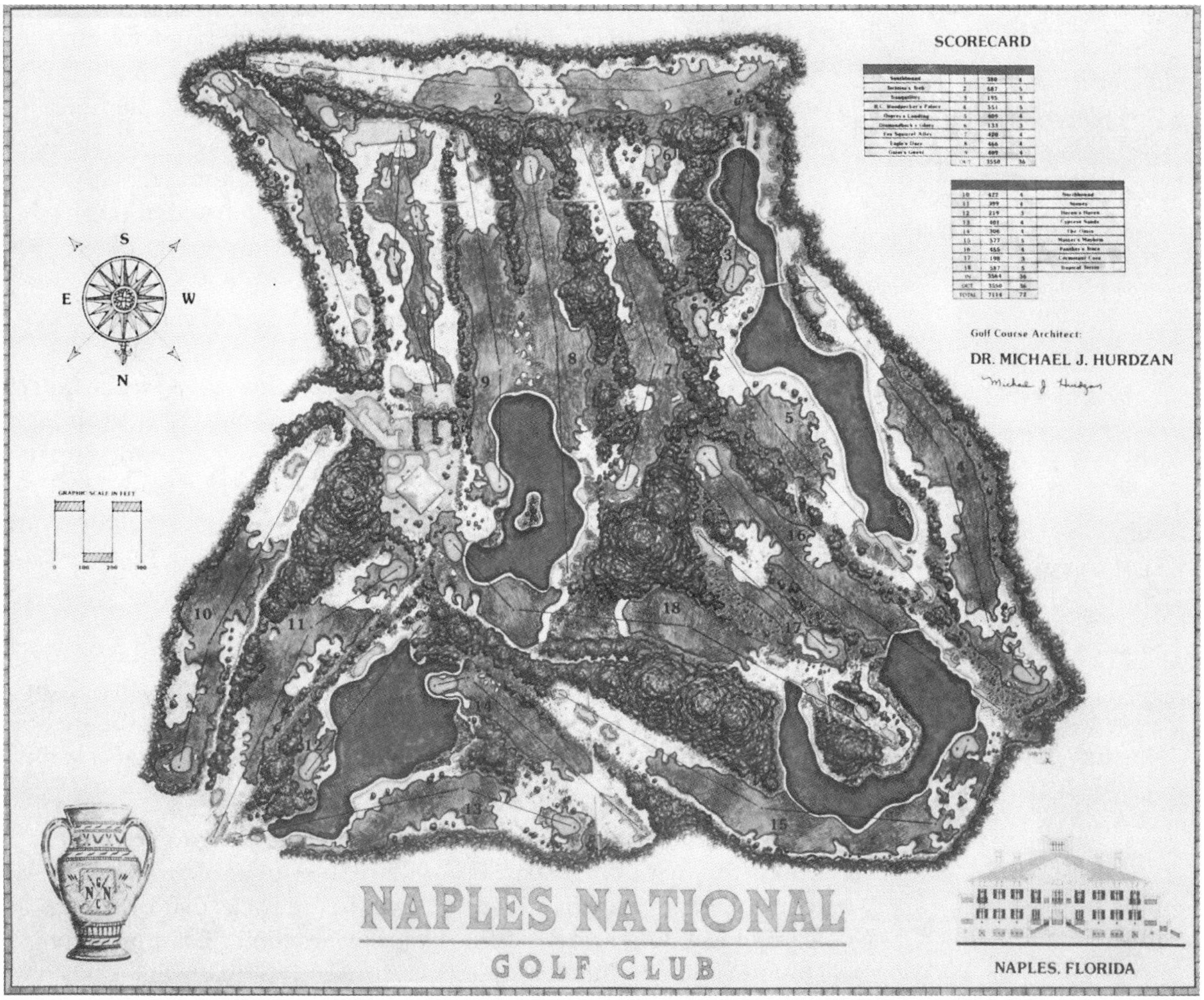

FIGURE 15-3
A routing plan for the Naples National Golf Club, by Dr. Michael Hurdzan, ASGCA.

COURTESY OF HURDZAN-FRY DESIGN.

green locations. The points are connected with straight lines. "We always note the elevation of tee points, landing areas, and the green locations. We call this our stick-and-ball drawing because that is essentially what it looks like."

4. "Our checklist is the list of constraints and priorities we develop for each project. Of course, we have the usual things to verify, but our feeling is that every site is unique."
5. "Our biggest mistakes have been trying to outguess how environmentalists will view projects." Hurdzan points out the wise saying that "all politics are local" and believes this is also true of environmental issues. "In one area, the hot button might be salamanders and at the next community it may be wildflowers." Guessing, in Hurdzan's view, is usually where projects can go astray.
6. "When planners have not done their homework, you will probably have a difficult time defending any routing that has been laid out. This is why we insist on a process." The Hurdzan-Fry philosophy is to

The course which demands the greatest number of placements from the tee, and the most diversity of shots, both from tee and to green, is the best.
—*George C. Thomas Jr.,* Golf Architecture in America

stir the spirit, exceed expectation, and, as he puts is, "defy understanding." Among his dislikes are designs that don't approach this level of thought. "I believe that each hole should have a distinctive and strong personality. It needs to become an unforgettable friend to the golfer."

7. "I am fascinated with all sorts of routings, not just those that are famous. Sometimes it is the out-of-the-way golf course that is refreshing and interesting." Among his own creations, an outright favorite is the Devil's Pulpit in Ontario, Canada.
8. "At the Devil's Pulpit, we gave our clients a choice of routing plans and some alternate green locations. Rather than choose, they instructed us to build the greens, after which they would make a decision on which to keep. This seemed sort of unusual, but it was an amazing commitment to doing what was right. Well, we ended up keeping the extra greens, and today the course can be played to these alternate greens, which makes for a interesting experience."

Bruce Charlton

Bruce is president of Robert Trent Jones II and has worked for the Jones Organization since 1981. His position has placed him directly in the spotlight of this world-renowned practice. Bruce is often the first on the scene when it comes to reviewing property for its potential as a finished course.

1. "Access is the most important. How are people going to get there? This is the first place I start. From there, we situate a clubhouse, and then the course begins to evolve." One of the tricks that Bruce has learned is to ask outright if the owner or developer has a preferred clubhouse site in mind. "You'd be surprised how many times this has all but been decided, but for some reason people think it might offend us to have a site already picked out. It's important for us to know what's in the client's mind, and there are usually a lot of good reasons why a particular site is preferred." On a few occasions, Charlton has started out by presenting clients with a plan showing clubhouse sites and nothing else. "Why not? Without an approved clubhouse location, a lot of time can get wasted," he points out.
2. "I go backward. I look for the best finishing holes and then the starting holes. Nothing is worse than a lackluster finish. The last three holes of each nine should be like a crescendo. They should be memorable. Once the finishing and starting holes are in place, we play with the others. Of course, by this time we have analyzed the elevations and studied the site for all sorts of conditions and the presence of great holes that need to be worked into the design."
3. Bruce draws centerlines right on a topo map, then follows up by placing tracing paper ("trash," as it is affectionately called) over the topo to further work out the details of optional routings. "Sometimes I don't even use a scale. I just work in a loose form until the site begins

to present some options." A useful term coined by Charlton is *airplane scale,* the creative use of maps scaled 1"=400' that fit easily on airplane tray tables and therefore allow routing work to continue while traveling.

4. "It's a mental checklist. The main ideal we stress is compass points for the par 3s—that is, having each par 3 play in a different direction. This is somewhat applied to the par 5s, too. We study left-to-right versus right-to-left holes. Our belief is that there should be one par 4 that is driveable, one par 5 that is reachable, and one definite three-shot par 5—although this is becoming harder and harder to achieve. In the final sequence, there should be a great chance of swings in a match and good risk-reward holes that are good gamble holes. In the closing holes, we usually make the hazards more intense and provide alternate routes and heroic shot opportunities."
5. "Personally, I have not done enough killer par 4s, the kind that takes every ounce of skill, not just length. It's relatively easy to design a long par 4 but difficult to make a shorter par 4 play really tough."
6. "Land planning can be very poor, especially when it requires routing through lots and across roads. This is the thing I dread most when it comes to routing."
7. "George C. Thomas's courses have always intrigued me. He was a master at changing directions almost every step of the way."

MOST COMMON MISTAKES MADE ON ROUTING PLANS

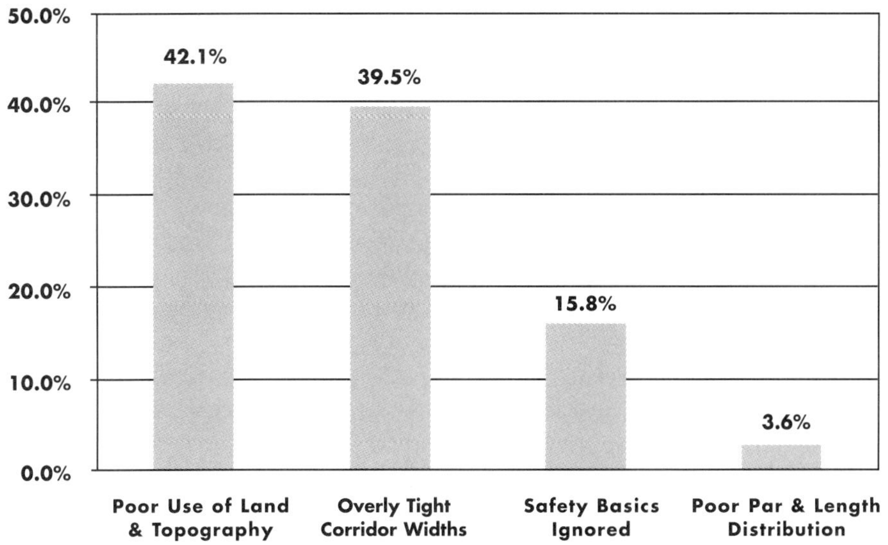

FIGURE 15-4
The four most common problems with routing plans, according to a survey of golf course architects and planners, are shown in their order of frequency.

8. "We did a project several years ago where the client wanted to look at options for an eventual complex of 72 holes, but it was important to consider the first and second 18 as separate phases. By the time we were done, considering that we were presenting multiple options and that within each plan there were multiple phasing choices, we had an exponential number of routing plans to render. I was up late, and one of these many plans—there must have been 30—somehow got an extra hole added to it. I called it a bonus hole."

Gil Martinez

Gil Martinez is president of GMA, a respected land planning firm responsible for energetic resort and community projects worldwide. In contrast to many planners, Gil is respected among golf course architects and widely used for his creative approaches to working with developers in an effort to get the most from all aspects of a project. (See Hole 6, "Real Estate: The Almighty Influence.")

1. "We begin by understanding the property constraints. Because our work revolves around real estate, we have to be efficient. Of course we look at drainage and where the water goes, and once you know this, you can see how wildlife uses the property. Visiting the property is essential; you've got to see the patient if you're going to operate. For a starting point, we must eventually find a clubhouse site. But it has to be tested to see if it works." One of Gil's favorite approaches is to test a clubhouse site by erecting scaffolding on the land to the height that the clubhouse is expected to be built. "This gives us a structure to climb and see the actual views that will be afforded. It also lets us visualize the mass of the clubhouse from areas of the property."
2. "We let the land drive the routing. My process is to assume a 7200-yard course and divide this by 18. My first pass is to route 18 holes of all equal size, about 450 yards each, just to see how the layout might go out and return. Very often this leads to the conclusion that we're better off with nine holes out and nine back. There's nothing wrong with that for most courses in today's world, especially where the site is difficult and rugged. Of course, I look at the topo when doing this preliminary routing study. Next I search for the par 3s, usually in tight areas where a longer hole could not fit as easily. And then I begin to balance the yardage and adjust my equal holes into par 3s, 4s and 5s. Of course, all of this has to make sense with the layout of streets and lots, and there has to be enough corridor width for the golf course to function properly."
3. Martinez does not use templates to lay out courses; he works over topo maps on tracing paper until ideas come together. Once a plan is articulated and passes some degree of acceptance by those involved, the tee, angle, and green points are staked in the field for a careful site walk-through. "This is a luxury we seldom do without. It tells us early on whether the plan will work or not."

When one has seen the golfers at Deal, St. Andrews, Westward Ho!, and Prestwick contenting themselves with greens which frequently violate some of these cherished principles, doubt arises in one's mind as to our wisdom in constructing as we do. Many of the finest greens in Britain lie there today, just as nature made them.
—Robert Hunter, The Links

4. "The list is there," Gil says, pointing to his head, "but it may be slightly different for every project, at least in terms of priority."
5. "Although we try not to make mistakes, everyone makes them, and we learn with each project."
6. "Putting the clubhouse on the high point of the property is a common mistake. It is usually a terrible place to put what amounts to a rather large building. Of course, when there are views to the ocean or forest, then this may make tremendous sense. In urban areas, it may be that the clubhouse needs to see just the golf course. I also have problems with single fairway routings when the land for the course is crowned—this creates a wall for a view." So what's Gil's biggest pet peeve? "Without a doubt, it's cramming too much onto a site. That is the biggest mistake developers make, because once it's built, it's there forever—it simply can't be fixed."
7. "A good routing plan needs to involve a good story line. People don't realize that the finished look of a golf course is just the skin; the routing is what's behind it all. The best routings are those that get into the thought process of the golfer and make people think."
8. "We once faxed a final routing plan down to Mexico after presenting a few options the month before. When we called back to talk through the final layout, we were told the guy we needed to speak with was out building the course!"

COMMON ERRORS

The most common errors in golf course routing are:

- Poor use of existing topography
- Poor use of existing vegetation
- Too many road crossings
- Failing to recognize that not enough land is available
- Long or difficult green-to-tee walks
- Poor balance between holes
- Back-to-back holes of similar length
- Poor variance in hole direction
- Disregard of morning and afternoon sun orientation
- Too many doglegs in one direction
- Too sharply angled doglegs
- Poor safety considerations

(Source: Not listed in any particular order; from a survey of golf course architects and planners conducted in 2001)

Les Furber

Having worked for Robert Trent Jones Sr. for 14 years and on his own for 21 years, Les, a Canadian golf architect, has seen it all. This interview was done by telephone, and I quickly realized that it's my loss to not have the opportunity to sit in the same room and share much more time with Les. For example, his story about working in Morocco with 200 military personnel and 200 civilians, each using wheelbarrows and shovels to build a course completely by hand, ranks among the most interesting I've ever heard about constructing golf courses in harsh locales. I would have loved to see Les describe how you build an entire green using manual labor in a vulnerable political climate—or, better yet, to hear in person his story about Mr. Jones's harrowing visit to Morocco during which an actual coup took place and his client, General Medbou, was killed by rebel forces just a few hundred yards away.

1. "For me, it involves studying the data and base information. The contours and mapping will suggest clubhouse sites. Once you look at these on paper, you can drive out on the site and see them in person. The first order of business is to find a place for all of the requirements: the clubhouse, parking and the start and finish holes. These are the things that come first."

FIGURE 15-5
Located in the Rocky Mountains at 5000 feet above sea level, this 455-yard par 4 plays much easier than it might appear. The elevation drops 120 feet from tee to the landing area and an additional 30 feet to a perched green. A medium- to short-iron approach shot allows the golf architect, Les Furber, ASGCA, to design a shallow green that creates a feeling of intimidation and deception.

SILVER TIP GOLF RESORT, ALBERTA, CANADA; PHOTO COURTESY OF LES FURBER

2. "I start by looking for good golf hole opportunities. And, of course, considering the flow of the land, the drainage, and the sunlight. I may draw as many as five alternatives for routings, and it's extremely crucial for me to visit the property. You don't get to appreciate the views by sitting in your office; I've learned that over the years."
3. Although Les runs a computer-literate office with all of the latest CAD software and capabilities, he still prefers to work schematically on tissue paper. "I draw and other people use the mouse," he explains. "We do not draw with the computer; we only use it to create working drawings once we have figured out the plan on paper." Les is also among the architects who do not rely on templates of holes. "I have a photographic memory of golf holes and take from my memory bits and pieces to fit the situation."
4. "My list is more of a list of taboos—finishing holes against the sun and things like that."
5. "I've put too much championship aspect into some layouts, especially at resorts where the idea is to have fun." With respect to workloads, Furber recalls his time with Robert Trent Jones Sr. and a valuable lesson learned. "I enjoyed working for Mr. Jones, and it made me realize the importance of delegating. Mr. Jones was great at this; he would give us direction and then let us perform. While running my own business, I've fallen into the realm of trying to do too much. Good golf course design takes a hands-on approach, and that's what I strive for now."

6. "Water features on the outside of doglegs do not enforce the integrity of golf holes. I believe blind holes slow play and should not be a part of designs. For uphill climbs, I try to design a par 5 where the golfer can spread out the elevation increase over three shots. This makes it less tiresome. I detest uphill par 3s because I believe it takes away all the thrill of making a hole-in-one. What good is this once-in-a-lifetime achievement if the poor guy who hit the ball doesn't get to see it go in?"
7. "My favorite routings are those with perhaps one extra par 3 or par 5. Instead of just four par 3s, I'll often add one on a nine because I firmly believe the 3s and 5s are the most memorable experiences in a round. Overall, I enjoy routings that are interesting and make you think with heroic and strategic holes."
8. Les has many humorous stories. Most are centered on the never-dull moments he spent working for Jones. "Once, when Mr. Jones was working for the king of Morocco, he was asked how many holes make up a golf course. Mr. Jones explained that golf courses were usually made up of 18 holes but that additional nines could be built if the demand was there. He said he had done 27-hole and 36-hole layouts for some clients. 'Then in Morocco, we shall have 45!' came the word from the king." And, so the story goes, 45 holes were built.

Pete Dye

I met Pete in the bar at the Double Eagle Golf Club outside Columbus, Ohio, just before we attended an event honoring the late Robert Trent Jones Sr. Although we had met before, I was reminded of how wonderfully honest Pete is in his opinions. He has an incredible knack of saying what he means, usually in a humorous way. For example, later that evening, during the tribute to Mr. Jones, when anyone who had ever worked for Jones was asked to stand, Pete called out, with his customary quick wit, "I applied for a job. Does that count?" (It might be noted that Alice Dye, an excellent golfer, was late coming off the finishing hole while I spoke with Pete, but this did not deter her from occasionally interjecting toward the end of our interview time. She will have you know that her comments, while they are attributed to Pete, are the sensible ones.)

1. "We begin with the clubhouse and, of course, there has to be good access for this area, and also the maintenance area. Owners will try like the devil to get you to put the clubhouse on the highest point on the property, and a lot of times you can't convince them this is wrong. It creates uphill finishing holes, and there is usually a much better location for it."
2. "We look at the property and use a topo map and aerial. We might find three or four ways to lay out the course, and then we walk the property without staking anything. We usually do this before going to the owner with any solutions. This is our time to test the various ideas. Once we have a basic routing plan, we discuss it with the client, and then we have the usual two, three, and four points put into the

ground for each hole so we can walk it and make adjustments." (By "two, three, and four points" Pete means the customary points used to lay out par 3s, 4s, and 5s respectively, with one point at the tee and green and points at each fairway landing point on the par 4s and 5s.)

3. "One of my quirks is that I work backward—it's a helluva lot more important to consider a golf hole from the green back than from the tee shot toward the green."
4. "No checklist, but we believe some things are more important than others. Balance, for example. At Crooked Stick, I must have been lucky with this, but if you look at the course there is a good balance of left-to-right and right-to-left holes, and an equal number of hazards on the right as on the left." One of Dye's theories, and I suspect he's onto something, is that golf course architects are highly influenced by where they played most of their golf during their first years with the game. During World War II, Dye ran the maintenance crew at Pinehurst and it was there, where he played nearly every day for almost half a year, that he became saturated with Donald Ross's style. "Ross would have a long par 4 and then a short one. A left-to-right hole might play into a green with a right-to-left opening. I'm sure these things stuck somewhere in me because they are things I seem to do without having to think about it."
5. "The first course we did, we crossed a creek 13 times! I have no idea what we were thinking, but back then we did a lot of forced carries that Alice and I still regret."
6. "Well, one thing that really bothers me is that the topo numbers are getting too damn small! My son, Perry, still has good eyesight, so we have him read the topo. Another thing today is how hard it is to evaluate what's going to happen to a golf course in the future. The strategy you set out to create might not be good several years ahead."
7. "Pinehurst No. 2 has tremendous variation—especially at the finish, where I think the routing of any course must show off its best face."
8. "The funniest thing I can remember to do with a routing was when we were working down in the Dominican Republic on the Teeth of the Dog. The client told us to create a great course and we could take our pick of the land we needed. We were clearing fairways along the cliffs above the ocean one afternoon when this guy, Rudolfo Escobar, who worked for our client, came running out to the site all out of breath. 'Mr. Dye,' he said in a trembling voice, 'our company owns more than 450,000 acres here, and somehow you've managed to build part of the golf course on land we don't own. Now I have to go and buy it!'"

Jay Morrish

Jay Morrish enjoys a distinguished career, having worked with many of the more prominent names in golf course design. His first position in the field was on the crew building Spyglass Hill in Pebble Beach, California. From there he worked for Robert Trent Jones Sr. and, later, with Fazio Golf Designs, Desmond Muirhead, and, finally, Jack Nicklaus. It was in the early days of Nicklaus's entrance to the design profession that Morrish gained a reputation as a frontrunner in the world of golf course architecture. In 1983, he formed his own firm and worked mainly with touring pro Tom Weiskopf, creating many celebrated designs throughout the world. Now, with all of his former partnerships behind him, he works from his Dallas-area office at what he calls "a more peaceful pace."

1. "I have a rule when beginning any project. I ask the owners to send me a contour map with 2-foot contours. Right away this tells me who's serious and who isn't. Anyone who's serious about building a golf course has no problem coming up with the mapping, even if the topo has to be flown from scratch." From this point, Morrish moves on to

FIGURE 15-6
The ninth hole at Stone Canyon Golf Club in Tucson, Arizona. Jay Morrish, ASGCA, considers it among the most striking examples of desert golf, with the land literally melting into the golf course and vice versa.

PHOTO COURTESY OF THE STONE CANYON GOLF CLUB

the task of beginning to put the pieces together. "I make sure we have a good idea of who's involved. It's important to have a handle on the engineering, the planning, and any wetlands work. Then, once all of the information is gathered, I focus on the clubhouse. Usually it's on a high point and somewhere in the center of things." Jay points out that clients typically want their clubhouse elevated where it has views and can be seen. "We can usually work with this unless it's too high up or creates a battle getting the finishing holes back home."

"My process revolves around templates. I have various scales—even metric—that I use regularly." When asked about a common dismissal of templates because they go against fitting holes to the land, Morrish has a quick response: "The templates I use are hinged so we can bend the doglegs, and we have all different lengths. It not only saves time but it allows me to see so many options. It confirms whether a course is doable or not. I can look at multiple options in a very short period of time, which I couldn't possibly accomplish without them."

4. "It's a mental checklist, but I go through all of the usual things like variation in par 3s and making sure we're being sensitive to the direction of the sun."
5. "My biggest mistakes have been to work on a few projects where the people in charge were clueless."
6. "People that are clueless."
7. "A favorite of mine is Double Eagle outside Columbus, Ohio. No two par 4s are in a row, and it's one of the few courses I've ever done that I've been able to attain that. But there, we really had our choice of the land, and the routing just fell together nicely. Any time a routing falls into place, it makes for a good start."
8. Morrish smiles about a course in Tennessee that he visited once to help fix. "Basically, it was missing a hole. This farmer simply went out there and graded the entire course without plans. What a mess, but it was a funny one."

Bob Lohmann

Bob Lohmann is president of Lohmann Golf Designs in Chicago, Illinois. He began his career with the firm of Killian & Nugent before starting his own practice. Like many of those interviewed, Bob is a past president of the ASGCA and active in supporting the golf course design profession through organizations, conferences, and seminars.

1. "Aside from the clubhouse, which is really where I think you have to begin looking at sites, we tend to look at green and tee sites. This is all done on the topo so we can understand the land before going out there and walking around." Bob relates an unusual trick he learned from architect Dick Nugent. "Dick would always use his fist as an approximate placeholder for a clubhouse. Of course, his fist is fairly big, so at 1"=200' scale, it represented a decent size. I can still picture him placing his fist on a topo map and quickly outlining the area, which amounted to about 6 acres."

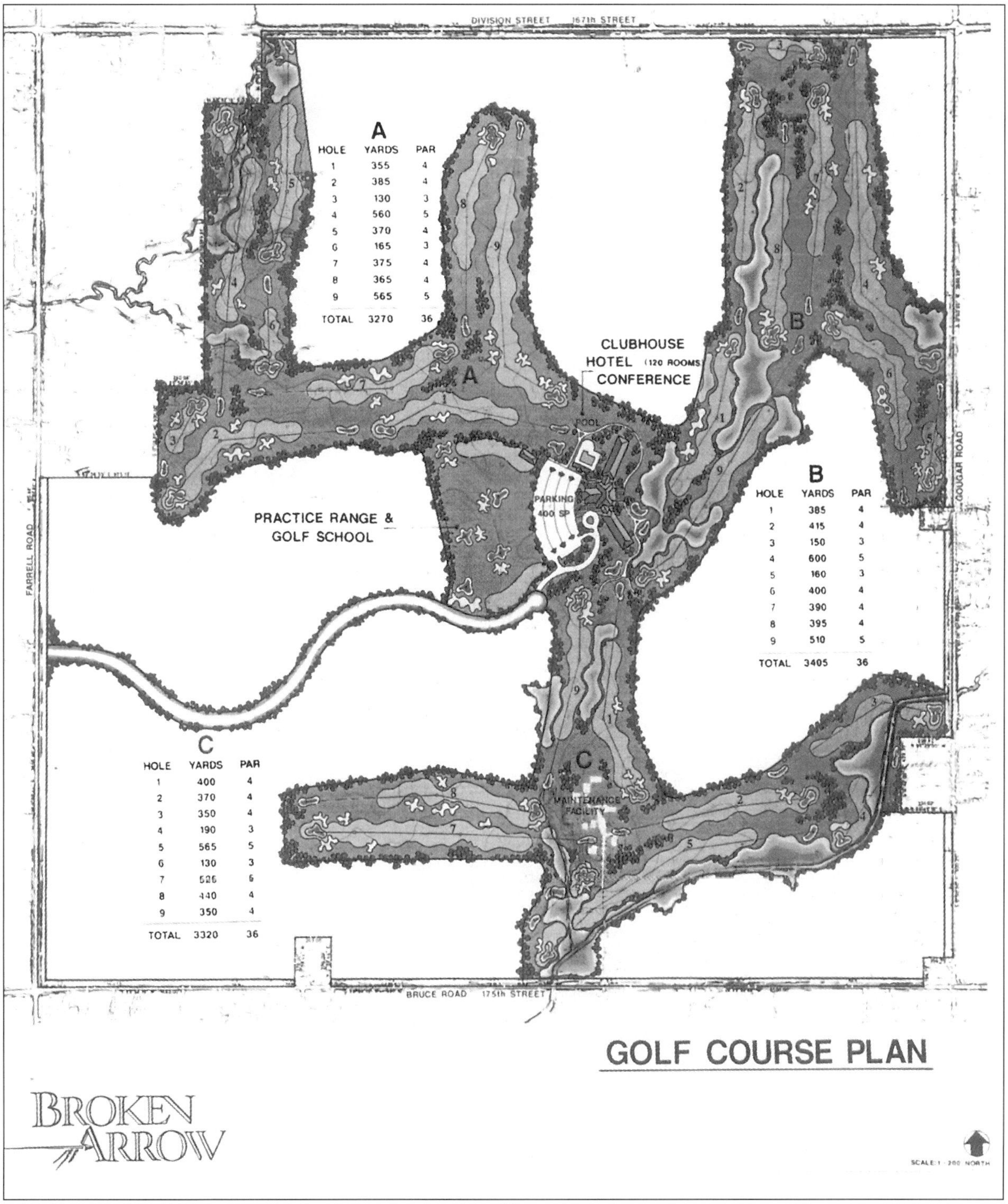

DIVISION STREET 167th STREET
A
HOLE YARDS PAR
1 355 4
2 385 4
3 130 3
4 560 5
5 370 4
6 165 3
7 375 4
8 365 4
9 565 5
TOTAL 3270 36
CLUBHOUSE
HOTEL (120 ROOMS)
CONFERENCE
POOL
PARKING
400 SP
PRACTICE RANGE &
GOLF SCHOOL
FARRELL ROAD
B
HOLE YARDS PAR
1 385 4
2 415 4
3 150 3
4 600 5
5 160 3
6 400 4
7 390 4
8 395 4
9 510 5
TOTAL 3405 36
COUGAR ROAD
C
HOLE YARDS PAR
1 400 4
2 370 4
3 350 4
4 190 3
5 565 5
6 130 3
7
8 440 4
9 350 4
TOTAL 3320 36
MAINTENANCE
FACILITY
BRUCE ROAD 175th STREET
GOLF COURSE PLAN
BROKEN
ARROW
NORTH

FIGURE 15-7

Routing plan for the Broken Arrow Golf Club, Lockport, Illinois, by Bob Lohmann, ASGCA. The unique 27-hole routing is in the midst of a residential development, extends in all directions, yet is not interrupted by road crossings. Even though frontage is maximized, the effect is a core-type routing.

COURTESY OF LOHMANN GOLF DESIGNS, INC.

The heart of golf lies in propelling the ball accurately from one situation to another. Each step in the journey should be hazardous.
—*John L. Low,*
Concerning Golf

2. "After we walk the site, we typically come back and begin laying out various options using a set of templates that we've made over the years. We have various hole lengths and sizes that are cut out of transparent plastic. It allows us to fit holes in and try different approaches."
3. "Once the templates are laid out and we feel this routing might be worthwhile, we'll trace it by putting tracing paper right over the templates and topo. These routing studies are then used later to come up with final options. Very often, we'll go back out to the site and repeat the process or check on areas that need further study."
4. "We do have a checklist, mainly for things like balancing the holes that go left against those that go right. Also for shot values, we take a lot of time making sure that we're creating the most interesting layout we can get." Bob also takes great pride in involving his entire design staff in critiquing routings. "It is not uncommon for four architects to look at each routing and make suggestions and improvements. It adds work but, in the long run, it makes for a better finished product."
5. "My biggest concern is when I see things are getting too tight. It's very important to be able to convince clients to do what's right. The mistakes we've made have always been in this area—that is, not doing a good job of convincing. This is the most important lesson I've learned: You have to gain the trust of those you're working for."
6. "Having the sun face early holes or finishing holes is a real problem. So is a lack of variation in holes. These are the two problems we see most in routings, especially plans we get that have already been routed by land planners."
7. Bob's favorite routings are the layouts that seem the most comfortable and offer the most variation. "Variation is key" is a common theme he uses when addressing those in the industry and his clients.
8. "There's always those great stories about presenting 17-hole layouts. I've done that, and it's something you really only want to do once in your life, I can assure you."

Dana Fry

In Texas, long ago, in a comforting Texan sort of twang, I was given the secret to how one finds enough time to play golf: "Everybody has the same amount of time; it's all in how you prioritize it." Dana Fry has found enough time to play golf. During the rest of his time, he designs golf courses. Dana first learned his craft working as a field designer for Tom Fazio and then joined Dr. Michael Hurdzan in Columbus, Ohio, in 1988. In a relatively short time, Dana has become a sought-after designer and a creative force in the world of golf course architecture.

1. "We begin at the clubhouse. Of course, we'll always ask the client if they have an idea of where the clubhouse should be. After all, they probably know the land better than we do at the early stages."
2. Dana admits that he couldn't read topo before he joined with Mike Hurdzan. "When I was a shaper in the field, we used sketches to build

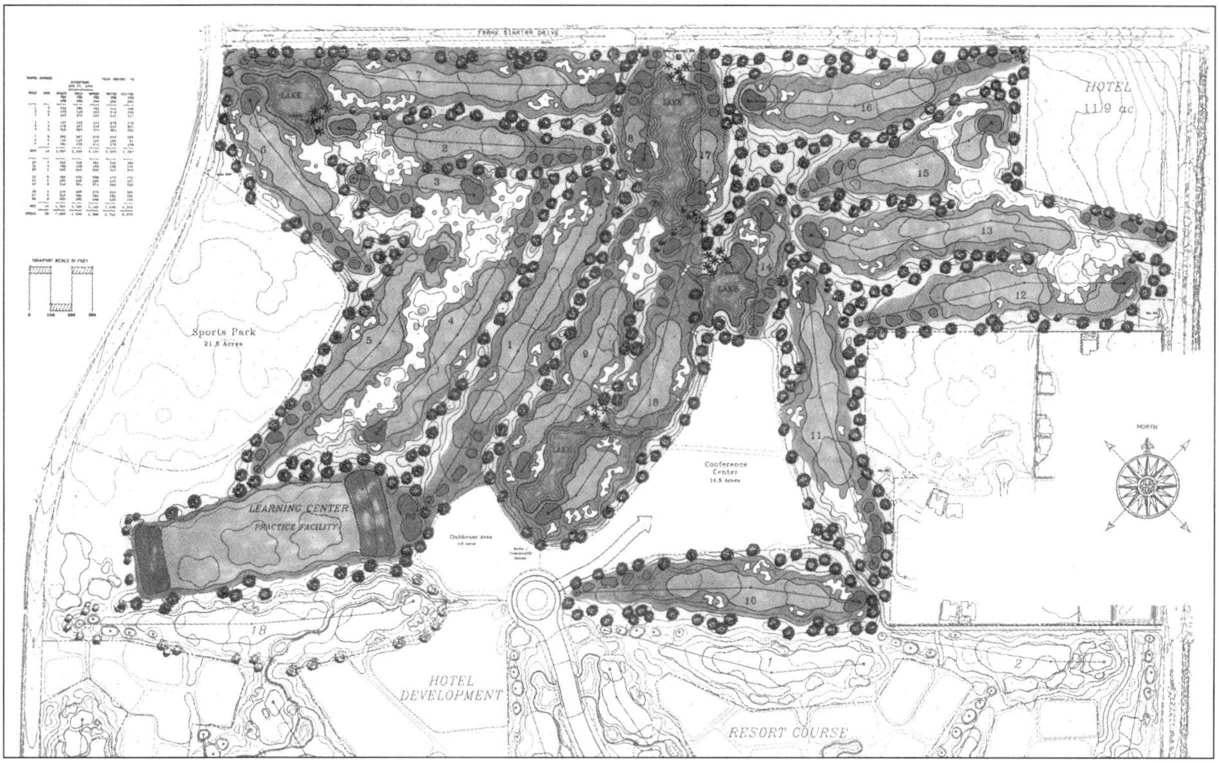

FIGURE 15-8
Routing plan by Dana Fry, ASGCA, for a resort course in Palm Desert, California.

COURTESY OF HURDZAN-FRY DESIGN.

from, but I soon learned the value of topo mapping and designing this way. Our process is to let the land dictate where the holes should go, and we strive for this in all our work." Like other offices with multiple designers, Hurdzan-Fry brings them together to look at routings and work as a team. "This is a tremendous benefit because what one of us might see could bring a whole new perspective to the routing."

3. "We don't use templates in our office. We just sketch routings on tracing paper that we lay over the contour maps."
4. Fry has no official checklist but spends a great deal of effort on safety issues. "It's one of the most important things we stress."
5. "My first projects probably were not as good as they could have been when it came to alternating shots into a green. This is why it's so important to have more than one designer looking at the routing plan. What may not be evident to one person is usually obvious to another."
6. "Sometimes things get thrust upon you. Being squeezed is an awful position to be in, especially when you don't have the power to put your foot down and do the right thing."
7. Fry has played all of the top 100 courses in the United States as rated by *Golf Digest*. In addition, he's played 95 of the top 100 courses in the world as rated by *Golf* magazine, so I was greatly interested in his comments about favorite routings. "Shinnecock Hills [Southampton, New York] simply has no weakness. It is as pure as a routing plan can get and a remarkable golf course in virtually every way."

8. "It's not particularly humorous, but there is an irony to Tom Doak's new Pacific Dunes course in Oregon. It sits right next to Bandon Dunes, which has achieved almost every possible high rating that a new course can receive, yet in my opinion Pacific Dunes is even better. Every hole fits the land perfectly. I think it will be interesting to see how it gets received."

Cabell Robinson

Cabell Robinson joined the office of Robert Trent Jones back in 1963 and was asked by Mr. Jones to run an office in Spain. Cabell initially refused, at which point Mr. Jones asked whether Cabell had ever been to Europe. "Nope," he answered, and so it was decided that he should at least give it a try. He traveled to Spain and later admitted he really liked it. "It was a whole lot more exciting than New Jersey, so I accepted the challenge," he notes. Today Robinson works in both the United States and Europe, managing his own firm. Including the work for Jones, he has completed 40 golf courses and has worked in 18 different countries.

1. "I begin at the clubhouse, unless there is some compelling reason not to."
2. "My first pass is to try for two out-and-back nines, but I'm definitely not opposed to one loop going out and back. I think in nine-hole segments." One of the greatest lessons Robinson learned, which came from working in the Jones organization, was not to focus too early on the details. "If you get into the small details too quickly, you lose sight of what really needs to be done, and that's getting a routing plan that works. That will allow you to move on to the next step."
3. "I do everything freehand, even without a scale. I work on tracing paper and might go through dozens of studies before things begin to work out."
4. "There's a checklist in my head, but I keep my mind open to new ideas. Besides the customary rules, I try to stay open to new ideas and don't let too many rules bog me down."
5. "I've made a lot. The good news is that there are probably no more left for me to make. I've used up my quota!"
6. "I don't care for it when courses are divided into halves. This is less interesting to the golfer."
7. "A golf course needs to adventure a person. Places like Pebble Beach are excellent at this; they take you on a journey, and they are intriguing. Some of the best routings in the world have conditions that we tend to shy away from nowadays. Greens you can't see on a par-4 or -5 tee are a good example. Every once in a while, a green you can't see is a nice thing because it adds a sense of surprise to the game. The same goes for blind shots. One or two make the game interesting."
8. "I accidentally presented a 19-hole course to some clients one time and quickly came up with the idea that we couldn't decide on which par 3 was better. I'm not sure if they bought it at the time, but it was the only thing I could come up with on the spur of the moment."

PART FOUR

The Finish

Presenting Routing Plans

HOLE NO.

16

Presentations are not just about unrolling a nicely colored plan and then sitting back to answer questions if they come. It is well documented that, at least in the eyes of most people, a routing plan can be confusing. Not only does the routing plan itself need to be crafted with clarity to communicate well but so does the overall presentation—including the format of the meeting, what will be said, and the form of the presentation itself.

The range of presentation types is broad. The plan may be a rough sketch shown to a longtime client at a one-on-one meeting. Obviously, the logistics and need for a more formal plan in this setting is nowhere what goes into a presentation before a planning commission that will ultimately vote on whether or not to allow a golf course to be built. Between these extremes are all of the reasons to create a routing plan. All presentations, big deals or small, are important. Once a plan is presented for the first time, it cannot be presented again for the first time. A good first impression is precious.

Very often when you say something is, it becomes.
—Vernon Swaback, of Swaback Partners, commenting on the gift of being able to articulate the essence of a project

No matter its level of intensity, a presentation is an opportunity. With a familiar client or group, it is an opportunity to continue to show one's depth and value. With a new client or group, it is an opportunity to generate confidence in one's abilities. Before a large group, it is an opportunity to promote golf and golf courses as excellent uses of land for recreation and open space.

Routing plans are not static. Even when they are pinned to a wall and its creators have left the room, people will study them and play around the course as if they are miniature golfers hitting shots across the brightly colored lake colored in front of the 15th green. The human being cannot help but follow sequentially numbered stops on a map. This compulsive behavior stems from our kindergarten days, when we learned to count. The routing plan is a map that sucks one in to its sequential points of interest. Follow the path. Where does it lead? What lies ahead? The map is a magnet.

Those who had benefit of hearing the golf course architect or planner point out the plan's key aspects will repeat them to others. The plan will develop a life of its own. While it may define the *physical* changes to take place, it represents *psychological* changes, too. The best routing plan presentations are expressions of how the golf course will play to the emotions.

LEVEL OF DETAIL

Routing plans are used for three primary purposes: (1) as a working tool to help determine whether or not projects are viable and the consequences of the options to the routing; (2) in a presentation to sell a golf course design; and (3) as a record of the finished course that will help players understand it.

Each of these purposes calls for a different level of detail or emphasis. Most attention is paid to reasons 1 and 2, as these are the *primary* uses of routing plans. The uses associated with reason 3 are considerably downstream.

Routing plans typically include the following details:

- Primary tee point
- Angle points
- Green points
- Centerlines
- Property limits
- Golf course limits

  Occasionally with safety envelopes for each hole expressed in some degree of detail.
- Other primary uses

  Access, clubhouse area, practice area, etc.
- Prominent site features and existing obstacles

  Natural or artificial water, ravines, wetlands, environmentally sensitive areas, etc., that are necessary for site evaluation and affect the routing.

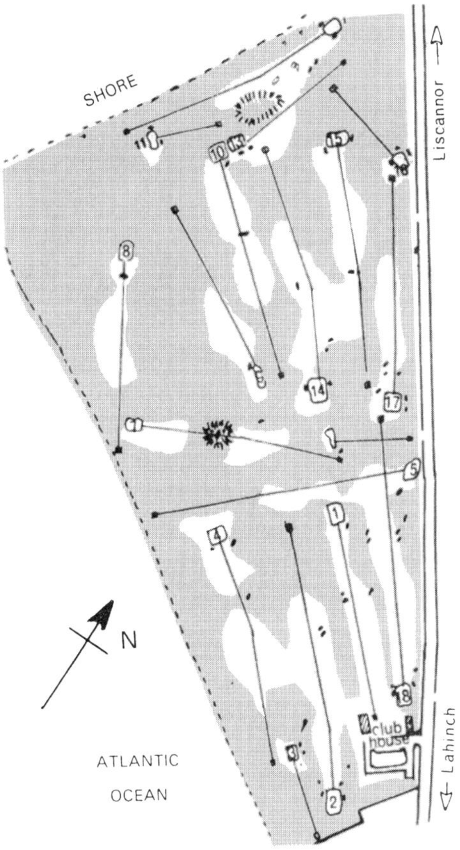

FIGURE 16-1
In their most rudimentary form, routing plans show not much more than the centerlines of holes. These examples were taken from scorecards where the function is simply to show the path of the golf course. Although such stick-figure plans are a viable means to show a golf course, they are not adequate to show the features and strategy, now expected by recipients of routing plans prepared by professionals.

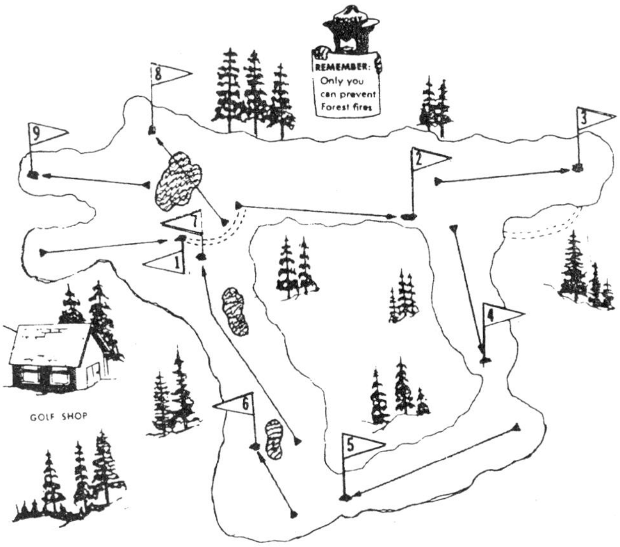

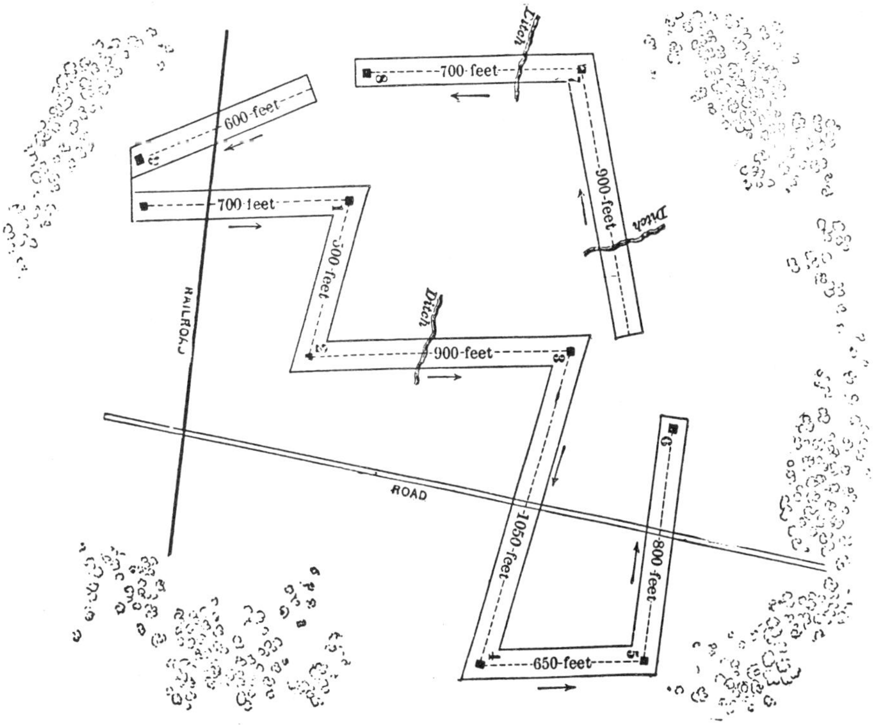

FIGURE 16-2
As scary as a routing plan presentation can get! This diagram appeared in *Outing* magazine in February 1899. It is indicative of early American courses, which were often nothing more than flags placed in a flat field. The emphasis was on the straight path from tee area to green area.

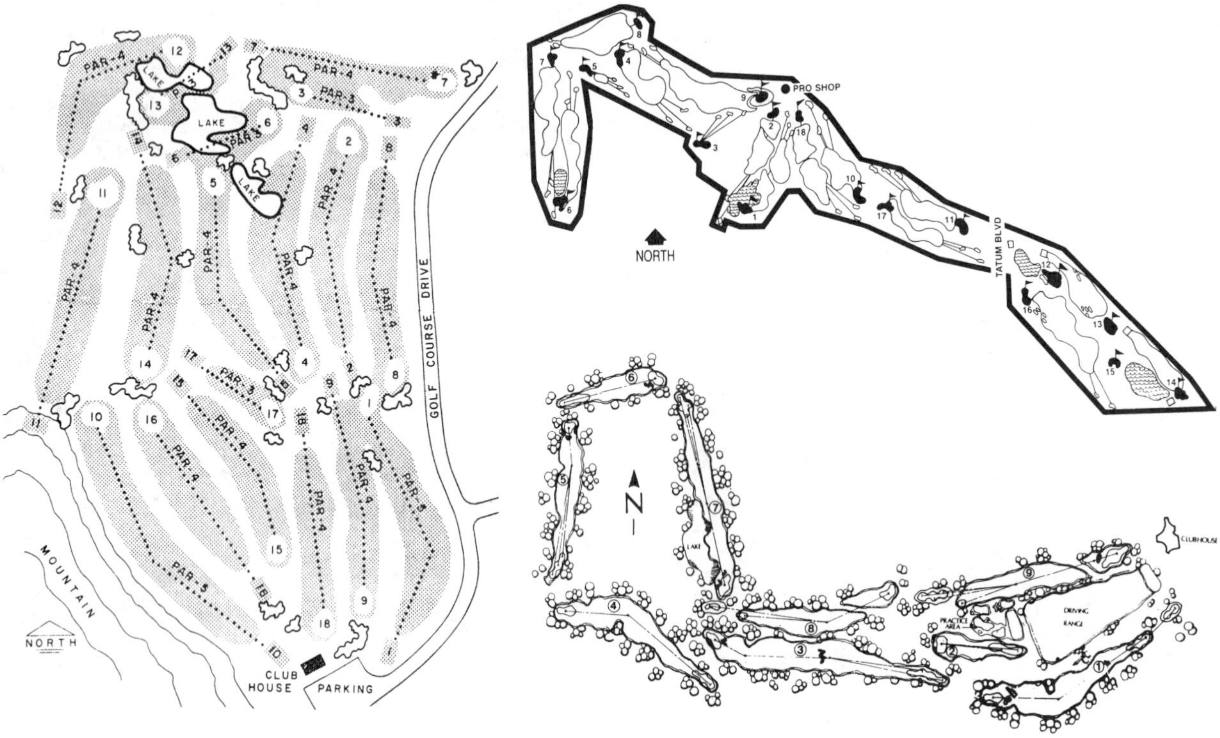

FIGURE 16-3
As it became more important to indicate more than just the path of golf holes, fairway limits and features were added to routing plans. In these examples taken from scorecards, the routings are shown in great detail despite their small size.

- Prominent site improvements
- Site orientation

  North, scale, prevailing wind, etc.
- Course scorecard

  Par, yardages, etc. (often accompanies the routing plan if not actually affixed to it)

Additional details can include but are not limited to the following:

- Additional tees and tee details

  Outlines of tee shapes, points, and centerlines of shots.
- Fairway, mowing, and rough delineations

  The limits of the improved turfgrass is the most common indication, but some plans, by way of color or texture, show differences in fairway mowed heights, roughs, etc.
- Contrasting roughs

  Waste areas, detention basins, tall grassy areas, etc.
- Hazards

  Sand bunkers, water hazards, ravines, shorelines, etc.
- Water

  All water features, natural or artificial.
- Terrain features

  Natural barancas, hillsides, forested areas, rock outcroppings, etc.
- Trees and vegetation

  Existing naturally and areas to be planted.

- Topo
  Shown by contour lines or by hatching.
- Green details
  Green outlines and perhaps even major contour variations within.
- Cart path alignments
- Project features
  Improvements such as residential areas, lots, roads, and structures.
- Clubhouse building and grounds
  In detailed form.
- Detailed notes and descriptions
  Often, the playing strategy of a golf hole is called out on a plan; also, a description of the course and holes can accompany the routing plan.
- Comparison chart
  Showing the variation and differences among the holes, either along with the scorecard or as a separate chart.

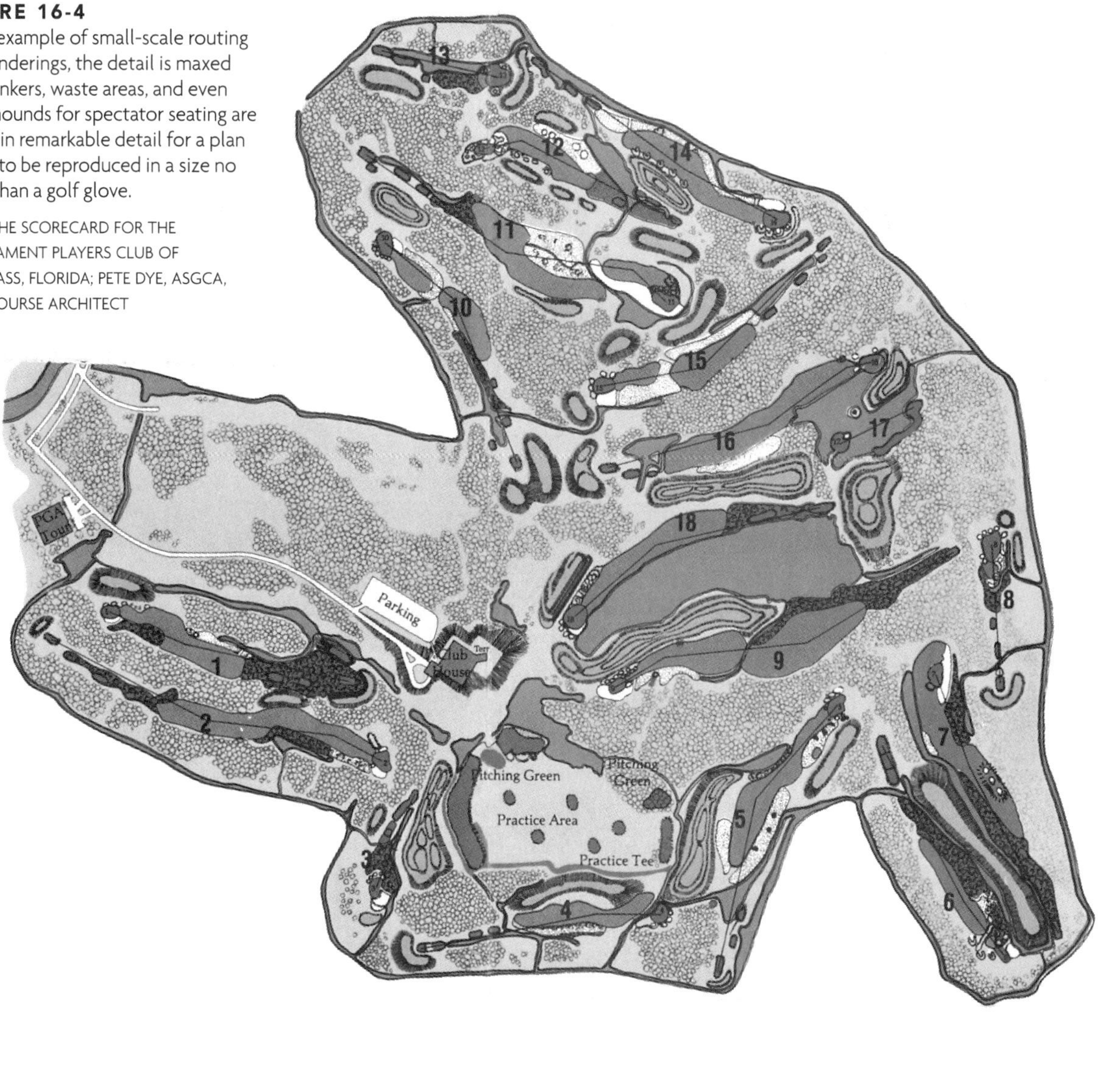

FIGURE 16-4
In this example of small-scale routing plan renderings, the detail is maxed out. Bunkers, waste areas, and even large mounds for spectator seating are shown in remarkable detail for a plan meant to be reproduced in a size no larger than a golf glove.

FROM THE SCORECARD FOR THE TOURNAMENT PLAYERS CLUB OF SAWGRASS, FLORIDA; PETE DYE, ASGCA, GOLF COURSE ARCHITECT

NAMING

Golf architects often name courses and even holes. And why not? Sculptors name their work. It is part of the joy of being an artist. Best name ever? How about Gog Magog Golf Club in Cambridgeshire, England? The club derives its name from the chalk hills on which the course lies; Gog and Magog are the two legendary giants whose roots reach back into ancient mythology.

Routing plans, of course, must all have adequate title blocks, drawing information, dates, etc. This information is essential, as it establishes the basics for anyone looking at the plan. A discussion of the three fundamental uses of routing plans summarizes their relationship to ideas covered in earlier chapters:

(1) Routing Plans as Working Tools: Routing plans for the purpose of planning and determining suitability are generally rough in format, almost sketchy. They are typically at 1"=200' scale, although 1"=400' scale is sometimes used for large sites or those with multiple courses. Regardless of the scale to which the plan is reduced, almost all routing plans are drawn at 1"=200' scale when working out options and determining feasibility.

Often, such plans are made up of just centerlines and points, with no regard for further detail. Working plans, however, can be more elaborate, and sketches can include fairway outlines and may even be colored to better show the sequence of holes and—always an important consideration—to increase readability.

Routing plans are used as working tools in these contexts: determining land suitability, siting evaluation, preliminary budget determination, general land planning, obtaining early client approval of approaches, obtaining entitlements, and similar needs. Rarely are roughly sketched plans used for making formal proposals, obtaining final permits, land/project marketing, or obtaining financing.

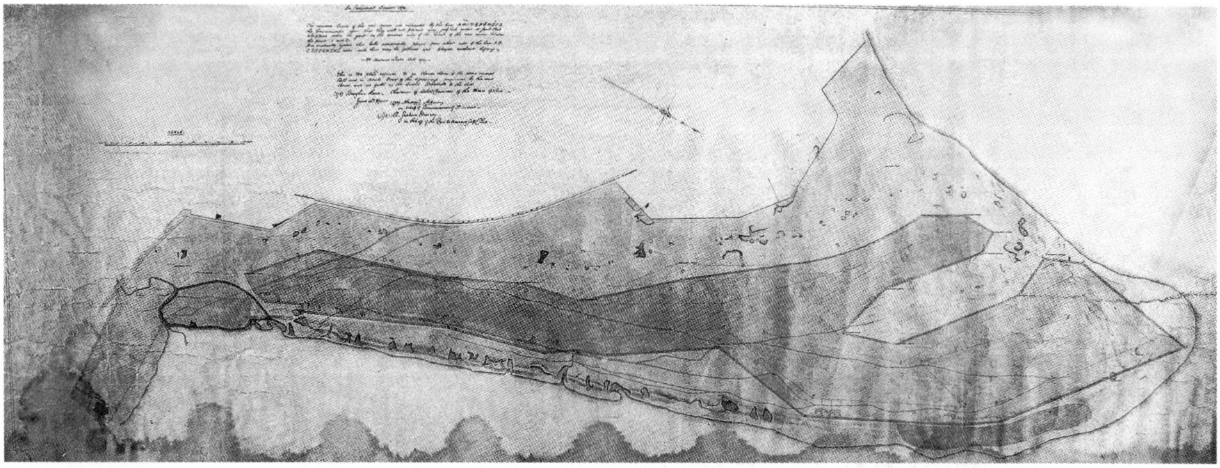

FIGURE 16-5

The New Course at St. Andrews is among the first, if not *the* first, routing plan ever drawn that depicted centerlines for each golf hole. Centerlines are now a staple of routing plans. The designer of The New Course was B. Hall Blyth, a civil engineer. Blyth's plan shows centerlines for The New Course. Blyth's original plan was about to be burned in a bonfire many years after The New Course was built but was saved at the last minute. (See "Subsequent Maps" in Hole 2) The plan now hangs proudly in the new clubhouse that serves the courses operated by the St. Andrews Links Trust.

COURTESY OF THE ST. ANDREWS LINKS TRUST

PRESENTATION FORMAT

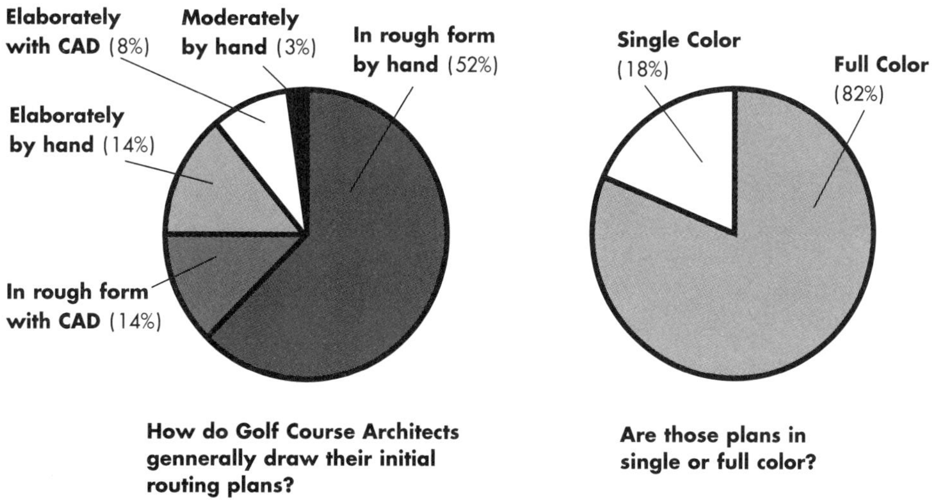

FIGURE 16-6
Golf course architects and planners answered these questions as part of a 2001 survey. The results show that most initial routing plans are loosely detailed yet rendered in color.

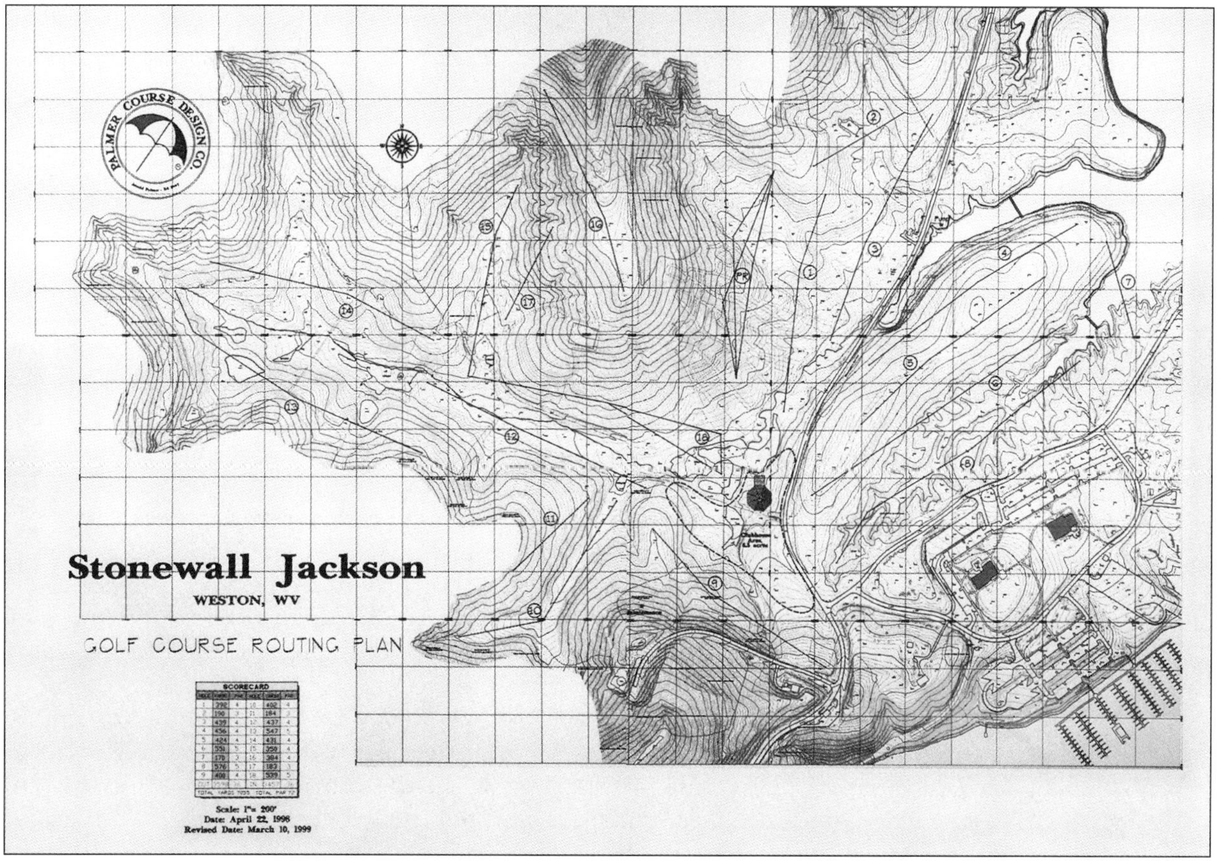

FIGURE 16-7
This routing plan, although generated using CAD software, is as simple as it gets. The plan consists of hole centerlines only and was created based on rough sketches drawn over the topographical mapping. From this plan, which is largely an in-house planning tool, the golf course architects will develop a more detailed plan for presentation purposes.

COURTESY OF PALMER COURSE DESIGN COMPANY

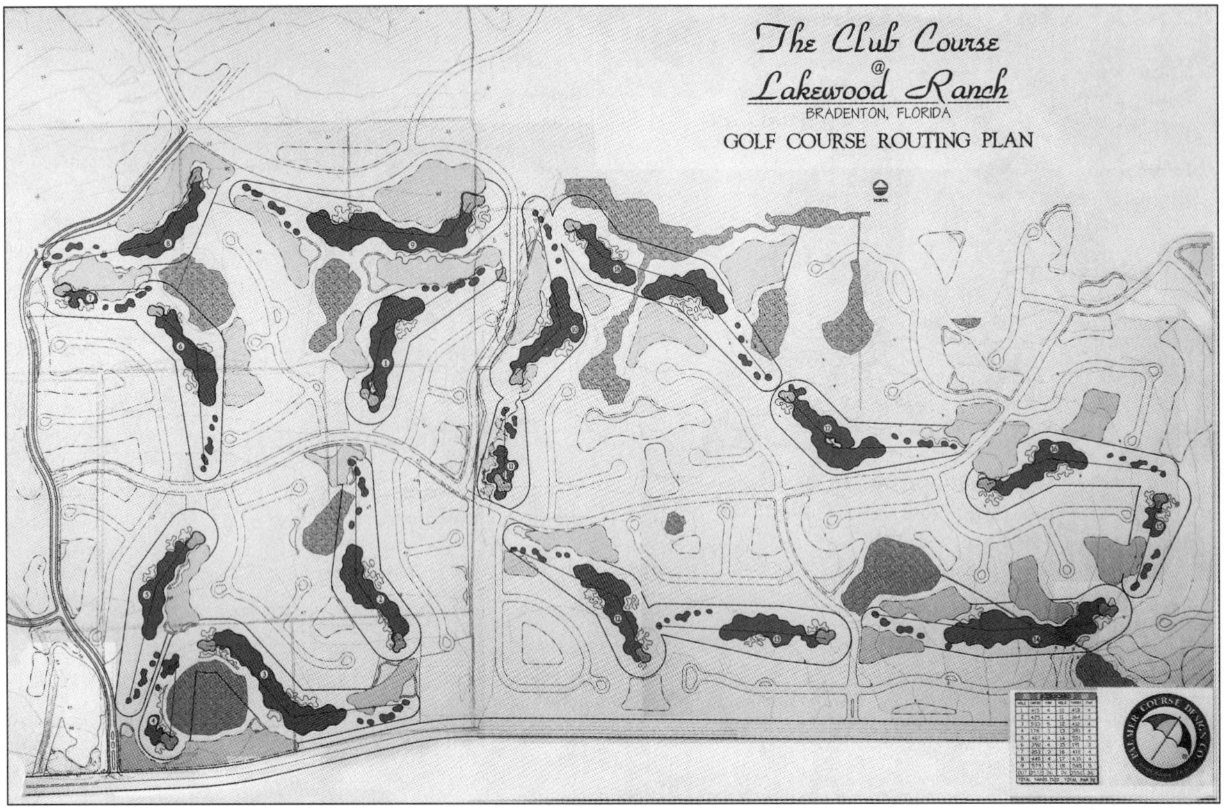

FIGURE 16-8
Example of a routing plan created for the purpose of determining land use.

COURTESY OF PALMER COURSE DESIGN COMPANY

(2) Routing Plans Presented to Sell a Design: Routing plans for the purpose of selling, especially to those outside the world of architects, planners, engineers, and so on, must be clear, exciting, and full of interest. They are usually in color and are almost always appreciated first in a formal setting, such as a meeting or presentation before a group. They are typically at 1"=200' scale, although 1"=100' scale is also popular. At 1"=100' scale, much detail can be put into a plan—almost too much for some situations. A par-5 hole at 1"=100' scale, for example, can be almost 20 inches long—the length of a small dog. If this scale is used, then the plan must be detailed enough to make the large holes look appropriate. The reverse is equally true. A plan at 1"=400', regardless of its use, cannot have too much detail, or it might be too confusing.

A nation writes its story in a book of deeds: history—and a book of art: painting, sculpture and architecture. The book of art is the most enduring and easily read.
—Unknown author

(3) Routing Plans of Finished courses: When a course is built, or almost ready to open, a final routing record plan is often useful to the marketing people whose job it is to promote the course and bring it to life on scorecards, sales brochures, and the framed print that hangs in the clubhouse like those still at St. Andrews almost 200 years after they were drawn.

Requests for such plans should not be ignored or thought of as too bothersome. It is essential that the person responsible for the design of a golf course represent it and record it for future generations. The changes that were likely made to the last routing plan—perhaps the one just

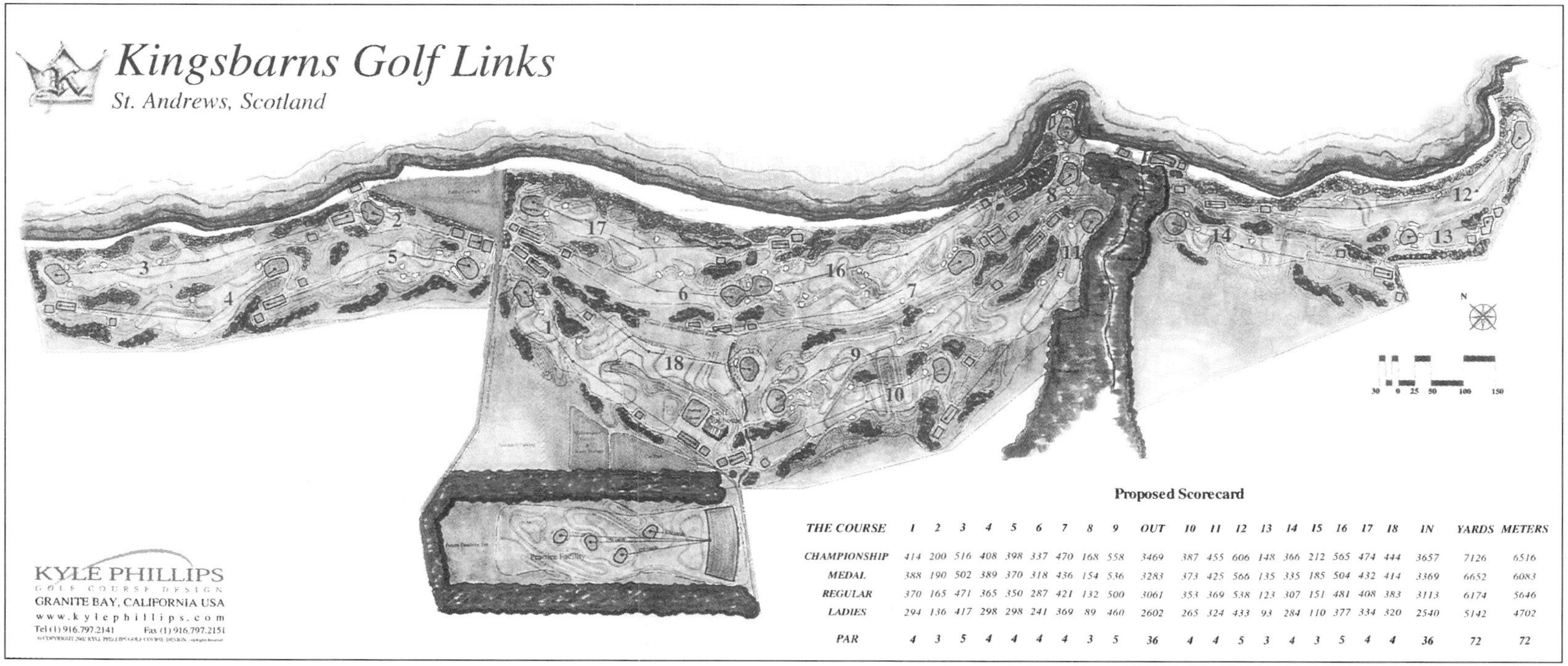

Kingsbarns Golf Links
St. Andrews, Scotland
1
2
3
4
5
6
7
8
9
10
11
12
13
14
16
17
18
N
30 0 25 50 100 150
Proposed Scorecard
THE COURSE 1 2 3 4 5 6 7 8 9 OUT 10 11 12 13 14 15 16 17 18 IN YARDS METERS
CHAMPIONSHIP 414 200 516 408 398 337 470 168 558 3469 387 455 606 148 366 212 565 474 444 3657 7126 6516
MEDAL 388 190 502 389 370 318 436 154 536 3283 373 425 566 135 335 185 504 432 414 3369 6652 6083
REGULAR 370 165 471 365 350 287 421 132 500 3061 353 369 538 123 307 151 481 408 383 3113 6174 5646
LADIES 294 136 417 298 298 241 369 89 460 2602 265 324 433 93 284 110 377 334 320 2540 5142 4702
PAR 4 3 5 4 4 4 4 3 5 36 4 4 5 3 4 3 5 4 4 36 72 72
KYLE PHILLIPS
GOLF COURSE DESIGN
GRANITE BAY, CALIFORNIA USA
www.kylephillips.com
Tel (1) 916.797.2141 Fax (1) 916.797.2151

FIGURE 16-9
Routing plan of Kingsbarns Golf Links, St. Andrews, Scotland.

COURTESY OF KYLE PHILLIPS, ASGCA, GOLF COURSE ARCHITECT

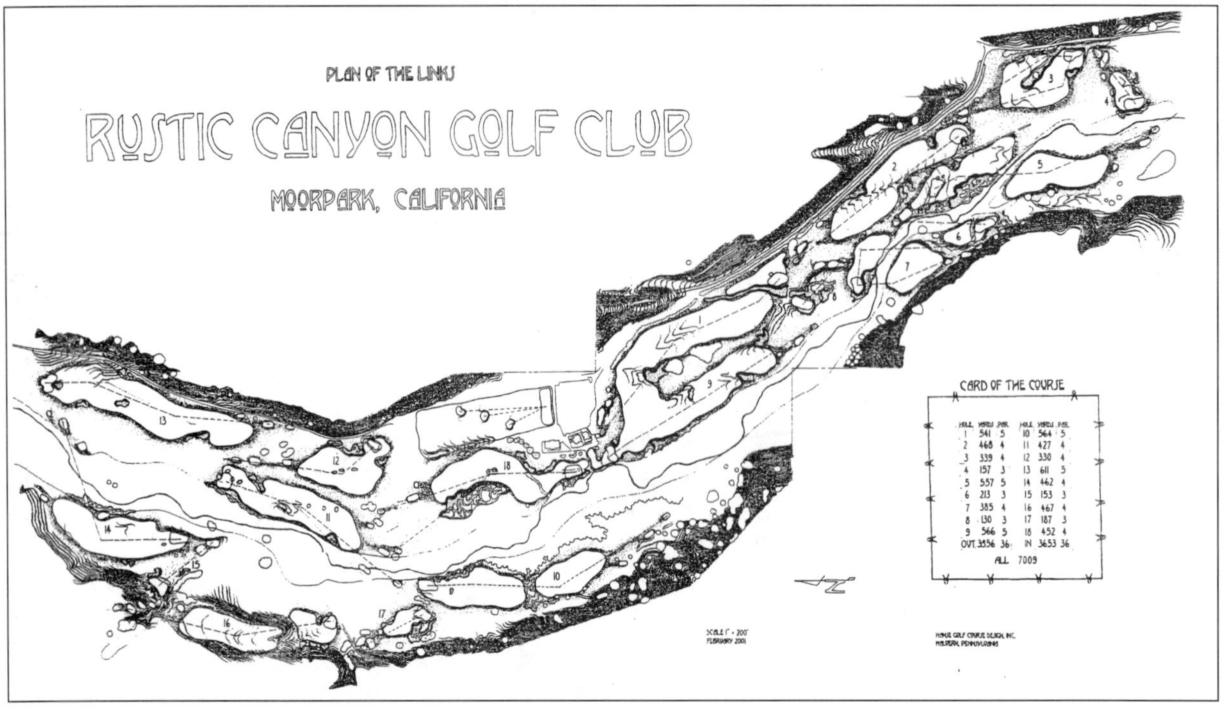

FIGURE 16-10
Routing plan of Rustic Canyon Golf Club, Moorpark, California.

COURTESY OF GIL HANSE, GOLF COURSE ARCHITECT, AND GEOFF SHACKELFORD, DESIGN CONSULTANT

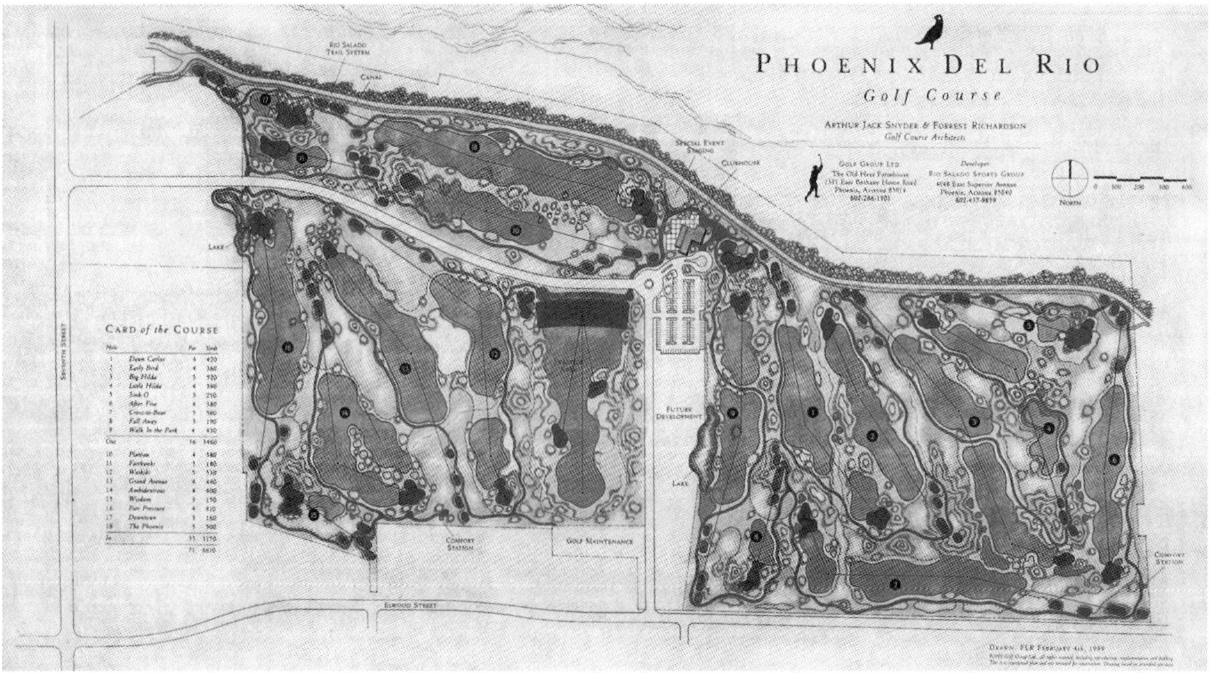

FIGURE 16-11
Routing plan of Del Rio Golf Club, Phoenix, Arizona.

ARTHUR JACK SNYDER, ASGCA, AND FORREST RICHARDSON, ASGCA, GOLF COURSE ARCHITECTS

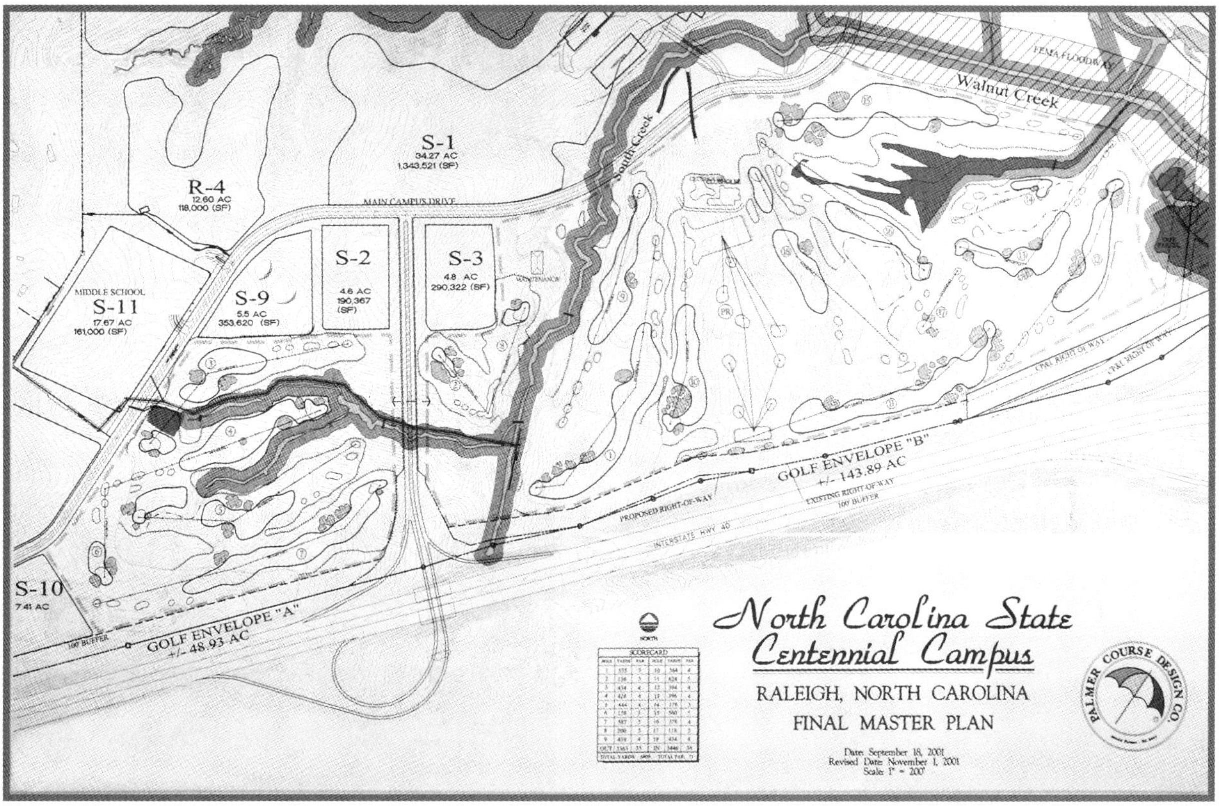

FIGURE 16-12
Routing plan for North Carolina State Centennial Campus.

COURTESY OF PALMER COURSE DESIGN COMPANY

before groundbreaking to finally seal the deal—must be brought up to date. The bunkers must be shown in the correct place, as must the fairway alignments that were adjusted to leave the towering tree, and so on. What a shame that many of the greatest architects never got around to doing this. The trend continues today. A majority, if not almost all, of the plans reproduced in this book were done *before* the courses they depict were built. (I hate to let you in on this secret, but the bunkers and yardages you have been studying are, in many cases, not what you will find if you visit.)

The Pickle Plan

One thing that routing plans are not is a series of pickles, blobs, hot dog shapes, or other rudimentary forms slapped onto a drawing. When you see such forms the plans are done, surely, by amateurs pretending to be versed in the art of routing courses. These examples rarely have centerlines, the primary ingredient of all plans. An exception is the in-house quick sketch of a golf course architect or able planner, who may make quick routing freehands. But even these have some semblance of good practice and form. They are for internal use and not for showing off.

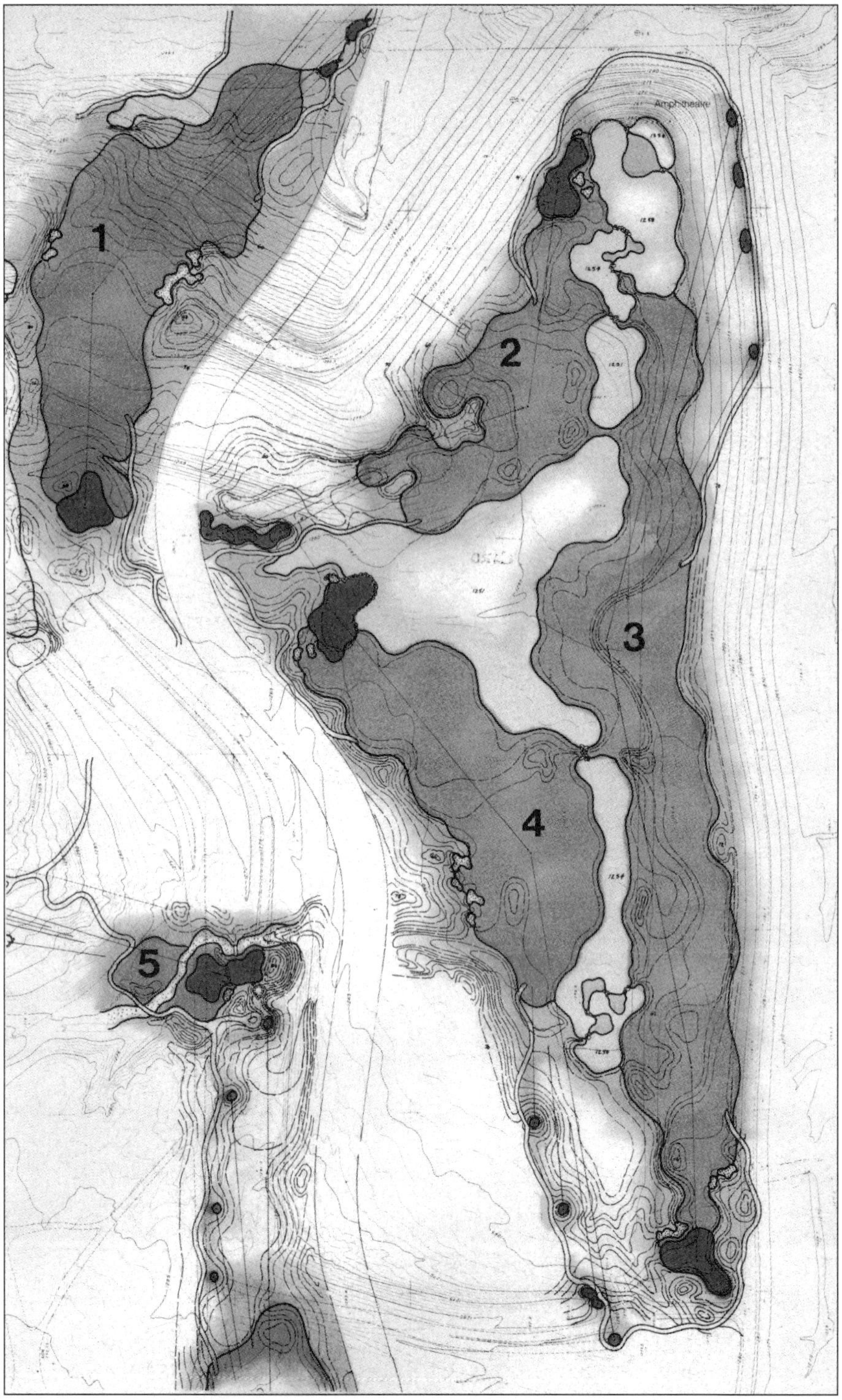

FIGURE 16-13
A portion of a routing plan drawn after the course was built. The plan was created using both the design plans and grading plans to form a highly accurate drawing of the course and its finished features.

FORREST RICHARDSON, ASGCA, GOLF COURSE ARCHITECT

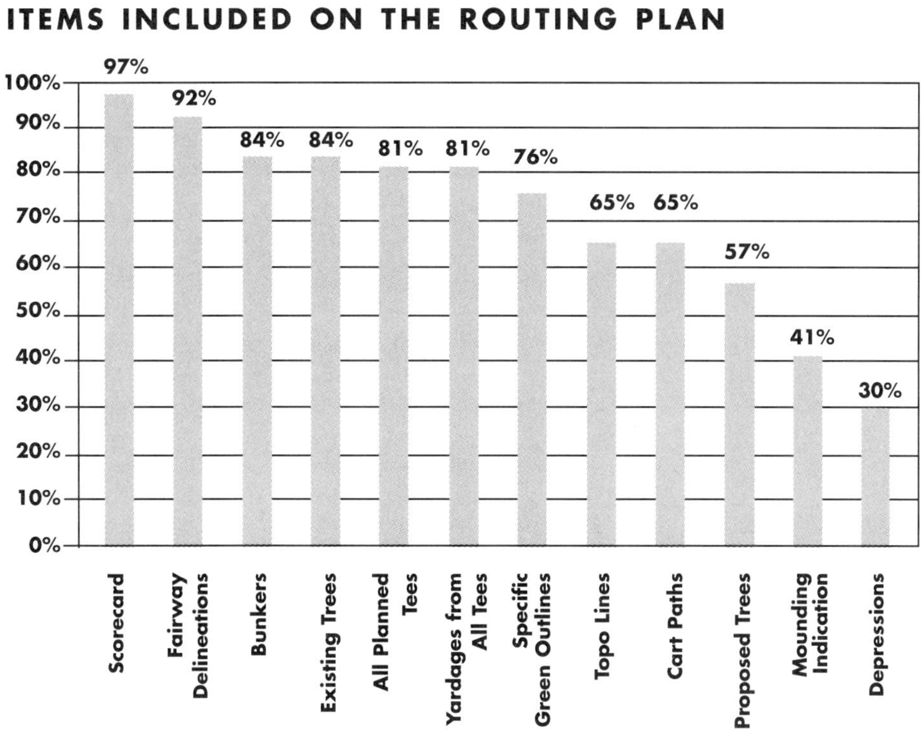

FIGURE 16-14
The chart lists the elements golf course architects and planners show on routing plans created for presentation purposes. The percentages reflect the proportion of respondents who regularly depict that element on their plans.

SOURCE: SURVEY CONDUCTED OF GOLF COURSE ARCHITECTS AND PLANNERS IN 2001

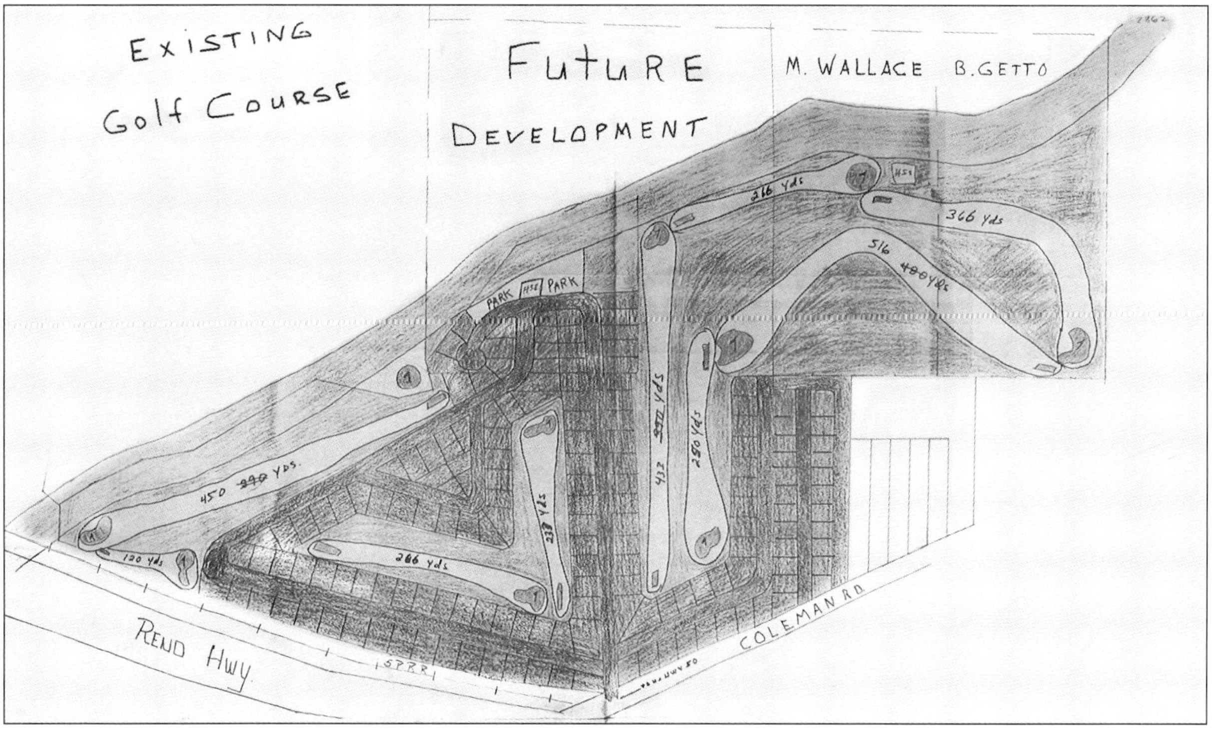

FIGURE 16-15
A client-created routing plan often looks like this. These plans say a lot about what is important to a client. In this case, it appears to be 9 holes crammed into an odd-shaped parcel with not much regard for playability, safety, or strategy.

PERSONAL COLLECTION OF THE AUTHOR

Detail: Enough or Too Much?

The element of detail is a question also of strategy. For projects with complicated entitlement requirements, it may be beneficial to *not* show much detail. Instead, the plan is often rudimentary, yet professional, and shows just the basic routing with other details to be worked out as the plan and project mature through the review and approval process. This approach is especially useful when presenting too much information might bog down the entitlement process. By keeping routing as an art form to be sculpted in the field to some degree, the approval process remains focused on broad-stroke planning issues, and the details of the golf course are reserved for a different set of discussions and eyes.

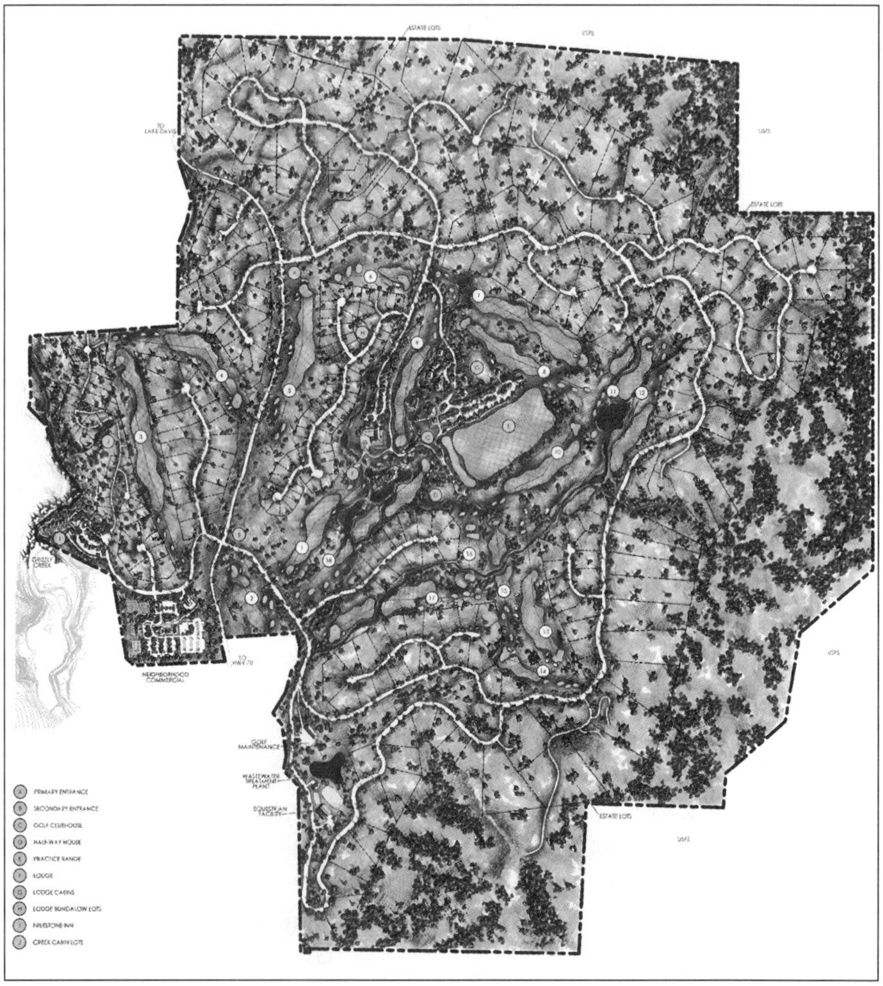

FIGURE 16-16
A master plan of a golf course community called Grizzly Ranch. The detail shows streets, landscaping around buildings, and individual lots.

COURTESY OF GAGE DAVIS ASSOCIATES

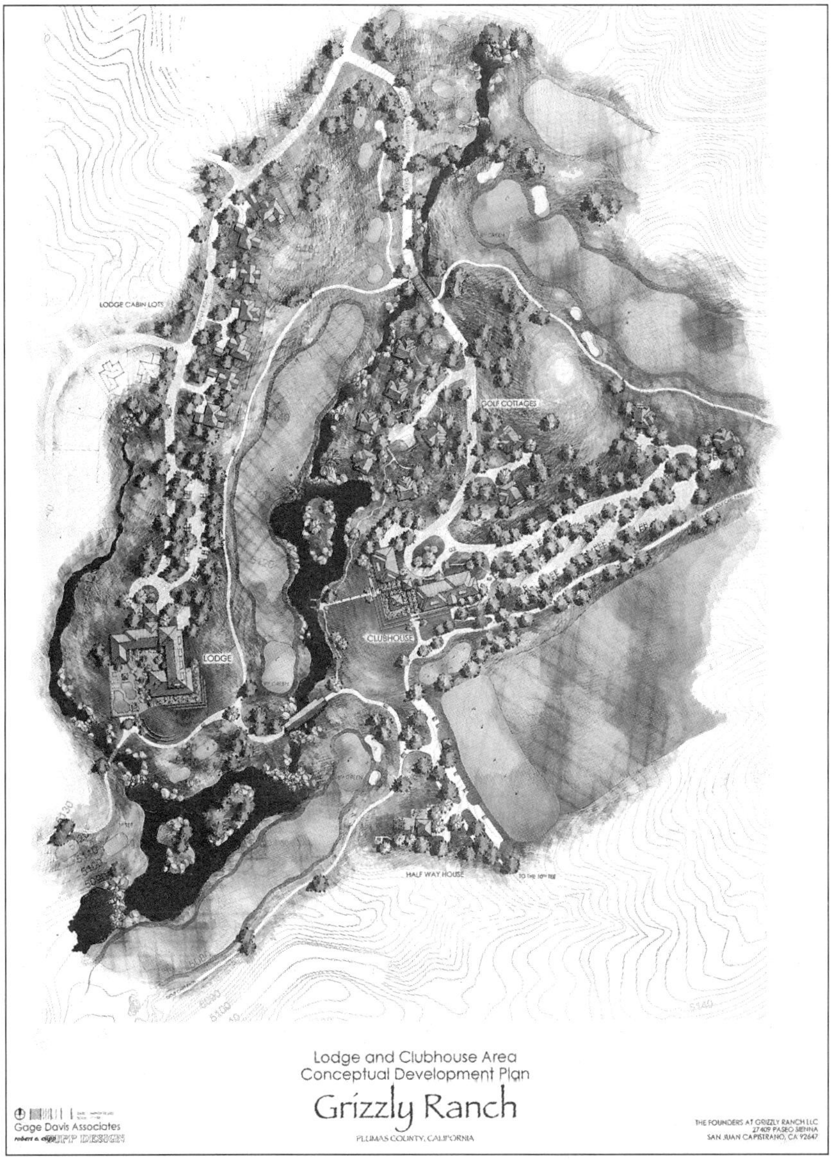

FIGURE 16-17
The clubhouse area of Grizzly Ranch (from Figure 16-16) enlarged and rendered in more detail.

COURTESY OF GAGE DAVIS ASSOCIATES

FIGURE 16-18
Because the clubhouse is an identifiable component of any golf project, integrating it with the presentation can be effective to illustrate how the course will integrate the clubhouse and its site. In this presentation plan for Grizzly Ranch, the clubhouse elevation has been created in the same illustrative style used in the master plan depicted in Figure 16-16.

COURTESY OF GAGE DAVIS ASSOCIATES

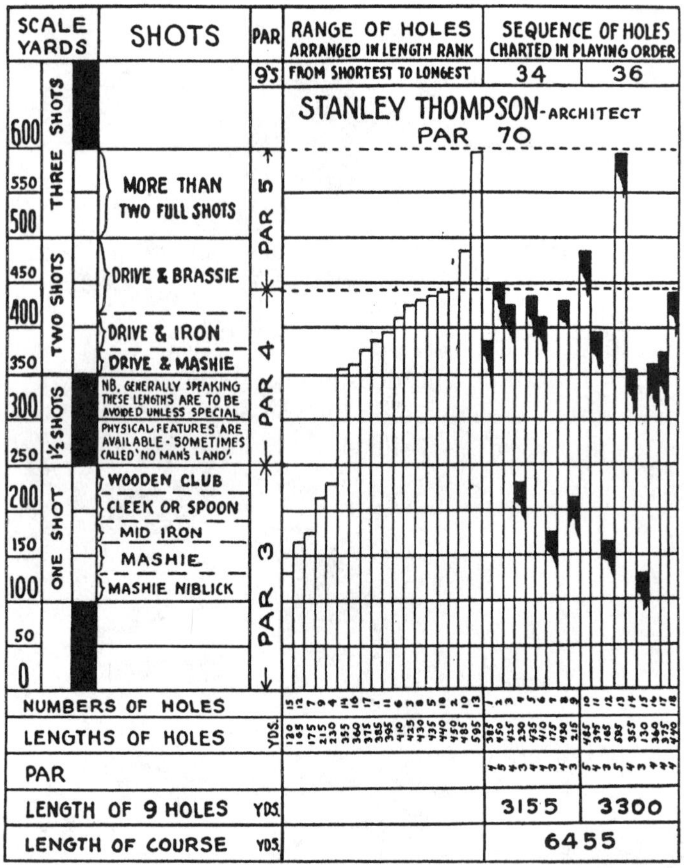

FIGURE 16-19
A chart showing how the 18 holes of a course stack up in terms of yardage, par, and shot sequence. It takes some time to absorb but is quite interesting.

ORIGINALLY PRINTED AS PART OF THE PROMOTION FOR THE JASPER PARK LODGE GOLF COURSE IN ALBERTA, CANADA; STANLEY THOMPSON, GOLF COURSE ARCHITECT; C. 1925

Calculations from Plans

Take-offs, quantified areas and dimensions *taken* from a plan, can be generated from routing plans provided enough detail is rendered. To satisfy the need to determine compatibility with regional restrictions or the golf course construction budget, it is often necessary to calculate approximate turf coverage, water surface area, average green size, and similar quantitative measures.

The Use of Color

Color is now commonplace. Even in early routing plans for presentation purposes, color was added in watercolors. The great (and very large, I might add) maps drawn of St. Andrews are spectacular in their soft and muted, sophisticated use of color. Their faded quality looks majestic. It gives the feeling that the plan cannot be argued with.

Color in modern CAD systems is a given. Only the office that does not purchase color cartridges prints in black and white. Copy machines are all moving to color capabilities. Diazo, the ammonia-based method of printing on sensitized paper via blueprinting, is unfortunately becoming a thing of the past. The staff at my local blueprinting shop, Techniprint Co. of Phoenix, which was established in 1947, seems close to locking the door when they see me approaching with an armful of old plans to have real blueprints run off. "Diazo is as dead as Caesar," I am told by Rick Jackson, their chief technologist. I remind Rick that he learned the business running blueprints and that the scent of ammonia is not so bad once you get used to it. Rick, and I'm now convinced the rest of the world, too, is obsessed with digital files, color reproduction, and the zesty ability to "do anything." Was the soft watercolor splashed onto hand-inked drawings of the 1800s as exciting for the technologists of that time? I'll bet so.

Color is powerful, to be sure. Its use must be tailored to match the need. If overused, it becomes a hindrance; if well used, it is a valuable communication tool. The best routing plan is one that can be reproduced in black and white. This does not mean that the best routing plans cannot also be great in color. But to be clear, color is not always a necessity. As with road maps, color should help, not obscure.

FIGURE 16-20

This routing plan, rendered in a CAD software program, allows quick calculations of areas defined by different layers. For example, as all of the greens are grouped into one layer of the digital file, their square footage can be instantly generated. This is especially useful for estimating costs, planning, and taking the plans to the final construction document stage.

COURTESY OF PALMER COURSE DESIGN COMPANY

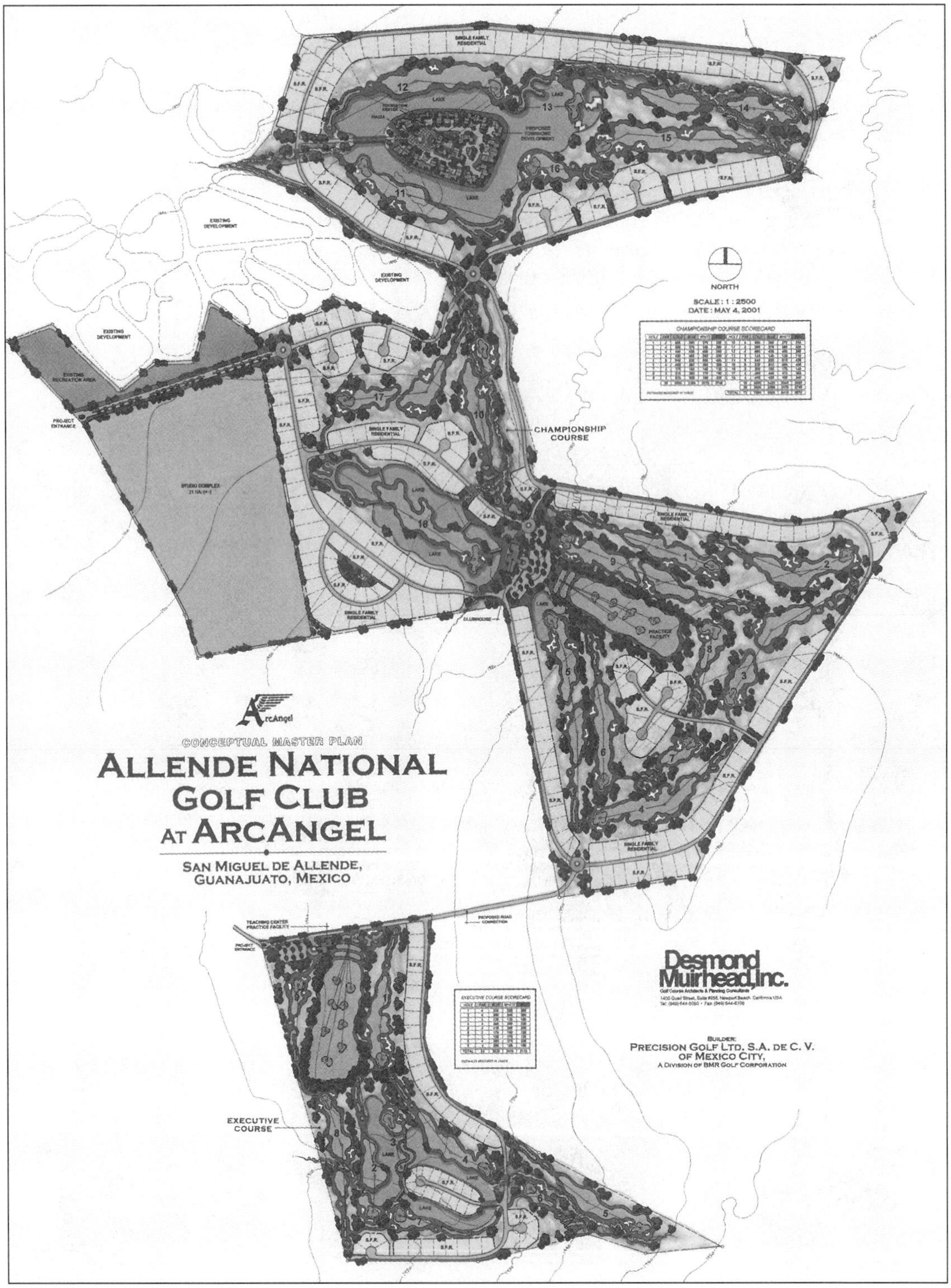

FIGURE 16-21

A master plan for a community located north of Mexico City, Mexico. The routing plan, which includes an 18-hole regulation course and a 9-hole executive-length course, is complicated, given the odd-shaped parcels that make up the project.

COURTESY OF DESMOND MUIRHEAD, INC.

Thoughtful Presentations — A Short Story

Presentations should leave a good impression. I will never forget the story of an English advertising man, Michael Peters, who was remarkably good at presentations. Faced with a major presentation to win the business of British Rail, Peters and his staff managed the following:

Their appointment with the brass at British Rail was scheduled for 9:00 A.M. However, on arriving at Peters's impressive office, the British Rail executives found disorganization. A receptionist was busy doing her nails and talking to a friend, who was sitting on the reception counter dangling her legs over the edge. The receptionist was not only preoccupied but also unfamiliar with the telephone extension system. Instead of getting up to let Peters know the British Rail people had arrived, she kept painting her nails, talking, and only occasionally trying lamely to work the phone system. After a few minutes, a young office clerk, sloppily dressed, entered and managed to ask if anyone wanted coffee or tea and took orders. Almost ten minutes later, he returned with assorted cups, many dirty, and no fresh cream. The British Rail executives began to show their displeasure. "Look, we're here to see Mr. Peters, and it's now going on 9:15," one remarked. They finally were led into a messy conference room with enough chairs for just four of the six representatives. Sitting at the conference table was an employee making a personal call about her boyfriend. To add insult to injury, the tea was cold, and one of the cups had a lipstick imprint that matched the unmistakable bright orange worn by the inefficient receptionist.

After waiting another ten minutes, the chief of British Rail stormed back into the lobby and demanded to see Mr. Peters immediately. He said that he was a busy person with important tasks. "We need to begin our meeting now, or we will have to depart and not consider Mr. Peters for this work."

Finally, Peters entered the conference room, followed by the receptionist, her friend, and the sloppy office clerk. The employee abruptly stopped talking on the phone. A crew of people came in with chairs, rags to wipe off the table, a fresh tea service—this time hot—and a smartly prepared presentation packet for each of the British Rail representatives. Peters introduced "his staff," explaining that each was a paid actor who had been acting out a planned script. The lesson, he told them, was that the treatment they received when they arrived was precisely how British Rail treats its customers—extremely poorly and with no regard for good, prompt service, not to mention clean cups and hot tea. Peters suggested that if British Rail truly wanted to win back the traveling public, they would have to reinvent themselves. They needed more than an advertising campaign; they needed to change.

I can assure you that Michael Peters can tell this story with more drama and accuracy than I can. I was not there. But the lesson has always stayed with me as an example of the power of making a point, even before you show them your stuff.

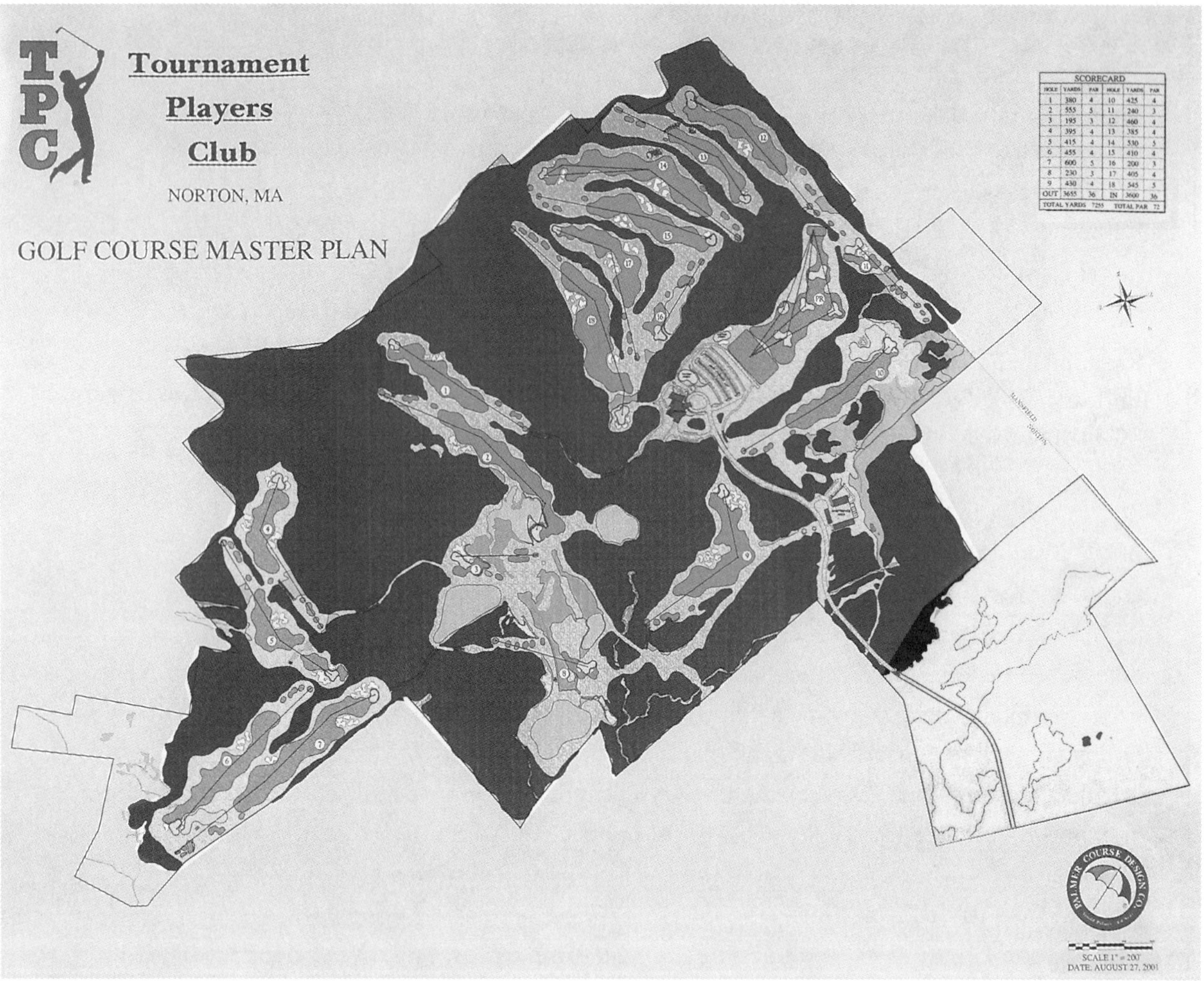

FIGURE 16-22
Routing plan for the Tournament Players Club at Norton, Massachusetts. The plan was drawn using CAD software, printed on a large-format ink-jet printer, and sent to multiple locations for use in presentations about the new course.

COURTESY OF PALMER COURSE DESIGN COMPANY

THE PRESENTATION

Presentations are not just visual. Formal presentations must be well choreographed. Even the small details must be thought of in advance. It does not look good to have no place to hang a large plan. The room's size is good to know in advance, also whether you will be inside or out, how many will attend, and who.

Many years ago, I was able to assist a good friend, Henry Delozier, land his first golf course management contract. The course he was vying to take over and transform had been designed as an open links-ish layout with no trees whatsoever. In addition to helping him draft his ideas for rerouting a few holes, I helped address his concerns about the lack of trees by explaining that several authentic links courses *do* have trees. Henry then decided to use his presentation to suggest planting some trees in clusters to help define the course better and provide needed shade. But instead of just talking about this, or merely indicating it on a plan, we armed him with an actual pine tree in a 15-gallon container, which he wheeled into the room as part of his presentation. He got the job, attributing his success, in part, to the memorable and creative act of bringing a simple but effective visual aid to the meeting.

The following are random but useful thoughts on the elements and conditions of presentations:

- Format

  Know the format for the presentation—the room, who will be attending, etc.
- Choreography

  The meeting should be planned; even for a relatively casual presentation, planning and scripting is important.
- Handouts

  Sometimes a good idea, sometimes not; it depends on the nature and type of meeting and who may need a record of the routing plan and ancillary information.
- Scale models

  An old technology, but an impressive tool; it brings out the model railroad mentality in all of us.
- Projection

  Plans and images projected in large scale can be impressive—and complicated; make sure the technology matches the audience and that you are not overproducing your presentation.
- On-site meetings

  The best way to obtain appreciation for a routing plan is to present it and then walk the land to show off views, terrain, features, etc.
- Speaking skills

  A necessary part of any presentation, which is why plans sent via the mail and discussed impersonally are so, well, impersonal.

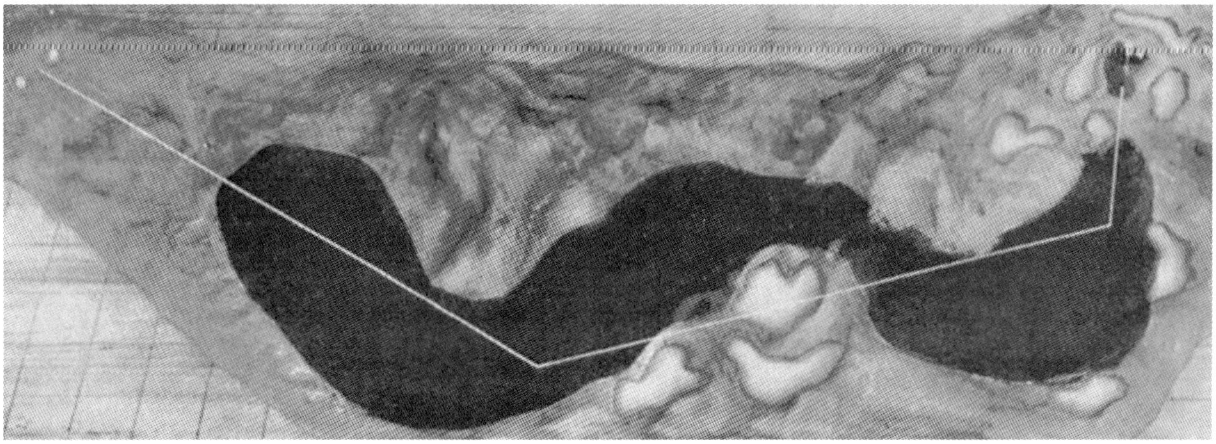

FIGURE 16-23

A. W. Tillinghast was famous for using clay models to articulate ideas. This historic photograph depicts the seventh hole at Garden City Golf Club, Garden City, New York, designed by Deverux Emmet. Tillinghast used the model to accompany an article on three-shot holes.

SOURCE: *GOLF ILLUSTRATED*, APRIL 1916

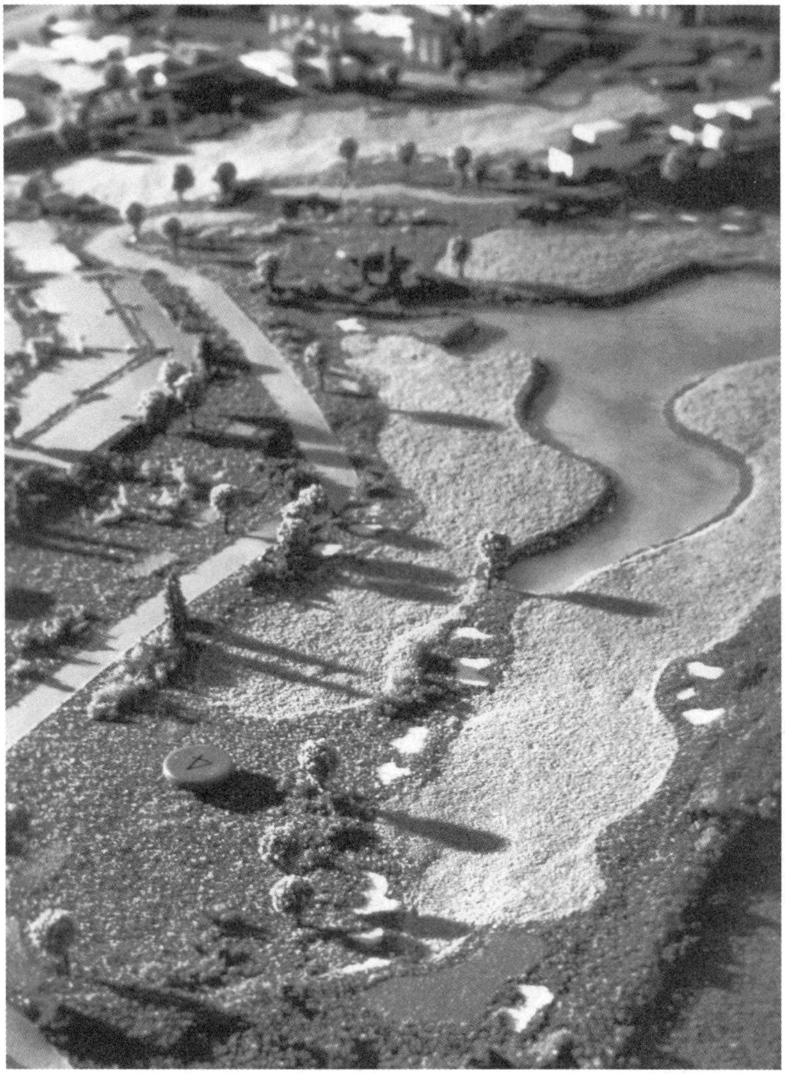

FIGURE 16-24
Close-up of a scale model of a golf course. Although time-consuming and sometimes costly, a scale model brings a routing plan to life. When properly detailed, a scale model can be a conversation piece. Viewers are able to move around, spend time in one area, and see the golf course as if it were already finished. Even the best efforts in three-dimensional digital art sometimes appear flat compared to architectural models.
PHOTO BY CRAIG WELLS

Presentations are taking on new looks as a direct result of technological advances and the access people have to computers. While not all of the following items are technological in nature, this list points out ancillary supports for routing plans that make them more dynamic and interactive:

- Site staking

  GPS equipment allows approximate points to be set in the field for occasions when a meeting at or near the site might be followed by a field trip to see the actual routing on the land.

- Computer-generated fly-throughs

  Amazing results are possible when plans are digitized and set in motion, allowing the viewer to fly through the finished project as if in a helicopter.

- Renderings

  Whether traditional or computer generated, renderings of holes and green settings can bring dimension to routing plans, which often appear flat no matter how much effort is made to make them come alive.

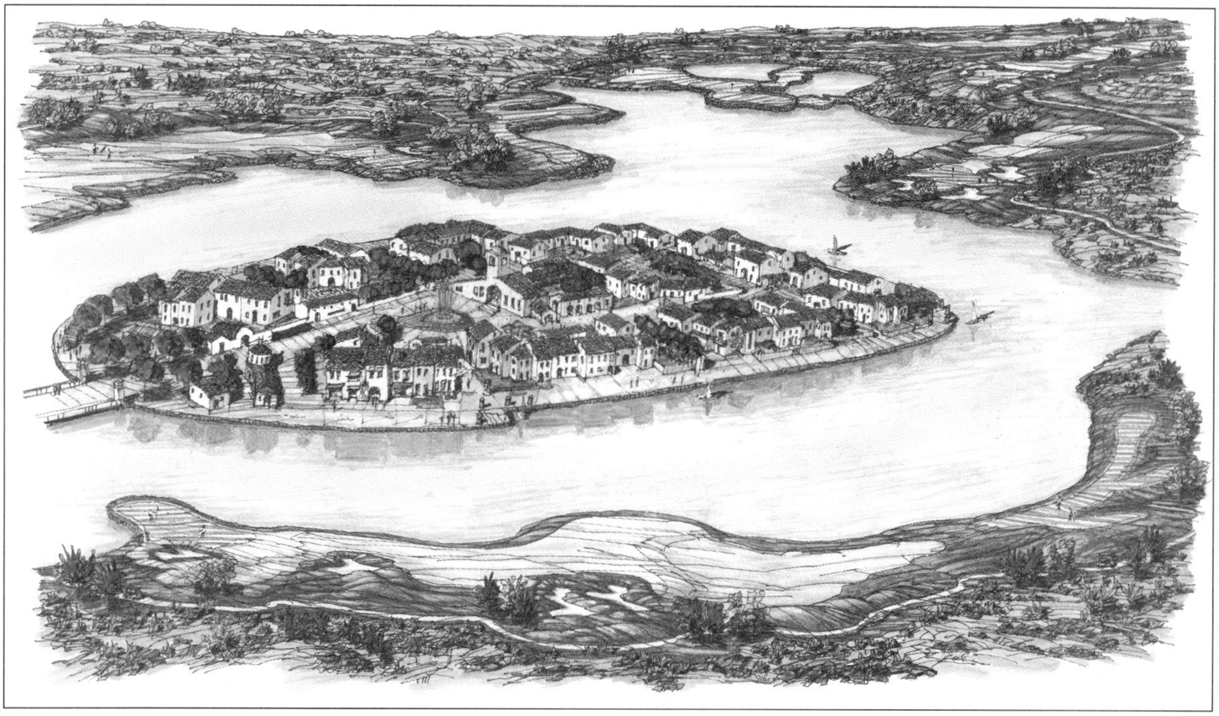

FIGURE 16-25
Rendering is an excellent method of conveying the feeling of a golf course project. In this example, an area of a routing plan has been enlarged and brought to life. The island centerpiece is from the routing plan of the golf course and community from Figure 16-21.
COURTESY OF DESMOND MUIRHEAD, INC.

FIGURE 16-26
Using specialized software programs, computer-generated renderings can be created and provided to clients for various marketing uses.
IMAGE COURTESY OF ©NICKLAUS DESIGN

STEP 1

STEP 2

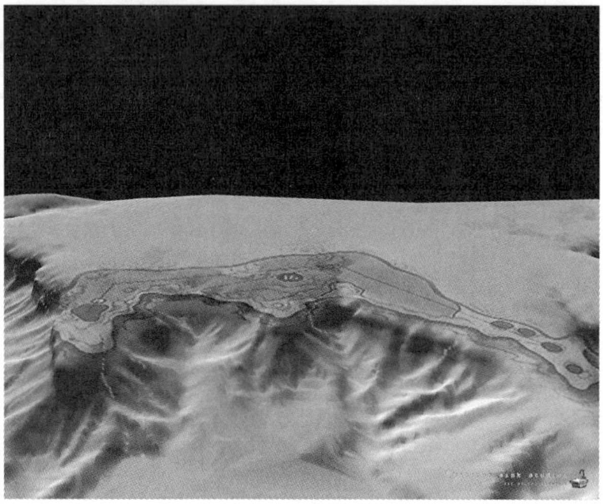

STEP 3

STEP 4

FIGURE 16-27
The progression of images shows how a digital computer model can be created to render a golf course or a portion of a course. (Step 1) A perspective photograph is taken of the site; (Step 2) The routing plan is digitized, put into the same perspective as the photograph, and layered over the photo image; (Step 3) The existing topographical data is imported to the computer model for use by the computer illustrator; (Step 4) The golf hole and features are rendered into place using the routing plan concept as a guideline. The finished rendering can be used to show how a golf hole will appear in its environment.

COURTESY OF KITCHEN SINK STUDIOS, LLC; EXAMPLE BASED ON THE 16TH HOLE OF THE ROUTING PLAN SHOWN IN FIGURE 7-2

The Augusta Proposal

In order to gain interest in Augusta, Bobby Jones commissioned a 20-page booklet touting the property and the design of the course. Titled "The Bobby Jones Golf Course by Dr. Alister MacKenzie," it included a preface from Dr. MacKenzie, a hole-by-hole description, a detailed description of the property and its trees, and a simplified routing plan. In his preface, MacKenzie listed four essentials that he and Jones agreed upon before routing Augusta:

1. A really great course must be pleasurable to the greatest possible number.
2. It must require strategy as well as skill, otherwise it cannot be enduringly interesting.
3. It must give the average player a fair chance and at the same time require the utmost from the expert who tries for the sub-par scores.
4. All natural beauty should be preserved, natural hazards should be utilized, and a minimum of [them] artificially introduced.

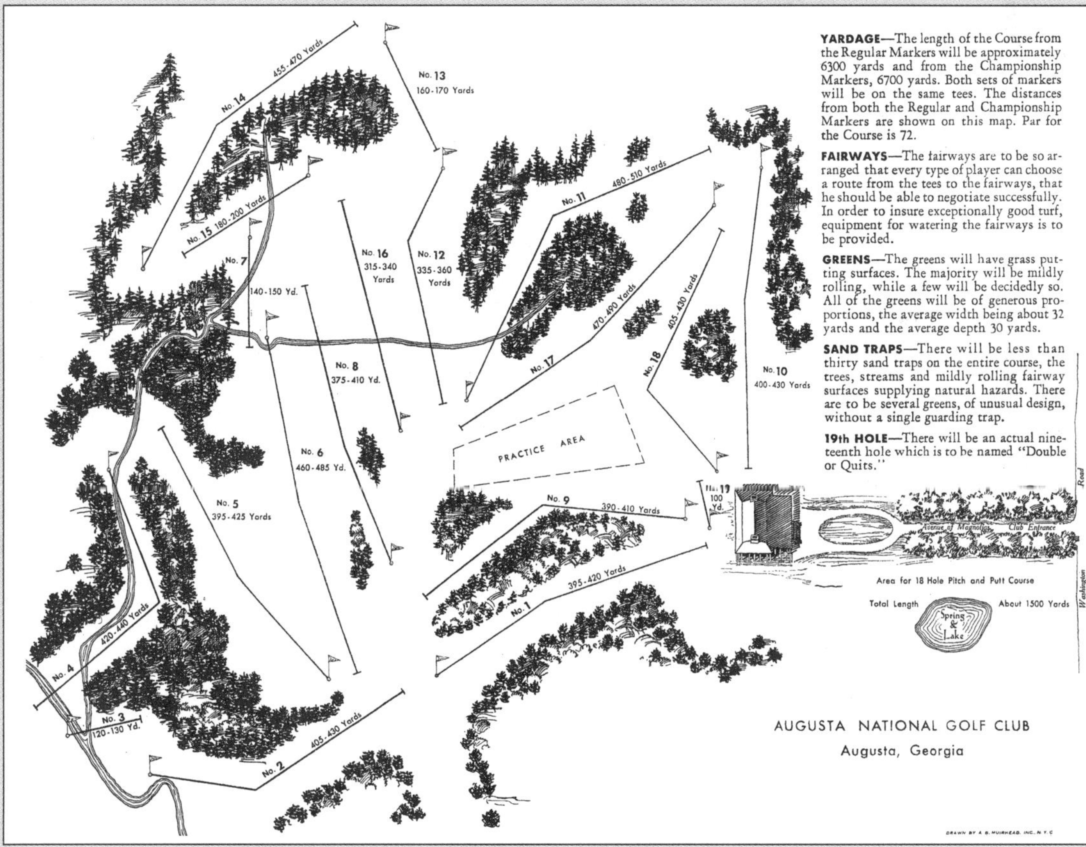

Although not drawn by Alister MacKenzie, the routing plan included in Bobby Jones's booklet selling the concept of Augusta captures the magic that became the "most beautiful golf course in all the world." Note the original inclusion of a 19th hole (a bye hole), which was dubbed "Double or Quits." Although this 100-yard shorty was never built, it received prominent attention both on the plan and in text presented to would-be members.

COURTESY OF USGA LIBRARY

Work expands to fill the time available for its completion.
—C. Northcote Parkinson, Parkinson's Law

- Written descriptions
  Of holes, the theme, etc.
- Theme books
  Substantial books describing the project and literally writing its story; such books may include imagery, landscape treatments, conceptual renderings, etc.
- Visual aids
  Actual plants, stone samples, etc. that constitute some of the construction materials or indigenous materials on a site.
- Representative imagery
  Photos of like projects, finished courses, and details that reinforce the routing and design.
- Web support
  An excellent way to follow up a presentation is by leaving those present with a Web address where they can log on and get more detailed information, perhaps even some of the studies that went into forming the option(s) presented.

New technology is changing continually. Nicolas Hower, who has spent his career following and practicing in the digital imaging field, says that "we're only at the beginning" when it comes to digital rendering of golf projects. According to Hower, we will soon see the full integration of GIS data with that of a golf course architect's field visits, and those layers of design will then be connected directly to technology that will be able to show the intent of the designer. "Right now, we are working within several separate steps," notes Kory Kapfer, Hower's partner. "Very soon, it will be possible to allow the golf course architect to literally describe his vision in whatever form is handy." That vision will then be built in a virtual form and can be rendered as routing plans, rendering, or animated fly-throughs. The golf developer will not only be able to see a project before it is built but also the technology will actually follow along as a course goes from the conceptual stage to final design and, eventually, construction.

For the present, Hower and Kapfer, plus others in the business of bringing technology to golf rendering, produce work in the aforementioned process of individual steps. With a combination of analog and digital media, the intent of projects is illustrated in new and engaging ways despite an ever-changing box of digital tools to draw from.

Never Assume Anything!

HOLE NO. 17

by Arthur Jack Snyder

Multiple considerations erupt even before you can design a routing plan for a golf course: the acreage of land available; whether the main axis of the property runs north and south or east and west; topography (lay of the land); soil conditions, including depth and quality, stony soil or rock beneath the surface; rock outcroppings; tree cover; drainage conditions; and numerous other items. Here we cover certain details that may be missed. They are just some of the surprises I've encountered during many years working with clients, difficult sites, shapers, contractors—and even a few *difficult* contractors!

SCALE

At the Wailea Golf Courses on the island of Maui in Hawaii, the views are so vast that they are apt to overpower anything we design. The slopes of the dormant volcano, Haleakala, which rises to 10,023 feet above sea level, tower above the courses on one side while the wide expanse of the Pacific Ocean is on the other. The islands of Lanai and Kahoolawe and the crescent-shaped crater of Molokini rise from the blue waters of the Pacific. Humpback whales can be seen in the winter months. There is much to draw the attention of golfers away from the golf course!

When I looked out over the expansive views, it became apparent that we would need to compensate, so to speak, for the tremendous impact of the scale of the ocean view. We decided to make the greens a little larger and the fairways somewhat wider than might normally be built. Also of great importance, lakes were placed on holes facing away from the shoreline where they didn't compete with the ocean; otherwise, they would appear to be little puddles by comparison. A spectacular and expansive view, especially from a high elevation, can be a wonderful attribute, but it needs to be dealt with during the routing process. The alignment of holes and the relationship of features must be well thought out.

FIGURE 17-1
At Wailea's Blue Course, careful attention was paid to aligning holes with ponds so that the expansive Pacific Ocean would not make the ponds look like tiny teacups.

PHOTO COURTESY OF WAILEA RESORT

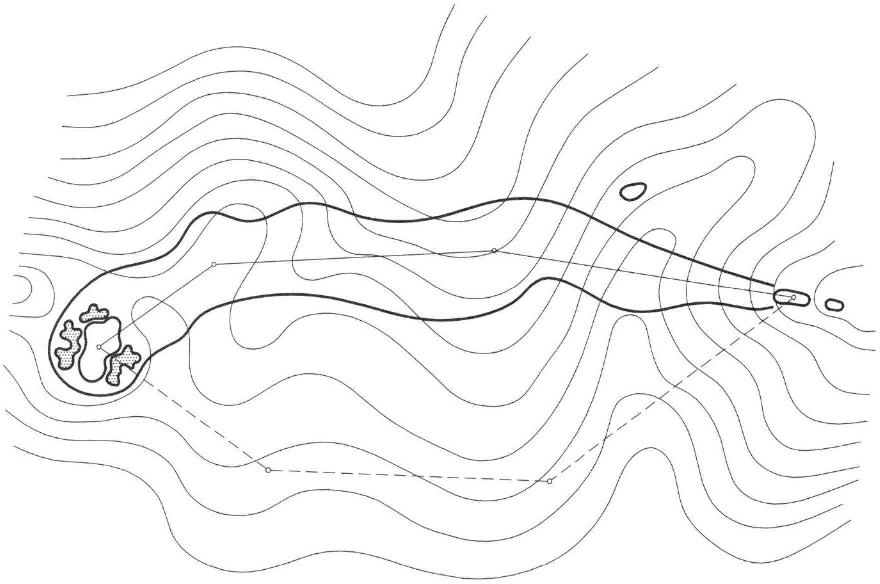

FIGURE 17-2
An example of creative problem solving through routing decisions. The conventional wisdom is to play with the contour; in this case, that would be around the hill to the left. But doing so would create three successive blind shots for the golfer. The better decision was to play up and over the hill. In doing so, only one partially blind shot occurs.

PROBLEM SOLVING

Occasionally, it is necessary to make decisions that completely affect the design of a hole. At the par-5 fourth hole on the Blue Course at Wailea, we were faced with the choice of going around or over a rise in the land. To go around it, the double dogleg to the right would slope to the left on all three shots. Additionally, the drive and second shot landing areas would be largely blind. Holes that bend to the right but slope to the left are usually uncomfortable.

The alternate route would involve hitting the drive uphill with an elevation rise of about 40 feet. Although the fairway turf disappears from sight, golfers at the far end of the drive landing area were visible. I determined that when the golfers disappeared from view, it would be safe for the golfers on the tee to hit their first shots. From the drive landing area, the second target area and green were fully visible, with only a slight downslope ahead and to the left. With this routing, the only problem was for golfers whose tee shot failed to reach the top of the rise. However, their second shot would be straight away, and most would be able to see when the preceding group was out of range. We decided to take the latter routing, which definitely made the hole much more playable and interesting.

Curiously, a fellow golf course architect of great prominence once criticized the hole and noted that I should have routed "with the contour" instead of up and over the rise. Little did he know that much thought had been put into the decision. What appeared to him an obvious solution, as I pointed out, would have made for a par-5 with at least two blind shots, and perhaps even more for the higher handicapper. By taking the approach up and over, we avoided play around a curve for what may have seemed like an endless journey.

What you do with your ball hasn't got anything to do with what the other fellow does with his. I can play in the morning and you a month from now.
—Will Rogers, from The Weekly, *Article #163, January 24, 1926*

MAKE IT INTERESTING

Henry Shelton was involved in golf course construction, and his company built many courses in the western United States during the 1950s, 1960s, and into the 1970s. He learned much about construction and earth moving while serving with the Seabees in the Pacific during World War II. He was a witty gentleman and had several favorite sayings, such as "let them know you've been here," "design wise," and "fluff it up and leave it soft." None of us quite knew what that meant, but if Henry said it, we knew it was important! Henry and I were about the same age. Even though I had been in close proximity to the game since age 11, I learned a lot about construction from him. He had quite a crew—how often do you see shaping being done with a motor grader? That blade was really humming.

I never had to worry about construction procedures when Henry was building one of my courses. He often made suggestions for adding interest, golfwise or aesthetically. Far too often, I feel golf course designers separate themselves from the people who carry out their designs in the field. Henry taught me that ideas can come from anyone, and it always pays to keep an open mind. Many times I shared designs with Henry before they were finished. Having built golf courses, he was a source of great insight and advice.

We had just one thing to worry about with Henry. He was left-handed, and we caught him (although rarely) changing the tilt on tees to help reduce the occurrence of left-handed slices! It was a sorry day for me, and for other designers, when Henry retired.

KEEP WHAT IS THERE

A prime consideration in golf course design is to change things as little as possible. In other words, make the golf course fit the land, not the land fit the course. Some of the greatest golf courses have attained their stature due to their features and the interesting stories that go along with what has been saved. I advise to always be aware of features that are already there, especially during the routing process. They may make the setting distinctive—a one-of-a-kind experience.

When it was decided to build a second course at Wailea (the Orange Course), I walked the land to see what was there. It was not an easy task. I recall returning from that expedition a bloody mess, with clothes tattered and torn from all the jaggy things growing there. But I did see things of extreme interest.

Imagine finding ancient walls laid up without mortar about a thousand years ago. Why were they built? No one really knows. The early settlers were seafarers who sailed from Polynesia for thousands of miles across open seas and landed on the most remote archipelago on Earth. If they had missed, they might have landed in Alaska! We decided to save the walls and worked them into the course design. Heavy equipment operators were told to keep their distance, as ground vibration may have caused them to tumble. However, when construction manager George

Biersdorf arrived at the site one morning, he discovered that one of the walls had disappeared. Nothing more than a low ridge of dust remained where it had been. A contractor who was building a hotel had been told he could take rock from the golf course site. Permission ended with this incident.

Several heiaus (place of worship) were also discovered at Wailea and were saved as features of the golf course. But one of the most interesting, yet scary, discoveries was a rock formation of unusual shape just off the fourth fairway. It was shaped like Botticelli's *Birth of Venus*. The high point of the "shell" was about 10 feet above ground and was about 20 feet wide. In the center, where Venus is in the painting, was a flat area about 2 feet above ground with a path leading up to it. It was a quiet late afternoon when I first stumbled upon this formation. Not a breath of air was moving. As I stood studying this amazing sight, I wondered if it had any significance. Was it used as a place of worship—or sacrifice?

FIGURE 17-3
The Wailea Resort, where Arthur Jack Snyder, ASGCA, created the first two courses in this once remote part of Maui, Hawaii, is on a lava-covered slope that leads to white sand beaches.

Every fresh hole we play should teach us some new possibility of using our strokes and suggest to us a further step in the progress of our golfing knowledge.
—*John L. Low,* Aspects of Golf Course Architecture

Suddenly the wind started blowing—hard. The branches of the surrounding heawe trees were tossed about in the gale, and through the resulting raspy wind I could imagine the ancient ones saying, "Who is this stranger? And what is he doing here?" The hair stood up on the back of my neck, and I rapidly departed.

More interesting rock formations were located between the 16th green and the 17th tee at the Orange Course. I had instructed the two bulldozer operators who were doing the clearing to watch for interesting rock formations and to save them until I could appraise their importance. They discovered two rocks about 3 feet tall and 18 inches thick standing on end. That was about the size of the Menehune, the Hawaiian version of the Irish leprechauns. About 50 feet farther down the slope of Mount Haleakala was a small rise in the grade where about 20 more rocks of the same size and shape, all standing on end, leaned slightly uphill toward the first two. As I stood studying this scene, an amazing revelation formed in my mind. The Menehune were said to work at night because the direct rays of the sun on their bodies would turn them immediately to stone. I developed the following theory:

This particular night, these two were working on the slope of Mount Haleakala. They were so happy at what they were doing that they lost track of time. Suddenly, one of them noticed that the sun was about to rise over the top of the mountain. They rapidly ran toward the village, their friends and relatives leaning toward them, urging them to hurry to safety. But they didn't make it. When they were about 50 feet from the village, the sun's direct rays fell upon them and the village, and all of them were turned to stone and remained as they are today.

Unfortunately, later remodeling of the Orange Course bulldozed this area. Only this story remains as evidence of its existence.

TIGHT SITES

A particularly tight site was The Phoenician in Phoenix, Arizona. The property consisted of rather odd-shaped land to begin with. It had tight little corners, and the rugged slopes of Camelback Mountain descended into the golf course property, its slopes significantly cutting down the usable acreage. In fact, we had only about 110 acres in total, and it was very tight due to the odd shapes. Bordering properties, existing lots, and future houses were apparently going to be quite vulnerable to missed tee shots or second shots. We had to figure out how to guide traffic away from the boundaries and still fit in a course of regulation length.

To complicate matters even more, we were told it would be necessary to retain runoff from the mountain, which would be considerable. I envisioned creating retention areas that would become muddy little holes if we just used them for detention, so I went to work trying to solve all of these issues. The eventual solution was to put water in the bottom of our retention areas and make them into lakes. And, to solve two problems at once, we put them along the boundaries of the property in strategic areas so people would aim away from the boundaries and thereby away from the houses. What at first seemed like two problems came together to actually *solve* two problems.

Although the yardages were relatively short at the Phoenician, we managed to get just over 6000 yards from the middle tees. But, as I have always preached, length is not everything in a golf course. Strategy of the play, tightness, and the accuracy required are all factors that can be used where length is not attainable.

There are in golf full shots and the other thing; it is the latter which should be associated with the typical short hole.

—*John L. Low,* Aspects of Golf Course Architecture

THE EASIEST WAY TO MOVE WATER IS WITH WATER

A popular belief is that you need about a grade of 1½ to 2 percent to effectively move water across a golf course. Wrong! There is a far easier way to move water, and it can be done with absolutely no grade at all. Often, the routing plan must accommodate an extremely flat site or a portion of a site that is relatively flat. When faced with this condition, the golf course architect may make design decisions that eventually will allow earth moving to help carry the drainage that occurs on the course to low points. Most of the time, this involves moving thousands of cubic yards of dirt so the land tilts from one end to the other, eventually meeting or exceeding the 1½ to 2 percent fall mentioned earlier.

Here is the easier way: Use water to move water. On a project that was nearly dead flat from one end to the other, we created long lagoons that could collect water from the entire length of the site and then conveniently discharge an excess at the lower end. This not only turned out to be a better and less costly solution than earth moving, it also provided the course with a theme, something to flow through the layout and create interest and charm.

THE UPHILL BATTLE

Routing uphill holes creates all sorts of havoc, but with a good plan of attack, you can make them work. At the Phoenician, we had the back end of Camelback Mountain intruding on the property. Making use of this dramatic, rocky mountain was essential. There was a good opportunity for an interesting downhill par-3 hole, but first we had to get up the mountain to a high enough elevation.

In order to make the climb, I decided to use a medium-length par 4. Normally, there is not a lot of rise on a tee from back to front, but to demonstrate the severity of the grade, we needed an 8-foot rise in elevation from the back to the front of this long main tee. Without the slope of the tee, it would have looked like you were hitting right into the hillside—far too ominous a tee shot.

We also needed to take into account how we might shape the fairway and green. We wound up angling the green from front right to back left in order to get a view into the green from along the right side. The green was planned to have two rises and three plateaus. This would allow visibility from the fairway and prevent the approach from looking like a great Chinese wall. We designed in a little escape route up and around the left side of the green. All this gave us a chance to ascend the upper side of Camelback Mountain, where we routed a spectacular downhill par 3 of about 150-yards. Keep in mind that this was all done during the routing. Otherwise we couldn't prove the holes could be built!

WEATHER OR NOT

The Volcano Golf and Country Club on the big island of Hawaii sits right on a ridge between two active volcanoes—Kilawaia, which is the most active volcano on earth, and Mauna Loa. The locals say that if you leave a putt on the lip, you can just wait for a few seconds for a tremor to knock it in.

The northeast side of the Hawaiian Islands are the windward side, which causes the moist tradewinds off the Pacific to be deflected upward into cooler air and causing condensation and mist or rain. The Volcanoes Course is located on both sides of a ridge that separates the northeast side of the course from the west side, which is as arid a desert as you will ever find.

Early in our work there, we figured out that we had better get over on the east side of the golf course and work first thing in the morning, as this area was literally a rain forest or jungle. Toward noon, it would start to rain until work had to be halted. The construction process was awkward; all of our equipment and operations moved to the west side in the afternoon, and it went back and forth like this during the entire job.

I always consider weather—prevailing winds, sunlight conditions, and rainfall—but never independently on two sides of a single golf course. This project opened my eyes to the fact that nature does not care about your plans for a golf course. Over the expanse of several hundred acres it is possible to have distinct weather patterns, a situation I had never anticipated.

WHERE'S THE BULLDOZER?

A lava tube is like a cave formed by a lava flow whose edges and top hardened while liquid lava was still flowing underneath. Having worked in Hawaii, it had been my pleasure to visit the Volcano National Park, and while there I learned about lava tubes and many other natural phenomena brought about by volcanic activity.

Never, however, did I expect to encounter such natural caverns during construction. We almost lost bulldozers a couple of times. Sometimes the tunnels were just a foot or two under the surface, and when the ground collapsed we had to make grade changes on the spot to compensate for the new elevations.

My advice is this: Make sure you truly know the land you are planning. If that means talking with the local experts, then do it. You can never assume what is on the surface is what is underneath.

FIGURE 17-4
A discovered lava tube is pointed out. The voids are created when molten lava flows out of natural tunnels formed by cooling lava. Obviously not delineated on topographical maps, such voids beneath the ground are disasters waiting to happen.

18 STAKES ON A SUNDAY AFTERNOON

White Mountain Country Club at Pinetop, Arizona, is 7600 feet above sea level in the White Mountains. At the time it was built, it was the second-highest golf course in the United States, built in the largest Ponderosa pine forest in the world. The original nine holes were built in 1955, mostly by my father. I ended up there that winter and quickly learned that it is not a good idea to assume that what works at one altitude is going to work at another. We made all sorts of interesting discoveries about how grass grows at different altitudes and in different climates.

I also recall the feeling of the local folks. "You're 180 miles from Phoenix and it will never be a success. You'll go broke in a very short time," they said. But with a big lumber mill only a few miles away, a lot of people were looking for golf. The course was such a success that within six months of opening, it was determined that we were going to need another nine holes.

That is when I got my feet wet in golf course design. Milt Coggins Sr. and Gray Madison, who were involved with the layout of the original nine, joined me, and we set out one day (it may not have been a Sunday), each with an armload of iron stakes and a compass. We actually paced, with no surveying equipment, and laid out another nine holes. It was rather hard to pace because the pine growth in places was so thick

The only thing worse than playing too tough a course is having to spend five hours or more playing that same course!
—Peter Oosterhuis

we couldn't pace accurately. I got to thinking, "Gee, we'd better put this thing on paper, survey it, and actually locate the stakes." Which I did. Fortunately, there had been a power line along the west side of the original nine, and we had used that as a reference base.

Later, after our trek in the woods, I took a transit (a surveying instrument) with a rod and a 100-foot tape and located all those stakes. This was quite a job, considering the dense growth. I discovered, among other things, that the par 3s were all too long and the par 4s were too short. It made for a pretty poor routing, so I relocated the stakes. The basic idea of the holes was the same, but I made it a more interesting and certainly more usable layout.

I learned that it is essential to understand property from the actual conditions shown on a survey as well as the ground. It is just not possible to do routings in the field without a survey because what we perceive might be completely different than what actually exists.

WATER WITCHES

A water witcher is a person who has a knack with branches—*Y*-shaped willow branches, to be exact. The witcher holds the two upper arms of the *Y* with each hand, and the straight branch that comes out ahead, which is maybe 2 feet long, moves up and down when underground water is encountered. I have seen witchers have to hold onto the branch

FIGURE 17-5
Historical photo of a water witcher, or dowser. Although techniques vary, generally two sticks or rods are held in each hand and are used by the witcher to detect the presence of water below ground. In this photo, the witcher is using a traditional *Y*-shaped branch that is held at both ends.

just to keep it from jumping out of their hands! The activity slows down in spots, and eventually the witcher pinpoints a spot where the water is most prevalent. They say, "Let's put down the well in this spot," and lo and behold—magic! Pow! Five hundred gallons a minute!

In the beginning, I was not so sure of this. Once I had a notion to hire two witchers. We weren't going to trust just one. I brought out this woman. She had located the first well on this project, so we sort of trusted her. She said, "There's an underground stream coming down here." So we put a stake there. And she came in from other angles right to the same spot. Before calling the second witcher, we took a chance and pow! another 500 gallons. You never know what you're going to get into.

BEING CREATIVE

Sometimes the routing of a course can create unusual situations. At Cave Creek in Phoenix, there were three greens that came fairly close together. Not too close, but they were all lined up. The thought struck me about 2:00 A.M., when I was working one of my usual all-nighters, that we could join these three greens together. St. Andrews has its double greens, and there are other double greens throughout the world, but here was a real opportunity to join three greens and create something unusual. They all came together, two from the north and one from the south.

Then I took it one step further. I designed two separate approaches to one green—two fairways—and I added a fourth green to the series so we would have an alternate green to use in conjunction with whichever of these fairway was in use. We could have a left-hand dogleg and a right-hand dogleg. The first reaction of my client was, "Of all the cock-eyed ideas in creation, this is the worst! Don't you dare put that in there." I responded that if they didn't want something unique but very playable, that was their choice. The next morning, I got a telephone call: "Hey, that's not a bad idea."

We did it—a huge green of about 27,000 square feet. Sometimes you have to push. If I had assumed that they would never buy it, it would have stayed in my head forever.

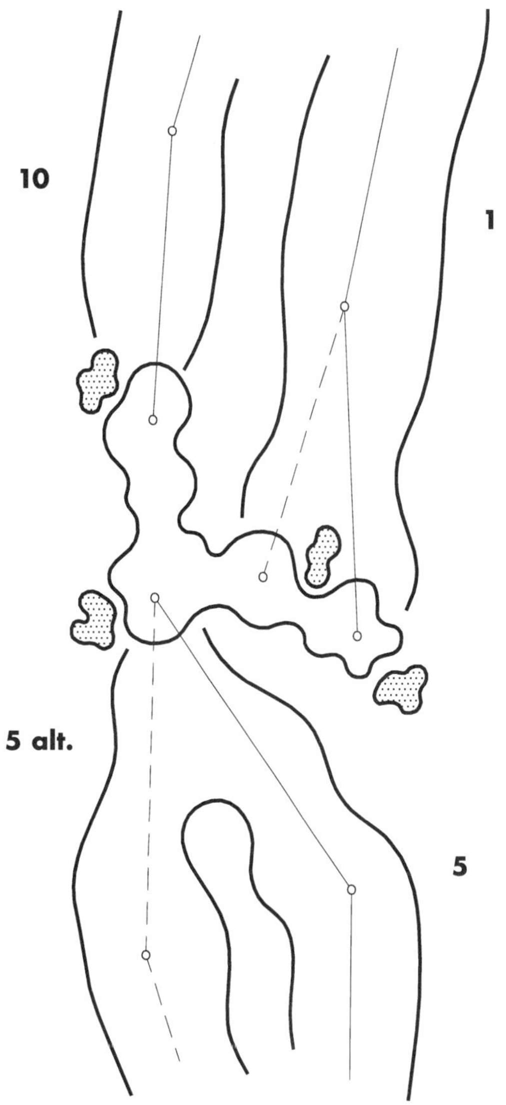

FIGURE 17-6
Plan showing the quadruple green at Cave Creek Park Golf Course in Phoenix, Arizona. Depending on which fairway of the fifth hole is in use, which is predicated on the position of the tees on the fifth hole, the green position of the first hole is set. When the left fairway of the fifth is in play, the pin for the first hole is right of the sand bunker.

FIGURE 17-7
Arthur Jack Snyder's father, Arthur A. Snyder, stands proudly in front of the Alcoma Country Club outside of Pittsburgh. At Oakmont, where he began as a caddy and later became a greenkeeper, he was influenced by Henry C. Fownes and William C. Fownes Jr., who created Oakmont despite having no background in golf architecture.

GOLF SHOULD BE FUN

Fun? You had to know my dad to appreciate his feeling for the game of golf. It was a lifesaver for the whole family that he got into it in the first place. I cannot imagine myself working in the steel mills of western Pennsylvania.

Golf is always an enjoyable game, and there are ways of making it fun without being outlandish. Some golf courses make beautiful pictures, but they are a job—a tour—and you are glad when it's over. You don't want to go back and play them. I say, let's make our golf courses interesting and challenging, but not too difficult. Challenging, but not too intimidating.

The routing plan is where a course begins to take shape. A golf course should not be so impossible or so intimidating that it is not fun. You can test this when you're looking at a routing plan. The game was not meant to be a chore. It's okay to make the golfer ask when the 18th hole is coming, but not because he can't wait for the round to be over. We want people to come back, time and time again. That is what the successful golf courses are built upon.

MAINTENANCE

One of the most important goals of designing a golf course is making it maintainable. The maintenance cost goes on forever, and designers sometimes fail to take this into account. Coming from a family of greenkeepers, I have always had my share of critics looking over my shoulder and commenting on my designs. "Boy, you better look at this a second time and give this a little more thought, because it's going to be a problem area," they say. Having been a superintendent myself at three golf courses and having set up maintenance programs at a number of others, I gained an early respect for maintenance.

Our roots go back to Oakmont, where my father was learning the business in 1911. Having Oakmont to learn on was important and highly instructional. Oakmont was a maintainable golf course, even though it had a couple hundred sand traps. The rolling mounds are graceful, and no slope is so steep that it presents problems. And guess what—it is one of the most challenging courses in the world. It proves that steep and severe are not requirements.

I'VE KNOWN JACK SNYDER since 1976, when I first rode my bicycle to his home to ask questions about golf course design. One of his favorite stories is to relate the warning his wife, Ruth, used to call out whenever I turned my metallic red ten-speed into the driveway: "Jack, it's that crazy kid on the bike again!"

Jack is a golf course architect, and he's been figuring out routing plans for more than 50 years. Most of what I know about golf course design has either come from Jack or been explained by him in one form or another. Having worked alongside him for the past several years, it's been great to get his opinions on what I've learned from other people and from reading. In this aptly titled chapter, Jack delves into some of the topics we've discussed on the many road trips taken to our job sites. My request was that he think about some of the unusual and interesting things he has learned about routing—specifically, assumptions he's made that didn't pan out.

My association with Jack (actually Arthur Jack Snyder) began getting serious in the mid-1980s, when I got the opportunity to design my first course. I needed Jack's help and wisdom then and have been forever grateful that he collaborated, allowing me to finally get into the world of golf course architecture. After this first project, Jack began needing my help—not for the wisdom part, but as hands and eyes to follow through on projects while he recovered from heart surgery.

Jack Snyder is a graduate of Pennsylvania State University, where he studied landscape architecture. His father, Arthur A. Snyder, began caddying at the Oakmont Country Club near Pittsburgh in 1907, and so began the Snyder family's involvement with golf. Jack and his brothers, Jim and Carl, literally grew up on a golf course. Eventually, they each became greenkeepers. All three are Class AA Life Members of the Golf Course Superintendents Association of America (GCSAA). Starting out as a caddie, Jack worked on a course maintenance crew and wound up teaching a course in golf course design while a senior at Penn State. He went on to become the golf course superintendent at Oakmont Country Club.

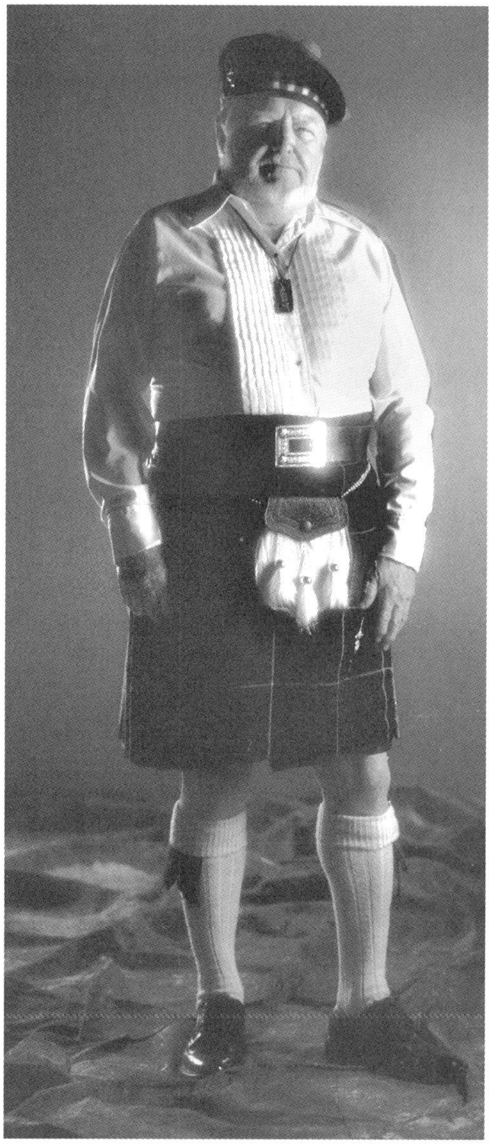

FIGURE 17-8
Golf course architect Arthur Jack Snyder, ASGCA, pictured in full Scottish regalia.

PHOTOGRAPH BY RICK GAYLE

Eventually the family moved out west, where he made the decision to pursue a life designing golf courses. He was among the early members of the American Society of Golf Course Architects (ASGCA) and is a past president. Jack has designed more than 75 courses.

Today, in his eighties, Jack is a constant source of knowledge and what seems to be an endless repertoire of stories about designing golf courses. I am forever grateful for his patience and willingness to work with me and to pass on what he learned in the many years he has been around, over, and on golf courses. His work has covered all types of courses and conditions, always, as he puts it, "To be fun and enjoyable." The lessons he shares are among my favorites of those he has handed down. They were picked for their relevance to routing. Trust me when I say there are hundreds more where these came from!

Lessons Learned from Cypress Point

HOLE NO.

18

Perhaps the greatest lesson that the Cypress Point Club can teach us is that golf is, above all, a matter of time. While the game itself may be played out over a matter of hours, the golf course knows nothing of this. It has taken its own sweet time to get where it is. The best courses will tell you this. In an unspoken language understood only between golf course and golfer, there is conversation about natural beauty, about daring attempts, and about timelessness. The Cypress Point Club on the Monterey Peninsula of California speaks this language better than any golf course in the world. It has the gift of being able to connect with the golfer. Indeed, it has the gift of being able to connect even with the nongolfer. Anyone who has ever laid eyes on its ribbons of grass, its secluded forests, its reach into the ocean, has sensed a wondrous feeling. The present seems insignificant when one realizes that nature has spent millions of years crashing against itself to make all this possible. And somehow, among these thoughts of scale and time, we must focus on the golf at hand. The golf moments are even smaller moments, even more insignificant. Yet they will stay with us forever.

We removed about fifteen acres more of trees than were necessary from a golfing point of view, for the purpose of opening out fresh vistas to the ocean and sand dunes, and increasing the beauties of the place.
—Alister MacKenzie, in The Fairway *(November 1928)*

The decision to end our round about routing with a look at the Cypress Point Club is both legitimate—and selfish. Legitimate, because this wondrous golf course is considered by many throughout the world as the best ever created. Selfish, because I am among the believers.

The business of routing golf courses today deals exclusively with those courses that are *built* and not the ancient layouts that *evolved* out of almost untouched linksland. As a result, it is appropriate that lessons be passed on from the best of the best of this first category. Cypress Point is a course that rose out of a vision, a concept, that had great regard for the land. The course was routed purposefully and with great care. It has captured the heart of nearly every golfer in the world through its stunning beauty, its perfect atmosphere, and its *remarkable routing.*

VISION

The destination known at the Monterey Peninsula—whose Pebble Beach Golf Links is perhaps the most famous golf course outside of St. Andrews—was once rugged coastline, hostile and seemingly inaccessible. Developer Samuel Morse saw it differently. The rugged parts would remain, and so too the enchanted forests and the one influence no one could change even if they wanted—the weather. What Morse saw was an attraction in the land that would captivate people. His dream came true through unmatched vision. In some ways, it was an easy sell. Everyone he introduced to the property fell in love with it. Many never left. Morse was always looking for ways to preserve open space land while carving out areas for people to build homes. This foresight paved the way for a special golf course—a course that preserves open space with a few limited home sites. Just down the coast from Pebble Beach, already a celebrated golf course, was Cypress Point, named for its cypress trees, blown into twists, each looking like a giant piece of living driftwood. In 1924—five years after the opening of Pebble Beach—the idea was born to create a special golf club in this area. Three individuals—Byington Ford, Roger Lapham, and the unforgettable Marion Hollins—were frontrunners for the project. Hollins was among the best women golfers in the United States, having claimed the U.S. Women's Amateur Title in 1921.

RANKING
Cypress Point has never ranked lower than fifth in *Golf Digest's* "100 Greatest Golf Courses in the World."

Originally, Seth Raynor, who learned from the legendary Charles Blair Macdonald, was selected by Hollins to design the course at Cypress Point. Raynor got as far as a preliminary routing scheme when he died suddenly in 1926. This is when Hollins and her cofounders turned to Alister MacKenzie. MacKenzie was known to those in the Pebble Beach area for his work in California. It was only natural that he was chosen to pick up where Raynor had left off.

Alister MacKenzie had developed a strong tie with Robert Hunter, who had overseen construction of MacKenzie's work. It was Hunter that MacKenzie entrusted with this most amazing site. Hunter, a talented designer in his own right, was always eager to assist—a refreshing collaboration among golf architects. Still, how truly outstanding that

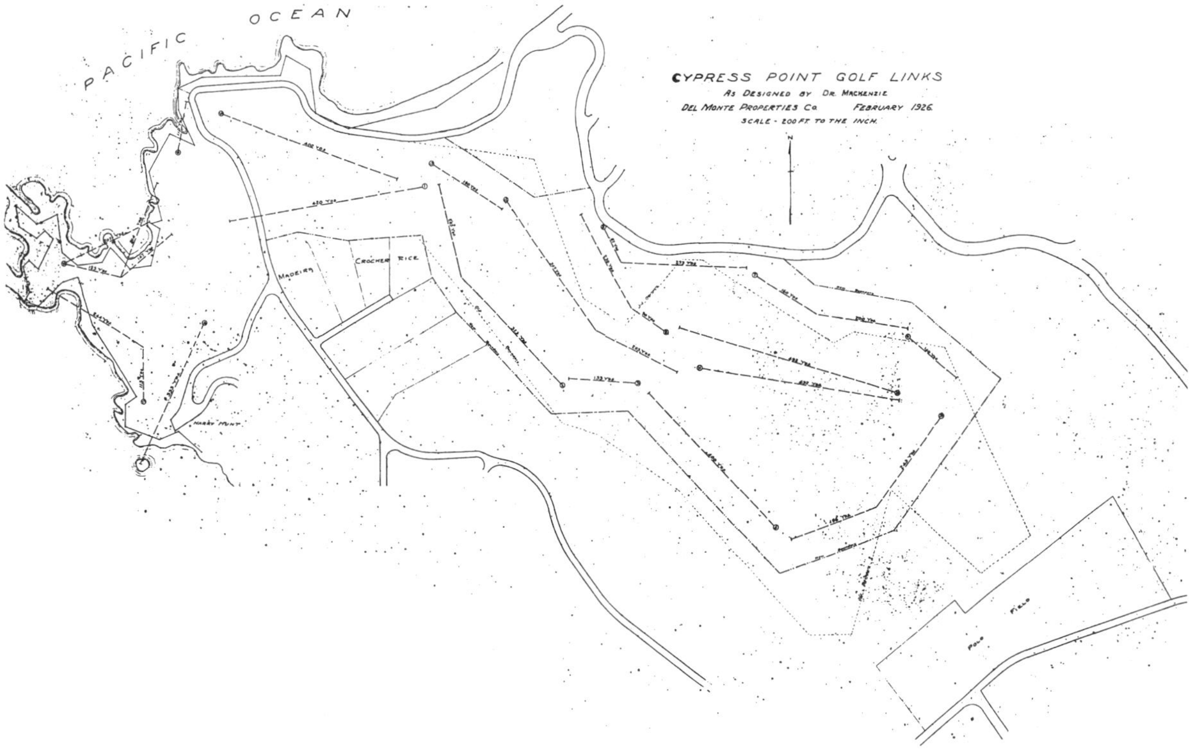

FIGURE 18-1
Dr. Alister MacKenzie's original routing plan of the Cypress Point Club (c. 1926) was a stick-figure plan that showed the centerlines of holes laid onto the property. Probably the boundary was the same, or similar to, that which Seth Raynor had been working with until his death earlier in the year. The holes are shown in their configuration before MacKenzie and Hunter made their now famous changes to the routing.

COURTESY OF CYPRESS POINT CLUB

these two talented men sought to work together for a common cause and not vie to control the work as his own. Both knew the potential of the course. Their writings before, during, and after its completion show their passion for the work. Although MacKenzie is credited with the course in most accounts, there is no doubt that Hunter is embedded in almost every detail.

THE ROUTING TAKES SHAPE

Raynor's original thoughts on the routing are mostly lost in history. Without question, though, it was Raynor who first set pencil to paper and worked out the feasibility of putting a golf course along the coast and back into the dunes and woods that rolled away from the sea. Raynor's plans were reportedly similar to those MacKenzie finally built. The ocean holes were well rehearsed by Raynor as he explained his ideas for a routing. There is the famous story about the 16th hole where Raynor, during one of his visits, expressed concern that the length might be too much for a par 3. Upon hearing this, Hollins set a ball down where the tees were planned, grabbed a club, and sent a shot sailing to the location where the green sits today. Such are the legends that make for good discussion at the end of a round—this particular one setting the stage for what may well be the most famous hole in all of golf. It is a shame we do not have a record of Raynor's reaction to Hollins's shot. By all accounts, Raynor was a true gentleman, and his questioning of the length was reasonable. We could use more Raynors

[A]s so many great architects and artists have proven, a diverse background is often the most valuable asset one can bring to a difficult job such as that of a golf architect.
—Geoff Shackelford, referring to Robert Hunter in Alister MacKenzie's Cypress Point Club

in today's make-it-long-and-tough design world. The optional detour area to the left of the 16th green was no doubt influenced by Raynor and carried out in its famous form by MacKenzie and Hunter.

Geoff Shackelford, in his book *Alister MacKenzie's Cypress Point Club,* notes that MacKenzie made two important visits to route Cypress Point. His preliminary stick-figure alignment of holes, dated February 1926, shows the course in a fashion similar to the only known presentation plan, which was drawn for MacKenzie by Albert Barrows the following month. Interestingly, a study of MacKenzie's preliminary plan shows property lines that were likely handed down to him from Raynor. The routing of the Cypress Point Club was destined to occur within the 170 or so acres of these boundaries.

Later, in 1927, MacKenzie made final changes that were then put into action by his man-in-the-field, Robert Hunter. Hunter himself made many other subtle changes to the routing after this point—most notably the shift of the 14th hole inland to its present position, where the routing so perfectly rises up one last time before allowing the golfer to begin the trek to the ocean. It was at the insistence of Samuel Morse that No. 14 be moved away from Seventeen-Mile Drive. Apparently Morse was the ultimate visionary, seeming to know how popular the scenic road would become.

REMAINING MYSTERIES

The final routing of the Cypress Point Club cannot be imagined any better than it is. If there were a way to make it better, then it would certainly not be fit for this planet. Whatever imperfections remain are certainly no worse than the mole that graced Marilyn Monroe's left cheek.

The most intriguing mystery at Cypress involves the continuing theories on what decisions were made along the stretch of holes at the ocean. During construction and even after completion of much of the golf course, both MacKenzie and Hunter wrote descriptions of the 16th as a par 4. By these accounts, the routing would have been 37 going *out* and 36 coming *in* for a total par 73. The ocean holes were likely to have played a big part in the routing. Except for the locations of tees and slight shifts in green sites, these holes were mostly nonadjustable. All movement had to lead up to them, and the holes that did were far less etched in stone.

Also somewhat a mystery is the March 1926 presentation plan by Barrows that formed a par 71. This play showed the holes playing as follows: *Out*—4, 5, 3, 4, 4*, 3*, 4*, 4, 4 = 35; and then *In*—5, 5*, 5*, 3*, 4, 3, 3, 4, 4 = 36. The asterisked pars show where par changes were later made in the final layout. The final routing ended up as: *Out*—4, 5, 3, 4, 5, 5, 3, 4, 4 = 37; and then *In*—5, 4, 4, 4, 4, 3, 3, 4, 4 = 35—quite opposite that of the presentation plan in terms of the front and back. How is it supposed that such a swing between nines occurred?

Could MacKenzie and Hunter have had plans up their sleeves to adjust the back-to-back par 5s on the front? Or, did they make any effort to change the 17th into a par 5? This latter idea has not been given much attention, but with ample room for a farther seabound tee at No. 17, per-

MEN'S SCORE CARD
CYPRESS POINT CLUB

HOLE	BLUE TEES	WHITE TEES	PAR	HANDICAP STROKES	HOLE	BLUE TEES	WHITE TEES	PAR	HANDICAP STROKES
1	420	407	4	5	10	477	477	5	16
2	544	531	5	1	11	433	423	4	4
3	161	156	3	17	12	411	403	4	2
4	384	371	4	7	13	361	339	4	14
5	490	471	5	11	14	387	381	4	8
6	521	511	5	3	15	139	124	3	18
7	160	159	3	15	16	233	217	3	6
8	338	318	4	9	17	375	362	4	10
9	291	291	4	13	18	339	324	4	12
Total Out	3309	3215	37		Total In	3155	3050	35	
					Total Out	3309	3215	37	
					Total	6464	6265	72	

Scorer ....

Attest ....

Date ....

Men's Par 72
Course Rating White 71.0 Blue 72.0

FIGURE 18-2
A scorecard from the Cypress Point Club teaches a fascinating lesson in how a great course is not made great by adhering to any particular set of standards or rules in terms of par order, sequence, or length

haps less opportunity to cut past the stand of cypress trees at the fairway, and maybe even less clearing along the cliffs, the 17th may well have been Cypress's answer to the Cape Hole, the popular 18th down the road at Pebble Beach. True, such a hole may have been a marginal par 5 in terms of length, but there is no question that a hole of even 460 yards in this era, especially one with the ocean to the slice side, would be a deciding hole toward the end of the round. One sure to tempt players to try for eagle.

It was well known that MacKenzie, even as late as 1931, was intent on convincing the Club to install an island tee at No. 18 that would lengthen the hole by as much as 50 yards. His design concept at the 18th called for a suspension bridge and was even taken to the engineering stage. This idea was vetoed by Samuel Morse as being too intrusive and possibly dangerous. So, if not at the 18th, then why not a tee way out at the 17th? No bridge would be required at 17.

His ability to accept suggestions from others made him an even better architect, perhaps the best who ever lived.

— *Geoff Shackelford, Alister MacKenzie's Cypress Point Club*

If the 17th had been made into a par 5 and if the 16th had been made a par 4, the series along the ocean might have been 3, 4, and then 5—perhaps a better-appearing series, certainly seeming more diverse to anyone looking at the scorecard from afar. Hollins was dead set against the 16th being anything but a stout par 3, and the 14th had been shifted away from the ocean, so the desire to explore a par 5 along the sea at the 17th may have been even stronger. Yet there is no decisive evidence to support this theory. Did MacKenzie give any thought to the 17th as a par 5? Sure. He undoubtedly thought of *all* the areas for what they *might* be. This is the job of any decent golf architect. MacKenzie—and Hunter—were as decent as could be.

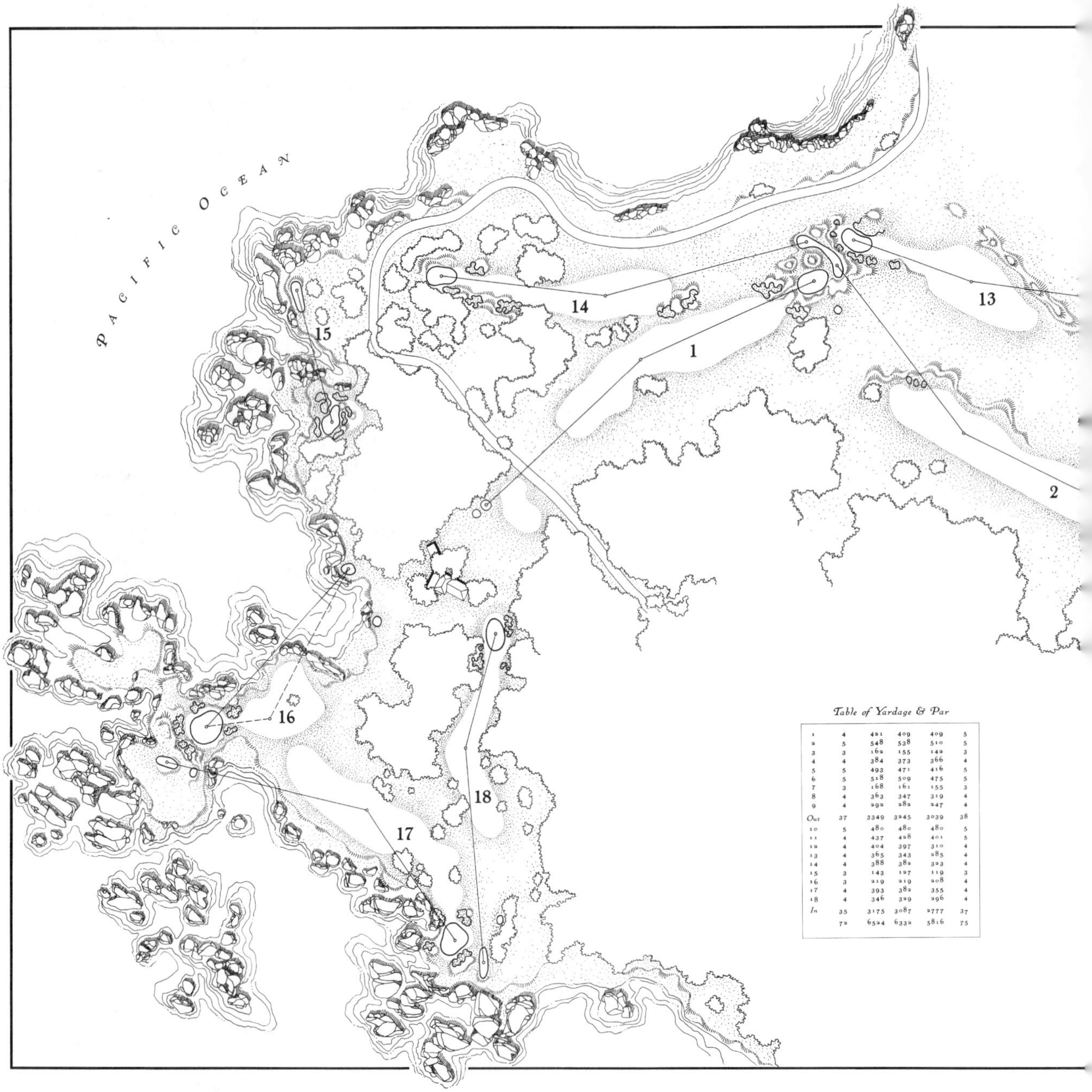

Table of Yardage & Par

1	4	421	409	409	5
2	5	548	538	510	5
3	3	162	155	142	3
4	4	384	373	366	4
5	5	493	471	416	5
6	5	518	509	475	5
7	3	168	161	155	3
8	4	363	347	319	4
9	4	292	282	247	4
Out	37	3349	3245	3039	38
10	5	480	480	480	5
11	4	437	428	401	5
12	4	404	397	310	4
13	4	365	343	285	4
14	4	388	382	323	4
15	3	143	127	119	3
16	3	219	219	208	4
17	4	393	382	355	4
18	4	346	329	296	4
In	35	3175	3087	2777	37
	72	6524	6332	5816	75

FIGURE 18-3
The Cypress Point Club.

DRAWN BY THE AUTHOR, 2002

ANTICIPATION

Seventeen-Mile Drive through the Del Monte Forest is the ultimate path to a golf course. Whether you are a member or just passing by the curves through the forest and open areas along the sea establish the absolute truth that the land is king when it comes to superlative golf.

The feeling of arriving at the Cypress Point Club is not due to a spectacular entry road, clubhouse, or pathway. None of this is necessary. The spectacle is understood by the aforementioned secret code between golfer and course. You know you have arrived just by the tranquility, the

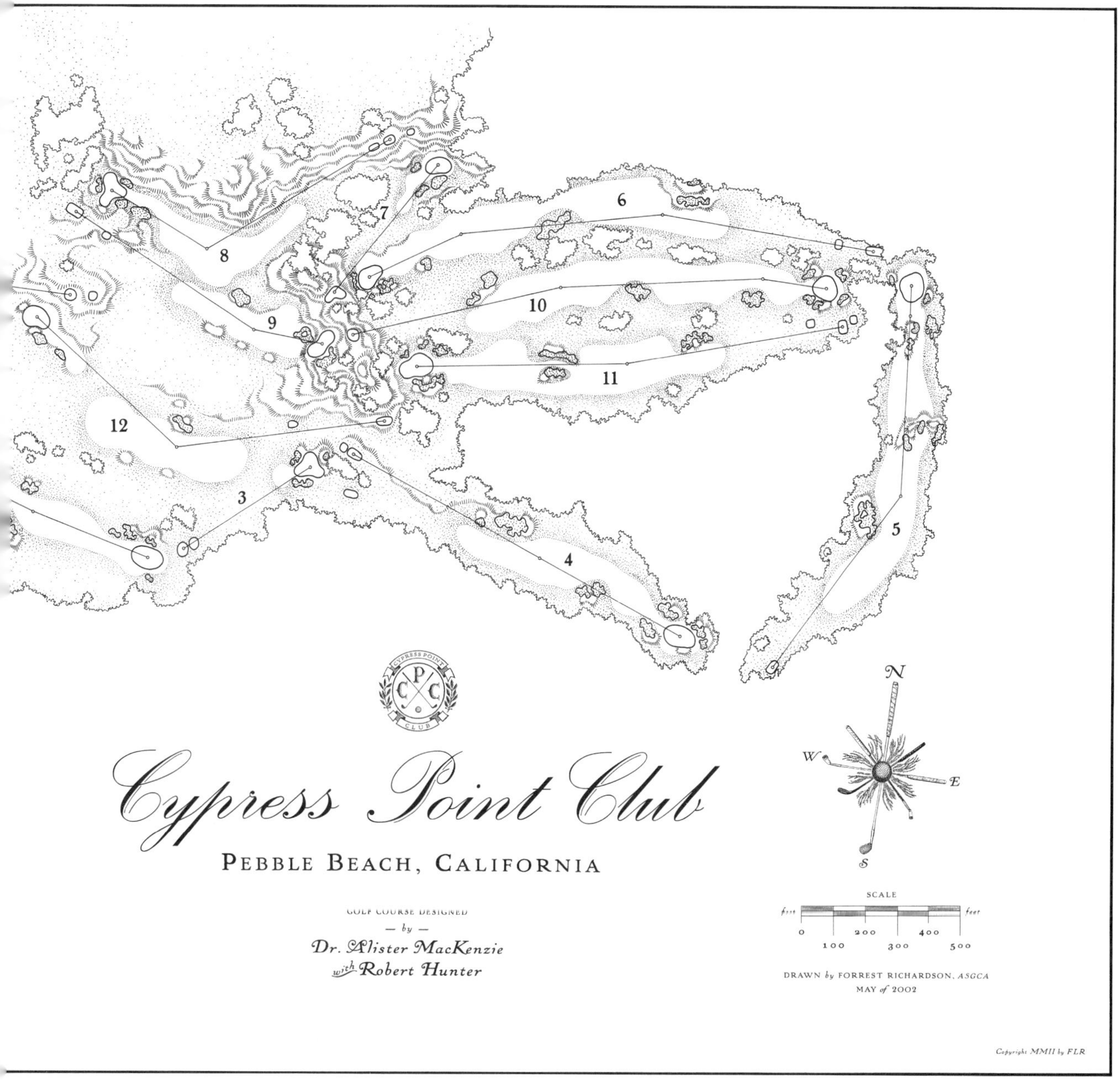

understated ambiance, the reserved attitude. It is the most comfortable spot in all of golf. The place has cradling arms, like those of a father holding his son and at the same time allowing him to peek out to the world. Although the clubhouse is set on a rise above the ocean, it looks out to the surf through trees and golf. How tempting it would have been to plop the clubhouse on the water's edge—and how wrong.

Although several accounts exist of life inside the old clubhouse, my thesaurus does not contain a list of words for *Cypress Point clubhouse,* and so it is with reverence that I leave this entirely to the imagination. Some things are best this way. This is one.

> *Monotony is the foe that golf course designers must everlastingly fight.*
> —Dr. Alister MacKenzie

COMPARISON OF PAR PATTERN FOR A 3-HOLE SERIES OF DIFFERENT PARS

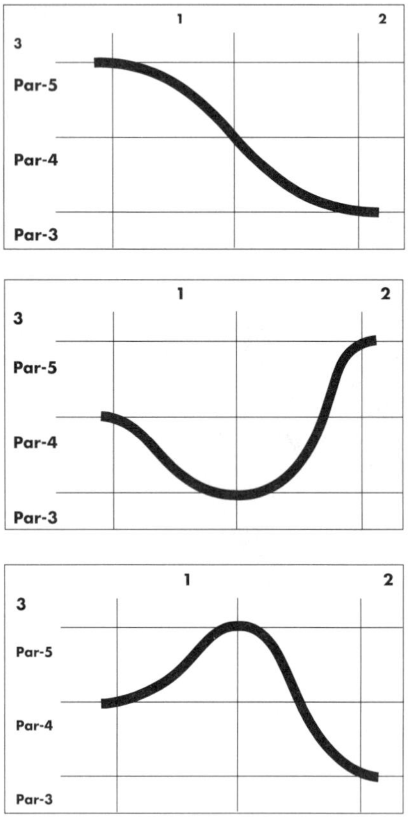

FIGURE 18-4
Which is a better sequence of par for three successive holes if each is to be a different par and the series is to begin with a par 4 or 5? In these charts, the sequence of three holes is explored. MacKenzie's openers at Cypress Point—par 4, 5, and then 3—form the most pleasing pattern of the three, which is represented by the lower graph.

Outside the clubhouse, the round of golf begins in simple form. There is a closeness to everything. A small practice putting green. It is simple, too. Paths lead uncontested to the parking lot, or to the clubhouse, or to wherever. No curbs, no obstacles, just finely cut turf surrounding a structure that looks like a very large house.

We are ready to play.

THE OPENING

The First Hole

Hole No. 1 plays tantalizingly away from the ocean, yet every one of your senses knows exactly in which direction it resides. The ocean is that stunning woman on the street, and here we are with an errand in the opposite direction. Well below the other side of the clubhouse, the ocean crashes onto rocks and forms the golf holes that, to the casually acquainted, command the most attention at Cypress Point. Still, even though we know there is greatness in the holes before the ocean, the anticipation of meeting this beauty is almost too much to bear. Why—why can't we play out *that* way?

The first hole is longish. It is not all that easy, yet it presents itself in a straightforward manner. It is there for the taking. We are leaving civilization and to prove this point, we are asked to play our tee ball across Seventeen-Mile Drive from a tee so personal that it may as well be the front porch of the modest golf shop. We are away now. Seventeen-Mile Drive is our threshold. We see into the doorway of the course—to Hole 14, some tees—but we cannot be bothered with them now. We are beginning a journey.

The Second Hole

We turn slightly in direction, but we plow on farther away from the ocean. There is room here to open up and take a breath. The first hole is now far behind. This par 5 allows us to look away from our rear-view mirror and concentrate on what is to come. Ahead we see a forest. The green fronts it like a welcome mat.

The Third Hole

We started with a par 4. Then a par 5. And now a par 3. Is there any better sequence of holes if each par of the three is to be different? How perfect is 4, 5, and then 3? Very perfect. Right off the bat, we have played one of each variety. It is as if we have seen the entire produce section in one aisle. We have experienced the forest and have seen the dunes. We are absorbing the textures.

The Fourth Hole

There is more to this course. We move onward, changing direction only slightly. The routing rises gradually. This par 4 gives us options to play left for a gamble and a much better approach. The forest is taller now, and darker. Sounds are deadened. The smack of the ball is quieter. It is time to focus on golf. But what lies ahead? Certainly we cannot continue away from the ocean much longer.

The Fifth Hole

The routing turns, and we sense that the rest of the course is distant. Or is it the other way around? Here, at the edge of the woods, maybe *we* are distant. There appears to be no golf to our right, only to our left. Through trees are greens, tees, and fairways. The novel we are playing has taken us away from the theme—the very title of the book—and has built characters and funneled our thinking on matters of golf and not of oceans, crashing waves, and heroic shots across them both. We want to read more of this book, and this par 5 will do nicely. It is a complex character, full of traps and vinegar.

There are three holes that play across the arm of the sea. There are others that are backed by magnificent vistas or forest and mountain bordered by Monterey pine and the weird cypress which abounds there. There are giant sand dunes which one plays over, along and sometimes unfortunately, into. It is a combination of brilliant green fairways, startlingly blue water, unbelievably white sand, with a superb achievement in golf architecture.

—Samuel Morse

The Sixth Hole

A turn back toward the ocean. At last! But curiously, the farther we descend this second-in-a-row par 5, the more out-of-touch the ocean becomes. As we move closer, we also get lower. The horizon is now only sand dunes and the tops of scraggly trees. Two par 5s in a row is simply a throwback to the days when par mattered not and the only importance was good golf. This was not unusual to MacKenzie. It is no more an oddity than two crescendos with but an accent between. Symbols bang and the music builds—twice. The green, backed by a dramatic sand dune backdrop, brings us out of the forest and into the open. From the putting surface, the ocean is vastly off limits. It hides beyond. There, but not.

MAKING THE TURN

The Seventh Hole

We are brought up among the dunes and their crystal-white sand. The breeze of the still-far-off ocean now in our face. *But we turn again.* How maddening! This time we play only slightly away. The quest for the ocean remains, but not until this second par 3 in the round is faced and brought to its knees. The hole is nearly identical in length to our first par 3, the 3rd. What was Mackenzie thinking? Or Hunter? Ah, it is a different hole altogether. With the rising terrain behind the green and tall pines upon it, things here look small. The green seems far away because of this, as does the valley of fairway that runs the length of the hole.

Cypress Point has a masterful relation to its site. It's full of subtlety.
—Desmond Muirhead

This is another peaceful spot. Quiet and reserved.

There are courses within courses at Cypress. The seventh reminds us of a highland meadow cleared from dense woodlands. But the dunes behind and that breeze give us cause to know better. This is no highland meadow. The forest we keep seeing is no different than it is along the spans of Seventeen-Mile Drive itself—there one minute and gone the next. The ocean is close by.

The Eighth Hole

Robert Hunter said of the eighth, "Here we enter the high dunes and to put this little hole in its place all we are required to do is to carry 240 yards over a huge dune and then we can kick the ball onto the green." What more is there to know? I will tell you. We have managed to reach the links portion of this routing. The bright white sand of the dunes is framed by clumps of tall grasses. Neither dune nor grass is a place for a golf ball. Absolutely neither.

How can this be? We are here at the eighth and yet it is only our third par 4? Par 4s are the very staple of golf courses. They rule in their plenty. MacKenzie has introduced us to his 5s, his 3s, and just two 4s. And this one speaks differently than most 4s. As Hunter explained, it is relatively short, although lengthened somewhat since originally built.

This may be the most spectacular of Cypress's inland holes. There are views from tee to green for which one gives thanks.

Our route has changed once again—we are headed to the coast. And how fitting that we have not even reached the halfway point. The water in the teapot has not begun to boil. It is still brewing.

The Ninth Hole

The most felicitous meeting of land and sea in creation.
—Robert Louis Stevenson, on the Monterey Peninsula

The routing turns away—again. The ninth may not be tall, but it is capable. It is the smallest of cactus needles in your hand, so small and so irritating that it must be dealt with. On paper, the ninth is a mere par 3½—a par 4 caught back in the "two hundreds." But we are again given four strokes to make a mark on a short one.

A most interesting psychological question is raised by this risky short hole: Does one take a chance before the turn to the in holes, or does one play conservatively and shoot for safety? Very likely the decision will influence the round as a whole. It is bound to influence how we play the balance of the holes—those we have been longing to meet.

The Tenth Hole

This hole seems familiar. We are backtracking, going up into the woods from an elevated tee at the back of the green we have just tried our darndest to master in two putts. Our tee shot marks the point at which we are supposed to be going back home. But this is off in yet another direction. MacKenzie is toying with us. We are the needle of his compass, and he has us pointed toward the South Pole! He has managed to challenge us not only through the design of each hole and the placement of the hazards but also through the direction we are headed and the things we see, or are kept from seeing. The treasure hunt continues. The turn is now behind us.

THE HEART OF THE COURSE

Now might be a good time to take a breather. What nice things we have seen. We started out on a rise above the ocean, but far enough away not to be bothered by mist or crashing waves. We headed off toward the forest, started coming back, but turned, and then turned again, and finally turned once more. We have seen the forest approaching, been deep within it, grabbed hold of the dunes that sit at its entrance, and are now back among towering trees. We have done this, mind you, in half of the tour. We have seen everything but those ocean holes we remember so well, whether from playing them many times before or from playing them mentally over the flat images in a coffee-table book.

> *Cypress Point is an adventure all the way.*
> *—Herbert Warren Wind*

The 11th Hole

MacKenzie's longest par 4 at the Cypress Point Club directs us to the most massive of dunes. The green could not be placed farther from us or it would be buried beneath this great sand structure. A hint of woods is still around us, but all who approach this great dune with its tiny green know full well what lies beyond.

The 12th Hole

We are out of the woods, at least the deep woods. From our perch between white sand and those now familiar clumps of weedy grass is a path out and around to the right that we are "told" to follow. Here it is, some 70 years after MacKenzie's passing—and he speaks so very clearly to us about what he expects of our golfing talent. No hole at Cypress Point is more simply laid out, yet none is more complex. While the openness may signal that we are out of the literal woods, the golf here has no relation to the metaphorical woods.

The 13th Hole

The 13th hole is the second of three successive dogleg right par 4s. Is this worse than had they been right, then left, then right? Is this worse than had they gone left, then right, then left? Such questions are trivial. Quite. They go where they are *supposed* to go. And it does not matter in any regard. This is a golf course, not a menu.

We are tied in the seventh inning now. This is the heart of our game and the reason everyone has come to partake.

FIGURE 18-5
"The most pleasant walk in all of golf," the walk to the 15th hole.
COURTESY OF CYPRESS POINT CLUB

The 14th Hole

This majestic hole plays up to an approach so remarkably guarded by trees that it appears the green is trying to hide something. Behind the shot to the green is a skyline framed by these very trees. Once we are on the green, the attention shifts toward the Pacific Ocean and those next holes nestled just a walk away.

When play is completed at the 14th, we cross Seventeen-Mile Drive—our threshold—and the finish is underway. There are only so many holes left in the adventure. This, of course, is true of any 18-hole layout after the 14th. But here at Cypress, the realization has a different ring. While only four to play, they are among the greatest in all the world of golf, and it is hard to contain the anticipation that has built while we were busy figuring things out during the past hour or more.

The Most Pleasant Walk in All of Golf

I had been putting what little money I had in ocean frontage, for the sole reason that there was only so much of it and no more, and that they wasn't making any more.
—Will Rogers, in a column published 13 April 1930

"The tees for the next hole shall be located close by to the green being played so that golfers will not have to endure long walks." Bah, humbug! If this rule were followed to the *T*, then the greatest of all walks in golf would be lost. The lesson learned from the walk from the edge of Seventeen-Mile Drive to the tees at the 15th hole is one of landscape, simplicity, and, foremost, intrigue. As the path curves slightly left—toward where we want to be—the eyes move slightly right—toward what they want to see. The ocean is before us, but it is to our right, which is open, permitting the farthest view. Humans seek the farthest view because it takes in the most area. Taking a cue from our ancestral wanderings and the associated threats to our safety, we seek information by looking outward. Our eyes scan as far as they can see through involuntary actions. This is why we look ahead and slightly right first, trying to see. Once the coast is clear, we look beyond the low-lying trees and brush that separate us from what is around to the left.

The ice plant, although technically a succulent, is anything but succulent to the golfer during play. Along the path, however, it serves us well, with its flowering blossoms cascading among the rocks that form the far western edge of California.

LOCAL RULE

Ocean holes 15, 16, and 17. Cliff and beach played as part of the course, and not water hazard. Deer prints can be repaired on greens only.

THE FINISH

Whoever said finishing holes should carry our memories of a course into the next round must have been thinking of the last four holes at the Cypress Point Club. This is the standard.

The 15th Hole

I am sure that there is no more beautiful spot in all of golf. A picture of this spot would do no better than trying to describe the taste of rhubarb pie to someone who's never eaten it. It is beyond words. The only thing is to tell you the bits that make sense from your easy chair. It is a short par 3. It gets much less attention than its big brother, a hole away. It is the calm before the storm, a sheltered bay, a harbor for golfers who have maneuvered out from the inlands and are preparing for their voyage. The 15th is everything a golf hole should be.

FIGURE 18-6

Although the wonder of Cypress Point begins long before the 15th hole, for many, the journey is defined upon reaching this first seaside hole. Although several routings have been valiantly attempted, there is unlikely to be a better meeting of ocean and golf than Alister MacKenzie created at this short par 3. The golfer is cradled in a contradiction of tranquil beauty and rough seas. The forces at work are both inspiring and terrifying. The golf is at the same time both easy and difficult.

COURTESY OF CYPRESS POINT CLUB; PHOTOGRAPH BY MARTIN MILLER

FIGURE 18-7
The 16th hole at The Cypress Point Club may have been thought of as a par 4 during its design phases, but it eventually became the most famous par 3 in the world. A study of the demands it places on the golfer can serve as a lesson about solving almost any strategic design problem in golf course architecture.

COURTESY OF CYPRESS POINT CLUB; PHOTOGRAPH BY MARTIN MILLER

The 16th Hole

Coming from our short par 3, we face a par 3 that is completely different. While a nominal iron would have done just a few steps earlier, an iron may not even enter the picture for this test. Our green is out there. No sheltered cove. No harbor. No calm.

This is a hole that captures all of the design strategies. It asks us to lay up. It beckons us to be heroic. It gives us a detour. It is open to the left. But it is all the while penal at its core.

Even when the play is safe, safety is not guaranteed. There is risk up until the end. And one wishes the end, at least the end marked by the sound of the ball rattling in the cup, would come soon. We are walking a tightrope made of rock, planted with grass and on which four golfers and a few caddies are making their way to the other side. There is no net.

The 17th Hole

We have wrestled with the two short holes, but we are still in a hold. The tee for the 17th hole is on the rocks and now more than ever are we truly out in the ocean. While our view from the green behind us was spectacular, it was also framed by terra firma. Peeks at the sea, both right and left, were our views. Here, though, we see forever along the coast. And that coast, at least part of it, is our fairway.

The climax to our story is here and now. The tee shot is a matter of dialing in the degrees and firing away. Calculations must be made for the wind—and the nerves. The copse that was cleverly left along the rocky ledge to the water is a reminder to play left. Too far, however, and it will bring the hazards at the green into play. Too far right, and the chances are good the line to the green will be out over the ocean and in from the right. Either way, these trees are an obstacle. If not now, then later. If you brought a student of golf course design to this tee only and pointed out these remaining trees and nothing else, it would be a brilliant lesson. MacKenzie and Hunter knew what they were doing because they knew what the golfer would be doing. They imagined the moments that have taken place every day since they last set foot here. They were clever men. An ordinary design would have cleared all the way to the water's edge. We know this because it is the way we see most golf holes along the water. The shoreline is open. Not here. The shoreline is full of complexity, and so is the golf.

HARDEST HOLE ON TOUR

When it was played as part of the Pebble Beach Pro-Am, Cypress Point's 16th hole was the most difficult of all the holes played by the PGA Tour.

The 18th Hole

The towering cypress trees line the parade route back home. They are crowding the street and waving. As if our journey has not been full of surprise enough, we are now asked to play an obstacle course of woods that are closer to us than those we left just seven or eight holes ago. This is the home stretch of the routing. As the fairway rises to the right of the clubhouse, we see signs of activity. The anticipation of coming home is in the air.

The above description of the Cypress Point Club could have been written long ago, for not much has changed. In 2001, many of the dunes were restored by thinning the growth that had taken over their slopes. There have been minor changes to the eighth and ninth holes and, recently, to the 15th hole, where a part of the green to the front right corner was built up where it had slowly been disappearing into the Pacific.

The Cypress Point Club is full of lessons on the art of routing a golf course. It breaks rules, breaks molds, and breaks the heart of all who expect outright perfection in their round of golf. The only perfection it can provide is the journey itself. What one does along the way is a blank book, one to be written by thousands of authors, each with a thousand plots waiting to unfold.

I am grateful to have the opportunity to conclude my round with a look at this wonderful golf course. I do not believe that Alister MacKenzie or Robert Hunter thought that the act of writing about Cypress Point would bring as much joy as playing the course. I am indebted for the opportunity they gave me, however unknowingly.

SPECIAL ACKNOWLEDGMENT

Many great writings mention the Cypress Point Club. The one dedicated to the subject in unparalleled fashion is *Alister MacKenzie's Cypress Point Club* by Geoff Shackelford. I am grateful for Geoff's writing and for his time spent discussing a few aspects of the routing that have been covered here. Also, my appreciation goes to the Club itself for making materials available to support this writing. The personal attention of head professional Jim Langley was invaluable and constant. Just as Cypress Point offers great lessons in routing golf courses, its personnel are the best of those connected to this great and wonderful game.

Few clubhouses in all of sport are as comfortable or as honestly charming.
—Herbert Warren Wind

A FEW OF THE LESSONS

- A golf course can be driven by a visionary other than the golf course architect.
- If a golf course is to be great, the most important element should probably be the golf course.
- The routing should take its lead from the land, not the other way around.
- A great routing can be the brainchild of not one mind, but several.
- Those involved in a great routing need not all be professional golf architects; they just need to be smart.
- The first routing is not always the best routing.
- Great routings can come from a team effort.
- When egos are left at the door, teamwork can take place.
- A course completed under budget can be a great course.
- A course completed ahead of schedule can be a great course.
- The name of a golf course is always best when based on authenticity.
- It is possible to have par 3s of identical length and still have a great course.
- A golf course does not need length to be great.
- Diversity of terrain and landscape is an asset.
- Golf shots that are varied throughout the round will win the hearts of golfers.
- A humble clubhouse can be a great clubhouse.
- Trees can be cleared for vistas, not just for the golf.
- Length can be worthwhile, but not without reason.
- A golf club where the staff enjoys going to work is a great asset.
- Continuing regard for an original design speaks volumes.
- Practice areas are not always possible or absolutely necessary.
- When a road bisects a property, not all is lost.
- Pars do not have to be even on each nine for the course to be great.
- Back-to-back par 5s can work out just fine.
- Back-to-back par 3s can work out just fine.
- Parallel holes can work out just fine.
- A routing does not have to return after nine holes, and it does not have to go way out and then turn back, either.
- A routing can have several successive holes that turn in one direction and still be regarded as excellent.
- The quality of work a golf course architect does is likely to be the quality of work he will be hired to do. (Bobby Jones made his decision to hire MacKenzie at Augusta after seeing the Cypress Point Club.)
- Long walks are not long when they go somewhere nice.
- An uphill hole to the clubhouse can work just fine.

Reflections on Routing

HOLE NO. 19

A musty book in adequate condition sits near the place where I do most of my writing. It was purchased for slightly too much. Although I own a new copy of the same book, I do not find it as satisfying as the musty one. The new copy smells of ink and factory glue, the old copy of yellowed pages and deteriorating cloth. The book is *The Mystery of Golf,* by Arnold Haultain. Haultain was able, back in 1908, to capture golf in a way that no author since has been able to. He speaks of what makes golfers tick. Why the game is so fascinating. How it captures the hearts of those who play it. And, appropriate to this discussion of routing, just what it is about the relationship of the golfer to the ground over which golf is played that that makes the game so mysterious. In *The Mystery of Golf,* Haultain describes his home course: "...hills, valleys, trees, a gleaming lake in the distance, a grand and beloved piece of bunting lending gorgeous colour to the scene; a hospitable clubhouse with spacious verandahs and armchairs; shower-baths; tea and toast; whisky and soda; genial companionship; and the ever delectable pipe."

It is no coincidence that half of these 45 words are devoted to the clubhouse. It is likely that, in the moments before and after his rounds, and even on days which no golf was played, Haultain was inspired to write about golf just by being at this 19th hole.

This is our 19th hole. Like all 19th holes, it is a metaphor for an opportunity—one last chance. The 19th hole of a golf course is a fictitious place in terms of play but a very real place in terms of completing play. At the 19th hole, one reflects on a round well played, parts of a round well played, or at least parts of a round that should have been well played. At the 19th hole there is time to appreciate the round of golf, to tell stories, and to create new ones.

Golf is a game, and talk and discussion is all to the interests of the game. Anything that keeps the game alive and prevents us being bored with it is an advantage. Anything that makes us think about it, talk about it, and dream about it is all to the good and prevents the game from becoming dead.
—Dr. Alister MacKenzie

At the 19th hole of this book, we can look at golf course routing with an eye toward the future. In a game that is so immeasurably dependent on the land, we can ponder how routings might be influenced by the land. In a game so revered for its traditions, we can ask which ones might be worth losing. And in a game so full of options, we can consider a few that might be worthwhile.

There are eight topics that I feel deserve attention in our 19th hole. They are listed here as a preface:

- The effect of golf equipment and golf balls
- Golf's use of land
- The time it takes to play golf
- Golf and the environment
- New technologies for routing and playing golf
- The cost of golf
- Golf's popularity
- Where golf course routing is headed

THE EFFECT OF GOLF EQUIPMENT & GOLF BALLS

It is true that some golfers are hitting the ball farther these days. I suspect that the term *these days* will apply no matter the year in which this paragraph is read. As equipment improves, it increases the likelihood of a golf ball traveling farther down a fairway. What has not necessarily improved is the golfer. I know this because the last group I was paired with had a healthy investment in golf clubs but no investment in improvement. They hit the ball with zest. It went far. And mostly, when it went far, it also went far off line.

The down side of balls traveling farther, whether from better club engineering or better ball design, is that golf courses are difficult to change—especially in terms of length. Think back to the safety envelopes covered in Hole 7, "Safety Considerations." If we route courses with these safety considerations in mind and we strive to be efficient in land use, where do we find extra length? Do we buy someone's backyard and plop a tee where the swimming pool used to be? Do we extend a green right up to the fence and forget the rule that says there should be about 100 feet from that line to the edge of the green? What do we do about the width of golf corridors?

If we figured that a ball travels 267 yards (800 feet) from the back tee to the angle point of a par-4 or par-5 hole, what do we do when the angle point changes due to length? How do we plan for some future event over which we have no control?

Might all this affect the safety cone and the safety envelope? Sure it will. And I'll tell you what else: It will affect the width, too. If a golf course architect establishes that the width of a corridor should be 350 feet based on a drive of a certain length, this width might be extended as the drive becomes longer.

These are the primary reasons that this issue is so relevant to routing. We may be able to shift hazards and tighten fairways later on, but we do not always have the luxury of adding length or the width to accommodate a new length. This is even more true on the many classic layouts where lengthening has occurred over the years and we are simply out of space. It is also costly to change golf courses. This is an important point, and one that ultimately drives the cost of a round or a membership to heights that prevent many from partaking.

I've seen more golf courses improved by hurricanes than by green committees.
—John LaFoy

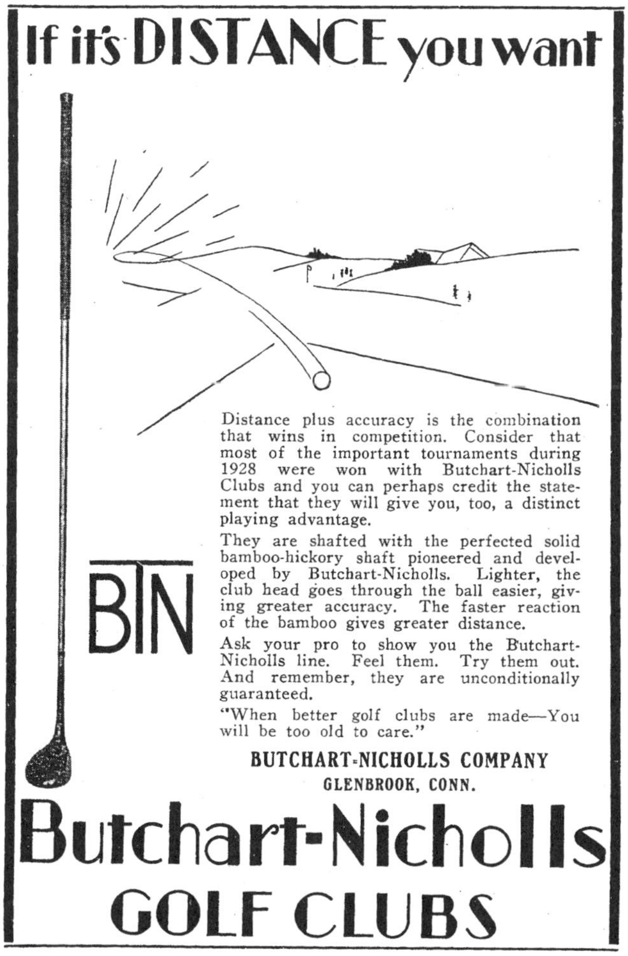

FIGURE 19-1
This old advertisement, except for the dated design, looks almost as if it could have appeared just last month in a popular golf magazine.

COURTESY OF THE USGA GOLF LIBRARY COLLECTION; C. 1929

There is hardly anything accidental in the modern golf course—it's all sort of nail-clipper precision.
—Desmond Muirhead

The Clubmakers

I spent time discussing the subject of club improvement with John Solheim, president of Karsten Manufacturing of Ping golf club fame. I have known John for many years. He is among the mere handful of golf equipment manufacturing executives who are passionate about the engineering and science of golf clubs and balls. That is refreshing. While I have a good handle on what golf course architects, planners, and developers of golf courses can—or cannot—do with respect to changes in equipment, I felt it appropriate to go to the source. John runs one of the companies that is helping golfers hit longer shots. With great anticipation, I asked John what he felt should be done in the face of longer shots. I wasn't sure what to expect of his answer.

"I feel that we need to find ways to bring back the premium of accuracy. There's no reason to encourage a driver at every par 4 or par 5. There are other tee shots in golf, and they need to be encouraged," he said. "Somehow we need to get people to think it's not macho to simply hit the ball a long way—golf shots need to be accurate. That's a great part of the game."

In some ways, John's comment surprised me. After all, he sells clubs. If consumers want to hit the ball farther at every par 4 or 5, the capitalistic equation says you give them what they want. But, like his father, Karsten Solheim, who founded Ping, John does not think like everyone else. It is his family's cleverness that built Ping into the major force it is today. He remains a voice for innovation and for thinking outside the box. It also occurred to me that Ping's brand is built on the element of accuracy; this is where engineering comes into play. In the early ads for Ping irons, the ugly ones with yellow backgrounds, it was the promise of accuracy that drove the golfer to check them out at the pro shop.

Solheim does point out that one of the attractions of bringing new players into the game is the equipment. "I don't feel we can take that away from young people any more than we would have wanted it taken away from us when we were learning the game and trying out new clubs and balls," he said. "Equipment is a big reason people get excited about golf."

I instantly recalled that many of my fondest memories as a young golfer are of buying a new club with money saved from delivering newspapers, and of trying out a new ball with a different feel. Many of my purchases were, admittedly, for extra length.

In our discussion about length, Solheim and I worked out the mathematics of an 18-hole, par-72 course. On such a layout (that is, one with four par 3s, four par 5s, and ten par 4s), it is expected that the scratch golfer will typically hit 14 full shots off the tee, these are *the drives*. These shots are expected at each par 4 and each par 5. We then expect that at least 18 shots will be taken from the fairway; these are the second shots on par 5s and all of the approach shots. To round out the full shots, we know that four shots to the par-3 greens will occur. This list of expected shots totals 36. The rest of the strokes are putts—36 if the scratch golfer shoots par. For a bogey golfer, we can safely say that the extra 18 shots (if this golfer is to shoot a 90 on the par-72 course) will be taken in the fairway or around the green. Assuming that about half of these extra shots will be full shots, it is interesting to conclude that, in a typical round of golf, the big tee shot accounts for about one-third of the total full shots, just one in five of the total strokes.

Primarily, the bulk of concern lies with the big tee shot. How wonderful it would be if we could put a premium on accuracy on at least some of those shots. Wouldn't it be better for clubmakers if there were two or more choices in driving clubs—one for outright length and one for accuracy? If we could divide up those big tee shots, we might be onto something. Solheim is genuine in his commitment to focusing on accuracy. To him, the approach to controlling length needs to be balanced.

The Golf Ball

Most people I spoke with favor some limitation on the golf ball. A USGA representative pointed out, quite matter-of-factly, that his organization already does so by publishing and enforcing rules on ball performance. The tone of his voice implied that they would continue to do so. The ball has always been somewhat of a constant. Once the manufacturing of balls went from a cottage industry to factory production, the romance of the ball-making craft was gone; now golf balls are just sold. Golf course routings—both those that have stood the test of time and ones not yet built

SHOTS TAKEN BY THE BOGEY GOLFER DURING AN 18-HOLE ROUND

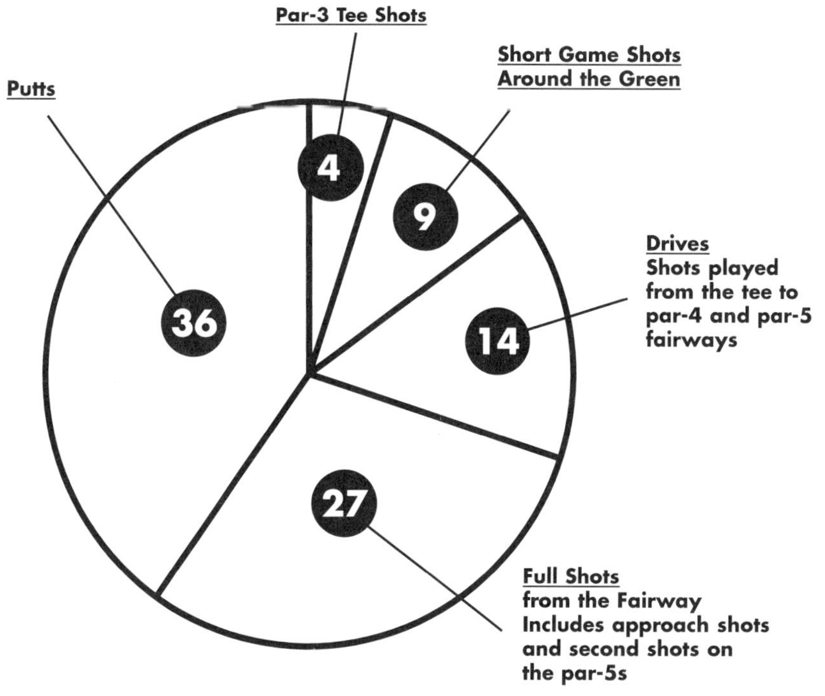

FIGURE 19-2
This chart cleverly shows the percentage of shots by category taken by a bogey golfer during an 18-hole round on a par-72 course with four par 3s, four par 5s, and ten par 4s. Note the percentage of full drives from the tee, shots that are usually executed with just one club: the driver. What a windfall to clubmakers it would be if some of these shots were made more interesting by requiring a yet-undiscovered club to be used to master their strategy!

—will each benefit from a limitation on the performance of golf balls. By the very nature of it being just one thing, instead of 14 like our club selection, it is a far easier target for standardization. Given the choice a golfer would certainly not part with his clubs for they are a personal weapon of sorts. But the ball, so long as it is sturdy and fairly good, can be made a commodity.

The Golfers

Statistics show that the average handicap has not changed substantially in the past 30 years. People vary the challenge of the game depending on the tees they play. A golf architect can design a course that offers great tests and is great fun from all sets of tees, with exciting placement of features and hazards. The problem, of course, is to convince golfers to play from the right tees—that is the set of tees that will suit their game and make the experience enjoyable.

Peter Oosterhuis, who contributed so graciously to this book, notes that there will always be Tigers out there. Tour professionals will always make strides to combat a course. That is their job.

The question is, is it entirely bad for the tour professional to be hitting long shots and reaching par 5s in two, or hitting irons from the tee to just in front of par-4 greens? Perhaps it just proves that par as a concept is destined to become meaningless; remember, once there was no concept of an ideal score. What would it be like if the long-hitting professional played into more greens from the tee than on the typical four par-3 holes during a round? Maybe we should actually be shortening courses for tournaments instead of lengthening them. This could actually be exciting and interesting. I would certainly rather have Tiger Woods than Joe Blow hitting these long shots into 350-yard par 4s. Tiger will be more accurate, I'll bet, than Joe.

Conclusion

Golf will always be a game of trying to do better. That is the soul of the game. We need to preserve our classic courses, but we must understand that trying to beat them will always be part of the game. I do believe we need to limit equipment—perhaps more than is currently being done—but we still need to allow for the excitement of newness and innovation. A difficult balancing act.

Solheim left me with this thoughtful observation: "Golf is a unique combination of something that's very old mixed with new technologies. It will always be this way, and it's what makes it such an appealing and interesting game."

THE USE OF LAND

The use of land per golf course increases as we seek more length, if that is indeed our mission. Because land costs money, the cost of golf rises as a result. Alternatively, some innovative ideas have emerged for reducing land consumption for golf. These are independent of whether we want more length or not.

Most of these new ideas have not caught on. Some of the best are no different than golf; they are just variations on the theme of golf. I divide the alternative golf course ideas into three categories: (1) *courses*—which are smaller, fewer in holes, but nonetheless courses; (2) *facilities*—which are not golf courses but practice areas, putting venues, simulators, etc; and (3) *new games*—which are derived from golf but played with different equipment or on different grounds.

MAKE GOLF DIFFICULT AGAIN

Make golf difficult again
Let's do all that we can
Let's answer the call
Stamp out this wretched ball
Let's stand together for once and for all
Make golf difficult again
Let's ban the NXT
And bring back the featherie
Let's do away with all technology

—Protest song sung by Ian MacCallister (a fictious golf architect) and cohorts in a 2001 TV commercial for the Titleist NXT golf balls

NXT SONG LYRICS WRITTEN BY CRAIG JOHNSON, NICK CALDENBAUGH AND JOHN PETRUNEY OF ARNOLD WORLDWIDE

Alternative Courses

Bill Amick, ASGCA, a Florida-based golf course architect, is a leader in promoting and understanding alternative courses. His accompanying routing plan for a combination compact course, Cayman ball course, and practice area is one such example. "The reason for such facilities is to reduce costs, land requirement, playing time, nonrenewable resources, and walking distance," says Amick. But the real benefit may be less obvious. "When we build these types of courses," he points out, "we're making the game a better fit for the majority of golfers." A majority of regulation courses, according to Amick, are mistaken in their notion that they fit the game that most golfers play.

By now, it may be obvious that the use of land is not the only reason to explore alternative courses, facilities, and games. They may also save time and resources and be a better match for existing golfers and the new golfers the game needs to sustain itself. The alternative course can take on many forms and shapes. It can be a par-3 course, a precision course, a four-hole course, a 12-hole course, or a combination of the above. I am always surprised at the tendency not to develop good ol' nine-hole courses. What is it with this aversion? Could it be that the "serious" golf course developer or private club builder would rather be caught dead than explain why he built a nine-hole course?

A few miles from my office is a small, insignificant nine-hole layout where 100,000 rounds are played every year, I'll bet. The land was paid off probably 50 years ago, and not more than six people can possibly work there. At $8.00 per round, plus the driving range, I'll bet it ranks as one of the greatest golf investments of all time.

Alternative Facilities

Golf needs alternative facilities, providing they are enjoyable. To provide just another practice range on which people whack balls without much reason is not positive. Overall, ranges should strive to be engaging, instructional, and entertaining.

Recently, I broke down and tried my hand at a golf course simulator. This particular one was located indoors and consisted of a hitting mat, a

COMPACT COURSE

Hole	Par	A	B	C	D	E	F	Club(s)
1	3	170	155	141	127	113	99	8 Iron
2	4	510	468	425	383	340	298	Driver + 5 Iron
3	3	251	230	209	188	167	146	7 Metalwood/2 Iron
4	4	393	360	328	295	262	229	Driver + Other Wedge
5	3	278	254	231	208	185	162	3 Metalwood
6	4	483	443	403	362	322	282	Driver + 7 Iron
7	3	125	114	104	93	83	73	Pitching Wedge
8	4	537	492	448	403	358	313	Driver + 9 Metalwood/3 Iron
9	3	197	180	164	147	131	115	6 Iron
10	4	456	418	380	342	304	266	Driver + 9 Iron
11	3	224	205	186	168	149	130	4 Iron
12	4	564	517	470	423	376	329	Driver + 5 Metalwood/1 Iron
	42	4188	3836	3489	3139	2790	2442	

FIGURE 19-3
Golf course architect Bill Amick, ASGCA, has mastered the art of the alternative course with this 12-hole compact course and adjoining 12-hole Cayman ball course. Amick, who has routed several Cayman courses, makes an interesting observation regarding new equipment advances. "Restoring the original challenge and balance to most par-72 courses would necessitate much longer holes and courses totaling near 8000-yards." The configuration in this example can be accommodated on less than 200 acres of land. The benefits are many; perhaps the most attractive is providing a forum in which new golfers can develop their game.

CAYMAN COURSE

Hole	Par	A	B	C	Club(s)
1	3	60	50	40	Wedge
2	4	235	196	157	Driver + 8 Iron
3	3	99	82	66	6 Iron
4	4	262	218	175	Driver + 4 Iron
5	3	139	115	93	3 Metalwood
6	4	190	175	140	Driver + Wedge
7	3	126	105	84	7 Metalwood/2 Iron
8	4	289	240	193	Driver + 3 Metalwood
9	3	85	71	57	8 Iron
10	4	249	207	166	Driver + 6 Iron
11	3	112	93	75	4 Iron
12	4	289	230	184	Driver + 7 Metalwood/2 Iron
	42	2135	1782	1430	

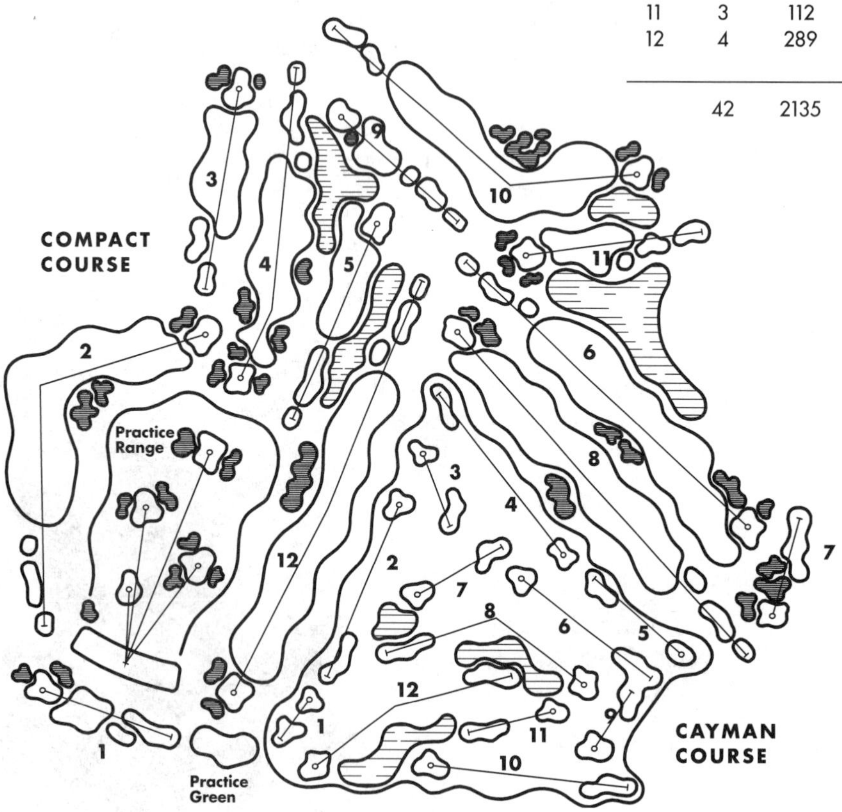

ARBITRARY VALUES

Golf architect George C. Thomas Jr. promoted the idea that par was too arbitrary and that it needed to be overhauled. His interesting view was that greens could be smaller and less emphasis placed on their size if putts would count for half a stroke only. This might also speed up play, as the counting of a putt for an entire stroke would be done away with and golfers would not take so much time worrying over half of the score to be counted. Accuracy from the fairway would be rewarded. In essence, hitting greens in regulation or less would come with an advantage. *Accuracy* would be rewarded until the point of reaching the green. In match play format, the idea that Thomas promoted can make for a very quick game. A hole may be decided early by concession or otherwise. (*Note:* A read of the chapter called "Arbitrary Values" in Thomas's *Golf Architecture in America* is a must if this sounds interesting. You might also find it worthwhile to try a game in which you apply the concept.)

canvas backdrop on which a golf hole was projected from the rear, and a series of sensors and wires to record my swing, the trajectory of the ball, and so on. I must admit that the experience was a good one. The technology associated with hitting real balls into a canvas backdrop and analyzing the shot by computer will get better and better, I suspect. The next generation of simulators will be more realistic, perhaps engaging all of the senses.

Simulators are just part of alternative facilities. There are practice range tees that form a circle around the same target, allowing shots to be played from several angles. There are practice holes without greens. There is an exciting concept called Extreme Golf, created by my friend Ted Claassen. In Extreme Golf you tee off from sand traps, begin holes from deep rough and play any number of "impossible" shots. There is even a concept, called Garts, that was invented by your dear author. (You play Garts like darts, but with a golf ball and wedge.) How terrific that people are finding ways to employ smaller pieces of land, to bring golf to people for less money, and to think outside of the box we call golf.

Alternative Games

My definition of *alternative games* is "games that are golflike but require different equipment"—either different implements or different balls. This makes the games golflike, but not golf.

One day, on an airplane, I took out a sheet and wrote down every means I could imagine to make a golf ball go straight. My idea was to think about the ways to reduce land required for a golf course, especially one winding through a residential community. At one point my menagerie of ideas ranged from tethers attached to the ball to devices

Golf beats us all, and that is the chief reason we shall never cease loving her, nor ever give up our attempt to subdue her.

—Robert Hunter, The Links

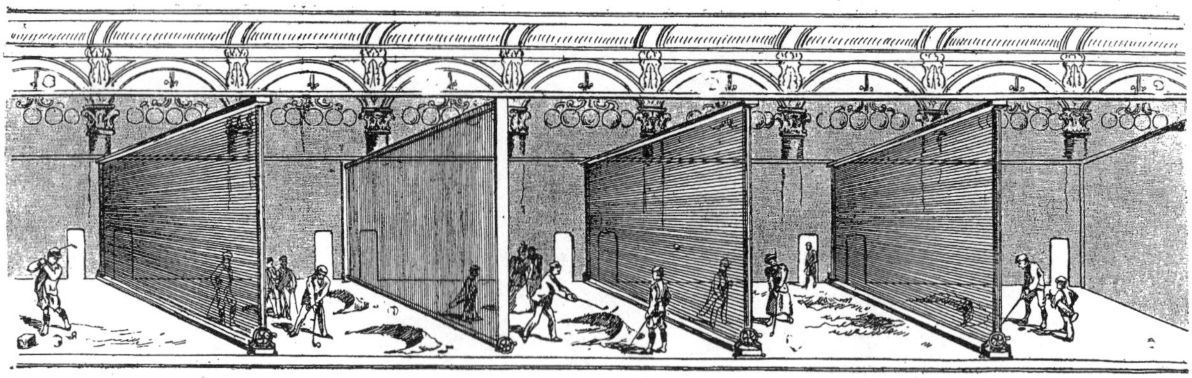

No. 1. Drive off Tee. *No. 2. Brassey Shot.* *No. 3. Lofting.* *No. 4. Approach.* *No. 5. On the Green, holing-out.*

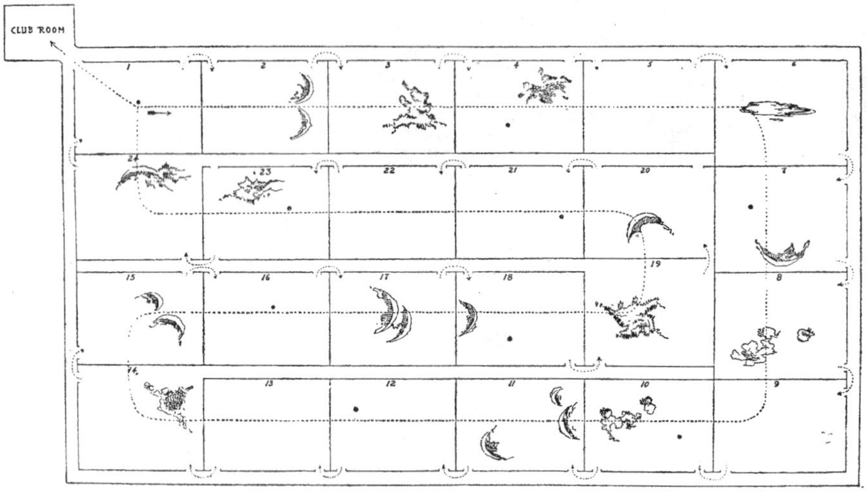

FIGURE 19-4
This concept from the turn of the last century was called Short Golf by its inventor, W. H. White, of Scotland. It envisions a room-to-room venue where golfers play shots, moving themselves from one situation to the next. The cutaway at top shows the individual rooms, separated by screening, where golfers play holes by going from room to room to play tee shots, fairway shots, sand shots, approaches, and, finally, putts.

COURTESY OF THE USGA GOLF LIBRARY ARCHIVE; FROM *THE GOLFER'S MAGAZINE*, NOVEMBER, 1898

that would make the ball self-destruct in flight should it be headed for someone's breakfast nook. I also conceived of a massive wind machine to guide balls. You name it, I wrote it down. I did not, however, think to change the shape of the golf ball. This was apparently too easy.

Enter Mr. Burton Silver, the New Zealander who invented GolfCross® in 1989. GolfCross began as a parody. Burton, you see, is an author and cartoonist; one of his books is entitled *The Kama Sutra for Cats*. GolfCross was to be a blend of New Zealand's two most popular sports, golf and rugby. "It began as a joke," he recalls. "We fashioned a little ball the shape of a football but the size of a golf ball, and we ventured out to take photos of people hitting it through goals. I was onto a book idea, so I thought."

One of those along was George Studholme, who happened to be an ex-greenkeeper. When positioned on a tee and tilted in the direction of the shot, the oblong "ball" went straight. When tilted on the tee, the ball went consistently to the side in an almost perfect curve. "George was the first to suggest maybe we were onto something," recalls Silver. "I did not know whether to take him seriously, but soon we all realized he really did think we had something."

GolfCross is played, as George later noted, "anywhere you can get a mower or a mob of sheep." This is because the odd-shaped ball is placed on a special tee (really a cup); thus, finely clipped turf is not essential. Because the ball, with its gyroscopic aerodynamics, goes almost wherever the player wants it to go, GolfCross courses can be extremely tight and narrow. In addition, there are no greens, which means no putting. In fact, there is no hole. Instead, the ball is hit into a goal that is a *V*-shaped upright net apparatus. It swings to face players as they reach what, in GolfCross, is called a *yard*. The yard is akin to a green, but the ball is still hit from the tee (or cup) and chipped into the goal, which is swung around in any of three positions to face the golfer.

"I am the worst possible messenger for this new game," admits Silver. "I mean, here I am, an author of parodies, and people are expected to take me seriously." Well, people are. GolfCross, while in its infant stage, is building steam. Silver has received calls from all over the world where land is tight and money to construct a full-blown golf course is unavailable. The features of GolfCross—hitting through a goal, not requiring improved fairways, requiring less mowing, and so on—mean that you can put a GolfCross course virtually anywhere. I believe the real benefit might be, however, in introducing the GolfCross ball to regular courses. It goes 90 percent as far as a regular golf ball. It goes dead straight when teed properly. And it could transform some courses into more suitable layouts if the GolfCross ball is used, let's say, from tee to green, and then replaced by a regular ball for putting. Of course I do not know what awful damage a GolfCross ball might do to a green should one of its pointed ends bombard the green head-on.

FIGURE 19-5
No, you are not seeing things. The GolfCross ball is elliptical in shape, weighs about 4 grams more than a golf ball, and goes literally wherever the player aims it when placed on a special tee. Why? The ball acts as a gyroscope, holding its rotation constant. It is not subject to the wild effects of spin that result when golf clubs strike regular golf balls.

FIGURE 19-6
A GolfCross course literally mowed out of farmland in New Zealand. Because the ball is always hit from a tee, there is no need for closely mowed fairways or improved greens. Instead of greens, GolfCross holes end at a yard, an area defined by markers where the golfer may rotate the goal net into any of three positions.

No one ever knows what's next, but they always do it.
—*George Carlin,* Napalm & Silly Putty

Other golflike games have been avoided here. The description of GolfCross is ample, I believe, to stir up creativity among those in the golf business. It certainly reduces land requirements. One can just look around and see that there are ways to preserve the uniqueness of golf, its traditions, and so on while allowing flexibility in bringing new ideas to the table, many with an emphasis to lessen the amount of land required for golf. Certainly not all ideas are good. That is why many remain just ideas.

Conclusion

Golf in its 18-hole standard is not likely to go away, nor should it. What is good for the game is the reinvention of old ideas and the discovery of new ones. These do not need to be sorted out here. The sorting will be accomplished in tidy fashion by the consumer. What we do need are fewer standards that prevent alternative ideas from at least being heard. Golf course architects and planners should twist some arms. The golf industry ought to bend a little. Developers who see marketing stumbling blocks should view them instead as marketing opportunities.

THE TIME IT TAKES TO PLAY

One of the great qualities of golf is that it *does* take a comparatively long time to play a full round of golf. In a world where we have abandoned the double-feature movie, shop with a click, and relegate lunch to munching down on the run, I find it wonderful to do something—this one thing—for a relatively long time. I tell people this, but often to no avail. People, young people especially, are used to quick, now, faster, get-it-over-with, and instant.

When golf "takes too much time to play," this can have several effects: (1) it can ruin the experience if it takes too long to suit one's personal taste; (2) it can mean fewer players will have access to popular courses; and (3) in a day and age full of responsibilities and diversions, it can mean that fewer people will take up and stay with the game. The young woman who sells me bagels at the corner bakery says she hates golf because it takes too much time, but she also admits to playing it whenever she gets invited because she loves every minute of it. What might happen if she could play in two hours instead of four?

The variables of the time it takes to play golf include: (a) the golfer; (b) the course; and (c) the game being played. Golf course managers have tried to corral the first variable. We send golfers out on the correct set of tees, and we even set up courses on busy days so that play proceeds from where we want it to. As for courses, we have tried all sorts of alternative lengths and ideas, but we come back to the consumer's desire for "real golf"—the course of 6800 yards with a par to match at 71 or 72. Most people feel fulfilled at 18 holes in the same way they feel fulfilled by watching a two-hour movie compared to a 45-minute "film."

We have not spent much time tinkering with the third variable—the game being played. Why is it that we assume that stroke play is the *only* way? Recall the story of Royal Worlington from Hole 4, "Types of Golf Courses." At this wonderful course, play occurs in an alternating shot format. The nine holes are regularly played in just under 1½ hours.

What games could be played on existing 18-hole regulation golf courses, perhaps on busy Saturday mornings? How about a required format such as that played at Royal Worlington? Or a version of the arbitrary values solution proposed by George C. Thomas Jr. (see p. 485). Why not set up courses (those on which it would work) to skip three or four holes on busy days? The possibilities are many.

One of my favorite ideas is from golf course architect Don Knott, who suggests one reallllllly long golf hole that is a par 72 all on its own. "No waits between holes," he points out. And who is to say that this might not work—if not as a par 72, then as a string of par 7s, 8s, and 9s over six or seven holes? Perhaps a wacky idea, but creative thought necessarily involves the unusual, the unthinkable, the impossible.

What has happened to the original concept of the game? The game started out as an obstacle course, played over natural terrain. It was the player's option to choose a route and strategy to get from point A to point B. . . . [O]ur modern courses are looking much more like a bowling alley, with narrow strips of fairway flanked by the occasional hazard.

—Don Knott, from his 1994 president's speech to the ASGCA

Conclusion

Golf was played at first, it is thought, as a combination of stroke and match play—a game of one against one and whoever gets less wins. Then it was played as match play. And then the idea of par—a standard—was adopted—and relatively recently, I might add. So what is next? I submit that golf has not seen all its games. Has not been invented to its absolute best. That ideas are lurking out there that can speed play and still keep the game enjoyable and golflike.

THE ENVIRONMENT

It is interesting to consider that an 18-hole golf course produces enough oxygen to meet the needs of a town of about 7000 people. Open space land is an essential balance to the network of pavement, concrete, and rooftops that cross the surface of the earth. This is not to say that golf courses belong everywhere, for they do not. But near towns, in communities, and on the outskirts of both, golf courses account for sustainable acreages that preserve open land, allow views, and permit wildlife to move from one area to another. They are also areas of recreation for the human species—playgrounds in which to renew souls, sanctuaries in which to communicate with each other, and sources of employment for millions of people.

A golf course can be an asset to the environment, and most are. A majority of golf courses are self-contained landscapes; what falls on them remains on them. In instances where golf courses convey drainage, they do so responsibly, often collecting runoff from streets and developments and filtering it before it moves downstream.

Speaking of downstream, I was once in a public meeting about a proposed golf course when a man got up and complained that he was "tired of these golf courses always being planned upstream of oceans and rivers." I nicely inquired if he might point out a location on a map—*any*

Why must a course be 18 holes? The game did not start that way. Any number of holes was acceptable for hundreds of years. Just imagine the number of new facilities that could be available if golfers accepted the concept of a 6-, 11-, or 15-hole course.

—Don Knott, from his 1994 president's speech to the ASGCA

map—that showed an area for development—*any development*—that would not have an ocean or river below it. Thankfully, he had not considered Lake Eyre (Australia), Lake Assal (Africa), the Dead Sea (Asia), the Valdes Peninsula (South America), Death Valley (North America), or the Bentley Subglacial Trench (Antarctica), for these are the only places on earth he could have cited. Everywhere else is above the oceans.

To many communities, a golf course represents an asset on which the sewage of those who live nearby can be safely discharged after it is treated. This is a common function of golf courses in the chain of a thriving town or community. What better method of returning water to the earth than through the natural filtration of the land and soil? Instead of merely dumping treated sewage, it is given a home. This efficient use of irrigation and recharging natural aquifers is just one of the many examples of a golf course assisting in making the overall environment more efficient in and around developed areas.

It is anticipated that golf courses will continue to play a role in the above ways. Routing courses must take into account all of the considerations discussed in order to be an asset to the community. Those who plan and develop golf courses will do well to heed this advice. The creativity of golf course routing, the blazing of new ideas, and the quest to find new ways to satisfy the needs of the golfer will all have better results if a high priority is placed on the environmental aspects of projects.

Conclusion

Golf began as a natural experience. Today, this trend to naturalness is stronger than ever. What has changed is the ability to build courses literally wherever there is a will. This has its drawbacks. But the ability is being harnessed to transform blighted sites into sustainable, enjoyable, useful areas. The future of golf is to find land that is compatible in many ways—environmentally is but one. The golf course of tomorrow is one of beauty for all that is fun for the golfer, profitable for the owner, and serves as an oasis among its neighbors.

NEW TECHNOLOGIES FOR ROUTING & PLAY

Ever-changing technologies will or may affect routing and the game of golf. The most promising are those to do with satellite communication and involving the principles of GIS.

Advances for Routing

One of the hard parts about routing is that the golf architects cannot always be on the site. Being on the site is often the determining factor in making a golf course exceptional. This hands-on and in-person requirement is often not met to the degree necessary. The main stumbling block is that golf course architects and planners cannot be everywhere at once. It is not practical to be traveling every few days.

One area of activity is likely to be in remote reconnaissance. Whether by satellite imagery, flying drones, or on-land robotic rovers, remote surveying of land will be a valuable asset to planners, architects, and developers. By guiding remote video cameras across a site, these professionals may eventually be able to tour the land without visiting the site each time there appears to be a need.

A scenario might be as follows: A client requests that a golf course architect log on to a site tour in which both the architect and developer will maneuver across a site, let's say in Central America. The golf architect is in Canada and the developer is in New Mexico. A local survey company has sent out a robot rover that is maneuvered across the site, transmitting data about elevation, soil conditions, and so on. It also sends real-time video of its travels, and both architect and client can follow along on a map that is projected in each of their conference rooms. For the golf perspective, perhaps the rover is driven up to a hilltop so the view can be taken in. For the development perspective, perhaps the area along a road is driven to assess access. Once this is done, both parties can determine if they wish to visit the site personally to evaluate it. Then, when the golf course architect and planner are doing heavy design work, they can "visit" the site at any time using the initial method. This, of course, can be extended to construction visits, allowing the golf course architect to see what is going on without the typical travel hassles. Will such technology take the place of in-person travel? No. But it is yet another tool to help make the routing and eventual course better.

Why not go out on a limb? That's where the fruit is.
— Will Rogers

FIGURE 19-7
The process of routing is being integrated with the physical construction of golf course projects. This bulldozer is equipped with Trimble's SiteVision® GPS System for earth moving, a satellite-based program that guides the earth-moving operator and eliminates much of the traditional surveying of points used to build golf courses. With an on-board display screen, the operator can refer to drawings and may also interact with the golf course architect in real time. Coordinates, including elevations, are monitored and verified as the shaping work progresses. The process of moving from routing plan to field verification and then to actual construction is being streamlined thanks to such innovation and technology.
COURTESY OF TRIMBLE NAVIGATION LIMITED

Golf is, in part, a game; but only in part. It is also in part a religion, a fever,a vice, a mirage, a frenzy, a fear, an abscess, a joy, a thrill, a pest, a disease, an uplift, a brooding, a melancholy, a dream of yesterday, and a hope for tomorrow.
—New York Tribune *(1916)*

Advances for Construction

Construction advances are related to routing, as they are the eventual step for a routing plan to be put to use. When a routing plan is created using GIS coordinates and programs, or when it is transferred to such a digital database, all are able to share the data. Design plans, staking points, and the fieldwork of clearing, grading, and shaping can be integrated.

For example: A digital routing plan based on GIS data can go from rough form to a design plan much more quickly when the points and planning work are all in the same file. Planners, engineers, environmental designers, building architects, landscape architects, and so on can each draw from the file and create plans that can be almost instantaneously seen by agencies, construction consultants, and others.

The real use of this technology is the integration of machinery with the final design data. A bulldozer or other blade grader can be equipped with GIS sensors that will tell the operator the correct orientation of blade and pitch that is required to meet the profile of the design. In some applications, the pitch of the equipment is completely controlled by the data and the operator is merely there in case something needs resolution.

Advances for Play

Golfers will soon carry cell phone–sized devices to indicate their distance, give course facts, and warn of approaching lightning. Might GPS change the way golf is played? Perhaps.

Think for a minute of the practice putting green. There are dozens of golfers, all going from point to point, pausing to see if anyone is in their way. What if—and this may take some getting used to—you designed an entire course this way? Imagine a large area of turf, hazards, tees, and greens. With the aid of GPS technology, a golf match could be carried out exactly like a simple game of "who's the best putter." You go first and decide on the target. There we go, off across the "course". Ah, you lose. Now it's my turn to pick the target, and I say we play around that lake and up to the top of the hill. Ah, we halve. Still my turn. This time we'll play down the right side of the orchard and…

Farfetched? Not with GPS technology mapping your position and instantly notifying the other golfers using the same "course." Once you lock-in a "hole," it organizes all the users. Because players cannot see everywhere across the area, the GPS sees for them.

Another area of technology addresses the growing need to accommodate both golfers with physical disabilities and the growing population of older golfers. The baby boomers who are maturing will be playing lots of golf, and for a longer time, perhaps, than we have seen in past years. It is likely that there will be more aged golfers than ever within the next two decades.

An interesting advancement is a new machine that looks like a golf club but is in reality a firing mechanism. You use it to shoot by placing it

FIGURE 19-8
Hand-held GPS devices the size of pagers are capable of indicating to players the exact yardage from their location to the target.

COURTESY OF GOLFLOGIX

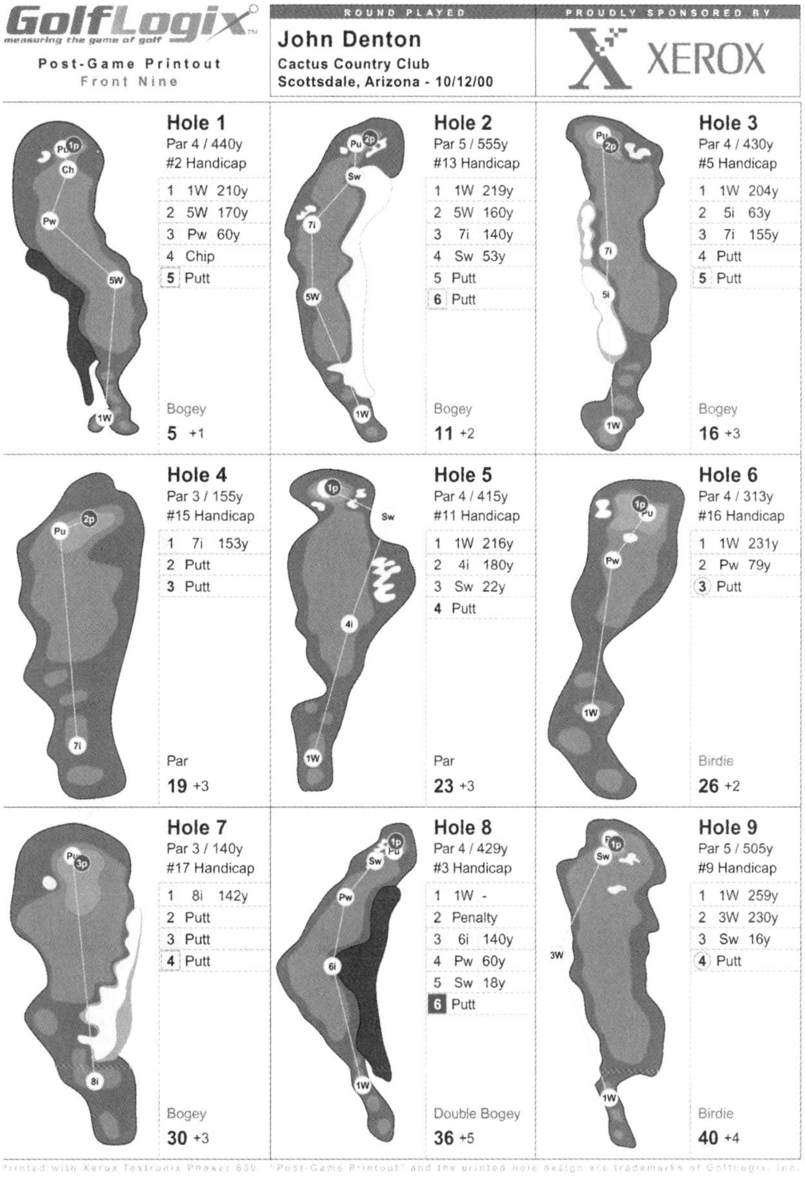

GolfLogix
measuring the game of golf
Post-Game Printout
Front Nine
ROUND PLAYED
John Denton
Cactus Country Club
Scottsdale, Arizona - 10/12/00
PROUDLY SPONSORED BY
XEROX
Hole 1
Par 4 / 440y
#2 Handicap
1 1W 210y
2 5W 170y
3 Pw 60y
4 Chip
5 Putt
Bogey
5 +1
Hole 2
Par 5 / 555y
#13 Handicap
1 1W 219y
2 5W 160y
3 7i 140y
4 Sw 53y
5 Putt
6 Putt
Bogey
11 +2
Hole 3
Par 4 / 430y
#5 Handicap
1 1W 204y
2 5i 63y
3 7i 155y
4 Putt
5 Putt
Bogey
16 +3
Hole 4
Par 3 / 155y
#15 Handicap
1 7i 153y
2 Putt
3 Putt
Par
19 +3
Hole 5
Par 4 / 415y
#11 Handicap
1 1W 216y
2 4i 180y
3 Sw 22y
4 Putt
Par
23 +3
Hole 6
Par 4 / 313y
#16 Handicap
1 1W 231y
2 Pw 79y
3 Putt
Birdie
26 +2
Hole 7
Par 3 / 140y
#17 Handicap
1 8i 142y
2 Putt
3 Putt
4 Putt
Bogey
30 +3
Hole 8
Par 4 / 429y
#3 Handicap
1 1W -
2 Penalty
3 6i 140y
4 Pw 60y
5 Sw 18y
6 Putt
Double Bogey
36 +5
Hole 9
Par 5 / 505y
#9 Handicap
1 1W 259y
2 3W 230y
3 Sw 16y
4 Putt
Birdie
40 +4

FIGURE 19-9
This printout demonstrates the integration of the GPS world to the golfer. The golfer carries a small GPS device (see Figure 19-8) and records the points where shots were taken on a course. These data are available on a printout on completion of the round. The chart shows where the golfer hit the shot and can be used to improve his understanding of his game and the course — or can simply be a keepsake of the experience.

COURTESY OF GOLFLOGIX

behind the ball and engaging a trigger. How wonderful that there may be something to sustain the weak older golfer who can no longer smash drives more than 100 yards. How awful it would be to have played golf, hitting 250-yard tee shots, and then being sent well to the front of the pack to hit dribblers no longer than a decent salad bar.

Conclusion

Technology is likely to do exciting things for golf. Golf can be made more fun and more interesting when technology meshes with the traditions of the game. This is another tough balancing act.

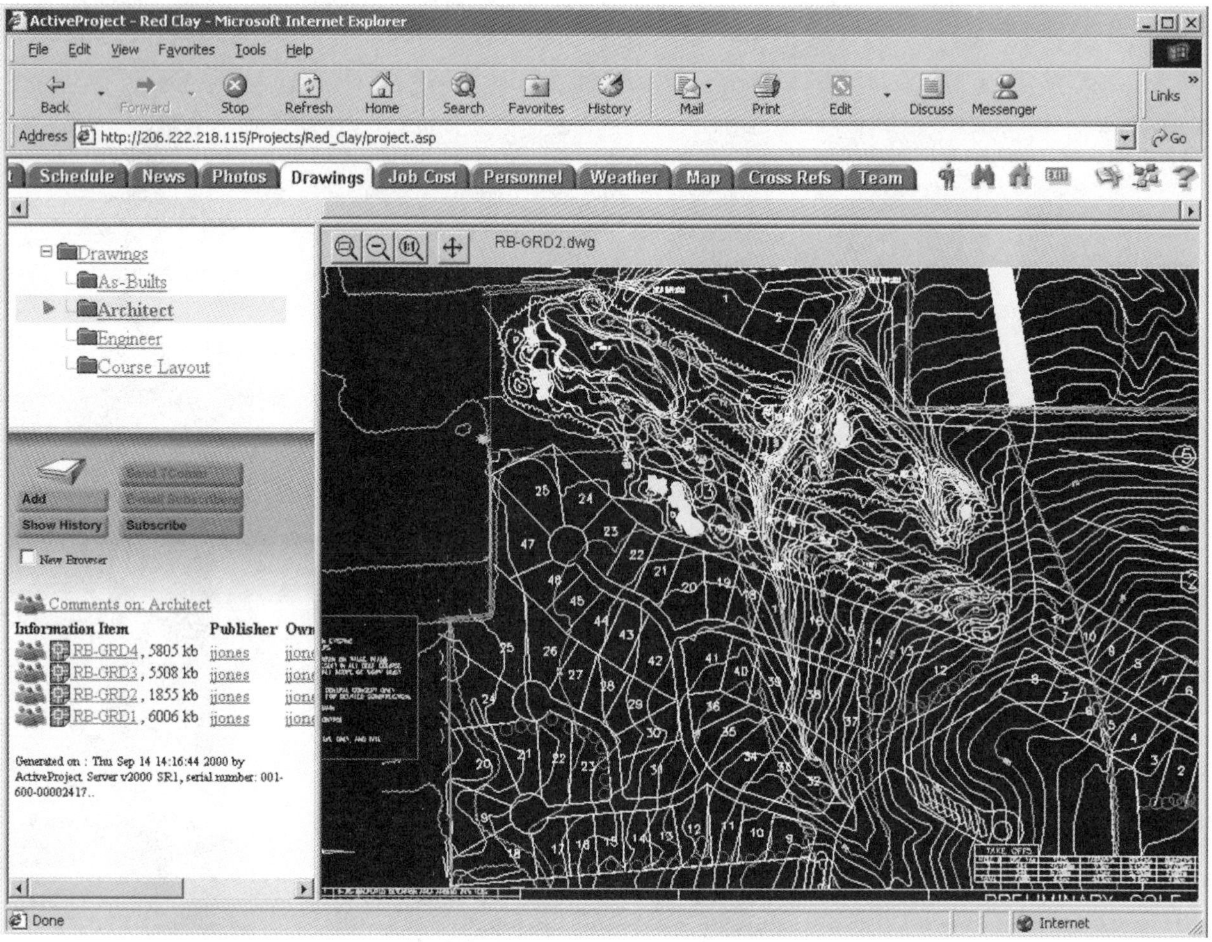

FIGURE 19-10
Technology is linking the golf architect with the disciplines of construction, management, and development. Projects are completed more quickly, in some respects, as a result of integrated databases that can be used in real time and simultaneously by various entities. In this example, a project is being managed by the client and contractor even though it is still on the drawing board of the architect.
COURTESY OF LANDSCAPES UNLIMITED

THE COST OF GOLF

Affordable golf is a round of 18 holes that costs about the same as a good steak dinner at a fairly nice restaurant. In 2001 dollars, this equates to about $2 per hole.

Golf has become, to many, way too expensive. This problem may be more one of people than of policy. To make policy, you need people on the other end who are willing to accept it. Certainly not all golf can be, or should be, accessible. The private club and the exclusive resort are private and exclusive for good reason. Often, these are easier propositions. More money can be made and therefore more money spent. At the affordable end, there is less money to be made and therefore, usually, less money to be spent. Quantity makes up the difference.

This causes a real problem. Not every community has a great and wonderful municipal or affordable daily-fee course. Because of this, the golfer who plays affordable lower end courses desires to be a part of the higher end, but it is almost never the other way around. The casual public golfer on a fixed income wants to play the likes of what he sees on TV, in golf magazines, and hears about when playing with others.

Perhaps every once in a while he will splurge on a course of such stature or one that resembles these images.

This is where creativity can play a role. Ideas, good routings, and good thinking do not cost much at all. Injecting these into *all* projects will assist in leveling the playing board. Remember, the Cypress Point Club was built for an aggressively low budget. Its designers used every strength they had to save costs and build with restraint. This strength was exerted with their mind, and it is their ideas and common sense that make the course so wonderful. Surely it had great land, but even that decision involved great minds and thought.

Architects need to continue the effort to bring accuracy to the forefront of courses. Lengthening holes is not the only answer; in fact, it's probably not a good idea in most situations.

—John Solheim, Karsten Manufacturing

Conclusion

Golf was always meant to pit golfer against opponent. The opponent is supposed to be a monster made up of land, the weather, the occasional fellow player, and one's inner self. Only in the last 20 years have we added the opponent of high cost. This is a good way to ruin a business. It can drive people away.

GOLF'S POPULARITY

"Building more courses for young golfers is a far more important issue than lengthening courses for the long hitters. Golf's future is with bringing people into the game and keeping them excited." John Solheim said that, and it cannot be said better. I am reminded that entire conferences have been concerned with these topics. Little did the organizers know that they just needed to send everyone a sheet with John's quote and we could all have saved the time and effort.

It is, admittedly, a simpler matter to identify a problem than to resolve it. Golf is made popular today by television and the lure of doing what the pros do and playing where they play. What should we do with this popularity? Is golf harnessing this attraction well?

What we need more of is the family outing, the mom who wants to spend four hours with her daughter but can never find the time. We need more grandparents who want to spend an entire weekend getting to know their kids' kids and need an excuse. We need more business executives who save time being efficient and then need a place to spend the banked hours. Golf can be the answer—not for everyone, but for many.

To meet these needs, golf must be fun. It must be accessible, reasonable, and also realistic. It must take people away and allow them to dream, escape, and feel better. Golf must meet the challenge if it is to live and breathe into this infant century.

Conclusion

The routings we devise today cannot be thought of as purely physical solutions. They must rise up and solve problems, must serve as breaks to

FIGURE 19-11
The future.

everyday life. They must transport golfers away from the hustle and bustle to sometimes soothing, sometimes mind-boggling venues that help erase worries and cares. Courses must be fun from the first day a new golfer steps out to try the game. But first, we must make sure our courses truly invite the new golfer, the youngster, the first-time player.

WHERE GOLF COURSE ROUTING IS HEADED

There is no appropriate introduction to the future. It simply arrives. The answer to the question of where golf may be headed is a loaded one indeed. A great deal depends on how the game is accepted by the next generation of golfers. As was proved by the ancient European games of kolf, choule, pall-mall, and mail à chicane, no game or pastime is immune from lack of interest and eventual abandonment. Each of these games was popular, the rage of their time. Yet, golf has endured. Maybe the answer to golf's future lies in an understanding of this endurance.

Golf continues, in my view, because it transcends the norm of playing and competing on a static playing board. But, so unlike the open-ended and uncontrolled activities of hunting, fishing, and hiking, golf marries the best of two extremes; on one hand, we have the playing board, with its rules, procedures, and format, but on the other, we have the feeling of being able to take our own path—to go wherever we like—and no official or rule prohibits this. Golf is the ultimate of individual games, for we can go about it as we damn well please. The bad decisions are ours to bear, the good ones ours to hold dear.

In golf, the player is both given carte blanche and bound to a certain strictness. This contract seems just perfect. The blank page that is a golf hole allows one to draw his own route—but there is still a page, still an element of staying within the lines, and still the surprise when what was deemed a good route is blocked by evil influences. How delightful a game it is. And, as many have pointed out, how maddening!

It would be presumptuous to make any blanket answer to such a broad question as "Where is golf course routing headed?" There may be no single answer. Whether routings will take golfers on journeys over new types of terrain, on old courses remodeled in new ways, across completely new types of courses, or even indoors, is a matter of many factors, only some of which have been discussed.

The art of routing a golf course is powerful. It elicits emotions. It surprises. It challenges. One moment it is about theater, and the next it is about the stage itself. It is storytelling in its highest form. Its greatest gift is allowing new stories to be written by a never-ending line of waiting actors. The magic of golf happens when we take golfers from point A to point B. That is the only known direction in which golf course routing is ever headed. Here's to point B!

Resources

The following resources are listed for convenience to the reader. Many of the organizations listed are referred to in this book.

American Society of Golf Course Architects (ASGCA)
221 North LaSalle Street
Chicago, Illinois 60601
(312) 372-6160
www.asgca.org
The premiere organization of professional golf course architects in North America; profiles of golf course architects, a library of designs, current news, etc.

American Society of Irrigation Consultants (ASIC)
221 North LaSalle Street
Chicago, Illinois 60601
www.asic.org
Organization of professionals within the irrigation industry. Founded to keep those within the industry informed of irrigation design, installation, and product application issues.

Americans with Disabilities Act (ADA)
www.usdoj.gov/crt/ada/adahom1.htm
The official Web site for the Americans with Disabilities Act of 1990; news, compliance information, and the Act itself.

British and International Golf Greenkeepers Association (BIGGA)
BIGGA House
Aldwark, Alne, York YO61 1UF
United Kingdom
+44 1347 833800
www.bigga.co.uk
The professional association of greenkeepers in the United Kingdom.

Club Managers Association of America (CMAA)
1733 King Street
Alexandria, Virginia 22314
(703) 739-9500
www.cmaa.org
An association of over 5000 members operating country, city, athletic, faculty, yacht, town, and military clubs.

European Golf Association (EGA)
Place de la Croix-Blanche 19
CH-1066 Epalinges
Switzerland
+41 21-784-35-32
www.ega-golf.ch
Organization whose membership is restricted to European national golf amateur golf associations or unions. Observes the Rules of Golf and amateur status as directed by the Royal & Ancient.

European Institute of Golf Course Architects (EIGCA)
Merrist Wood House, Worplesdon
Guildford, Surrey GU3 3PE
United Kingdom
+44 1483 884036
www.eigca.org
The organization of professional golf course architects in Europe; members' profiles, news, education, and library.

First Tee
World Golf Village
425 South Legacy Trail
St. Augustine, Florida 32092
(904) 940-4300
www.thefirsttee.com
Organization committed to making the game of golf accessible and affordable to kids and minority youth.

Golf Course 1
www.golfcourse1.com
An affiliated Web site of the ASGCA. A resource for golf course developers and owners of new courses and remodeling projects.

Golf Course Builders Association of America (GCBAA)
727 O Street
Lincoln, Nebraska 68510
(402) 476-4444
www.gcbaa.org
A nonprofit trade organization of golf course builders and suppliers; includes member directory, certification information, application form, and news.

Golf Course Superintendents Association of America (GCSAA)
1421 Research Park Drive
Lawrence, Kansas 66049-3859
(785) 841-2240
www.gcsaa.org
The professional organization for golf course superintendents; career opportunities, learning center, resource center, news, and more.

Golf Course.com
www.golfcourse.com
An online magazine and database useful for finding golf course locations, prices, policies, public reviews, and so on.

GolfCross
www.golfcross.com
Alternative format of golf using an oval golf ball that is pitched into netting structures resembling American football goal posts as opposed to rolling the ball into a hole. This Web site contains all the information one could hope for about GolfCross.

Golf Digest
www.golfdigest.com
The official Web site of *Golf Digest;* includes course reviews, travel information, instructional tips, features from the magazine, and news (recommend www.golfdigest.com/courses).

Golf Online
www.golfonline.com
The official Web site of *Golf* magazine; includes articles, travel information, instruction, and the golfcourse.com database.

Golf Range Association of America (GRAA)
www.golfrange.org
Organization dedicated to the advancement of the golf range and practice facility industry; includes a national Top 100 list, *Golf Range* magazine, golf range directory, and membership information.

Golf Traveler www.misc.traveller.com/golf
A database of course scorecards and course information.

Golfing Scotland
Gateway East, Technology Park
Dundee DD2 12W
Scotland
+44 1382 429000
www.scottishgolf.com
Directory of courses and practice ranges, news, and webcam for Scottish courses.

Irrigation Association
6540 Arlington Boulevard
Falls Church, Virginia 22042-6638
www.irrigation.com
Association whose mission is to provide information about improving the products and practices used in the irrigation industry. Included are directories, conservation and water management resources, a search engine, and education and job opportunities.

Japanese Society of Golf Course Architects
www.jsgca.com
Organization of leading golf course architects in Japan.

John Wiley & Sons, Inc.
111 River St.
Hoboken, NJ 07030
(201) 748-6000
www.wiley.com
Global publisher focusing on scientific, technical, and medical journals; textbooks; and professional and consumer books as well as subscription services.

Ladies Professional Golf Association (LPGA)
100 International Golf Drive
Daytona Beach, Florida 32124-1092
(386) 274-6200
www.lpga.com
The organization of female professional golfers (includes club pros) in the United States; LPGA Tour news updates, information on touring and teaching pros, history, and pro shop.

Land Trust Alliance
1331 H Street, NW, Suite 400
Washington, DC 20005-4734
(202) 638-4725
www.lta.org
The leading organization promoting and fostering the private land conservation movement by encouraging voluntary land conservation across the United States.

Michigan State University Turfgrass Information Center
www.lib.msu.edu/tgif
Database of over 76,000 publicly available turfgrass educational materials.

National Club Association (NCA)
www.natlclub.org
Association that provides legal advice and lobbyist services for private and recreational clubs.

National Golf Course Owners Association (NGCOA)
1470 Ben Sawyer Boulevard, Suite 18
Mt. Pleasant, South Carolina 29464
(843) 881-9956
Information source for member golf course owners, offering them data critical to their success in the golf industry; includes ADA and IRS information, upcoming association events, and *Golf Business* magazine.

National Golf Foundation (NGF)
1150 South US Highway One, Suite 401
Jupiter, Florida 33477
www.ngf.org
(561) 744-6006
The leading organization dedicated to researching the entirety of the golf industry; directory of member companies, infosearch, golf directory, course construction activity, and news.

Pace Manager Systems
4804 Elmdale Drive
Rolling Hills Estates, California 90274
(310) 791-7348
www.pacemanager.com
Pace Manager seeks to cure the problem of slow play on today's courses by finding its cause and proposing solutions.

PGA Tour
112 TPC Boulevard, Sawgrass
Ponte Vedra Beach, Florida 32082
www.pgatour.com
The organization of touring professionals (male, female, and senior) in the United States; tournament schedules, leaderboards, headlines, course travel information, and online store.

Professional Golfers Association of America (PGA)
100 Avenue of the Champions
Palm Beach Gardens, Florida 33410
www.pga.org
Organization of professional golfers (including club pros) within the United States; tournament headlines, schedules, and golf instruction.

Remodeling University
www.remodelinguniversity.org
An affiliated site of the ASGCA. The leading resource for golf course developers and owners on remodeling, renovation, and restoration projects.

Royal & Ancient Golf Club of St. Andrews (R&A)
St. Andrews, Fife, KY169JD
Scotland
www.randa.org
Leading legislative body of golf in Europe; site includes European tour news, information on St. Andrews, rules of golf, and frequently asked questions. Also included is information about the British Golf Museum.

Shivas Irons Society
P.O. Box 22239
Carmel, CA 93922
www.shivas.org
A society dedicated to exploring the "beautiful and mysterious" side of golf, providing opportunities for personal and social transformation. Based Michael Murphy's novel *Golf in the Kingdom.*

Society of Australian Golf Course Architects (SAGCA)
www.sagca.org.au
The organization of professional golf course architects within Australia; members' profiles, golf and the environment, news journal, and contacts.

St. Andrews Links Trust
Pilmour House
St. Andrews, Fife, KY169SF
Scotland
+44 1334 466666
www.standrews.org/uk
The official Web site of the "Home of Golf." Information on all six St. Andrews golf courses, online booking, history, and store.

United States Golf Association (USGA)
P.O. Box 708
Far Hills, New Jersey 07931
(908) 234-2300
www.usga.org
The governing body for golf within the United States; information on USGA championship tournaments, rules of golf, handicapping, equipment, foundation for people with disabilities, *Golf Journal* magazine, news, and contacts.

Urban Land Institute (ULI)
1025 Thomas Jefferson Street NW
Suite 500 West
Washington, D.C. 20007
(202) 624-7000
Organization dedicated to providing leadership and guidance with respect to responsible and environmentally enhancing land planning issues, techniques, and strategies.

World Golf Village
21 World Golf Place
St. Augustine, Florida 32092
www.wgv.com

Home of the World Golf Hall of Fame and Golf Museum.
World Scientific Congress of Golf
www.golfscience.org
A collection of documented golf scientific research projects by authors around the globe.

Bibliography

Barclay, James A. *The Toronto Terror: The Life and Works of Stanley Thompson, Golf Course Architect.* Chelsea, Mich.: Sleeping Bear Press, 2000.

Behrend, John, and Peter N. Lewis. *Challenges & Champions: The Royal & Ancient Golf Club.* St. Andrews, Fife, Scotland: Royal & Ancient Golf Club of St. Andrews, 1998.

Chapman, Kenneth G. *Kenneth G. Chapman's The Rules of the Green: A History of the Rules of Golf.* Chicago: Triumph Books and the USGA, 1997.

Colt, H. S., and C. H. Alison. *Some Essays on Golf Course Architecture.* New York: Charles Scribner's Sons, 1920, and Droitwich, Worcestershire, England: Grant Books, 1993.

Cornish, Geoffrey S., and Ronald E. Whitten. *The Architects of Golf.* New York: HarperCollins, 1993.

———. *The Golf Course.* New York: Rutledge Press, 1981, 1982, 1984, 1987.

Mulvihill, David A., et al. *Golf Course Development in Residential Communities.* Washington, D.C.: Urban Land Institute, 2001.

Cotton, Henry. *Henry Cotton's Guide to Golf in the British Isles.* Manchester, Greater Manchester, England: Cliveden Press, 1969.

Davis, Spencer H. Jr., Steven R. Langlois, and Louis M. Vasvary. *The Dictionary of Golf.* New York: Carlton Press, 1990.

Davis, William H. *Great Golf Courses of the World.* New York: Golf Digest, 1974.

de St. Jorre, John. *Legendary Golf Clubs of Scotland, England, Wales, and Ireland.* Wellington, Fla.: Edgeworth Editions, 1998.

Doak, Tom. *The Anatomy of a Golf Course.* New York: Lyons & Burford, 1992.

Doak, Tom, Dr. James S. Scott, and Raymund M. Haddock. *The Life and Works of Dr. Alister MacKenzie.* Chelsea, Mich.: Sleeping Bear Press, 2001.

Garrity, John. *America's Worst Golf Courses: A Collection of Courses Not Up to Par.* New York: Collier Books, 1994.

Graves, Robert Muir, and Geoffrey S. Cornish. *Golf Course Design.* New York: John Wiley & Sons, 1998.

Gillum, John. *The Sacred Nine.* Suffolk, England: The Royal Worlington & Newmarket Golf Club, 1992.

Green, Robert, and Brian Morgan. *Classic Holes of Golf: A Grand Tour of the World's Most Challenging, Historic, and Beautiful Golf Holes.* New York: Prentice Hall, 1989.

Hawtree, Fred. *Aspects of Golf Course Architecture.* Droitwich, Worcestershire, England: Grant Books, 1998.

Hobbs, Michael. *Golf in Art.* Edison, N.J.: Chartwell Books, 1996.

Hoffman, Davy. *America's Greatest Golf Courses.* New York: Gallery Books, 1987.

Hunter, Robert. *The Links.* New York: Charles Scribner's Sons, 1926, and Chelsea, Mich.: Sleeping Bear Press, 1999.

Hurdzan, Michael J. *Golf Course Architecture: Design, Construction, and Restoration.* Chelsea, Mich.: Sleeping Bear Press, 1996.

Jarrett, Tom. *St. Andrews Golf Links: The First 600 Years.* Edinburgh, Lothian, Scotland: Mainstream Publishing, 1995.

Joy, David. *St. Andrews and The Open Championship: The Official History.* Chelsea, Mich.: Sleeping Bear Press, 1999.

Kroeger, Robert. *The Golf Courses of Old Tom Morris.* Cincinnati, Ohio: Heritage Communications, 1995.

Lewis, Peter N., Elinor R. Clark, and Fiona C. Grieve. *A Round of History at the British Golf Museum.* St. Andrews, Fife, Scotland: Royal & Ancient Golf Club of St. Andrews, 1998.

Lewis, Peter, Fiona C. Grieve, and Keith Mackie. *Art and Architecture of the Royal and Ancient Golf Club.* St. Andrews, Fife, Scotland: Royal & Ancient Golf Club of St. Andrews, 1997.

Longstaff, J.R. *The First Hundred Years of Bishop Aukland Golf Club: 1894–1994.* Bishop Aukland, Durham, England: Bishop Aukland Golf Club, 1994.

Lyle, Sandy, and Bob Ferrier. *The Championship Courses of Scotland.* Kingswood, Tadworth, Surrey: World's Work, 1982.

Macdonald, Charles Blair. *Scotland's Gift: Golf.* New York: Charles Scribner's Sons, 1928, and Stamford, Conn.: Classics of Golf, 1985.

MacKenzie, Alister. *Golf Architecture.* London: Simpkin, Marshall, Hamilton, Kent & Co., 1920; Stamford, Conn.: Classics of Golf, 1988; and Droitwich, Worcestershire, England: Grant Books, 1982.

———. *The Spirit of St. Andrews.* Chelsea, Mich.: Sleeping Bear Press, 1995.

Muirhead, Desmond, and Guy L. Rando. *Golf Course Development and Real Estate.* Washington, D.C.: Urban Land Institute, 1994.

Muirhead, Desmond, and Tip Anderson. *St. Andrews: How to Play the Old Course.* Newport Beach, Calif.: Newport Press, 2000.

Pace, Lee. *Pinehurst Stories: A Celebration of Great Golf and Good Times,* 2nd ed. Pinehurst, N.C.: Pinehurst, 1999.

Peper, George, and the editors of *Golf* magazine. *The 500 World's Greatest Golf Holes.* New York: Artisan, 2000.

Price, Charles. *The World of Golf: A Panorama of Six Centuries of the Game's History.* New York: Random House, 1962.

Redmond, John. *Great Golf Courses of Ireland.* Dublin, Ireland: Gil & Macmillan, 1992.

Robertson, James K. *St. Andrews: Home of Golf.* St. Andrews, Fife, Scotland: J. & G. Innes, 1967.

Ross, Donald J. *Golf Has Never Failed Me: The Lost Commentaries of Legendary Golf Course Architect Donald J. Ross.* Chelsea, Mich.: Sleeping Bear Press, 1996.

Scott, Tom. *The Concise Dictionary of Golf.* New York: Mayflower Books, 1978.

Shackelford, Geoff. *Alister MacKenzie's Cypress Point Club.* Chelsea, Mich.: Sleeping Bear Press, 2000.

———. *The Captain: George C. Thomas and His Architecture.* Chelsea, Mich.: Sleeping Bear Press, 1997.

———. *The Golden Age of Golf Design.* Chelsea, Mich.: Sleeping Bear Press, 1999.

———. *Masters of the Links: Essays on the Art of Golf and Course Design.* Chelsea, Mich.: Sleeping Bear Press, 1997.

Shapiro, Mel, Warren Dohn, and Leonard Berger. *Golf: A Turn-of-the-Century Treasury.* Secaucus, N.J.: Castle, 1986.

Stobbs, John. *An ABC of Golf.* London: Stanley Paul, 1964.

Swift, Duncan. *The Golfer's Reference Dictionary Illustrated.* Dearborn, Mich.: Schaefer's Publishing, 1999.

Thomas, George C. *Golf Architecture in America.* Chelsea, Mich.: Sleeping Bear Press, 1997.

Tillinghast, A. W. *The Course Beautiful.* Warren, N.J.: Treewolf Productions, 1995.

———. *Reminiscences of the Links: A Treasury of Creative Essays and Vintage Photographs on Scottish and Early American Golf.* Warren, N.J.: Treewolf Productions, 1998.

Ward-Thomas, Pat, Herbert Warren Wind, Charles Price, and Peter Thomson. *The World Atlas of Golf: The Great Courses and How They Are Played.* New York: Random House, 1976.

Wilde, Judith, and Richard Wilde. *Visual Literacy: A Conceptual Approach to Graphic Problem Solving.* New York: Watson-Guptill Publications, 1991.

Index

Note: For the convenience of the reader, golf courses bestowed royal status have been listed without reference to "royal" preceding their names.